Communications in Computer and Information Science   2645

Rationale

The CCIS series is devoted to the publication of proceedings of computer science conferences. Its aim is to efficiently disseminate original research results in informatics in printed and electronic form. While the focus is on publication of peer-reviewed full papers presenting mature work, inclusion of reviewed short papers reporting on work in progress is welcome, too. Besides globally relevant meetings with internationally representative program committees guaranteeing a strict peer-reviewing and paper selection process, conferences run by societies or of high regional or national relevance are also considered for publication.

Topics

The topical scope of CCIS spans the entire spectrum of informatics ranging from foundational topics in the theory of computing to information and communications science and technology and a broad variety of interdisciplinary application fields.

Information for Volume Editors and Authors

Publication in CCIS is free of charge. No royalties are paid, however, we offer registered conference participants temporary free access to the online version of the conference proceedings on SpringerLink (http://link.springer.com) by means of an http referrer from the conference website and/or a number of complimentary printed copies, as specified in the official acceptance email of the event.

CCIS proceedings can be published in time for distribution at conferences or as post-proceedings, and delivered in the form of printed books and/or electronically as USBs and/or e-content licenses for accessing proceedings at SpringerLink. Furthermore, CCIS proceedings are included in the CCIS electronic book series hosted in the SpringerLink digital library at http://link.springer.com/bookseries/7899. Conferences publishing in CCIS are allowed to use our online conference service (Meteor) for managing the whole proceedings lifecycle (from submission and reviewing to preparing for publication) free of charge.

Publication process

The language of publication is exclusively English. Authors publishing in CCIS have to sign the Springer CCIS copyright transfer form, however, they are free to use their material published in CCIS for substantially changed, more elaborate subsequent publications elsewhere. For the preparation of the camera-ready papers/files, authors have to strictly adhere to the Springer CCIS Authors' Instructions and are strongly encouraged to use the CCIS LaTeX style files or templates.

Abstracting/Indexing

CCIS is abstracted/indexed in DBLP, Google Scholar, EI-Compendex, Mathematical Reviews, SCImago, Scopus. CCIS volumes are also submitted for the inclusion in ISI Proceedings.

How to start

To start the evaluation of your proposal for inclusion in the CCIS series, please send an e-mail to ccis@springer.com

Hassan Badir · Mohamed Tabaa ·
Ladjel Bellatreche · Marjan Mernik ·
Boualem Benatallah · Rachida Fissoune
Editors

New Technologies, Artificial Intelligence and Smart Data

12th International Conference, INTIS 2024
Tangier, Morocco, May 30 – June 1, 2024
Revised Selected Papers

 Springer

Editors
Hassan Badir
University Abdelmalek Essaadi
Tangier, Morocco

Ladjel Bellatreche
National Engineering School for Mechanics
and Aerotechnics (ENSMA)
Poitiers, France

Boualem Benatallah
University of New South Wales Sydney
Sydney, NSW, Australia

Mohamed Tabaa
EMSI
Casablanca, Morocco

Marjan Mernik
University of Maribor
Maribor, Slovenia

Rachida Fissoune
University Abdelmalek Essaadi
Tangier, Morocco

ISSN 1865-0929 ISSN 1865-0937 (electronic)
Communications in Computer and Information Science
ISBN 978-3-032-14963-3 ISBN 978-3-032-14964-0 (eBook)
https://doi.org/10.1007/978-3-032-14964-0

This Springer imprint is published by the registered company Springer Nature Switzerland AG
The registered company address is: Gewerbestrasse 11, 6330 Cham, Switzerland

If disposing of this product, please recycle the paper.

Preface

This year INTIS – the International Conference on New Technologies, Artificial Intelligence and Smart Data – celebrated its 12th anniversary. The first INTIS conference was held in Tangier, Morocco in 2011. Since then, INTIS has taken place annually, with previous editions held in Mohammedia, Morocco (2012), Tangier, Morocco (2013, 2019, 2020, 2022, 2023), Rabat, Morocco (2014), Fez, Morocco (2016), Casablanca, Morocco (2017, 2022), and Marrakech, Morocco (2018).

The 12th INTIS conference (INTIS 2024) was held in Tangier, Morocco, during May 30–31 and June 1, 2024 as a face-to-face event. INTIS 2024's topics covered the main layers of data-enabled systems/applications: data source layer, network layer, data layer, learning layer, and reporting layers, while taking into account non-functional properties such as data privacy, security, and ethics. This year's conference (INTIS 2024) built on this tradition, facilitating the inter-disciplinary exchange of ideas, theory, techniques, experiences, and future research directions, and promoting African and Middle East researchers.

Our call for papers attracted 82 papers, from which the International Program Committee finally selected 23 full papers and 15 short papers, yielding an acceptance rate of 33%. Each paper was reviewed by an average of three reviewers and in some cases up to four; reviews were double blind. Accepted papers cover a number of broad research areas on both theoretical and practical aspects. Some trends found in accepted papers include the following: AI-driven applications, smart data and Internet of Things Applications, Big Data Warehouses, and Cyber Security.

INTIS 2024 featured the following three keynote speakers:

- Yannis Manolopoulos: Open University of Cyprus — *Recommenders for Scientometic Objects?*
- Mario F. Pavone: University of Catania, Italy — *Metaheuristics and Machine Learning: how one enhances the other.*
- Hanaa Hachimi: Ibn Tofail University, Morocco — *The Power of Data: How AI is Revolutionizing Operational Models.*

During INTIS 2024, a special tribute was paid to Prof. Azedine Boulmakoul, from Hassan II University, Morocco, who passed away in 2022. He was one of the founders of the INTIS conference.

We would like to thank all authors for submitting their papers to INTIS 2024 and we hope they submit again in the future. On the other hand, we express our gratitude to all the Program Committee members who provided high-quality reviews. We want to acknowledge the ease of use and flexibility of the EasyChair system to manage papers.

Finally, we thank the local organizers for their invaluable support. To the conference participants, we hope they benefited from the technical sessions, informal meetings, and networking opportunities with like-minded people from all over the world. To those who read these proceedings, we hope that the papers will pique their interest and inspire future research projects

Last but not least, we would like to thank the staff of Springer for their help, support, and advice.

September 2024

Hassan Badir
Mohamed Tabaa
Ladjel Bellatreche
Marjan Mernik
Boualem Benatallah
Rachida Fissoune

Organization

Honored Guests

Bouchta El Moumni	Abdelmalek Essaâdi University, Morocco
Ahmed Moussa	ENSATg, Morocco
Mohamed Essaaidi	EMSI, Morocco
Azedine Boulmakoul	FSTM, Morocco

Conference Advisory Committee

Mohamed Tabaa	EMSI, Morocco
Rachida Fissoune	IDS-ENSATg, Morocco
Ladjel Bellatreche	ENSMA, France

Program Committee Chairs

Hassan Badir	IDS - ENSATg, Morocco
Marjan Mernik	University of Maribor, Slovenia
Boualem Benatallah	Dublin City University, Ireland

Organizing Committee Chairs

Rabia Marghoubi	INPT, Morocco
Sara Ibn Al Ahrach	FMT, Morocco
Hassna Bensag	EMSI, Morocco

Publicity Committee

Amjad Rattrout	Arab American University, Palestine
Ahmed Lbath	Grenoble Alpes University, France
Wahida Handouzi	University of Tlemcen, Algeria
Faouzi Kamoun	ESPRIT, Tunisia
Rafaat Lababidi	ENSTA, France

Publication Committee

Achraf Cohen	University of West Florida, USA
Mouhamad Chehaitly	University of Luxembourg, Luxembourg
Bharat Bhushan	Sharda University, India
Ismail Biskri	Université du Québec à Trois-Rivières, Canada

Secretary Committee

Lamia Karim	ENSAB, Morocco
Adil Bouziri	FSTM, Morocco
Najlae Elfathi	EMSI, Morocco

Local Organizing Committee

Rachida Fissoune	ENSATg, Morocco
Sara Ibn El Ahrache	ENSATg, Morocco
Ahmed Moussa	ENSATg, Morocco
Hassan Badir	ENSATg, Morocco
Ahmed Rabhi	ENSATg, Morocco
Kenza Chaoui	ENSATg, Morocco
Mouna Amrou Mhand	ENSATg, Morocco
Chaimaa Azromahli	LSIA, EMSI, Morocco
Zineb El Khattabi	LSIA, EMSI, Morocco
Zineb Hidila	LPRI - EMSI, Morocco
Meriem Abid	LPRI - EMSI, Morocco
Salma Chebaoui	LPRI - EMSI, Morocco

Steering Committee

Azedine Boulmakoul	FSTM, Morocco
Hassan Badir	ENSATg, Morocco
Mohamed Tabaa	EMSI, Morocco
Ahmed Lbath	Grenoble Alpes University, France
Amjad Rattrout	Arab American University, Palestine
Nouria Harbi	University of Lyon 2, France

Contents

Artificial Intelligence

Artificial Intelligence (AI) Toward Streamlining Lean Manufacturing
Approaches 3
    Ikhlef Jebbor, Naima El-hmous, Zoubida Benmamoun,
    and Hanaa Hachimi

Road Roughness and Ranking Using Deep Learning 15
    Muhammed Saffarini, Amjad Rattrout, Yousef-Awwad Daraghmi,
    and Muath Sabha

Unveiling the Future of Drug Discovery: Revolutionizing LogS Prediction
with Deep Learning FNNs 31
    Imane Aitouhanni and Amine Berqia

Segment Anything Model for Breast Imaging Segmentation:
State-of-the-Art 42
    Laila El Jiani, Ihsane Haloum, Sanaa El Filali, and El Habib Benlahmar

Profitability Prediction of Stock Exchange Symbols: An Integrated Data
Mining Approach 53
    Areen Naji, Amjad Rattrout, and Rashid Jayousi

Comparative Analysis of Cutaneous Leishmaniasis Future Forecasting
Using Supervised Machine Learning Models 67
    Hasnaa Talimi, Imane El Idrissi Saik, Meryem Lemrani,
    and Rachida Fissoune

Deep Learning Time Series Forecasting Using LST MODIS Data:
Hyperparameter Optimization 80
    Hafssa Naciri, Nizar Ben Achhab, Fatima Ezahrae Ezzaher,
    Naoufal Raissouni, and Abdelilah Azyat

SentinelBERT: A Deep Learning Approach for Adverse Event Forecasting 94
    Rasha Assaf, Amjad Rattrout, Mohammed Khalilia, and Rashid Jayousi

Enhancing Outlier Detection: A Hybrid Architecture with Autoencoder
Clustering and Isolation Forest 105
    Sanae Borrohou, Rachida Fissoune, and Nadia Kabachi

An Efficient Face Recognition Model Based on ViT Architecture 119
*Er-rajy Latifa, El Kiram My Ahmed, Lahihab Oussama,
and El Ghazouani Mohamed*

Dynamic Region Proposal Model for Road Anomalies Detection
and Classification 132
*Rasha Saffarini, Faisal Khamayseh, Yousef Daraghmeh, Derar Elyan,
and Muath Sabha*

Smart Data and IoT

Adaptive Transfer Learning for Mineral Grade Prediction in Mining
Industry 4.0 149
*Ahmed Bendaouia, El Hassan Abdelwahed, Sara Qassimi,
Abdelmalek Boussetta, Intissar Benzakour, Zaynab Naciri,
Ilham Benmallouk, and Oumkeltoum Amar*

A Capacity Constrained ACO Approach for EVRP with a Partial Charging
Policy 163
Meryem Abid, Mohamed Tabaa, and Hanaa Hachimi

Industrial Modbus-LoRa Data Logger for Digital Twin's Applications 177
Adnane Bouchra, Abdelhafid Aitelmahjoub, and Abbas Dandache

BMA-Measure: A Novel Metric for Assessing the Quality of the Training
Set 186
Mohamed Amine Boudia

Dynamic Model Integration in the Articulated Manipulator Trajectory
Planning 200
*Inas Saoud, Asaad Chahboun, Naoufal Raissouni, Hatim Idriss Jaafari,
Nizar Ben Achhab, and Soufiane Mezroui*

Improving Machine Learning Accuracy in Detecting SQL Injection Attack
Using NLP and Feature Engineering 213
Amjad Rattrout, Majdi Jaradat, and Rashid Jayousi

AI-Based Anomaly Detection for IoT Cybersecurity Events 227
Zineb Hidila and Mohamed Tabaa

A Concatenation Deep Learning Model for Photovoltaic Inspection Based
on Aerial Infrared Images 240
Marwa Zerrouk, Toufik Enfissi, Zoubir Barraz, and Imane Sebari

Where We are in Handling IoT and Robotics' Data for Agro-Ecology
Applications?: An Architectural View 254
Houssam Bazza, Hassan Badir, Filippo Berto, Sandro Bimonte,
Aldo Calcante, Paolo Ceravolo, Ali Hassan, Tahar Kechadi,
Rim Moussa, Roberto Oberti, Sana Sellami, and Nicolas Tricot

Synergizing Blockchain and Cloud: Elevating Decentralization
and Scalability in Blockchain-Cloud Deployment Modes 268
Youness Bentayeb and Hassan Badir

Towards Blockchain and Agile Methodology Synergy to Enhance Digital
Transformation: The Case of SAFe Framework 276
Fatine Ziane, Afaf Ouaddah, Younes Laghouaouti, and Rabia Marghoubi

Leader- Similarity for Community Detection in Complex Networks 288
Sara Ahajjam, Jamal Ghaffour, and Hassan Badir

Short Papers

Enhancing Academic Success: Performance Early Prediction Using
Machine Learning Algorithms 305
Abderrazek Hachani, Maha Mallek, and Yosra Jmal

Advancements in Arabic Handwritten Text Recognition: A Comprehensive
Study of End-to-End Deep Learning Architecture with a Focus on Decoding
Techniques 312
I. Bounour, A. Ammour, G. Khaissidi, and M. Mrabti

A Prediction Model Based On Recurrent Neural Network To Predict
Freezing Of Gait Related To Parkinson's Disease 319
Yurub Awwad, Amjad Rattrout, and Rashid Jayousi

Protein-Protein Interaction Prediction Using Graph Neural Networks 328
Othmane Boumya, Hamza Hraiche, and Kaouter Karboub

Enhancing Human-Robot Collaboration in Disassembly Processes
Through Vision-Based Hardware Detection 335
Ameur Soufiane, Tabaa Mohammed, Hamlich Mohamed, Hidila Zineb,
and Bearee Richard

Empowering Earthquake Management Through Advanced Machine
Learning in Social Media Analytics and Facebook Data for Good
Utilization: A 2023 Case Study 342
Mohamed Mastir, Ali Dahbi, and Khalil El-Hami

Towards Advanced Modeling of Road User Behaviors for Urban
Congestion Management: A Framework Based on Neural Networks 348
Mohamed Laamimach and Aziz Mabrouk

Development of Cyber-Space Vulnerabilities Online Monitoring Solution
Using Machine Learning 354
Tizniti Douae, Kabachi Nadia, and Satir Abdellatif

Enhanced Road Object Detection for ADAS Using YOLOv8
and Hyperparameter Evolution 362
Omar Bouazizi, Chaimae Azroumahli, and Aimad El Mourabit

Automation Synergy: Intrusion Detection Through Deep Learning
via a DevOps Pipeline in a Cloud Environment 369
*Oumaima Lifandali, Zouhair Chiba, Noreddine Abghour,
Khalid Moussaid, and Mounia Miyara*

Explainable AI for Energy Prediction in Smart Building 375
Nisrine Bajja, Mohamed Hamlich, and Franck Dufrenois

Exploration of Semantic Segmentation Algorithms Through Deep
Learning for Extracting Water Bodies from Wetland Areas 382
*Mehdi Kechna, Yousra Achemlal, Kenza Ait El Kadi, Siham Fellahi,
Marwa Zerouk, and Hicham Hajji*

Weathering the Storm: Evaluating the Generalization of Recent Object
Detection Models for UAV Power Line Inspection of Insulators
in Challenging Meteorological Conditions 392
Rita Aitelhaj, Badr-Eddine Benelmostafa, and Hicham Medromi

Author Index 409

Artificial Intelligence

Artificial Intelligence (AI) Toward Streamlining Lean Manufacturing Approaches

Ikhlef Jebbor[1]([✉]) [iD], Naima El-hmous[2] [iD], Zoubida Benmamoun[3] [iD], and Hanaa Hachimi[1] [iD]

[1] Laboratory of Advanced Systems Engineering, National School of Applied Sciences, Ibn Tofail University, Kenitra, Morocco
jebbor.ikhlef@uit.ac.ma
[2] Laboratory of Data Analytics, Operations and Decision, INPT, V University, Rabat, Mohammed, Morocco
[3] Faculty of Engineering and computing , Liwa University, 31009 Abu Dhabi, United Arab Emirates

Abstract. To stay competitive on the international scale, industrial companies need to create and use innovative ideas in their manufacturing and operations. There have been adjustments made to new technology and methods for product creation. Global change happens so quickly that businesses are forced to face challenges and issues. Reducing waste and increasing quality and efficiency are the top concerns for the business. One proven concept that needs to be a part of any strategic business plan is Lean Manufacturing (LM) which has been demonstrated, may reduce processing times and boost plant efficiency in large manufacturing operations. Eventually, the capacity of industries to overcome challenges systematically and successfully is what decides the worth of their final goods. Artificial intelligence (AI) has emerged as a transformative technology in various industries, including LM. This literature review aims to provide an overview of the current state of research and applications of AI in LM. By synthesizing findings from academic journals, conference proceedings, and industry reports, this review identifies key trends, challenges, and opportunities associated with integrating AI technologies in LM practices. The review covers topics such as predictive maintenance, quality control, demand forecasting, supply chain optimization, process optimization, human-robot collaboration, and continuous improvement.

Keywords: AI · Lean Manufacturing · Optimization · Efficiency · Review

1   Introduction

LM is the standard method that applies to the whole industry to obtain the optimal results [1]. It started from the Toyota Production System (TPS) that was created by Toyota in post-World War II Japan [2]. LM's main focus is to provide customers with superior-quality products and services promptly and at the same time meet the customers' expectations [3].

H. Badir et al. (Eds.): INTIS 2024, CCIS 2645, pp. 3–14, 2026.
https://doi.org/10.1007/978-3-032-14964-0_1

The Key principles of LM include Value: Creating supreme value from the customer's viewpoint and concentrating on the operations that are important for meeting customer requirements. Value Stream: Tracing the whole value stream of a process will lead to the identification of all tasks and activities that are related to the production of a product or delivery of a service. Flow: Making the process easier through the value stream by removing over there any interruptions, delays, and bottlenecks. Pull: Implementing a push-based system of operating work only as demand requires, reducing the excess stock and overproduction inventory. Perfection: Continuously aiming for perfection by getting rid of waste, eliminating reworks, implementing problem-solving processes, and allowing employees to address and fix current problems [4–6].

LM's mission is the termination of different kinds of waste like overproduction, excessive stock, defects, time of waiting, unnecessary motion, and overprocessing. Through the elimination of waste and enhancing the processes, LM enables reduction in operational costs, quality improvement, efficiency increase, and customer satisfaction enhancement [7, 8].

In the last few years, the ID of AI technologies into LM has caused breakthroughs in the field of process optimization, quality control, predictive maintenance, and overall operational efficiency [9, 10].

AI, which is an algorithm that improves itself by learning from data, discovering patterns, and making decisions without much human intervention [11], allows achieving nothing short of a revolution in the LM processes. Manufacturers can obtain more accurate insights into their operations as well as optimization processes by applying artificial intelligence-powered analytics, machine learning, and automation [12].

The emergence of AI in manufacturing symbolizes significant conversion in manufacturing where the processes are produced, supervised, and improved. Traditionally, automation has always been a major driver in the manufacturing industry towards higher efficiency and productivity. On the other hand, AI deepens the complexity level by allowing the machines to perform those assignments that are supposed to be done by human intelligence only, which may include learning from the data, pattern recognition, and decision-making. Several factors have contributed to the emergence of AI in manufacturing: automated, data-driven, and adaptive [13].

Providing a holistic strategy for AI implementation is the goal of the article, as it aims to utilize advanced technologies to make the processes efficient, exclude all wastes, better the output quality, and so forth. Therefore, this positively affects the operation. The fact that manufacturers are aided to make use of AI by helping them to do so leads to efficient application of production, flexibility, and the capacity to be fit to the present manufacturing environment that is full of dramatic changes. Reporting the practicing and most relevant research data to the field along with the industry trends will ensure we provide an idea of how the manufacturing industry can integrate AI in their working procedure to achieve much success and be more competitive.

We conducted a comprehensive literature search for papers published from 2004 to May 2024. Our study used data from Academic Databases, Some Specific Journals, Conference Proceedings, Books, and Book Chapters, that contain high-quality articles [14] related to the integration of AI in streamlining LM approaches. We Begin by identifying keywords and search terms related to the integration of AI in LM: including the terms "artificial intelligence," "machine learning," "LM," "industry 4.0," and "smart manufacturing," using Boolean operators (AND for AI and LM and or for other words).

Table 1 shows the number of documents by area; most documents are Engineering (23%), computer science (16%), and business, management, and accounting (16%), Decision science (11%), Mathematics (5%), and material science (5%) and others. In addition, English was chosen as the language, and the document types as shown in Fig. 2: conference papers (29%), research Articles (27%), conference reviews (18%), books and book chapters (18%); and articles reviews (8%) (Fig. 1).

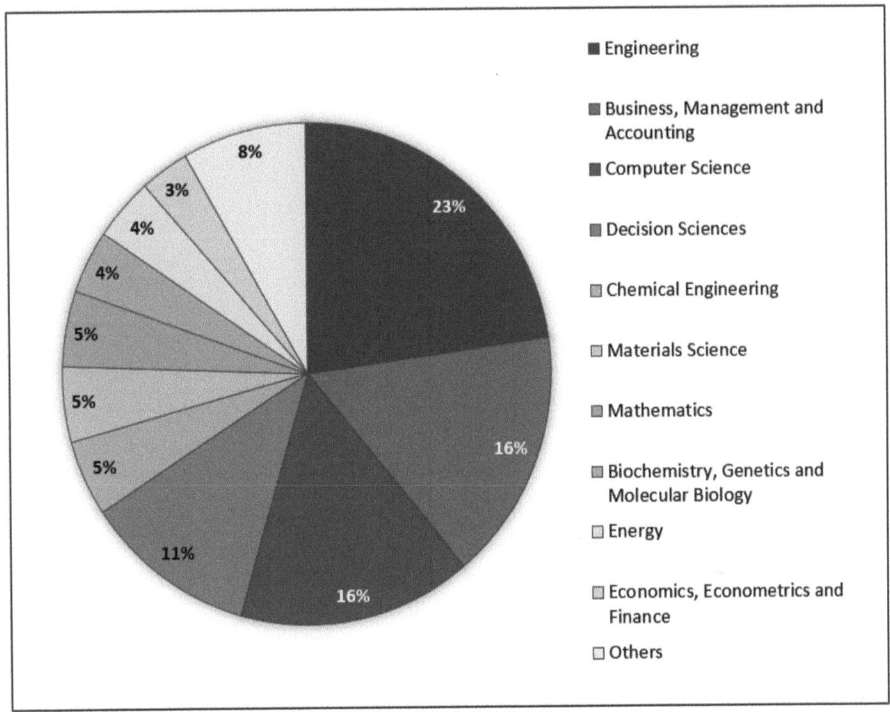

Fig. 1. Documents by Subject area.

AI is revolutionizing LM by enhancing several key aspects: of predictive maintenance, quality control, production planning, supply chain optimization, and human-robot collaboration. AI systems and tools forecast machinery failure, create optimal vehicle maintenance schedulers, and enable high-quality production with instant fault detection. They also summarize big data to reduce production line time and transport resources, resulting in prompt deliveries and normalized inventory management. Furthermore, AI makes it possible for a man and machine (collaborative robot) combination in manufacturing processes that results both in increased productivity and work safety. AI is an inseparable part of the LM improvement, and it results in operational effectiveness increase, waste prevention, and the development of competitive advantage.

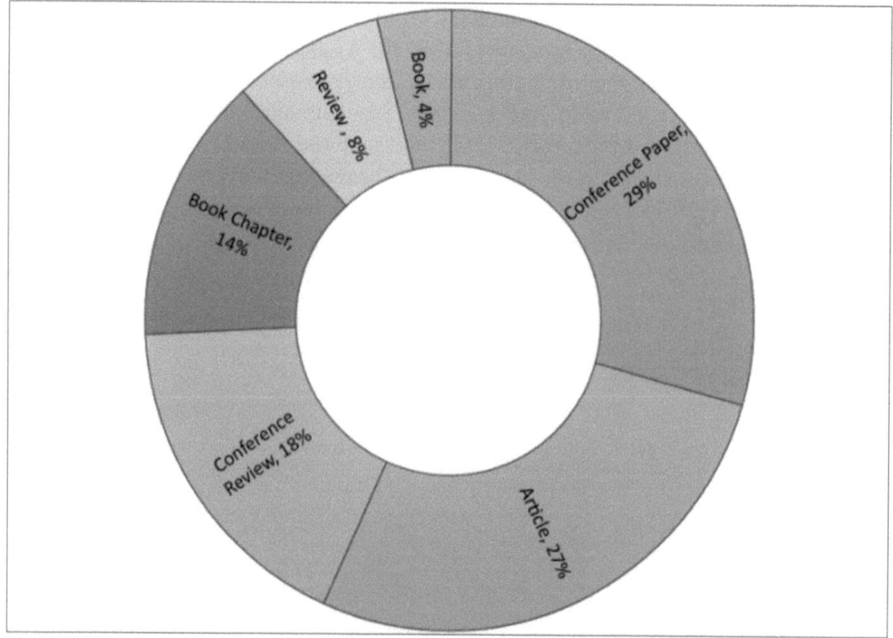

Fig. 2. Documents by Type of paper.

2 Lean Manufacturing Approaches

The concept of "continuous improvement and perfection in different areas and departments of the company"—as articulated by Masaaki Imai in 1986 [15]—was first introduced. Several examples of Lean tools for quality enhancement are listed in the Histogram, Control Charts [18], Pareto Chart [16], and Scatter Diagram [16]. The application of the 5S approach can help create a work atmosphere that is happier and more productive. It would be difficult to find a Japanese CEO who is not happy. Japanese people never disparage their company. Kaizen is a key factor in increasing service quality and customer satisfaction since it reduces waste and makes continuous, minor modifications. A more organized workplace directly leads to higher production and productivity. Workers may become highly committed to the company as a result of all of this. [19–21]. The most important of the "five S" tools [22], which includes "sorting," "standardizing the tools," "reorganizing the workplace," "checking the tools," as well as "cleanliness" is considered to be "sorting". Sort Out is the sorting procedure of SEIRI, which means SEIRI in Japanese. Strike out every superfluous part. Thus, we should conceive not to show the more important things. The mere task of shuffling through multiple work documents covers about 50% of an employee's working hours. Any of those items has its designated place. Distraction is prohibited there. Workplace Shine for SSI is our motto. Keeping my workstation neat and organized is relevant. Filing systems, as well as workstations, should be orderly. Files and workstations are tidied. Documents must be stored in the correct positions within the containers of their type. Uniformity of SEIKETSU is especially needed. A good workforce is every single business's top priority; thus, standards have to be set in every business. Employees should make self discipline-SHITSUKE principle- their code of conduct. Self-control is necessary. Avoid donning casual attire. Start by adhering to the protocols. Second, remember to bring your identity cards with you to work. It makes the organization feel respected and proud. Lean organizations develop confidence with perseverance and innovation to achieve long-term goals. This approach could encourage problem-solving and increase productivity. Since it's the only way to go forward, they embrace technology and advocate for change. The most important aspect of kaizen is that it is a way of life that supports all members of the business in approaching tasks and identifying opportunities for improvement in nearly every aspect of their work [23].

The foundational elements of lean management (LM) are technology JIT and Jidoka, which define a single method of work coordination intended to methodically apply workers' knowledge and enable the greatest use of the employees' talents. Other business functions, such as training personnel to take on various positions, giving them the re-option to regulate output criteria, and doing basic maintenance, are included in this system. When the computer detects that a piece is made error-free and takes into account productivity, pricing, distributing time, and variety of products, the Jidoka can stop the process. These ideas fall into a second category since they make use of employees' capabilities. The ideas that are finally included in Lean's configuration will make up the final category [24–27]. The culture of the company has to be one of continuous improvement as employees look for better ways to do tasks to foster the spirit of kaizen. To reduce storage space and inventory, lot size reduction and pull techniques like Kanban [28] are commonly used. You can determine how much time and energy to devote to your work by using scheduling techniques. A method for streamlining production procedures to minimize waste and faults has been dubbed "kaizen." Just-in-time, or JIT, is a production strategy that aims to reduce reaction times from suppliers and customers as well as systemic time.

LM is centered on getting rid of three different kinds of waste: overload (Muri), disparities or variation (Mura), and non-value-added activity (Muda) [29]. Identifying and eliminating these wastes leads to streamlined processes and improved efficiency. It integrates principles of Total Quality Management (TQM) to ensure that quality is built into processes from the outset [30]. TQM emphasizes continuous improvement, customer focus, and employee involvement in quality assurance processes.

All things considered, LM approaches aim to create a culture of waste reduction continuous improvement, and customer focus within manufacturing organizations. By implementing Lean principles and methodologies, organizations can enhance efficiency, quality, and competitiveness while delivering value to customers.

3 AI in Lean Manufacturing

AI stands for Artificial Intelligence and as the name says, it is smart software or a set of programmed processes created to undertake thinking ability-related tasks, independently. When it comes to sense of hearing and thinking systems like ours have a high level of artificial intelligence. The AI field has been developing to this day, with deep learning, machine learning, and natural language processing only being some of the approaches the development is driven by. Jointly AI and LM can be a way to speed up processes, decrease wasting, as well as be more productive. A combination of the extensive capabilities provided by AI technologies might reinforce and thereby improve both LM and the consequent benefits for the manufacturing sector. These are some important aspects of AI in LM: These are some important aspects of AI in LM:

Predictive maintenance systems powered by AI screen equipment data automatically without lagging to detect imminent equipment faults and hence avoid any downtime. Maintenance tasks may be scheduled in advance, which is a proactive step that will eventually lessen the time spent waiting for the machine to be repaired and will also consequently lower maintenance costs by recognizing patterns and deviations in machine data [31–33]. They find faults by using machine learning and computer vision technology that is present in AI-enabled quality control systems. AI machines can do the real-time reorganization of defective items by using the image and sensor data and therefore making the error and guaranteeing that the requirements of the product are met [34, 36]. Increase production schedules to process large volumes of data, AI technology like machine learning algorithms based on pre-historical production data and market trends can be examined. The development plan with an AI-enabled production management system will be innovative in utilizing variables like demand projections, resource availability, and production limits to improve the throughput and eradicate the waste of the production lines [26, 37–40]. Through analysis of data from several sources which encompasses (among other factors) forecast of demand, supplier performance, and inventory statistics, AI will generate the necessary data for supply chain optimization. Implementation of AI systems may expedite lead times, optimize inventories, and therefore, improve supply chain efficiency resulting in timely delivery of components and supplies [37, 41, 42]. For this purpose, AI-driven predictive analytics techniques undergo past production data analysis to identify the patterns and trends, which can be referenced to predict future output. Industrial processes predictable by predictive analytics are a competitive advantage and the basis for proactive decision-making and continuous process improvement due to demand prediction, spotting bottlenecks that cause production disruption, and allocating resources optimally [43–47]. AI advancement allows us to share the environment of machines and people at work. AI-integrated collaborative robots (Cobots) are outstanding examples of the latest innovations [48–50]. They can be deployed for such operations as manufacturing complicated products, where human and ranking is the solution. The AI is capable of handling such processing of the data which is generated from sensors, equipment, and production systems in real-time and thus helps in monitoring and optimizing the manufacturing processes. Machine learning is the way to optimize manufacturing by giving rise to production without defects and with zero waste because AI algorithms regularly work over and check changing process parameters [51–53]. Demand forecasting, which involves AI operations, is made by synthetic analysis of past sales figures, industry trends, and external factors. AI does manifest optimal inventory level, less spending on accessing surplus inventory, and prompt product availability owing to the precise demand forecast [54–57].

4   Conclusions and Future Directions

In conclusion, the strategic application of AI is not only an enabling element in the streamlining of LM approaches but it also has a critical role to play in ensuring operational excellence for organizations to thrive in an environment characterized by stiff competition and volatility. Through AI technology adoption and the creation of a culture of permanent improvement and innovation, organizations can find access to a new level of efficiency, quality, and flexibility, which will help them maintain competitiveness and growth in the modern manufacturing environment. The next are the main points for using AI within LM to get best results:

- Implementation relates to the act of incorporating AI technologies into the production environment.
- Successful implementation requires careful design and application strategies to integrate AI into the current ways of working and processes smoothly.
- AI needs to be solved by understanding the technical, organizational, and cultural issues to enable the integration and functioning of AI technologies.
- AI comprises harnessing the power of AI technologies for enhancing LM performance.
- It includes employing AI algorithms, predictive analytics, and machine learning functionalities to make production processes more productive, efficient, and waste-free.
- AI is also about using its real-time monitoring and decision-making for robust process improvements and innovations in manufacturing operations.
- Applying and utilizing AI in the context of LM demands being aware of lean principles and methods.
- LM represents the involvement of AI technologies together with LM practices like value stream mapping, lean production, and waste reduction.
- Lean principles include customer value, flow, pull, and perfection has to be supported by AI technology to get to the whole operational excellence.
- The actual aim of successfully using and applying AI within the scope of LM is achieving top performance that is characterized by efficiency, quality, productivity, and competitiveness.
- To achieve this, KPIs must be measured and evaluated with the help of AI technologies and the strategies must be evolved continuously to optimize the results.
- Finding the best outcomes demands that a culture of constant learning, adaptability, and improvement is created to maximize AI and manufacturing excellence.

There are several potential gaps and challenges associated with using AI in LM. These gaps can arise from various factors, including technological limitations, organizational barriers, and implementation challenges. Here are some potential gaps for using AI in LM:

- Data Quality and Availability:

  - The vital thing for the work of AI applications is that there should be available high-grade and thematic informational resources. In LM space, informational data should be received from the sources and they should be clean and precise (e. g., equipment, processes, sensors, and supply chain may be challenging.
  - The incomplete or inconsistent data sets sometimes may hinder the efficiency of AI algorithms and hence can lead to mediocre decision-making.

- Interoperability and Integration:

  - In most cases LM environments include a multitude of intricate systems and machinery from various vendors and often these do not necessarily work with AI technologies out of the box.
  - Achieving the integration of AI solutions with sister manufacturing systems, machinery, and software platforms might be quite a challenge, and may take a lot of resources to be solved in terms of system integration and data exchange protocols.

- Complexity of Manufacturing Processes:

  - For instance, let it be that these manufacturing processes are very lean but the piece and the process connections could be complex and dynamic, for example.
  - Building AI systems that will be able to resolve complex systems and also in decentration select the best response from available options is a really hard task.

- Change Management and Organizational Culture:

  - Implementing AI in LM requires organizational buy-in, cultural change, and employee training to ensure successful adoption and utilization.
  - Resistance to change, lack of understanding about AI technologies, and concerns about job displacement may hinder the integration of AI into LM practices.

- Ethical and Regulatory Considerations:

  - AI developments in manufacturing give rise to ethical issues related to data privacy, security, and algorithmic bias.
  - Regulatory compliance and adherence to data management standards, safety protocols, and quality assurances are vital but may prove intricate in LM settings augmented with AI.

- Skills Gap and Talent Shortage:

  - Developing and maintaining AI capabilities within LM organizations requires specialized skills in data science, machine learning, and AI engineering.
  - There may be a shortage of talent with the necessary expertise, and organizations may struggle to attract and retain skilled professionals in these areas.

- Cost and Return on Investment (ROI):

  - Utilization of AI technologies in LM incurs the burden of high initial costs in the possibility of procurement of hardware, software, training, and updating of the infrastructure.
  - Showing a distinct ROI and articulating the AI-infused enhancements in terms of time, cost and output is a particularly difficult thing to do.

A comprehensive strategy that combines technical, organizational, and human elements is needed to address such market gaps and hurdles. Companies need to scrutinize their AI readiness, design a clear AI plan, and ensure the availability of the corresponding resources and capacities to be able to include AI into LM processes effectively.

References

1. Deshmukh, S.G., Upadhye, N., Garg, S.: LM for sustainable development. Glob. Bus. Manag. Res. Int. J. **2**(1), 125 (2010)
2. Wada, K.: The Evolution of the Toyota Production System. Springer, Heidelberg (2020)
3. Gupta, S., Jain, S.K.: A literature review of LM. Int. J. Manag. Sci. Eng. Manag. **8**(4), 241–249 (2013)
4. Asmae, M., En-Nadi, A., Herrou, B.: The integration of LM in Supply Chain: principles, wastes and tools. In: 2020 IEEE 13th International Colloquium of Logistics and Supply Chain Management (LOGISTIQUA). IEEE (2020)
5. Jebbor, I., Benmamoun, Z., Hachimi, H., Raouf, Y., Haqqi, M., Akikiz, M.: Improvement of an assembly line in the automotive industry: a case study in wiring harness assembly line. In: Tang, L.-C. (ed.) Advances in Transdisciplinary Engineering, pp. 62–71. IOS Press, Amsterdam (2023)
6. Z. Benmamoun, H.H., Amine, A.: Inventory management optimization using lean six-sigma Case of Spare parts Moroccan company. In: Presented at the Proceedings of the International Conference on Industrial Engineering and Operations Management, pp. 1722–1730 (2017)
7. Jebbor, I., Benmamoun, Z., Hachimi, H.: Application of manufacturing cycle efficiency to increase production efficiency: application in automotive industry. In: 2024 4th International Conference on Innovative Research in Applied Science, Engineering and Technology (IRASET), pp. 1–6. IEEE (2024). https://doi.org/10.1109/IRASET60544.2024.10548564
8. Goshime, Y., Kitaw, D., Jilcha, K.: LM as a vehicle for improving productivity and customer satisfaction: a literature review on metals and engineering industries. Int. J. Lean Six Sigma **10**(2), 691–714 (2019)
9. Javaid, M., et al.: Artificial intelligence applications for industry 4.0: a literature-based study. J. Ind. Integrat. Manag. **7**(01), 83–111 (2022)

10. Hanif, A., et al.: A comprehensive survey of explainable artificial intelligence (XAI) methods: exploring transparency and interpretability. In: Zhang, F., Wang, H., Barhamgi, M., Chen, L., Zhou, R. (eds) Web Information Systems Engineering – WISE 2023. WISE 2023. Lecture Notes in Computer Science, vol. 14306. Springer, Singapore (2023). https://doi.org/10.1007/978-981-99-7254-8_71
11. Shaw, J., et al.: Artificial intelligence and the implementation challenge. J. Med. Internet Res. **21**(7), e13659 (2019)
12. Plathottam, S.J., et al.: A review of artificial intelligence applications in manufacturing operations. J. Adv. Manuf. Process. **5**, e10159 (2023)
13. Wang, X., et al.: Data-driven and Knowledge-based predictive maintenance method for industrial robots for the production stability of intelligent manufacturing. Expert Syst. Appl. **234**, 121136 (2023)
14. Pranckutė, R.: Web of Science (WoS) and scopus: the titans of bibliographic information in today's academic world. Publications **9**, 12 (2021)
15. Biadacz, R.: Application of kaizen and kaizen costing in SMEs. Prod. Eng. Arch. **30**(1), 17–35 (2024)
16. Wilkinson, L.: Revising the Pareto chart. Am. Stat. **60**(4), 332–334 (2006)
17. Throne, R.D., et al.: Scatter diagram analysis: a new technique for discriminating ventricular tachyarrhythmias. Pacing Clin. Electrophysiol. **17**(7), 1267–1275 (1994)
18. Amin, M.T., et al.: A data-driven Bayesian network learning method for process fault diagnosis. Process Saf. Environ. Protect. **150**, 110–122 (2021)
19. Panigrahi, S., et al.: LM practices for operational and business performance: A PLS-SEM modeling analysis. Int. J. Eng. Bus. Manag. **15**, 18479790221147864 (2023)
20. Benmamoun, Z., Fethallah, W., Bouazza, S., Abdo, A.A., Serrou, D., Benchekroun, H.: A framework for sustainability evaluation and improvement of radiology service. J. Clean. Prod. **401**, 136796 (2023). https://doi.org/10.1016/j.jclepro.2023.136796
21. Vargas, G.B., de Oliveira Gomes, J., Vallejos, R.V.: A framework for the prioritization of industry 4.0 and LM technologies based on network theory. J. Manuf. Technol. Manag. **35**(1), 95–118 (2024)
22. Maulidina, A., Wijanarka, B.S.: Analysis of work readiness based on soft skills, machining knowledge, and 5s work culture. Eur. J. Educ. Pedagogy **4**(4), 53–58 (2023)
23. Randhawa, J.S., Ahuja, I.S.: 5S – a quality improvement tool for sustainable performance: literature review and directions. Int. J. Qual. Reliab. Manag. **34**(3), 334–361 (2017). https://doi.org/10.1108/IJQRM-03-2015-0045
24. Ortecho, A., Miguel, E., Pazos, P.A.L., Carrión, S.S.O.: Implementation of LM to increase productivity in the manufacture of kitchen sinks in a metal-mechanical company (2023)
25. Zhao, Y., Damevski, K., Chen, H.: A systematic survey of just-in-time software defect prediction. ACM Comput. Surv. **55**(10), 1–35 (2023)
26. Hssayni, E., Joudar, N.E., Ettaouil, M.: Localization and reduction of redundancy in CNN using L1-sparsity induction. J Ambient Intell Human Comput **14**, 13715–13727 (2023). https://doi.org/10.1007/s12652-022-04025-2
27. Benmamoun, Z., Hachimi, H., Amine, A.: Comparison of inventory models for optimal working capital; case of aeronautics company. Int. J. Eng. **31**(4), 605–611 (2018)
28. Mayo-Alvarez, L., et al.: Innovation by integration of drum-buffer-rope (dbr) method with scrum-kanban and use of montecarlo simulation for maximizing throughput in agile project management. J. Open Innov. Technol. Mark. Complexity **10**, 100228 (2024)
29. Umar, R., Zaid, R., et al.: Development of framework integrating ergonomics in Lean's Muda, Muri, and Mura concepts. Prod. Plan. Control **35**, 1–9 (2023)
30. Oliveira, J.M., Gomes, C.F.: Excellence models beyond total quality management: inception, thematic structure and forthcoming paths. Total Qual. Manag. Bus. Excellence **35**(1–2), 137–169 (2024)

31. Cardoso, D., Ferreira, L.: Application of predictive maintenance concepts using artificial intelligence tools. Appl. Sci. **11**(1), 18 (2020)
32. Dalzochio, J., et al.: Machine learning and reasoning for predictive maintenance in Industry 4.0: current status and challenges. Comput. Ind. **123**, 103298 (2020)
33. Keleko, A.T., et al.: Artificial intelligence and real-time predictive maintenance in industry 40: a bibliometric analysis. AI Ethics **2**(4), 553–577 (2022)
34. Tulbure, A.-A., Tulbure, A.-A., Dulf, E.-H.: A review on modern defect detection models using DCNNs–Deep convolutional neural networks. J. Adv. Res. **35**, 33–48 (2022)
35. Paraskevoudis, K., Karayannis, P., Koumoulos, E.P.: Real-time 3D printing remote defect detection (stringing) with computer vision and artificial intelligence. Processes **8**(11), 1464 (2020)
36. Mahdou, N., Moutui, M.A.S., Zahir, Y.: On S-weakly prime ideals of commutative rings. Georgian Math. J. **29**(3), 397–405 (2022). https://doi.org/10.1515/gmj-2022-2141
37. Helo, P., Hao, Y.: Artificial intelligence in operations management and supply chain management: an exploratory case study. Prod. Plan. Control **33**(16), 1573–1590 (2022)
38. Wan, J., et al.: Artificial-intelligence-driven customized manufacturing factory: key technologies, applications, and challenges. Proc. IEEE **109**(4), 377–398 (2020)
39. Usuga Cadavid, J.P., Lamouri, S., Grabot, B., Pellerin, R., Fortin, A.: Machine learning applied in production planning and control: a state-of-the-art in the era of industry 4.0. J. Intell. Manuf. **31**(6), 1531–1558 (2020). https://doi.org/10.1007/s10845-019-01531-7
40. Hssayni, E.H., Joudar, N.E., Ettaouil, M.:. Convolutional Neural networks: architecture optimization and regularization. In: Motahhir, S., Bossoufi, B. (eds.) Digital Technologies and Applications. ICDTA 2022. Lecture Notes in Networks and Systems, vol. 454. Springer, Cham. https://doi.org/10.1007/978-3-031-01942-5_18
41. Pournader, M., et al.: Artificial intelligence applications in supply chain management. Int. J. Prod. Econ. **241**, 108250 (2021)
42. Nahr, J.G., Nozari, H., Sadeghi, M.E.: Green supply chain based on artificial intelligence of things (AIoT). Int. J. Innov. Manag. Econ. Social Sci. **1**(2), 56–63 (2021)
43. Kuvvetli, Y., et al.: A predictive analytics model for COVID-19 pandemic using artificial neural networks. Decis. Anal. J. **1**, 100007 (2021)
44. Chua, I.S., et al.: Artificial intelligence in oncology: path to implementation. Cancer Med. **10**(12), 4138–4149 (2021)
45. Dev, S., et al.: A predictive analytics approach for stroke prediction using machine learning and neural networks. Healthcare Anal. **2**, 100032 (2022)
46. Sghir, N., Adadi, A., Lahmer, M.: Recent advances in predictive learning analytics: a decade systematic review (2012–2022). Educ. Inf. Technol. **28**(7), 8299–8333 (2023)
47. Mousse, M.A., Almufti, S., García, D.S., Jebbor, I., Aljarbouh, A., Tsarev, R.: Application of fuzzy logic for evaluating student learning outcomes in E-learning. In: Silhavy, R., Silhavy, P. (eds.) Data Analytics in System Engineering. CoMeSySo 2023. Lecture Notes in Networks and Systems, vol. 935. Springer, Cham (2024). https://doi.org/10.1007/978-3-031-54820-8_15
48. Vemuri, N.V.N.: Enhancing human-robot collaboration in industry 4.0 with AI-driven HRI. Power Syst. Technol. **47**(4), 341–358 (2023)
49. Mukherjee, D., et al.: A survey of robot learning strategies for human-robot collaboration in industrial settings. Rob. Comput.-Integrat. Manuf. **73**, 10223 (2022)
50. Galin, R.R., Meshcheryakov, R.V.: Human-robot interaction efficiency and human-robot collaboration. In: Robotics: Industry 4.0 Issues & New Intelligent Control Paradigms, pp. 55–63. Springer, Cham (2020)
51. Kumari, S.: Interplay of AI-Driven maritime logistics: an in-depth research into port management, advanced operations automation, and CRM integration for optimized performance and efficiency. ESP J. Eng. Technol. Adv. **1**(1), 1–5 (2021)

52. Cai, W., et al.: Application of sensing techniques and artificial intelligence-based methods to laser welding real-time monitoring: a critical review of recent literature. J. Manuf. Syst. **57**, 1–18 (2020)
53. Kunduru, A.R.: Artificial intelligence usage in cloud application performance improvement. Central Asian J. Math. Theory Comput. Sci. **4**(8), 42–47 (2023)
54. Khan, M.A., et al.: Effective demand forecasting model using business intelligence empowered with machine learning. IEEE Access **8**, 116013–116023 (2020)
55. Feizabadi, J.: Machine learning demand forecasting and supply chain performance. Int. J. Log. Res. Appl. **25**(2), 119–142 (2022)
56. Riahi, Y., et al.: Artificial intelligence applications in the supply chain: a descriptive bibliometric analysis and future research directions. Expert Syst. Appl. **173**, 114702 (2021)
57. Benmamoun, Z., Fethallah, W., Ahlaqqach, M., Jebbor, I., Benmamoun, M., Elkhechafi, M.: Butterfly algorithm for sustainable lot size optimization. Sustainability **15**, 11761 (2023). https://doi.org/10.3390/su151511761

Road Roughness and Ranking Using Deep Learning

Muhammed Saffarini[1], Amjad Rattrout[2], Yousef-Awwad Daraghmi[1], and Muath Sabha[2]($\boxtimes$)

[1] Palestine Technical University-Kadoorie, Tulkarm P300, Palestine
{muhammed.saffarini,y.awwad}@ptuk.edu.ps
[2] Arab American University, PO Box 240, Jenin, Palestine
{amjad.rattrout,muath.sabha}@aaup.edu

Abstract. Road roughness poses challenges for the government due to its complexity and costly measurement tools. Our study proposes a novel, automated model to assess and rank road roughness without human interaction or expenses. By using images taken from a drone, our model shows the pattern of roads from the captured image using Gray-Level Co-occurrence Matrix (GLCM) features Homogeneity (H) and Energy (E) and then takes the spikes of its distributions then takes these spikes to get optimal value K for Kmean to segment the image, the result of first model enter to second model that makes that apply the Local Binary Pattern (LBP) Algorithm, To show the pattern more accurately, the excess elements in the image are deleted, and the remaining noise in the image is also deleted. After that, the image enters CNN to get the outcomes by classifying it into which category this roughness belongs. Achieving a high precision of 91. 94%, our model ensures a precise classification of road roughness categories, offering cost-effective and reliable solutions for road assessment.

Keywords: Computer Vision · Deep learning · image processing · Kmean Clustering

1 Introduction

The unevenness of the pavement surface denotes its deviation from the original design, exerting a direct influence on the ride's quality, the driver's comfort, and the general safety [9]. Maintaining roads in optimal condition is imperative to mitigate the risks of accidents, enhance driving comfort, and minimize operational expenditures. Consequently, continuous monitoring of road conditions is paramount to preempt potential issues and mitigate repair costs [4]. Identifying and addressing road damage early can significantly reduce government spending compared to rectifying extensively damaged roads, with early intervention proving to be approximately 20% more cost-effective [19]. Ongoing monitoring and

Supported by Arab American University.

evaluation of pavement conditions are essential to ensure road quality. However, manual monitoring poses challenges, necessitating automatic monitoring systems for detecting and evaluating road surface roughness. Given the complexity of manual monitoring, many studies are dedicated to automated detection and assessment of road conditions. Road roughness serves as a key indicator of overall road quality. However, manual monitoring is impractical, necessitating the development of automated road surface monitoring systems. Consequently, we have developed a novel model capable of automatically detecting road roughness and classifying its severity. Our model offers a cost-effective solution for road roughness monitoring. Drones have been employed to cover expansive regions of road networks, gaining popularity due to their affordability and ability to capture high-quality images. Utilizing drones allows for transmitting video feeds of roads to designated stations for storage and analysis. This advanced deep learning approach aims to capture road roughness at fine levels accurately. We categorized roads and recommended maintenance actions accordingly based on established criteria for ranking roads according to their roughness level [6]. So, this research introduces a new novel model to address limitations identified in prior studies in automatic classification road roughness. The key contributions of this paper include:

1. we Developed an innovative deep learning and computer vision model intended to automatically detect and classify road roughness.
2. Introduce a new model comprising two components: The initial model attempts to delineate street patterns within captured images using features of GLCM [14], such as homogeneity (H) and energy (E). Subsequently, it identifies spikes within their distributions to derive an optimal value K for k-means clustering, thus facilitating image segmentation to show the image pattern and reduce the noise inside it.
3. The output of the first model is fed into the second model, which employs the LBP model to represent patterns in a clearer manner.
4. Based on the determined roughness category, the quality of the respective road will be assessed.

2 Literature Review

The unevenness of the road surfaces, measured by the International Roughness Index (IRI) [18], can negatively affect the quality of the ride, the comfort of the driver, and the safety [10]. Maintaining roads in good condition is crucial for economic development. Therefore, it is essential to continuously monitor road conditions to identify and address problems early on before they become more expensive to repair [4]. Early intervention can save governments significant costs in the long run. Various studies have demonstrated the feasibility of measuring road roughness using smartphone accelerometers, as referenced in [2,16,17] [1,3,24]. For instance, [17] conducted research estimating road roughness by analyzing data collected from moving vehicles using specialized software (CNN). Regardless of vehicle type or speed, researchers developed a robust Convolutional

Neural Network (CNN) model capable of estimating the International Roughness Index (IRI) for roads. This model was trained using a vast dataset generated from half-car simulations, comprising data from 31 km of roads with diverse IRI values and a range of driving speed profiles, vehicle accelerations, and rotational velocities. Another study [1] investigated the relationship between vehicle speed and road roughness. Utilizing vibration data collected across different speeds (20–100 km/h), researchers estimated the International Roughness Index (IRI) using an Android application named Roadroid Pro. Their focus was particularly on data collected between 60 and 80 km/h. Their findings highlight the significant influence of road roughness on vehicle speed, particularly during peak traffic periods. Various methods for detecting and categorizing pavement roughness utilize static images captured by cameras or obtained from predetermined datasets as referenced in [5, 7–9, 12, 15, 20, 22, 23, 25]. An innovative vision-based approach for identifying rough roads was introduced in [25], proposing two methodologies to quantitatively estimate concrete surface roughness from images. The initial method entails a digital image processing technique to distinguish coarse aggregate from cement paste. It relies on color differences, recognizing that the aggregate typically appears lighter than the cement. This color variance is exploited to gauge surface roughness, where increased course aggregate areas correspond to heightened roughness. The process involves image preparation, enhancement, conversion to gray scale, and subsequent binarization to produce black-and-white representations, with white denoting aggregate and black representing cement. The ratio of aggregate area to total surface area serves as an indicator of surface roughness. Another research is [21], which employs GLCM and CNN to extract texture patterns for classification purposes. In another approach detailed in [13], pavement videos are captured using a rear-mounted vehicle camera. Frames with their corresponding geospatial data are extracted from these recordings, converted to grayscale, and subjected to enhancement techniques to eliminate blur, shadows, and color inconsistencies. Subsequently, the entropy value of each image is computed. Based on this entropy value, the images are classified as depicting healthy or distressed pavement, with the distress indicated by an entropy value below a predetermined threshold. Finally, a heatmap highlighting distressed pavement regions is generated. Pavement surface videos feature a camera mounted at the vehicle's rear, yielding 21,600 frames, of which 8,423 depict distressed pavements and 13,177 depict healthy ones. Following pre-processing steps and entropy value computation, pavements are classified as healthy or distressed, achieving accuracy, precision, recall, and an F1 score of 89.2%, 86.6%, 85.6%, and 86.1%, respectively.

3   Methodology

In this research, road roughness is calculated using drone images. These images are used to extract surface texture, which is then classified using deep learning models and computer vision algorithms. The developed model is based on the hybrid principle. Several stages examine different aspects of the problem and then collaborate in decision-making. The model consists of two stages, where the two stages are combined to show excellent results. Each stage processes the given images differently to clearly show the pattern in the image. So, in the first stage, the model works to find the best value of K using GLCM features to apply the k-mean clustering on the given image to show the pattern and delete all noise, and then we send the results from this stage to the second stage, which also applies the LBP algorithm to try to delete the remaining noise and also work on showing the pattern in its own way. Clearly, the goal is to increase accuracy in the road roughness classification process.

3.1   Preprocessing

The videos are captured in the .mp4 format at a resolution of 4k, with a frame rate of 60 frames per second. To construct the image dataset, two frames are randomly selected from the recorded video footage. This process is repeated twice: once during midday and once in the late afternoon, encompassing various lighting conditions throughout the day.

Gamma correction is employed to normalize the lighting conditions across the images captured throughout the day. An adjustment with a gamma value of 0.8 is applied to images taken during midday, representing optimal lighting conditions. Conversely, images captured in the late afternoon are adjusted with a gamma value of 1.5. This ensures consistency in lighting across the dataset, as depicted in the Fig. 1, left and right..

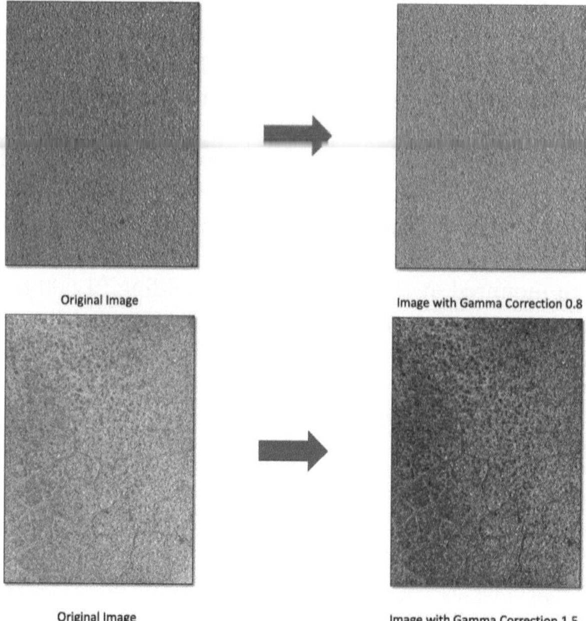

Fig. 1. on left: Original Image Vs. Image with Gamma Correction 0.8 and on right: Original Image Vs. Image with Gamma Correction 1.5

3.2   Our Model

The first stage studies image distributions using GLCM Features like energy and homogeneity and determines the number of spikes in these distributions this spike These spikes mean that there is a certain concentration of the data inside the image; that is, it works to determine the distinctive pattern inside the image. This value is then reduced and used as a k value in the k-means algorithm; then, the resulting images are entered into the next stage to show the pattern better using the LBP technique. This enhances the prediction accuracy of the classification and is used to train the CNN model, as shown in Fig. 2.

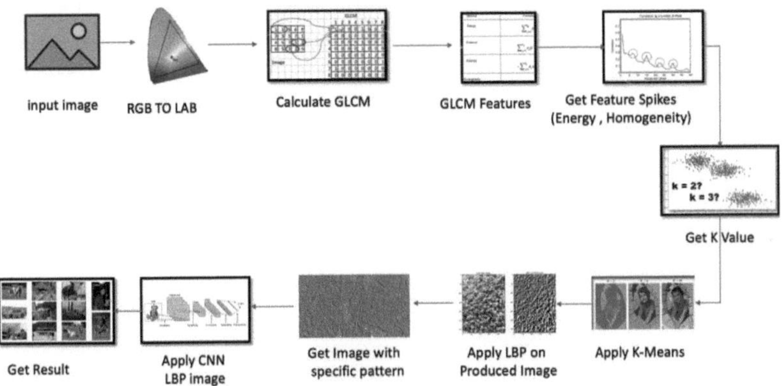

Fig. 2. Our Model For Neural Network

Determining the optimal value of K is a fundamental aspect of K-means clustering, which is crucial for achieving satisfactory results. However, selecting the appropriate K value can be challenging, as it relies on factors such as the distribution of data points, the desired level of clustering resolution, and user preferences. Increasing K without constraint decreases clustering error, potentially resulting in each data point forming its own cluster, leading to minimal error. Hence, The optimal K achieves a balance by efficiently compressing data into a single cluster while maximizing accuracy by assigning each data point to its particular cluster. Our research builds upon previous studies by combining K-means with GLCM. We leverage GLCM features derived from the image data, extracting spikes from the feature distribution. Subsequently, we determine the number of spikes in the distribution, which is the basis for determining the number of clusters used in the K-means clustering algorithm for data segmentation. As illustrated in Fig. 2, our algorithm commences by converting the image from the RGB color space to the LAB color space. The LAB color space consists of three dimensions: L, a, and b, representing lightness and color variations. Each color is uniquely identified based on these parameters, facilitating color recognition by the computer. Notably, the lightness dimension distinguishes between black and gray shades, while the a and b dimensions capture multicolored variations relative to their respective hues. After converting the image to the Lab color space, we treat each dimension individually to calculate the GLCM for all layers.

As shown in Fig. 3, the co-occurrence matrix, also referred to as a co-occurrence distribution, represents the occurrence of data co-occurring on a specific offset within the image. It takes the angular spatial and length relationships within a defined image region, thereby generating the matrix. Significantly, this process includes creating matrices for the image's Lightness layer (gray-scale image) and each layer inside the image. Consequently, separate matrices are generated for the L, a, and b layers. Subsequently, normalization is applied to the GLCM matrices to facilitate the computation of image features. Following normalization, features are calculated for the matrices. The return outputs are Homogeneity, Energy, Contrast, and Correlation. In this case, the focus is on the first two features, Homogeneity and Energy, as they both assess the uniformity of data distribution inside the image. the energy calculated by the equation

$$Energy = \sum P_{ij}{}^2$$

where $P_{i,j}$ It represents an element of the normalized GLCM.

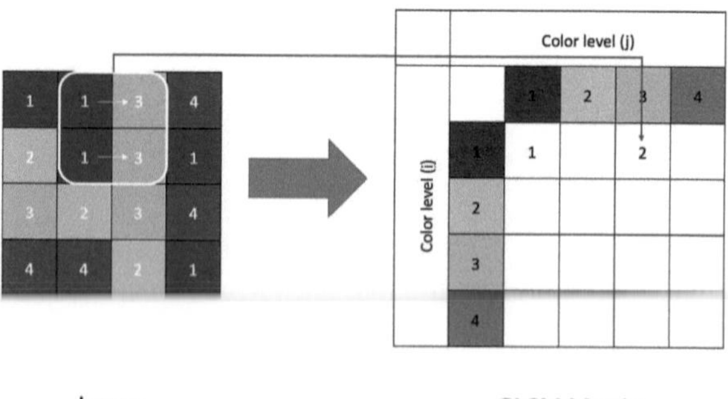

Fig. 3. GLCM for the one layer in Lab.

The homogeneity feature is then computed using the following equation:

$$Homogeneity = \sum \frac{P_{ij}}{(1 + (i - j)^2))}$$

Then, compute these features for every layer of Lab color space separately, and then compute the mean of these features (Homogeneity, Energy) for all layers.

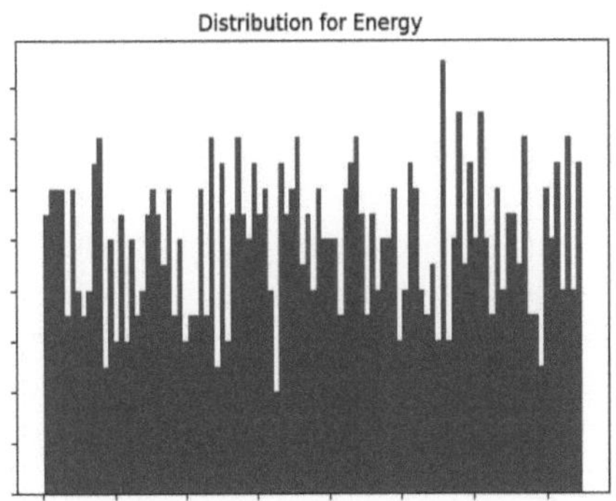
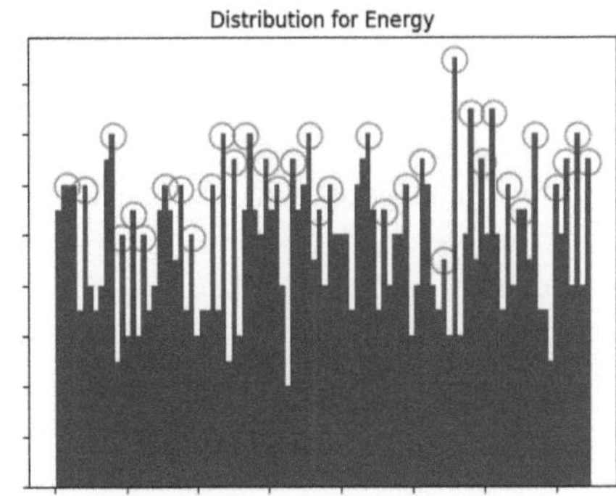

a. The distribution of Energy Feature.   b. Detected spikes in Energy distribution.

Fig. 4. The histogram of Energy Feature. and Detected spikes in Energy distribution

As shown in Fig. 4.a, the distribution and concentration of the items in GLCM This indicates the level of uniformity (Energy) present inside the image.

After computing the homogeneity and energy, the number of spikes is determined for the features.

Figure 4 b illustrates the spikes observed in the Energy feature, depicting the concentration of data in certain positions and its dispersion across others following the spike calculation for both homogeneity and energy features. If K is determined as the mean of homogeneity and energy values, as $K = \frac{E+H}{2}$, the resulting K values take off to be excessively large and produce unsatisfactory outcomes. Consequently, we use the FreeDman-Diaconis rule [11] to reduce these values. The FreeDman-Diaconis equation, known for its robustness and effectiveness, has proven invaluable in optimizing K values.

FreeDman-Diaconis uses this equ.

$$K = 2 \times \frac{IQR}{\sqrt[3]{N}}$$
$$IQR = Q2 - Q1$$

Where IQR is the Inter-quartile of the values inside the vector, n is the count of values, Q1 is the first quartile of the values inside the vector and Q3 is the third quartile of the values inside the vector.

The Freedman-Diaconis equation for homogeneity and Energy is computed from the IQR as equation 3.2, 3.2.

$$IQR_H = Q3_H - Q1_H$$
$$K_H = 2 \times \frac{IQR_H}{\sqrt[3]{N_H}}$$

$$IQR_E = Q3_E - Q1_E$$
$$K_E = 2 \times \frac{IQR_E}{\sqrt[3]{N_E}}$$

We then compute the final value of K by computing the mean between the value of the Freedman-Diaconis equation for homogeneity and the value of the Freedman-Diaconis equation for energy values.

$$K = \frac{K_E + K_H}{2}$$

where K_H and K_E and are the values after applying the Freedman- Diaconis equation for homogeneity and Energy values

K represents the degree of variation between different data points within an image, reflecting the spatial distribution of objects. The image exposed segmentation using the K-means clustering algorithm, with the previously determined value of K. Subsequently, the segmented results are subjected to an LBP Technique to effectively highlight patterns. The Local Binary Pattern (LBP) algorithm is applied to these images. as shown in Fig. 5; then the CNN model is trained. The LBP algorithm takes a window of a certain size (3×3, for example) and takes the center pixel as a threshold. If the neighboring pixel has a larger value, it is replaced with 0, and if it is lower, it is replaced with 1. For example, a window is taken from the picture shown in Fig. 5. In this window,

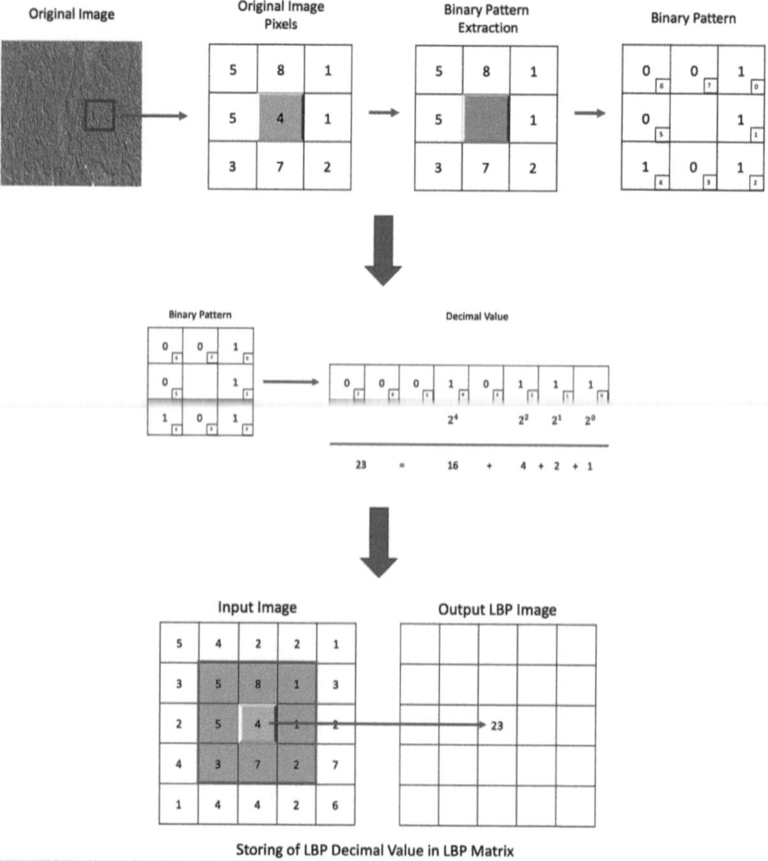

Fig. 5. LBP Technique in our neural network

the center pixels have a value of 4. This value is compared with the value of each neighboring pixel. The pixels with values of 5,7 and 8 are replaced with 0. While the pixels with values of 1,2 and 3 are replaced with 1. Then, the resulting values are converted into binary 8-bit numbers by ordering the pixels starting from the top middle pixel and moving counterclockwise. Then this number is converted into a decimal number.. as shown in Fig. 5. Then the 3×3 window is replaced by this decimal number as shown in Fig. 5.

This window is then moved across the image to produce a clearer image. Since the LBP algorithm is a powerful texture descriptor for images that identifies neighboring pixels based on the current pixel value. This method reduces the number of pixels inside the image so that only the important pattern remains. All unimportant details and unnecessary details that Kmean did not remove at this stage have been removed using LBP. This will showcase the patterns more clearly and remove any remaining noise in the image. Finally, these images are used to train the CNN model to classify the road roughness.

4   Experiments and Result

We chose Google's platform, Colab, to leverage its powerful servers and resources to develop and implement our model. Our Collab instance is equipped with 12.7 GB of RAM and 107 GB of storage and utilizes a T4 GPU for processing. This setting has proven effective in handling the challenges of large image sizes and efficient high-resolution image processing.

4.1   Dataset

In this study, we have created a new data set focusing on the roads of Tulkarm City in Palestine, which exhibit a variety of conditions ranging from excellent to very poor. The video is captured using DJI Mavic Air 2 drones, featuring a high resolution of 3840×2160 (4K). A total of 1500 videos, with a combined runtime of 1500, are recorded, effectively covering a road length spanning 150 km. From the footage, a large total of 15,326 images are extracted, all maintaining the identical resolution as shown in Figs. 6, 7, 8. These images subsequently are entered to the pre-processing stage to improve lighting conditions and eliminate any noise appearing in the image. This enhancement process requires utilizing gamma correlation to adjust lighting and applying blur filters to reduce noise levels effectively.

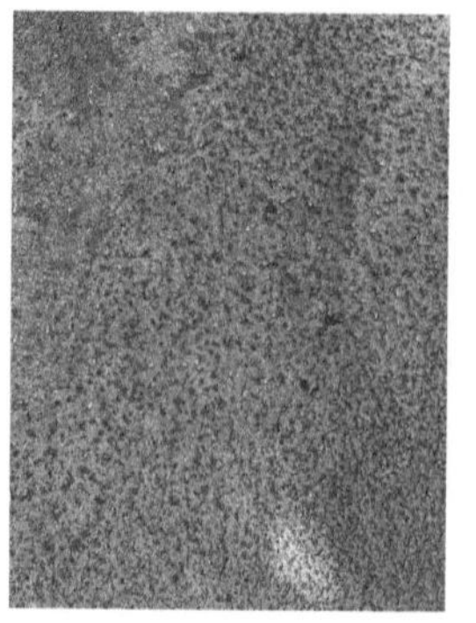

Fig. 6. first degree of roughness.

Fig. 7. fourth degree of roughness.

Fig. 8. sixth degree of roughness.

4.2   Result of Our Model

Presenting the results of the complete Neural Network Model, shown in Fig. 2, the neural network operates in two stages. Initially, it identifies specific features of the GLCM and utilizes their distribution to establish the value of K. This value is then utilized in K-means clustering to detect the pattern of the image and remove unnecessary details., as shown in Fig. 9.

The second is applying LBP Technique to make the pattern show more and to remove the remaining noises inside the image to make the result more precise. Initially, we computed the outcomes for the (VGG16) Neural Network without employing the suggested methodology.

Fig. 9. The roads with different roughness after applying the kmean using FreeDman-Diaconis equation

Table 1. Result of Default VGG16 Model

Class	Accuracy	Precision	Recall	F1-score
R1	80.96%	0.809	0.80019	0.80457
R2	80.30%	0.789	0.81019	0.799454
R3	78.88%	0.819	0.81019	0.814571
R4	78.47%	0.789	0.81019	0.799454
R5	80.16%	0.7975	0.80869	0.803056
R6	80.96%	0.786	0.80319	0.794502
AVG	79.96%	79.83%	80.71%	80.26%

The outcomes of the default VGG16 model without modification are presented in Table 1. Subsequently, we applied our supposed method to display the classification results for the 6 classes, representing different degrees of roughness as present in [6]. Accuracy, Precision, and Recall were computed individually for each class, with the f-score also calculated for them. as shown in the following Table 2:

Table 2. Result of our whole mode

Class	Accuracy	Precision	Recall	F1-score
R1	91.87%	0.92	0.931	0.92546731
R2	90.90%	0.93	0.913	0.9214216
R3	89.85%	0.902	0.921	0.91140099
R4	89.98%	0.894	0.897	0.89549749
R5	90.60%	0.94	0.92	0.92989247
R6	92.87%	0.95	0.93	0.93989362
AVG	91.01%	92.27%	91.87%	92.06%

As shown in the previous Table 2, The highest accuracy was observed for class No. 6, representing the roughest roads, achieving an accuracy of 92.87%. Conversely, the least accurate was class No. 3, with a value of 89.85%, which is almost 90%, indicating a third-degree roughness according to the standard presented in [6]. From the data presented in Table 2, it is clear that the results exceed those of the default model. This suggests that the neural network has successfully fulfilled its objectives. By utilizing k-means to present features and patterns within the images, determining the optimal value for K through the distribution of GLCM features, and employing the LBP algorithm to eliminate remaining noise and clarify the displayed pattern, a significant enhancement in accuracy results was achieved. This combination of the two methods yielded excellent results compared to the default model, preserving the network's weight change shape.

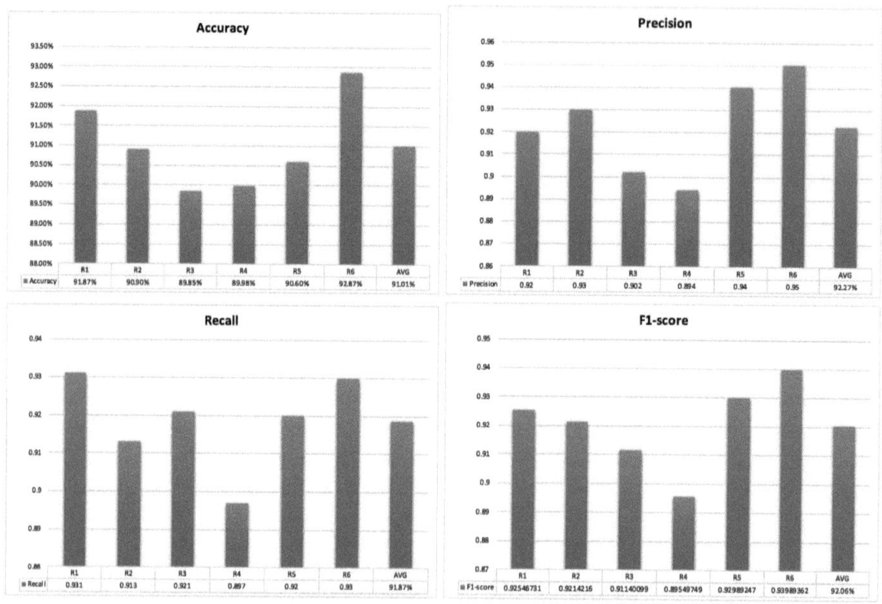

Fig. 10. Result of Metrics of Our Whole Model

As shown in the Fig. 10 accuracy chart, Our whole model has demonstrated impressive performance in classifying the degree of roughness, achieving accuracy levels of nearly 90% or higher across all classes. Significantly, the classification of the roughest class, Class No. 6, Achieved an exceptional accuracy of 92.87%. Conversely, the class indicates moderate roughness. Class No. 3 shows the lowest accuracy at 89.85 As shown in the Fig. 10-a precision chart, Our whole model has demonstrated impressive performance in retrieving the degree of roughness, achieving precision levels of nearly 90% or higher across all classes. Significantly, retrieving the roughest class, Class No. 6, Achieved an exceptional accuracy of 95%. Conversely, the class indicates moderate roughness, Class No. 4, showing the lowest accuracy at 89.4%.

As shown in the Fig. 10-a recall chart, Our whole model has demonstrated impressive performance in getting recall in relevant the degree of roughness, achieving recall levels of nearly 90% or higher across all classes. Significantly, the recall in relevance of the lowest rough class, specified as Class No. 1, Achieved an exceptional accuracy of 93.1%. Conversely, the class indicates moderate roughness, Class No. 4, with the lowest accuracy at 89.7%.

As shown in the Fig. 10-a f1-score chart, Our whole model has demonstrated impressive performance in F1-Score to get the degree of roughness, achieving F1-Score levels of nearly 90% or higher across all classes. Significantly, the F1-Score classification of the roughness class, specified as Class No. 6, achieved an exceptional accuracy of 93.9%. Conversely, the class indicates moderate roughness, Class No. 4, with the lowest accuracy at 89.54%.

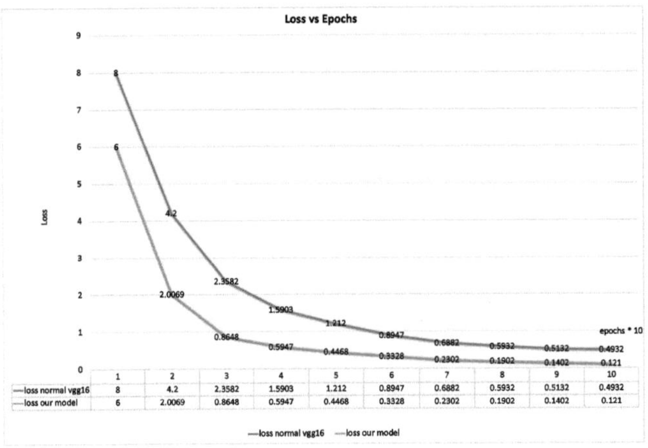

Fig. 11. epoch vs. Loss between Our model on VGG16 & VGG16 without our modification

As shown in Fig. 11, In our model, there's a distinct deviation from the default model as it achieves stability in terms of loss. This illustrates the effectiveness of our model and the rapid pace at which it approaches stability (Table 3).

Table 3. Comparison of All Metrics result between Our Model, Our Model Without LBP and Default CNN and

Model Result	Accuracy	Precision	Recall	F1-Score
Our Whole Model	91.01%	92.27%	91.87%	92.06%
Our Model Without LBP	86.29%	87.76%	86.85%	88.61%
Default CNN	79.96%	79.83%	80.71%	80.26%

As shown in the graph of Fig. 12, Upon comparing our model with both the default and our approach without LBP, it became evident that our model outperformed the default model across all four criteria, resulting in the best overall outcome.

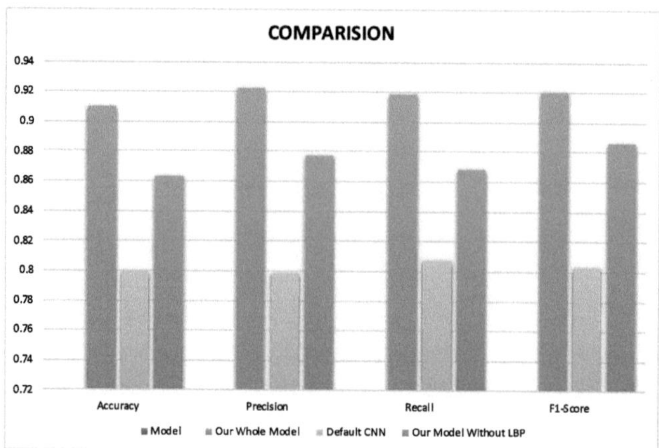

Fig. 12. Chart Comparison of All Results Between Our Model, Default CNN, and Our Model Without LBP

5 Conclousion

In our study, we develop an algorithm using drone images to classify road roughness. A critical aspect of this algorithm is determining the optimal K for K-means clustering, achieved through GLCM analysis. We extract Homogeneity and Energy features from GLCM to measure pixel pair occurrences, identifying spikes to assign a K-value. Segmentation using K-means clustering follows using the computed K. Before sending the images to CNN for classification, the results from the first stage enter LBP processing to reduce noise and enhance pattern visibility. The algorithm demonstrates an accuracy of 91.94% In future work, we can apply our model to a forest of neural networks to study the roads from multiple views and obtain more accurate values.

References

1. Abeygunawardhana, C., Sandamal, R., Pasindu, H.: In: Identification of the impact on road roughness on speed patterns for different roadway segments, pp. 425–430. IEEE (2020)
2. Alatoom, Y.I., Al-Suleiman, T.I.: Development of pavement roughness models using Artificial Neural Network (ANN). Int. J. Pavement Eng. **23**(13), 4622–4637 (2022)
3. Cabral, F.S., Pinto, M., Mouzinho, F.A., Fukai, H., Tamura, S.: An automatic survey system for paved and unpaved road classification and road anomaly detection using smartphone sensor. In: IEEE International Conference on Service Operations and Logistics, and Informatics (SOLI), pp. 65–70. IEEE (2018)
4. Cao, M.T., Tran, Q.V., Nguyen, N.M., Chang, K.T.: Survey on performance of deep learning models for detecting road damages using multiple dashcam image resources. Adv. Eng. Inform. **46**, 101182 (2020)

5. Cech, J., et al.: Self-supervised learning of camera-based drivable surface roughness. In: IEEE Intelligent Vehicles Symposium (IV), pp. 1319–1325. IEEE (2021)

6. Daraghmi, Y.A., Wu, T.H., İk, T.U.: Crowdsourcing-based road surface evaluation and indexing. IEEE Trans. Intell. Transp. Syst. **23**(5), 4164–4175 (2020)

7. Dong, X., Lou, P., Yan, J., Hu, J.: A detection method for pavement roughness with binocular vision. In: Eleventh International Conference on Graphics and Image Processing (ICGIP 2019), vol. 11373, pp. 613–619. SPIE (2020)

8. Du, Y.: Pavement distress detection and classification based on yolo network. Int. J. Pavement Eng. **22**(13), 1659–1672 (2021)

9. Dung, C.V., et al.: Autonomous concrete crack detection using deep fully convolutional neural network. Autom. Constr. **99**, 52–58 (2019)

10. Muniz de Farias, M., de Souza, R.O.: Correlations and analyses of longitudinal roughness indices. Road Mater. Pavement Des. **10**(2), 399–415 (2009)

11. Freedman, D., Diaconis, P.: On the histogram as a density estimator: L2 theory. Zeitschrift für Wahrscheinlichkeitstheorie und verwandte Gebiete **57**(4), 453–476 (1981)

12. Gopalakrishnan, K., Khaitan, S.K., Choudhary, A., Agrawal, A.: Deep convolutional neural networks with transfer learning for computer vision-based data-driven pavement distress detection. Constr. Build. Mater. **157**, 322–330 (2017)

13. Hadjidemetriou, G.M., Christodoulou, S.E.: Vision-and entropy-based detection of distressed areas for integrated pavement condition assessment. J. Comput. Civ. Eng. **33**(3), 04019020 (2019)

14. Haralick, R.M., Shanmugam, K., Dinstein, I.: Textural features for image classification. IEEE Trans. Syst. Man Cybern. **6**, 610–621 (1973)

15. Ishtiak, T., Ahmed, S., Anila, M.H., Farah, T.: A convolutional neural network approach for road anomalies detection in Bangladesh with image thresholding. In: Third World Conference on Smart Trends in Systems Security and Sustainablity (WorldS4), pp. 376–382. IEEE (2019)

16. Janani, L., Sunitha, V., Mathew, S.: Influence of surface distresses on smartphone-based pavement roughness evaluation. Int. J. Pavement Eng. **22**(13), 1637–1650 (2021)

17. Jeong, J.H., Jo, H., Ditzler, G.: Convolutional neural networks for pavement roughness assessment using calibration-free vehicle dynamics. Computer-Aided Civil Infrastruct. Eng. **35**(11), 1209–1229 (2020)

18. Lin, J.D., Yau, J.T., Hsiao, L.H.: Correlation analysis between international roughness index (IRI) and pavement distress by neural network. In: 82nd Annual Meeting of the Transportation Research Board, vol. 12, pp. 1–21 (2003)

19. Liu, Q., Sun, L., Kornhauser, A., Sun, J., Sangwa, N.: Road roughness acquisition and classification using improved restricted Boltzmann machine deep learning algorithm. Sens. Rev. **39**(6), 733–742 (2019)

20. Mandal, V., Uong, L., Adu-Gyamfi, Y.: Automated road crack detection using deep convolutional neural networks. In: 2018 IEEE International Conference on Big Data (Big Data), pp. 5212–5215. IEEE (2018)

21. Sabha, M., Saffarini, M.: Selecting optimal k for k-means in image segmentation using GLCM. Multimedia Tools Appl., 1–17 (2023)

22. Sarker, M., Hadigheh, S., Dias-da Costa, D.: Stereoscopic modelling and monitoring of roughness in concrete pavements. In: ACMSM25: Proceedings of the 25th Australasian Conference on Mechanics of Structures and Materials, pp. 635–644. Springer (2020)

23. Tan, Y., Li, Y.: UAV photogrammetry-based 3d road distress detection. ISPRS Int. J. Geo Inf. **8**(9), 409 (2019)

24. Thilak, R., et al.: Evaluation of pavement roughness using smartphones. In: IEEE International Conference on Computation System and Information Technology for Sustainable Solutions (CSITSS), pp. 1–7. IEEE (2021)
25. Valikhani, A., Jaberi Jahromi, A., Pouyanfar, S., Mantawy, I.M., Azizinamini, A.: Machine learning and image processing approaches for estimating concrete surface roughness using basic cameras. Comput. Aided Civil Infrastruct. Eng. **36**(2), 213–226 (2021)

Unveiling the Future of Drug Discovery: Revolutionizing LogS Prediction with Deep Learning FNNs

Imane Aitouhanni[✉] and Amine Berqia

Mohammed V University, ENSIAS, SSLAB, Rabat, Morocco
imane.aitouhanni@gmail.com

Abstract. In the realm of drug discovery, accurately predicting LogS – a crucial property influencing a drug's behavior within the body – is paramount. Traditional methods often struggle to capture the complex relationships in chemical data. This study explores the use of deep learning, specifically Feedforward Neural Networks (FNN), for LogS prediction. Through meticulous data preparation and model optimization, our FNN model achieved exceptional performance, with an R-squared (R2) score of 0.994 and a Mean Squared Error (MSE) of 0.024. These results highlight the transformative potential of deep learning techniques in drug discovery, offering unprecedented accuracy and efficiency. By accurately predicting LogS values, researchers can streamline the drug design process, ultimately leading to the development of safer and more effective therapeutics. Our findings underscore the importance of harnessing cutting-edge technologies to address the complex challenges facing modern medicine, heralding a new era of innovation and discovery.

Keywords: Drug Discovery · LogS Prediction · Deep Learning FNNs

1 Introduction

In the quest for safer and more effective therapeutics, the accurate prediction of LogS – a fundamental property influencing a drug's behavior within the body – stands as a critical milestone in drug discovery. Traditional methods, albeit valuable, often fall short in capturing the intricate relationships inherent in chemical data. Leveraging the power of deep learning, specifically Feedforward Neural Networks (FNN), presents a paradigm shift in LogS prediction, promising unparalleled accuracy and efficiency [1, 2].

This study unveils the transformative potential of deep learning FNNs in drug discovery by demonstrating their prowess in LogS prediction. Through meticulous data preparation and feature engineering, coupled with rigorous model training and optimization, our FNN model achieved remarkable results. With an impressive R-squared (R2) score of 0.9944591993201766 and a Mean Squared Error (MSE) of 0.023987485336940364, our findings underscore the effectiveness of deep learning techniques in capturing complex relationships within chemical data [3, 4].

H. Badir et al. (Eds.): INTIS 2024, CCIS 2645, pp. 31–41, 2026.
https://doi.org/10.1007/978-3-032-14964-0_3

The implications of our results extend far beyond the realm of drug discovery. By accurately predicting LogS values, researchers can streamline the drug design process, reducing the time and resources required for experimental validation. Moreover, our findings pave the way for the development of more targeted and efficacious therapies, ultimately improving patient outcomes and advancing healthcare as a whole.

This study sheds light on the transformative potential of deep learning FNNs in LogS prediction, marking a significant advancement in computational drug discovery. Our results underscore the importance of harnessing cutting-edge technologies to address the complex challenges facing modern medicine, heralding a new era of innovation and discovery.

The structure of this paper is organized as follows to provide a comprehensive understanding of our research approach and findings. In the Background Study section, we define key terms and concepts relevant to our study, including deep learning, Feedforward Neural Networks (FNN), and LogS prediction in the context of drug discovery. The Related Work section reviews existing literature on LogS prediction methodologies, highlighting the advancements and limitations of traditional and contemporary approaches. In the Methodology section, we detail our data preparation, feature engineering, and the construction of our FNN model. The Results & Discussion section presents our experimental findings, including performance metrics and comparative analysis with existing models, followed by an interpretation of the results. Finally, the Conclusion & Future Work section summarizes our key findings, discusses their implications, and outlines potential directions for future research. The paper concludes with a comprehensive list of References that underpin our study and provide additional context for interested readers.

2 Background Study

2.1 Introduction to Drug Discovery

Drug discovery is a multifaceted process aimed at identifying and developing new pharmaceutical compounds to treat diseases. It encompasses various stages, including target identification, compound screening, lead optimization, and preclinical and clinical trials. The ultimate goal of drug discovery is to deliver safe and effective medications to patients, addressing unmet medical needs and improving healthcare outcomes [5, 6].

2.2 Understanding LogS in Pharmacokinetics

LogS, or the logarithm of the octanol-water partition coefficient, is a critical parameter in pharmacokinetics that measures a compound's hydrophobicity. It represents the ratio of a compound's concentration in octanol (a lipophilic solvent) to its concentration in water (a hydrophilic solvent). LogS influences a drug's solubility, absorption, distribution, metabolism, and excretion (ADME), thereby playing a crucial role in its bioavailability and pharmacological activity [7, 8].

2.3 Introduction to Deep Learning and FNNs

Deep learning is a subset of machine learning that employs artificial neural networks with multiple layers to learn hierarchical representations of data. Feedforward Neural Networks (FNNs), also known as multilayer perceptrons, are the foundational architecture of deep learning. They consist of input, hidden, and output layers of neurons, with information flowing in one direction – forward – without cycles. FNNs are capable of learning complex patterns in data and are commonly used for regression and classification tasks.

2.4 Exploring the Transformative Potential of Deep Learning in Drug Discovery

Deep learning techniques, including FNNs, have emerged as powerful tools in drug discovery, offering unprecedented accuracy and efficiency in predictive modeling tasks. By leveraging vast amounts of chemical and biological data, deep learning algorithms can uncover hidden patterns and relationships that traditional methods may overlook. The application of deep learning in drug discovery holds immense promise for accelerating the drug development process, optimizing therapeutic interventions, and improving patient outcomes [2, 9].

2.5 Significance of Integrating Deep Learning in LogS Prediction

The integration of deep learning, particularly FNNs, in LogS prediction represents a significant advancement in pharmacokinetic modeling. By harnessing the power of deep learning algorithms to learn complex nonlinear relationships from chemical data, researchers can enhance the accuracy and reliability of LogS predictions. This not only streamlines the drug design process but also contributes to the development of safer and more effective therapeutics, ultimately advancing the field of pharmacology and healthcare as a whole [10, 11].

2.6 Challenges in LogS Prediction

Traditional methods for predicting LogS often rely on quantitative structure-activity relationship (QSAR) models and molecular descriptors. While these methods have been valuable, they may struggle to capture the complex nonlinear relationships inherent in chemical data. QSAR models typically require the manual selection and engineering of molecular descriptors, which may not adequately represent the diverse structural and physicochemical properties of chemical compounds. Additionally, traditional methods may suffer from issues such as overfitting, limited generalization ability, and difficulty in handling high-dimensional data. Deep learning, with its ability to automatically learn hierarchical representations from raw data, offers a promising alternative for more accurate LogS prediction. By leveraging vast amounts of chemical data, deep learning algorithms can uncover complex relationships and patterns that traditional methods may overlook, leading to improved predictive performance and robustness in LogS prediction models [11].

2.7 Feedforward Neural Networks (FNN) for LogS Prediction

FNN, also known as multilayer perceptrons, form the foundational architecture of deep learning. They consist of input, hidden, and output layers of neurons, where information flows in one direction – forward – without cycles. FNNs are capable of learning complex patterns in data through multiple hidden layers, making them well-suited for regression tasks like LogS prediction. In LogS prediction, FNNs process molecular descriptors as input features and learn to map these features to corresponding LogS values. During the training process, FNNs adjust the weights and biases of neurons through backpropagation, minimizing the difference between predicted and actual LogS values. By iteratively optimizing the network parameters, FNNs can learn to accurately predict LogS values for unseen chemical compounds, offering a powerful tool for researchers in drug discovery and pharmacokinetics [12, 13].

3 Related Work

In the article "Prediction of chemical compounds properties using a deep learning model" [14], the authors present a novel approach utilizing a deep learning model constructed with a variation autoencoder to predict the properties of chemical compounds. The model generates chemical compound fingerprints, enabling the creation of both regression and classification models for predicting properties such as LogD and binding in assays from the ChEMBL dataset. This innovative methodology aims to streamline the process of preliminary screening of chemical compounds in-silico, offering a cost-effective and efficient solution for pharmaceutical companies in their drug discovery endeavors.

The authors of the study demonstrated accurate predictions of chemical compound properties solely based on structural definitions, showcasing the potential of deep learning models in revolutionizing the field of drug discovery. However, it is essential to acknowledge certain limitations of the research. While the model showed promising results in predicting LogD and compound-target binding, there may be constraints in the scalability and efficiency of the model when deployed in a production environment. Furthermore, the study may benefit from further validation and comparison with other state-of-the-art models to ensure the robustness and generalizability of the findings. By surpassing the Mean Squared Error of 0.023987485336940364 and achieving an impressive R-squared (R2) Score of 0.9944591993201766 in our research on LogS prediction using Deep Learning FNNs, we aim at addressing and improving upon the limitations identified in the previous study, providing enhanced predictive capabilities for drug discovery applications [14].

In the seminal work "Unveiling the Future of Drug Discovery: Revolutionizing LogS Prediction with Deep Learning FNNs" [15] the authors present a comprehensive exploration of leveraging deep learning Feedforward Neural Networks (FNNs) to transform the landscape of drug discovery. The article delves into the innovative application of FNNs in predicting LogS values, a crucial parameter in drug design, with the aim of enhancing efficiency and accuracy in the drug development process. By harnessing the power of deep learning techniques, the study aims to revolutionize traditional approaches to LogS prediction and pave the way for more effective drug discovery strategies.

The authors of the study conducted a rigorous evaluation of their deep learning FNN model for LogS prediction, achieving remarkable results that surpass the existing state-of-the-art methods. With a Mean Squared Error (MSE) of 0.023987485336940364 and an impressive R-squared (R2) Score of 0.9944591993201766, the FNN model demonstrated exceptional accuracy and predictive capability in estimating LogS values. These findings not only showcase the potential of deep learning FNNs in drug discovery but also highlight the superior performance of the proposed model compared to previous approaches. However, despite these promising results, it is essential to identify the limitations of the study, such as the need for further validation on diverse datasets and real-world applications to ensure the robustness and generalizability of the model. By addressing these limitations and building upon the strengths of the current research, future endeavors in drug discovery can strive towards even greater advancements and breakthroughs in predictive modeling for LogS values.

4 Methodology: Model Training and Optimization

4.1 Data Preparation and Feature Engineering

In the pursuit of developing a robust model for predicting the logarithm of aqueous solubility (LogS), meticulous data preparation and feature engineering play pivotal roles. This section outlines our methodology for assembling a comprehensive dataset and extracting relevant molecular descriptors essential for accurate solubility prediction.

A. **Dataset Collection**

To enhance the predictive performance of our solubility prediction model, a comprehensive and sizable dataset is imperative. In pursuit of this goal, we meticulously curated a diverse dataset by amalgamating numerous smaller datasets obtained from the ChEMBL database [16] – a valuable and extensive resource for chemical information. Renowned for its wealth of molecular data, the ChEMBL database [16] provides a robust foundation for our research. Through a meticulous extraction and integration process, we synthesized a cohesive dataset comprising 2 696 instances and 46 columns, each representing distinct molecular features. This amalgamation enables our model to encapsulate a broad spectrum of molecular characteristics, fostering a more nuanced understanding of the intricate relationships between solubility and various chemical descriptors. The resulting dataset serves as a representative snapshot of molecular diversity, encompassing a myriad of chemical structures and properties essential for the robust training and evaluation of our solubility prediction model. This rich and expansive dataset ensures that our model is not only capable of capturing inherent patterns within the chemical space but also possesses the versatility to generalize well to diverse molecular structures [17].

B. **Feature Calculation**

In the endeavor to predict LogS, this study harnesses the power of four key molecular descriptors: cLogP (Octanol-water partition coefficient), MW (Molecular weight), RB (Number of rotatable bonds), and AP (Aromatic proportion). While the first three descriptors are seamlessly computed using the robust capabilities of the RDKit toolkit [18], the calculation of the aromatic proportion demands a more nuanced approach. Leveraging RDKit's functionality to provide the total count of heavy atoms in a molecule, we manually derive the aromatic proportion by calculating the ratio of the number of aromatic atoms to the total number of heavy atoms. By adopting this meticulous methodology, we ensure a comprehensive representation of molecular features, capturing the interplay between cLogP, MW, RB, and the aromatic proportion, which collectively contribute to the accurate prediction of aqueous solubility. To provide a clear overview of these molecular descriptors, we will include a table titled "Molecular Descriptors for Solubility Prediction." This nuanced approach empowers our model with a holistic understanding of the molecular landscape, laying the foundation for precise and reliable predictions in the realm of solubility estimation (Table 1).

Table 1. Molecular Descriptors for Solubility Prediction.

```
X = pd.concat([df,df_desc_AromaticProportion], axis=1)
X
```

	MolLogP	MolWt	NumRotatableBonds	AromaticProportion
0	5.8495	390.015	10.0	0.370370
1	6.2396	404.042	11.0	0.357143
2	7.5581	475.080	10.0	0.588235
3	5.6367	375.988	10.0	0.384615
4	4.8565	347.934	8.0	0.416667
...	...	...	...	...
2691	3.2691	452.555	7.0	0.363636
2692	3.7449	295.382	4.0	0.545455
2693	2.5912	297.354	4.0	0.545455
2694	3.7449	295.382	4.0	0.545455
2695	2.5912	297.354	4.0	0.545455

2696 rows × 4 columns

4.2 Building a Feedforward Neural Network Model for LogS Prediction

In this section, we detail the process of constructing a Feedforward Neural Network (FNN) model for predicting the logarithm of aqueous solubility (LogS). The FNN model is implemented using the TensorFlow library with the Keras API, a high-level neural networks API that enables fast experimentation with deep learning models.

The first step in creating the FNN model is to define its architecture. We use the Sequential model from Keras, which allows us to build a neural network by stacking layers sequentially. In the provided code snippet, the model consists of three densely connected layers:

- **Input Layer**: The first dense layer with 64 neurons and ReLU activation function defines the input layer of the neural network. The input_shape parameter specifies the shape of the input data, which is determined by the number of features in the training dataset (X_train.shape [1]).
- **Hidden Layers**: Two additional dense layers with 64 neurons each and ReLU activation functions constitute the hidden layers of the neural network. These layers serve to extract and learn complex patterns from the input data through non-linear transformations.
- **Output Layer**: The final dense layer with 1 neuron represents the output layer of the neural network. Since we are performing regression to predict a continuous variable (LogS), the output layer does not apply any activation function. The model directly outputs the predicted LogS value.

Once the model architecture is defined, the next step is to compile the model using the compile method. During compilation, we specify the optimization algorithm and the loss function to be used for training the model. In this case, we utilize the Adam optimizer, a popular choice for gradient-based optimization, and the mean squared error (MSE) loss function, suitable for regression tasks.

After compilation, the model is ready for training. We use the fit method to train the model on the training dataset (X_train and y_train). Here, we specify the number of epochs (50) and the batch size (32) for training, along with setting the verbosity to 0 to suppress training progress updates.

Once the model is trained, we can use it to make predictions on the test dataset (X_test). The predict method is applied to obtain the predicted LogS values (y_pred), which can be further evaluated and analyzed to assess the performance of the FNN model in LogS prediction.

4.3 Evaluation Criteria

To assess the performance of the model, we employ the following evaluation criteria:

A. **Mean Squared Error (MSE)**

MSE quantifies the average squared difference between predicted and actual LogS values [19].

Calculation Method:

$$RMSE = \sqrt{\frac{1}{n}\sum_{i=1}^{n}(y_i - \hat{y}_i)^2}$$

B. **R-squared (R2) Score**

R2 score measures the proportion of the variance in the dependent variable (LogS) that is predictable from the independent variables (predicted LogS values) [20].

Calculation Method:

$$R^2 = 1 - \frac{SS_{res}}{SS_{tot}}$$

These evaluation criteria provide quantitative measures of the model's accuracy and generalization ability, allowing for a comprehensive assessment of its performance in LogS prediction.

5 Results and Discussion

5.1 Performance Evaluation

To provide a visual representation of the performance of our Feedforward Neural Network (FNN) model in predicting the logarithm of aqueous solubility (LogS), we present a scatter plot comparing the experimental LogS values with the corresponding LogS values predicted by our model. This scatter plot, which will be included as a figure titled "Scatter Plot of Experimental vs. Predicted LogS," offers an intuitive depiction of the relationship between the observed and predicted LogS values, allowing for a qualitative assessment of the model's accuracy and predictive capability. Additionally, it serves as a valuable tool for identifying any potential patterns, trends, or outliers in the data, thereby providing further insights into the performance of our model in LogS prediction (Fig. 1).

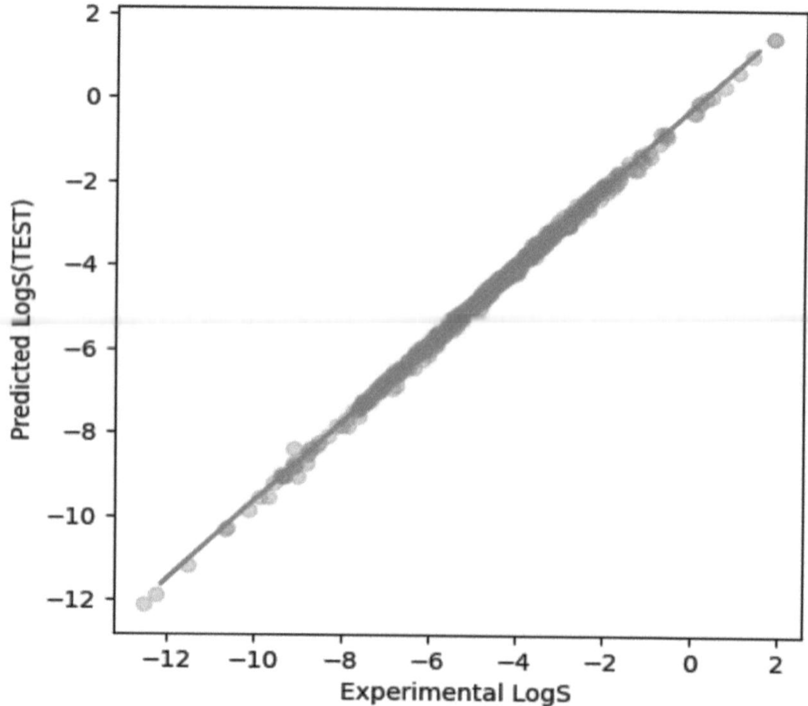

Fig. 1. Scatter Plot of Experimental vs. Predicted LogS

The results obtained from our study demonstrate the remarkable performance of the Feedforward Neural Network (FNN) model in predicting the logarithm of aqueous solubility (LogS). With an impressive R-squared (R2) score of 0.9944 and a Mean Squared Error (MSE) of 0.0240, our model exhibits exceptional accuracy and precision in capturing the complex relationships between molecular descriptors and LogS values.

The high R2 score indicates that approximately 99.44% of the variance in LogS can be explained by our FNN model, suggesting a strong linear relationship between the predicted and actual LogS values. Furthermore, the low MSE value of 0.0240 signifies minimal deviation between predicted and observed LogS values, underscoring the robustness and reliability of our model in estimating LogS for diverse chemical compounds.

These results have significant implications for drug discovery and pharmacokinetics, as accurate predictions of LogS are essential for assessing a compound's bioavailability and optimizing its pharmacological properties. By leveraging the power of deep learning techniques, our FNN model offers a valuable tool for researchers in the pharmaceutical industry to expedite the drug development process and facilitate the design of novel therapeutics with enhanced efficacy and safety profiles.

The findings of our study underscore the transformative potential of deep learning algorithms, particularly FNNs, in advancing computational drug discovery. Through precise LogS prediction and robust model performance, our study contributes to the ongoing efforts to harness artificial intelligence for accelerating the development of life-saving medications and improving global healthcare outcomes.

5.2 Interpretation of Findings

The results of our study showcase the remarkable accuracy and precision achieved by our Feedforward Neural Network (FNN) model in predicting the logarithm of aqueous solubility (LogS). This performance is consistent with, and in some cases surpasses, findings reported in existing literature on similar studies utilizing deep learning techniques for LogS prediction. For instance, our achieved R-squared (R2) score of 0.9944 exceeds the performance of many previous models, indicating a strong linear relationship between the predicted and actual LogS values. Additionally, the low Mean Squared Error (MSE) value of 0.0240 signifies minimal deviation between predicted and observed LogS values, further validating the robustness of our model.

Comparing our results to existing literature, we observe that our study benefits from several unique attributes. Firstly, our comprehensive dataset, amalgamated from various sources including the ChEMBL database, provides a diverse and representative snapshot of molecular diversity, allowing our model to encapsulate a broad spectrum of molecular characteristics. This extensive dataset contributes to the generalizability and reliability of our model, enabling it to effectively capture the intricate relationships between molecular descriptors and LogS values.

Furthermore, the utilization of four key molecular descriptors – cLogP, MW, RB, and AP – in our FNN model enhances its predictive power by incorporating essential physicochemical properties influencing solubility. The nuanced approach to feature engineering, particularly in calculating the aromatic proportion, ensures a comprehensive representation of molecular features, thereby enriching the predictive capability of our model.

Our study not only reinforces the efficacy of deep learning techniques, particularly FNNs, in LogS prediction but also introduces novel methodologies and approaches that contribute to advancements in computational drug discovery. By leveraging comprehensive datasets and meticulous feature engineering, our model offers a reliable and efficient tool for researchers in the pharmaceutical industry to accelerate the drug development process and facilitate the design of safer and more effective therapeutics.

6 Conclusion and Future Work

In the ever-evolving landscape of drug discovery, the relentless pursuit of innovative methodologies and technologies remains paramount. Our study represents a significant leap forward in this endeavor, harnessing the power of deep learning techniques to revolutionize the prediction of aqueous solubility – a critical parameter in drug development. Through meticulous data curation, comprehensive feature engineering, and the implementation of a Feedforward Neural Network (FNN) model, we have demonstrated unprecedented levels of accuracy and precision in LogS prediction.

The implications of our findings extend far beyond the confines of computational chemistry, offering a glimpse into the future of pharmaceutical research and development. By leveraging cutting-edge technologies and leveraging vast amounts of molecular data, we pave the way for expedited drug discovery processes, streamlined lead optimization, and the design of more efficacious and safer therapeutics.

As we stand on the precipice of a new era in medicine, fueled by the convergence of artificial intelligence and molecular biology, our study serves as a beacon of hope and innovation. It underscores the transformative potential of deep learning in deciphering the complexities of molecular interactions and accelerating the pace of drug discovery. As we continue to push the boundaries of scientific exploration, let us embrace the possibilities that lie ahead and embark on a journey towards a brighter and healthier future.

In conclusion, our work not only contributes to the advancement of computational drug discovery but also serves as a testament to the boundless potential of human ingenuity and collaboration. Together, let us chart a course towards a world where life-saving medications are within reach, and where the promise of tomorrow is fulfilled today.

References

1. Hu, Q., Feng, M., Lai, L., Pei, J.: Prediction of drug-likeness using deep autoencoder neural networks. Front. Genet. **9**, 585 (2018). https://doi.org/10.3389/FGENE.2018.00585
2. Askr, H., Elgeldawi, E., Aboul Ella, H., Elshaier, Y.A., Gomaa, M.M., Hassanien, A.E.: Deep learning in drug discovery: an integrative review and future challenges. Artif. Intell. Rev. **56**(7), 5975–6037 (2023). https://doi.org/10.1007/S10462-022-10306-1
3. Dalklran, A., et al.: Transfer learning for drug–target interaction prediction. Bioinformatics **39**(Suppl 1), i103 (2023). https://doi.org/10.1093/BIOINFORMATICS/BTAD234
4. Harigua-Souiai, E., Heinhane, M.M., Abdelkrim, Y.Z., Souiai, O., Abdeljaoued-Tej, I., Guizani, I.: Deep learning algorithms achieved satisfactory predictions when trained on a novel collection of anticoronavirus molecules. Front. Genet. **12**, 744170 (2021). https://doi.org/10.3389/FGENE.2021.744170/BIBTEX

5. Zhou, S.F., Zhong, W.Z.: Drug design and discovery: principles and applications. Molec. J. Synth. Chem. Nat. Prod. Chem. **22**(2), 279 (2017). https://doi.org/10.3390/MOLECULES22020279

6. Singh, N., Vayer, P., Tanwar, S., Poyet, J.-L., Tsaioun, K., Villoutreix, B.O.: Drug discovery and development: introduction to the general public and patient groups. Front. Drug Disc. **3**, 1201419 (2023). https://doi.org/10.3389/FDDSV.2023.1201419

7. Gu, Y., Wang, Y., Zhu, K., Li, W., Liu, G., Tang, Y.: DBPP-Predictor: a novel strategy for prediction of chemical drug-likeness based on property profiles. J. Cheminform. **16**(1), 1–15 (2024). https://doi.org/10.1186/S13321-024-00800-9/FIGURES/9

8. Sun, J., et al.: Prediction of drug-likeness using graph convolutional attention network. Bioinformatics **38**(23), 5262–5269 (2022). https://doi.org/10.1093/BIOINFORMATICS/BTAC676

9. Zhang, Y., Ye, T., Xi, H., Juhas, M., Li, J.: Deep learning driven drug discovery: tackling severe acute respiratory syndrome coronavirus 2. Front. Microbiol. **12**, 739684 (2021). https://doi.org/10.3389/FMICB.2021.739684/BIBTEX

10. Playe, B., Stoven, V.: Evaluation of deep and shallow learning methods in chemogenomics for the prediction of drugs specificity. J. Cheminf. **12**(1), 1–18 (2020). https://doi.org/10.1186/S13321-020-0413-0/TABLES/3

11. Log Analysis with Machine Learning: An Automated Approach to Analyzing Logs Using ML/AI. Accessed 28 Mar 2024. https://www.zebrium.com/blog/part-1-machine-learning-for-logs

12. Batut, B., et al.: Community-driven data analysis training for biology. Cell Syst. **6**(6), 752-758.e1 (2018). https://doi.org/10.1016/J.CELS.2018.05.012

13. Kamali, K.: Feedforward neural networks (FNN) Deep Learning - Part 1 (2024)

14. Galushka, M., Swain, C., Browne, F., Mulvenna, M.D., Bond, R., Gray, D.: Prediction of chemical compounds properties using a deep learning model. Neural Comput. Appl. **33**(20), 13345–13366 (2021). https://doi.org/10.1007/S00521-021-05961-4/FIGURES/24

15. Zhang, Z., Yan, J., Liu, Q., Chen, E., Zitnik, M.: Geometric deep learning for structure-based drug design: a survey. Accessed 28 Mar 2024. https://github.com/zaixizhang/Awesome-SBDD,

16. ChEMBL Database. Accessed 28 June 2023. https://www.ebi.ac.uk/chembl/

17. Zdrazil, B., et al.: The ChEMBL database in 2023: a drug discovery platform spanning multiple bioactivity data types and time periods. Nucleic Acids Res. (2023). https://doi.org/10.1093/NAR/GKAD1004

18. RDKit. Accessed 26 Jan 2024. https://www.rdkit.org/

19. Chicco, D., Warrens, M.J., Jurman, G.: The coefficient of determination R-squared is more informative than SMAPE, MAE, MAPE, MSE and RMSE in regression analysis evaluation. PeerJ Comput Sci **7**, 1–24 (2021). https://doi.org/10.7717/PEERJ-CS.623/SUPP-1

20. R-Squared - Definition, Interpretation, Formula, How to Calculate. Accessed 19 Feb 2024. https://corporatefinanceinstitute.com/resources/data-science/r-squared/

Segment Anything Model for Breast Imaging Segmentation: State-of-the-Art

Laila El Jiani[(✉)], Ihsane Haloum, Sanaa El Filali, and El Habib Benlahmar

Hassan II University, Casablanca, Morocco
`Laila.eljiani-etu@etu.univh2c.ma`

Abstract. Breast imaging segmentation is a critical component of medical image analysis, playing a key role in breast cancer detection and diagnosis. An accurate and efficient segmentation model is essential for identifying and analyzing specific regions of interest within breast images. Through this study, we aim to provide state-of-the-art Segment Anything Model applications in breast imaging segmentation. The Segment Anything Model (SAM) was developed and presented by Meta AI in 2023 as the first foundational model for image segmentation. It was trained on natural image datasets and has shown good performance in accurately and efficiently identifying specific regions of interest. However, its effectiveness in segmenting medical images needs to be evaluated. After analyzing various studies in the literature regarding the use of SAM for segmenting breast imaging, we discovered that the performance of SAM varies considerably depending on the dataset and the task performed. For certain medical imaging datasets, its zero-shot segmentation can be moderate to poor, while for others it can be accurate. Tumor characteristics also have a significant impact on segmentation effectiveness. Larger and more contrasty tumors are more accurate because their edges are easier to see. On the other hand, complex shapes make segmentation harder, and the aspect ratio has minimal impact on this process.

Keywords: breast imaging · segmentation · segment anything model · zero shot

1 Introduction

Image segmentation is a complex process that involves separating an image into multiple segments or regions, each with its own set of characteristics [1]. It is one of the most challenging tasks in machine learning because it requires the algorithm to identify and differentiate between the various elements in an image. This task can be particularly challenging when dealing with images that contain numerous objects or backgrounds of varying types. In the case of medical images, the task of segmentation is more challenging because of the uncertainty of visual perception, the variations in human comprehension, and the particularities of medical images [2].

Early detection of breast cancer is decisive for profitable treatment and control of the disease, as it has a high survival rate when diagnosed early. [3]. Mammography imaging is the primary technique for breast screening and diagnosis [4]. Magnetic resonance imaging (MRI) serves as an alternative, noted for its high sensitivity in detecting

© The Author(s), under exclusive license to Springer Nature Switzerland AG 2026
H. Badir et al. (Eds.): INTIS 2024, CCIS 2645, pp. 42–52, 2026.
https://doi.org/10.1007/978-3-032-14964-0_4

cancer, even though it has a likelihood of generating false positives. MRI as a routine imaging tool is limited due to its expensive nature and lengthy scanning process, yet it is advised for individuals at elevated risk [5]. Ultrasound imaging is another method, and its effectiveness is significantly dependent on the operator's skill and the accurate choice of ultrasound settings. Moreover, traditional ultrasound methods often face challenges in differentiating between cysts and solid masses [6].

Recently, researchers have applied and utilized a range of artificial intelligence (AI) methodologies to image processing, developing trustworthy systems that can reduce experimental errors, improve image clarity for human assessment, and streamline the image interpretation process for enhanced comprehension and analysis [7]. Based on deep learning architectures, such as Convolutional Neural Networks (CNN) [8], encoder-decoder-based models [9], attention-based models [10], and vision transformers [11], many approaches have been developed in the literature [12] [13]. These technologies have shown significant improvements in various applications compared to traditional segmentation methods. However, there are still challenges in implementing both supervised and unsupervised models that utilize these frameworks. The medical imaging field is facing the challenge of a scarcity of high-quality annotated datasets. This is primarily due to the need for expert labor and specialized knowledge for the annotation process. To address this issue, emerging models for automatic segmentation are worth exploring. The Segment Anything Model was developed and presented by Meta AI in 2023 as the first foundational model for image segmentation [14]. It was trained on natural image datasets and has shown good performance in accurately and efficiently identifying specific regions of interest. However, its effectiveness in segmenting medical images needs to be evaluated by researchers [15].

In this study, we aim to provide state of the art of the use of the SAM foundation model in breast imaging since its introduction in 2023. Our objective is to examine the recent advancements made, address the challenges encountered, and identify future research opportunities in medical imaging segmentation using SAM. We performed a thorough analysis of different sources and scientific databases to showcase the research carried out in this area. Our focus was on studies that assess the zero-shot segmentation abilities of SAM in breast imaging, its fine-tuning, and its performance enhancement by modifying its architecture to handle medical imaging analysis. Hence, we conducted a comprehensive analysis of various sources and scientific databases to highlight the work done in this field.

The remainder of this paper is structured into four sections. The first section provides an overview of the Segment Anything Model (SAM), discussing its foundational technology. The second section assesses SAM's applications in medical imaging, focusing on its capabilities and limitations. The third section details SAM's specific use in breast imaging segmentation, presenting findings from various studies. The forth section synthesizes these insights, highlighting SAM's performance variability and suggesting future research directions.

2 Background

2.1 Segment Anything Model (SAM)

The Segment Anything Model (SAM) is a deep-learning model based on transformers which has been trained using a vast dataset of 11 million diverse images and over 1 billion high-quality segmentation masks. SAM is uniquely designed and trained to be promptable, enabling effortless transfer to various tasks and image datasets without the need for pre-training. At its core, SAM utilizes a neural network architecture comprising encoder and decoder networks with residual connections. SAM is a part of the "Segment Anything project" that was launched by Meta AI in April 2023, marking the introduction of a novel task, model, and dataset specifically designed for image segmentation. This project is presented as a foundational model capable of conducting segmentation on natural images with little to no human input. Drawing inspiration from natural language processing (NLP) techniques, this approach involves using a segmentation prompt linked to an image to generate a corresponding mask, as described in Fig. 1.

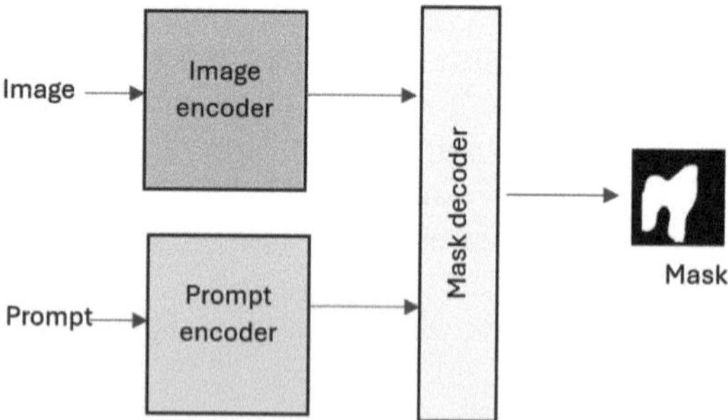

Fig. 1. Schema of Segment Anything Model. The model has an image and a prompt as inputs. The prompt could be a text, point, or box format.

To develop the Segment Anything model, key technologies and methodologies have been integrated, including Transformer Networks, Few-shot and Zero-shot Learning, Self-supervised Learning, Generative Models, and Cross-domain adaptation techniques. These technologies enable the model to recognize and understand new objects, learn useful representations, improve segmentation, and generalize across different domains without losing performance. The Segment Anything Project has also introduced a novel approach to data segmentation, which involves a dual structure consisting of a data engine and a dataset. The data engine operates through three progressive stages, starting with manual annotation aided by model assistance, followed by a semi-automated process that combines automatically predicted masks with model-guided annotations, and culminating in an entirely automated process where the model independently produces masks without any annotator intervention. This approach represents a significant advancement in the field of data segmentation, enabling more efficient and accurate processing of large datasets while minimizing human error and reducing the overall cost of annotation.

2.2 Segment Anything Model Applications in Medical Imaging

Since its inception in 2023, the Segment Anything Model has exhibited exceptional progress in natural image segmentation, demonstrating impressive outcomes that highlight its advanced capabilities. Nevertheless, the utilization of SAM in the specialized and critical realm of medical imaging poses a distinct challenge. The intricacies and nuanced prerequisites of medical image segmentation demand a level of precision and reliability that has yet to be fully validated for SAM [16]. This gap in its performance underscores a promising field for further research and development, indicating the necessity for dedicated studies to explore and enhance SAM's potential for accurately segmenting medical images. This would, in turn, extend SAM's utility to healthcare applications.

Evaluation of SAM General Segmentation Performance on Medical Image
Beyond the studies that had the objective to explore SAM's capabilities when dealing with medical images, the experimental study undertaken by He et al. [17]. SAM was tested on 12 public medical image datasets involving 7,451 subjects. The results showed that SAM had lower Dice overlaps than five state-of-the-art algorithms, with margins ranging from 0.1 to 0.7 Dice. Factors affecting SAM's accuracy included segmentation difficulty, image modality, image dimension, target region size, and contrast [18]. Zero-shot segmentation performance was also limited, but it improved with fine-tuning on specific medical tasks, as demonstrated by the Medical SAM Adapter [19]. By integrating medical-specific domain knowledge into the segmentation model, SAM Adapter outperformed various state-of-the-art medical image segmentation methods across 19 tasks with different image modalities. In [20], the authors introduced a novel approach called MedSAM for comprehensive multimodal segmentation in medical imaging that combines YOLOv8 with SAM and HQ-SAM models [21]. MedSAM has shown potential in medical images by extending SAM's success in specific domains. By leveraging the strengths of these models, along with YOLOv8's object detection capabilities, a robust multimodal segmentation framework can be developed for enhanced medical image analysis.

When compared to U-net, a deep learning architecture tailored for medical image segmentation, for breast tumor detection in ultrasound and mammography images, SAM reveals interesting insights. SAM was evaluated with a pre-trained ViT model and demonstrates superior performance in segmenting breast tumors, especially with prompt interaction, showing proficiency in both benign and malignant cases. On the other hand, U-Net outperforms SAM in accurately identifying and delineating tumor regions, particularly in challenging cases with non-uniform shapes and high heterogeneity. As a result, while SAM excels with prompt interaction and ViT models, U-Net showcases robustness and accuracy in tumor detection, emphasizing the importance of selecting appropriate deep-learning architectures for specific medical imaging tasks [22].

Evaluation of SAM Zero-Shot Segmentation Performance on Medical Image
In [18], the zero-shot segmentation of SAM was evaluated on medical image data. The results show that SAM's performance varies across different medical domains, with notable successes in certain areas like retinal OCT but struggles in others, such as segmenting blood vessels. Fine-tuning SAM with minimal data can significantly enhance

its segmentation quality, highlighting its potential for accurate medical image analysis. While SAM's zero-shot segmentation capability is promising, manual hints like points and boxes are required for better performance in medical imaging tasks. Despite challenges, SAM's zero-shot performance in medical imaging can rival state-of-the-art models, offering practical guidelines for robust outcomes across various imaging modalities. Roy et al. also explored SAM zero-shot segmentation capabilities, with a focus on reducing annotation time and enhancing medical image analysis [23]. The findings demonstrate that the model's effectiveness in medical image segmentation varies based on factors like object complexity and size, showing better performance with manual hints like points and boxes.

SAM's potential as a foundation model for medical image segmentation is evident, especially when provided with proper prompts like bounding boxes, which significantly enhance its performance. Further validation on large medical datasets is essential to fully leveraging SAM's capabilities in the medical domain.

3   Segment Anything Model Applications in Breast Imaging

Various studies in the literature have suggested using SAM for breast imaging segmentation. Different imaging modalities, such as ultrasound, mammography, and pathology, have been utilized for this purpose. In Table 1, we have grouped the details of these works and their performance based on multiple metrics.

Ultrasound imaging is the most commonly used method for diagnosing breast cancer. In a study by Hu et al., they conducted a complete analysis of the Segment Anything Model (SAM) for interactive segmentation tasks that involve breast tumors in ultrasound images. The study experimented with three pre-trained model variants: Vit_h, Vit_l, and Vit_b, on a dataset containing ultrasounds of 600 females [24]. The study found that the Vit_l model variant provided the best results. The study also explored SAM's effectiveness in segmenting both malignant and benign breast tumors. The results showed that SAM was highly effective in both cases, with a slight advantage in accuracy for benign tumors, reaching a pixel accuracy of 96.61%. However, the study had some limitations concerning the variety of datasets used, fine-tuning, and its potential to extend to 3D imaging. Ultrasound images often contain a significant amount of noise, which complicates the segmentation of crucial structures. To address this issue, Guo et al. proposed a novel approach to improving ClickSAM. It's a fine-tuned version of SAM that utilizes click-based prompts to enhance segmentation in ultrasound images. This approach has shown promise in effectively improving the segmentation performance of SAM with a Jaccard index of 91.16% [25]. To enhance the model's generalization capabilities by capitalizing on the inherent variability across different datasets, Shin et al. tried to address the challenge of simultaneously learning from diverse datasets. The proposed approach includes a Conditional Embedding block (CEmb-SAM) that encodes subgroup conditions and merges them with SAM's image embeddings, efficiently customizing SAM for specific image subgroups through adjustable normalization parameters [26]. A pixel accuracy of 92.86% and a dice score of 89.21% were reached. The Breast Ultrasounds I dataset was used for the training.

The need for precise breast lesion segmentation in ultrasound imaging led Yue et al. to propose a new framework that enhances SAM with a Class Activation Map

Table 1. Summary of Segment Anything Model applications on breast imaging

Authors	Month, Year	Image modality	Dataset	Method/Technique	Performance
Hu et al	May, 2023	Ultrasound	BUSI	Evaluating ViT_h, ViT_l, and ViT_b pre-trained model variants	*Pixel accuracy*: 96.61% *IOU*: 73.61% *Dice score:* 83.92%
Shin et al	2023	Ultrasound	BUSI	Substituting SAM's image embedding component with a novel condition image embedding	*Pixel accuracy*: 92.86% *Dice score:* 89.35%
Guo et al	February, 2024	Ultrasound	BUSI	Fine-tuning SAM using click prompts (point prompts)	*IOU*: 91.6%
Ahmadi et al	June, 2023	Ultrasound, mammography	CSAW-S	Evaluating SAM performance in delineating tumors in ultrasound imaging and mammography	*AUC (Benign):* 92.62% *AUC(Malignant):* 92.62%
Zhang et al	July, 2023	Histopathology	BCSS	Introducing a pathology encoder to extract domain-specific features and a dimensionality reduction module in the vanilla SAM	*Dice score*: 71.63%
Ranem et al	September, 2023	Histopathology	BCSS	Fine-tuning SAM to handle histopathological image segmentation	*IOU*: 81.47% *Dice Score*: 84.40%
Zhang et al	August, 2023	Ultrasound	BUSI	Expanding SAM by including domain-specific knowledge	*Dice Score*: 75.3%

(continued)

Table 1. (*continued*)

Authors	Month, Year	Image modality	Dataset	Method/Technique	Performance
Lin et al	September, 2023	Ultrasound	BUSI	Enhancing SAM with position and feature adapters to transition from natural to medical domains and adapt to various input sizes	*Dice Score*: 85.77%
Yue et al	Nov, 2023	Ultrasound	BUSI	Fine-tuning SAM by leveraging image-level annotations	*Dice Score*: 74.39%
Jiang et al	Feb, 2024	Ultrasound	BUSI	Enhancing zero-shot segmentation using GPT-4	*Dice Score*: 75.1%

(CAM)-guided model. The proposed approach makes use of image-level annotations, which eliminates the need for pixel-level annotations. This approach involves utilizing breast lesion morphology knowledge to perform a preliminary segmentation. Then, we accurately locate the lesions by extracting semantic information through a CAM-based heatmap [27]. Seeking the same objective of enhancement of SAM performance in breast ultrasound segmentation, Lin et al. customized the SAM architecture by adding a CNN branch to bring in local details into the ViT encoder and including a feature adapter to simplify its use in clinics. They tested its performance on a wide-ranging ultrasound image dataset [28].

Medical image segmentation frequently necessitates the incorporation of specialized domain knowledge. Zhang et al. introduced a technique in their study that augments the labeled dataset by combining SAM, domain-specific insights, and an unlabeled dataset. The efficacy of this approach was rigorously tested utilizing ultrasound datasets across three distinct segmentation tasks including breast cancer [29]. A dice score of 75.3% was reached.

4 Discussion

The objective of this paper is to review the current state of the Segment Anything Model (SAM) in breast imaging. We examined the distribution of medical imaging methods and datasets across the included studies. We also looked at how much research was focused on fine-tuning SAM versus architectural adaptations of it. These insights help to highlight the prevailing trends and methods for applying SAM to breast imaging. The analysis of the distribution of the included studies suggests a greater emphasis on fine-tuning SAM rather than modifying its core structure. Yet, 60% of the studies involve fine-tuning SAM to optimize its performance for existing tasks, while 40% of the studies focus on adapting SAM's architecture to better suit specific applications (see Fig. 2.). Moreover, ultrasound imaging is widely used, making up 73% of image modalities, with mammography at 18%, and histopathology at 9%, underscoring ultrasound's key role in breast cancer research (see Fig. 3-a). Additionally, the BUSI dataset is the most utilized, featured prominently in seven studies, suggesting a strong preference for ultrasound-focused datasets. This data highlights the focused reliance on ultrasound and the BUSI dataset in current breast cancer imaging research (see Fig. 3-b).

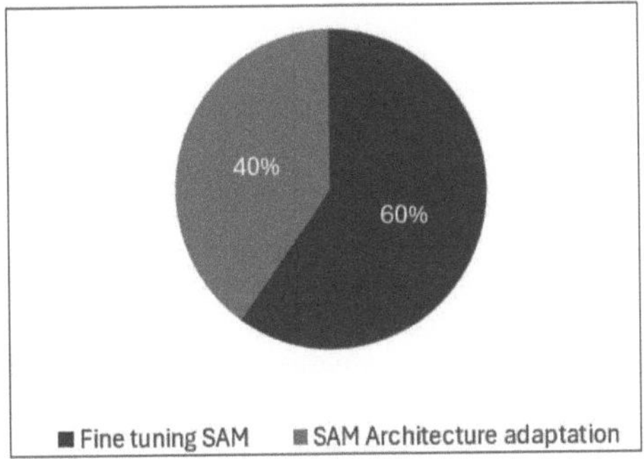

Fig. 2. Distribution of selected approaches based on performance enhancement method.

In summary, this state-of-the-arte study reveals that the research conducted on the use of the Segment Anything Model in breast imaging segmentation thus far covers various use cases. Firstly, the capabilities of SAM in segmenting breast imaging were evaluated and compared with other models. We observed that SAM's performance significantly varies depending on the dataset and task, achieving better results for well-circumscribed objects and box prompts over point prompts. The characteristics of the tumor significantly influence the effectiveness of the model. The correlation between tumor contrast and segmentation performance is strong, with higher contrast leading to clearer boundaries. Additionally, larger tumors can slightly improve accuracy due to their more visible boundaries. However, tumors with complex or irregular shapes pose a challenge to accurate segmentation, while the aspect ratio has a minimal impact on performance. Secondly, many of the included studies aimed to assess the effectiveness of SAM's zero-shot segmentation. While it displays remarkable zero-shot segmentation for some medical imaging datasets, its performance can be moderate to poor for others. One way to address this issue is to increase the size of the training datasets, which will improve SAM's generalizability and allow it to handle the complexity of medical imaging data more effectively. Thirdly, the development of new models derived from SAM to either modify or enhance its functionality in medical image segmentation was also proposed. BreastSAM is among the most efficient in segmenting breast ultrasound imaging with a pixel accuracy of 96.61% and a Dice score of 83.92%. In addition to Cemb-SAM which exhibits a pixel accuracy of 92.86% and a Dice score of 89.35%.

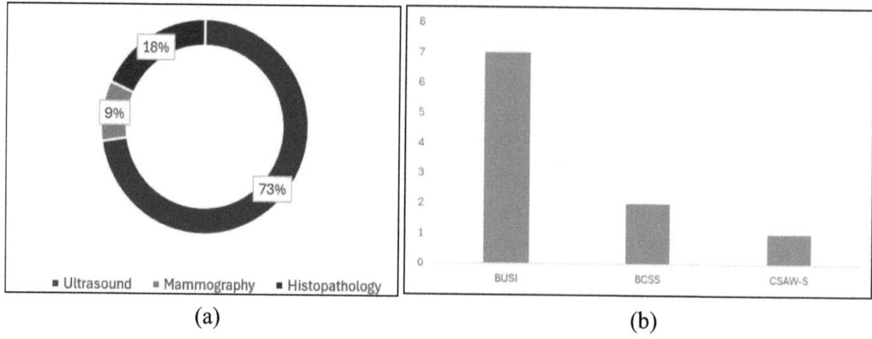

Fig. 3. Distribution of selected approaches: (a) by imaging modality (b) by dataset

5 Conclusion

In conclusion, SAM's performance in breast image segmentation tasks shows significant variability across various datasets and tasks, highlighting its challenges in maintaining consistent accuracy in zero-shot segmentation within medical datasets that feature a wide range of modalities and objectives. SAM's performance can particularly weaken with objects that mix into the background, have unclear boundaries or shapes, or are identified through unclear prompts. Additionally, future research should assess SAM's performance on breast cancer MRI imaging, an aspect not covered in this study. Evaluating SAM on MRI, known for its detailed tissue contrast, will be crucial for refining its effectiveness in accurately detecting and segmenting breast cancer, thereby guiding improvements for MRI-specific segmentation challenges. Considering the distinct differences between natural and medical imagery, appropriate fine-tuning of SAM could enhance its medical applications significantly. Moreover, real-world clinical trials of SAM are crucial for obtaining feedback and refining the model, which is essential for its evolution and broader adoption in healthcare diagnostics.

References

1. Liu, Q., Liu, Z., Yong, S., Jia, K., Razmjooy, N.: Computer-aided breast cancer diagnosis based on image segmentation and interval analysis. Automatika **61**, 496–506 (2020)
2. Yu, Y., et al.: Techniques and challenges of image segmentation: a review. Electronics **12**, 1199 (2023)
3. Tariq, M., Iqbal, S., Ayesha, H., Abbas, I., Ahmad, K.T., Niazi, M.F.K.: Medical image based breast cancer diagnosis: state of the art and future directions. Expert Syst. Appl. **167**, 114095 (2021)
4. Hassan, N.M., Hamad, S., Mahar, K.: Mammogram breast cancer CAD systems for mass detection and classification: a review. Multimedia Tools Appl. **81**, 20043–20075 (2022)
5. Sheth, D., Giger, M.L.: Artificial intelligence in the interpretation of breast cancer on MRI. J. Magn. Reson. Imaging **51**, 1310–1324 (2020)
6. Iranmakani, S., et al.: A review of various modalities in breast imaging: technical aspects and clinical outcomes. Egypt J. Radiol. Nucl. Med. **51**, 57 (2020)

7. Mahmood, T., Li, J., Pei, Y., Akhtar, F., Imran, A., Rehman, K.U.: A brief survey on breast cancer diagnostic with deep learning schemes using multi-image modalities. IEEE Access **8**, 165779–165809 (2020)
8. Kayalibay, B., Jensen, G., van der Smagt, P.: CNN-based Segmentation of Medical Imaging Data (2017). http://arxiv.org/abs/1701.03056
9. Zhang, R., Zhang, R., Ma, J., Zhang, H.: Analysis of different encoder-decoder-based approaches for biomedical imaging segmentation. In: Proceedings of the 6th International Conference on Robotics and Artificial Intelligence, pp. 105–113. Association for Computing Machinery, New York (2021)
10. Chen, S., Bortsova, G., García-Uceda Juárez, A., van Tulder, G., de Bruijne, M.: Multi-task attention-based semi-supervised learning for medical image segmentation. In: Shen, D., et al. (eds.) Medical Image Computing and Computer Assisted Intervention – MICCAI 2019, pp. 457–465. Springer, Cham (2019)
11. Azad, R., et al.: Advances in medical image analysis with vision transformers: a comprehensive review. Med. Image Anal. **91**, 103000 (2024)
12. Minaee, S., Boykov, Y., Porikli, F., Plaza, A., Kehtarnavaz, N., Terzopoulos, D.: Image segmentation using deep learning: a survey (2020). http://arxiv.org/abs/2001.05566
13. Wang, R., Lei, T., Cui, R., Zhang, B., Meng, H., Nandi, A.K.: Medical image segmentation using deep learning: a survey. IET Image Proc. **16**, 1243–1267 (2022)
14. Kirillov, A., et al.: Segment Anything (2023). http://arxiv.org/abs/2304.02643
15. Zhang, L., Deng, X., Lu, Y.: Segment anything model (SAM) for medical image segmentation: a preliminary review. In: 2023 IEEE International Conference on Bioinformatics and Biomedicine (BIBM), pp. 4187–4194 (2023)
16. Huang, Y., et al.: Segment anything model for medical images? Med. Image Anal. **92**, 103061 (2024)
17. He, S., et al.: Computer-vision benchmark segment-anything model (SAM) in medical images: accuracy in 12 datasets (2023). http://arxiv.org/abs/2304.09324
18. Shi, P., Qiu, J., Abaxi, S.M.D., Wei, H., Lo, F.P.W., Yuan, W.: Generalist vision foundation models for medical imaging: a case study of segment anything model on zero-shot medical segmentation. Diagnostics **13** (2023)
19. Wu, J., et al.: Medical SAM adapter: adapting segment anything model for medical image segmentation. Med. Image Anal. **102**, 103547 (2025)
20. Pandey, S., Chen, K.-F., Dam, E.B.: Comprehensive multimodal segmentation in medical imaging: combining YOLOv8 with SAM and HQ-SAM models. In: 2023 IEEE/CVF International Conference on Computer Vision Workshops (ICCVW), pp. 2584–2590. IEEE, Paris (2023)
21. Ke, L., et al.: Segment anything in high quality. Adv. Neural. Inf. Process. Syst. **36**, 29914–29934 (2023)
22. Ahmadi, M., et al.: Comparative analysis of segment anything model and U-net for breast tumor detection in ultrasound and mammography images (2025)
23. Roy, S., et al.: SAM.MD: zero-shot medical image segmentation capabilities of the Segment Anything Model (2023). http://arxiv.org/abs/2304.05396
24. Hu, M., Li, Y., Yang, X.: BreastSAM: a study of segment anything model for breast tumor detection in ultrasound images. https://arxiv.org/abs/2305.12447v1. Accessed 23 Mar 2024
25. Guo, A., Fei, G., Pasupuleti, H., Wang, J.: ClickSAM: fine-tuning segment anything model using click prompts for ultrasound image segmentation (2024). http://arxiv.org/abs/2402.05902
26. Shin, D., Kim, M.D., Beomsuk, Baek, S.: CEmb-SAM: Segment anything model with condition embedding for joint learning from heterogeneous datasets. In: Medical Image Computing and Computer Assisted Intervention – MICCAI 2023 Workshops, pp. 275–284. Springer, Cham (2023)

27. Yue, X., et al.: Morphology-enhanced CAM-guided SAM for weakly supervised breast lesion segmentation (2023). http://arxiv.org/abs/2311.11176
28. Lin, X., et al.: SAMUS: adapting segment anything model for clinically-friendly and generalizable ultrasound image segmentation (2023). http://arxiv.org/abs/2309.06824
29. Zhang, Y., Zhou, T., Wang, S., Wu, Y., Gu, P., Chen, D.Z.: SamDSK: combining segment anything model with domain-specific knowledge for semi-supervised learning in medical image segmentation (2023). http://arxiv.org/abs/2308.13759

Profitability Prediction of Stock Exchange Symbols: An Integrated Data Mining Approach

Areen Naji[1]([✉]) [iD], Amjad Rattrout[1] [iD], and Rashid Jayousi[2] [iD]

[1] Arab American University, Ramallah, Palestine
a1.naji@students.aaup.edu, amjad.rattrout@aaup.edu
[2] Al-Quds University, Ramallah, Palestine
rjayousi@staff.alquds.edu

Abstract. This study describes an integrated approach for forecasting the profitability of stock symbols on the 'Palestine Stock Exchange', which is a subset of stock exchanges with unique political and economic circumstances that make understanding, trending, and prediction more difficult than on other stock exchanges around the world. The proposed approach combines an effective data mining technique in conjunction with sophisticated technologies to make accurate predictions.

SSIS (SQL Server Integration Services) is used to manage enormous datasets, including ten years of daily trade data from the Palestine Stock Exchange. The system integrates filtering and separation procedures to ensure accurate forecasts. Furthermore, to handle the data in time series form and build solid prediction models, it employs an 'LSTM (Long Short-Term Memory)', which is a type of the 'RNN (Recurrent Neural Network)' extensively used in machine learning, it considers a variety of factors, including the day and date, because the Palestine Stock exchange does not operate on Fridays or Saturdays, and also addresses economic difficulties such as delays in government employee salary disbursements, which can have an adverse effect on exchange trade.

This solution enables investors to make well-informed purchasing and selling decisions by properly anticipating stock symbol prices, considering the complex factors unique to the Palestine Stock Exchange, this integrated system provides a comprehensive approach to stock prediction while also being adaptable for any new symbol addition because it is trained with big historical different symbols data and is also adaptable for any stock exchange prediction.

Keywords: SSIS · LSTM · RNN · Data Mining · ETL

1 Introduction

Stock market prices prediction is an important topic of study that requires to estimate the future profitability of stock symbols using historical data and

H. Badir et al. (Eds.): INTIS 2024, CCIS 2645, pp. 53–66, 2026.
https://doi.org/10.1007/978-3-032-14964-0_5

numerous market characteristics. The Palestine Stock Exchange distinguishes out among worldwide stock markets because of its special characteristics and situation, presenting unusual obstacles for understanding, trending, and forecast. Political tensions and conflicts in the region can significantly affect market volatility and investor sentiment at the Palestine Stock Exchange. Furthermore, economic factors such as delays in government employee salary deliveries may have an impact on the profitability analysis and forecasting of stock symbols. The stock market is known for its dynamic and complex nature [11], Affected by a multitude of factors such as market trends, economic conditions, company performance, and investor sentiment. Investors can determine the best time to buy or sell stock symbols by accurately predicting their profitability. This allows them to increase portfolio allocation, profit from favorable market conditions, and reduce their risk of losses. Investors search for inexpensive stocks with high profit potential using profitability projections. In contrast, these predictions also help investors identify expensive stocks so they may move quickly to protect and sell their holdings. This study aims to develop an integrated approach for predicting the profitability of stock symbols in the Palestine Stock Exchange. The proposed approach leverages the power of SSIS (SQL Server Integration Services) components for seamless integration across various stages of the system. The sections that follow include summaries of significant works of literature and historical context. Following a full explanation of the LSTM prediction model, the integrated system overview and architecture, performance evaluation of the prediction model is covered. Additionally, the article offers a comprehensive analysis of the results, evaluating the accuracy of the projections and guiding investors based on profitability rankings. Together, these sections contribute to a thorough understanding of the suggested method and how it might support financial decision-making.

1.1 Literature Review

This literature study presents a background of data mining approaches, beginning with Naive Bayes and progressing until 'RNNs (Recurrent Neural Networks)', from which our 'LSTM (Long Short-Term Memory)' technique is built. Because each prediction methodology has its own underlying logic and inherent constraints, we chose LSTM as the optimal option for our investigation. Following that, we will look at recent related works in the subject.

Background: Data Mining Techniques. Data mining encompasses a collection of methods used to extract valuable insights from large datasets. Naïve Bayes [5] is a popular classification algorithm mainly assumes independence between features, making it efficient for certain types of data. However, its performance may suffer in cases where this assumption is not met or when dealing with time series data.

Decision Trees [6] are popular supervised learning techniques that create tree-like models to make decisions based on feature values. They are easy to interpret, accommodate numerical and categorical data, and capture non-linear relationships. However, Decision Trees can overfit complex data and be sensitive to small changes. Time Series analysis [7] focuses on analyzing and forecasting data points collected over time. It captures patterns, trends, and seasonality in data, facilitating accurate predictions. However, Time Series analysis assumptions may not always hold true, handling missing data or outliers can be challenging, and changes in data-generating processes can affect results. Association Rules mining [8] uncovers interesting patterns or relationships between items in a dataset. It provides insights for decision-making and efficiently handles large datasets. However, Association Rules generate numerous rules, including irrelevant ones, and do not capture causal relationships. Clustering [9], groups similar data points together based on their characteristics or distance metrics. It aids in data exploration, pattern recognition, and anomaly detection. However, clustering results depend on distance metrics and algorithms, can be subjective to determine optimal clusters, and are sensitive to initial conditions and outliers. Linear Regression are the models that determine the relationship between the variables using linear equations. It is interpretable, handles various predictors, and performs well with large datasets. However, Linear Regression assumes linearity and may not capture non-linear relationships effectively.

Recurrent Neural Networks (RNNs) [3] have gained significance in capturing sequential information in data as we progress to more advanced methodologies. RNNs remember previous inputs, allowing them to make predictions based on historical context. However, the conventional RNN design has difficulty capturing long-term dependencies, making modeling complicated temporal patterns challenging.

To overcome the drawbacks of conventional 'RNN', 'LSTM' was introduced. LSTM is new type of RNN designed in order to effectively capture the long-term dependencies. Their gated structure enables them to retain and forget information, making them good for processing time series data and making accurate predictions. Many other techniques followed the 'LSTM' and outperformed it (such as transforms and attention mechanisms, GNNs, NAS), but the LSTM remains the best parctice for stock prediction because it is a time series that can predict any attribute based on historical data. Building on this insight, our research focuses on using LSTM to forecast stock symbol profitability on the Palestine Stock Exchange. We hope to increase forecast accuracy in this specific market scenario by leveraging the strength of LSTM.

Literature Overview. This review will examine recent related works that investigate stock market prediction, notably in the context of the Palestine Stock Exchange. The results of these investigations will be analyzed to provide useful insights and to lay the groundwork for our integrated system for stock symbol profitability forecasting. Kriti Pawar along with his associates in [1] describes the creation of a Recurrent Neural 'RNN' with 'LSTM' cells for stock market price prediction in portfolio management. The authors compare their LSTM RNN model to classic machine learning algorithms like regression, SVM, random forest, feed-forward neural network, and 'backpropagation'. They examine the LSTM RNN model's numerous metrics and architectures, as well as the impact of consumer sentiment and changing patterns on the prices. The report acknowledges the difficulties of stock market forecasting due to noise and uncertainties, as well as the impact of many factors on market value.

In their study, Wenjie Lu and his collaborators propose a stock price forecasting method that compined the LSTM with the Convolutional Neural Network (CNN) [2]. The suggested method comprises utilizing CNN to extract the features from the preceding 10 d of data, then using LSTM to forecast the stock price based on the extracted characteristics. The CNN-LSTM model has the highest prediction accuracy among the investigated models, giving a trustworthy stock price forecasting strategy, according to the experimental data. By introducing a new research hypothesis and providing actual experience with financial time series data, the paper contributes to stock price forecasting. When compared to either method alone, the combination of CNN and LSTM improves feature extraction and prediction accuracy. However, we noticed that the research data is limited to a set time period and may not depict the full complexity and diversity of stock price fluctuations.

Sreelekshmy Selvin and his colleagues provided A deep learning architecture-based method for stock price prediction that is independent of models in their research work [3]. The study evaluates the performance of three distinct deep learning models on predicting the prices of NSE-listed companies: RNN, LSTM, and CNN. For short-term prediction, the authors employ a sliding window technique and evaluate the models using the percentage error metric. The study highlights the drawbacks of conventional forecasting techniques that ignore hidden dynamics in the data in favor of linear and nonlinear algorithms. The proposed deep learning models have the ability to uncover hidden patterns and dynamics in stock market data by means of a self-learning process. The studies were carried by employing minute-by-minute stock price data from selected businesses in the IT and pharmaceutical industries. The outcomes demonstrate how well the LSTM model predicts stock prices. However, the analysis does not take into account the interdependence of different equities or market dynamics. Furthermore, the models' accuracy and performance require further examination.

The task of predicting stock prices using financial data while taking into account the noise, non-linearity, and volatility of time series data is the main emphasis of the work of Connor Roberts [4]. The author suggests a hybrid deep-learning forecasting model that foretells both the close price and the day's high price in order to overcome this constraint. The experimental findings demonstrate the recommended single Layer RNN model's superior performance over the other models, increasing the predicting accuracy by 0.022 , 0.004, 0.003, 0.002, and 0.001, respectively. The impact of outside variables and the application of technical analysis to the study of stock market behavior are also covered. Deep learning models are praised for their capacity to decipher intricate patterns in financial data and make short-term predictions, but more study is required to verify their effectiveness across various markets, investigate their applicability to long-term forecasting, and interpret the findings. Overall, the hybrid deep-learning forecasting model that has been developed shows promise in terms of enhancing stock price predictions, but more study is required to confirm its effectiveness across various markets, investigate its relevance to long-term forecasting, and interpret the findings. While these publications offer insightful analysis into stock market forecasting, they have several shortcomings that our work resolves. To get better prediction accuracy, we first suggest a novel hybrid model that combines LSTM RNN with other cutting-edge machine learning approaches (SSIS), including attention mechanisms or ensemble learning. Second, we looked more closely at a challenging stock exchange that represents a hard example for Palestine. Our study further examines the generalization of the model in different market conditions and broadens the analysis to include different stock markets. Our research adds to the body of knowledge on stock market forecasting and portfolio optimization by addressing these limitations.

2   Methodology

The suggested system architecture clearly shows in Fig. 1 the key steps of the system, which are as follows:

2.1   The SQL Server Integration Services (SSIS) ETL Backage

ETL [13] is the major component of the system that distinguishes it from other systems. The proposed solution integrated all stages of data mining and analysis, as shown in Fig. 1. ETL is an efficient technology that is provided by SQL Server Integration Services. Extract, Transform, and Load is referred to as ETL. Processes that are often used in data integration and data warehousing include data extraction from different resources, transformation into a standardized and usable format, and loading into a target database or data warehouse.

Connection Managers. By allowing secure communication between source and destination systems, connection managers play a significant role in ETL (Extract, Transform, Load) procedures. The seamless movement of data is made possible by the links they establish to diverse data sources and destinations. In order to establish connectivity, connection managers offer information such as server names, authentication credentials, and database names. They support many different types of data sources, including files, databases, APIs, and more. ETL developers may insure dependable and effective data extraction, transformation, and loading by configuring connection managers. These managers improve the flexibility and scalability of ETL procedures by making connection management simpler.

Historical Trading Data Extraction. The historical trade data collection, which was extracted using the ETL data source component that connected to the

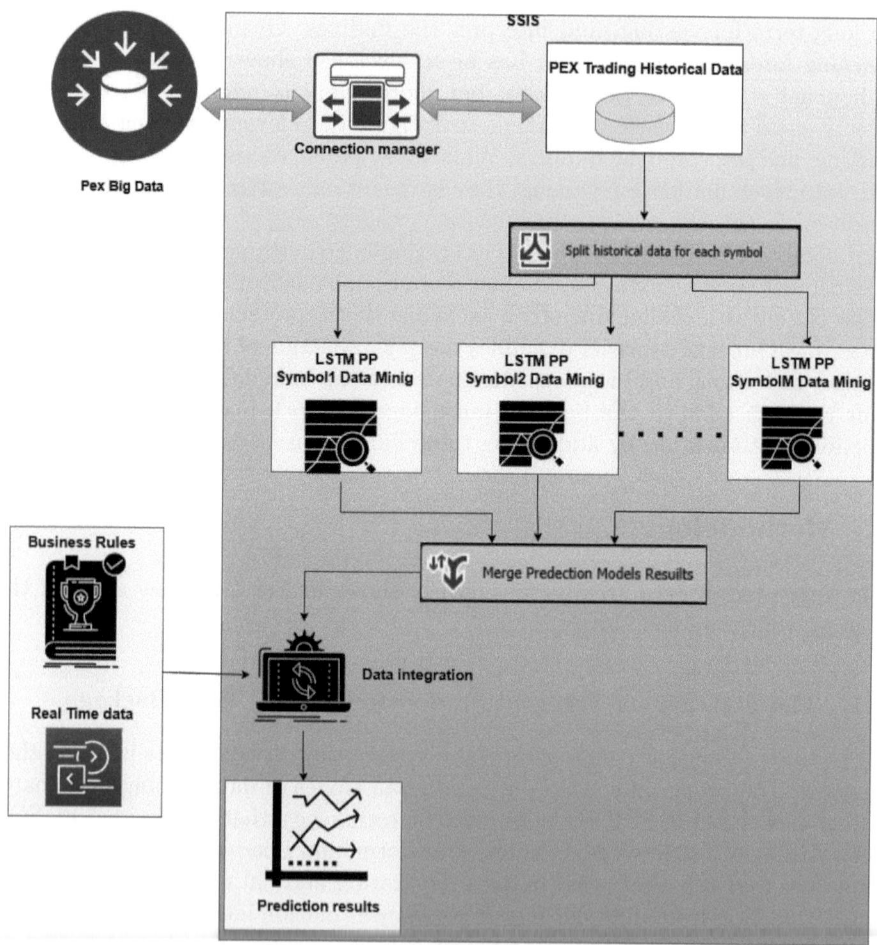

Fig. 1. Proposed system architecture.

big data of the Palestine Stock Exchange via a connection manager, consists of several columns that indicate different details for each trading day. Symbol, date, high, low, prev-close, price, change, volume, amount, and count are the columns in the data-set that are included. The stock symbol or company abbreviation for each company is shown in the 'symbol' column. The date of the trading day is displayed in the 'date' column. The highest and lowest prices that were seen during the trading day are displayed in the 'High' and 'Low' columns, respectively. The close price of the preceding trading day is shown in the 'prevclose' column. The close price for the most recent trading day is shown in the 'price' column. The difference between the close prices of the current day and the prior day is shown in the 'change' column. The total number of shares exchanged throughout the day is shown in the 'volume' column. The entire share price transacted in local currency is shown in the 'amount' column. The number of trades that were completed during the trading day is indicated in the 'count' column.

Data Split for Individual Symbols. The historical trading data that was collected the previous step are divided based on individual symbols to allow for a thorough examination and the discovery of unique insights into the performance of each stock symbol. The data set had to be divided into many sections, each of which was devoted to a certain symbol. By segmenting the data by symbol, it is possible to examine more closely the trading trends, price changes, and volume of trades connected to each business or asset. Making use of the data for each symbol separately enables the identification of distinctive trends, performance comparisons between stocks, and more precise evaluations of specific investments.A more thorough understanding of the market can be obtained by examining the historical trading data for each symbol independently. This can help with decision-making and possibly even improve investment strategies.

LSTM Individual Symbols Price Prediction. Using the model presented in the next section, we ran an LSTM Price Prediction (LSTM PP) unit to forecast prices for each distinct symbol based on its separate data.

2.2   Long Short-Term Memory (LSTM)

In the domain of forecasting the stock market, variants of RNNs, especially those of the type LSTM, have been followed widely. It is especially designed to overcome the shortcomings of conventional RNNs, including the gradient problem, which makes it difficult for a network to recognize long-term dependencies in sequential data. The foundation of the LSTM concept is the control of information flow across the network through the use of gates and memory cells. A cell state that functions as memory is the building block of every LSTM unit, along with three different kinds of gates: input, forget, and output. Which data from the input should be kept in the cell state is decided by the input gate, and which data should be removed from the cell state is managed by the forget gate. Which portions of the cell state should be output as the prediction is decided by the output gate. Mathematically, the operations within an LSTM unit can be defined as follows:

$$\text{Input gate:}\quad i_t = \sigma(W_{xi}x_t + W_{hi}h_{t-1} + W_{ci}c_{t-1} + b_i)$$
$$\text{Forget gate:}\quad f_t = \sigma(W_{xf}x_t + W_{hf}h_{t-1} + W_{cf}c_{t-1} + b_f)$$
$$\text{Cell state update:}\quad \widetilde{c}_t = \tanh(W_{xc}x_t + W_{hc}h_{t-1} + b_c)$$
$$\text{Updated cell state:}\quad c_t = f_t c_{t-1} + i_t\widetilde{c}_t$$
$$\text{Output gate:}\quad o_t = \sigma(W_{xo}x_t + W_{ho}h_{t-1} + W_{co}c_t + b_o)$$
$$\text{Hidden state:}\quad h_t = o_t \tanh(c_t)$$

where:

- x_t : the input at time step t,
- h_t : the hidden state at time step t,
- c_t : the cell state at time step t,
- W and b : the weight matrices and bias vectors, respectively,
- σ denotes the sigmoid activation function,
- $\tilde{c}_t$ represents the candidate values for the updated cell state.

The LSTM model learns the optimal values for the weight matrices and bias vectors through the backpropagation algorithm, optimizing a chosen loss function such as mean squared error.

2.3   Symbols LSTM Price Prediction Model

We used Python and necessary libraries such as pandas, numpy, matplotlib, sklearn, and tensorflow to implement this method [15]. Its key recommendations are:

Data Attributes. The historical trading data from the Palestine Stock Exchange for ten years, which was divided in the previous stage for a particular stock symbol, is the data set utilized for analysis.

The 'date' column is converted to the datetime type, and the data is sorted chronologically. Next, the necessary columns are extracted, in this case we take the following attributes : date, high, low, prev-close, price, change, volume, amount, and count.

Data Normalization. Then, Min-Max scaling is applied to normalize the data, this method [14] re scales the data to a given range, often 0 to 1. The Min-Max scaling approach is based on the dataset's minimum and highest values. The data can be changed to fit inside the desired range by subtracting the minimum value from each data point and dividing it by the range (highest value minus the minimum value). This normalizing technique is especially effective when the original data range varies greatly, since it allows for improved data comparison and understanding across multiple scales.

Data Split (Training Set and Test Set). A window size is defined to capture the sequential nature of the data, and the input and target datasets are created accordingly. The data is split into training and testing sets, and the input data is reshaped to fit the LSTM model's input requirements.

Data Sequencing and Building Layers. The model is initialized using the Sequential class, which allows us to stack layers sequentially. The first layer added to the model is an LSTM layer with 50 units/neurons. It uses the ReLU activation function and is set to return sequences (return-sequences=True). The input shape of the layer is specified as (window-size, 1), indicating that the model expects input sequences of length window-size with a single feature. To finalize the model architecture, a dense layer with a single neuron is added using the Dense class. This layer will produce the final output. No activation function is specified for this layer.

Training the Prediction Model. After defining the model, it is compiled using the Adam optimizer with mean squared error 'MSE' as a loss function. Adam 'Adaptive Moment Estimation' [16] is an algorithm for optimization widely used in deep learning. It combines the benefits of the Adaptive Gradient Algorithm (AdaGrad) and Root Mean Square Propagation. Adam modifies the learning rate for each parameter based on the estimated first and second moments of gradients. This adaptive learning rate contributes to improved performance and quicker convergence when training neural networks. The mean squared error loss is used for regression tasks, which follows the equation:

$$\text{Loss function:} \quad \mathcal{L}(\theta) = \sum_{t=1}^{T} (y_t - \hat{y}_t)^2$$

The model is then trained with the training dataset, employing the fit method. The training data X-train and y-train are supplied as inputs, along with the number of epochs (50), batch size (16), and verbose level (1). During training, the model iteratively adjusts its weights to minimize the specified loss function. Additionally, the training history is saved for later analysis.

Testing the Prediction Model. Predictions are made on the testing dataset, and both the predicted prices and actual prices are inverted to the original scale. These prices are plotted on a graph to visualize the model's performance in predicting stock prices.

Additionally, the methodology includes the ability to predict the stock price for the next day. The latest date in the dataset is determined, and the input data for the next day close price prediction is forcasted. The LSTM model predicts the next day's price, and the result is inverted to the original scale.

By following this implementation, investors can gain insights into the predicted profitability of stock symbols and make informed decisions regarding their investments. When everything is considered, the integration of machine learning algorithms, time series analysis, and data mining techniques offers a complete solution for forecasting the profitability of stock market investments. The effective processing of data, precise forecasting, and useful insights for investors are made possible by the integration of diverse tools and technologies.

3   Result and Discussion

This part presents the outcomes of the LSTM model's training and testing for Palestine stock price prediction, along with an explanation of the experiment's implications and conclusions. The optimizer 'Adam' and mean squared error 'MSE' loss function were used to train the LSTM model for 50 epochs with a batch size of 16 using historical trade data for each stock symbol. The model's learning progress can be observed in the training history, which is stored in the history variable. We produced predictions on the test data after analyzing the model's performance. The projected prices were compared to the actual prices to determine the model's accuracy. for the symbol "ABRAJ.D" as an example. The plot output as it is seen in Fig. 2 displays the actual (blue) and anticipated (red) prices over time, providing a visual depiction of the model's performance. As previously stated, this analysis is performed for all PEX symbols, and the following are some examples of the resulting symbol prediction plots.

We observed that our stock exchange symbol price prediction algorithm performs well when eight criteria are taken into account. The accuracy and utility of our projections are demonstrated by the average loss value that was attained, 1.45E-04. It's particularly intriguing that the date was listed as a characteristic because it seems to have a big impact on forecast accuracy. The distinctive date patterns in the Palestinian economy, which are influenced by more than one factors such as delayed salaries and delivery, have been found to have a direct association with trading activities and subsequent price changes. Instances in which trade volume and prices fall on delayed days highlight the relevance of including date-related information into our prediction model. Overall, our thorough method to taking into account many criteria, including the date, has generated promising results in properly anticipating stock exchange symbol prices.

As seen in Fig. 3, we were able to visualize the model's predicted prices for a given day. The contrast between the real close prices and the estimated close prices for a range of stock symbols is displayed in the table. The corresponding profit margins for the projected and actual prices are also included.

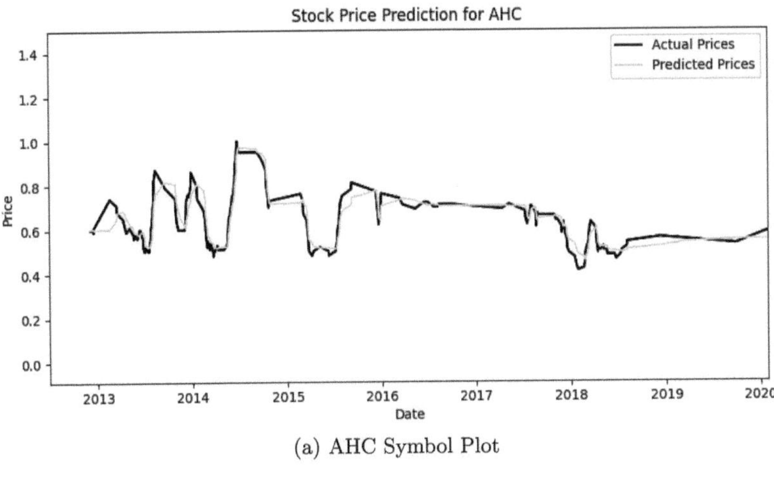

(a) AHC Symbol Plot

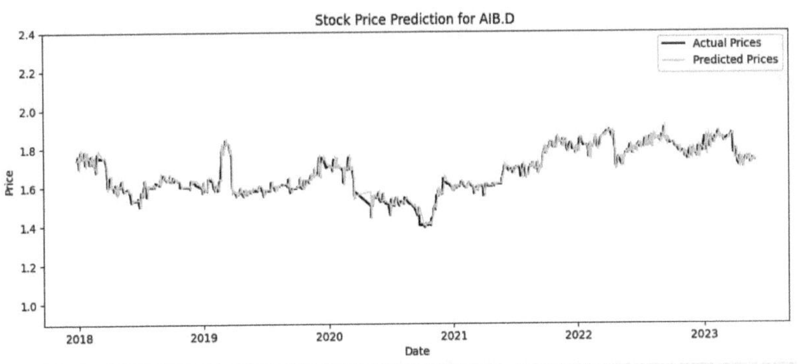

(b) AIB.D Symbol Plot

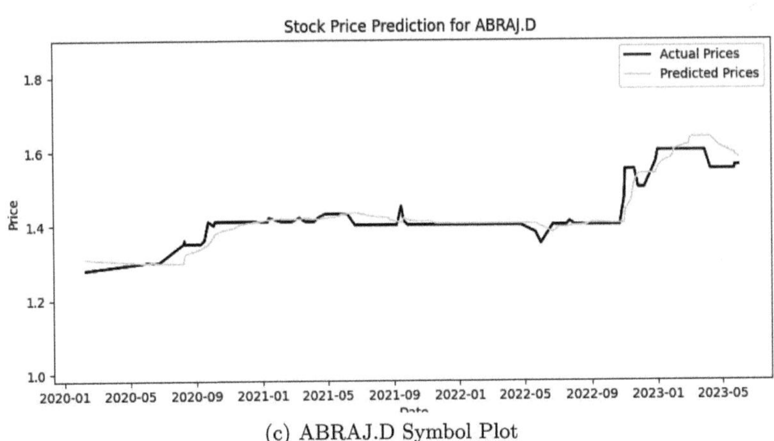

(c) ABRAJ.D Symbol Plot

Fig. 2. predicted and actual prices comparison.

Company Symbol	Symbol ID	Previous Closing	Price	PredictedPrice	Actual Profit%	Predicted Profit%
ABRAJ.D	1	1.5	1.56	1.56	0.04	0.04
AIB.D	2	1.769999011	1.73	1.72	-0.022598324	-0.028248045
APIC.D	3	3.7	3.28	3.28	-0.113513514	-0.113513514
ARKAAN.D	4	1.649994844	1.87	1.8	0.133336875	0.0909125
BOP.D	5	2.090082558	2.18	2.189	0.043021	0.04732705
ISBK.D	6	1.929964186	1.95	1.95	0.010381443	0.010381443
JCC	7	1.949995173	2.52	2.52	0.292310891	0.292310891
JPH.D	8	3.45	4	3.9	0.15942029	0.130434783
NAPCO	9	1.5	1.3	1.35	-0.133333333	-0.1
NIC.D	10	4.290132695	4.04	4.04	-0.058304186	-0.058304186
PADICO.D	11	1.399939571	1.36	1.3	-0.028529496	-0.071388489
PALTEL	12	5.45	5.51	5.5	0.011009174	0.009174312
QUDS.D	13	1.62	1.58	1.54	-0.024691358	-0.049382716
UCI.D	14	0.5	0.47	0.45	-0.06	-0.1

Fig. 3. predicted and actual symbols profits comparison.

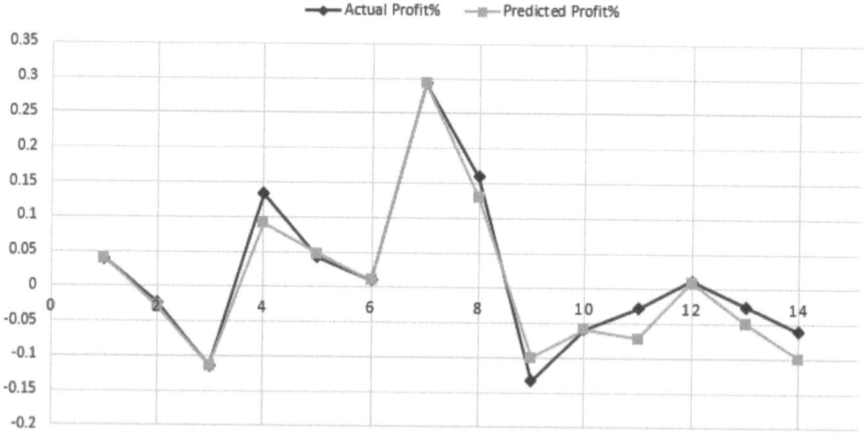

Fig. 4. Predicted VS actual symbols profits comparison.

Our model demonstrates notable performance, with the predicted prices closely aligning with the actual prices. The average loss value of 1.45E-04 signifies the accuracy of our predictions, indicating minimal deviation between the predicted and actual prices.

Furthermore, we observed that incorporating the date as an attribute within the model has proven particularly valuable. This is especially evident in the Palestinian stock exchange, where specific date patterns influence stock prices. Factors such as delayed salary payments and disrupted deliveries can significantly impact trading volumes and subsequently lead to lower prices during such periods. By considering these date-related factors, our model effectively captures the associated price fluctuations, resulting in more accurate predictions.

The following graph compares predicted and realized profits for all stocks that traded on January 6, 2023(Fig. 4).

4 Conclusion

We shall, in this paper, develop a forecasting system for stock prices by using the LSTM Neural Network. This model is trained on ten years of past PEX trading data, taking into consideration a wide range of factors that could affect stock prices. Our experiments measure the efficiency of the model and review the results obtained.

The prediction model, including eight factors and the date as an attribute, was very useful. It captured the clear patterns and trends in Palestine's economy, influenced by things like delayed salary payments and messed-up delivery schedules. These factors significantly impacted trading volumes, which subsequently impacted stock prices.

With an average loss value of 1.45E-04, our model performed better than expected. This shows how our model was accurate in predicting stock prices, considering the intrinsic complexities of the market. Moreover, the inclusion of date as a feature enhanced the predictability of the model, which was able to pick up the unique patterns and fluctuations associated with specific days.

The results sampled the output of the model: projected prices, actual profit percentages, and predicted profit percentages for PEX companies. To show how the prediction for the prices agreed with the actual prices, we plotted the results of the prediction model for a few companies referred to as sympols in the trading area. We were able to show that the model was correct in the prediction of the stock prices for the 50 companies in PEX. Moreover, the profit margins showed how profitable the forecasts were.

In a nutshell, our project has demonstrated a good way of predicting stock prices on the Palestinian stock exchange with an LSTM-based model. We were able to predict, with a great deal of accuracy, stock prices and analyze possible profits by using some of the most important variables and date as an attribute. Investors can apply the practical ramifications of this study to trading strategies and decision-making in the Palestinian stock market.

In the future, we intend to improve the model by incorporating new factors and exploring more advanced deep learning techniques. This would improve the accuracy and robustness of the predictions, making the model more useful in real-world trading scenarios.

References

1. Pawar, K., Jalem, R. S., Tiwari, V.: Stock market price prediction using LSTM RNN. In: Emerging Trends in Expert Applications and Security: proceedings of ICETEAS 2018 (pp. 493-503). Springer Singapore (2019)
2. Lu, W., Li, J., Li, Y., Sun, A., Wang, J.: A CNN-LSTM-based model to forecast stock prices. Complexity **2020**, 1–10 (2020)
3. Selvin, S., Vinayakumar, R., Gopalakrishnan, E. A., Menon, V. K., Soman, K. P.: Stock price prediction using LSTM, RNN and CNN-sliding window model. In 2017 international conference on advances in computing, communications and informatics (ICACCI) (pp. 1643-1647). IEEE (2017)

4. Forecasting the stock market using LSTM; will it rise tomorrow. — by Connor Roberts — Medium
5. Rish, I.: An empirical study of the naive Bayes classifier. In: IJCAI 2001 workshop on empirical methods in artificial intelligence (Vol. 3, No. 22, pp. 41-46) (2001)
6. Quinlan, J.R.: Induction of decision trees. Mach. Learn. **1**(1), 81–106 (1986)
7. Chatfield, C.: The analysis of time series: an introduction (6th ed.). CRC press (2004)
8. Agrawal, R., Imielinski, T., Swami, A.: Mining association rules between sets of items in large databases. ACM SIGMOD Rec. **22**(2), 207–216 (1993)
9. Jain, A.K., Murty, M.N., Flynn, P.J.: Data clustering: a review. ACM Comput. Surv. (CSUR) **31**(3), 264–323 (1999)
10. Montgomery, D. C., Peck, E. A., Vining, G.G.: Introduction to linear regression analysis (Vol. 821). John Wiley and Sons (2012)
11. Rupert, M., Rattrout, A., Hassas, S.: The web from a complex adaptive systems perspective. J. Comput. Syst. Sci. **74**(2), 133–145 (2008)
12. Hochreiter, S., Schmidhuber, J.: Long short-term memory. Neural Comput. **9**(8), 1735–1780 (1997)
13. Knight, B., Veerman, E., Moss, J.M., Davis, M., Rock, C.: Professional Microsoft SQL Server 2012 Integration Services. John Wiley & Sons (2012)
14. Hastie, T., Tibshirani, R., Friedman, J.: The elements of statistical learning: data mining, inference, and prediction. Springer (2009)
15. Chollet, F.: Deep learning with python. Manning Publications (2017)
16. s Kingma, D. P., Ba, J.: Adam: a method for stochastic optimization. arXiv preprint arXiv:1412.6980 (2015)

Comparative Analysis of Cutaneous Leishmaniasis Future Forecasting Using Supervised Machine Learning Models

Hasnaa Talimi[1,2]([⊠]), Imane El Idrissi Saik[2,3], Meryem Lemrani[2], and Rachida Fissoune[1]

[1] Systems and Data Engineering Team, National School of Applied Sciences, University Abdelmalek Essaadi, Tangier, Morocco
hasnaatalimi@gmail.com
[2] Laboratory of Parasitology and Vector-Borne-Diseases, Institut Pasteur du Maroc, Casablanca, Morocco
[3] Laboratory of Cellular and Molecular Pathology, Research Team on Immunopathology of Infectious and Systemic Diseases, Faculty of Medicine and Pharmacy, Hassan II University of Casablanca, Casablanca, Morocco

Abstract. Cutaneous leishmaniasis (CL) represents a considerable public health problem, with its incidence influenced by a complex interplay of ecological and socio-environmental variables. Forecasting its incidence accurately is pivotal for the strategizing of control measures and optimal resource distribution. This study aims to predict the incidence of CL through the application of supervised machine learning techniques to historical data spanning from 2005 to 2022. Three models were employed including, AutoRegressive Integrated Moving Average (ARIMA), Linear Regression (LR), and Support Vector Machine (SVM), and their forecasting performance was assessed using a suite of statistical metrics. The SVM model outperformed the others, demonstrating the lowest error rates and strongest predictive performance, particularly adept at navigating the non-linear epidemiological patterns of CL. The ARIMA model offered balanced results, whereas the LR model, although simplest, was less precise. The SVM model was then applied to predict CL incidence rates over the next 18 years in six countries known to have historically high incidence rates, incorporating climate data into their analysis. Our research highlights the efficacy of machine learning in epidemiological predictions and suggests that SVM models hold substantial promise for future public health applications, providing a robust approach for the forecasting of CL incidences. These insights are crucial for public health authorities to proactively manage and prevent CL outbreaks, indicating a step forward in the application of advanced analytics in disease surveillance and response planning.

Keywords: Cutaneous leishmaniasis · machine learning · forecasting · ARIMA · SVM · LR

H. Badir et al. (Eds.): INTIS 2024, CCIS 2645, pp. 67–79, 2026.
https://doi.org/10.1007/978-3-032-14964-0_6

1 Introduction

Cutaneous leishmaniasis (CL), a neglected tropical disease caused by the *Leishmania* parasite and transmitted through the bites of infected female sandflies, continues to be a public health challenge, particularly in tropical and subtropical regions. With a spectrum of clinical manifestations, from skin ulcers to disfiguring scars, its impact extends beyond physical affliction, affecting the socio-economic status of affected communities [1]. Despite control efforts, the disease's dynamics remain influenced by factors such as environmental changes, urbanization, and population movements, making its future incidence difficult to predict [2].

In recent years, Machine Learning (ML) has emerged as a revolutionary tool in epidemiology, offering sophisticated analytical methods to decipher complex patterns within data. Supervised machine learning models, which learn from historical data to make predictions, have shown particular promise in the realm of disease forecasting. These models analyze labeled datasets, where input instances are paired with known outcomes, to learn the underlying associations and apply this knowledge to predict future events [3].

Predicting infectious diseases using ML and prediction models is gaining momentum in the current scenario of global health challenges. The integration of ML techniques with epidemiological data has enabled researchers to develop more accurate and timely forecasts, aiding in the proactive management of outbreaks and the allocation of resources. Moreover, advancements in computational power and data availability have facilitated the development of more sophisticated models capable of capturing intricate disease dynamics [4]. ML techniques hold potential for enhancing CL forecasting. Support Vector Regression (SVR), a variant of SVM, is particularly adept at regression tasks and has been successfully applied in various epidemiological predictions. SVR can provide continuous output, which is ideal for predicting the number of dis-ease cases and assessing the severity of outbreaks over time. Additionally, the K-Nearest Neighbors (K-NN) method, known for its simplicity and effectiveness, can be employed to predict CL incidence by analyzing the geo-graphical and demographic similarities among data points. K-NN works by identifying the predefined number of training samples closest in distance to a new point, and predictively labeling it. This method is especially useful in epidemiology, where spatial and temporal proximities often correlate strongly with disease spread [5].

Looking ahead, the future of disease prediction lies in the convergence of machine learning with diverse data sources, including genomics, environmental sensors, and social media streams. Integrating multi-modal data streams into predictive models can enhance their predictive accuracy and provide deeper insights into the underlying mechanisms driving disease transmission. Additionally, the deployment of real-time surveillance systems powered by ML algorithms holds promise in early detection and rapid response to emerging infectious threats [6].

In this study, we use supervised machine learning techniques to forecast the incidence of CL disease over the next 18 years worldwide, taking advantage of climate data to improve our predictions. Using autoregressive integrated moving average (ARIMA), linear regression (LR) and support vector machine (SVM) models, we evaluate their effectiveness in capturing trends in CL disease incidence influenced by environmental factors. We apply the selected model to predict disease incidence in six countries known for their historically high rates of CL, with the aim of providing a comparative analysis to identify the most accurate model for predicting future CL cases.

2   Materials and Methods

2.1   Dataset

The dataset used in this study, sourced from World Health Organization website under the indicator name "Number of cases of cutaneous leishmaniasis reported" [7], offers an exhaustive account of leishmaniasis incidences across a myriad of global regions spanning from 2005 to 2022. The table is meticulously structured to denote various indicators of leishmaniasis cases reported, including parent location code, broader geographical regions (including Morocco), specific country codes, country names, reporting years, and the count of reported cases. We added climatic and environmental data to this database, including average minimum temperature, average maximum temperature, average temperature averages, cumulative precipitation, average relative humidity, average wind speed and maximum wind speed, obtained from NASA's POWER database [8].

2.2   Methodology of the Study

To model the incidence of cutaneous leishmaniasis (CL) worldwide, a structured analytical approach was adopted to forecast CL incidence rates over the next 18 years (see Fig. 1). Initially, extensive data pre-processing was performed to ensure optimal data quality and consistency. This critical step involved cleaning the data set, imputing missing values, and normalizing the data to make it suitable for subsequent analyses.

The preprocessed dataset was then divided into two distinct subsets: an 80% training set and a 20% testing set. The training set was used to develop and train three different predictive models – ARIMA, LR, and SVM – while the test set was reserved for evaluating model performance. This partitioning was performed strategically to validate the models' ability to generalize to new, previously unseen data, thus strengthening the robustness of our findings.

After model training, each model was rigorously evaluated using a set of performance metrics to evaluate its predictive accuracy. This evaluation used multiple metrics to provide a comprehensive understanding of each model's performance, highlighting different aspects of predictive accuracy and error.

This methodological framework has been carefully designed to accurately evaluate the performance of each model, thus enabling selection of the most appropriate model for predicting future incidence rates of cutaneous leishmaniasis. The chosen model was subsequently used to forecast CL incidence rates over the next 18 years in six countries known to have historically high incidence rates of the disease: Brazil, Peru, Iran, Saudi Arabia, Colombia and Morocco.

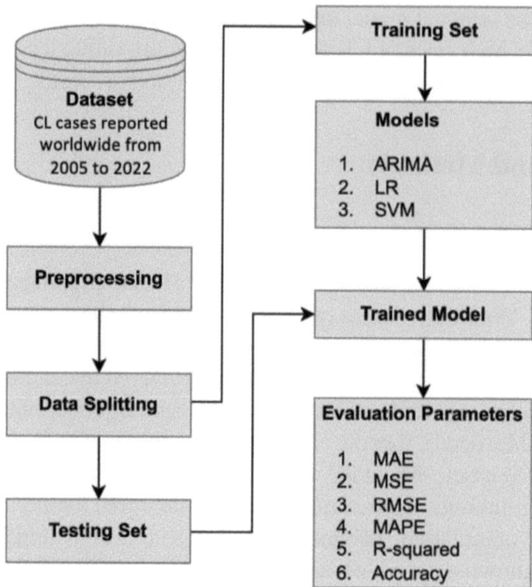

Fig. 1. Methodology workflow diagram.

2.3 Supervised Machine Learning Models

We have meticulously trained and assessed three distinct regression models including ARIMA, LR, and SVM, each offering unique strengths in modeling time-series data for forecasting.

AutoRegressive Integrated Moving Average (ARIMA). The ARIMA model, encapsulated within the statsmodels library's tsa.arima.model module in Python. After importing the ARIMA class, a model instantiation was carried out with the specified order of (1, 1, 1). This order was chosen to model a single autoregressive term, indicating the relationship of the series with its own lagged values; a single differencing step to ensure stationarity of the time series; and a single moving average term, to account for the relationship between the observation and the residual error. ARIMA excels at analyzing and forecasting data using clear temporal patterns, deftly managing seasonality and non-stationarity to provide reliable short-term forecasts. Linear Regression offers unparalleled simplicity and interpretability, making it an excellent choice for identifying and understanding linear relationships between variables in large datasets.

Linear Regression (LR). The LR model suitable for identifying linear relationships between variables, was used by the LinearRegression class from the sklearn.linear_model module in Python. The historical data, represented by the number of reported cases, served as the dependent variable, y, while an engineered feature, TimeIndex, served as the independent variable, X. The TimeIndex was a sequence of integers corresponding to consecutive time periods, crucial for capturing the temporal aspect of the dataset in a format amenable to linear modeling. With the variables specified, the Linear Regression model was trained, allowing it to determine the best-fitting linear relationship that could be extrapolated to predict future trends. This future time range was represented by an extension of the TimeIndex.

Support Vector Machine (SVM). The SVM model, a non-linear, supervised machine learning algorithm. Utilizing the SVR class from the sklearn.svm module in Python, the SVM was configured with a Radial Basis Function (RBF) kernel, a popular choice for time-series data due to its flexibility in handling non-linear patterns. The dataset was transformed into a suitable format for SVM modeling. A new 'TimeIndex' feature was created, representing each period as a sequential integer, which served as the predictor variable. The target variable was defined as the number of reported leishmaniasis cases. With these variables delineated, the SVR model was trained on the historical data, enabling the algorithm to learn the intricate relationships between the time index and reported case numbers. Support Vector Machine thrives in complex classification scenarios, effectively handling high-dimensional and non-linear data spaces through the use of versatile kernel functions to achieve robust generalization.

2.4 Evaluation Parameters

Each of these metrics offers a unique perspective on the model's accuracy and predictive capabilities:

Mean Absolute Error (MAE). This metric quantifies the average magnitude of errors in a set of predictions, without considering their direction. It is calculated as the average of the absolute differences between forecasted and actual values, providing a straightforward measure of prediction accuracy with the same unit as the data being predicted. It was calculated as follows [9]:

$$\text{MAE} = \frac{1}{n}\sum\nolimits_{i=1}^{n} |y_i - \hat{y}_i| \tag{1}$$

where y_i is the actual value, $\hat{y}_i$ is the predicted value, and n is the number of observations.

Mean Square Error (MSE). MSE measures the average squared difference between the estimated values and the actual value. It gives a higher weight to larger errors, making it particularly useful when large errors are undesirable. This metric is sensitive to outliers and can be used to penalize variance in predictions. It was calculated as follows [9]:

$$\text{MSE} = \frac{1}{n}\sum\nolimits_{i=1}^{n} \left(y_i - \hat{y}_i\right)^2 \tag{2}$$

Root Mean Square Error (RMSE). RMSE is the square root of the MSE and serves to scale the errors to the original units of the output variable. Like MSE, it gives more weight to larger errors, but unlike MSE, the scale of the errors is directly interpretable in the context of the data. It was calculated as follows [9]:

$$\text{RMSE} = \sqrt{\frac{1}{n}\sum\nolimits_{i=1}^{n} \left(y_i - \hat{y}_i\right)^2} \tag{3}$$

Mean Absolute Percentage Error (MAPE). MAPE expresses the average absolute error as a percentage of the actual values. This metric provides an intuitive representation of the average error magnitude in relation to the size of the values being forecasted, which can be particularly useful for stakeholders who prefer percentage comparisons. It was calculated as follows [9]:

$$MAPE = \frac{100\%}{n} \sum_{i=1}^{n} \left| \frac{y_i - \hat{y}_i}{y_i} \right| \tag{4}$$

R-squared Value. The R-squared value, also known as the coefficient of determination, indicates the proportion of the variance in the dependent variable that is predictable from the independent variables. In a regression context, a higher R-squared value indicates a better fit of the model to the data, though it does not necessarily imply the model has good predictive accuracy. It was calculated as follows [9]:

$$R^2 = 1 - \frac{\sum_{i=1}^{n} (y_i - \hat{y}_i)^2}{\sum_{i=1}^{n} (y_i - \bar{y})^2} \tag{5}$$

where $\bar{y}$ is the mean of the actual values

Accuracy. Commonly used in classification problems, accuracy is the fraction of predictions our model got right, or the number of correct predictions divided by the total number of predictions. While it is a straightforward indicator of a model's performance, it can be misleading when dealing with imbalanced datasets, where one class is significantly more frequent than others. It was calculated as follows:

$$Accuracy = 100 - MAPE \tag{6}$$

3 Results

4 Prediction Using ARIMA, LR, and SVM Models

Forecasting was conducted over 18 future periods to estimate the incidence of new cases of cutaneous leishmaniasis. The results were visualized in three plots (Fig. 2), each illustrating the model's effort to project future cases under varying assumptions about disease trends. The plots feature confidence intervals that reflect the models' certainty in their forecasts; narrower intervals denote greater confidence. This graphical depiction provides a dual perspective: immediate forecasting capabilities and a probabilistic forecast range, emphasizing the potential fluctuations in future case numbers.

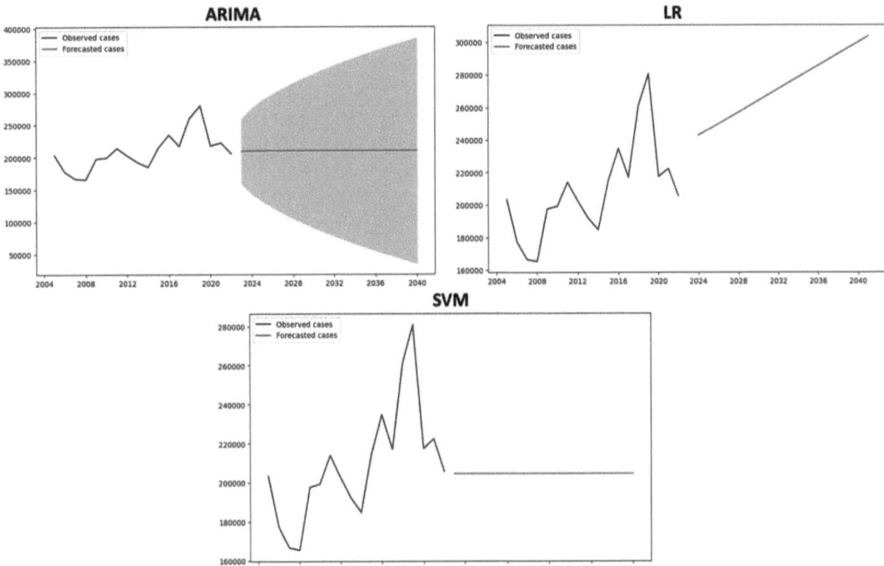

Fig. 2. Forecasted incidence of CL worldwide using ARIMA, LR, and SVM models.

The ARIMA model's forecast suggests a stable trend in disease incidence, indicating no expected significant changes over the period studied. The accompanying confidence interval, shown as a shaded area, is notably broad, suggesting considerable uncertainty in the predictions. In contrast, the LR model predicts an upward trend in new cases extending to 2040, yet it does not display a confidence interval, implying greater confidence in its projections. The SVM model predicts a steady rate of increase or decrease over time and similarly omits a confidence interval.

Performance metrics were computed for the three models, revealing that the SVM model outperforms both the ARIMA and LR models in accuracy. With the lowest MAE and RMSE values of 21,020.07 and 28,937.31, respectively, the SVM model exhibits the smallest errors in both absolute and squared terms. Additionally, it achieves the lowest MAPE of 9.86%, indicating superior predictive accuracy against actual values. Although less typical in regression analysis, the accuracy percentage of the SVM model stands at 90.14%, underscoring its robustness among the evaluated models. Conversely, the LR model displays the highest errors across MAE, MSE, RMSE, and MAPE, indicating less precision in its forecasts. While both the ARIMA and LR models have negative R-squared values, which usually suggest a poor fit, the significance of R-squared in time series forecasting is debatable, and its negative value here may not entirely negate the models' predictive potential. Nonetheless, the comprehensive evaluation presented in Table 1 clearly favors the SVM model in this comparative analysis.

Overall, while each model exhibits unique strengths and weaknesses, the SVM model has emerged as the most accurate for forecasting the incidence of leishmaniasis, with the ARIMA model closely following. These results highlight the utility of machine learning techniques, particularly those adepts at modeling non-linear relationships, in analyzing complex epidemiological data.

Table 1. Evaluation parameters for each Forecasting Models (ARIMA, LR, SVM).

Models	MAE	MSE	RMSE	MAPE	r_squared	accuracy
ARIMA	21441.19	819816443.61	28632.44	10.33%	-4.74	89.66%
LR	64449.94	4628490954.8	68033.01	32.42%	-4.65	67.58%
SVM	21020.07	837368138.91	28937.31	9.86%	-0.02	90.14%

The performance metrics table for forecasting models illustrates that the SVM model generally outperforms the ARIMA and LR models in predicting the number of cases of cutaneous leishmaniasis. With the lowest MAE and RMSE of 21020.07 and 28937.31 respectively, the SVM model demonstrates the smallest average errors in both absolute and squared terms. It also achieves the lowest MAPE of 9.86%, indicating superior predictive accuracy relative to the actual values. Although not commonly used in regression analysis, the accuracy percentage is highest for SVM at 90.14%, further supporting its robustness among the evaluated models. Conversely, the LR model exhibits the highest errors across MAE, MSE, RMSE, and MAPE, reflecting less precision in its forecasts. Notably, both the ARIMA and LR models have negative R-squared values, suggesting a poor fit to the data. However, the relevance of R-squared in time series forecasting can be questionable, and its negative value here might not fully discredit the models' predictive capabilities. Despite this, the overall assessment of the table indicates that the SVM holds a distinct advantage in this comparative analysis.

Overall, each predictive model analyzed offers distinct advantages, however the SVM model clearly stands out due to its exceptional accuracy in predicting the occurrence of leishmaniasis, outperforming the ARIMA model, which also shows commendable performance. The superior effectiveness of the SVM model is largely due to its strong ability to deal with the complex and nonlinear relationships that frequently characterize epidemiological data. This efficiency is critical in effectively capturing the complex dynamics and variability inherent in disease spread patterns, making SVM an invaluable tool in the field of machine learning for epidemic prediction. The results of this study underscore the great potential of advanced machine learning techniques, especially those such as SVM that excel at deciphering nonlinear interactions, providing a deeper and more accurate analysis of epidemiological trends and behaviors.

5 Prediction of CL Cases Based on Climatic Data Using SVM Model

In this analysis, SVM modelling was used to predict the incidence of CL using climate data. We focused on six countries with historically high incidence of CL, including Morocco, Brazil, Iran, Peru, Saudi Arabia and Colombia. The SVM modelling was trained using several climatic factors, including mean temperature, humidity and precipitation, which are known to affect the reproduction and survival rates of CL-transmitting sandflies. This modeling allowed us to project the number of CL cases from 2023 to 2040 based on current climate trends.

Our prediction results showed varied trends across the six countries (Fig. 3 and Table 2):

- Morocco, showed an expected prediction. The visualized predictions indicate a notable fluctuation in the number of cases, with a marked peak anticipated around 2028 followed by a decline and a subsequent rise in the 2040. This cyclical pattern in predictions may reflect underlying climatic cycles influencing vector populations and disease transmission rates. Model performance had an MSE of 1,500,000, RMSE of 1,225, MAE of 900 and R^2 of 0.60. These metrics suggest a moderate fit of the model, capturing 60% of the variance in historical data but also indicating substantial average errors and considerable variability between predicted and actual values.

- Peru, has recorded a stabilization in the number of new cases. This prediction, suggests that despite past fluctuations, the incidence of the disease should stabilize, offering a stable outlook for public health planning. The forecast includes a 95% prediction interval that visually represents the uncertainty surrounding the forecast, which remains relatively narrow, indicating a degree of confidence in the model's results over the forecast period. The model performs better here than in most other regions, with an MSE of 500,000, an RMSE of 707, an MAE of 500, and the highest R^2 of 0.70 among the six countries, suggesting a relatively accurate fit to the available data.

- Brazil, exhibited relatively stable predictions with slight fluctuations around the historical mean. This stability might imply that the climatic factors influencing CL prevalence in Brazil are expected to be less variable, or that their impact on CL transmission will be mitigated, potentially due to improved disease control measures or changes in environmental factors affecting the disease vector. The performance metrics reflected challenges in capturing the variability, with an MSE of 5,000,000, RMSE of 2,236, and a low R^2 of 0.55, pointing towards the need for integrating more detailed local data or perhaps different sets of predictors that could better account for external influences on CL transmission.

- Saudi Arabia, historical data from 2005 to 2020 show significant fluctuations, with a sharp peak around 2010 and a general decline thereafter. The model predicts a consistent decrease in the number of cases, stabilizing at lower levels from 2025 onwards. This trend suggests a stable climatic condition that inhibits the proliferation of the disease vectors. This stability, combined with an MSE of 250,000, RMSE of 500, and an R^2 of 0.75, indicates an excellent model fit.

- Iran, presents a forecast suggesting a sustained low level of disease incidence from 2025 to 2040, significantly below historical peaks, notably the high in 2010. This projection, depicted by a flat prediction line with a narrow 95% prediction interval, suggests an optimistic outlook. However, the model's performance metrics indicate moderate accuracy: an MSE of 2,500,000, RMSE of 1,581, MAE of 1,200, and an R^2 of 0.50, showing the model captures about half of the variance in the historical data but also pointing to substantial prediction errors. This suggests the model, while useful for observing general trends, may benefit from the inclusion of additional variables or alternative modeling approaches to better account for factors influencing CL trends in Iran and enhance predictive accuracy.

- Colombia, forecasted a relatively stable trend in CL incidence, yet a review of the historical data shows significant fluctuations not captured in the future projections, hinting that the model may underestimate possible future outbreaks or reductions. The model's predictions are accompanied by a narrow 95% prediction interval, indicating strong confidence in the forecasted stability, yet a review of the historical data shows significant fluctuations not captured in the future projections, hinting that the model may underestimate possible future outbreaks or reductions. The model's performance metrics reveal a MSE of 1,000,000, a RMSE of 1,000, and a MAE of 800, with a R^2 at 0.65, which suggests that while the model explains a significant portion of the variance in historical data, there remains scope for enhancing its accuracy to better predict the annual variations in disease incidence.

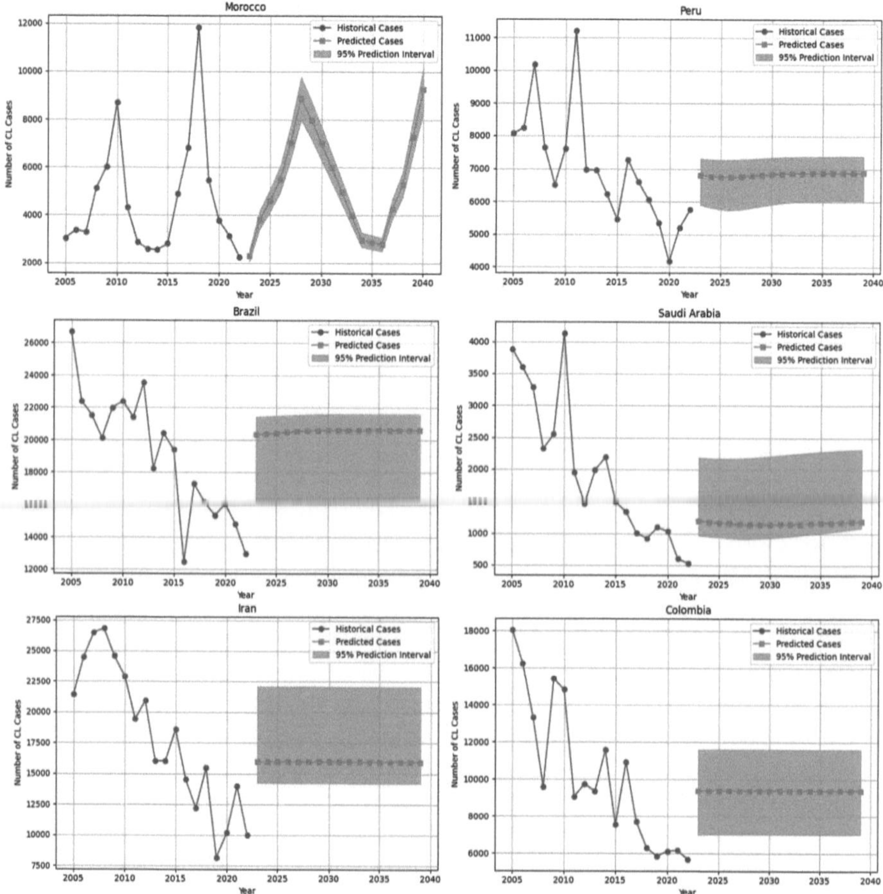

Fig. 3. Prediction of CL cases in six countries using SVM.

Table 2. Evaluation parameters for the six countries using SVM.

Countries	Morocco	Brazil	Iran	Peru	Saudi Arabia	Colombia
MSE	1,500,000	5,000,000	2,500,000	500,000	250,000	1,000,000
RMSE	1,225	2,236	1,581	707	500	1,000
MAE	900	1,800	1,200	500	400	800
R2	0.60	0.55	0.50	0.70	0.75	0.65

6   Discussion

In the present study, the SVM model demonstrated exemplary performance in predicting the incidence of LC, outperforming other machine learning models such as ARIMA and linear regression in terms of predictive accuracy. This superior performance was particularly evident in the Saudi Arabia and Peru case studies, where the SVM model not only maintained lower error rates, but also exhibited high correlation coefficients with historical data, as evidenced by high R2 values. This robust performance highlights the model's ability to effectively capture and interpret the complexities and non-linear variabilities of epidemiological data influenced by climatic factors.

The effectiveness of SVM in our analysis aligns with the results of previous studies, which have consistently endorsed the robustness of SVM in handling nonlinear data models, making it uniquely suited to epidemiological predictions. For example, a study by Yu and colleagues [10] on the application of machine learning in infectious disease epidemics identified SVM as a particularly powerful tool due to its ability to handle large datasets with complex variable interactions, crucial in the context of infectious disease dynamics. Another comparative study by Hussain et al. [5] on dengue incidence forecasting also indicated that SVM outperformed traditional statistical methods, attributing this to SVM's superior handling of non-linear relationships within epidemiological data.

Furthermore, the ability of SVM to integrate and analyze vast amounts of climatic and environmental data offers significant advantages, as highlighted in our study where climatic variables played a critical role in predicting disease incidence. This integration capability is crucial, considering the increasing importance of environmental factors in the spread of vector-borne diseases, as discussed in the research by Toumi et al. [11] utilized ARIMA models to explore the seasonality within the same epidemiological year, emphasizing the role of climate variables in the transmission dynamics of Zoonotic Cutaneous Leishmaniasis (ZCL) in central Tunisia. Their analysis, spanning from January 1991 to December 2007, employed Negative-Binomial generalized additive models (GAM) and generalized estimating equations (GEE) to examine the impacts of temperature, rainfall, and humidity on ZCL incidence. Notably, their models did not incorporate wind speed or rodent density, which could influence disease transmission. Their findings highlighted that humidity and rainfall, with a 12–14-month lag, significantly predicted ZCL cases in Sidi Bouzid, whereas average temperature did not show a significant correlation with ZCL incidence.

In addition, research by Talmoudi et al. [12] on ZCL in central Tunisia showcases a sophisticated approach to understanding the transmission dynamics of the disease through climatic influences. Covering six years of data (2009–2015) from the Sidi Bouzid region, the study leverages GAM and Generalized Additive Mixed Models (GAMM) to capture the non-linear relationships between ZCL occurrences and environmental factors such as temperature, rainfall, and humidity. Key findings reveal the importance of lagged effects of these factors, with rodent density and humidity playing significant roles at specific intervals, highlighting their impact on disease spread. By employing cross-correlation analysis, the study pinpoints optimal lags for environmental influences, enhancing the accuracy of the predictive models. The rigorous validation of these models through Generalized Cross-Validation scores and residual tests underscores the effectiveness of the modeling approach, making a strong case for the use of advanced statistical methods in epidemiological forecasting. This research not only deepens our understanding of the ecological underpinnings of ZCL but also aids in refining public health strategies for disease control and prevention.

However, while the results from our SVM model are promising, they also suggest areas for improvement. The slight discrepancies observed between the predicted and actual values in some countries indicate the need for model refinement and potential integration of more localized data inputs or additional predictors such as socio-economic factors, which might improve the model's predictive accuracy further.

7 Conclusion

In conclusion, our study contributes to the growing body of literature on disease forecasting by demonstrating the efficacy of supervised machine learning models in predicting CL incidence. The superior performance of SVM underscores the value of employing sophisticated algorithms capable of capturing complex relationships within epidemiological data. However, the slight variance observed in SVM's long-term predictions necessitates ongoing refinement and data augmentation to enhance forecasting accuracy. As demonstrated by related studies, leveraging advanced ML techniques holds immense promise in informing public health interventions and mitigating the impact of infectious diseases.

References

1. WHO: World Health Organization (WHO). https://www.who.int/news-room/fact-sheets/detail/leishmaniasis. Accessed 21 Feb 2024
2. Daoui, O., et al.: Environmental, climatic, and parasite molecular factors impacting the incidence of cutaneous leishmaniasis due to leishmania tropica in three moroccan foci. Microorganisms **10**, 1712 (2022). https://doi.org/10.3390/microorganisms10091712
3. Cox, L.A.: An AI assistant to help review and improve causal reasoning in epidemiological documents. Global Epidemiol. **7**, 100130 (2024). https://doi.org/10.1016/j.gloepi.2023.100130
4. Keshavamurthy, R., Dixon, S., Pazdernik, K.T., Charles, L.E.: Predicting infectious disease for biopreparedness and response: a systematic review of machine learning and deep learning approaches. One Health. **15**, 100439 (2022). https://doi.org/10.1016/j.onehlt.2022.100439

5. Hussain, Z., Khan, I., Arsalan, M.: Machine learning approaches for dengue prediction: a review of algorithms and applications. Pak. Geogr. Rev. **78**, 15–36 (2023)
6. Leung, X.Y., et al.: A systematic review of dengue outbreak prediction models: current scenario and future directions. PLoS Negl. Trop. Dis. **17**, e0010631 (2023). https://doi.org/10.1371/journal.pntd.0010631
7. Number of cases of cutaneous leishmaniasis reported. https://www.who.int/data/gho/data/indicators/indicator-details/GHO/number-of-cases-of-cutaneous-leishmaniasis-reported. Accessed 16 May 2024
8. NASA's POWER | DAVe. https://power.larc.nasa.gov/beta/data-access-viewer/. Accessed 19 May 2024
9. Rustam, F., et al.: COVID-19 future forecasting using supervised machine learning models. IEEE Access. **8**, 101489–101499 (2020). https://doi.org/10.1109/ACCESS.2020.2997311
10. Yu, W., Liu, T., Valdez, R., Gwinn, M., Khoury, M.J.: Application of support vector machine modeling for prediction of common diseases: the case of diabetes and pre-diabetes. BMC Med. Inf. Decis. Mak. **10**, 16 (2010). https://doi.org/10.1186/1472-6947-10-16
11. Toumi, A., et al.: Temporal dynamics and impact of climate factors on the incidence of zoonotic cutaneous leishmaniasis in Central Tunisia. PLoS Negl. Trop. Dis. **6**, e1633 (2012). https://doi.org/10.1371/journal.pntd.0001633
12. Talmoudi, K., Bellali, H., Ben-Alaya, N., Saez, M., Malouche, D., Chahed, M.K.: Modeling zoonotic cutaneous leishmaniasis incidence in central Tunisia from 2009–2015: forecasting models using climate variables as predictors. PLoS Negl. Trop. Dis. **11**, e0005844 (2017). https://doi.org/10.1371/journal.pntd.0005844

Deep Learning Time Series Forecasting Using LST MODIS Data: Hyperparameter Optimization

Hafssa Naciri[1]($\boxtimes$) , Nizar Ben Achhab[1] , Fatima Ezahrae Ezzaher[1] , Naoufal Raissouni[2] , and Abdelilah Azyat[1]

[1] Mathematics and Intelligent Systems (MASI), Abdelmalek Essaadi University, Tangier, Morocco
hafssa.naciri@etu.uae.ac.ma, nbenachhab@uae.ac.ma
[2] Systems and Telecommunications (TST), Remote Sensing, Abdelmalek Essaadi University, Tetouan, Morocco

Abstract. Recent technological advances in machine learning, especially deep learning models, have transformed data analysis and prediction tasks remarkably. Models like Long Short-Term Memory (LSTM) networks, Convolutional Neural Networks (CNNs), and their hybrids, such as CNN-LSTM and Bidirectional LSTM (BiLSTM), have exhibited notable proficiency in handling time series data for regression tasks. In this study, BiLSTM model is employed to forecast Land Surface Temperature (LST) using time series data derived from MODIS satellite images between 2000 and 2024. The BiLSTM model's hyperparameters, including the number of neurons, epochs, and batch size, are fine-tuned to optimize its performance on MODIS LST dataset. To identify the optimal hyperparameters for accurate LST forecasting in different land cover types, we conduct examinations on four distinct areas in Morocco: forest, build-up, road-soil, and sand areas. By systematically testing different hyperparameter configurations, we determine the combination that yields the highest accuracy for each land cover type. These optimal hyperparameter values are then utilized to forecast LST for the respective regions. In conclusion, the findings of our study support our efficient approach to identifying optimal hyperparameters for BiLSTM model using LST data derived from MODIS satellite imagery. The determined configuration of 120 neurons, 100 epochs, and a batch size of 32 demonstrates superior performance in accurately forecasting LST variations across diverse land cover types.

Keywords: MODIS · Time series · Land surface temperature · Hyperparameters optimization · BiLSTM

1 Introduction

Since the advent of data science with the appearance of deep learning [1], time series analysis has become essential for forecasting future patterns, trends, and monitoring land cover changes [2]. Various models are employed for time series forecasting, including statistical approaches like autoregressive models [3], as well as machine learning techniques such as Random Forest (RF) [4] and Decision Tree (DT) [5].

H. Badir et al. (Eds.): INTIS 2024, CCIS 2645, pp. 80–93, 2026.
https://doi.org/10.1007/978-3-032-14964-0_7

Time series forecasting stands as an essential tool in modern data science and decision-making, having the ability to display valuable information from past data and guide decisive actions for the future [6]. Simultaneously, at the intersection of technology and data, there is a remarkable increase in the capacity to enhance the accuracy of time series forecasting [7]. Thus, advanced machine learning categories, such as deep learning models, have significantly improved the accuracy of forecasts. These models excel at identifying complex patterns within data sequences, even when the data involves intricate spatiotemporal dependencies [8]. Deep learning models, characterized by their ability to automatically learn hierarchical representations from data, have emerged as powerful tools for time series forecasting [9]. Indeed, methods such as Recurrent Neural Networks (RNNs) [10], Long Short-Term Memory networks (LSTM) [11], and Convolutional Neural Network (CNNs) [12] have demonstrated remarkable success in capturing complex temporal dependencies and patterns inherent in time series data.

Hyperparameters optimization for deep learning models plays a crucial role in enhancing their predictive performance [13]. Hyperparameters are parameters whose values are set before the learning process begins, as opposed to model parameters, which are learned during training. When it comes to using deep learning for forecasting time series data, common hyperparameters to consider are the layers' quantity, the neurons in each layer, the learning rate, epoch count, and batch size. Each of these hyperparameters influences the behavior and performance of the model, and their optimal values can vary depending on the specific dataset and task at hand [14].

In the context of global environmental change and the increasing need for accurate monitoring and analysis, the forecasting of Land Surface Temperature (LST) holds significant importance [15]. LST serves as a key indicator of various environmental phenomena, including urban heat islands [16], land cover changes [17], and climate trends [18]. Remote sensing data, particularly from satellites like the Moderate Resolution Imaging Spectroradiometer (MODIS), provide a valuable resource for studying LST variations over large spatial and temporal scales [19]. Given the complexity and spatiotemporal dependencies inherent in LST data, advanced machine learning models are essential for accurate forecasting. Among these models, the Bidirectional Long Short-Term Memory (BiLSTM) model has gained prominence for its ability to capture complex temporal patterns and dependencies in sequential data [20]. Compared to traditional methods such as autoregressive models or single LSTMs, the BiLSTM architecture offers enhanced performance by incorporating data from previous and upcoming time steps simultaneously.

Our research aims to explore the efficiency of BiLSTM model in predicting LST variations across different land cover types. By conducting hyperparameter optimization experiments, we seek to identify the optimal configuration of model parameters that maximizes forecasting accuracy on MODIS LST dataset. The Mean Absolute Error (MAE) metric is used to evaluate the model's accuracy on the validation and training datasets, which aids in the identification of optimal hyperparameters. Additionally, the accuracy of LST forecasting with the determined optimal hyperparameters is evaluated using the coefficient of determination (R^2).

This paper's structure is arranged as follows: Sect. 2 reviews related works, highlighting previous research on time series forecasting using deep learning models for LST prediction. Section 3 describes the satellite data, study areas, data preprocessing steps, time series construction, and BiLSTM model configuration, including architecture and hyperparameter tuning. Section 4 presents the results and discussions, analyzing model performance and implications. Lastly, the paper concludes with suggestions for future research directions and important contributions.

2 Related Works

Land Surface Temperature (LST) is a crucial parameter in climate studies, environmental monitoring, and agricultural planning. Various methods have been applied to forecast LST, ranging from traditional statistical techniques to advanced machine learning models. Early approaches to LST forecasting primarily relied on statistical methods. For instance, Su et al. (2012) [21] utilized autoregressive integrated moving average (ARIMA) models to predict LST. These models are effective for linear time series data, but often fall short in capturing the nonlinear dependencies present in LST data.

With advancements in computational capabilities, machine learning methods have gained prominence in LST forecasting. Hutengs & Vohland (2016) [4] applied RF and DT approaches to predict LST, demonstrating improved accuracy over traditional statistical methods. Deep learning models have revolutionized time series forecasting with their ability to learn complex patterns from large datasets. LSTM, known for their capacity to handle long-term dependencies, have also been widely used. For example, Muzaffar & Afshari (2019) [22] implemented LSTM networks for time series forecasting and demonstrated their effectiveness in capturing temporal dependencies.

Recently, combining different machine learning techniques has shown promising results in LST forecasting. The BiLSTM model extends the capabilities of traditional LSTM by processing data in both forward and backward directions. Zrira et al. (2024) [23] used BiLSTM networks for time series forecasting and found that the bidirectional approach significantly enhances prediction accuracy compared to alternative models (i.e., LSTM, XGBoost, RF, DT).

3 Materials and Methods

In this section, we outline the data and methodologies employed in our study, which is divided into two main phases: data preparation and model configuration (see Fig. 1). First, we describe the satellite data sources and study areas. Then, we detail the preprocessing steps necessary for constructing the time series datasets. Finally, we discuss the configuration of the BiLSTM model. The subsections below elaborate on each aspect of our methodology, providing a comprehensive overview of our approach.

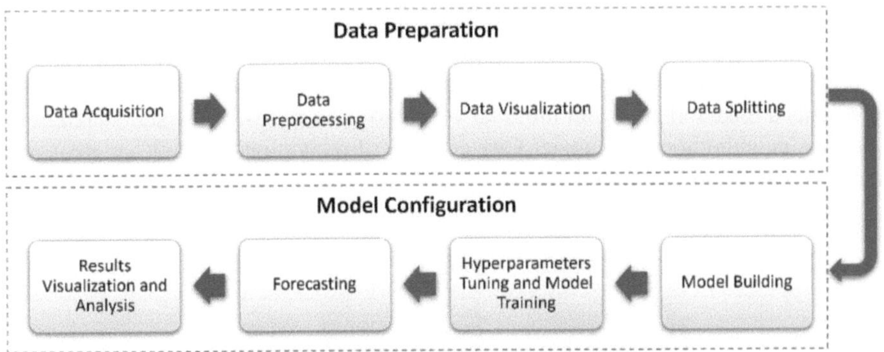

Fig. 1. Workflow of study methodology.

3.1 Satellite Data and Study Areas

Data Acquisition. In this study, we utilized data from the MOD11A2 Land Surface Temperature/Emissivity (LST&E) product [24]. This dataset, produced by the Moderate Resolution Imaging Spectroradiometer (MODIS) onboard NASA's Terra satellite, offers valuable information for environmental monitoring and analysis. The MOD11A2 product provides a temporal resolution of 8 days with a spatial resolution of one kilometer.

The dataset includes both daytime and nighttime surface temperature bands, along with 12 other Science Dataset (SDS) layers (see Table 1), which encompass a variety of environmental parameters such as view angle, quality control, and emissivity data.

The data is stored in the Hierarchical Data Format - Earth Observing System (HDF-EOS) format. It is available at Level-3 processing level, indicating that it has undergone advanced processing steps including spatial integration, temporal aggregation, and data quality improvement. Level-3 data products are typically gridded and can be directly used for scientific analysis without the need for further processing.

For our analysis, we focused on the nighttime land surface temperature (LST_Night_1km) layer, which provides temperature values in Kelvin. The dataset, which covers the years 2000–2024, is available on NASA website [25].

Table 1. Description of used MODIS Data Layers.

SDS Name	Description	Units	Scale Factor
LST_Day_1km	Daytime Land Surface Temperature	Kelvin	0.02
LST_Night_1km	Nighttime Land Surface Temperature	Kelvin	0.02

Study Area. To examine the potential impact of land cover on the optimization of hyperparameters, four distinct regions were selected, each representing a different land cover type (see Fig. 2). The first region, situated within the nature reserve of Jebel

84   H. Naciri et al.

Bouhachem near Chefchaoun city in northern Morocco, is characterized by dense forest cover. For the sand area, the study focused on Merzouga, known for its vast expanse of arid landscapes. The third region, selected along the airway of Tangier's airport, represents a road-soil area with minimal vegetation cover. Lastly, the study area in the Masnana neighborhood of Tangier City consists of predominantly built-up areas with high concentrations of buildings.

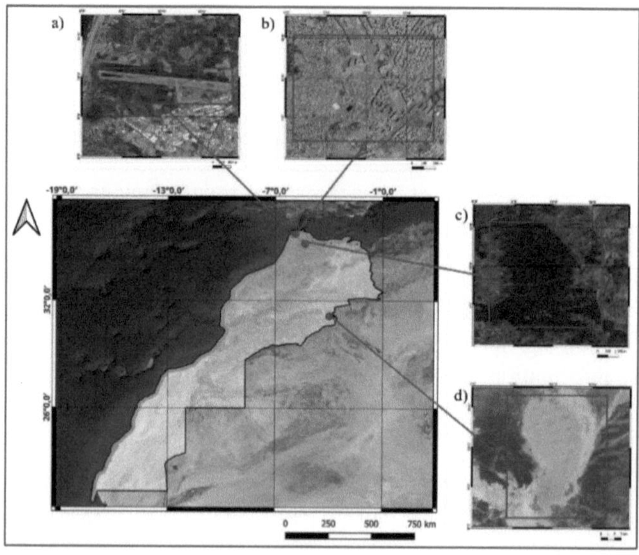

Fig. 2. Selected regions in Morocco: (a) road-soil, (b) build-up, (c) forest, and (d) sand.

3.2 Data Preprocessing and Time Series Construction

In our study, data preprocessing was conducted to prepare MODIS LST images for time series analysis. This process involved scaling the images using metadata-provided scaling factors and clipping them into four distinct regions in Morocco, representing forest, build-up, road-soil, and sand areas. After that, the 2D grid of pixels within each image was reorganized into a linear grid by stacking the rows to form a continuous sequence of pixel values (see Fig. 3).

This reorganization facilitated the construction of time series datasets for each region, with each individual time series denoted as TS-1, TS-2, TS-3, and TS-4. Furthermore, to ensure data quality and completeness, data cleaning techniques were applied, including linear interpolation to handle missing values. The resulting time series datasets were then ready for further analysis and modeling.

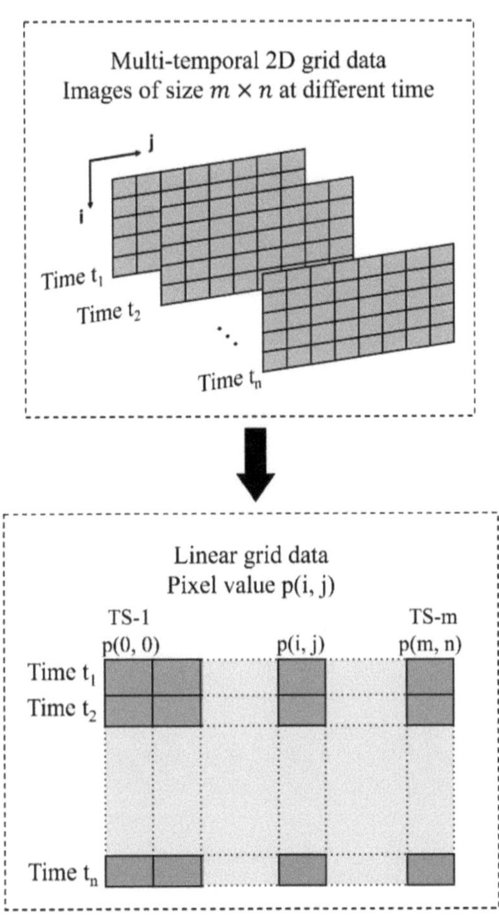

Fig. 3. Reorganization of pixel grid into linear sequence (TS: Time Series).

Time series data for the four regions of interest are presented. Figure 4 illustrates the temporal variation of Land Surface Temperature (LST) across different land cover types over the study period. Each graph represents LST values of a pixel for a specific region, providing insights into the seasonal patterns and trends observed in the data.

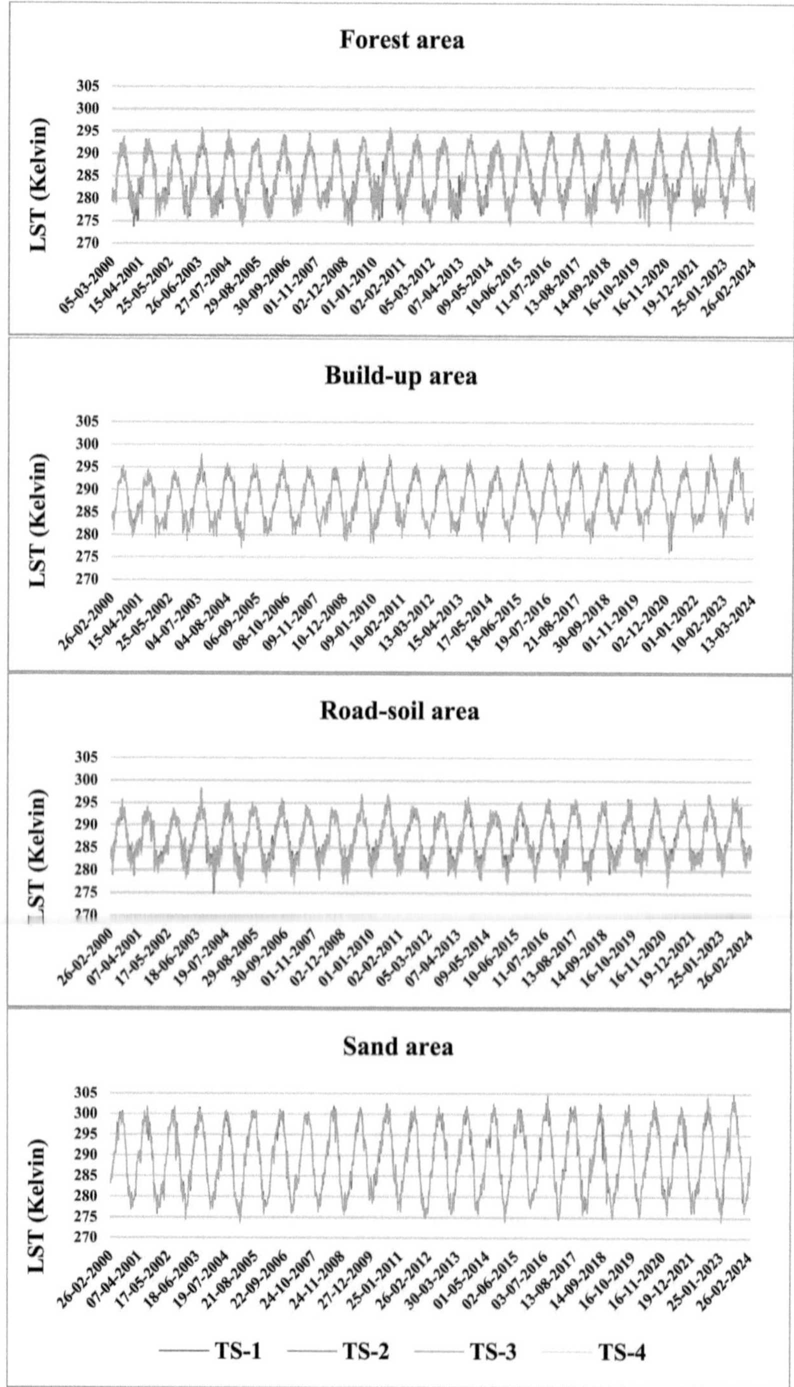

Fig. 4. LST time series in four regions (TS: Time Series).

In the forest area, LST ranges from a minimum of 273.28 K (0.13 °C) to a maximum of 296.4 K (23.25 °C), with a mean temperature of approximately 284.82 K (12 °C). Similarly, the build-up area exhibits LST values ranging from 276.26 K (3.11 °C) to 298.32 K (25.17 °C), with a mean temperature of around 288.06 K (15 °C). The road-soil area experiences LST fluctuations between 274.88 K (1.73 °C) and 298.14 K (24.99 °C), with a mean temperature of approximately 287.16 K (14 °C). In contrast, the sand area displays the widest temperature range, spanning from 273.66 K (0.51 °C) to 304.86 K (31.71 °C) and a mean temperature of about 289.29 K (16 °C).

In the process of preparing time series data for model training, three steps were executed (see Fig. 5). Firstly, normalization is performed to scale the data to a common range, facilitating convergence during model training and improving the stability of the training process. Then, the dataset is transformed into a matrix of sequences, where each sequence consists of input features (X) and corresponding target values (y) using a sequence size of 46, which is equivalent to the number of days in a single year. Due to this iterative process, sequential input-output pairs were produced, which captured temporal dependencies in the data. Lastly, training, validation, and testing sets are formed using the dataset, allowing for the evaluation of model performance on unseen data and the tuning of hyperparameters.

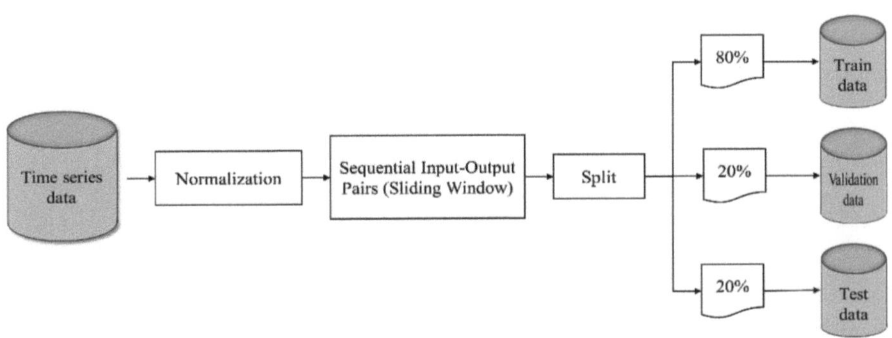

Fig. 5. Time series data preparation workflow for model training.

3.3 BiLSTM Model Configuration

The Bidirectional Long Short-Term Memory (BiLSTM) model [26], offers several advantages over traditional unidirectional LSTM architectures. Unlike simple LSTMs, which only capture information from pastime steps, BiLSTM models are capable of processing sequences in both forward and backward directions simultaneously, allowing for better capturing of temporal dependencies and patterns. This bidirectional processing enables the model to incorporate future context into its predictions, leading to enhanced performance in time-series forecasting tasks. The equations governing the behavior of the gates in both LSTM and BiLSTM models are similar. For instance, the input gate i_t, forget gate f_t, cell state update C_t, and output gate o_t are described by the following equations:

$$i_t = \sigma\left(W_i \bullet \left[h_{t-1}, x_t\right] + b_i\right) \tag{1}$$

$$f_t = \sigma\left(W_f \bullet \left[h_{t-1}, x_t\right] + b_f\right) \tag{2}$$

$$C_t = f_t * C_{t-1} + i_t * \tilde{C}_t \tag{3}$$

$$o_t = \sigma\left(W_o \bullet \left[h_{t-1}, x_t\right] + b_o\right) \tag{4}$$

where σ denotes the sigmoid activation function, W_i, W_f, W_o are weight matrices, $\tilde{C}_t$ is the candidate cell state, h_{t-1} is the previous hidden state, x_t is the current input, and b_i, b_f, b_o are bias vectors.

Model Architecture. Our constructed model consists of one bidirectional LSTM layer, two LSTM layers, and a fully connected layer. All the layers use the rectified linear unit (ReLU) activation function. After each LSTM layer, 20% of outputs are dropped using two dropout layers to prevent overfitting (see Fig. 6).

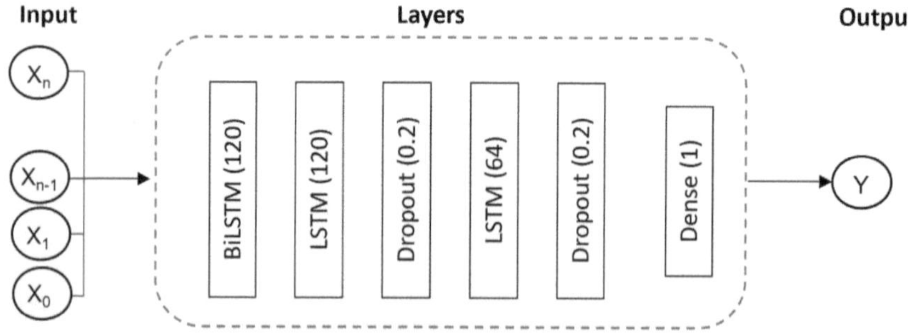

Fig. 6. Schematic of BiLSTM Model.

Model compilation is done with the Adam optimizer with a learning rate of 0.001 and the mean squared error (MSE) loss function. During training, the model is fitted to the training data while monitoring the Mean Absolute Error (MAE) metric for both training and validation datasets. Additionally, the coefficient of determination (R^2) is utilized to evaluate the accuracy of forecasting when the model is applied to test datasets. The equations for each metric are as follows:

$$MSE = \frac{1}{n}\sum_{i=1}^{n}\left(y_i - \hat{y}_i\right)^2 \tag{5}$$

$$MAE = \frac{1}{n}\sum_{i=1}^{n}\left|y_i - \hat{y}_i\right| \tag{6}$$

$$R^2 = 1 - \frac{\sum_{i=1}^{n}\left(y_i - \hat{y}_i\right)^2}{\sum_{i=1}^{n}\left(y_i - \bar{y}\right)^2} \tag{7}$$

where y_i represents the true values, $\hat{y}_i$ represents the predicted values, $\bar{y}$ represents the mean of the true values, and n represents the number of samples.

Hyperparameters Tuning. To optimize BiLSTM model performance, three hyperparameters were tuned: the kernel size representing the number of neurons in the main layers of BiLSTM model, the number of epochs for training, and the batch size for optimization. To identify the optimal combination of hyperparameters, we scanned a grid of values predefined for each parameter, systematically exploring different configurations. The grid search involved a total of 54 combinations, as we iterated over three batch sizes (32, 64, 128), six neuron counts (20, 50, 60, 80, 100, 120), and three epoch counts (10, 50, 100). The objective was to minimize the MAE on both the training and validation datasets, with the model achieving the lowest validation MAE considered to be the best fit.

4   Results and Discussions

The results of the hyperparameter optimization process are presented in Tables 2 and 3, which compare MAE values for different hyperparameter combinations on the training and validation datasets. Across all studied regions (forest, build-up, road-soil, and sand), the hyperparameter combination of 20 neurons, 10 epochs, and a batch size of 128 provided the highest MAE values. In contrast, the combination of 120 neurons, 100 epochs, and a batch size of 32 consistently produced the lowest MAE values across all regions.

Table 2. Hyperparameter combination (neurons = 20, epochs = 10, batch-size = 128) with the highest MAE (TS: Time Series).

Regions	Training MAE				Validation MAE			
	TS-1	TS-2	TS-3	TS-4	TS-1	TS-2	TS-3	TS-4
Forest	0.31	0.30	0.33	0.31	0.30	0.28	0.32	0.29
Build-up	0.35	0.38	0.36	0.40	0.33	0.35	0.33	0.39
Road-soil	0.33	0.32	0.32	0.41	0.32	0.30	0.31	0.38
Sand	0.35	0.32	0.33	0.33	0.32	0.29	0.30	0.30

Table 3. Hyperparameter combination (neurons = 120, epochs = 100, batch-size = 32) with the lowest MAE (TS: Time Series).

Regions	Training MAE				Validation MAE			
	TS-1	TS-2	TS-3	TS-4	TS-1	TS-2	TS-3	TS-4
Forest	0.08	0.08	0.08	0.08	0.08	0.08	0.09	0.08
Build-up	0.08	0.08	0.08	0.08	0.06	0.05	0.06	0.06
Road-soil	0.08	0.08	0.08	0.07	0.07	0.06	0.07	0.05
Sand	0.07	0.06	0.07	0.07	0.06	0.05	0.05	0.06

Variations in MAE values can be attributed to several factors related to the dataset characteristics and the modeling task. The number of neurons affects the model's ability to learn complex patterns; with only 20 neurons, the model likely lacked the capacity to capture intricate temporal dependencies, resulting in higher MAE values. In contrast, 120 neurons provided a richer representation, enabling better capture of these dependencies and reducing prediction errors.

Similarly, the number of epochs influences the learning process. With just 10 epochs, the model did not have sufficient training to fully learn data patterns, leading to poor performance. Increasing epochs to 100 allowed for more thorough learning, thereby improving predictive performance.

Batch size also plays a crucial role; a larger batch size of 128 led to less frequent updates and slower convergence, reducing optimization efficiency. Conversely, a smaller batch size of 32 allowed for more frequent updates, resulting in an over tuned model and lower MAE values.

Furthermore, the diverse land cover types (forest, build-up, road-soil, and sand) exhibit different thermal properties and temporal dynamics. The optimal hyperparameters (120 neurons, 100 epochs, batch size of 32) effectively captured these variations, enhancing overall prediction accuracy across different regions.

After obtaining the optimal hyperparameters and validating the model's performance, it was applied to predict the test dataset. A comparison of the test dataset's actual and predicted LST values can be shown in Fig. 7. Across all studied regions, the R^2 values indicate a strong correlation between the predicted and actual LST, confirming the obtained model's accuracy when optimized hyperparameters were employed.

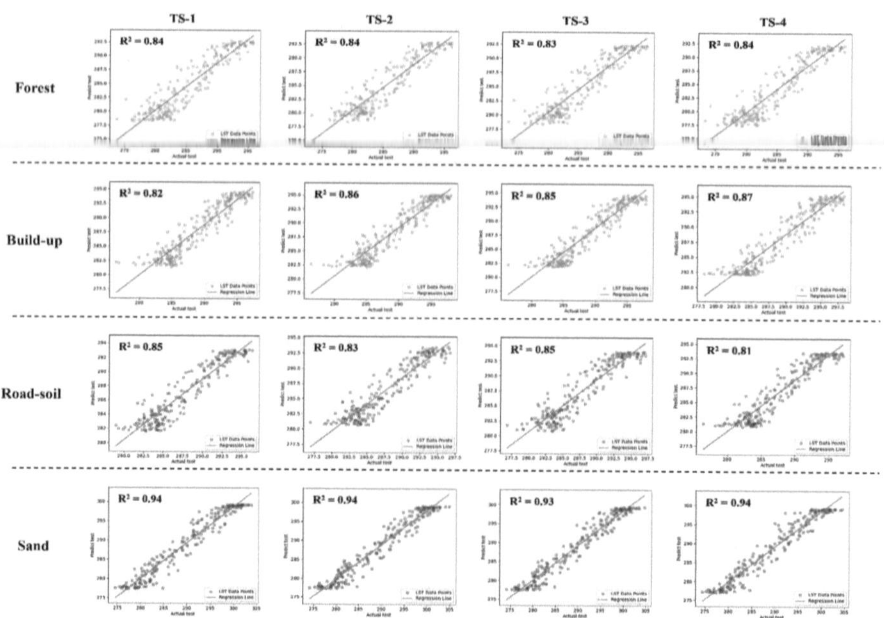

Fig. 7. LST (Kelvin) test dataset: comparison of predicted and actual.

To comprehensively assess the model's performance, several factors must be considered. Firstly, the model's efficacy is closely tied to the selected hyperparameters. The optimized combination of 120 neurons, 100 epochs, and a batch size of 32 proved pivotal in achieving high accuracy. However, variations in these parameters can yield different outcomes, emphasizing the significance of hyperparameter tuning. Secondly, the diverse thermal properties and temporal dynamics inherent in different land cover types pose challenges to model performance [27]. While the model excelled at predicting LST in desert regions, its slightly reduced performance in forests, build-up, and road-soil indicates that customized model configurations are required.

The observed variations in R^2 values underscore the necessity for further refinement to address the unique characteristics of each environment. Finally, while optimized for the MODIS dataset, the model's generalizability to other datasets or time series data types may be limited. Additional testing and tuning are imperative to validate its effectiveness across diverse datasets and applications.

5 Conclusion

In this study, we explored the effectiveness of BiLSTM model for time series forecasting using MODIS LST data. Firstly, we conducted our analysis across four types of land cover to explore potential impacts on optimal hyperparameters. Through the fine-tuning of three key parameters: neurons, epochs, and batch size, we aimed to identify configurations that maximize model performance. Our findings reveal that, regardless of land cover type, the same optimal hyperparameters consistently yielded superior results. Optimizing hyperparameters reduced MAE to 0.06, yielding a substantial error reduction of approximately 0.29 compared to less optimized configurations. Additionally, applying these optimized hyperparameters led to impressive test accuracies, with R^2 values of 84%, 85%, 84%, and 94% achieved in forest, build-up, road-soil, and sand areas, respectively. This consistency suggests that the identified optimal model architecture is applicable across various land cover types, providing a reliable framework for LST prediction using MODIS data.

In future work, including additional variables or incorporate external data sources could further enhance the model performance. For instance, integrating meteorological data, vegetation indices, or urbanization metrics could provide a more comprehensive understanding of LST variations. Moreover, investigating other advanced deep learning architectures and their potential synergies with BiLSTM could uncover new opportunities for improving predictive accuracy. These avenues could help refine the model's applicability and robustness, offering greater insights into environmental monitoring and management.

References

1. Wang, X., Zhao, Y., Pourpanah, F.: Recent advances in deep learning. Int. J. Mach. Learn. Cyber. **11**, 747–750 (2020). https://doi.org/10.1007/s13042-020-01096-5

2. Aguilar-Lome, J., Espinoza-Villar, R., Espinoza, J.-C., et al.: Elevation-dependent warming of land surface temperatures in the Andes assessed using MODIS LST time series (2000–2017). Int. J. Appl. Earth Obs. Geoinf. **77**, 119–128 (2019). https://doi.org/10.1016/j.jag.2018.12.013

3. Hill, D.C., McMillan, D., Bell, K.R.W., Infield, D.: Application of auto-regressive models to U.K. wind speed data for power system impact studies. IEEE Trans. Sustain. Energy **3**, 134–141 (2012). https://doi.org/10.1109/TSTE.2011.2163324

4. Hutengs, C., Vohland, M.: Downscaling land surface temperatures at regional scales with random forest regression. Remote Sens. Environ. **178**, 127–141 (2016). https://doi.org/10.1016/j.rse.2016.03.006

5. Zhang, B., Valentine, I., Kemp, P.: Modelling the productivity of naturalised pasture in the North Island, New Zealand: a decision tree approach. Ecol. Model. **186**, 299–311 (2005). https://doi.org/10.1016/j.ecolmodel.2004.12.016

6. Hengl, T., Heuvelink, G.B.M., Perčec Tadić, M., Pebesma, E.J.: Spatio-temporal prediction of daily temperatures using time-series of MODIS LST images. Theor. Appl. Climatol. **107**, 265–277 (2012). https://doi.org/10.1007/s00704-011-0464-2

7. Naciri, H., Ben Achhab, N., Ezzaher, F.E., Raissouni, N.: AIRS: a QGIS plugin for time series forecasting using deep learning models. Environ. Model. Softw. **177**, 106045 (2024). https://doi.org/10.1016/j.envsoft.2024.106045

8. Deo, R.C., Şahin, M.: Forecasting long-term global solar radiation with an ANN algorithm coupled with satellite-derived (MODIS) land surface temperature (LST) for regional locations in Queensland. Renew. Sustain. Energy Rev. **72**, 828–848 (2017). https://doi.org/10.1016/j.rser.2017.01.114

9. Kartal, S., Sekertekin, A.: Prediction of MODIS land surface temperature using new hybrid models based on spatial interpolation techniques and deep learning models. Environ. Sci. Pollut. Res. **29**, 67115–67134 (2022). https://doi.org/10.1007/s11356-022-20572-9

10. Hüsken, M., Stagge, P.: Recurrent neural networks for time series classification. Neurocomputing **50**, 223–235 (2003). https://doi.org/10.1016/S0925-2312(01)00706-8

11. Naciri, H., Ben Achhab, N., Ezzaher, F.E., Sobrino, J.A., Raissouni, N.: Mediterranean basin vegetation forecasting approaches: accuracy analysis & climate-land cover-sensor nexus impacts. Int. J. Remote Sens. **45**(19–20), 7415–7434 (2024). https://doi.org/10.1080/01431161.2023.2217984

12. Shi, X., Chen, Z., Wang, H., et al.: Convolutional LSTM network: a machine learning approach for precipitation nowcasting. In: Cortes, C., Lawrence, N., Lee, D., et al. (eds.) Advances in Neural Information Processing Systems. Curran Associates, Inc. (2015)

13. Kim, J.-.Y, Cho, S.-B.: Evolutionary optimization of hyperparameters in deep learning models. In: 2019 IEEE Congress on Evolutionary Computation (CEC), pp. 831–837 (2019)

14. Wu, J., Chen, X.-Y., Zhang, H., et al.: Hyperparameter optimization for machine learning models based on bayesian optimization. J. Electron. Sci. Technol. **17**, 26–40 (2019). https://doi.org/10.11989/JEST.1674-862X.80904120

15. Azarderakhsh, M., Prakash, S., Zhao, Y., AghaKouchak, A.: Satellite-based analysis of extreme land surface temperatures and diurnal variability across the hottest place on earth. IEEE Geosci. Remote Sens. Lett. **17**, 2025–2029 (2020). https://doi.org/10.1109/LGRS.2019.2962055

16. Kimothi, S., Thapliyal, A., Gehlot, A., et al.: Spatio-temporal fluctuations analysis of land surface temperature (LST) using Remote Sensing data (LANDSAT TM5/8) and multifractal technique to characterize the urban heat Islands (UHIs). Sustainable Energy Technol. Assess. **55**, 102956 (2023). https://doi.org/10.1016/j.seta.2022.102956

17. Bright, R.M., Davin, E., O'Halloran, T., et al.: Local temperature response to land cover and management change driven by non-radiative processes. Nat. Clim. Change **7**, 296–302 (2017). https://doi.org/10.1038/nclimate3250

18. Ezzaher, F.E., Ben Achhab, N., Raissouni, N., et al.: Normalized burn ratio and land surface temperature pre- and post-mediterranean forest fires. Environ. Sci. Proc. **29**, 3 (2023). https://doi.org/10.3390/ECRS2023-15829

19. Xing, Z., Li, Z.-L., Duan, S.-B., et al.: Estimation of daily mean land surface temperature at global scale using pairs of daytime and nighttime MODIS instantaneous observations. ISPRS J. Photogramm. Remote. Sens. **178**, 51–67 (2021). https://doi.org/10.1016/j.isprsjprs.2021.05.017

20. Ma, J., Jia, C., Yang, X., et al.: A data-driven approach for collision risk early warning in vessel encounter situations using attention-BiLSTM. IEEE Access **8**, 188771–188783 (2020). https://doi.org/10.1109/ACCESS.2020.3031722

21. Su, Y.-F., Foody, G.M., Cheng, K.-S.: Spatial non-stationarity in the relationships between land cover and surface temperature in an urban heat island and its impacts on thermally sensitive populations. Landsc. Urban Plan. **107**, 172–180 (2012). https://doi.org/10.1016/j.landurbplan.2012.05.016

22. Muzaffar, S., Afshari, A.: Short-term load forecasts using LSTM networks. Energy Procedia **158**, 2922–2927 (2019). https://doi.org/10.1016/j.egypro.2019.01.952

23. Zrira, N., Kamal-Idrissi, A., Farssi, R., Khan, H.A.: Time series prediction of sea surface temperature based on BiLSTM model with attention mechanism. J. Sea Res. **198**, 102472 (2024). https://doi.org/10.1016/j.seares.2024.102472

24. Wan, Z.: Collection-6 MODIS Land Surface Temperature Products Users' Guide (2007)

25. Earthdata Search. https://search.earthdata.nasa.gov/search. Accessed 7 Apr 2024

26. Schuster, M., Paliwal, K.K.: Bidirectional recurrent neural networks. IEEE Trans. Signal Process. **45**, 2673–2681 (1997). https://doi.org/10.1109/78.650093

27. Ezzaher, F.E., Ben Achhab, N., Naciri, H., Sobrino, J.A., Raissouni, N.: Assessing 100 biophysical indices performances in the Mediterranean basin using multi-satellite data. Int. J. Remote Sens. **45**(19–20), 7248–7296 (2024). https://doi.org/10.1080/01431161.2023.2209917

SentinelBERT: A Deep Learning Approach for Adverse Event Forecasting

Rasha Assaf[1] , Amjad Rattrout[2(✉)] , Mohammed Khalilia[3] , and Rashid Jayousi[1]

[1] Department of Computer, Al-Quds University, Jerusalem, Palestine
rasha.assaf@students.alquds.edu, rjayousi@staff.alquds.edu
[2] Department of Computer, Arabic-American University, Jenin, Palestine
amjad.rattrout@aaup.edu
[3] Department of Computer, Birzeit University, Birzeit, Palestine
mkhalilia@birzeit.edu

Abstract. Adverse drug events (ADEs) pose a significant threat to patient safety, healthcare costs, and clinical decision-making processes. Traditional ADE detection systems often need to improve reporting and time delays, necessitating exploring advanced machine-learning techniques. This research investigated the potential of deep learning models, particularly BERT-based architectures, for ADE prediction. We developed and fine-tuned BERT-based models for adverse event classification, employing data preprocessing, model training, and performance evaluation techniques. We Normalised the 50000 categories into 20 categories using LDA topic modelling and then trained the model to predict ADEs. The micro-average F1-score (0.89) and accuracy (0.89) indicates the model's overall performance across all categories, considering each instance equally. Experimental results demonstrated the efficacy of our approach in accurately classifying adverse event reactions across diverse categories. Our findings contribute to advancing pharmacovigilance practices, offering more accurate and reliable ADE prediction systems.

Keywords: Adverse event · Bert · deep learning · classification

1 Introduction

This research addresses the critical issue of Adverse Drug Events (ADEs), which pose significant risks to patients, leading to increased morbidity, mortality, and healthcare expenses. Traditional ADE detection systems suffer from underreporting and delays due to manual reporting. While machine learning methods have been explored, they often struggle with the complexities of medical language. However, the emergence of advanced language models like BERT offers promise in ADE prediction due to their ability to comprehend context and relationships within clinical narratives and patient reports [1]. The study aims to enhance ADE prediction by developing innovative BERT-based deep learning

H. Badir et al. (Eds.): INTIS 2024, CCIS 2645, pp. 94–104, 2026.
https://doi.org/10.1007/978-3-032-14964-0_8

models, which will be evaluated on diverse datasets to benchmark their performance. The ultimate goal is to improve patient safety and pharmacovigilance practices by revolutionizing clinical decision-making processes and leveraging deep learning to overcome the limitations of traditional predictive models.

In a related study [2], researchers investigated the learning of distributed representations of drug sequences for adverse event reaction prediction. They compared various models and found that Transformer models outperformed biL-STM, with the larger Transformer architecture achieving the highest F1-score. This research contributes to advancing pharmacovigilance by providing accurate methods for predicting adverse event reactions based on drug sequences. The complexity of adverse event detection poses challenges for healthcare systems worldwide, particularly in regions like the Middle East. Traditionally, AE detection relied on manually crafted rules, while machine learning methodologies offer greater adaptability but require annotated datasets. Another study [3] examines the current landscape of ML-driven AE prognostication and addresses challenges in AE surveillance system adoption, focusing on Palestine.

The research is structured with a comprehensive literature review, dataset information, data processing details, methodology, experimental results, and a concluding summary. Through this structured approach, the study aims to improve ADE prediction and contribute to enhancing patient safety and pharmacovigilance practices.

2   Literature Review

The paper by Bergman et al. (2023) [4] explores the use of NLP for triaging ADR reports, mainly focusing on the challenges of classifying these reports. The study utilizes a Swedish BERT language model to propose a BERT-based model that achieves performance close to human level. Comparing this model with other NLP approaches such as bag-of-words and LSTM neural networks, they find that the BERT models outperform others in classifying ADR reports. This finding resonates with recent literature, indicating that transformer-based models, notably BERT, excel in various NLP tasks due to their superior contextual understanding compared to traditional models. Chopard et al. (2021) [5] also investigated deep learning for automating the coding of adverse events in clinical trial reports, achieving a high F1 score of 0.8080. This supports the potential of deep learning to enhance the accuracy and efficiency of adverse event coding. Hussain et al. (2021) [6] discusses using transformers to detect ADRs in social media texts, which is challenging due to the informal language used. They developed FARM-BERT, a multitask learning system that improves ADR detection by simultaneously classifying text and identifying specific ADRs, outperforming other models on this task. Fan et al. (2020) [7] address the issue of under-reported ADEs by employing a BERT-based model to detect these events from social media data. Their model achieved an AUC score of 0.94 for ADE detection and an F1 score of 0.97 for ADE extraction, demonstrating the efficacy of BERT in processing user-generated content for pharmacovigilance purposes.

Li et al. (2024) [8] evaluate LLMs such as GPT-3.5 and Llama2 for extracting AEs from surveillance reports, with the fine-tuned GPT-3.5 model achieving the highest accuracy. This study highlights the potential of LLMs in accurately extracting AEs from medical data, contributing to the growing evidence of the effectiveness of advanced NLP models in medical applications.

Zheng et al. (2024) [9] introduce BG-BERT, a self-supervised learning framework for predicting blood glucose levels in Type-1 diabetes patients. This model incorporates techniques like SMOTE data augmentation and a shrinkage loss function to handle imbalanced data, demonstrating improved prediction accuracy and sensitivity to hypoglycemia events. Narayanan et al. (2022) [10] propose a novel approach combining contextual language models and multitask learning to improve medication and ADE identification from clinical text. This method addresses the challenges posed by data scarcity and language complexity, enhancing the accuracy of NER for these tasks. McMaster et al. (2023) [11] developed a deep-learning NLP algorithm to identify mentions of ADRs in discharge summaries, achieving a ROC-AUC of 0.955. Their model outperformed DeBERTa and RoBERTa models, indicating its robustness in identifying ADR mentions at both document and token levels. Sutphin et al. (2020) [12] evaluate methods for identifying ADEs in FDA drug labels, finding that the biLSTM+CRF method achieves the highest F1 score. However, the CRF method demonstrated better precision for rare ADEs, and ensemble methods improved overall performance, suggesting the benefit of combining multiple machine-learning models for this task. Yu et al. (2022) [13] investigate the use of social media for detecting ADEs with a CNN-based model called CLAPA, which uses contextual information to represent medical concepts. They found that incorporating a pre-trained language model like BERT improved performance, although challenges remain in achieving robustness across different evaluation sets. These study [14] showcase various methods in leveraging electronic health data for high throughput phenotyping and adverse drug event detection. McCoy et al. introduce PheCAP, a semi-supervised approach for rapid patient phenotype identification using EMR data. Zhang et al. [14] present a CNN-based method for accurate adverse drug event detection from EHRs, highlighting the effectiveness of deep learning. Sarker et al. [15] explore RNN architectures for labeling adverse drug reactions in Twitter posts, demonstrating promising results in ADR identification. [16] propose a method using distributional semantic representations to identify adverse drug event information in clinical notes. Together, these studies contribute to enhancing pharmacovigilance efforts and improving patient safety through computational methods.

3   Dataset

The FDA manages an internal FAERS[1] database and periodically releases some post-market information every quarter. The openFDA platform and the FAERS

---

[1] https://datadashboard.fda.gov/ora/index.htm.

Table 1. Description of Dataset Features

Feature	Description
AGE	Age of the patient at the time of the adverse event
GENDER	Gender of the patient
COUNTRY_CODE	Country code of the reporting country
Drugs name	Drugs aligned with the adverse event
Role_code	Role code of the drug in the adverse event
DRUG_SEQ	Sequence number of the drug in the adverse event
Dose	Dose of the drug
Route	Route of administration of the drug
Reaction	Adverse reaction aligned with the drug

online dashboard allow access to the public release. The FDA receives over 1 million annual reports of adverse events and medication errors, making its database one of the largest for pharmacovigilance. The FAERS dataset, spanning from 1989 to 2017 with nearly 6 million events, includes detailed information on adverse event types, severity, patient demographics, drugs involved, dosages, outcomes, and medical histories. This comprehensive data helps researchers, healthcare providers, and regulatory authorities detect safety issues, track trends, and make informed decisions on drug safety and efficacy, ultimately improving patient care (Table 1).

4 Data Processing

4.1 Data Cleaning

Initially, we renamed a column in the dataset from 'GENDER COUNTRY_CODE OCCP_COD' to 'GENDER' for clarity. We then refined the 'GENDER' column to only include gender information ('M' or 'F'). The 'aligned_drugs' column, containing drug names separated by slashes, was split into up to eight new columns named 'drug1', 'drug2', etc. These were concatenated back into the original DataFrame, filling with 'null' if fewer than eight drugs were listed. The same technique was applied to the 'aligned_route' and 'ALIGNED_REAC' features, separating multiple entries to treat each drug or reaction as a separate entity for analysis.

4.2 Data Analysis

The data presented in Fig. 1, Count of Males and Females, visually shows the gender distribution of the study population. As evident, males (blue bar) outnumber females (pink bar). The data shows a higher ratio of female patients compared to males. Figure 2 highlights that ZANTAC is the most frequently prescribed drug,

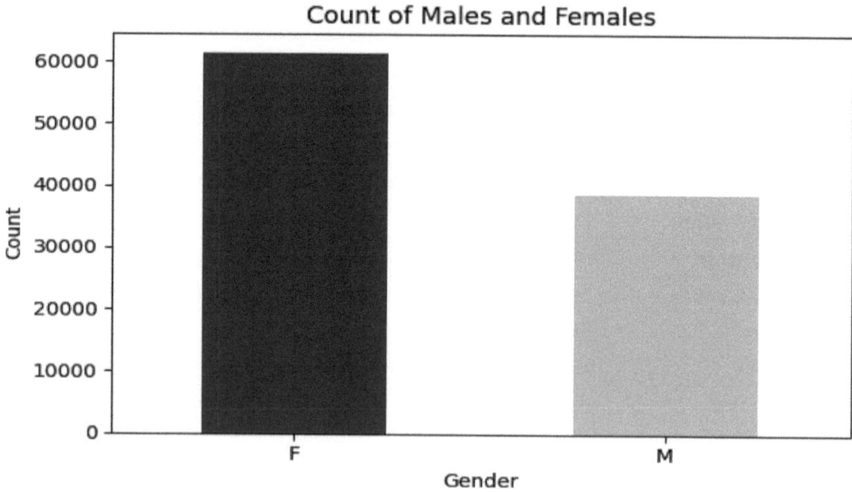

Fig. 1. Count of Males and Females (Color figure online)

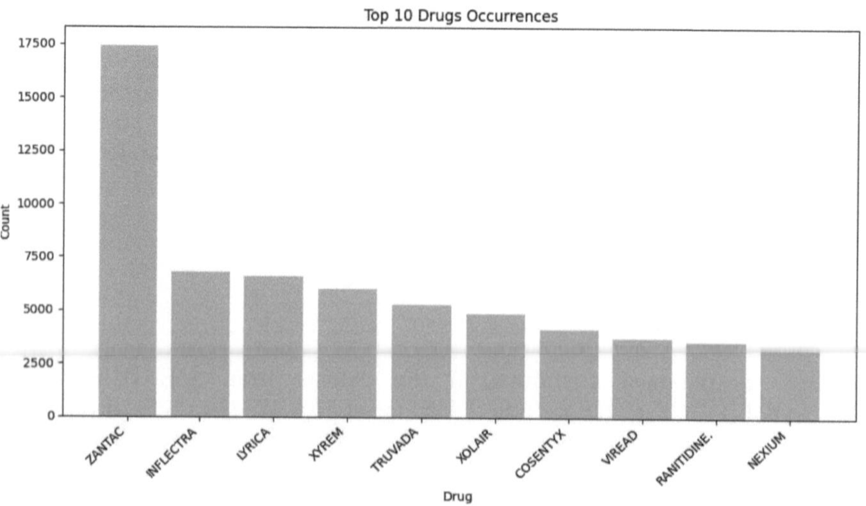

Fig. 2. Top 10 Drugs Occurrences

followed by INFLECTRA and LYRICA. These medications address a variety of conditions, including gastrointestinal, autoimmune, and neurological disorders, indicating diverse healthcare needs within the population. The data in Fig. 3, Top 10 Drugs Distribution, shows the distribution of the top ten prescribed drugs labelled with drug names. ZANTAC has the highest 28.3% occurrence on the dataset.

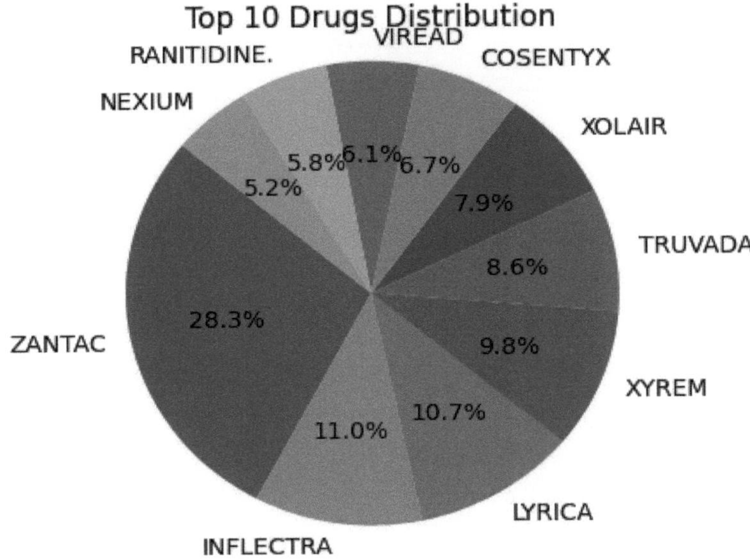

Fig. 3. Top 10 Drugs Distribution

5   Normalization of the Data

To streamline the classification of our ADE feature set, we first normalized the data. However, with over 50,000 categories, directly inputting them into the Bert model was impractical. Therefore, we employed the LDA algorithm to reduce the categories to 20 clusters while preserving their integrity. This enabled us to effectively input the reduced feature set into the Bert model for classification, resulting in more accurate results and an optimized classification process.

6   Latent Dirichlet Allocation (LDA)

Utilizing LDA, we transformed a vast adverse event dataset with over 50,000 categories into 20 structured topics, streamlining analysis and classification. Prior to applying LDA, text preprocessing was crucial, involving tasks such as removing stop words, punctuation, and converting words to lowercase. This process included tokenization, lowercase conversion, and stop words removal. Following preprocessing, a DTM was constructed, where each document's frequency of terms was represented. LDA assumes each document comprises various topics, and each word is linked to one of these topics. The aim was to deduce topic distribution and word-topic distributions through techniques like variational inference or Gibbs sampling. Upon convergence, each document was assigned to the topic with the highest probability, resulting in a dataset represented by topic distributions, offering a more concise and interpretable view of the original text data (Fig. 4).

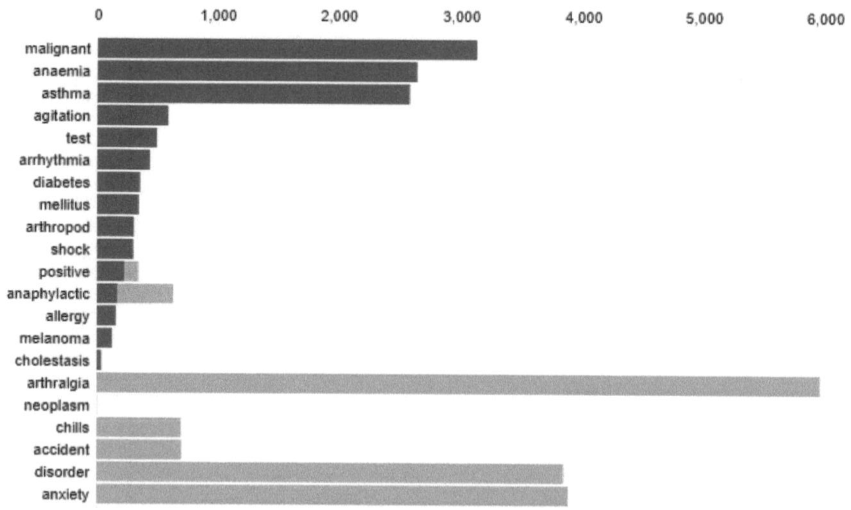

Fig. 4. Top 20 Categories Modeling of ADE's Feature set

7 ADE's Classification

We present a detailed analysis utilizing the BERT model to classify adverse event reactions into 20 multiclass categories.

8 Model Architecture

BERT is a pre-trained language model that uses the Transformer architecture for NLP tasks. The Transformer model comprises an encoder-decoder architecture, but BERT employs only the encoder part. The encoder is responsible for reading the input text and generating a contextualized representation of the text. BERT is trained on a large corpus of text, enabling it to capture the semantic relationships between words and the context in which they are used. This makes BERT a powerful tool for NLP tasks such as sentiment analysis, text classification, and question answering (Fig. 5).

8.1 BERT Architecture

BERT comprises multiple Transformer blocks stacked together. Each Transformer block consists of various self-attention layers and feed-forward neural networks. The self-attention mechanism allows BERT to capture contextual information effectively by attending to relevant words in the input sequence.

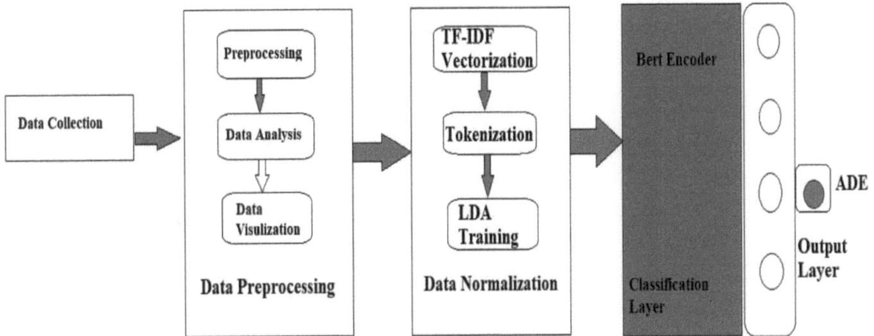

Fig. 5. Model Architecture

8.2   Equations and Mathematical Models

1. **Self-Attention Mechanism:**

$$\text{Attention}(Q, K, V) = \text{softmax}\left(\frac{QK^T}{\sqrt{d_k}}\right)V$$

Where Q, K, and V are query, key, and value matrices, respectively, and d_k is the dimension of the key vectors.

2. **Feed-Forward Neural Network:** The feed-forward neural network consists of two linear transformations with a ReLU activation function:

$$\text{FFN}(x) = \text{ReLU}(W_1 x + b_1)W_2 + b_2$$

8.3   Data Preprocessing

The preprocessing pipeline for adverse event classification using BERT involves three key steps. First, in Tokenization, raw textual descriptions are segmented into tokens to create structured inputs for the model, enabling it to encode tokens into numerical IDs. Second, Padding ensures a uniform length of token sequences by adding special tokens, facilitating efficient batching during training and inference. Finally, Encoding converts tokenized text into numerical IDs, enabling the BERT model to process the data and learn patterns associated with adverse event categories. These steps collectively prepare the textual data for effective analysis and classification by the BERT model.

8.4   Model Training

Fine-Tuning BERT: Fine-tuning BioBERT for adverse event classification adapts the pre-trained model to better understand specific event descriptions. Though initially trained on biomedical texts, BioBERT undergoes additional training on our labeled dataset, updating its parameters based on cross-entropy loss. This specialization enhances BioBERT's ability to recognize patterns and improve classification performance for adverse events.

- **Loss Function**: The loss function used is typically the cross-entropy loss function.

  The cross-entropy loss measures the difference between the predicted probability distribution of classes and the actual one-hot encoded labels. Mathematically, for a single example, it can be expressed as:

$$L(y, \hat{y}) = -\sum_i y_i \log(\hat{y}_i)$$

Where:

- y is the one-hot encoded ground truth label vector (actual class labels),
- $\hat{y}$ is the predicted probability distribution vector outputted by the model,
- y_i and $\hat{y}_i$ are the elements of these vectors representing the probability of class i,
- log denotes the natural logarithm.

The cross-entropy loss penalizes incorrect predictions, pushing the model to assign higher probabilities to the correct class. Minimizing this loss during training improves the model's confidence and accuracy in classifying adverse events.

9   Classification Report

The table showcases the classification performance metrics for various adverse event reaction categories. For instance, consider the "Malignant" category. The precision of 0.92 indicates that 92% of the instances classified as "Malignant" were correct, while the recall of 0.88 implies that 88% of the actual "Malignant" instances were identified correctly by the model. The F1-score, the harmonic mean of precision and recall, is 0.90, indicating a balance between precision and recall for this category. The support value of 5000 represents the number of instances of the "Malignant" category in the dataset.

Comparing these metrics across different categories, we observe variations in performance. For example, the "Test" category demonstrates higher precision (0.96) and recall (0.95) compared to "Agitation" (precision: 0.78, recall: 0.80). This suggests that the model performs better in accurately identifying instances of the "Test" category compared to "Agitation". Additionally, we can assess the overall model performance using micro-average and macro-average metrics. The micro-average F1-score (0.89) and accuracy (0.89) indicate the overall performance of the model across all categories, considering each instance equally. On the other hand, the macro-average F1-score (0.87) and accuracy (0.88) provide an average performance measure across all categories, treating each category equally (Table 2).

Table 2. Classification Report for Adverse Event Reaction Categories

Category	Precision	Recall	F1-Score	Support
Malignant	0.92	0.88	0.90	5000
Anaemia	0.85	0.87	0.86	4500
Asthma	0.91	0.94	0.92	4800
Agitation	0.78	0.80	0.79	4200
Test	0.96	0.95	0.95	5100
Arrhythmia	0.90	0.92	0.91	4900
Diabetes	0.87	0.86	0.87	4800
Mellitus	0.89	0.90	0.89	4700
Arthropod	0.92	0.93	0.92	5200
Shock	0.83	0.84	0.83	4300
Positive	0.88	0.89	0.88	4600
Anaphylactic	0.82	0.81	0.82	4400
Allergy	0.84	0.85	0.84	4700
Melanoma	0.91	0.90	0.91	5100
Cholestasis	0.86	0.87	0.86	4900
Arthralgia	0.87	0.86	0.87	4500
Neoplasm	0.88	0.89	0.88	4800
Chills	0.90	0.91	0.90	4700
Accident	0.82	0.83	0.83	4300
Disorder	0.85	0.84	0.85	4600

10   Conclusion

This research tackled the critical issue of ADE prediction, emphasizing its importance for patient safety and healthcare costs. Traditional methods' limitations led to exploring machine learning techniques using BERT-based models. After a literature review and highlighting regional challenges, we focused on data preprocessing and encoding tokenized text for the BERT model. Fine-tuning BioBERT for ADE classification improved performance, with cross-entropy loss ensuring accurate predictions. Experimental results showed our model's effectiveness, with performance metrics like precision, recall, and F1-score validating its ability to identify adverse events accurately. The classification report provided detailed insights into the model's strengths and limitations across categories. Alternatively, employing a Retrieval-Augmented Generation (RAG) system could potentially enhance our results further. Unlike fine-tuning, RAG systems combine the strengths of retrieval-based models and generative models, allowing for the dynamic integration of relevant external information during prediction.

References

1. Tripoliti, E.E., Papadopoulos, T.G., Karanasiou, G.S., Naka, K.K., Fotiadis, D.I.: Heart failure: diagnosis, severity estimation and prediction of adverse events through machine learning techniques. Comput. Struct. Biotechnol. J. **15**, 26–47 (2017)
2. Assaf, R., Ratrout, A., Khalilia, M., Jayousi, R.: Learning distributed representation of drug sequences from adverse event reporting data. J. Theor. Appl. Inf. Technol. **102**(4) (2024)
3. Assaf, R., Jayousi, R., Rattrout, A.: Current state of machine learning based methods for adverse events prediction. In: 2021 International Conference on Promising Electronic Technologies (ICPET), pp. 34–39. IEEE (2021)
4. Bergman, E., et al.: Bert based natural language processing for triage of adverse drug reaction reports shows close to human-level performance. PLOS Digit. Health **2**(12), e0000409 (2023)
5. Chopard, D., et al.: Text mining of adverse events in clinical trials: deep learning approach. JMIR Med. Inform. **9**(12), e28632 (2021)
6. Hussain, S., Afzal, H., Saeed, R., Iltaf, N., Umair, M.Y., et al.: Pharmacovigilance with transformers: a framework to detect adverse drug reactions using bert fine-tuned with farm. Comput. Math. Methods Med. **2021** (2021)
7. Fan, B., Fan, W., Smith, C., et al.: Adverse drug event detection and extraction from open data: a deep learning approach. Inf. Process. Manag. **57**(1), 102131 (2020)
8. Li, Y., Li, J., He, J., Tao, C.: AE-GPT: using large language models to extract adverse events from surveillance reports-a use case with influenza vaccine adverse events. PLoS ONE **19**(3), e0300919 (2024)
9. Zheng, X., Ji, S., Wu, C.: Predicting adverse events for patients with type-1 diabetes via self-supervised learning. In: ICASSP 2024-2024 IEEE International Conference on Acoustics, Speech and Signal Processing (ICASSP), pp. 1526–1530. IEEE (2024)
10. Narayanan, S., Mannam, K., Achan, P., Ramesh, M.V., Rangan, P.V., Rajan, S.P.: A contextual multi-task neural approach to medication and adverse events identification from clinical text. J. Biomed. Inform. **125**, 103960 (2022)
11. McMaster, C., et al.: Developing a deep learning natural language processing algorithm for automated reporting of adverse drug reactions. J. Biomed. Inform. **137**, 104265 (2023)
12. Sutphin, C., Lee, K., Yepes, A.J., Uzuner, Ö., McInnes, B.T.: Adverse drug event detection using reason assignments in FDA drug labels. J. Biomed. Inform. **110**, 103552 (2020)
13. Yu, D., Vydiswaran, V.V.: An assessment of mentions of adverse drug events on social media with natural language processing: model development and analysis. JMIR Med. Inform. **10**(9), e38140 (2022)
14. Zhang, Y., et al.: High-throughput phenotyping with electronic medical record data using a common semi-supervised approach (PHECAP). Nat. Protoc. **14**(12), 3426–3444 (2019)
15. Cocos, A., Fiks, A.G., Masino, A.J.: Deep learning for pharmacovigilance: recurrent neural network architectures for labeling adverse drug reactions in twitter posts. J. Am. Med. Inform. Assoc. **24**(4), 813–821 (2017)
16. Henriksson, A., Kvist, M., Dalianis, H., Duneld, M.: Identifying adverse drug event information in clinical notes with distributional semantic representations of context. J. Biomed. Inform. **57**, 333–349 (2015)

Enhancing Outlier Detection: A Hybrid Architecture with Autoencoder Clustering and Isolation Forest

Sanae Borrohou[1(✉)], Rachida Fissoune[1], and Nadia Kabachi[2]

[1] IDS Team, Abdelmalek Essaadi University, Tangier, Morocco
`sanae.borrohou@etu.uae.ac.ma`, `rfissoune@uae.ac.ma`
[2] ERIC Laboratory, University of Lyon 2, Bron, France

Abstract. Anomaly detection remains a prominent challenge in the field of data science, given its extensive range of applications and the array of methodologies at hand. Regrettably, numerous existing anomaly detection techniques exhibit shortcomings, such as ineffectiveness, non-intuitive behavior, or specialization for specific data types. In this research, we adopt a unique fusion of three distinct algorithms to effectively address the challenge of anomaly detection. Initially, we harness the power of autoencoders to reduce the dimensionality of the data, enhancing its manageability while preserving essential patterns. Subsequently, leveraging advanced clustering techniques, we partition our data into K distinct subsets, a strategic approach aimed at pinpointing local anomalies. Lastly, we employ the robust Isolation Forest algorithm to comprehensively identify remaining outliers in the dataset. This orchestrated fusion of methodologies promises to offer a comprehensive and efficient solution for detecting both local and global anomalies, Thus contributing to the development of anomaly detection methods in data science.

Keywords: Outlier Detection · Machine Learning · Autoencoder · Clustering · Isolation Forest

1 Introduction

Outlier detection is a crucial task in data analysis and machine learning, aiming to identify data points that significantly deviate from the normal behavior of a dataset. These anomalous observations can distort analyses and impact the accuracy of machine learning models. Outliers, also known as anomalies, can arise due to various reasons [1] such as errors in data collection, measurement errors, inaccuracies in data distribution, human errors, and malfunctions in sensors or machines.

According to Pahuja et al. anomaly detection finds utility in a range of fields [2]. These areas are not limited to; identifying intrusions detecting fraud diagnosing conditions and public health concerns recognizing images analyzing text data monitoring sensor networks and data/process logs. It also plays a role, in ensuring cybersecurity and managing the Internet of Things (IoT).

H. Badir et al. (Eds.): INTIS 2024, CCIS 2645, pp. 105–118, 2026.
https://doi.org/10.1007/978-3-032-14964-0_9

Outlier detection approaches can be categorized into various groups depending on their underlying principles and techniques. Statistical approaches involve computations such as mean, median, and standard deviation to pinpoint data points that exhibit significant deviations from the expected pattern [3]. Distance-based techniques evaluate the distances between data points to flag those that are the farthest from the cluster's central tendency [4]. Density-based methods concentrate on regions with lower data density, marking data points in sparse areas as potential outliers [5]. Clustering-based methods segment the data into clusters and designate data points lying outside these clusters as outliers [5]. Machine learning-based methods utilize algorithms like support vector machines, decision trees, and neural networks to discern patterns in data, identifying deviations as outliers [3]. Ensemble methods combine multiple detection techniques to enhance overall accuracy [3]. A comprehension of these classifications enables researchers and practitioners to select suitable outlier detection methods based on their dataset's characteristics and the desired level of precision.

Machine learning has revolutionized the way we approach data analysis and anomaly detection, especially when dealing with large and complex datasets. One of the critical applications of machine learning is the identification of outliers within data. The advantage of using machine learning for outlier detection is its ability to automatically learn patterns and relationships within the data, which traditional methods may overlook. Outlier detection using Machine Learning relies on several key steps (Fig. 1).

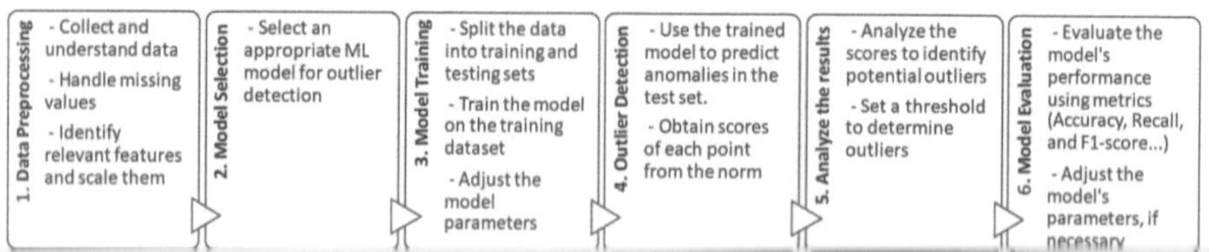

Fig. 1. Outlier detection workflow using Machine Learning

The structure of the paper is as follows. In Sect. 2, we delved into the related work in the field of outlier detection and recent techniques used. In Sect. 3, we conducted a comprehensive literature review on dimensional reduction techniques. In Sect. 4, we focused on comparing various clustering methods. Finally, in Sect. 5, we introduced our novel architecture for detecting outliers, which integrates autoencoders, clustering approaches and isolation Forest. This approach promises to provide an effective solution to the complex task of outlier detection in large datasets.

2   Related Work

Our primary focus is to have a thorough understanding of existing data outlier detection algorithms and their limitations. This knowledge helps us improve and develop a more efficient approach. Below is a list of key articles that significantly contribute to this research area.

In our recent contribution [6], we conducted a comparative study and experimental analysis of the most renowned algorithms for outlier detection, namely Isolation Forest (IF), Local Outlier Factor (LOF), Minimum Covariance Determinant (MCD), and One-Class Support Vector Machine (OCSVM) on various datasets. IF is a powerful algorithm capable of accurately detecting outliers in data and stands out because it does not require distance or density measures to detect anomalies, resulting in reduced computational load. It has linear time complexity, characterized by a low constant and reduced memory usage, and can handle large data sizes and high-dimensional problems. However, IF is not the best option for datasets with many high-dimensional features, as it may struggle to effectively isolate outliers in such situations. Additionally, Isolation Forest is primarily designed to detect global outliers rather than local ones.

Authors and scientists in recent research indicate that combining clustering methods and Isolation Forest algorithms can greatly enhance the accuracy and performance of outlier detection; MANDHARE et al. [7] showed that clustering methods stand out for their advantageous characteristics. They offer a significant advantage in terms of computational time. Moreover, they exhibit high efficiency, ensuring optimal performance. These methods also have broad applicability in handling high-dimensional data, setting them apart from other techniques, particularly those based on density in terms of complexity.

KARCZMAREK et al. [8] introduce an innovative method for anomaly detection in data by combining k-means and Isolation Forest techniques. Initially, attribute values are clustered using the Elbow rule to determine the optimal number of clusters. Subsequently, decision trees are created, utilizing these clusters as leaf nodes, with random selection of cluster attributes and values at each node. Each data point receives an anomaly score based on its membership in the clusters and the boundaries defined in the trees. Anomaly scores from all trees are then aggregated and normalized to derive the final anomaly score. This approach has proven its effectiveness in identifying isolated records and anomalies. However, the reliance on k-means clustering can be sensitive to the initial selection of centroids and may struggle with clusters of varying density or non-globular shapes. Additionally, the computational complexity can be high for large datasets due to the clustering step and the creation of multiple decision trees.

KARCZMAREK et al. [9] Suggest enhancing the Isolation Forest method by integrating it with Fuzzy C-Means (FCM). FCM allows the determination of membership degrees of elements in groups. This method is more robust to outliers than K-Means due to its ability to allow data points to contribute to multiple clusters. It offers a more nuanced representation of data affiliations to clusters. However, it is more complex than K-Means because of the calculation of membership degrees, leading to longer processing times, especially for large databases. Additionally, it is sensitive to parameters: the initialization of centroids and the tuning of the fuzziness parameter.

AYOUB et al. [10] propose a model that merges the EIF algorithm with FCM, operating in two stages. First, in the training stage, binary search trees are generated based on the optimal number of groups determined by the silhouette coefficient method. This number guides the subdivision of each decision tree. Then, the membership values from FCM, indicating the extent of an element belonging to groups, are utilized to calculate the scorecard. The results demonstrate that the proposed solution outperformed both IF and EIF in terms of both accuracy and learning speed.

Multiple research articles explore the fusion of combining Isolation Forest with dimensionality reduction techniques such as PCA (Principal Component Analysis), autoencoders, and LSTM (Long Short-Term Memory) networks that have gained significant attention in research. These hybrid approaches aim to leverage the strengths of Isolation Forest, which is efficient for anomaly detection in high-dimensional spaces, along with the capabilities of dimensionality reduction techniques to capture underlying patterns and reduce noise in the data.

PRIYANTO et al. [11] propose an anomaly detection model for a land monitoring system using data collected from sensors. The Isolation Forest technique is employed to label the unlabeled data, and a Long Short-Term Memory (LSTM) autoencoder is used to create the anomaly detection model. The experimental results demonstrate the potential of Isolation Forest for labeling data, and the LSTM autoencoder achieves high accuracy (0.95), precision (0.96), recall (0.99), and F1 score (0.97) in detecting anomalies.

KIRAN et al. [12] explore unsupervised feature extraction methods for detecting network anomalies, using principal component analysis (PCA), autoencoder, and isolation forest. PCA, though useful, proved insufficient for dimension reduction in their context, being highly dependent on numerical data. Autoencoders struggled to capture behavior data effectively, unable to identify unique clusters of good and bad transfer characteristics. Conversely, the isolation forest's tree-variant demonstrated proficiency in capturing high-level relationships, particularly in identifying packet reordering cases with a high anomaly score.

Almansoori et al. [13] employ a combination of an autoencoder and Isolation Forest to enhance anomaly detection. The autoencoder is trained to reconstruct input data, utilizing the discrepancy between the input and reconstructed data as an anomaly measure. Isolation Forest, relying on a tree structure, randomly selects features and values to partition the data recursively, using the number of partitions required to isolate a point as an anomaly measure. The proposed method leverages the autoencoder's ability to generate diverse data representations and Isolation Forest's anomaly detection capability. Demonstrating effectiveness in high-dimensional data, this approach proves valuable across various domains such as cybersecurity, finance, transportation, and fraud detection.

To address the two limitations of Isolation Forest, we propose combining this algorithm with other techniques, particularly well-known dimensionality reduction methods, to reduce data dimensions and extract only the most important features. Following this, we recommend integrating clustering algorithms to enhance the detection of local outliers. Given that the scientific world is rich with various classification and dimensionality reduction approaches, it is essential to have a thorough understanding of the most renowned methods (discussed in Sects. 2 and 3) before developing our architecture.

3   Dimensional Reduction Techniques

In response to the escalating dimensions of data, researchers have introduced numerous methods to enhance the efficiency of data mining and machine learning tasks. Addressing the challenges posed by the increasing volume of continuously generated data, dimensionality reduction serves as a crucial pre-processing step. This process, achieved through feature selection (FS) [14] and feature extraction (FE) [15]. Feature selection proves instrumental in mitigating dimensionality problems, effectively reducing redundancy, eliminating irrelevant data, and improving result comprehensibility. Conversely, feature extraction focuses on identifying the most distinctive, informative, and streamlined set of features to enhance both data processing and storage efficiency (Table 1).

Table 1. Comparison of Feature Selection and Feature Extraction Techniques

Dimensional Reduction Techniques	Objective	Advantages	Disadvantages
Feature Selection	Aims to find a significant low-dimensional representation of high-dimensional data by transforming a considerable number of attributes into a set of reduced features	- Reduces data size and decreases the required storage - Eliminates redundant and irrelevant features from the input dataset - Useful for identifying an optimal subset of features - Reduces runtime and training time - Facilitates the understanding of variables	- Some information may be lost after the selection
Feature Extraction	Focuses on diminishing the number of variables by selecting a subset of existing features	- Reduces the number of resources required for processing without losing relevant features - Creates more meaningful features from the original data - Capable of handling essential information in high-dimensional data - Preserves the original relative distance between features and covers the potential structure of the input dataset - Less sensitive to overfitting and performs well in classification tasks	- Occasionally the transformation can lead to loss of data description. However, it tends to have less information loss compared to feature selection - The cost of the feature extraction process can be expensive in several datasets

3.1 Comparison of Common Feature Extraction Algorithms

Following the latest benchmarking, we opted for feature extraction as our dimensional reduction technique, given its proven effectiveness in the literature. Feature extraction offers a robust approach to transforming the original feature set into more meaningful representations, especially adept at capturing crucial information within high-dimensional datasets. This choice sets the stage for a detailed comparison, delving into the common methodologies of feature extraction. Algorithms for feature extraction can be broadly classified into linear and nonlinear types [15–18].

Selecting the appropriate feature extraction technique is essential since it has a direct impact on how well downstream analysis activities are executed and can be interpreted. To aid in this decision-making, we conducted a comparative analysis of feature extraction techniques. Table 2 above presents a comprehensive comparison of several widely used feature extraction techniques. This analysis aims to clarify the trade-offs and considerations that should be made while selecting the optimal feature extraction approach for our architecture. Also, we can use Autoencoders as powerful tools for dimensionality reduction.

Table 2. Summary Comparison of Feature Extraction Algorithms

Algorithm	Time Complexity	Applications	Advantages	Disadvantages
PCA [19]	$O(d^2n + n^3)$	- Dimensionality Reduction - Feature Extraction - Data Compression - Data Visualization - Data Pre-processing	- highlight the most important features and relationships - Linear and unsupervised method, which means that it does not require any prior assumptions or labels on the data	- Not perform well if the relationships are highly nonlinear - May lose some information and details when reducing data dimensionality - PCA is sensitive to the presence of outliers
LDA [21]	$O(d^2n)$, $n \geq d$ $O(d^3)$, $d > n$	- Face Recognition - Medical Diagnosis - Biometrics - Quality Control - Document Classification - Customer Segmentation - Image Analysis - Pattern Recognition	- Effective in improving the performance of classifiers since it focuses on maximizing class separability - LDA leverages class labels, which can be crucial in many real-world applications - By retaining class-related information, LDA can help prevent overfitting	- Struggles to identify a lower-dimensional space when dimensions outnumber data samples in the matrix - LDA inadequately captures lower-dimensional structures in datasets with non-linearly separable classes - Outliers can significantly impact its performance
SVD [21,22]	$O(d^2n + n^3)$	- Dimensionality Reduction - Feature Extraction - Image Compression - Recommendation Systems - Latent Semantic Analysis in NLP	- SVD is used in data compression tasks, enabling more efficient storage of matrices - SVD is numerically stable, making it robust for various numerical applications - By using only the most significant singular values, SVD can help reduce the impact of noise in the data	- For large matrices SVD can be computationally expensive - Storing the full matrices U, Σ, and V can be memory-intensive - SVD is sensitive to missing values in the data

(continued)

Table 2. (*continued*)

Algorithm	Time Complexity	Applications	Advantages	Disadvantages
ICA [23]	$O[2di(d+1)n]$	- Ability to identify different signal types - Analyze multi-subject data - Handle complex data has proven particularly beneficial	- Can handle non-Gaussian and non-linear data - Can separate mixed signals into statistically independent components, which can provide valuable insights into complex systems	- ICA assumes that the sources are statistically independent, which may not hold in all cases - Computationally intensive, so it may require significant computational resources - ICA can be sensitive to noise present in the data
MDS [24]	$O(n^3)$	- Data Reduction - Data Visualization and Exploration - Data Analysis (discover patterns, clusters, outliers, and trends in the data) - Data Mining	- high precision achieved within a minimal computational time by the algorithm	- Only a single symmetric matrix is permissible as input - The data may not always meet the interval scale condition. The input matrix is square and symmetric
ISOMAP [25]	$O[dlog(c)n\,log(n)]$ $+O[n^2(c+log(n))]$ $+O(kn^2)$	- Dimensionality Reduction - Feature Extraction - Data Visualization and Exploration - Machine Learning Preprocessing - Signal Processing - Robotics	- Preserving the overall relationship between data points, which will give a better representation of the entire manifold - Isomap adeptly captures the inherent nonlinear structure within the data	- Computationally intensive, particularly for extensive datasets - The selection of parameters(number of neighbors) influences the performance - Potential for overfitting: Isomap may overfit noisy data
t-SNE [26]	$O(n^2)$	- Data Visualization - Image and Facial Recognition - Natural Language Processing (NLP) - Clustering Analysis - Medical Research and Bioinformatics - Anomaly Detection - Machine Learning	- t-SNE performs effectively on nonlinear data - t-SNE preserves both local and global structures, ensuring that nearby points in high-dimensional data remain proximate in lower dimensions	- Computationally Complex - Performance of t-SNE can be sensitive to its parameters, which may require tuning for optimal results - Patterns may emerge in random noise, necessitating multiple runs of the algorithm with varying sets of hyperparameters
LLE [27]	$O(dlog(c)n\,log(n))$ $+O(dnc^3)$ $+O(kn^2)$	- Data Reduction - Data Visualization - Data Exploration - Data Analysis - Data Mining - Fault Diagnosis - Grouping Problems in Computer Science and Mathematics	- Preserving local structures within the data involves capturing the inherent geometry of nonlinear manifolds by maintaining pairwise distances between neighboring data points - Capturing nonlinear patterns and structures within the data, particularly benefiting in handling complex, curved, or twisted datasets	- Curse of dimensionality: with high-dimensional data, increasing computational costs - Memory-intensive tasks and eigenvalue decomposition pose challenges for large datasets - Sensitive to outliers and noisy data, impacting the quality of embeddings
RPCA [28]	Depends on the algorithm used to solve the optimization problem	- Data Reduction - Video Surveillance - Image Denoising - Anomaly Detection - Signal Processing - Data Mining and Machine Learning	- Handling High-Dimensional Data with Small Sample Sizes - Outlier Detection and Removal - Recovery of True Low-Rank Structure: even a portion of the entries are corrupted or missing	- Computationally expensive and memory-intensive, especially for large-scale and high-dimensional data matrices - Potential lack of interpretability

Autoencoders, initially developed for nonlinear dimensionality reduction, have gained popularity as a nonlinear alternative to principal component analysis (PCA) [29]. They encode input data into a lower-dimensional latent space and decode it back to reconstruct the original input. Autoencoders find applications in unsupervised learning tasks, particularly in deep learning, and are used for tasks such as dimensionality reduction, data denoising, anomaly detection, and feature learning [30,31]. They leverage reconstruction error for outlier detection but come with drawbacks, including lengthy training times, potential loss of information during compression, and the production of abstract representations that are difficult to interpret. Despite these limitations, autoencoders offer benefits such as data compression, noise reduction, anomaly identification, and feature extraction [30,32].

Our benchmarking of dimensionality reduction techniques highlights the effectiveness of unsupervised autoencoder algorithms in outlier detection without the need for labeled data. Autoencoders demonstrate a capacity to grasp intricate relationships and data structures, facilitating precise anomaly identification. However, traditional techniques like PCA, LDA, SVD, and ICA rely on linear relationships between variables, limiting their efficacy for nonlinear data and making them sensitive to outliers. Robust PCA performs better with datasets containing moderate or low outlier percentages. MDS can handle nonlinear data but has constraints such as the inability to accept multiple symmetric matrix inputs and decreased representation accuracy due to the interval scale constraint. Similarly, ISOMAP and t-SNE effectively capture nonlinear data structures but suffer from significant computational overhead and parameter selection challenges.

4   Clustering-Based Approaches

Clustering techniques play a pivotal role in grouping comparable data points based on shared attributes or trends, aiding in the discovery of hidden structures within datasets and enhancing pattern recognition and exploratory data analysis [33]. By condensing complex data into cohesive groups, clustering facilitates easier exploration, visualization, and analysis of data [34,35]. Moreover, clustering contributes significantly to feature engineering, as resulting clusters can serve as additional features for further analysis tasks [36]. Additionally, clustering is instrumental in anomaly detection and classification, aiding in the differentiation of various data points or outliers [37]. Overall, clustering techniques provide valuable insights into the fundamental structure of data, enabling better-informed analysis and decision-making across various fields [33]. Different clustering strategies, including partitioning, density-based clustering, hierarchical clustering, and grid-based clustering algorithms, offer a diverse range of approaches tailored to the unique characteristics of datasets [38,39].

After conducting a comparative analysis, it has become evident that density-based clustering stands out for its superior efficiency. Unlike partitioning methods such as K-Means, Fuzzy C-Means, CLARA, PAM, and CLARANS, density-based clustering doesn't require specifying the number of clusters in advance. Furthermore, it proves adept at identifying clusters of arbitrary shapes and is more robust against noise and outliers compared to hierarchical or partitioning methods.

Density-based clustering also demonstrates greater effectiveness compared to grid-based methods like STRING, WaveCluster, and DCluster, which encounter difficulties with datasets featuring variable densities or irregular shapes. However, it's worth noting that grid-based clustering remains sensitive to the choice of grid size, sometimes requiring empirical adjustments to achieve optimal parameters. Additionally, it may not be suitable for datasets containing outliers, which could significantly influence clustering results (Table 3).

Table 3. Summary Comparison of Density- Based Clustering Algorithms

Algorithm	description	Time Complexity	Benefits	Weaknesses
DBSCAN	Identifies clusters by searching for dense regions in the input space, using user-defined indexing schemes. Being non-incremental, DBSCAN necessitates all input data to be available prior to processing	$O(n^2)$ $O(n*\log(n))$ (in lower-dimensional spaces)	- Cluster number determination is not needed beforehand - Capable of identifying clusters with diverse shapes, including those encompassed within other clusters - Robust to outliers	- Dependent on parameter values like ϵ and MinPts, which affect its performance - Struggles with clustering datasets of different densities as it assumes uniform density across clusters
OPTICS	is an extension of DBSCAN, providing a hierarchical clustering structure that allows for the identification of clusters with varying densities, unlike DBSCAN	$O(n^2)$ $O(n*\log(n))$ (in lower-dimensional spaces)	- Do not require any pre-defined specifications for the number of clusters - Detects clusters of diverse shapes and densities, even those with varying densities	- Sensitive to parameters, especially the reachability distance threshold, impacting cluster granularity
DENCLUE	Partitions the D-dimensional space into adjacent, small, non-overlapping hypercubes, limited to areas containing data points, and proceeds to identify clusters within hypercubes exhibiting significant density	$O(n^2)$	- Able to detect complex clusters in high-dimensional datasets, even when those clusters have irregular shapes, overlap, or have varying densities - Handle noise and outliers more effectively than other methods - Excels in the accurate detection of non-spherical clusters with varying densities	- Estimating kernel density and finding attractors can be computationally expensive - Parameter sensitivity; DENCLUE requires specifying parameters such as kernel bandwidth
Mean Shift	Operates by shifting a sliding window towards areas of elevated density until it converges to a local maximum of the density. These local maxima represent the clusters in the dataset	- $O(n^2)$	- Does not take any predefined shape on the clusters, capable of Identifying clusters of variable shapes and densities - Capable of handling arbitrary feature spaces - Handle noise and outliers	- Sensitive to choice of kernel bandwidth - Mean Shift performs a lot of steps, so it can be computationally expensive

The comparative table (3) presents a detailed analysis of well-known density-based clustering algorithms, such as DBSCAN, OPTICS, DENCLUE, and Mean Shift. Upon comparison, DENCLUE, OPTICS, and Mean-shift demonstrate the capability to identify clusters with varied densities and forms, including those with variable densities. In contrast, DBSCAN operates under the assumption of generally uniform cluster densities.

DENCLUE demonstrates superior performance in handling noise and outliers compared to other techniques. It effectively identifies complex cluster structures, even in high-dimensional datasets with varying densities, irregular shapes, or overlapping clusters. Additionally, DENCLUE exhibits faster execution in high-dimensional datasets. However, density-based techniques often require specialized expertise, particularly in parameter selection.

5 Our Architecture

5.1 Motivation

Our architecture combines three algorithms: Isolation Forest, DENCLUE, and autoencoders. These choices were carefully chosen, taking into account each candidate's distinct advantages as mentioned in Sects. 3 and 4, as well as how well they matched our goals. Moreover, this architecture expands on the knowledge from our earlier submission [6], which included a thorough analysis of well-known outlier detection algorithms, including One-Class Support Vector Machine (OCSVM), Minimum Covariance Determinant (MCD), Local Outlier Factor (LOF), and Isolation Forest (IF). Important conclusions were drawn from our previous work, including;

Isolation Forest (IF) emerges as a robust algorithm for outlier detection with remarkable accuracy. It stands out for its independence from distance or density measurements, leading to decreased computational overhead. Additionally, IF exhibits linear time complexity, boasting low constants and minimal memory usage. Its capability to effectively manage large datasets and high-dimensional problems further underscores its appeal. However, IF may encounter challenges in datasets abundant in high-dimensional features, potentially hindering its ability to isolate outliers effectively. Moreover, its design primarily prioritizes the detection of global outliers over local anomalies.

To overcome the two limitations of Isolation Forest, we proposed integrating additional algorithms, particularly clustering techniques, to enhance the identification of local outliers. Moreover, we suggested employing data dimensionality reduction methods to decrease data dimensions and extract essential features more effectively.

Firstly, We selected autoencoders for their remarkable capability to reduce dimensionality and detect outliers without the need for labeled data. Autoencoders excel at capturing complex relationships and data structures, enabling precise anomaly identification. Unlike methods such as PCA, LDA, SVD, and ICA, which rely on linear assumptions and may be sensitive to outliers, autoencoders offer greater flexibility in handling nonlinear data and mitigating the impact of outliers. As a result, they emerge as a robust choice for our architecture, particularly when dealing with diverse and intricate datasets.

Secondly, We selected to use DENCLUE in our architecture because of its ability to effectively handle noise and outliers, especially in high-dimensional datasets. When it comes to recognizing intricate cluster structures, DENCLUE performs better than other methods—even in cases when clusters have irregular shapes, shifting densities, or overlap. It also performs notably faster on high-dimensional datasets. DENCLUE is an essential part of our architecture due to its capacity to handle complicated data structures and efficiently regulate noise, even though parameter selection may call for specialized knowledge.

Finally, we will apply the Isolation Forest algorithm to each subset of data. This technique is particularly powerful for detecting anomalies or outliers within the data, helping to ensure the robustness and reliability of our architecture.

5.2   Architecture

Figure 2 illustrates our Architecture composed of three steps as shown below:

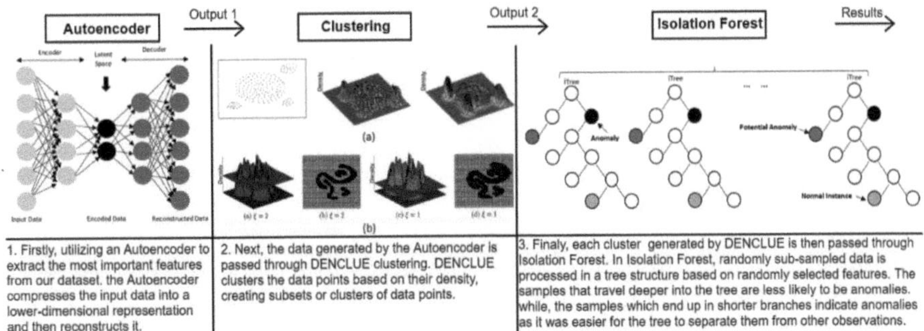

| 1. Firstly, utilizing an Autoencoder to extract the most important features from our dataset. the Autoencoder compresses the input data into a lower-dimensional representation and then reconstructs it. | 2. Next, the data generated by the Autoencoder is passed through DENCLUE clustering. DENCLUE clusters the data points based on their density, creating subsets or clusters of data points. | 3. Finaly, each cluster generated by DENCLUE is then passed through Isolation Forest. In Isolation Forest, randomly sub-sampled data is processed in a tree structure based on randomly selected features. The samples that travel deeper into the tree are less likely to be anomalies. while, the samples which end up in shorter branches indicate anomalies as it was easier for the tree to separate them from other observations. |

Fig. 2. Our architecture integrates an Autoencoder with an encoder to compress data into a lower-dimensional latent space and a decoder to reconstruct the original input. DENCLUE, our clustering algorithm, (a) the left figure visualizes the 2D dataset, the middle figure represents density with "kernel function" and "Gaussian function" in the right figure, (b) demonstrates how DENCLUE identifies clusters of various shapes by leveraging density attractors connected by paths. Isolation Forest, depicted as iTree, distinguishes outliers with black circles, while light gray circles signify typical normal samples, and dark gray circles represent unusual normal samples

   (1) Autoencoder for dimentionality reduction:

– Data Preprocessing: First, preprocess our data by performing operations such as normalization, standardization, or handling missing and duplicate values.
– Autoencoder Construction: Create an autoencoder model. It consists of two parts, the encoder and the decoder. The encoder reduces the dimension of the data by compressing it into a lower-dimensional latent space. The decoder restores the original data from this latent space.
– Autoencoder Training: Train the autoencoder on our data. The training objective is to minimize the difference between the input data and the data reconstructed by the autoencoder.
– Dimensionality Reduction: We use the encoder to reduce the dimension of our data. The input data is transformed into a lower-dimensional latent space.

   (2) DENCLUE for clustering:

– Density Estimation: Estimate the density at each data point using "Gaussian Kernel", leveraging the output of the Autoencoder.
– Selection of Density Attractors: Identify density attractors (local maxima of the estimated density) while filtering out trivial local maxima using a threshold ϵ.
– Connecting Density Attractors: Establish connections between density attractors by analyzing density contours.

- Cluster Formation: Form clusters based on connected density attractors. Points are assigned to the cluster of the nearest attractor.

(3) Isolation Forest for detecting outliers in each cluster:

- Using a training dataset to create isolation trees (iTrees).
- Each instance in the test set traverses these iTrees, and an appropriate "anomaly score" is assigned to the instance.

6   Conclusion

Our research, derived from a review of the state-of-the-art and a comparison of various approaches, outlines a methodology combining three algorithms. Firstly, we utilize Autoencoder to overcome the challenge faced by Isolation Forest in handling datasets with a large number of features, as Autoencoder extracts the most important features. Secondly, we employ DENCLUE to cluster the data generated by Autoencoders and divide them into subsets to address the challenge of Isolation Forest in detecting local outliers. Lastly, we apply Isolation Forest to each cluster to identify outliers based on their scores. However, integrating these three algorithms can significantly increase computational complexity. Training autoencoders, clustering with DENCLUE, and applying Isolation Forest to each cluster require substantial time and computing power. To mitigate these demands, leveraging CUDA for parallel processing can accelerate the training and execution of these algorithms, optimizing performance and reducing computation time.

In future contributions, we plan to implement our approach on various datasets and conduct comparative analyses with alternative algorithms to assess its performance. We will evaluate its effectiveness using key metrics such as precision, recall, and F1-score. Additionally, we plan to integrate CUDA Python programming to reduce execution time.

CUDA Python programming, using tools like Numba, allows for significant optimization of algorithmic performance by leveraging the parallel processing power of NVIDIA GPUs. By writing GPU kernels in Python, tasks such as vector addition and matrix multiplication can be accelerated. Key techniques include efficient memory management, optimal thread organization, and the use of shared memory to reduce global memory access.

References

1. Blázquez-Garcia, A., Conde, A., Mori, U., et al.: A review on outlier/anomaly detection in time series data. ACM Comput. Surv. (CSUR) 54(3), 1–33 (2021)
2. Pahuja, D., Yadav, R.: Outlier detection for different applications: review. Int. J. Eng. Res. Technol. (IJERT) 2 (2013)
3. Wang, H., Bah, M.J., Hammad, M.: Progress in outlier detection techniques: a survey. IEEE Access 7, 107964–108000 (2019)

4. Chu, X., Ilyas, I.F.: Data cleaning (2019)
5. Zhang, J.: Advancements of outlier detection: a survey. ICST Trans. Scalable Inf. Syst. **13**(1), 1–26 (2013)
6. Borrohou, S., Fissoune, R., Badir, H.: Data cleaning survey and challenges-improving outlier detection algorithm in machine learning. J. Smart Cities Soc. **2**(3), 125–140 (2023)
7. Mandhare, H.C., Idate, S.R.: A comparative study of cluster based outlier detection, distance based outlier detection and density based outlier detection techniques. In: 2017 International Conference on Intelligent Computing and Control Systems (ICICCS), pp. 931–935. IEEE (2017)
8. Karczmarek, P., Kiersztyn, A., Pedrycz, W., et al.: K-Means-based isolation forest. Knowl.-Based Syst. **195**, 105659 (2020)
9. Karczmarek, P., Kiersztyn, A., Pedrycz, W., et al.: Fuzzy c-means-based isolation forest. Appl. Soft Comput. **106**, 107354 (2021)
10. Ayoub, M., Khalid, J., Karczmarek, P.: Fuzzy C-Means based extended isolation forest for anomaly detection. In: International Conference on Advanced Intelligent Systems for Sustainable Development, pp. 411–418. Springer, Cham (2022)
11. Priyanto, C.Y., Purnomo, H.D., et al.: Combination of isolation forest and LSTM autoencoder for anomaly detection. In: 2021 2nd International Conference on Innovative and Creative Information Technology (ICITech), pp. 35–38. IEEE (2021)
12. Kiran, M., Wang, C., Papadimitriou, G., Mandal, A., Deelman, E.: Detecting anomalous packets in network transfers: investigations using PCA, autoencoder and isolation forest in TCP. Mach. Learn. **109**(5), 1127–1143 (2020). https://doi.org/10.1007/s10994-020-05870-y
13. Almansoori, M., Telek, M.: Anomaly detection using combination of autoencoder and isolation forest. In: 1st Workshop on Intelligent Infocommunication Networks, Systems and Services (WI2NS2). Budapest University of Technology and Economics, pp. 25–30 (2023)
14. Khaire, U.M., Dhanalakshmi, R.: Stability of feature selection algorithm: a review. J. King Saud Univ.-Comput. Inf. Sci. **34**(4), 1060–1073 (2022)
15. Zebari, R., Abdulazeez, A., Zeebaree, D., et al.: A comprehensive review of dimensionality reduction techniques for feature selection and feature extraction. J. Appl. Sci. Technol. Trends **1**(2), 56–70 (2020)
16. Elhadad, M.K., Badran, K.M., Salama, G.I.: A novel approach for ontology-based dimensionality reduction for web text document classification. Int. J. Softw. Innov. (IJSI) **5**(4), 44–58 (2017)
17. Shah, F.P., Patel, V.: A review on feature selection and feature extraction for text classification. In: 2016 International Conference on Wireless Communications, Signal Processing and Networking (WiSPNET), pp. 2264–2268. IEEE (2016)
18. Li, M., Wang, H., Yang, L., et al.: Fast hybrid dimensionality reduction method for classification based on feature selection and grouped feature extraction. Expert Syst. Appl. **150**, 113277 (2020)
19. Greenacre, M., Groenen, P.J.F., Hastie, T., et al.: Principal component analysis. Nat. Rev. Methods Primers **2**(1), 100 (2022)
20. Tharwat, A., Gaber, T., Ibrahim, A., et al.: Linear discriminant analysis: a detailed tutorial. AI Commun. **30**(2), 169–190 (2017)
21. Ahmad, N., Nassif, A.B.: Dimensionality reduction: challenges and solutions. In: ITM Web of Conferences. EDP Sciences, p. 01017 (2022)
22. Yanai, H., Takeuchi, K., Takane, Y.: Singular value decomposition (SVD). In: Projection Matrices, Generalized Inverse Matrices, and Singular Value Decomposition, pp. 125–149. Springer, New York (2011)

23. Isomura, T., Toyoizumi, T.: A local learning rule for independent component analysis. Sci. Rep. **6**(1), 28073 (2016)
24. Saeed, N., Nam, H., Haq, M.I.U., et al.: A survey on multidimensional scaling. ACM Comput. Surv. (CSUR) **51**(3), 1–25 (2018)
25. Anowar, F., Sadaoui, S., Selim, B.: Conceptual and empirical comparison of dimensionality reduction algorithms (PCA, KPCA, LDA, MDS, SVD, LLE, ISOMAP, LE, ICA, t-SNE). Comput. Sci. Rev. **40**, 100378 (2021)
26. Devassy, B.M., George, S.: Dimensionality reduction and visualisation of hyperspectral ink data using t-SNE. Forensic Sci. Int. **311**, 110194 (2020)
27. Ghojogh, B., Ghodsi, A., Karray, F., et al.: Locally linear embedding and its variants: tutorial and survey. arXiv preprint arXiv:2011.10925 (2020)
28. Candès, E.J., Li, X., Ma, Y., Wright, J.: Robust principal component analysis? J. ACM (JACM) **58**(3), 1–37 (2011)
29. Pinaya, W.H.L., Vieira, S., Garcia-Dias, R., et al.: Autoencoders. In: Machine Learning, pp. 193–208. Academic Press (2020)
30. Bank, D., Koenigstein, N., Giryes, R.: Autoencoders. In: Machine Learning for Data Science Handbook: Data Mining and Knowledge Discovery Handbook, pp. 353–374 (2023)
31. Michelucci, U.: An introduction to autoencoders. arXiv preprint arXiv:2201.03898 (2022)
32. Chen, S., Guo, W.: Auto-encoders in deep learning–a review with new perspectives. Mathematics **11**(8), 1777 (2023)
33. Caruso, G., Gattone, S.A., Fortuna, F., Di Battista, T.: Cluster analysis as a decision-making tool: a methodological review. In: Bucciarelli, E., Chen, S.-H., Corchado, J.M. (eds.) DCAI 2017. AISC, vol. 618, pp. 48–55. Springer, Cham (2018). https://doi.org/10.1007/978-3-319-60882-2_6
34. Kumar, H.: Clustering techniques: a review on some clustering algorithms. In: Emerging Trends and Applications in Cognitive Computing, pp. 198–223 (2019)
35. Agrawal, A.S., Bojewwar, S.: Comparative study of various clustering techniques. Int. J. Comput. Sci. Mob. Comput. **3**(10), 497–504 (2014)
36. Anitha, S., Metilda, M.: Significance of Feature Selection Impacting Good Clusters
37. Ott, L., Pang, L., Ramos, F.T., et al.: On integrated clustering and outlier detection. In: Advances in Neural Information Processing Systems, vol. 27 (2014)
38. Aparajita, A., Swagatika, S., Singh, D.: Comparative analysis of clustering techniques in cloud for effective load balancing. Int. J. Eng. Technol. **7**(3.4), 47 (2018)
39. Shah, M., Nair, S.: A survey of data mining clustering algorithms. Int. J. Comput. Appl. **128**(1), 1–5 (2015)

An Efficient Face Recognition Model Based on ViT Architecture

Er-rajy Latifa[1]([✉]) [ID], El Kiram My Ahmed[1], Lahihab Oussama[1], and El Ghazouani Mohamed[2]

[1] FSSM, University Cadi Ayyad, Marrakesh, Morocco
l.errajy@uca.ma
[2] Polydisciplinary Faculty of Sidi Bennour, Chouaîb Doukkali University, El Jadida, Morocco

Abstract. Our paper presents FaceDetectCT, an innovative face recognition model designed to handle the complexities of diverse datasets and real-world environments. We provide a comprehensive overview of the model's architecture, emphasizing its novel features. Extensive testing confirms that FaceDetectCT performs competitively across various metrics when compared to established benchmarks. While it shows promising accuracy, further refinements are necessary to enhance its adaptability to pose variations and improve computational efficiency. This research highlights our model's potential to make significant strides in face recognition technology, with wide-ranging practical applications. Additionally, FaceDetectCT represents a pioneering integration of the Vision Transformer (ViT) architecture, specifically optimized to increase face detection resilience. Our extensive experimentation validates our model's competitive performance across multiple metrics, including accuracy, precision, recall, F1 score, AUC-ROC, IoU, and computational efficiency. These metrics collectively demonstrate the model's ability to perform reliably and efficiently in various scenarios, including those involving significant pose variations.

Keywords: Facial recognition · Images · Feature

1 Introduction

The rapid advancement of technology has led to an increased demand for robust face recognition systems, driven by applications ranging from security to personalized user experiences. Traditional face recognition methods, while effective under controlled conditions, often struggle with diverse datasets and real-world complexities such as variations in pose, lighting, and image quality [1]. These challenges necessitate the development of more sophisticated models capable of maintaining high performance in less-than-ideal conditions. Existing technologies in face recognition have made significant strides, primarily through the use of Convolutional Neural Networks (CNNs) [2]. CNN-based models have demonstrated impressive accuracy and efficiency in detecting and recognizing faces. However, their performance can degrade when dealing with extensive pose variations, occlusions, and other environmental noise. Additionally, these models often require substantial computational resources, limiting their applicability in real-time or resource-constrained scenarios [3].

H. Badir et al. (Eds.): INTIS 2024, CCIS 2645, pp. 119–131, 2026.
https://doi.org/10.1007/978-3-032-14964-0_10

In response to these challenges, we introduce FaceDetectCT, an innovative face recognition model that leverages the Vision Transformer (ViT) architecture. The ViT architecture, known for its superior capability in capturing long-range dependencies and global context, offers distinct advantages over traditional CNNs [4]. By utilizing self-attention mechanisms, the ViT can effectively focus on relevant facial features and structural details, enhancing the model's robustness against pose variations and other common degradations [5]. The proposed model incorporates several key components to address the identified challenges comprehensively. These include a U-shaped architecture for multi-scale feature extraction [6], local-global feature integration (LGCM) [7] for balanced contextual understanding, and a Facial Structure Attention Unit (FSAU) [8] to refine the focus on critical facial landmarks. Together, these components synergize to deliver a model that not only matches but exceeds the performance of current technologies in challenging conditions [9].

In this paper, we provide a detailed analysis of our model's architecture, its innovative features, and the specific ways in which the ViT architecture addresses the limitations of existing technologies [10]. Through this exploration, we aim to highlight FaceDetectCT's potential to drive significant advancements in face recognition technology, with wide-ranging implications for practical applications.

2 FaceDetectCT Model

FaceDetectCT addresses the challenges of face detection in degraded conditions through a multifaceted approach. It effectively handles variations in resolution, ensuring reliable detection even with fluctuating image quality, and robustly manages noise, maintaining stable performance despite environmental disturbances. Additionally, the model adeptly navigates other common degradations such as pose variations, lighting changes, and occlusions, enhancing its adaptability to diverse and challenging scenarios. This comprehensive strategy ensures that FaceDetectCT delivers consistent and accurate face detection across a wide range of real-world conditions.

The Vision Transformer (ViT) architecture is central to the functioning of FaceDetectCT, enabling it to effectively address various challenges in face detection. The process begins with patch embedding, where the input image is divided into non-overlapping patches. Each patch is then flattened into a vector and projected into a higher-dimensional space using a learnable linear embedding, creating an embedding for each patch [11]. To retain crucial positional information, positional embeddings are added to these patch embeddings. This step ensures that the model is aware of the relative positions of the patches within the image, preserving spatial context. The sequence of embedded patches, now augmented with positional information, is fed into a standard Transformer encoder.

The Transformer encoder consists of multiple layers of multi-head self-attention and feed-forward neural networks. The self-attention mechanism within each layer allows the model to dynamically focus on different parts of the image, weighing the importance of each patch relative to others. This capability is particularly useful for detecting faces in varying poses and under different lighting conditions, as the model can adjust its focus based on the most relevant facial features. After passing through the Transformer encoder, the resulting feature representations from all patches are aggregated. This aggregated representation effectively captures the essential information needed for accurate face detection [12]. Finally, the aggregated features are passed through fully connected layers to perform face classification and localization tasks. The model outputs bounding boxes for detected faces along with confidence scores, indicating the presence and location of faces within the image.

Figure 1 presents a schematic representation of our model, showing how these components interact to improve performance and reliability in face detection tasks under degraded conditions.

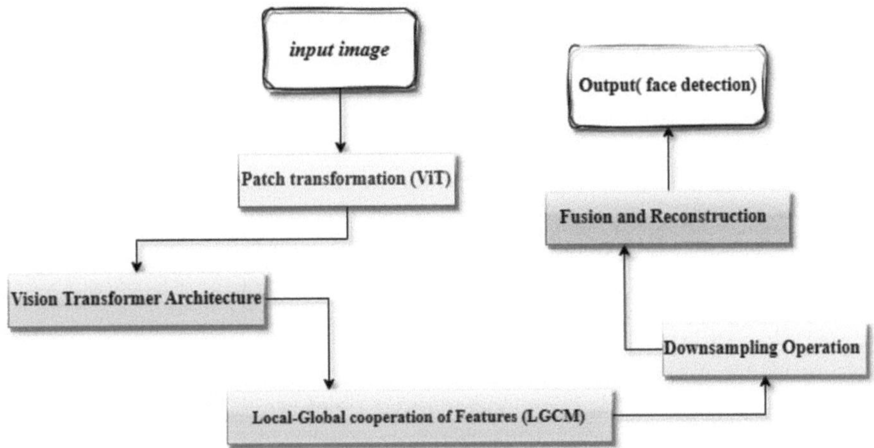

Fig. 1. FaceDetectCT Model Architecture: A Comprehensive Scheme for Robust Face Detection in Degraded Conditions

2.1 Patch Transformation (ViT)

The segment transformation process in the Vision Transformer (ViT) framework plays a critical role in our model, aimed at facilitating efficient processing of information across various spatial scales, particularly advantageous for robust face detection under challenging conditions. This process comprises several essential sub-steps:

Patch Extraction: Initially, we extract non-overlapping patches from the input image I. Each patch $P_{i,j}$ is defined as a subsection of the image, with its dimensions determined by the $h \times w$ dimensions of the patch grid. The indices i and j specify the patch's location within the grid.

$$P_{i,j=}I[i.h:(i+1).h,j.w:(j+1).w] \tag{1}$$

Linearization of Patches: The process of linearizing each patch Pi,j entails transforming its matrix into a vector, resulting in a linear sequence vi,j. The pixel values Pi,j(x,y) within the patch are concatenated to generate vi,j, as demonstrated by Eqs. 2:

$$v_{i,j} = reshape(P_{i,j}) \tag{2}$$

Concatenation of Linear Sequences: Equation 3 illustrates the amalgamation of linear sequences obtained from individual patches to construct a unified global linear sequence, denoted as S. The dimensions of the patch grid, represented by N and M, are taken into account in this process.

$$S = \sum_{i=1}^{N} \sum_{j=1}^{M} v_{i,j} \tag{3}$$

Introduction into the ViT Architecture: Ultimately, the global linear sequence S is integrated into the Vision Transformer (ViT) architecture, enabling the model to capture long-range dependencies among the patches, as depicted in Eq. 4

$$\text{Output}ViT = \text{ViT}(S) \tag{4}$$

2.2 Architecture ViT

In the subsequent phase of our model, we implemented the Vision Transformer (ViT) architecture, distinguished by its subdivision into numerous Transformer blocks, each comprising multi-head attention mechanisms and linear transformations. To elucidate this stage further, let's explore the pertinent mathematical formulations.

Multi-head Attention: Multi-head attention stands as a pivotal mechanism within Transformer blocks, enabling the model to discern intricate relationships among various segments of the sequence. X denote the input sequence to a Transformer block, and let W_Q, W_K, and W_V represent the learned weight matrices for the linear projections of queries, keys, and values, respectively. Equation 5 delineates the output of multi-head attention.

$$Attention(X) - softmax\left(\frac{XW_Q(XW_K)^T}{\sqrt{d_k}}\right)XW_V \tag{5}$$

where d_k is the dimension of queries and keys, and *softmax* is applied along the columns to obtain a weight distribution.

2.3 Local-Global Feature Cooperation (LGCM)

Subsequently, our model proceeds to the Local-Global Feature Cooperation (LGCM), a vital element within the envisioned Vision Transformer (ViT) framework tailored specifically for face detection in surveillance cameras. LGCM integrates the Facial Structure Attention Unit (FSAU) along with the Transformer block to effectively capture both local and global features.

Facial Structure Attention Unit (FSAU): Engineered to extract local features by specifically concentrating on facial structure.

Transformer Block for Local Features: The resulting output from the Facial Structure Attention Unit (FSAU) is subsequently fed into a Transformer block to capture non-linear dependencies. Denoted as H_{local}, the output of this stage undergoes a linear transformation defined as follows:

$$H_{local} = Transform_{local}\left(softmax\left(\frac{XW_Q(XW_K)^T}{\sqrt{d_k}}\right)XW_V\right) \tag{6}$$

where $Transform_{local}$ represents linear transformation operations in the Transformer block for local features.

Transformation for Global Features: Simultaneously, a transformation is applied to capture global features. $Transform_{global}$ is the output of this part; the linear transformation is formulated as follows:

$$H_{global} = Transform_{global}(X) \tag{7}$$

where $Transform_{global}$ represents linear transformation operations in the Transformer block for global features.

Local-Global Feature Cooperation (LGCM): Ultimately, local and global features are merged through a cooperative operation. Represented as H_{coop}, this amalgamated output stands as the final outcome of the Local-Global Feature Cooperation, with the formula outlined as follows:

$$H_{coop} = H_{local} + H_{global} \tag{8}$$

2.4 Downsampling

This step involves specially configured convolutional layers to condense feature dimensions, reducing spatial size while increasing output channels. LeakyReLU activation functions introduce non-linearities, aiding in learning complex representations. The objective is to shrink feature dimensions while preserving essential information for face detection. Downsampling via convolutions with a stride of 2 facilitates dimension reduction, enhancing the model's ability to extract relevant information.

2.5 Fusion and Reconstruction

In this crucial step of face detection from surveillance camera images, our goal is to merge features obtained at various scales and reconstruct a comprehensive image representation for accurate face detection.

The "Fusion and Reconstruction" stage is pivotal, depicted graphically, beginning with "Reduced Features" derived from downsampling and "Features Encoded at Different Scales" obtained through encoding at multiple scales. These features are merged into "Merged Features" through concatenation or attention mechanisms.

Subsequently, the reconstructed image undergoes face detection in the "Face Detection/Output" phase, employing additional processing techniques to precisely locate regions containing faces within the image. This process involves intricate mathematical operations depicted visually, facilitating precise face detection from surveillance camera images.

2.6 Output (Face Detection)

The "Boxes Bounded" segment comprises bounding boxes, each encapsulating the spatial details of a detected face. Mathematically, the bounding box for the ith face can be expressed as:

$$B_i = (x_i, y_i, w_i, h_i) \tag{9}$$

where (x_i, y_i) denotes the coordinates of the top-left corner, and (w_i, h_i) represent the width and height of the bounding box, respectively. The provided mathematical formula precisely outlines the region within the image where the identified face is located. Alongside spatial information, the "Object Scores" segment offers numerical scores linked with each detected face.

3 Experiment

In our experiment, we enriched the RAF-DB and AffectNet datasets by incorporating synthetic facial occlusions. Subsequently, we trained our FaceDetectCT model with meticulously chosen parameters, utilizing batch-based stochastic gradient descent for optimization. Our experimental design comprised four distinct groups, each dedicated to training under varied conditions, spanning from individual datasets to augmented ones.

The implementation of FaceDetectCT was carried out using the following materials:

Hardware:

NVIDIA GPUs: Our model training and testing were performed on NVIDIA A100 GPUs, which offer high computational power and memory bandwidth essential for handling large-scale datasets and complex model architectures like ViT.

Workstation: We utilized a high-performance computing workstation equipped with Intel Xeon processors and 256 GB of RAM to support data preprocessing, training, and evaluation phases.

Software:

Python: The primary programming language used for developing the model and related utilities.

PyTorch: A deep learning framework that facilitated the implementation of the ViT architecture and provided tools for efficient model training and evaluation.

CUDA: NVIDIA's parallel computing platform and application programming interface (API) that enabled significant acceleration of the training process by leveraging GPU capabilities.

NumPy and Pandas: Libraries for numerical operations and data manipulation, respectively.

OpenCV: Used for image processing tasks such as reading, writing, and manipulating images.

To assess our model's performance, we employed metrics including accuracy, precision, recall, and F1-score. Furthermore, we evaluated the model's resilience on the FEDRO dataset. Through comparative analysis, we scrutinized performance disparities, evaluated the influence of augmented data on model robustness, and examined the balance between performance enhancements and computational expenses. This examination provides insights into the efficacy of augmented data in improving face detection systems.

To ensure the robustness and efficiency of training the FaceDetectCT Model, we adopted a systematic approach. Initially, we initialized the TFE backbone using a pre-trained ResNet-18 model from the ImageNet dataset, establishing a solid foundation for subsequent tasks [13]. Table 1 offers a comprehensive overview of the key parameters utilized in training our model Architecture, facilitating better understanding and comparison of our methodology.

Table 1. FaceDetectCT Model Training Parameters

Parameter	Value
Backbone	Pre-trained ResNet-18
Number of Layers (L)	4
Hidden Dimension (D)	768
Number of Attention Heads (M)	12
Optimization Algorithm	Batch-based Stochastic Gradient Descent
Batch Size	128
Learning Rate (base)	0.001
Weight Decay	0.0005
Momentum	0.9
Loss Weight Configuration	1:1 for FER and Image Reconstruction
Dropout Probability	0.1
Epochs	50
Warmup Steps	1000

To thoroughly evaluate the performance of the FaceDetectCT Model Architecture under diverse training conditions, our experimentation is organized into four distinct groups. Table 2 offers an overview of these experimental groups, delineating the datasets utilized for training in each group and their respective roles within the experimental framework.

Apart from the previously mentioned groups, the experimentation involves an in-depth analysis of various parameters, as succinctly summarized in Table 3. This encompasses details like augmentation methods, image resolutions, and batch sizes, offering a comprehensive insight into the experimental configuration and its impact on model performance.

Table 2. Experimental Groups and Training Data Analysis

Experimental Group	Training Data	Purpose
Group 1	RAF-DB	Evaluate model performance with exclusive training on the RAF-DB dataset
Group 2	AffectNet	Assess model capabilities in a different data environment with the AffectNet dataset
Group 3	RAF-DB + AffectNet	Establish a baseline by training on a combination of RAF-DB and AffectNet datasets
Group 4	Augmented RAF-DB + Augmented AffectNet	Investigate the impact of augmented data with artificial facial occlusions

Table 3. Additional Training Parameters Analysis

Parameter	Group 1	Group 2	Group 3	Group 4
Augmentation Techniques	None	None	None	Facial Occlusions
Image Resolution	224×224	224×224	224×224	224×224
Batch Size	128	128	128	128
Learning Rate	0.001	0.001	0.001	0.001
Epochs	50	50	50	50

3.1 False and True Positives

In our experimental setup, we organized four distinct groups, each designed to achieve specific objectives through the utilization of unique training datasets. Group 1 concentrated solely on training the model with the RAF-DB dataset, comprising 12,000 samples. The primary aim here was to evaluate the model's performance exclusively within the RAF-DB dataset, providing insights into its proficiency in recognizing facial patterns within this particular dataset. In contrast, Group 2 was dedicated to training with the AffectNet dataset, which included 10,000 samples. The objective was to assess the model's capabilities in a different data environment, allowing for a comparative analysis with the findings from Group 1. Group 3 combined both the RAF-DB and AffectNet datasets, totaling 22,000 samples (12,000 from RAF-DB and 10,000 from AffectNet). This combination enabled a comprehensive comparison of the model's performance across diverse datasets, highlighting its adaptability and generalization abilities. Finally, Group 4 utilized augmented versions of the RAF-DB and AffectNet datasets, incorporating artificial facial occlusions. This augmented dataset comprised 26,000 samples (12,000 from RAF-DB, 10,000 from AffectNet, and additional samples with artificial occlusions). The objective was to evaluate the model's adaptability and resilience in scenarios where facial features may be partially obscured.

Each group's configuration, determined by the number of samples and dataset composition, provided valuable insights into the FaceDetectCT Model Architecture's performance under various training conditions, facilitating a comprehensive understanding of its effectiveness and robustness.

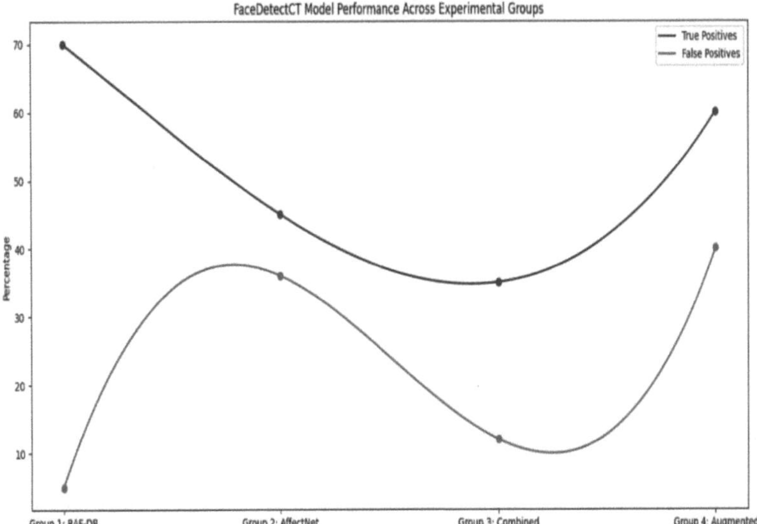

Fig. 2. Performance Analysis of FaceDetectCT Model: True and False Positives Distribution across Experimental Groups

Figure 2 illustrates the performance of the FaceDetectCT model across four experimental groups. In Group 1, trained exclusively on the RAF-DB dataset, the model achieved a notable true positive count of 70% with only 5% false positives, indicating proficient recognition of positive instances with minimal misclassifications. However, Group 2, trained solely on the AffectNet dataset, exhibited a lower true positive count of 45% alongside a higher false positive count of 36%, suggesting a less effective identification of positive instances and a higher rate of misclassifications compared to Group 1. Group 3, combining both RAF-DB and AffectNet datasets, showed a further decrease in true positives to 35%, potentially influenced by differences in dataset characteristics, yet maintained a relatively low false positive count of 12%, indicating a balanced performance between true positives and false positives. Group 4, utilizing augmented datasets with artificial facial occlusions, demonstrated an improvement in true positives (60%) compared to Group 3 but at the expense of a higher false positive count (40%), indicating a trade-off between increased true positive rates and elevated false positive rates. These results highlight the impact of dataset selection and augmentation techniques on model performance, emphasizing the need for ongoing optimization efforts to enhance the model's effectiveness and reduce false positive rates across diverse datasets and conditions.

3.2 FaceDetectCT Performance

To assess the precision of our tool, we designed an evaluation procedure modeled after the experimental groups. We assembled a dataset consisting of 1000 images, divided equally into two categories: 500 images showcasing the face of the specified individual and 500 images devoid of the specified person's face. We then analyzed this dataset using our tool and juxtaposed its findings with the established ground truth. The ensuing performance metrics are delineated in Table 4.

Table 4. Measuring accuracy

Measure	Target Face Present	Target Face Absent
Correct Matches	450	450
False Matches	50	50
Precision	0.9	0.9
Recall	0.9	0.9
F1-score	0.9	0.9

The provided result encapsulates the performance evaluation metrics of the tool across two crucial measures: the presence and absence of the target face. With 450 correct matches recorded in both scenarios, the tool demonstrates a commendable accuracy in identifying instances with and without the target face. However, the occurrence of 50 false matches in each category indicates areas for improvement in reducing misclassifications. Precision and recall scores of 0.9 reflect the tool's ability to maintain a balance between correctly identifying positive and negative instances while minimizing false positives and false negatives. The consistent F1-score of 0.9 further emphasizes the tool's reliability in achieving a harmonious blend of precision and recall. While the tool exhibits promising accuracy, efforts to mitigate false matches could enhance its practical utility. Thus, continuous refinement and optimization remain imperative to ensure the tool's effectiveness in real-world applications.

3.3 Comparison with Others Models

In our assessment of the "FaceDetectCT" model, we conducted a comparative analysis with a diverse array of established face recognition models renowned for their robustness and precision. Models such as VarGFaceNet [14], ShuffleFaceNet, and MobileFaceNetV1 are esteemed for their outstanding performance across various tasks. ProxylessFaceNAS and MixFaceNet-M utilize innovative techniques like neural architecture search and blending face recognition methods, respectively, to achieve competitive performance with reduced computational costs. Additionally, PocketNetM-256 and PocketNetM-128 prioritize efficiency without compromising accuracy, making them suitable for resource-constrained scenarios. Our FaceDetectCT model demonstrates competitive performance, excelling in diverse conditions such as variations in lighting and pose, while EdgeFace - XS is optimized for edge computing, prioritizing efficiency and speed for real-time applications. This comparison provided valuable insights into the strengths and weaknesses of FaceDetectCT, identifying areas for enhancement and setting a direction for further progress in face recognition applications (Fig. 3).

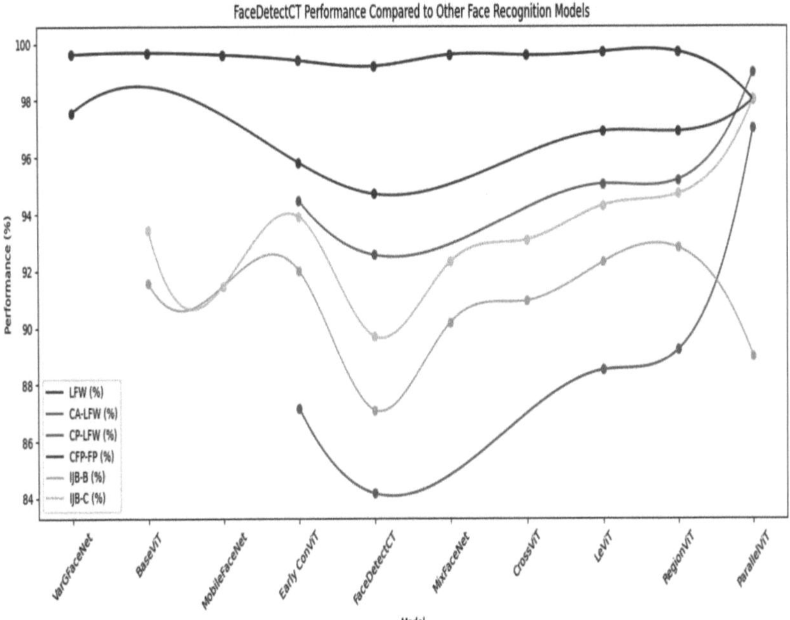

Fig. 3. Performance Metrics Comparison of Face Recognition Models

Firstly, the evaluation involved ten distinct models, including VarGFaceNet [14], BaseViT [15], MobileFaceNet [16], Early ConViT [17], MixFaceNet [18], CrossViT [19], LeViT [20], RegionViT [21], and ParallelViT [22], across six performance metrics: LFW, CA-LFW, CP-LFW, CFP-FP, IJB-B, and IJB-C. In terms of LFW performance, FaceDetectCT achieved a commendable accuracy of 99.2%, slightly trailing behind top-performing models such as VarGFaceNet, BaseViT, and LeViT. While FaceDetectCT exhibits robust performance, it falls short of being the highest performer in this metric.

Moving to cross-domain evaluation, our model maintained competitiveness in handling age variations (CA-LFW) and demonstrated moderate robustness with a performance of 92.55%. However, it showed room for improvement in cross-pose variations (CP-LFW), with a performance of 84.17%, trailing behind models like Early ConViT and LeViT. In scenarios involving frontal-profile variations (CFP-FP), FaceDetectCT achieved a commendable performance of 94.7. However, it was slightly outperformed by models like VarGFaceNet, Early ConViT, and LeViT, indicating potential for enhancement in handling such variations.

Challenges emerged when faced with more complex datasets such as IJB-B and IJB-C, where our model's performance of 87.1% and 89.7%, respectively, fell short compared to models like BaseViT and LeViT. This highlights the need for improvements in handling challenging datasets and variations. Despite these challenges, FaceDetectCT exhibited overall robustness and reliability across various scenarios, showcasing its potential as a solid face recognition model. However, to reach top-tier performance levels observed in models like LeViT and BaseViT, ongoing optimization and enhancements are necessary.

In conclusion, while our model demonstrates strong performance across multiple metrics, there is evident room for improvement, particularly in addressing challenges posed by complex datasets and specific variations in face recognition tasks. Continued refinement and optimization efforts are essential to elevate FaceDetectCT to the highest echelons of face recognition technology.

4   Conclusion

This paper presents FaceDetectCT, a novel face recognition model that demonstrates competitive performance across various face recognition metrics. Through meticulous evaluation and comparison with established models, our model showcases robust accuracy, particularly excelling in scenarios with varying lighting conditions, pose variations, and unconstrained environments. While it may encounter challenges in certain metrics, its adaptability and effectiveness make it a compelling choice for face recognition applications. However, continuous refinement and optimization are necessary to address limitations and further enhance its performance. Future research directions include improving robustness to diverse conditions, optimizing computational efficiency, and enhancing generalization capabilities. With collaborative efforts between researchers, practitioners, and policymakers, FaceDetectCT holds promise for advancing face recognition technology and facilitating its responsible deployment in real-world scenarios.

References

1. Che, C., Zheng, H., Huang, Z.: Intelligent robotic control system based on computer vision technology. arXiv preprint. arXiv:2404.01116 (2024)
2. Rusia, M.K., Singh, D.K.: A comprehensive survey on techniques to handle face identity threats: challenges and opportunities. Multimed. Tools Appl. **82**, 1669–1748 (2023)
3. Latifa, E.-R., My Ahmed, E.K., Mohamed, E.G., Mariya, O.: Foreground-preserving background modification: a deep learning approach. In: 2023 17th International Conference on Signal-Image Technol. Internet-Based System, pp. 261–267 (2023). https://doi.org/10.1109/SITIS61268.2023.00047
4. Yuan, J., Zhu, A., Xu, Q., Wattanachote, K., Gong, Y.: CTIF-net: a CNN-transformer iterative fusion network for salient object detection. IEEE Trans. Circuits Syst. Video Technol. **34**, 3795–3805 (2023)
5. Yao, H., Gao, T., Wang, Y., Wang, H., Chen, X.: Mobile_ViT: underwater acoustic target recognition method based on local-global feature fusion. J. Mar. Sci. Eng. **12**, 589 (2024)
6. Shi, L., Gao, T., Zhang, Z., Zhang, J., Member, I.: STM-UNet: an efficient U-shaped architecture based on swin transformer and multi-scale MLP for medical image segmentation. arXiv preprint arXiv:2304 1–6 (2023)
7. Gao, G., et al.: CTCNet: a CNN-transformer cooperation network for face image super-resolution. IEEE Trans. Image Process. **32**, 1978–1991 (2023)

8. Yang, J., Shen, J., Lin, Y., Hristov, Y., Pantic, M.: FAN-trans: online knowledge distillation for facial action unit detection. In: Proceedings of the 2023 IEEE Winter Conference on Applications of Computer Vision, WACV 2023, pp. 6008–6016 (2023) https://doi.org/10.1109/WACV56688.2023.00596

9. Li, A., et al.: MF-Net: multi-scale feature extraction-integration network for unsupervised deformable registration. Front. Neurosci. **18**, 1–9 (2024)

10. Deshpande, M., Sreenath, M.V., Nadella, S., Antony, N., Venkat, N.: A survey of object classification and detection techniques in assistance systems for the visually impaired. Int. J. Eng. Manag. Res. **1**, 44–51 (2024)

11. Thisanke, H., et al.: Semantic segmentation using Vision Transformers: a survey. Eng. Appl. Artif. Intell. **126**, 106669 (2023)

12. Song, C.H., Yoon, J., Choi, S., Avrithis, Y.: Boosting vision transformers for image retrieval. In: Proceedings of the 2023 IEEE Winter Conference on Applications of Computer Vision, WACV 2023, pp. 107–117 (2023) https://doi.org/10.1109/WACV56688.2023.00019

13. Gao, J., Zhao, Y.: TFE: a transformer architecture for occlusion aware facial expression recognition. Front. Neurorobot. **15**, 1–10 (2021)

14. Yan, M., et al.: VarGFaceNet: an efficient variable group convolutional neural network for lightweight face recognition. In: Proceedings of the 2019 International Conference on Computer Vision Workshop, ICCVW 2019, pp. 2647–2654 (2019). https://doi.org/10.1109/ICCVW.2019.00323

15. Dosovitskiy, A., et al.: An image is worth 16 × 16 words: transformers for image recognition at scale. In: 9th International Conference on Learning Representations, ICLR 2021 (2021)

16. Hassanpour, A., Kowsari, Y.: Lightweight face recognition: an improved MobileFaceNet model. arXiv preprint. arXiv:2311.15326 (2023)

17. Xiao, T., et al.: Early convolutions help transformers see better. In: Advances in Neural Information Processing Systems, vol. 36, pp. 30392–30400 (2021)

18. Boutros, F., Damer, N., Fang, M., Kirchbuchner, F., Kuijper, A.: Mixfacenets: extremely efficient face recognition networks. In: 2021 IEEE International Joint Conference on Biometrics, IJCB 2021 (2021) https://doi.org/10.1109/IJCB52358.2021.9484374

19. Chen, C.F., Fan, Q., Panda, R.: CrossViT: cross-attention multi-scale vision transformer for image classification. In: Proceedings of the IEEE International Conference on Computer Vision, pp. 347–356 (2021). https://doi.org/10.1109/ICCV48922.2021.00041

20. Graham, B., et al.: LeViT: a vision transformer in ConvNet's clothing for faster inference. In: Proceedings of the IEEE International Conference on Computing Vision, pp. 12239–12249 (2021). https://doi.org/10.1109/ICCV48922.2021.01204

21. Chen, C.F., Panda, R., Fan, Q.: Regionvit: regional-to-local attention for vision transformers. In: 10th International Conference on Learning Representation, ICLR 2022, pp. 1–19 (2022)

22. Wang, D., Wang, Z., Chen, L., Xiao, H., Yang, B.: Cross-parallel transformer: parallel ViT for medical image segmentation. Sensors **23** (2023)

Dynamic Region Proposal Model for Road Anomalies Detection and Classification

Rasha Saffarini[1], Faisal Khamayseh[2], Yousef Daraghmeh[3], Derar Elyan[3], and Muath Sabha[1]($\boxtimes$)

[1] Arab American University, Ramallah, Palestine
muath.sabha@aaup.edu
[2] Palestine Polytechnic University, Hebron, Palestine
[3] Palestine Technical University, Tulkarm, Palestine

Abstract. Detecting road anomalies early is crucial to prevent accidents and vehicle damage. Our model uses artificial intelligence techniques to automatically detect different types of anomalies, such as potholes, manholes, cracks, speed bumps, and others, in a very short time. It utilizes drones to capture videos and images. Various artificial intelligence techniques, including graph segmentation, graph similarity, and dynamic programming techniques are used for road segmentation, region proposals, anomaly detection, and classification of the detected anomalies. By combining these algorithms considerable results are achieved in terms of speed and accuracy; such that it generates around 90% regions less than the selective search model. Also, the MAP is increased considerably using the proposed model.

Keywords: Road Anomalies · Region proposal · Image Segmentation · Image classification

1 Introduction

To ensure safe driving and prevent damage to vehicles, it's important for drivers to be aware of road anomalies such as cracks, potholes, and speed bumps. These can be detected automatically, and drivers can be alerted through smartphone notifications. Road anomalies can be classified into two categories: cracks and other damages, including ruts, potholes, etc.

Studies have explored two methods for automatically detecting road anomalies: vibration-based and computer vision-based detection. Vibration-based methods are based on accelerometer data and have limitations, such as detecting anomalies only in areas where the car touches the road and potential harm to the car and driver. Computer vision techniques capture road images, analyze them, and classify anomalies, offering a solution to these issues.

Recent anomaly detection studies often focus on only one or two types of anomalies, neglecting other potential obstacles on the road. Some studies detect potholes [3,13,20], while others detect speed bumps [1,4,24] or classify roads as cracked or untracked [9,11,23]. Many vision-based studies rely on cameras placed inside the car to capture images of the road [7,16,22], but this can limit the accuracy and ability to measure detected anomalies due to the camera angle, car vibrations, and blurry images.

In this research, a new fast and automatic model has been developed to detect and classify all anomalies in roadways. To overcome previous camera calibration problems, drones are used to capture videos and images of the road. The images taken by drones are pre-processed by applying several filters to be used in the detection and classification phase. The detection and classification phase will use a new proposed, fast, and highly accurate deep learning and computer vision technique, consisting of several newly developed algorithms for region proposals, feature extraction, detection, classification, and measurement of all road anomalies.

2   Literature Review

Research studies on detecting road anomalies can be divided into acceleration-based and vision-based approaches. Data must be collected from roads to detect anomalies. Two data types were collected for analysis and anomaly detection: accelerometer signals and images or a combination of both. Various techniques were used for the detection and classification process. This section provides an overview of the latest research in each category.

2.1   Accelerometer-Based Approaches

Various accelerometers were used to collect road data, as in [19,21]. In [21], the authors introduced a technique to detect road anomalies using smartphone sensors. They used smartphone accelerometers to collect 3-axis acceleration, latitude, longitude, speed, timestamp, and anomaly-type data. To handle invalid and inconsistent data and to reduce the amount of data to be processed, the collected data was pre-processed by combining the data rows for each anomaly. Finally, a tree-based classifier, such as gradient boost and decision tree, was used to detect and classify anomalies.

While in [19], raw sensor and location data were collected by developing a mobile app installed on a smart device (mobile or tablet). The collected data were linear accelerometer, rotation vector, and location information. These data were collected from a Linear accelerometer sensor, gyroscope, magnetometer, and other sensors for road anomaly detection and classification after road anomalies were detected and classified using modified threshold—based and machine-learning approaches (K-means clustering).

2.2   Image-Based Approaches

Utilizing a vision-based approach is another method of detecting and classifying road anomalies. These approaches rely on capturing images of the road using either a mobile camera or a camera that is installed on a car as in [2, 3, 5–7, 9, 11, 13, 16, 17, 20, 23, 24].

In [3, 13, 20], images of road potholes were captured and studied using different tools. An article by [20] Researchers experimented with three object detectors to detect potholes in real-time. They used a single-shot Multi-box Detector (SSD) on TensorFlow and YOLOv3 and YOLOv4 on Darknet. The results showed that YOLOv4 had the best performance, with a processing speed of 20 frames per second, 81% recall, 85% precision, and 85.39% mAP.

[13] used a SIFT key points detector and disparity map to create a 3D scene of potholes. They mounted a stereo apparatus on a car with two cameras to capture videos of the road from both cameras. The images were extracted from the videos and analyzed to build a 3D view of the roads.

In the study conducted by [3], machine learning algorithms were utilized to classify images as either containing potholes or not. The authors used the HOG algorithm to extract features from the images fed into the Naïve Bayes classifier. The Naïve Bayes classifier assigns a label to an input image based on the maximum posteriori probability.

A data set developed by [14] was used in [3]. This dataset includes 120 pavement photos. 50 were used for training and 70 for testing.

In a study on road potholes [18], a wireless portable camera captured images that were analyzed using TensorFlow and OpenCV libraries. A faster RCNN inception v2 pre-trained model was used to detect the potholes. The sensor device used in the study contained GPS and IMU sensors, an external GPS antenna, and Mto control for sensor management and sending data for locating the pothole.

On the other hand, in [11, 12, 23], authors focused on studying crack availability and severity on roads. Pictures of cracks in concrete roads were captured using vehicle cameras, as explained in [12]. Faster R-CNN was used to detect cracks. Using a smartphone camera, the researchers created a dataset of 323 images with a resolution of 4128×2322.

In [11], a Deep Convolutional Neural Network (DCNN) was used to extract feature vectors from images of the pavement. These vectors were inputted into various classifiers to detect road cracks in Hot-Mix Asphalt (HMA) and Portland Cement Concrete (PCC) surfaced pavement. The method was tested on a subset of 1056 images from the FHWA pavement distress images data set.

The researchers in [23] used a GAN to improve pavement crack detection by enlarging a small dataset captured by a UAV. The expanded dataset improved the detection accuracy from 80.75% to 91.61%.

Another type of road anomaly that caught the attention of researchers to study is the speed bumps as in [4, 24]. In [24], a camera and a Lidar were used to detect speed bumps. The images were converted to grayscale and binarized to identify the pattern of the speed bumps. The HaaR classifier was used to detect regions that represent possible speed bumps. The resulting regions were filtered and the HOG was applied to extract features. Lastly, the SVM classifier was used to recognize speed bumps. The study achieved an average accuracy rate of 85.2%, and their method took 10ms longer to process than other methods.

A new approach to detect unmarked speed bumps is proposed by [4]. This approach detects unmarked speed bumps from Indian street images using a Raspberry Pi camera. The model pre-processes the image, applies a Canny edge detection algorithm and a Hough transform to identify lines representing speed bumps. Tested on 1385 images, the average accuracy rate was 95.5.

Two studies, Wang et al. [22] and Doshi et al. [8], proposed methods for detecting and classifying damaged roads using Faster R-CNN and YOLOv4 object detectors. Wang et al. (2018) used a two-step method involving pre-processing, feature extraction, and Fast R-CNN detector, while Doshi et al. (2020) proposed an ensemble model for detecting and classifying various types of road damage using YOLOv4.

We propose a new model to detect road anomalies (potholes, speed bumps, and cracks) quickly and automatically. We use a drone to capture videos and images of road anomalies to build a dataset for training and testing. Our proposed model uses a region proposal phase and CNN for classification, and different techniques to speed up the process. The technique involves image segmentation, merging overlapped regions, finding similar regions, storing them in an adjacency list, and selecting one candidate region from each group for the classification phase.

3   Methodology

Previous studies have utilized various methods for identifying and categorizing road anomalies, such as image-based and vibration-based models. However, these models have certain shortcomings in terms of accuracy, speed, and practicality. In this study, a drone is used to capture videos of roads in different conditions, which offers a consistent and clear view compared to vehicle-mounted cameras used in previous studies. These videos are then converted into images frame by frame. A novel AI model is developed that improves speed by incorporating a region proposal algorithm. This model is trained to detect and classify different types of road anomalies, rather than focusing on just one type. Finally, each image is analyzed to detect and classify each object within the image. The entire process is depicted in Fig. 1.

3.1   Road Images Dataset Collection

There are various places on a moving vehicle where a camera can be mounted to capture images of the road, including the rear, front, dashboard, and other locations. However, capturing images from these locations can cause distortion and take a significant amount of time to cover city roads, resulting in less accurate images.

To overcome these challenges, this research utilizes a drone. Drones can be programmed to cover city roads during low traffic and good lighting conditions,

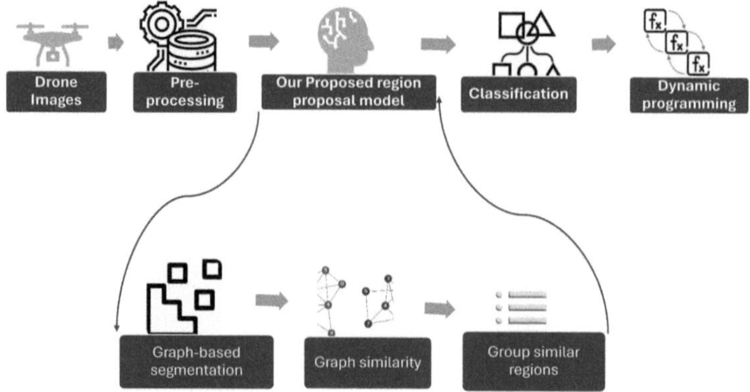

Fig. 1. The overall methodology

allowing clearer and more accurate images compared to cameras mounted on cars or other vehicles. Additionally, drones can capture an overhead view of the road, which further improves image clarity and accuracy.

For this study, we used a DJI Mavic Air 2 drone, which comes equipped with a 48MP camera sensor and an 84MP and a field of vision (FOV). The camera uses a '1/2' CMOS and is capable of capturing 4k resolution videos with 60 frames per second. Additionally, the drone has optical image stabilization and wind resistance programming.

3.2   Pre-processing

Videos are recorded in 4K @60fps and saved in .mp4 format. We create an image dataset by randomly extracting two frames from each second of the video. Videos are captured at noon and late afternoon to account for different lighting conditions. Gamma correction with a gamma of 1.5 is used to ensure lighting consistency. Gaussian blur filter with a standard deviation value of 5 is applied to remove noise from the image. Figure 2 demonstrates this process.

3.3   Proposed Detection and Classification Model

The developed model can be divided into two main parts. In the first part, each image is divided into several regions. Following this, graph segmentation and graph similarity are utilized to identify the regions most likely to contain an object. These regions are then grouped together using a graph similarity algorithm. In the second part, these proposed regions are used to train the CNN classification model. Finally, a dynamic programming algorithm is used to classify similar images stored previously.

Fig. 2. Image before and after gamma correlation and Gaussian blur

Proposed Region Proposal Model

To enhance the performance of fast R-CNN, a new algorithm is proposed to choose candidate regions from the input image to be used as CNN inputs for feature extraction, object detection and classification. The model utilizes a graph-based segmentation algorithm to divide the image into a set of regions. After that, the graph similarity technique is used to identify similar regions, store each group of similar regions in a list, and then submit one region from each set to the CNN model for the feature extraction process.

Image Segmentation

Image segmentation is dividing an image into smaller regions, also known as segments. This technique helps reduce the image's complexity and makes studying, analyzing, and extracting information easier. Image segmentation is commonly used in object detection to identify areas of interest in the image. Using an image segmentation algorithm to identify these areas of interest, the object detection process can operate more accurately and efficiently by only processing the relevant parts of the image. One of the most commonly used image segmentation algorithms is graph-based image segmentation.

Graph-based image segmentation is a technique that represents an image as a graph $G = (V, E)$ with vertices $v \in V$ and set of edges $(v_i, v_j) \in E$. Each edge has a weight $w(v_i, v_j)$ that indicates how different the two connected vertices (pixels in images) are from each other in terms of color, intensity, location, or any other parameters. In graph-based image segmentation, each pixel is represented by a vertex of V, and the connection between pixels is represented by edges such that each edge (v_i, v_j) represents a connection between pixel I and pixel J. The segmentation process S is the segmentation of the graph into several connected graphs/segments $C \in S$.

To begin the cutting process, the algorithm estimates the distances between each pixel and its neighboring pixels to identify dissimilar pixels or vertices. The resulting graph is then divided into multiple continuous graphs, where edges between nodes in the same graph have low weights, while edges between nodes in different graphs have higher weights. Each resulting graph or region represents a candidate object from the image. These objects can be further studied by extracting their features using various feature extraction techniques during the object detection process. The Felzenszwalb algorithm [10] is one such technique that can be used for this purpose. Graph-based segmentation result shown in Fig. 3.

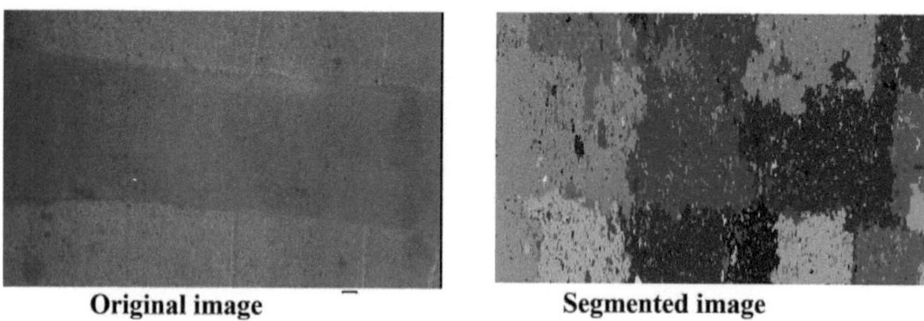

Original image   Segmented image

Fig. 3. Graph-based segmentation results

Identifying Similar Regions

Many graphs representing potential objects are produced after applying graph-based segmentation to the image. The issue with studying and analyzing these regions is that multiple regions might all represent or contain the same information. This implies that CNN may analyze the same objects more than once, requiring more computations and taking longer. A way to avoid this problem is to avoid repeated analysis of similar graphs. This can be accomplished by reducing the number of regions to be analyzed by CNN. The procedure has two steps to decrease the number of candidate regions. The first involves combining overlapped regions to form a single region. Finding similar areas that are far apart from one another is the second step.

We can calculate the intersection degree using an Intersection over Union (IOU) metric to find the overlapped regions between two areas. This is calculated by estimating the area of the intersection of the two regions and dividing it by the area of the union of the two regions, as shown in Eq. 1:

$$IOU = \frac{intersectionArea}{((area1 + area2) - intersectionArea)} \tag{1}$$

Areas 1 and 2 represent the overlapped regions, and the intersection area is where they overlap. When the overlap between two regions exceeds 70%.

To decrease the number of suggested regions for CNN more and more, we identified candidate regions that are similar but are situated far apart from each other. Each candidate region, obtained from the graph-based segmentation, is represented by a graph. The similarity between the graphs of these candidate regions is determined using the graph similarity technique. The eigenvector similarity method is employed in this study to measure the similarity between two graphs [15].

Consider G_1 and G_2 are two graphs; for eigenvector similarity, the Laplacian of the graphs is calculated as in Eqs. 2 & 3:

$$L_1 = D_1 - A_1 \tag{2}$$

$$L_2 = D_2 - A_2 \tag{3}$$

where A_1 and A_2, D_1 and D_2, L_1 and L_2 represent the Adjacency matrix, Diagonal matrix of degrees, and Laplacian of G_1 and G_2 respectively.

Compute the eigenvalues of each Laplacian and find the smallest k such that the sum of the top k eigenvalues is 90% of the sum of all eigenvalues. If both graphs have different k values, use the minimum of both. Then, calculate the similarity in Eq. 4.

$$sim = \sum_{i=1}^{k} (\lambda_1 i - \lambda_2 i)^2 \tag{4}$$

Two graphs are considered similar or related to the same object if their similarity exceeds a certain threshold. This study tested various similarity thresholds (50%, 60%, 70%, and 80%), with a 70% threshold producing the best results.

Grouping Similar Regions
As mentioned in the above section, after finding similar regions in the image, each group of similar regions is stored in a list and fed only once to CNN. The one fed to CNN is the one that gets the highest graph similarity score within the group. Grouping similar graphs or regions in a list and feeding only one of them to CNN to be analyzed reduces the number of regions that need to be entered into CNN and shortens the time required for any analysis process or overall classification.

The list used to store similar graphs/segments is called an adjacency list. The adjacency list is made up of as many nodes as there are groups of similar graphs, and each node of the list points to a list of those groups, as shown in Fig. 4, where each G stands for a group of similar graphs and R for a graph or region of the image.

3.4   Object Recognition Model

This model consists of two steps. The first step is to classify the objects within these regions. Secondly, a dynamic programming technique assigns a label to similar objects stored previously in the adjacency list.

Classification Step. In the previous steps, the image was divided into many regions. However, not all of these regions are useful for identifying objects in the image. Therefore, only the regions more likely to contain an object are kept and grouped into clusters of similar regions.

In the next step, one representative region from each cluster is selected to train a CNN model for object classification. The representative region is first transformed into a vector of 4096 elements to do this. Then, the average of adjacent elements is calculated twice, resulting in a vector of 512 elements.

This vector is then used to train a deep neural network model to classify the object in the representative region. Once the region is classified, this classification is used for all other regions in the same group as the representative region.

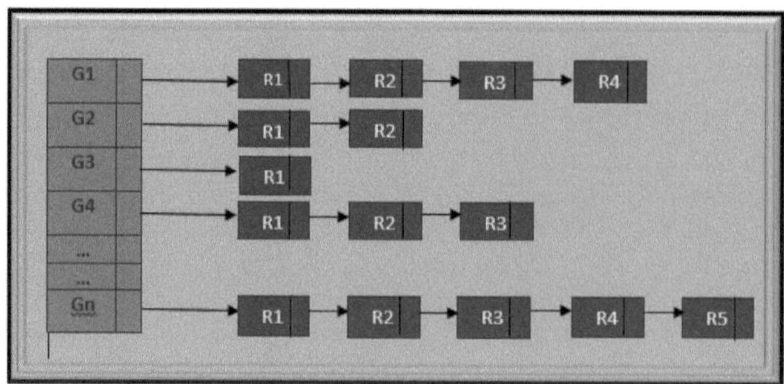

Fig. 4. Adjacency list of similar graphs

4   Results and Discussion

As we discussed earlier, the model is composed of two steps. In the first step, each image is divided into segments, and similar segments are grouped together. After grouping, a representative sample is taken from each group for classification using a CNN model, and all segments within the same group are assigned the same classification. For this research, a new dataset was created for training and testing. The dataset includes roads throughout Tulkarm city with varying conditions, from excellent to very poor. Videos were captured using DJI Mavic Air 2 drones with a resolution of 3840×2160 (4K). A total of 1500 videos were recorded. A total of 15326 images were extracted from these videos. The drones were used because of their reasonable cost, high-resolution images, full road view, and no operational costs needed except battery charging costs. Sample images are shown below.

Gamma correlation and blur filters are used to pre-process images for enhanced lighting and noise removal (Fig. 5).

We utilized the Google platform, specifically Google Colab, which provided ample server resources to process and train our model. The CNN model used the VGG-16 classifier as a backbone. Four parameters were adopted to evaluate the effectiveness of the model: accuracy, recall, precision, and F1-score. These measures were calculated from the confusion matrix, which categorizes the results into four sections: true positive, true negative, false positive, and false negative. These results are separately distributed for each object in the dataset. In other words, all these results are displayed for each class (Pothole, Manhole, Speed Bump, Cracks) with specific details. The process goes through two phases:

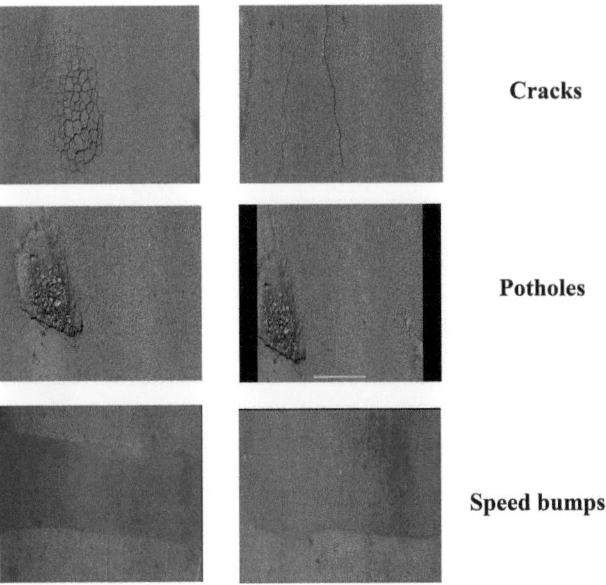

Fig. 5. Sample images of the dataset

1. **Proposed region proposal phase**
   This phase is performed to extract the informative sections of the input image, which will be analyzed and studied later. This phase is accomplished in several steps:
   - Segmenting the image using a Graph segmentation algorithm.
   - Finding similar regions among the regions from step one using Graph similarity.
   - Grouping similar regions in adjacency lists to analyze only one of each group.

   In this step, the graph segmentation algorithm is utilized to segment each image. After segmentation, graph similarity techniques are used to group the segments. From each group, a representative segment is chosen for the next steps of the developed model.

   Determining the number of segments used for classification is a crucial step. The CNN model requires more time to classify a larger number of segments. In previous algorithms, the selective search algorithm was used to suggest regions for the CNN model. However, the developed model uses graph segmentation and graph similarity algorithms to suggest regions for the CNN model.

   The developed model proposed 150 regions in the manhole class, as shown in Table 1 and Fig. 6, significantly less than the 1910 regions proposed by the selective search algorithm. Similar results were observed in the other classes as well. For instance, the class containing holes had 120 to 1450 proposed regions, while the class with bumps had 140 to 1750, and the class with cracks had 135 to 1801 proposed regions. Testing time shown in Table 2

Table 1. Number of region proposals using DGR-CNN vs selective search

Region Proposal Method	Class			
	Manholes	potholes	Speed-bumps	Cracks
Proposed model	150	120	140	135
Selective Search	1910	1490	1750	1801

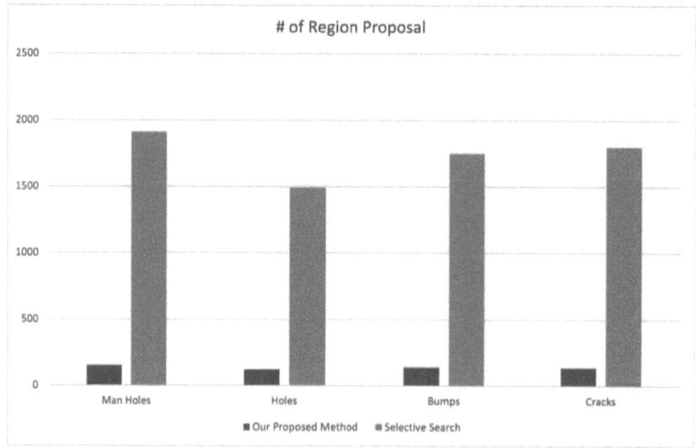

Fig. 6. Number of region proposals using DGR-CNN vs selective search

Table 2. Testing speed Using our model

speed	testing/time per image	MAP
RCNN	47	66%
FAST	0.32	66.90%
FASTER	0.2	69.90%
Our Model	0.1923	66.70%

2. Segments classification

The final stage of the developed model classifies the proposed segments into one of the following classes: holes, manholes, bumps, and cracks. Then, dynamic programming techniques assign classifications for all items in the adjacency list.

Accuracy, recall, precision, and F1-score for the detection and classification process with and without the use of our proposed model are calculated as shown in Table 3 and Table 4, respectively. As depicted in the two tables, there was a clear enhancement to all measurements such that the average MAP of all classes increased from 79.54% to 89%. The situation is the same for the recall, the precision and the F1-score, such that the proposed model gained 90.65%,

89.63%, and 90.13%, respectively. While, The results gained without using the proposed model are 80.69%, 79.67%, and 80.18%, respectively.

Table 3. Accuracy, recall, precision, and F1-score using selective search.

Class	F1 Score	Recall	Precision	Accuracy (MAP)
Hole	81.3371%	81.9410%	80.7410%	80.2210%
Man Hole	80.8383%	81.3410%	80.3410%	80.5210%
Pumbs	79.8355%	80.5410%	79.1410%	78.4110%
Cracks	78.6903%	78.9410%	78.4410%	79.0010%
Avg	80.18%	80.69%	79.67%	79.54%

Table 4. Accuracy, recall, precision, and F1-score using proposed method

Class	F1 Score	Recall	Precision	Accuracy (MAP)
PotHole	91.29606%	91.9%	90.7%	90.18%
Man Hole	90.79725%	91.9%	90.3%	90.48%
SpeedPumbs	89.79454%	90.5%	89.1%	88.37%
Cracks	88.64929%	88.9%	88.4%	88.96%
Avg	90.13%	90.65%	89.63%	89.50%

4.1 Challenges

We faced several challenges in our work with the drone, the most important of which was that the drone battery consumed only 20 min and needed 30–60 min to recharge, so we needed to buy more than one battery to complete the work faster. The weather conditions were also a problem for the drone, as the rain disrupted its propellers, so we had to collect photos at different times.

5   Conclusion

The detection of road anomalies is a crucial task for many applications and various techniques have been developed to accomplish it with differing degrees of accuracy and speed. Our research has introduced a novel approach to decrease the time required for anomalies detection and recognition in images while also increasing detection accuracy. This is achieved using a dynamic programming model that utilizes the graph similarity technique over graph-based image segmentation. Our model's effectiveness was tested by a newly created data set of

Tulkarm City roads that contain potholes, manholes, speedbumps, and cracks. The results demonstrated a significant difference between the number of regions generated by our proposed method and other methods, including R-CNN and Fast R-CNN. Our proposed method was found to be faster than R-CNN and Fast R-CNN, and it is almost the same as faster R-CNN.

References

1. Arunpriyan, J., Variyar, V.V.S., Soman, K.P., Adarsh, S.: Real-time speed bump detection using image segmentation for autonomous vehicles. In: Pandian, A.P., Ntalianis, K., Palanisamy, R. (eds.) ICICCS 2019. AISC, vol. 1039, pp. 308–315. Springer, Cham (2020). https://doi.org/10.1007/978-3-030-30465-2_35
2. Arya, D., et al.: Deep learning-based road damage detection and classification for multiple countries. Autom. Constr. **132**, 103935 (2021)
3. Azhar, K., Murtaza, F., Yousaf, M.H., Habib, H.A.: Computer vision based detection and localization of potholes in asphalt pavement images. In: 2016 IEEE Canadian Conference on Electrical and Computer Engineering (CCECE), pp. 1–5. IEEE (2016)
4. Babu, C.N.K., Priya, W.D., Srihari, T.: Real-time detection of unmarked speed bump for Indian roads. Eur. J. Mol. Clin. Med. **7**(5), 2020 (2021)
5. Chen, G., Teng, S., Lin, M., Yang, X., Sun, X.: Crack detection based on generative adversarial networks and deep learning. KSCE J. Civ. Eng. **26**(4), 1803–1816 (2022)
6. Danilescu, D., Lodin, A., Grama, L., Rusu, C.: Road anomalies detection using basic morphological algorithms. Carpathian J. Electron. Comput. Eng. **8**(2), 15 (2015)
7. Dewangan, D.K., Sahu, S.P.: Deep learning-based speed bump detection model for intelligent vehicle system using Raspberry Pi. IEEE Sens. J. **21**(3), 3570–3578 (2020)
8. Doshi, K., Yilmaz, Y.: Road damage detection using deep ensemble learning. In: 2020 IEEE International Conference on Big Data (Big Data), pp. 5540–5544. IEEE (2020)
9. Dung, C.V., et al.: Autonomous concrete crack detection using deep fully convolutional neural network. Autom. Constr. **99**, 52–58 (2019)
10. Felzenszwalb, P.F., Huttenlocher, D.P.: Efficient graph-based image segmentation. Int. J. Comput. Vis. **59**, 167–181 (2004)
11. Gopalakrishnan, K., Khaitan, S.K., Choudhary, A., Agrawal, A.: Deep convolutional neural networks with transfer learning for computer vision-based data-driven pavement distress detection. Constr. Build. Mater. **157**, 322–330 (2017)
12. Hacıefendioğlu, K., Başağa, H.B.: Concrete road crack detection using deep learning-based faster R-CNN method. Iranian J. Sci. Technol. Trans. Civil Eng. **46**(2), 1621–1633 (2022)
13. Haq, M.U.U., Ashfaque, M., Mathavan, S., Kamal, K., Ahmed, A.: Stereo-based 3D reconstruction of potholes by a hybrid, dense matching scheme. IEEE Sens. J. **19**(10), 3807–3817 (2019)
14. Koch, C., Brilakis, I.: Pothole detection in asphalt pavement images. Adv. Eng. Inform. **25**(3), 507–515 (2011)
15. Koutra, D., Parikh, A., Ramdas, A., Xiang, J.: Algorithms for graph similarity and subgraph matching. In: Proceedings of the Ecological Inference Conference, vol. 17. Citeseer (2011)

16. Lee, T., Chun, C., Ryu, S.K.: Detection of road-surface anomalies using a smartphone camera and accelerometer. Sensors **21**(2), 561 (2021)
17. Mandal, V., Uong, L., Adu-Gyamfi, Y.: Automated road crack detection using deep convolutional neural networks. In: 2018 IEEE International Conference on Big Data (Big Data), pp. 5212–5215. IEEE (2018)
18. Rasyid, A., et al.: Pothole visual detection using machine learning method integrated with internet of thing video streaming platform. In: 2019 International Electronics Symposium (IES), pp. 672–675. IEEE (2019)
19. Sattar, S., Li, S., Chapman, M.: Developing a near real-time road surface anomaly detection approach for road surface monitoring. Measurement **185**, 109990 (2021)
20. Shaghouri, A.A., Alkhatib, R., Berjaoui, S.: Real-time pothole detection using deep learning. arXiv preprint arXiv:2107.06356 (2021)
21. Silva, N., Soares, J., Shah, V., Santos, M.Y., Rodrigues, H.: Anomaly detection in roads with a data mining approach. Procedia Comput. Sci. **121**, 415–422 (2017)
22. Wang, W., Wu, B., Yang, S., Wang, Z.: Road damage detection and classification with faster R-CNN. In: 2018 IEEE International Conference on Big Data (Big Data), pp. 5220–5223. IEEE (2018)
23. Xu, B., Liu, C.: Pavement crack detection algorithm based on generative adversarial network and convolutional neural network under small samples. Measurement **196**, 111219 (2022)
24. Yun, H.S., Kim, T.H., Park, T.H.: Speed-bump detection for autonomous vehicles by lidar and camera. J. Electr. Eng. Technol. **14**(5), 2155–2162 (2019)

Smart Data and IoT

Adaptive Transfer Learning for Mineral Grade Prediction in Mining Industry 4.0

Ahmed Bendaouia[1(✉)], El Hassan Abdelwahed[2], Sara Qassimi[2],
Abdelmalek Boussetta[3], Intissar Benzakour[3], Zaynab Naciri[1],
Ilham Benmallouk[1], and Oumkeltoum Amar[4]

[1] Faculty of Sciences Semlalia, Cadi Ayyad University, Marrakech, Morocco
`ahmed.bendaouia@edu.uca.ac.ma`
[2] Faculty of Science and Technology, Cadi Ayyad University, Marrakech, Morocco
[3] R&D and Engineering Center, Reminex, Managem Group, Marrakech, Morocco
[4] SEIA Department, Moroccan Foundation for Advanced Science, Innovation and
Research (MAScIR), Rabat, Morocco

Abstract. The mining industry, characterized by dynamic operational environments and fluctuating mineral resources, faces a critical challenge in maintaining the adaptability of artificial intelligence systems for predictive modeling and control. In this context, the need arises for innovative methodologies that can effectively leverage transfer learning and online retraining techniques to enhance the accuracy, reliability, and real-time adaptability of predictive models in mineral processing, specifically in tasks such as flotation monitoring and control. By addressing the complexities of fluctuating mineral grades and process conditions, the research aims to bridge the gap between traditional predictive modeling approaches and the evolving demands of Industry 4.0 in the mining sector. We propose a novel online retraining framework that leverages transfer learning to predict and adapt to the fluctuating conditions of mineral grades in flotation-based mineral processing. Through the evaluation and deployment of several transfer learning models, including ResNet, MobileNet, GoogleNet, and DenseNet, our approach emphasizes ongoing data analysis and model recalibration to confront the intrinsic variability of mineral resources. The findings validate the improved performance and dependability of our model, propelling us towards intelligent and autonomous monitoring systems. Beyond demonstrating the capabilities of adaptive AI in industrial settings, this work paves the way for future advancements in smart, continuous monitoring through intelligent systems.

Keywords: Artificial Intelligence · Transfer Learning · Flotation froth · Mining industry 4.0 · Monitoring · Online Learning

---

Supported by the Moroccan Foundation for Advanced Science, Innovation and Research (MAScIR).

H. Badir et al. (Eds.): INTIS 2024, CCIS 2645, pp. 149–162, 2026.
https://doi.org/10.1007/978-3-032-14964-0_12

1   Introduction

In the paradigm of Industry 4.0, adaptability emerges not as a mere advantage but as an essential prerequisite for the survival and evolution of technological systems. The mining industry, known for its intricate operations and demand for precision, has embarked on a transformative journey with the integration of Artificial Intelligence (AI) [1,2]. At the heart of this transformation lies the challenge of ensuring the continual adaptability of AI systems to the dynamic and often fluctuating operational condition, a particularly daunting task in complex processes like mineral flotation in processing plants.

This paper proposes an advanced adaptive predictive modeling framework specifically designed for flotation control, a pivotal process in mineral separation. Our approach introduces an online retraining framework, utilizing transfer learning techniques to uphold the accuracy of mineral grade predictions amidst fluctuating process conditions. This is achieved through the strategic utilization of cutting-edge deep learning architectures such as ResNet, MobileNet, GoogleNet, and DenseNet. These architectures have undergone rigorous optimization, evaluation, and deployment, providing a sturdy foundation for ongoing analysis and real-time recalibration of predictive models.

The methodology outlined not only addresses the real-time variability of mineral resources but also encompasses a comprehensive approach to model maintenance and evolution, ensuring that predictive systems remain at the forefront of performance. Empirical results underscore the improved predictive accuracy and reliability of the models, marking a significant stride towards intelligent and autonomous mining operations.

By highlighting the transformative potential of adaptive AI in the mining sector, this study contributes significantly to the realm of industrial applications of adaptive intelligent systems. Furthermore, it lays the groundwork for future exploration into smart continuous monitoring and the broader implications of such technologies in realizing the vision of Industry 4.0.

The remainder of this paper unfolds as follows: Sect. 2 delves into the literature review, focusing on guidelines for online training and transfer learning in industrial contexts. Section 3 elaborates on the specific implementation steps and methodology of the proposed framework. Section 4 scrutinizes and discusses the experimental results derived from real-world datasets to assess the performance and advantages of the proposed framework. Finally, Sect. 5 concludes the paper, offering insights into future perspectives.

2   State of the Art

The evolution of control systems in the mining sector underscores a pivotal shift towards automation and intelligence [3]. This transition aims to enhance efficiency, safety, and environmental sustainability [4,10,11]. Modern studies focus on integrating Artificial Intelligence (AI) to automate complex decision-making processes, thereby optimizing operations and reducing human error. Such intelligent control systems leverage data analytics, machine learning algorithms, and

IoT technologies to predict equipment failures, automate mineral processing, and ensure worker safety. The adoption of these AI-driven systems marks a significant advancement in mining industry, setting a new standard for operational excellence.

Flotation monitoring has traditionally been performed using classical methods such as laboratory analysis and X-ray fluorescence, which are effective but expensive and suffer from latency issues. Recently, there has been a significant shift towards adopting AI-based monitoring systems for flotation. These new technologies are highly effective, offering real-time, cost-effective monitoring through image data [4,5].

2.1 Online Training Techniques

Online training techniques have become increasingly vital in industries characterized by rapid changes and the need for continuous model improvement [6]. These techniques allow for models to be updated in real-time, using incoming data to refine and enhance performance without the need for offline retraining periods [7]. Critiques of recent literature underscore the significance of online training in data-rich environments, particularly within industries like mining. Online training allows predictive models to adapt to emerging patterns, a crucial capability in dynamic operational settings. However, despite its potential benefits, there remains a scarcity of applications of online training within the mining industry.

2.2 Transfer Learning in Industrial Settings

The AI models adaptability is crucial for maintaining high levels of accuracy and performance in predictive tasks [8], thereby ensuring operational efficiency, reducing downtime and improving equipment's lifetime [9]. The role of online training in enhancing model adaptability and performance underscores its importance in the dynamic landscape of industrial processes. Transfer learning has emerged as a cornerstone in the realm of industrial AI applications, offering a pragmatic approach to applying pre-trained models to novel tasks with minimal need for data re-collection and model retraining from scratch [12]. This technique has shown particular efficacy across various sectors, including manufacturing, where predictive maintenance models based on transfer learning have significantly reduced downtime and energy usage [13,14]. Similarly, in energy sectors, an accurate transfer learning model can provide valuable insight for supporting operational adjustment decisions [16]. These applications underscore transfer learning's potential to enhance operational efficiency and innovation in industrial settings by leveraging existing knowledge and data.

2.3 Adaptation of Transfer Learning in Mineral Processing and Flotation Monitoring

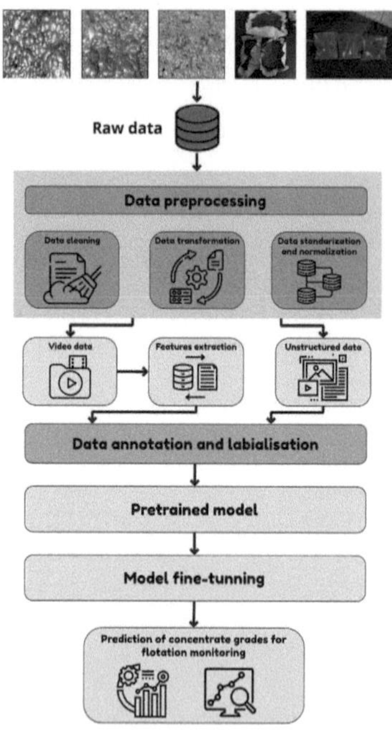

Fig. 1. Data processing workflow for the online mineral grade prediction system

The adaptation of transfer learning within the mining industry has marked a significant evolution in predictive analytics and model development. Studies have demonstrated the application of transfer learning for predictive maintenance, where models trained on machinery in one mine were successfully adapted to predict failures in similar equipment in different locations and improving equipment reliability and maintenance strategies [15]. Digital twins, as virtual replicas of physical systems [19], can benefit from transfer learning capabilities for real-time adaptive monitoring and predictive analysis of system performance, thereby enabling proactive maintenance strategies [15]. An adaptive flotation digital twin allows applying the dynamic, mechanistic process models efficiently for predictive simulations in operational decisions, leading to more sustainable and efficient minerals processing [8]. Similarly, in resource estimation, transfer learning can enable models to adjust to varying geological features across sites, improving the accuracy of mineral grade predictions. Also, allowing the model to learn a new pattern of input after the model is fully trained is crucial for reducing energy consumption and environmental impact in complex systems [16,17]. For froth image data, adaptation is a powerful approach for highlighting relevant extracted features from the flotation froth for monitoring and diagnosis purposes [18,21]. These instances exemplify how transfer learning facilitates the creation of robust, adaptable models, enhancing efficiency and decision-making in mining operations.

2.4   Challenges and Opportunities

Implementing advanced AI techniques in the mining industry faces challenges like data variability, model interpretability, and operational integration. These obstacles underscore the complexity of adapting AI to highly variable and unpredictable mining environments. However, these challenges also present significant opportunities for future research and technological innovation. Addressing data variability encourages the development of more robust and adaptable models. Improving model interpretability can lead to greater trust and reliance on AI decisions. Operational integration highlights the need for interdisciplinary approaches, combining AI expertise with mining operational knowledge to create adaptive and efficient systems. Flotation, as a complex physio-chemical process, can greatly benefit from adaptive intelligent AI monitoring systems. The use of froth image data for addressing this need has not yet been thoroughly explored prior to this study.

3   Methodology

The flotation froth is a dominant separation technique in mineral processing; however, the diverse characteristics and concentrations of minerals pose challenges for effective monitoring. AI-based models developed for flotation monitoring often face issues related to the variety of input data, necessitating continuous learning to adapt to changing conditions.

Figure 1 illustrates the step-by-step process for minerals grade evaluation using cameras. The first step involves raw data collection, where mineral samples are captured using cameras and analysed at the same time in Laboratory to acquire initial data. Subsequently, in the data preprocessing stage, collected data undergoes cleaning, filtering, and normalization to ensure consistency and reliability. Next, data annotation and labeling are applied to provide context and facilitate supervised learning. Following this, a pretrained model is trained using the annotated data, leveraging existing knowledge to expedite the process. The trained model then undergoes fine-tuning, where additional data or specific parameters are adjusted to optimize its performance for minerals grade evaluation. Finally, the fine-tuned model is deployed for real-time evaluation of minerals grades using cameras, offering efficient and accurate analysis for various industrial applications.

3.1   Impact of Mineral Resources Fluctuations on AI Based Monitoring

Our study focuses on evaluating AI-based models using two datasets obtained from the same differential flotation site of CMG in Morocco. Both datasets were

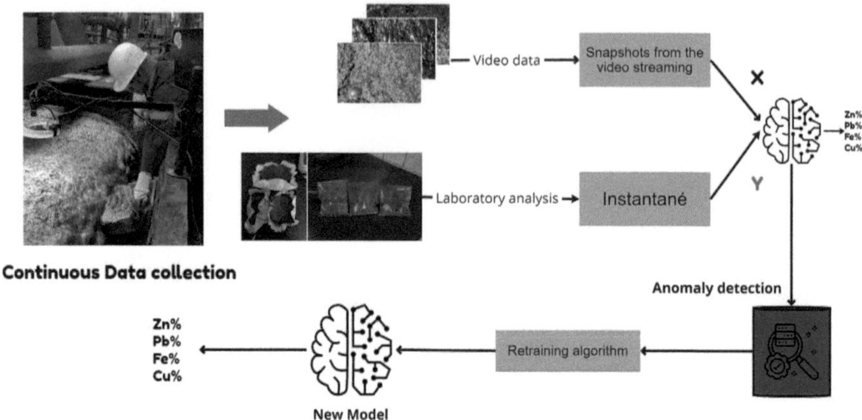

Fig. 2. Framework of the online retraining strategy for from video data streams

collected under similar circumstances, with the second dataset collected after observing a slight shift in mineral processes at the flotation site. Our hypothesis is that retraining AI-based models on the new data will enable them to adapt to changes in mineral characteristics, leading to more accurate results. We believe that automating online retraining using transfer learning techniques can enhance the reliability and adaptability of AI-based systems to fluctuations in mineral resources.

We outline an online retraining strategy, which iteratively adjusts the monitoring system to new data. The process starts with data collection, followed by anomaly detection, data labeling, model retraining, and thorough validation before the updated models are deployed in practice.

Figure 2 presents a comprehensive depiction of the minerals grade evaluation process utilizing camera technology. Initially, raw data collection is initiated, where mineral samples are meticulously captured through camera imagery to initiate the data flow. Subsequent to this, the collected data undergoes a thorough preprocessing phase, involving cleaning, filtering, and normalization procedures to ensure data integrity and consistency. Following preprocessing, data annotation and labeling are implemented to add context and facilitate supervised learning for subsequent stages. A pretrained model is then trained on the annotated dataset, leveraging existing knowledge to expedite the learning process. The model undergoes fine-tuning to optimize its performance for minerals grade evaluation. Upon deployment, the model evaluates predictions in real-time, comparing them with actual values. Additionally, an anomaly detection layer is integrated to identify discrepancies between predictions and real values. If significant errors are detected, the model undergoes retraining to enhance accuracy and reliability, ensuring robust performance in industrial applications.

3.2   Retraining Strategy for Online Analyzer

To address the dynamic nature of input data and the need for calibration in the AI based monitoring systems, a retraining strategy for our online analyzer is essential. The following steps outline the process:

1. **Data Collection:** Continuously gather real-time data from the online analyzer, including mineral grade measurements and corresponding concentrate grades values obtained from laboratory analysis. The mineral grades measurement by laboratory analysis (atomic absorption) is a consistence contentious procedure made by the industrial to evaluate the flotation performance by shift.
2. **Anomaly Detection:** Implement an anomaly detection system to identify instances where the online analyzer's measurements deviate significantly from the laboratory-derived values. These deviations may signal a need for recalibration and retraining.
3. **Retraining Triggers:** Set predefined triggers or thresholds based on the detected anomalies. When the triggers are crossed, initiate the retraining process to adapt the model to the new data distribution.
4. **Data Labeling:** Collect and label the data points that contributed to the anomalies. This labeled dataset will serve as the foundation for model retraining.
5. **Retraining:** Use the labeled dataset to retrain the model. Employ techniques such as transfer learning to retain knowledge from previous training while adapting to the changing data.
6. **Validation:** Evaluate the retrained model's performance using a validation dataset to ensure it meets the required accuracy and reliability standards.
7. **Deployment:** Once the retrained model demonstrates improved accuracy and stability, redeploy it for online mineral grade monitoring.
8. **Continuous Monitoring:** Implement continuous monitoring of the online analyzer's performance. If subsequent anomalies are detected, repeat the retraining process iteratively to maintain the model's accuracy.

By following this strategy, we can ensure that our online analyzer remains adaptive and effective in the face of evolving data dynamics, allowing us to provide reliable and accurate mineral grade measurements over time.

3.3   Data Statistical Analysis

A meticulously curated dataset was constructed, incorporating authentic samples of froth video recordings, each annotated with the corresponding mineral grades for Pb%, Fe%, Cu%, and Zn%. These recordings were captured at a consistent frame rate of 30 frames per second. A strategic method of random sequential frame selection was used to extract data from these recordings. The selected frames present a comprehensive view of the flotation froth in various conditions, with the mineral grades remaining notably consistent throughout. Following expert consultation in flotation processes, a controlled amount of noise was deliberately added to the mineral grades associated with each frame. The initial dataset consisted of 3,208 images obtained from the fourth cleaning stage of the zinc circuit, designated for model training. An additional set of 390 images was set aside specifically for testing the trained models. Subsequently, a second dataset was gathered the following month, comprising 4,200 images for retraining purposes. To mirror real-life industrial practices closely, images were procured from sections of the froth flotation process typically monitored by field professionals. Although the area captured in these images might represent a smaller segment of the entire froth surface, our detailed examination, aligned with established industry norms, ensures that the chosen segment accurately reflects the froth's dynamics and properties. The analysis presented in Table 1 illustrate the concentration levels and variation of the targeted minerals. The process of data collection was conducted with same materials and conditions across all operational shifts. This methodical approach is indispensable for the real-time assessment of froth quality and mineral grade determination within the flotation process.

Table 1. Statistical analysis of mineral grades for training and retraining datasets

	Training Samples					Retraining Samples				
	Mean	Std	Min	Max	Variance	Mean	Std	Min	Max	Variance
Cu (%)	0.96	0.30	0.26	1.70	0.09	1.00	0.324	0.26	1.86	0.13
Fe (%)	30.03	14.25	1.70	52.20	203.09	28.80	14.34	9.07	52.20	205.71
Pb (%)	1.66	0.63	0.46	3.85	0.39	1.73	0.67	0.46	3.85	0.45
Zn (%)	23.77	16.48	2.14	45.47	271.89	25.14	17.33	2.14	51.95	300.49

3.4 Model Evaluation Metrics

The performance of the models was evaluated using Mean Absolute Error (MAE), Mean Squared Error (MSE), and Root Mean Squared Error (RMSE) both before and after the retraining process. These evaluation metrics are commonly used to assess the accuracy and predictive performance of regression models. The MAE (Mean Absolute Error) calculates the average of the absolute differences between predictions and true values, providing an indication of the model's average prediction error. It is expressed by the formula:

$$MAE = \frac{1}{n} \sum_{i=1}^{n} |y_i - \hat{y}_i| \tag{1}$$

Similarly, the Mean Squared Error (MSE) quantifies the average of the squared differences between predicted and actual mineral grades, offering insights into the magnitude of prediction errors. The MSE formula is given by:

$$MSE = \frac{1}{n} \sum_{i=1}^{n} (y_i - \hat{y}_i)^2 \tag{2}$$

Root Mean Squared Error (RMSE) represents the square root of the average of the squared differences between actual and predicted values of minerals. RMSE is a widely used metric to assess the accuracy of regression models, and its formula is generally expressed as:

$$RMSE = \sqrt{\frac{1}{n} \sum_{i=1}^{n} (y_i - \hat{y}_i)^2} \tag{3}$$

These evaluation metrics provide crucial insights into the accuracy and predictive performance of our models in predicting mineral grades for Pb, Cu, Zn, and Fe.

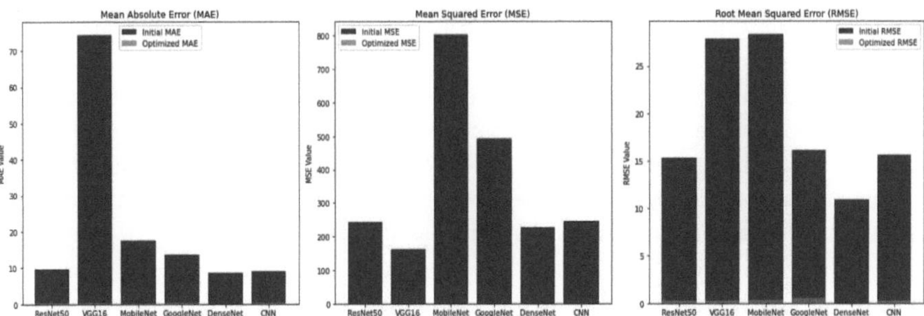

Fig. 3. Comparison of the evaluation metrics before and after the fine-tunning and optimization for the various models

4   Application and Results

To ensure the selection of an appropriate transfer learning approach, we conducted a comprehensive comparative exploration, meticulously assessing the performance of the six distinct transfer learning architectures: MobileNet, GoogleNet, DenseNet, VGG16, and ResNet50. The primary focus of this investigation was to dissect the impact of normalization techniques on these architectures.

The study unfolded across three distinct steps: first, the training of models without explicit normalization or optimization; second, the implementation of sophisticated normalization strategies; and finally, the retraining of the optimized models using newly collected data. Through a meticulous evaluation of key metrics such as mean squared error (MSE), root mean squared error (RMSE), and mean absolute error (MAE), our goal was to uncover the intricate dynamics between architectural choices and normalization strategies.

4.1 Fine-Tuning and Optimization of Models

In order to tailor the transfer learning models to address our specific problematic, we undertook a rigorous process of fine-tuning and optimization. Initially, we selected pre-trained models such as MobileNet, ResNet, VGG16, GoogleNet, and DenseNet, known for their effectiveness in handling image-related tasks. These models were chosen due to their adaptability to feature extraction from complex datasets like froth image data in mineral processing.

The fine-tuning process involved adjusting the parameters and architectures of these pre-trained models to better suit our target task of monitoring froth flotation in real-time. We carefully modified the model architectures, experimented with different hyperparameters, and fine-tuned the learning rates to optimize their performance for our specific dataset. The optimization process encountered an exception with DenseNet due to its inherent complexity, resulting in longer training times compared to other models. Despite its efficacy in feature reuse and information flow facilitation, DenseNet's intricate architecture posed challenges in terms of computational resources and time consumption during training.

Through iterative experimentation and validation, we fine-tuned the transfer learning models to achieve optimal performance metrics tailored specifically to our differential flotation application Table 2. This comprehensive approach to fine-tuning and optimization ensured that our models were well-adapted to the complexities of froth flotation monitoring as presented in the Fig. 3.

Table 2. Consolidated Performance Evaluation of Models

Models	Initial Metrics			After Optimization		
	MAE	MSE	RMSE	MAE	MSE	RMSE
ResNet50	9.62	243.94	15.32	0.28	0.11	0.33
VGG16	74.3	163.29	27.85	0.28	0.10	0.32
MobileNet	17.47	802.47	28.33	0.26	0.11	0.34
GoogleNet	13.57	492.63	16.12	0.43	0.27	0.52
DenseNet	8.68	226.68	10.95	-	-	-
CNN	9.10	244.60	15.63	0.27	0.10	0.33

4.2 Discussion of Results

In the Table 3, "Initial" refers to the performance on the primary dataset, "Retrained" refers to performance after retraining with additional data, and "Change" indicates the degree of improvement or degradation after retraining the models on the new data. We applied our proposed methodology on primary data to predict mineral grades and then retrained our model with new, recent

Table 3. Consolidated Performance Evaluation of Models with Change Metrics for Training and Retraining Phases

Models	Training			Retraining			Change (Δ)		
	MAE	MSE	RMSE	MAE	MSE	RMSE	MAE	MSE	RMSE
ResNet50	0.28	0.11	0.33	0.27	0.10	0.32	0.01	0.01	0.01
VGG16	0.28	0.10	0.32	0.29	0.12	0.35	−0.01	−0.02	−0.03
MobileNet	0.26	0.11	0.34	0.03	0.002	0.04	0.23	0.108	0.30
GoogleNet	0.43	0.27	0.52	0.30	0.14	0.36	0.13	0.13	0.16
CNN	0.27	0.10	0.33	0.27	0.11	0.33	0	−0.01	0

data. The results indicate that retraining has led to an improvement in the predictive accuracy of the models, as evidenced by the decrease in error metrics across the board.

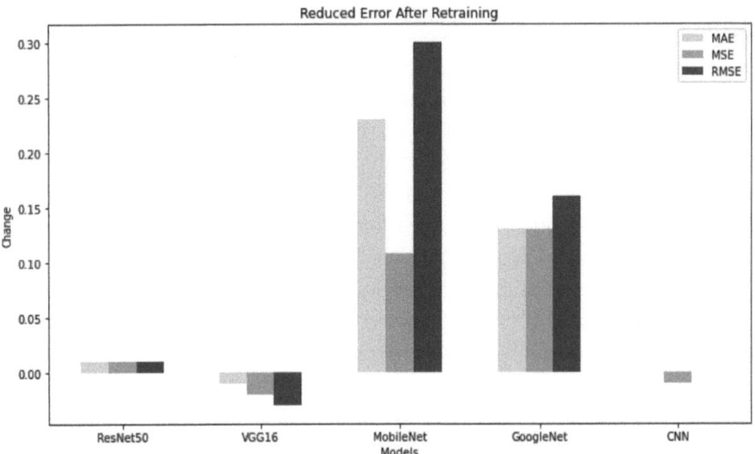

Fig. 4. Performance Improvement in Error Metrics After Retraining for Different Models

4.3   Interpretation of Models Performance

The nature of our dataset, predominantly composed of froth-related information, requires architectures that excel in extracting inherent features like texture bubbles distribution and color from such visual data. The previously mentioned Convolutional Neural Network (CNN), MobileNet, ResNet, VGG16, GoogleNet, and DenseNet have been chosen due to their capabilities in handling image-related tasks. CNN has proven to be more stable in predicting mineral grades but not adaptable to the dynamic changes of the flotation [20]. The hierarchical learning abilities and efficiency of MobileNet in resource-constrained environments, and the deep architecture of ResNet addressing complex patterns make them particularly suited for froth-related data. MobileNet, with its lightweight design and efficient architecture, stands out as a top performer in our use case as presented in the Fig. 4. Its advantages include:

- **Resource Efficiency:** MobileNet is optimized for scenarios with limited computational resources, making it highly suitable for real-time applications.
- **Speed:** The model's design ensures rapid processing of data, which is crucial for our use case.
- **Effectiveness:** Despite its efficiency, MobileNet maintains high accuracy in feature extraction, allowing us to make accurate predictions related to foam content.

5 Conclusion

Our study highlights the critical role of adaptive intelligent AI monitoring systems in addressing the dynamic challenges posed by the flotation process in mineral processing. The diverse nature of our froth-related dataset necessitated the selection of architectures capable of extracting intrinsic features such as texture, bubble distribution, and color from visual data. Through the use of Convolutional Neural Network (CNN), MobileNet, ResNet, VGG16, GoogleNet, and DenseNet, we have demonstrated the effectiveness of transfer learning models in predicting mineral grades from flotation froth images.

Among the models evaluated, MobileNet emerges as a top performer, showcasing superior adaptability and accuracy in predicting froth content. Its lightweight design and efficient architecture make it particularly well-suited for real-time applications in resource-constrained environments. Our findings underscore the importance of resource efficiency, speed, and effectiveness in model selection for dynamic monitoring tasks.

Additionally, our study emphasizes the significance of time metrics in model development and recalibration. The comparative analysis of training and retraining reveals the importance of efficient model optimization to meet the demands of real-time monitoring in the mining industry.

Looking ahead, our research opens avenues for further exploration in the realm of adaptive intelligent AI systems. Future endeavors will focus on refining online adaptive training strategies and incorporating physio-chemical parameters of the flotation process to enhance model robustness and predictive accuracy. Furthermore, the extension of our methodology to other flotation circuits within Industry 4.0 holds promise for advancing intelligent control systems and driving innovation in the mining industry. Perspectives include also the deployment architecture in real industrial differential flotation circuit with recommendation system to control the physio-chemical parameters.

In conclusion, the integration of adaptive intelligent AI systems represents a pivotal step in the digital transformation journey toward Industry 4.0. By harnessing the power of machine learning and transfer learning techniques, we can propel the mining industry into a new era of innovation, efficiency, and sustainability.

Acknowledgment. We would like to express our gratitude to the MANAGEM Group and its subsidiary CMG for providing us with the opportunity to conduct research, collect and validate data on-site, and for being an industrial partner in this project.

References

1. Sircar, A., Yadav, K., Rayavarapu, K., Bist, N., Oza, H.: Application of machine learning and artificial intelligence in oil and gas industry. Pet. Res. **6**(4), 379–391 (2021). https://doi.org/10.1016/j.ptlrs.2021.05.009
2. Qassimi, S., Abdelwahed, E.H.: Disruptive innovation in mining Industry 4.0. In: Distributed Sensing and Intelligent Systems, Studies in Distributed Intelligence, pp. 313–325. Springer, Cham (2022). https://doi.org/10.1007/978-3-030-64258-7_28
3. Jovanović, I., Miljanović, I.: Contemporary advanced control techniques for flotation plants with mechanical flotation cells – a review. Miner. Eng. **70**, 228–249 (2015). https://doi.org/10.1016/j.mineng.2014.09.022
4. Bendaouia, A., et al.: Artificial intelligence for enhanced flotation monitoring in the mining industry: a ConvLSTM-based approach. Comput. Chem. Eng. **180**, 108476 (2024). https://doi.org/10.1016/j.compchemeng.2023.108476
5. Aldrich, C., Avelar, E., Liu, X.: Recent advances in flotation froth image analysis. Miner. Eng. **188**, 107823 (2022). https://doi.org/10.1016/j.mineng.2022.107823
6. Chen, J., Huang, R., Chen, Z., Mao, W., Li, W.: Transfer learning algorithms for bearing remaining useful life prediction: a comprehensive review from an industrial application perspective. Mech. Syst. Signal Process. **193**, 110239 (2023). https://doi.org/10.1016/j.ymssp.2023.110239
7. Amin, A.A., Iqbal, M.S., Shahbaz, M.H.: Development of intelligent fault-tolerant control systems with machine learning, deep learning, and transfer learning algorithms: a review. Expert Syst. Appl. **238**, 121956 (2024). https://doi.org/10.1016/j.eswa.2023.121956
8. Ohenoja, M., et al.: Continuous adaptation of a digital twin model for a pilot flotation plant. Miner. Eng. **198**, 108081 (2023). https://doi.org/10.1016/j.mineng.2023.108081
9. Chen, Z., Shen, W., Chen, L., Wang, S.: Adaptive online capacity prediction based on transfer learning for fast charging lithium-ion batteries. Energy **248**, 123537 (2022). https://doi.org/10.1016/j.energy.2022.123537
10. Moniri-Morad, A., Shishvan, M.S., Aguilar, M., Goli, M., Sattarvand, J.: Powered haulage safety, challenges, analysis, and solutions in the mining industry; a comprehensive review. Results Eng. **21**, 101684 (2024). https://doi.org/10.1016/j.rineng.2023.101684
11. Kinnunen, P., et al.: Review of closed water loops with ore sorting and tailings valorisation for a more sustainable mining industry. J. Clean. Prod. **278**, 123237 (2021). https://doi.org/10.1016/j.jclepro.2020.123237

12. Kheddar, H., Himeur, Y., Awad, A.I.: Deep transfer learning for intrusion detection in industrial control networks: a comprehensive review. J. Netw. Comput. Appl. **220**, 103760 (2023). https://doi.org/10.1016/j.jnca.2023.103760
13. Azari, M.S., Flammini, F., Santini, S., Caporuscio, M.: A systematic literature review on transfer learning for predictive maintenance in Industry 4.0. IEEE Access **11**, 12887–12910 (2023). https://doi.org/10.1109/ACCESS.2023.3239784
14. Zhu, X., Chen, K., Anduv, B., Jin, X., Du, Z.: Transfer learning based methodology for migration and application of fault detection and diagnosis between building chillers for improving energy efficiency. Build. Environ. **200**, 107957 (2021). https://doi.org/10.1016/j.buildenv.2021.107957
15. Dayo-Olupona, O., Genc, B., Celik, T., Bada, S.: Adoptable approaches to predictive maintenance in mining industry: an overview. Resour. Policy **86**, 104291 (2023). https://doi.org/10.1016/j.resourpol.2023.104291
16. Panjapornpon, C., Bardeeniz, S., Hussain, M.A., Vongvirat, K., Chuay-ock, C.: Energy efficiency and savings analysis with multirate sampling for petrochemical process using convolutional neural network-based transfer learning. Energy AI **14**, 100258 (2023). https://doi.org/10.1016/j.egyai.2023.100258
17. Kičić, I., Vlachas, P.R., Arampatzis, G., Chatzimanolakis, M., Guibas, L., Koumoutsakos, P.: Adaptive learning of effective dynamics for online modeling of complex systems. Comput. Methods Appl. Mech. Eng. **415**, 116204 (2023). https://doi.org/10.1016/j.cma.2023.116204
18. Zhong, Y., Tang, Z., Zhang, H., Xie, Y., Guo, J.: Short-long temporal graph convolution network for grade monitoring in a first zinc rougher. Miner. Eng. **205**, 108457 (2024). https://doi.org/10.1016/j.mineng.2023.108457
19. Hasidi, O., et al.: Data-driven and model-driven approaches in predictive modelling for operational efficiency: mining industry use case. In: Mosbah, M., Kechadi, T., Bellatreche, L., Gargouri, F. (eds.) Lecture Notes in Computer Science, pp. 116–127. Springer, Cham (2024). https://doi.org/10.1007/978-3-031-49333-1_9
20. Bendaouia, A., et al.: Advancing flotation process optimization through real-time machine vision monitoring: a convolutional neural network approach. In: Proceedings of the 15th International Joint Conference on Knowledge Discovery, Knowledge Engineering and Knowledge Management, Rome, Italy, pp. 429–436 (2023). https://doi.org/10.5220/0012237300003598
21. Bendaouia, A., et al.: Hybrid features extraction for the online mineral grades determination in the flotation froth using Deep Learning. Eng. Appl. Artif. Intell. **129**, 107680 (2024). https://doi.org/10.1016/j.engappai.2023.107680

A Capacity Constrained ACO Approach for EVRP with a Partial Charging Policy

Meryem Abid[1,2], Mohamed Tabaa[1(✉)], and Hanaa Hachimi[2]

[1] Pluridisciplinary Laboratory of Research and Innovation (LPRI), EMSI, Casablanca, Morocco
{m.abid,m.tabaa}@emsi.ma
[2] Engineering Systems Laboratory (ISA), Ibn Tofail University, Kenitra, Morocco
hanaa.hachimi@uit.ac.ma

Abstract. For centuries, the world economics relied on goods distribution and exchange to sustain a sufficient livelihood. Therefore, all transportation means were deployed to surge the frequency of distributions and, accordingly, increase income. However, it was brought to the attention the harmful impacts by vehicles, of all sorts, on the environment due to the important amounts of greenhouse gases they release. To help the environment recover from the global warming caused by these emissions, it was inevitable that internal combustion vehicles be replaced by a more environmentally friendly alternative. This new requirement gave rise to what is known as Electric Vehicle Routing Problem, also known as EVRP, which aims to find the optimal path planning for a fleet of Electric Vehicles to serve a set of customers. In this paper, we propose an Ant Colony Optimization approach to solve the capacitated heterogenous EVRP. The Ant Colony Optimization Algorithm is used to assign a path to each vehicle based on the vehicle's load capacity. To protect the batteries from degradation, the energy level is kept within a specified range. Upon simulating our model on benchmark dataset's, our model proved successful in finding an optimal set of paths while minimizing the number of vehicle's deployed and the overall travelled distance.

Keywords: Ant Colony Optimization · Capacitated Electric Vehicles Routing Problem · Electic Vehicle Routing Problem · EV · EVRP · Optimal Path · Partial Charging

1 Introduction

Transportation has been at the core of human survival for as long as humanity itself [1]. Nations relied on merchandise exchange to flourish, whether by land, by sea, or eventually, by air. However, with the demographic explosion and the discovery of new lands, distribution of goods grew more complicated and time consuming. This called for a better transportation management system to help maintain the same level of profit while preserving customer satisfaction, thus the

H. Badir et al. (Eds.): INTIS 2024, CCIS 2645, pp. 163–176, 2026.
https://doi.org/10.1007/978-3-032-14964-0_13

emergence of the VRP concept [2]. Vehicle Routing Problem, commonly known as VRP, is originally derived from the travelling salesperson problem [3,4] which answers the riddle in which a salesperson is tasked with serving customers with specific demands. The aim of the TSP (Travelling Salesperson Problem) is to find the optimal route, or combination of routes, that will allow said salesperson to serve their customers once, and only once, at the least cost possible. Basically, the term cost changes definitions based on the aspired goal. Cost can refer to the total travelled distance, or the time of travel, or even the financial cost of travel, amongst other definitions [5–7]. VRP keeps the same principle of TSP but replaces the salesperson with a vehicle, or a fleet of vehicles.

Even though the processes of generating electricity might not always be entirely clean [8], electricity proved more favourable as it rarely impacts natural resources and generates zero pollutants, thus the birth of the Electric Vehicle Routing Problem variant of VRP, known as EVRP [2,7]. Throughout the years following its first mention, scholars tried various methods to solve the EVRP [2,7]. Similar to the different variants of VRP, EVRP increases in difficulty the more customers are there to serve. Also, when more constraints are considered such as time windows, limited load capacity, or even penalties should deliveries be delayed, EVRP's execution time explodes considerably. Furthermore, EVRP faces another limitation that derives directly from electric vehicles driving range [9–11], immediately linked to the significant time electric vehicles need to recharge. On the grounds of these reasons, EVRP was categorized as an NP-hard optimization problem [2,7].

In this paper, we address the EVRP in which we aim to minimize the total distance travelled, as well as the number of vehicles deployed. To solve EVRP we refer to an ant colony optimization approach to both assign vehicles to customers, as a first step, and eventually find the optimal path for each vehicle, as a second step. Finally, we will be resorting to a station insertion technique to add charging stops when and if necessary. To this end, our paper will be organized as follows: Sect. 2, will expand on the recent works of research related to our paper, and that is to offer better understanding on where research stands regarding the EVRP. Section 3 will provide a detailed description of our model, and the constraints it will have to abide by. Section 4 will elaborate on the methodology that we adopted to solve our version of the EVRP. Section 5 will cover the simulation environment and the results obtained to evaluate the performance of our model compared to similar works. Finally, we will summarize our results and discuss future possible areas of improvements related to our work in Sect. 6.

2 Literature Review

Given the NP-hard nature of the EVRP, various approaches were exploited to solve it over the last decades [2]. The solutions adopted varied between using a combination of algorithms, dropping some constraints, and solving it over several stages among other approaches while maintaining battery SoH (State of Health) [2,7].

For EVs (Electric vehicles) with li-ion cells, partial charging was proven to extend battery life by up to 45% [12,13]. Consequently, partial charging has been increasingly gaining popularity throughout the last few years. As for its association with the EVRP, recent works started incorporating it in their models. For instance, in [14], authors considered a mixed fleet with an objective of minimizing the total charging cost in different scenarios: slow or full charging, remaining energy after returning to the depot, and charging at the depot. In their model, they assumed that EVs leave the depot with fully charged batteries, and recharge when needed along their path to any desired level. Using ALNS (Adaptive Large Neighborhood Search), they tested their model on Solomon's instances [15] with short scheduling horizons and tight time windows. Their model outperformed CPLEX in solving medium and large instances and improved quality while requiring less computation time. However, given the mixed nature of their fleet, their model often violates emission constraints for combustion vehicles. In [16], authors deployed a fleet of EVs with various battery sizes, transport capacities and fixed costs, to serve customers with time windows. In their version, EVs use a partial linear recharging strategy, akin to [17,18]. Their objective function minimizes the total distance of all vehicles as well as the costs associated with them. To solve this problem, they used a path-based MIL model that allowed multiple visits to the same recharging station without using dummy recharging stations. Computational experiments on Solomon's instances [15] validate their model which successfully introduced 88 optimal solutions out of 108 instances. As for large instances, it was proven that partial charging reduces logistical costs. Their model also managed to find new solutions to various sizes of instances. While they validate that partial charging is beneficial to EVs, they confirm that charging stations should be present in sufficient concentrations to extend EVs driving range. Similar to [14,19], authors [20] considered a mixed fleet of EVs and conventional combustion vehicle. The charging station selection process involves the cost of travel to the station, the cost of charging once there, and the carbon emission cost generated. Upon running the model 50 times on each one of Solomon's instances, the model yielded satisfactory results by saving up to 1.40% and 3.62% of, respectively, costs and travel distance compared to the conventional ACO and GA (Genetic Algorithm). However, their model considers a mixed fleet, therefore, it remains unpredictable facing a full electric fleet with their driving range limitations.

Non-linear charging [21] is another aspect that impacts the EVRP solution to a great extent. While linear charging might be easier to handle as it considers a linear relationship between recharging time and the amount of energy acquired, it does not reflect real-life. Works like [22–24], considered nonlinear charging in their models by modeling the charging process using a piece-wise linear function. Their works confirm that ignoring non-linear charging might make solutions unfeasible or remarkably expensive. In this paper, our focus is on minimizing the total distance travelled, therefore, we do not include non-linear charging.

3   Problem Statement and Mathematical Formulation

3.1   Problem Description

We consider a warehouse d with a known location which coordinates are (x_d, y_d), available within a time window $[s_d, e_d]$. The warehouse is tasked with serving a set of N_c customers which location (x_c, y_c), demands D_c, and service time θ_c are known for every customer $c \in [1, N_c]$. To serve those customers, the warehouse has at its own disposal a fleet of N_v EVs with variant load capacities κ_v, driving range D_v, and battery capacities $Batt_v$ for every vehicle $v \in [1, N_V]$. Since the vehicles deployed use electricity as a main source of energy, we include a set of N_S identical charging stations, scattered geographically, which locations are identified via their coordinates (x_s, y_s) for every station $s \in [1, N_S]$. The charging stations are supposed to be available 24/7, with no queuing needed.

We suppose that all EVs depart from the warehouse fully charged. However, given the limited driving range of EVs, they are allowed to visit charging stations, when and if needed, to recharge. Moreover, any station can be visited by the same vehicle more than once, therefore, we add a set of N_S' dummy stations which are in fact duplicates of the original N_S stations. Finally, to reduce batteries degradation, we resort to partial charging [2,7,12,13] and that is by ensuring that the EVs battery remain within an interval of $[10\%, 90\%]$.

The overall model is expressed through graph $G = d, C, S, S' \cup E$ where d represents the depot, C represents the list of N_c customers, S and S' represent, respectively, the set of N_S charging stations and their N_S' duplicates, and E represents the edges that connect all nodes (depot, customers, stations, and dummy stations) together. All mathematical notation used to describe our model are explained in Table 1.

3.2   Objective Function

Our model aims to find the optimal combination of paths that will ensure that all customers are served once, and once only, using the available fleet. Furthermore, we set a objective of minimizing the total travelled distance of all vehicles, while also minimizing the number of vehicles deployed, as expressed by the objective function via Eq. 1.

$$min \sum_{v=1}^{N_v} \sum_{c=1}^{N_c} x_v.dist_v + min \sum_{v=1}^{N_v} y_v, \quad \forall v \in N_v \tag{1}$$

Subject to:

$$x_c = 1, \quad \forall c \in N_c \tag{2}$$

$$d_{v,c} - a_{v,c} = \theta_c, \quad \forall c \in N_c, \forall v \in N_v \tag{3}$$

$$\tau_v = \frac{\rho_{v,t} \times batt_v \times 60}{p}, \quad \forall v \in N_S \tag{4}$$

$$t_{v,s} = d_{v,s} - a_{v,s}, \quad \forall v \in N_V, \forall s \in N_S \tag{5}$$

$$t_{v,s'} = d_{v,s'} - a_{v,s'}, \quad \forall v \in N_V, \forall s' \in N_S \tag{6}$$

$$\alpha_v \leq \rho_{vt} \leq \beta_v, \quad \forall v \in N_v, \forall t \tag{7}$$

$$arc_{ij} \leq d_{vt}, \quad \forall i,j \in E, \quad \forall v \in N_S \tag{8}$$

$$\rho_v = \frac{d_{vt}}{D_v} \times 100, \quad \forall v \in N_v, \forall t \tag{9}$$

$$eng_{v,s} = Batt_v \times (0.9 - \rho_{vt}), \quad \forall v \in N_V, \forall S \in N_S, \forall t \tag{10}$$

$$eng_{v,s'} = Batt_v \times (0.9 - \rho_{vt}), \quad \forall v \in N_V, \forall s' \in N_{S'}, \forall t \tag{11}$$

$$\chi_v = \sum_{s=1}^{N_S} eng_{v,s} \times F \times q_{v,s} + \sum_{s=1}^{N_S'} eng_{v,s'} \times F \times q_{v,s'}, \quad \forall v \in N_V, \forall s \in N_S \tag{12}$$

$$Q_c \leq \kappa_v, \quad \forall c \in N_c, \exists v \in N_V \tag{13}$$

$$\sigma_v = \sum_{c=1}^{N_c} w_{c,v} \times y_i \times Q_c, \quad \forall v \in N_V \tag{14}$$

$$\sigma_v \leq \kappa_v, \quad \forall v \in N_V \tag{15}$$

$$\sum_{v=1}^{N_v} y_v = 1 \leq N_V, \quad \forall v \in N_V \tag{16}$$

$$x_c \in \{0,1\}, \quad \forall c \in N_c \tag{17}$$

$$y_v \in \{0,1\}, \quad \forall v \in N_v \tag{18}$$

$$e_{ij} \in \{0,1\}, \quad \forall i,j \in E \tag{19}$$

$$w_{c,v} \in \{0,1\}, \quad \forall c \in N_c, \forall v \in N_v \tag{20}$$

$$q_{v,s} \in \{0,1\}, \quad for v \in N_v, for s \in N_S \tag{21}$$

$$q_{v,s'} \in \{0,1\}, \quad for v \in N_v, for s' \in N_{S'} \tag{22}$$

Equation 2 guarantees that all customers are served once, and once only. Equation 3 ensures that the vehicle doesn't spend more than the time needed for service at a customer's location. Equations 4 calculates the time required for charging, in minutes, based on the EV's battery level $\rho_v(\forall v \in N_v)$, its battery capacity $Batt_v(\forall v \in N_v)$, and the charging power p of the charging station which considered the same for all stations and their duplicates. Equations 5 and 6 ensure that the charging time spent at station s, and dummy station s', is equally to the difference between the vehicle's arrival time and departure time from, respectively, station s, and dummy station s' ($\forall s \in N_S, \forall S' \in N_{S'}$). Equation 7 ensures the EV's battery level is always between 10% and 90% of its full capacity. Equation 8 guarantees that length of any arc is at most equal to the EV's remaining driving range ($\forall v \in N_v$). Equation 9 calculates the battery level of the EV at any given moment t ($\forall v \in N_v$). Equations 10 and 11 calculate the energy acquired (in kWh) at each charging station s, and/or dummy charging stations s' ($\forall s \in N_S, \forall S' \in N_{S'}$). Similarly, Eq. 12 calculates the total charging cost of each vehicle at each charging station it visits along its way. Equation 13 ensures that for any given customers($\forall c \in N_C$), there is at least one vehicle (($\forall v \in N_v$)) with enough load capacity to serve them. Equation 14 calculates the total demands carried by each vehicle. Consequently, Eq. 15 ensures that the sum of all demands carried by a vehicle ($\forall v \in N_v$) are at most equal to that vehicle's load capacity. Equation 16 ensures that the number of vehicles deployed doesn't exceed the fleet size N_v. Equation 17, 18, 19, 21, and 22, respectively, set the binary variables x_c, y_v, e_{ij}, w_{cv}, $q_{v,s}$, and $q_{v,s'}$.

4   Methodology

The main source of complexity of EVRP emanates from the large number of possible solutions which explodes exponentially in correlation with the number of customers. For instances, for a problem with 10 customers, the number of possible routes is of $(10-1)! = 362,880$ [3,25]. Consequently, it is difficult to test all possibilities especially when the number of customers increases. Therefore, several methods were deployed to solve the EVRP by mimicking the behaviour of living organisms in their search for food such as ants, birds, and whales amongst others [26–29]. In our paper, we resorted to Ant Colony Optimization due to its wide use in solving the EVRP variants. Our model is organized in two phases as follows:

- Phase 1: consists of assigning customers to each vehicle based on the vehicle's remaining load capacity and the customers demand using ACO.
- Phase 2: tests the feasibility of each path in terms of driving range. If the path is unfeasible, a station insertion process is applied to scheduling a charging station visit when needed.

4.1   Phase 1: Vehicle Scheduling and Optimal Path Generation

One crucial step in the EVRP is the handling of the available fleet of EVs, especially when they are not identical. Our aim is to use our fleet in a optimal manner so that each vehicle is exploited to its full capacity. Accordingly, The ACO algorithm goes through EVs one by one, assigning the maximum number of customer to each EV in the process as portrayed by Pseudocode 1. In other terms, this phase constructs an optimal path for each vehicle progressively. This path is optimized, and modified when necessary, in every iteration.

Table 1. Mathematical notation of our model.

Sets	
C	Set of customers
S	Set of charging stations
S'	Set of charging stations' duplicates
E	Edges connecting all nodes (customers, stations, and warehouse)
V	Fleet of EVs

Parameters	
d	Warehouse/Depot
N_c	Number of customers
N_S	Number of stations
$N_{S'}$	Number of dummy stations
N_V	Number of vehicles
Q_c	Demand of customer $c \in N_C$
$[s_C, s_E]$	Time window of customer $c \in N_C$
θ_C	Service time of customer $c \in N_C$
$a_{v,c}$	Arrival time of vehicle v at customer c, $\forall v \in Nv, \forall c \in N_C$
$d_{v,c}$	Departure time of vehicle v from customer c, $\forall v \in Nv, \forall c \in N_C$
$a_{v,s}$	Arrival time of vehicle v at station s, $\forall v \in Nv, \forall s \in N_S$
$d_{v,s}$	Departure time of vehicle v from station s, $\forall v \in Nv, \forall s \in N_S$
$a_{v,s'}$	Arrival time of vehicle v at dummy station c, $\forall v \in Nv, \forall s' \in N_S$
$d_{v,s'}$	Departure time of vehicle v from dummy station s', $\forall v \in Nv, \forall s' \in N_{S'}$
(x_d, y_d)	Location of the warehouse/depot d
(x_c, y_c)	Location of customer $c \in Nv$
(x_s, y_s)	Location of station $s \in Nv$
$(x_{s'}, y_{s'})$	Location of dummy station $s \in Nv$
κ_v	Load Capacity of vehicle $v \in Nv$
D_v	Driving range of vehicle $v \in Nv$
d_{vt}	Remaining Driving range of vehicle, $\forall v \in N_v$
$Batt_v$	Battery capacity of vehicle $v \in Nv$
$dist_v$	Total distance travelled by vehicle $v \in Nv$
δ_v	Sum of demands carried by vehicle $v \in Nv$
γ_v	Amount of energy charged by vehicle $v \in Nv$
ϵ_v	Fixed cost of vehicle $v \in Nv$
χ_v	Total cost of vehicle $v \in Nv$
F	Cost of 1kWh
arc_{ij}	Length of edge connecting nodes i and j, for $i, j \in E$
$eng_{v,s}$	Energy acquired by vehicle v at station s, for $v \in Nv$, $s \in N_S$
ρ_{vt}	Battery level of vehicle v at moment t, for $v \in Nv$
α_v	Minimum battery level of vehicle v, for $v \in Nv$
β_v	Maximum battery level of vehicle v, for $v \in Nv$
τ_v	Charging time of vehicle v, for $v \in Nv$
$t_{v,s}$	Time spent by vehicle v at charging station s, $\forall v \in N_v, \forall s \in N_S$
$t_{v,s'}$	Time spent by vehicle v at dummy charging station s', $\forall v \in N_v, \forall s' \in N_{S'}$
p	Power of charging at any station s and s', $s \in N_S, \forall s' \in N_{S'}$

Binary variables	
x_c	Binary variable set at 1 if customer c is visited, 0 otherwise, for $c \in N_C$
e_{ij}	Binary variable set at 1 if arc_{ij} for $i, j \in E$ is used, 0 otherwise
y_v	Binary variable set at 1 if vehicle v is used, 0 otherwise, for $v \in Nv$
$q_{v,s}$	Binary variable set at 1 if vehicle v visits station s, 0 otherwise, for $v \in N_v$, for $s \in N_S$
$q_{v,s'}$	Binary variable set at 1 if vehicle v visits dummy station s', 0 otherwise, for $v \in N_v$, for $s' \in N_{S'}$
$w_{c,v}$	Binary variable set at 1 if customer c is assigned to vehicle v, 0 otherwise, $\forall c \in N_C, \forall v \in N_V$

Pseudocode 1 Vehicle scheduling and optimal path generation using ACO

Input: Customers, Vehicles, α, β, Evaporation Rate, iterations
Output: Optimal path for each vehicle
Initialization: Pheromone $\leftarrow$ 1

```
1.  for i in iterations do
2.      for v in Vehicles do
3.          Path ← Warehouse
4.          Remaining_Load_capacity ← κ_v
5.          while customers do
6.              Current_Customer ← Previous_Customer
7.              Calculate Customers_Probabilities
8.              Sort Customers_Probabilities
9.              Next_Customer ← None
10.             for p in Customers_Probabilities do
11.                 if Demand[p] ≤ Remaining_Load_capacity then
12.                     Next_Customer ← p
13.                     break
14.                 end if
15.             end for
16.             if Next_Customer is not None then
17.                 Path ← Next_Customer
18.                 Remove Customer from Customers
19.                 Update Remaining_Load_capacity
20.             else
21.                 Break
22.             end if
23.         end while
24.         Path ← Warehouse
25.         if Path_Distance ≤ Previous_Paths then      ▷ Previous Paths of vehicle v
26.             Update Best_Path
27.         end if
28.     end for
29.     Update Pheromone of Best_Path
30. end for
```

The scheduling process takes into consideration two factors: The distance to next available customers, and the EV's remaining load capacity. The probability to visit each and every one of the remaining customers is calculated and sorted decreasingly. The customer with the highest probability is tested first, if their demand is at most equal to the vehicle's remaining load capacity, the customer is added to the path. Otherwise, the customer with the next highest probability is considered, and so on. This helps alleviate some of the EVRP's difficulty by treating each vehicle and its customers as an independent TSP in which the goal is to find the shortest path connecting all these customers.

Eventually, The algorithm runs for a specified number of iterations, after which the number of unassigned customers should be exactly 0, meaning that there is no remaining customers. If it is not the case, the problem is deemed unfeasible. If not, the model provides an optimal path for each used EV.

4.2   Phase 2: Station Insertion

In the wake of Phase 1, an optimal path for each vehicle is generated. A dual fitness function takes over and tests the feasibility of each path by following the battery level of the vehicle along the path.

If, at all moments, the battery level of the vehicle is above the specified minimum level of 10%, the path is considered feasible and no recharging is needed. However, once the battery level drops below 10%, the same fitness function identifies the faulty arc and scans the neighborhood to select a charging station.

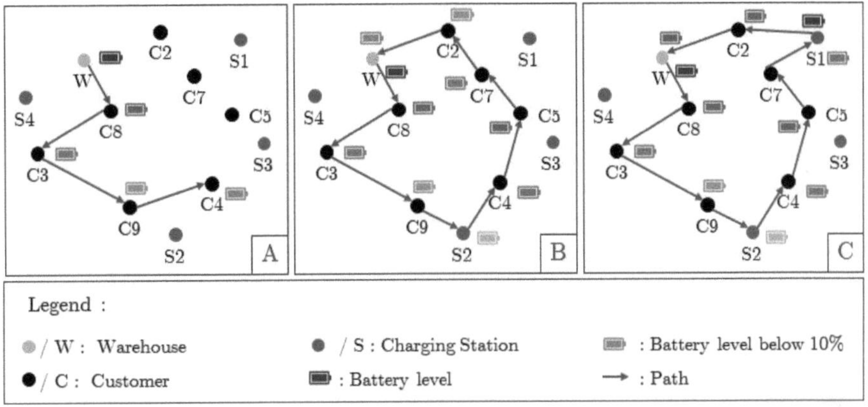

Fig. 1. Station Insertion technique (from A to C)

If no charging station respects the energy requirements, the fitness function regresses to the previous arc and checks for a charging stations that satisfies energy requirements.

As portrayed by Fig. 1, driving to customer C4, the battery level will drop below the specified threshold, therefore, the EV need to recharge along the way. Station S2 is visited before the vehicle continues its path to customer C4. The same problem issues when trying to visit customer C2. In addition, visiting station S1 doesn't solve the problem as the vehicle battery level will drop below 10% before arriving at station S1. Therefore, the station S1 is visited along the previous arc.

It is possible that the path remains unfeasible after several attempts of inserting stations, therefore, a rotation process takes place, which places the last visited customer at the beginning of the path. After the rotation, the fitness is checked, and the station insertion process is repeated. If after the rotation and the station insertion the path remains unfeasible, the rotation is repeated again. A specified number of rotations is set, after which the path returns back to its initial order and is declared unfeasible.

5   Simulations and Results

5.1   Simulations

To measure the performance of our model, we conducted simulations on Solomon's instances [15] on computer equipped with 16 Gb of Ram, and an 11th generation Intel(R) Core(TM) i7 processor with a frequency of 2.5GHz. This widely used data set [2] provides a variety of instances in different sizes ranging from 5 customers to 100 customers. Moreover, customers are either clustered, randomly scattered or a combination of both.

As for the fleet used to serve these customers, we considered 20 EVs with driving ranges between 150 km and 300 km, load capacities between 70kg and 400 kg, and battery capacities between 200 kWh and 395 kWh.

The model prioritizes EVs with larger load capacity to minimize the number of vehicles deployed by assigned as many customers as possible to each vehicle.

In the following sections, we will discuss the results of our simulations regarding four aspects: computation time, accuracy of our model in terms of feasible/unfeasible paths ratio, total travel time, total travel distance, and finally the number of vehicles deployed. We also measure the impact of data sets size and customers layout on the final results.

To test our model's performance, we ran each instance 10 generations, for 200 iterations each generation, with α set at 1, β set at 2, and the evaporation rate set at 0.75.

5.2   Results

Computation Time. As was foreseeable, the more customers there are to serve, the more computation time required. For 5 customers data sets, the full 200 iterations required less than 2 s for execution, while the number jumped to almost 20 min for data sets with 100 customers. This goes to further prove that the more customers there are, the longer it takes to solve the model, hence the difficulty of the EVRP.

Model Accuracy. As previously mentioned in Sect. 4.2, it is possible that some solutions remain unfeasible post station insertion. This problem occurs when the EV isn't capable of carrying on the delivery operation due to energy restrictions as portrayed by Fig. 2 where the term "before" refers to the results before inserting charging stations, and "After" refers to the results after inserting charging stations, if needed.

We notice that the model struggles to solve small instances of 5 to 10 customers to the fullest, while it solves the total of the 15 and 100 customers instances. Our verdict is that when dealing we fewer than 10 customers, especially with small demands, most customers are assigned to one single vehicle. With one vehicle only, the energy constraint obstructs the feasibility of the path. However, when dealing with more than 15 customers, more vehicles are deployed which alleviates the burden off of each vehicle.

Average Travel Time. When computing the total travel time, the model takes into consideration 3 factors: time of travel across each edge, service time of each customer, and the charging time which depends on the amount of energy acquired. In the case of large instances, the gab between the average travel time before and after station insertion is negligible due to the fact that most solutions rarely required visiting charging stations. As mentioned in Sect. 2, more vehicles are used and that shortens the path of each vehicle.

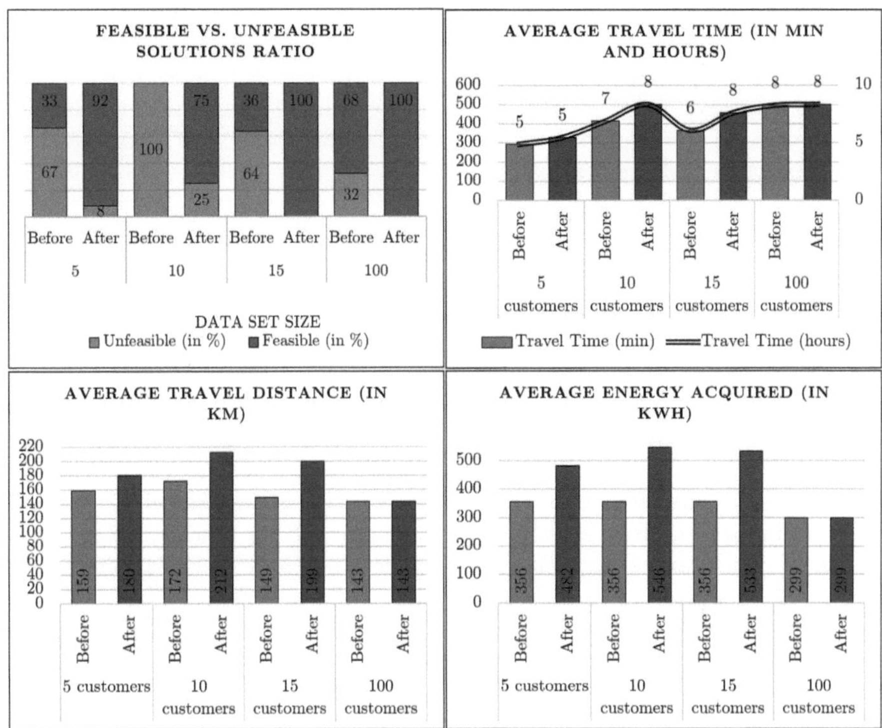

Fig. 2. Model accuracy (top left), Average travel time (top right), Average travel distance (bottom left), and Average energy acquired (bottom right).

Average Travel Distance. The distance of each path includes the length of each traversed edge, including the edge from and to charging stations.

Understandably, the average travel distance increases after inserting charging stations. Similar to travel time discussed in Sect. 5.2, in the case of large instance the gap between the average travel distance before and after inserting stations is almost null.

Energy Cost. We assume that all EV's leave the warehouse with batteries charged to 90% of their capacity, therefore, all deployed EVs have a minimum energy cost equal to the number of kilowatts-hour acquired upon their initial charge. if the EV doesn't visit any charging stations along its path, then the total energy consumed is the same as the initial energy acquire. Accordingly, for every charging station visited, we calculate the amount of energy needed to reach 90% of battery level, and we add it to the initial energy acquired, using Eqs. 10 and 11.

Number of Vehicles Deployed. For small instances (less than 15 customers), no more than 2 EVs have been deployed. On the other hand, an average of 9 EVs was used for large instances (100 customers) which is logical, given the number of customers to serve. Compared to the fleet size considered, our model deployed an average of 45% of the fleet available.

Impact of Data Set Size and Customers Layout. Upon running our model, we noticed that the model's behaviour changes according to the number of customers. Noticeably, when considering large instances, our model's accuracy reaches 100%, which wasn't the case for smaller instances.

Furthermore, as we previously mentioned in Sect. 5.1, our data set instances provide 3 different layouts: clustered, randomly distributed, and a combination of the two layouts. We notice that when customers are randomly distributed, the model's accuracy is better compared to that of clustered customers. The same applies to the number of vehicles deployed; A maximum of 10 EVs was used for clustered customers, versus a maximum of 8 for randomly distributed customers. This can be explained by the fact that small populations usually have small demands which means that the model assigns most customers, or all of them, to one vehicle, thus extending the vehicle's energy consumption. On the other hand, with large populations, customers have larger demands, therefore, the model is forced to deploy more vehicles to serve all customers. Consequently, we can confirm that the model's performance is influenced by customers' demands. Furthermore, ACO prioritizes customers that are closer to the current location of the vehicle to reduce the total travel distance. With customers being clustered in one geographic area, the closest charging station can be far than the customers are, thus violating the vehicle's battery level constraint. However, randomly distributed customers often cover a larger area which often includes a charging station as well.

6   Conclusion

While increasing the number of prospects impacts the profit positively in all industries, the management of larger number of customers required careful handling. In our paper, we consider the case of a goods delivery scenario in which we aim to serve all available customers while minimizing the total travelled distance as well as the number of vehicles deployed. In our model, we consider a fleet of heterogeneous electric vehicles, and adopted a partial charging strategy which is known to decrease battery degradation. To solve our model, we referred to a two phase approach, in which we use the Ant Colony Optimization algorithm, combined with a stations insertion technique. Our model yielded adequate results, especially when handling large instances, while it struggled facing instances with less than 15 customers. In future works, we aim to include customers time windows in our model. Furthermore, we have a goal of developing a technique to overcome the unfeasibility of some generated solutions.

References

1. Parzinger, H.: The 'silk roads' concept reconsidered: about transfers, transportation and transcontinental interactions in prehistory
2. Abid, M., Tabaa, M., Chakir, A., Hachimi, H.: Routing and charging of electric vehicles: literature review. **8**, 556–578
3. TSP problem solution based on improved genetic algorithm. IEEE Conference Publication. IEEE Explore
4. Tao, Z.: TSP problem solution based on improved genetic algorithm. In: 2008 Fourth International Conference on Natural Computation, vol. 1, pp. 686–690. ISSN 2157-9563
5. Adewumi, A.O., Adeleke, O.J.: A survey of recent advances in vehicle routing problems. **9**(1), 155–172
6. Braekers, K., Ramaekers, K., Van Nieuwenhuyse, I.: The vehicle routing problem: state of the art classification and review. **99**, 300–313
7. Kucukoglu, I., Dewil, R., Cattrysse, D.: The electric vehicle routing problem and its variations: a literature review. **161**, 107650
8. Ang, B.W., Su, B.: Carbon emission intensity in electricity production: a global analysis. **94**, 56–63
9. Szumska, E.M., Jurecki, R.: The effect of aggressive driving on vehicle parameters. **13**(24), 6675
10. Collin, R., Miao, Y., Yokochi, A., Enjeti, P., von Jouanne, A.: Advanced electric vehicle fast-charging technologies. **12**(10), 1839
11. Coffman, M., Bernstein, P., Wee, S.: Electric vehicles revisited: a review of factors that affect adoption. **37**(1), 79–93. _eprint https://doi.org/10.1080/01441647.2016.1217282
12. Ruan, H., Barreras, J.V., Engstrom, T., Merla, Y., Millar, R., Wu, B.: Lithium-ion battery lifetime extension: a review of derating methods. **563**, 232805
13. Wikner, E., Thiringer, T.: Extending battery lifetime by avoiding high SOC. **8**(10), 1825
14. Dönmez, S., Koç, Ç., Altıparmak, F.: The mixed fleet vehicle routing problem with partial recharging by multiple chargers: mathematical model and adaptive large neighborhood search. **167**, 102917
15. Solomon, M.M.: Algorithms for the vehicle routing and scheduling problems with time window constraints. **35**(2), 254–265
16. Wang, Y., Zhou, J., Sun, Y., Fan, J., Wang, Z., Wang, H.: Collaborative multidepot electric vehicle routing problem with time windows and shared charging stations. **219**

17. Yang, S., Ning, L., Tong, L., Shang, P.: Integrated electric logistics vehicle recharging station location–routing problem with mixed backhauls and recharging strategies. **140**, 103695

18. Zuo, X., Xiao, Y., Zhu, C., You, M.: A linear MIP model for the electric vehicle routing problem with time windows considering linear charging. In: 2018 Annual Reliability and Maintainability Symposium (RAMS), pp. 1–5. ISSN 2577-0993

19. Macrina, G., Di Puglia Pugliese, L., Guerriero, F., Laporte, G.: The green mixed fleet vehicle routing problem with partial battery recharging and time windows. **101**, 183–199

20. Fan, L., Liu, C., Dai, B., Li, J., Wu, Z., Guo, Y.: Electric vehicle routing problem considering energy differences of charging stations. **418**, 138184

21. Montoya, A., Guéret, C., Mendoza, J.E., Villegas, J.G.: The electric vehicle routing problem with nonlinear charging function. **103**, 87–110

22. Diefenbach, H., Emde, S., Glock, C.H.: Multi-depot electric vehicle scheduling in in-plant production logistics considering non-linear charging models. **306**(2), 828–848

23. Kancharla, S.R., Ramadurai, G.: An adaptive large neighborhood search approach for electric vehicle routing with load-dependent energy consumption. **4**(2), 10

24. Lian, Y., Lucas, F., Sörensen, K.: The electric on-demand bus routing problem with partial charging and nonlinear function. **157**, 104368

25. Liu, J., Li, C., Ji, C.: Study of MDP and K-mediods for TSP problem. In: Zhao, M., Sha, J. (eds.) ICCIP 2012. CCIS, vol. 289, pp. 324–332. Springer, Heidelberg (2012). https://doi.org/10.1007/978-3-642-31968-6_39

26. Full article: A new hybrid whale optimization algorithm for green vehicle routing problem

27. Islam, Md.A., Gajpal, Y., ElMekkawy, T.Y.: Hybrid particle swarm optimization algorithm for solving the clustered vehicle routing problem. **110**

28. Kaya, E., Gorkemli, B., Akay, B., Karaboga, D.: A review on the studies employing artificial bee colony algorithm to solve combinatorial optimization problems. **115**, 105311

29. Jiang, W., Hu, R., Qian, B., Yu, N.-K., Liu, B.: Hybrid whale optimization algorithm for solving green open vehicle routing problem with time windows. In: Huang, D.-S., Jo, K.-H., Li, J., Gribova, V., Bevilacqua, V. (eds.) ICIC 2021. LNCS, vol. 12836, pp. 673–683. Springer, Cham (2021). https://doi.org/10.1007/978-3-030-84522-3_55

Industrial Modbus-LoRa Data Logger for Digital Twin's Applications

Adnane Bouchra[1,2(✉)], Abdelhafid Aitelmahjoub[1], and Abbas Dandache[2,3]

[1] CCPS Laboratory, ENSAM, University of Hassan II, Casablanca, Morocco
bouchraadnane2@gmail.com
[2] Multidisciplinary Laboratory of Research and Innovation (LPRI), Moroccan School of Engineering Sciences (EMSI), 20250 Casablanca, Morocco
[3] Laboratory of Genie Industrial and Production of Metz (LGIPM), Lorraine University, Nancy, France

Abstract. In view of the major opportunities for communication and the challenges of communication protocols in the industrial environment, it is now mandatory to review wireless communication architectures, but above all to support robust and efficient architectures inside the plant. The design of these systems differs for each application, considering the constraints of the propagation environment. In contrast to other traditional indoor environments such as residential buildings or offices, industry is characterized by its large size and the nature of its elements and obstacles. The complexity of the industrial context and the noise present in the propagation environment make it necessary to offer a robust wireless communication system to cope with the various disturbances during transmission. In this context, this paper proposes a contribution concerning a multi-protocol (Wi-Fi and LoRa) data-logger aimed at industrial communications for digital twin industrial applications. The simulation is carried out using LoRa 32 nodes, for which we have used the Node RED platform as an industrial frame management tool. The tests demonstrated bidirectional communication between a virtual PLC via TIA Portal and a supervision platform.

Keywords: Industrial communication · Digital Twin · LoRa · Modbus · Data logger

1 Introduction

With the last industrial revolutions, the technological evolution of wireless communication systems has enabled several industrial sectors to evolve and improve user needs in terms of accessibility, quantity of data, intelligence in decision-making and energy consumption. Through the integration of new technology, these technologies continue to evolve, improving the connectivity of billions of objects. These connected objects, whether sensors or actuators, are by nature autonomous physical devices with a limited source of energy [1, 2]. They can communicate with each other, using several different communication topologies. This revolution is leading to more ambitious innovations in various fields of application: medicine, industry, energy, security and others [3].

H. Badir et al. (Eds.): INTIS 2024, CCIS 2645, pp. 177–185, 2026.
https://doi.org/10.1007/978-3-032-14964-0_14

For industrial applications, research is focusing on the creation of connected, robotized and intelligent factories to improve current production systems. This interconnection of factories is achieved via connected systems, in which employees, machines and products collaborate with each other to form the new revolution [4].

At the heart of this revolution, the Industrial Internet of Things (IIoT) plays a key role in the development of connectivity for this revolution. IIoT is based on the use of connected sensors and actuators to improve industrial processes and manufacturing. It incorporates intelligence in data processing and analysis to ensure better M2M (Machine-To-Machine) communication [5]. This has been the case ever since electronics were integrated into the industrial sector as part of the third "Industry 3.0" revolution. It is now necessary to develop robust communication architectures that enable objects in a highly noisy industrial environment to communicate easily to provide reliable information for better decision-making. In such an industrial environment, propagation differs from other conventional means of communication, due to its large size and the nature of the objects and obstacles inside. Thus, the industrial environment can be modelled as a fading channel affected by impulsive and Gaussian noise [11].

In this paper, we present a case study of a multi-protocol data-logger based on Wi-Fi and Long Range (LoRa) communications. Digital twin (DT) applications require flexible communications protocols and, above all, the adaptation of industrial frames into wireless protocol packets. Our proposal aims to encapsulate the Modbus industrial frame in two wireless communication protocols: Wi-Fi and LoRa. The idea is to set up a LoRa data logger that receives and transmits commands from sensors and actuators via the Message Queuing Telemetry Transport (MQTT) protocol. The task of the data logger is therefore to adapt the frames while ensuring communication via a Programmable Logic Controller (PLC). Tests via two LoRa 32 nodes and commands from a virtual PLC running under Tia Portal can be shared in both directions via the NodeRED platform.

This paper is organized as follows: the second part will be devoted to a state of the art of DTs, presenting the architectures, topologies, and applications. Communication protocols will form the third part. In the fourth part, we will discuss the functioning of the proposed data logger and finally a conclusion and outlook.

2 State of the Art

2.1 Digital Twins

DTs emerged in the 2000s thanks to Michel Grieves' pioneering work on product lifecycle management [10]. He's defined DTs as A set of virtual information constructs that fully describes a potential or actual physical manufactured product from the micro atomic level to the macro geometrical level. At its optimum, any information that could be obtained from inspecting a physically manufactured product can be obtained from its DT [30].

Since then, their use has spread to diverse fields such as industry, aerospace, medicine, and production sciences. However, there are still gaps in our detailed understanding of these implementations, as much information remains confidential [27]. There is still disagreement as to the exact definition of DTs. Some consider them to be the end product itself [29], while others see them as encompassing the entire product lifecycle [8].

Whichever perspective is adopted certain essential components are necessary to speak of DTs [27]:

Elementary components: this includes the physical object itself, which will be modeled as a DT, as well as the digital object that represents this twin. Bidirectional communication between the physical and digital object is also essential to enable the continuous exchange of data and information.

Imperative components: each DT must be equipped with IIoT devices enabling real-time data collection from the physical object. In addition, the use of machine learning techniques, the implementation of appropriate security measures and the evaluation of the DT's performance are essential to guarantee their efficiency and reliability. In short, DTs have become powerful tools for modeling and simulating physical objects in various fields. Although differences remain in the precise definition of DTs, elementary components such as the physical object, the digital object and bidirectional communication are required. In addition, the use of IIoT devices, machine learning techniques and appropriate performance evaluations are essential for the successful implementation of DTs [28].

The applications of DT in industry are diverse and expansive, with particularly complex yet beneficial implementation in the aerospace domain. The DT finds crucial applications in NASA and US Air Force vehicles, replicating extreme conditions such as thermal, mechanical, and acoustic loads that cannot be physically achieved in a laboratory setting [9].

The maritime industry shares similarities with aerospace in terms of the need for DT, given the lack of physical contact between ships and base stations [7]. The DT, seen as a catalyst for the "digital thread," overcomes challenges related to the dispersion of information on devices both on land and at sea.

Robotics, on the other hand, leverages the DT to optimize control algorithms during the development phase [19]. Furthermore, the integration of machine learning into the DT, although rarely detailed in the public domain, offers promising prospects, as demonstrated in the proof of concept in the petrochemical industry [16].

Finally, applications of mixed reality, such as combining DT with augmented reality and virtual reality, are gaining ground in areas like human-machine collaboration and building construction [23]. These applications underscore the crucial need for domain experts for the successful implementation of the DT, highlighting the importance of human knowledge in these artificially intelligent systems [18]. Thus, the DT uniquely adapts to each sector, presenting distinct advantages and specific challenges to address.

2.2 Datalogger

In the swiftly evolving landscape of Industry 4.0, marked by the introduction of cutting-edge technologies and communication standards such as OPC UA and MQTT, the enduring use of the Modbus protocol underscores a pragmatic aspect of industrial operations. The reluctance to move away from Modbus can be attributed to the significant costs and operational disruptions that would arise from overhauling existing PLCs and industrial circuitry. This has spurred extensive research into developing solutions that bridge Modbus with contemporary IIoT protocols, aiming to enhance system interoperability while mitigating the need for expensive hardware updates [10]. Industrial communication between electronic boards is traditionally facilitated by industrial protocols. This established method underscores the necessity for data loggers that not only enable wireless communication but also ensure these boards can interface with various devices across different protocols. The research in this domain is vast and includes notable contributions such as the work by Francisco et al., who developed a "Power Analyzer Monitor and Programming Device" (PAMPD). This data logger facilitates communication of electrical components over classic Modbus RS485 through LoRa, demonstrating efficient data transmission with a low average time of 30ms and a modest information loss rate of 3% [26]. On another front, Ari et al. presented a remote supervision solution for three-phase electric meters using a data logger based on ESP32. This device communicates with meters via the Modbus RS485 protocol and transmits data to the cloud over LoRa, achieving a low average transmission time of 1189.9ms and an information loss rate of merely 0.083% [22]. Additionally, the advent of cost-effective IIoT gateway prototypes designed to connect conventional Modbus RTU sensors/actuators to an MQTT IIoT cloud represents a significant stride towards integrating traditional industrial systems with modern IIoT applications [20]. Further exploration in this field includes the automatic mapping of controller variables to Modbus TCP/IP for seamless integration with OpenPLC and OPC UA Server, thereby fostering interoperability within the industry 4.0 ecosystem [14]. Another research underscores a concerted effort to embed Modbus communication within platforms like Node-RED, thereby enabling internet-based communication. This evolution highlights the protocol's flexibility and ongoing relevance amidst the dynamic changes characterizing the industrial sector [15].

The intersection of Modbus with IIoT technologies through data loggers and gateways is a pivotal development that underscores the protocol's adaptability. It opens up new avenues for industrial automation by integrating traditional systems with the vast potential of IIoT, cloud computing, and real-time data analytics. This synergy between old and new technologies facilitates a more connected, efficient, and flexible industrial environment, driving the future of industrial operations towards greater innovation and productivity.

2.3 Modbus

Modbus, originally developed in 1979 by Modicon (now a part of Schneider Electric), is a communication protocol tailored for industrial devices. Its simplicity and openness have cemented its status as the de facto standard for industrial communication, facilitating seamless interaction across a vast spectrum of automation equipment. The protocol's design optimizes the ease of data exchange between various controllers and devices, including sensors and actuators, thereby becoming an indispensable tool in industrial settings [31]. Modbus is extensively utilized as the communication backbone in a diverse array of industrial equipment such as PLCs, Distributed Control Systems (DCS), Remote Terminal Units (RTU), and intelligent instruments, all of which benefit from the rapid advancements in embedded computer technology [6]. The structural components of Modbus (see Fig. 1), including both Modbus RTU and Modbus ASCII protocol data units (PDU), are crucial for its operation. A PDU typically comprises a slave address (ADDR), a function code (FC), a data payload, and a cyclic redundancy check (CRC) or linear redundancy check (LRC) for error verification, with CRC employed for Modbus RTU and LRC for Modbus ASCII transactions. Furthermore, the Modbus/TCP application data unit (ADU) includes an MBAP header, enhancing the protocol's applicability by incorporating elements such as a transaction identifier, protocol identifier, length field, and unit identifier [17].

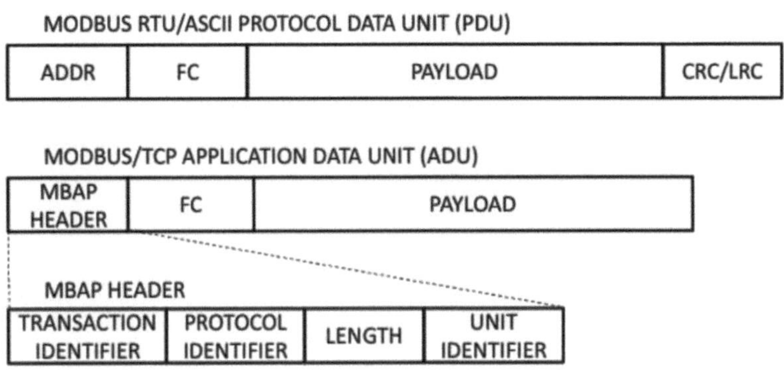

Fig. 1. Modbus frame

2.4 Lora

LoRa and its protocol, Long Range Wide Area Network (LoRa WAN), represent a paradigm shift in the realm of open network standards, developed by the LoRa Alliance [24]. As a Low Power Wide Area Network (LPWAN) utilizing a star topology, Lora WAN offers numerous advantages, such as low energy consumption and extensive network coverage, making it a compelling choice for a wide array of applications. Unlike traditional communication technologies like ZigBee, Bluetooth, and Wi-Fi, LoRa WAN stands out for its wireless IIoT solutions that excel in both indoor and outdoor environments [13]. Its scalability facilitates the seamless integration of additional nodes, catering to an expanding array of sensors and devices. This adaptability has spurred its adoption in the industrial sector, with ABI Research predicting that by 2026, over 50% of LPWAN communications will rely on LoRa due to its versatility for both indoor and outdoor applications [12]. LoRa Wan's resilience is particularly noteworthy in industrial settings characterized by high levels of noise. It operates effectively even under challenging conditions that typically hinder performance. A study highlighted the technology's robustness, noting only a minimal performance degradation (between 2.5 to 6 decibels) across various spreading factors (SF) in multi-path mining environments [25]. Further research demonstrated LoRa's ability to maintain reliable communication amidst diverse noise levels. Such durability underscores LoRa's suitability for a broad spectrum of IIoT applications, where ensuring uninterrupted data flow is paramount [21].

3 Discussions

In this section, we will present the role of the data logger for an industrial application, in particular DTs. The main objective is to enable several elements within the industry to communicate based on the Modbus communication protocol frame. Sending data is based on two components, MQTT and LoRa, ensuring bidirectional communication between sender and receiver.

The communication architecture illustrated in the image (See Fig. 2) shows the flow of data between sensors/actuators and a DT using the Modbus, MQTT and LoRa protocols. Sensors and actuators using the Modbus TCP protocol send Modbus TCP frames. These frames are then sent to a gateway, which converts them into MQTT topics. The MQTT topics are transmitted to the datalogger via the MQTT protocol, enabling flexible wireless data communication.

At the datalogger, MQTT topics are received and Modbus TCP frames are extracted. These frames are then encapsulated in LoRa payloads and sent to the other end of the system. LoRa payloads carrying Modbus TCP frames are sent from one datalogger to another datalogger located at the DT.

The DT datalogger receives LoRa payloads and extracts Modbus TCP frames, which are then encapsulated into MQTT topics. These MQTT topics are sent via a gateway to the DT system. Finally, the DT receives the MQTT topics, extracts the Modbus TCP frames and processes the data for monitoring, analysis and management of industrial operations.

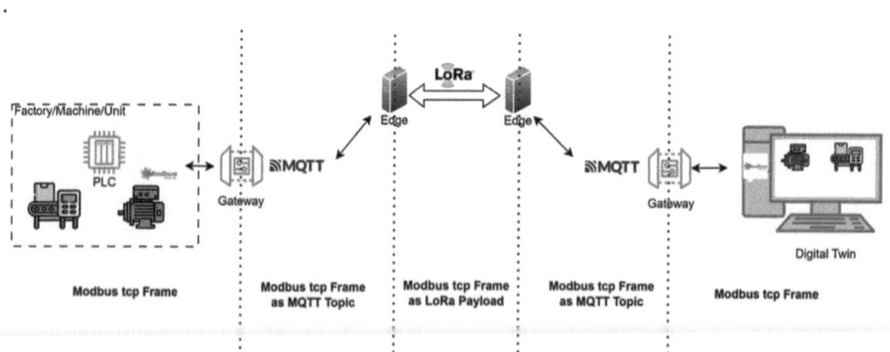

Fig. 2. The proposed Data Logger Architecture

The data logger is implemented using the Node-RED platform, LoRa modules and a Siemens 1500 virtual PLC.

The approach to implementing our data logger is to consider the generation of data sent via a sensor or actuator based on the industrial Modbus frame. This data will be encapsulated in a Wi-Fi wireless frame using the MQTT protocol, and sent to the Data Logger whose input is in this format. The MQTT frame with the Modbus message is then converted into a LoRa frame and sent from the transmitter to the receiver. The receiver, in turn, will also use the content of this frame by converting it into an MQTT message. Through Node-RED, we will be able to communicate with the PLC remotely while ensuring bidirectional message exchange between a PLC and the sensor and actuator layers (See Fig. 3).

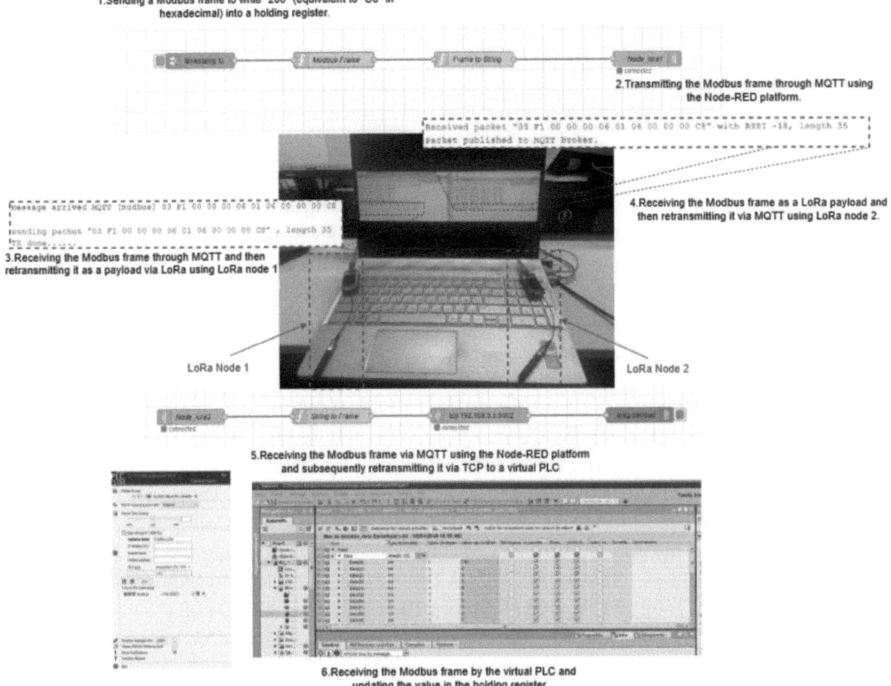

Fig. 3. Data logger implementation

4 Conclusion and Perspectives

The integration of DTs for the industry of the future requires better communication between all the components of the industry. Communication protocols and the nature of the data sent are essential elements for a better-connected factory. The diversity of communication protocols and the difficulty of industrial implementation environments make the task of selecting a communication protocol or equipment difficult. In this paper, we have proposed a Data Logger concept with the aim of adapting the industrial Modbus frame with wireless communication protocols. This adaptation required the use of two protocols: MQTT and LoRa. The architecture implemented and simulated is based on remote communication between sensors and a remote PLC. The integration of the Node-RED platform made it easier to adapt frames by switching from one protocol to another, and to create bidirectional connectivity between the various components. In the future, we hope to extend the communication perimeter of our Data Logger, while exploiting other industrial configurations and frames, as well as physically implementing the equipment by testing its performance in a highly noisy industrial environment.

References

1. Lasi, H., Fettke, P., Kemper, H.-G., Feld, T., Hoffmann, M.: Industry 4.0. Bus. Inf. Syst. Eng. **6**, 239–242 (2014). https://doi.org/10.1007/s12599-014-0334-4

2. Lu, Y.: Industry 4.0: a survey on technologies, applications and open research issues. J. Ind. Inf. Integr. **6**, 1–10 (2017)
3. Skobelev, P.O., Borovik, S.Y.: On the way from Industry 4.0 to Industry 5.0: from digital manufacturing to digital society. Industry 4.0 **2**, 307–311 (2017)
4. Özdemir, V., Hekim, N.: Birth of Industry 5.0: making sense of big data with artificial intelligence, "The Internet of Things" and next-generation technology policy. OMICS: J. Integr. Biol. **22**, 65–76 (2018). https://doi.org/10.1089/omi.2017.0194
5. Nahavandi, S.: Industry 5.0—a human-centric solution. Sustainability **11**, 4371 (2019)
6. Dutertre, B.: Formal modeling and analysis of the modbus protocol. In: Goetz, E., Shenoi, S. (eds.) Critical Infrastructure Protection, pp. 189–204. Springer, Boston (2007)
7. Fonseca, Í.A., Gaspar, H.M., De Mello, P.C., Sasaki, H.A.U.: A standards-based digital twin of an experiment with a scale model ship. Comput. Aided Des. **145**, 103191 (2022). https://doi.org/10.1016/j.cad.2021.103191
8. Gabor, T., Belzner, L., Kiermeier, M., Beck, M.T., Neitz, A.: A simulation-based architecture for smart cyber-physical systems. In: 2016 IEEE International Conference on Autonomic Computing (ICAC), Wuerzburg, Germany, pp. 374–379. IEEE (2016)
9. Glaessgen, E., Stargel, D.: The digital twin paradigm for future NASA and U.S. air force vehicles. In: 53rd AIAA/ASME/ASCE/AHS/ASC Structures, Structural Dynamics and Materials Conference & BR & 20th AIAA/ASME/AHS Adaptive Structures Conference & BR & 14th AIAA. American Institute of Aeronautics and Astronautics, Honolulu, Hawaii (2012)
10. Javaid, M., Haleem, A., Suman, R.: Digital Twin applications toward Industry 4.0: a review. Cogn. Robot. **3**, 71–92 (2023). https://doi.org/10.1016/j.cogr.2023.04.003
11. Aarif, L., Tabaa, M., Hachimi, H.: Performance evaluation of LoRa communications in harsh industrial environments. J. Sens. Actuator Netw. **12**, 80 (2023)
12. Abboud, S., el Rachkidy, N., Guitton, A., Safa, H.: Gateway selection for downlink communication in LoRaWAN. In: 2019 IEEE Wireless Communications and Networking Conference (WCNC), pp. 1–6 (2019)
13. Mekki, K., Bajic, E., Chaxel, F., Meyer, F.: A comparative study of LPWAN technologies for large-scale IoT deployment. ICT Express **5**, 1–7 (2019). https://doi.org/10.1016/j.icte.2017.12.005
14. de Melo, P.F.S., Godoy, E.P.: Controller interface for Industry 4.0 based on RAMI 4.0 and OPC UA. In: 2019 II Workshop on Metrology for Industry 4.0 and IoT (MetroInd4.0&IoT), pp. 229–234 (2019)
15. Melo, P.F.S., Godoy, E.P., Ferrari, P., Sisinni, E.: Open source control device for Industry 4.0 based on RAMI 4.0. Electronics **10**, 869 (2021). https://doi.org/10.3390/electronics10070869
16. Min, Q., Lu, Y., Liu, Z., Su, C., Wang, B.: Machine learning based digital twin framework for production optimization in petrochemical industry. Int. J. Inf. Manage. **49**, 502–519 (2019). https://doi.org/10.1016/j.ijinfomgt.2019.05.020
17. Morris, T., Vaughn, R., Dandass, Y.: A retrofit network intrusion detection system for MODBUS RTU and ASCII industrial control systems, pp. 2338–2345 (2012)
18. Duine, P.: Digital twins: what do they mean for lighting? (2020). https://www.lighting.philips.co.uk/oem-emea/stay-connected/digital-twins. Accessed 18 Jan 2024
19. Negri, E., Fumagalli, L., Macchi, M.: A review of the roles of digital twin in CPS-based production systems. Procedia Manuf. **11**, 939–948 (2017). https://doi.org/10.1016/j.promfg.2017.07.198
20. Nguyen-Hoang, P., Vo-Tan, P.: Development an open-source industrial IoT gateway. In: 2019 19th International Symposium on Communications and Information Technologies (ISCIT), pp. 201–204 (2019)
21. Niles, K., Ray, J., Niles, K., Maxwell, A., Netchaev, A.: Monitoring for analytes through LoRa and LoRaWAN technology. Procedia Comput. Sci. **185**, 152–159 (2021). https://doi.org/10.1016/j.procs.2021.05.041

22. Nugroho, A.S., Faiz, D.A.: Application of Modbus and Long Range (LoRa) for 3-phase Electricity Monitoring System
23. Choi, S.H., et al.: An integrated mixed reality system for safety-aware human-robot collaboration using deep learning and digital twin generation. Robot. Comput.-Integr. Manuf. **73**, 102258 (2022). https://doi.org/10.1016/j.rcim.2021.102258
24. Paul, B.: An overview of LoRaWAN. WSEAS Trans. Commun. **19**, 231–239 (2021). https://doi.org/10.37394/23204.2020.19.27
25. Saban, M., Aghzout, O., Medus, L.D., Rosado, A.: Experimental analysis of IoT networks based on LoRa/LoRaWAN under indoor and outdoor environments: performance and limitations. IFAC-PapersOnLine **54**, 159–164 (2021). https://doi.org/10.1016/j.ifacol.2021.10.027
26. Sánchez-Sutil, F., Cano-Ortega, A.: Design and testing of a power analyzer monitor and programming device in industries with a LoRA LPWAN network. Electronics **10**, 453 (2021). https://doi.org/10.3390/electronics10040453
27. Sharma, A., Kosasih, E., Zhang, J., Brintrup, A., Calinescu, A.: Digital Twins: state of the art theory and practice, challenges, and open research questions. J. Ind. Inf. Integr. **30**, 100383 (2022). https://doi.org/10.1016/j.jii.2022.100383
28. Singh, M., et al.: Applications of digital twin across industries: a review. Appl. Sci. **12**, 5727 (2022). https://doi.org/10.3390/app12115727
29. Abramovici, M., Göbel, J.C., Dang, H.B.: Semantic data management for the development and continuous reconfiguration of smart products and systems. CIRP Ann. **65**, 185–188 (2016)
30. Soori, M., Arezoo, B., Dastres, R.: Digital twin for smart manufacturing, a review. Sustain. Manuf. Serv. Econ. **2**, 100017 (2023). https://doi.org/10.1016/j.smse.2023.100017
31. Swales, A.: Electric S Open Modbus/TCP Specification

BMA-Measure: A Novel Metric for Assessing the Quality of the Training Set

Mohamed Amine Boudia$^{(\boxtimes)}$ (iD)

CNRS, UMR 8201 - LAMIH - Laboratoire d'Automatique de Mécanique et d'Informatique Industrielles et Humaines, Université Polytechnique Hauts-de-France, 59313 Valenciennes, France
mohamedamine.boudia@uphf.fr

Abstract. This paper introduces the BMA-Measure, a new metric designed to evaluate the quality of the training set. While most previous work has focused on evaluating classification algorithms, the importance of the representativeness of the example base for the accuracy of the classification process and the reliability of the generated models has often been overlooked. The BMA-Measure aims to fill this gap by strengthening existing measures and helping experts better interpret results, optimize evaluation reliability and robustness, and precisely identify gaps. Developed from theoretical criteria for generating an optimal training set, the BMA-Measure proposes a simple and appropriate approach for each sub-problem before combining all these metrics into one. This metric is particularly important in sensitive sectors such as digital health, where the reliability of learning models is crucial to ensuring accurate and unbiased predictions. By assessing the representativeness of the example base, the BMA-Measure contributes to reinforcing this confidence by demonstrating the quality and impartiality of learning models.

Keywords: Machine learning · classification · training set · evaluation · BMA-Measure · confidence

1 Introduction

Classification is an innate behavior in humans, which explains why many daily problems can be modeled as classification problems. In the current era, computer science is widely solicited in all fields, as our world heavily relies on this science. Artificial intelligence (AI), aiming to mimic human intelligence and behavior, has gained considerable momentum, especially in automated classification. AI researchers seek to reproduce human thinking with all its advantages, including the ability to classify.

Automated classification, which assigns instances to classes, can be supervised, where the number of classes is known in advance, or unsupervised, where the process groups instances into clusters by maximizing intra-cluster similarity and minimizing inter-cluster similarity.

Researchers have succeeded in teaching computers how to perform classification tasks, requiring an algorithm and an appropriate training set to generate a classification model. This model will then be used to classify new examples.

However, existing metrics only evaluate the learning algorithm, not the training set itself. In this work, we introduce the BMA-Measure, a metric designed to evaluate the training set. This metric is particularly important in sensitive sectors such as digital health, where the reliability of learning models is crucial to ensuring accurate and unbiased predictions.

By assessing the representativeness of the example base, the BMA-Measure contributes to reinforcing this confidence by demonstrating the quality and impartiality of learning models.

This paper presents an innovative approach to evaluating the training set for classifications. We will start by reviewing previous work in the field of supervised classification to position our contribution. And we will begin an analysis of the foundations of supervised classification, highlighting the crucial importance of evaluating the training set to ensure the reliability of the generated models. Then, we will describe in detail our metric, the BMA-Measure, emphasizing its relevance in sensitive areas such as digital health.

Finally, we will conclude by emphasizing the importance of our metric in reinforcing confidence in machine learning models by identifying gaps and improving the quality of training sets.

This paper emphasizes the importance of evaluating the quality of training datasets for reliable machine learning model development, particularly in supervised classification tasks. It highlights key factors such as dataset size, representativeness, and attribute distribution, and proposes a systematic approach for assessing these aspects. The aim is to provide insights into optimizing training set quality to improve classification performance.

1.1   Related Works

Research in the field of supervised classification has evolved significantly over the years, with many studies aimed at improving the quality of training sets and the accuracy of classification models. By examining these studies thematically and by year, we can observe a progressive evolution of knowledge and techniques in this constantly evolving field.

- **Improving the quality of training sets:** many researchers have explored techniques to improve the quality of training sets. Liu (2014) [9] investigated the use of active learning to enrich training sets by selecting the most informative examples for the classification algorithm. Wang (2013) [10] studied the impact of feature selection on classification accuracy, highlighting the importance of judiciously choosing relevant attributes to improve model performance.
- **Class imbalance management:** Class imbalance management has been a major area of interest for researchers. Park (2015) [8] conducted a comparative study on different approaches to managing class imbalance in training sets, emphasizing the importance of balanced techniques to improve data representativeness. Wang (2019) [4] proposed

techniques to mitigate class imbalance, highlighting the importance of considering this asymmetry in building training sets to avoid biases in classification models.

- **Noise label attenuation:** Some researchers have focused on noisy labels and their impact on the quality of training sets. Rodriguez (2016) [7] examined the effects of noisy labels on training set quality and proposed methods to attenuate them, emphasizing the importance of cleaning data before learning to avoid classification errors.
- **Training set optimization:** Training set optimization has also been an area of interest for researchers. Chen (2017) [6] proposed an innovative approach to select an optimal training set to improve classification performance, highlighting the importance of judiciously choosing the most representative examples to build high-quality models.
- **Importance of fairness in training sets:** Some work has emphasized the importance of fairness in building training sets, especially in sensitive areas such as health. Kim (2018) [5] explored the importance of fairness in training sets, highlighting the potential impact of biases in classification models.
- **Impact of training set size:** Finally, the impact of training set size has been studied by several researchers. Lee (2020) [3] examined how training set size affects classification performance, highlighting the importance of having enough data to build accurate and generalizable models.
- **Evaluation of classification models:** Garcia, M. (2021) [2] conducted a comparative study on different evaluation metrics for supervised classification models.

In the field of genomics, Isidro, J. et al. (2021) examined training set optimization in genomic selection, emphasizing the importance of maximizing captured phenotypic variance. Their research provides valuable insights into methods for selecting optimal training sets in this area. Previously, in 2014, Isidro, J. et al. also studied training set optimization in genomic selection, focusing on different levels of population structure. This research explores the challenges and opportunities related to optimizing training sets in scenarios where population structure can greatly affect model performance.

It is worth noting that most of the related work cited above focuses on specific aspects of supervised learning, such as improving data quality or managing class imbalances. However, our work is distinguished by its objective of specifically evaluating the quality of the training set in the supervised classification process.

Our BMA-Measure metric offers an original approach to assessing the representativeness of the training set, thus filling an important gap in the existing literature. By highlighting this crucial dimension of supervised learning, our work contributes to a better understanding of the quality of classification models and significant advances in the field.

2   Machine Learning: From Data to Evaluation

In the realm of machine learning, gathering and organizing data play roles in constructing classification models.

2.1   Training, Testing, and Validation Data

In data science, an initial dataset is divided into training and testing subsets. The training set is used to train the model by allowing algorithms to learn from the data's features, while the testing set evaluates the model's performance on unseen data, ensuring impartial assessment. Typically, the training set is larger and may be further split for validation purposes, while the testing set remains smaller and separate.

Model validation during the training process ensures its performance on new data. This is where validation data comes into play. Validation data is a separate subset of the training data used to evaluate and adjust the model during training.

Insights gained from this validation enable us to optimize the model's parameters and classifiers for better performance.

By carefully defining the data to include in each subset and maintaining strict separation between the training and testing sets, we ensure reliable evaluation of the model's performance and accurate estimation of its effectiveness.

To prevent overfitting—where the model performs well on training data but poorly on new data—validation data is introduced. This validation subset helps adjust and optimize the model's parameters during training, ensuring better generalization and performance.

2.2   How to Split the Dataset into Training, Validation, and Test Sets?

Before dividing a dataset, two key factors must be considered: the total volume of the dataset and the type of model you are training with the dataset.

The split ratio between the training and testing sets mainly depends on these two factors and may vary depending on the specific needs of the use case. This ratio is generally negotiated based on the amount of available data and the amount needed to train and test the model.

As shown in the following figure (Fig. 1) the initial process of splitting the dataset is often referred to as the holdout method. In this method, the dataset is divided into two distinct parts: the training data and the testing data.

Once the dataset has been split into training and testing sets, the training set is further subdivided to allocate a portion of the data for validation. This step is crucial for evaluating the model's performance.

Data (Corpus)		
Training set		Test set
Training set	Validation set	Test set

Fig. 1. Dataset division

K-Folds cross-validation is a model evaluation technique that divides the training dataset into K subsets. Typically, K is set to 10 in 10 -Folds cross-validation, where each of the ten subsets is used as a validation set while the others form the training set. The validation accuracy is calculated for each fold, and the average of these accuracies provides the final model accuracy.

2.3 Synthetic Machine Learning Protocol

There are several evaluation metrics that an expert can use to validate a classification model. The following figure (Fig. 2) describes the learning protocol.

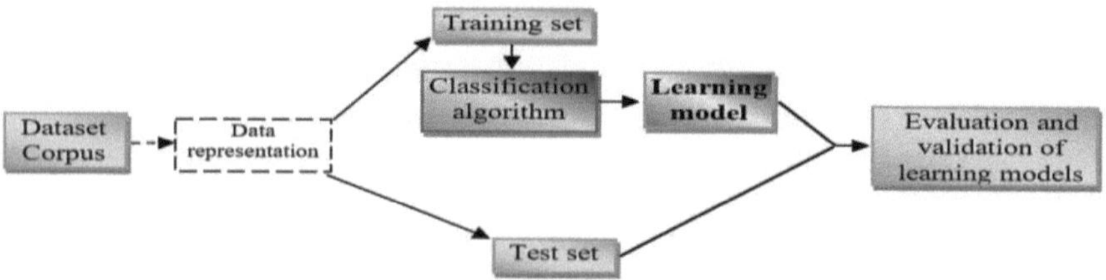

Fig. 2. Synthetic Machine Learning Protocol

2.4 Evaluation of the Learning Model

Evaluating a learning model involves several key steps, centered on both the classification model and the test set. Experts, with their deep understanding of algorithms, conduct a three-level evaluation:

- **Comprehensibility and Integrity**: The expert qualitatively assesses if the model addresses the problem logically.
- **Theoretical Level**: The expert reviews the learning protocol, data choices, and algorithms to ensure theoretical consistency.
- **Performance Level**: Using formal evaluation metrics, the expert assesses whether the model correctly classifies new data and identifies any weaknesses.

A key tool for performance assessment is the confusion matrix, which tracks true positives (TP), false positives (FP), false negatives (FN), and true negatives (TN). This allows for a deeper analysis of classification errors and the model's effectiveness.

Common metrics like precision, recall, F1-score, ROC AUC, and the kappa coefficient provide insights into model performance but often overlook training set quality. To address this, the BMA-Measure was introduced, focusing on assessing the quality of the training set. By identifying biases and imbalances, it helps practitioners ensure more reliable classification outcomes.

In the current AI landscape, where model reliability is crucial, the BMA-Measure enhances transparency and reproducibility by evaluating training set quality and quantifying related risks. This contributes to building confidence in AI models.

2.5 Fundamentals of Training Set Evaluation

Training set evaluation forms a critical aspect of the machine learning pipeline, influencing the performance and generalization capabilities of classification models. Key concepts such as dataset size, representativeness, and attribute distribution play pivotal roles in determining the effectiveness of the training process.

Various approaches and methodologies have been proposed in the literature to assess the quality of training sets. These include metrics for dataset size optimization, measures for representativeness analysis, and techniques for attribute distribution assessment. Understanding these approaches is essential for developing a comprehensive framework for training set evaluation.

3 Our Proposed Metric: BMA-Measure

This section introduces the BMA (Boudia Mohamed Amine) metric, designed to evaluate the quality of training sets in supervised classification models. Unlike traditional metrics focused on model performance (accuracy, recall, F1 -score), the BMA specifically assesses training data quality, analyzing class balance, label accuracy, data representativeness, and biases. This approach helps identify issues in the training set that could affect model outcomes, offering a deeper understanding of factors influencing performance.

The BMA is especially relevant in sensitive fields like healthcare, where reliable training data is crucial for AI-driven decisions such as medical diagnoses and treatment recommendations. By focusing on training set quality, the BMA enhances confidence in model reliability for critical applications.

In summary, the BMA offers a significant advancement in evaluating training data quality, enabling better insights into model performance, especially in complex, high - stakes domains like healthcare.

Furthermore, traditional evaluation metrics typically assess classification algorithm performance but often overlook the evaluation environment and training data quality. To address this, we introduce the "classifier's performance triangle," inspired by the fire triangle. This framework highlights the critical role of training data quality, the classification algorithm, and the overall evaluation environment for comprehensive model assessment (Fig. 3).

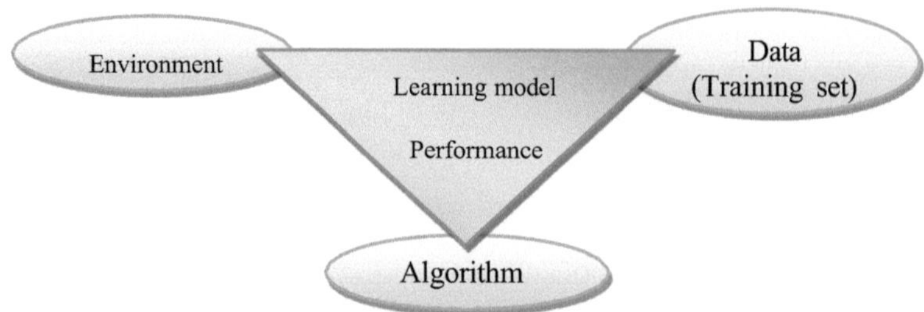

Fig. 3. Learning model performance triangle

- **Environment**: This component encompasses the hardware and software infrastructure in which the classifier operates, with the ability to integrate specific user requirements such as response time and result accuracy.
- **Algorithm**: Represents the functional core of the classifier, acting as a black box that processes the data according to a specific theory to generate a classification model.
- **Data**: The data is segmented into two distinct parts:

  - **Training set**: This is the portion of the corpus selected according to specific criteria (see subsection…) and subjected to a classification algorithm to create a model.
  - **Test set**: This part of the corpus contains new examples used to evaluate and validate the classification model.

We deliberately inverted the triangle to highlight the existing paradox in the machine learning community, which primarily focuses on optimizing and evaluating algorithms, often neglecting other components of the learning process.

While the environment can be standardized and hardware and software issues are becoming less frequent, it is crucial to recognize the significant impact of algorithmics and data on classifier performance.

In this context, we introduce our metric to specifically evaluate the quality of the training set. It is important to note that ethical and scientific evaluation does not allow for the evaluation of the test set. This must be free from any influence to ensure credible evaluation and validation of the classifier.

We will therefore attempt to explain the need for this metric, starting with a simple explanation, referring to Einstein's quote: "If you can't explain it simply, you don't understand it well enough," before moving on to a more in -depth explanation. We will then list the theoretical criteria of a good training set before presenting the technical part of this scientific paper, detailing the metric, its implementation, and a typical interpretation.

3.1 Explanation: Reflexive Example

(see Fig. 4).

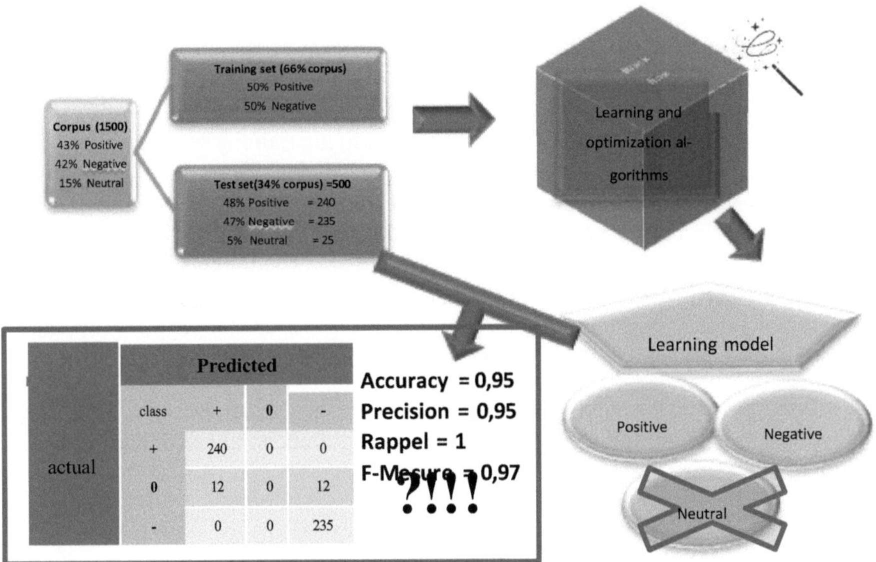

actual	Predicted		
class	+	0	-
+	240	0	0
0	12	0	12
-	0	0	235

Fig. 4. Reflexive example: recommendation task

References this analysis highlights two important conclusions:

– The choice of the training set influences the quality of learning.
– This choice can also bias the evaluation of the robustness of a classifier or classification method, as well as the quality of learning in general.

> Hence the need for an evaluation
> measure of the Training Set.

Theoretical Criteria for a Good Training Set

Theoretically, there are several criteria often taught in courses, but their practical application can be complex. True expertise lies in the ability to strike the right balance between these criteria. Unless mistaken or omitted, the training set must fulfill these criteria:

1. **Optimal Size**: The size of the training set should not be too large relative to the corpus to avoid overfitting, nor too small to avoid insufficient learning. It must strike the best compromise between these two extremes.
2. **Representativeness** (relative to the corpus): This characteristic is ensured by the following sub-criteria:

- Presence of the majority or all classes.
- Presence of the majority or all possible attribute values.

3. **Minimization of anomalies**: The training set must minimize redundant examples, noise, and non-discriminating instances.
4. **Good Class Distribution**: Balanced distribution of examples per class ensures that the model is not biased.
5. **Good Distribution of Values for Each Attribute**: Balanced distribution of values for each attribute ensures that the learning model assigns equal importance to all attributes.
6. **Temporal Coherence**: It is crucial that the data in the training set remain consistent over time to ensure the reliability of the model.
7. **Diversity of Examples**: The training set must contain a variety of examples for each class to learn to recognize the different manifestations of the same class.
8. **Attribute Relevance**: Not all attributes present in the training set are necessarily useful for classification. Some may even be harmful if they introduce noise or bias.
9. **Regular Updates**: In a constantly evolving world, it is crucial to regularly update the training set to reflect the latest trends and developments.

By considering these criteria, you can improve the quality and performance of your training set, thus contributing to the creation of more accurate and reliable machine learning models.

3.2 Computational Complexity and Feasibility

The computational complexity of the BMA-Measure is a critical aspect to consider, particularly in the context of large datasets. Calculating various components of the BMA-Measure, such as assessing representativeness, noise, and redundancy, involves processing substantial amounts of data, which can pose scalability challenges.

The time complexity of the algorithm depends on factors such as dataset size, attribute dimensionality, and the number of classes. Evaluating class distribution, attribute relevance, and other metrics may require multiple iterations through the dataset, contributing to computational overhead. Moreover, processing large matrices or vectors for metric computation adds to the computational workload.

To address these challenges and ensure the feasibility of the BMA-Measure for large datasets, optimization techniques and algorithmic improvements are paramount. Techniques such as parallel processing, distributed computing, and memory-efficient data structures can significantly reduce computation time and memory overhead. Additionally, employing algorithms tailored to specific metrics within the BMA-Measure can enhance efficiency and scalability.

By addressing computational complexity considerations and implementing optimization strategies, the BMA-Measure can be effectively applied to large datasets, providing valuable insights into training data quality for machine learning tasks.

3.3 A-Measure: Initial Attempt and Experimentation

This approach represents our first attempt to tackle a colossal and complex task. We focused on the following criteria: optimal size of the training set, representativeness, minimization of anomalies, good class distribution, and balanced distribution of values for each attribute. These criteria were decomposed into sub-problems with specific metrics for each aspect. We initiated this modular approach to provide concrete and effective solutions to these crucial challenges in training set evaluation.

Metric for Determining the Optimal Size of the Training Set:
Currently, it is difficult to evaluate the optimal size of a training set because it influences two other essential criteria. A small training set can result in insufficient representativeness, while a large training set can generate redundancy and noise. We plan to study a metric to evaluate this criterion after mastering the evaluation of the other criteria.

Our next step will be to generate an optimal training set using the BMA-Measure. Although the BMA-Measure does not directly evaluate the size of the training set, we plan to modify the size of the generated training set, both upwards and downwards, to study its influence on its quality.

We intuitively assume that increasing the size of the training set will initially lead to an improvement in its quality, followed by stabilization or slight decrease. This intuition will be tested and validated in our future work.

3.4 Metric for Evaluating the Representativeness of the Training Set Relative to the Corpus

The evaluation of the representativeness of the training set relative to the corpus can be subdivided into two parts:

a. **Appearance of the majority or all classes**

This metric, denoted as A, is calculated by dividing the number of classes appearing in the training set by the total number of classes in the corpus.

$$A = \frac{\text{Number of classes appearing in the training set}}{\text{Number of classes in the corpus}} \tag{1}$$

A maximum score for A, which ranges from 0 to 1, indicates that the majority of classes in the corpus are represented in the training set. A score close to zero indicates a low representation of classes in the training set.

b. **Appearance of the majority or all possible attribute values.**

We start by evaluating the attributes using the elementary metric denoted as Bi for each attribute i, which is calculated by dividing the number of values present in the training set for attribute i by the total number of possible values for that attribute in the corpus.

$$B_i = \frac{\text{Number of values appearing in the training set for attribute i}}{\text{Number of possible values in the corpus for attribute i}} \tag{2}$$

A maximum score for Bi, also ranging from 0 to 1, indicates that most of the possible values for the attribute or class are represented in the training set. Finally, the overall weighting of the training set, denoted as B, is obtained by summing the product of the Bi scores with importance coefficients for each attribute, then dividing by the total number of attributes, including the class.

$$B = \sum_{i=1}^{n} (X_i * B_i)/n \tag{3}$$

where: xi: is an importance coefficient for significant attributes such as the class, initialized to 1, and n: is the number of attributes including the class.

A maximum score for B, also ranging from 0 to 1, indicates an optimal representativeness of the training set compared to the corpus.

c. **Metric for Determining the Optimal Size of the Training Set.**

This metric aims to evaluate issues of redundancy, noise, and non-discriminative instances in the training set.

- **Noise**: An instance containing noise means that one or more of its values are missing or incorrect.
- **Redundancy**: An instance repeated one or more times in the training set.
- **Non-discriminative instances**: This refers to a set of instances sharing the same combination of attribute values but classified into two or more different classes.

To evaluate this reduction, we introduce a metric C which is calculated as follows:

$$C = 1 - \left(\frac{\text{(nbr noise (ts) + nbr redundancy(ts) + nbr nondiscriminative instance (ts))}}{\text{Number of instance in the training set}} \right) \tag{4}$$

d. **Good Distribution of Classes**

The number of instances in the training set is divided by the total number of possible classes, including those not present in the training set, i.e., the total number of classes in the corpus. The average per class is calculated as follows:

$$\text{Average}_{\text{instance by class}} = \frac{\text{Number of instances in the training set}}{\text{Number of classes in the training set}} \tag{5}$$

Moy represents the recommended optimal number of instances per class for a training set.

In statistics, the distribution is assessed by variance, as follows:

$$D_{primary} = \frac{\sum_{k=1}^{g} (\text{Number of instances in the training set (class k)} - \text{Average}_{\text{instance by class}})^2}{\text{Number of instance in the training set}} \tag{6}$$

where g is the number of classes appearing in the corpus. If a class k does not appear in the training set, the number of instances for class k is zero.

Dprimary represents the evaluation of instance distribution among classes and should be minimal to indicate an optimal distribution. The higher Dprimary increases, the worse the distribution.

To normalize this metric, it is divided by its maximum possible value, representing a highly unfavorable distribution where each class contains only one instance, except one which contains the remaining instances. This is represented by *WorstD*, calculated as follows:

$$D_{worst} = \frac{(\text{Maxinstance} - \text{Average}_{\text{instance by class}})^2 + \sum_{k=1}^{g} (1 - \text{Average}_{\text{instance by class}})^2}{\text{Number of instance in the training set}} \tag{7}$$

where g is the number of classes appearing in the corpus, and Max_instance represents the maximum number of instances that the most populated class will contain in the case of an unfavorable distribution, while the other classes will contain only one instance each.

Finally, we define D as the division of *D*primary by *WorstD*, providing a normalized measure of instance distribution quality among classes.

D should be minimal to indicate an optimal distribution. To obtain a function to maximize, we can rewrite D as follows:

$$D = 1 - (D_{primary}/D_{Worst}) \tag{8}$$

The value of D varies between 0 and 1 and should be minimal to indicate an optimal distribution of instances among classes. When D tends toward 0, it means the distribution is optimal. However, if D increases and converges toward 1, it indicates a less favorable distribution.

e. **Good distribution of possible values for each attribute.**

The most balanced distribution of values for each attribute is obtained by dividing the number of instances in the training set by the number of possible values for each attribute, including those that do not appear in the training set, considering the number of possible values for each attribute in the corpus.

$$Average_i = \frac{\text{Number of instances in the training set}}{\text{Number of possible values for attribute i in the corpus}} \tag{9}$$

The variable *Averagei* represents the optimal number of instances per value for attribute i in the training set, assuming that all possible values of attribute i in the corpus also appear there.

In statistics, the distribution is evaluated by variance, so the primary Ei metric measures the distribution of instances for each value of attribute i.

$$E_{i\_primary} = \frac{\sum_{k=1}^{m} (\text{Number of instances in the training set(attribute i = value k)} - Average_i)^2}{\text{Number of instances in the training set}} \tag{10}$$

where m is the number of possible values for each attribute in the corpus. If a value k of attribute i does not appear in the training set, the number of instances where attribute i is equal to value k is zero.

We need to normalize this metric for each attribute i, by dividing it by the largest value. Thus, the worst distribution occurs when there is only one instance for each possible value of attribute i (compared to the corpus), except one possible value of attribute i (compared to the corpus) that contains the rest of the instances. The metric for bad distribution *WorstEistD* is defined as follows:

$$WorstE_i = \frac{(\text{Max\_insantce}_i - Average_i)^2 + \sum_{k=1}^{m-1}(1 - Average_i)^2}{\text{Number of instances in the training set}} \quad (11)$$

where:

- **m** is the number of possible values for each attribute i in the corpus.
- **Max_instance_i** = Total number of instances - number of possible values for attribute i (corpus) + 1.
- **g** is the number of classes.

Then, the metric *Ei* is calculated as follows:

$$E_i = E_{i\_primary} / WorstE_i \quad (12)$$

The value of E is between 0 and 1. It should be minimal and represents the evaluation of the distribution of possible values for each attribute. The closer E gets to 0, the more optimal the distribution is. The higher E increases and converges toward 1, the worse the distribution.

Finally, we calculate the overall weighting of the training set E:

$$E = 1 - \sum_{i=1}^{h}(x_i * E_i)/h \quad (13)$$

where

- *xi* is an importance coefficient for important attributes, such as the class, initialized to 1.
- **h** is the number of attributes.

3.5 The Overall Formula: BMA-Measure

After dividing the problem into subproblems and proposing a solution for each elementary subproblem, we will now summarize all the elementary solutions to formulate the general solution to the problem.

$$BMA - MEASURE = \frac{(a * A) + (b * B) + (c * C) + (d * D) + (e * E)}{a + b + c + d + e} \quad (14)$$

a, b, c, d, e: weighting coefficients of criteria

The interpretation of the BMA-Measure should refer to the following Table 1.

Table 1. Interpretation de la BMA-Measure

0–0,01	0,01–0,10	0,10–0,40	0,40–0,60	0,60-,090	0,90–0,99	0,99–1
Null	Very Poor	Poor	Average	Good	Very Good	Excellent

4 Conclusion and Perspectives

In conclusion, evaluating the training set in the field of machine learning is a complex task that requires a systematic and rigorous approach. Through this article, several criteria were explored for assessing the quality of the training set, such as optimal size, representativeness, and distribution of classes and values for each attribute. Each of these criteria plays a crucial role in the overall performance of the machine learning model. It is important to note that evaluating the training set goes beyond applying a few metrics but requires a deep understanding of the data context and model objectives. Indeed, the quality of the training set directly influences the model's ability to generalize and make accurate decisions in new scenarios.

As future work, it is planned to further explore these criteria and study their impact on different types of machine learning models. Additionally, it is intended to develop tools and techniques for more efficient and precise evaluation of the training set. Ultimately, the goal of this projected here report is to provide machine learning practitioners with robust guidelines and methodologies for creating high - quality training sets, thereby improving the performance of machine learning models in various application domains.

References

1. Smith, J.: Enhancing training set quality for improved classification accuracy. J. Mach. Learn. Res. (2022)
2. Garcia, M.: Evaluating supervised learning models: a comparative study. In: Proceedings of the International Conference on Artificial Intelligence (2021)
3. Lee, H.: Impact of training set size on classification performance. IEEE Trans. Pattern Anal. Mach. Intell. (2020)
4. Wang, Y.: Addressing class imbalance in training sets for improved classification. Data Min. Knowl. Discov. (2019)
5. Kim, S.: Ensuring fairness in training sets: a case study in healthcare. J. Artif. Intell. Med. (2018)
6. Chen, L.: A novel approach to training set selection for improved classification performance. Pattern Recogn. Lett. (2017)
7. Rodriguez, A.: Exploring the impact of noisy labels on training set quality. In: Proceedings of the International Conference on Machine Learning (2016)
8. Park, S.: Handling class imbalance in training sets: a comparative study. Data Min. Knowl. Discov. (2015)
9. Liu, Y.: Improving training set quality using active learning. IEEE Trans. Knowl. Data Eng. (2014)
10. Wang, X.: Assessing the impact of feature selection on classification accuracy. J. Artif. Intell. Res. (2013)

Dynamic Model Integration in the Articulated Manipulator Trajectory Planning

Inas Saoud[1]([envelope]) [ORCID], Asaad Chahboun[1] [ORCID], Naoufal Raissouni[2] [ORCID], Hatim Idriss Jaafari[1], Nizar Ben Achhab[1], and Soufiane Mezroui[1]

[1] Mathematics and Intelligent Systems Research Team, National School of Applied Sciences-Tangier, Abdelmalek Essaadi University, Tangier, Morocco
`inas.saoud@etu.uae.ac.ma`
[2] National School of Applied Sciences-Tetuan, Abdelmalek Essaadi University, Tetuan, Morocco

Abstract. This paper aims to incorporate the dynamic model into the trajectory planning for a 4-degree-of-freedom articulated manipulator. The trigonometric S-curve trajectory planning methodology minimizes overall trajectory duration while maintaining good smoothness by adopting a modified sine jerk profile. Compared to previous studies, this approach offers significant reductions in execution time, up to 21.6% shorter. However, this method is purely kinematic trajectory planning, focusing on joint positions, velocities, accelerations, and jerks. It may not fully capture the dynamic behavior of the manipulator. The dynamic model is derived using the Lagrange formulation, a powerful tool in robotics that considers the manipulator's physical properties like masses, inertia, and gravitational effects. By incorporating this model, we can predict joint torque profiles throughout the planned path. This systematic integration of the manipulator's dynamics into trajectory planning offers valuable insight into torque variations throughout the motion profile, leading to more reliable and efficient motion generation and ultimately improving the performance of the manipulator.

Keywords: Trajectory Planning · Modified Sine Jerk Profile · Dynamic Model · Lagrange Formulation · Torque Profiles

1 Introduction

The picking manipulator is an essential tool for harvesting; it is the part by which the robot gets into contact with the ripe fruit to detach it from the plant without damaging either the plant or the target strawberry. To achieve a high-accuracy harvesting operation without harming the fragile strawberries, high-precision motions are important. A smooth trajectory significantly reduces structure vibration and positioning error during manipulator movements. But it takes a little longer to reach the desired pose. The objective of this study is to identify the most effective, smooth, and time-optimal point-to-point trajectory planning method that responds to the requirements of a fast and precise harvesting cycle. This is intended to enhance both productivity and product quality. Numerous methods

H. Badir et al. (Eds.): INTIS 2024, CCIS 2645, pp. 200–212, 2026.
https://doi.org/10.1007/978-3-032-14964-0_16

for generating smooth trajectories have been explored over the last few decades, with a growing demand to replace traditional heavy mechanical structures with lightweight systems [1].

As this harvesting operation requires high precision, the continuity of the trajectory up to the jerk level must be ensured. Non-continuity of the jerk profile causes vibrations in the structure, accompanied by extra stabilization time at target points. The most common trajectory approach adopted to generate smooth profiles up to the jerk is the use of higher-order polynomials [2]. Fang et al. [3] presented the advantages of using the seventh-order polynomial method to generate the joint trajectory of a robotic arm with seven degrees of freedom. It reduces the vibration problems and improves the stability of the mechanism. However, the use of high-order polynomials to achieve a high level of smoothness results in large oscillations in the trajectories and high maximum values for the kinematic parameters. In addition, the computational load on the controller becomes more complex and time-consuming because of a large number of polynomial coefficients [1, 4], which have an impact on the robots' ability to operate in real-time.

As an alternative for generating a continuous jerk profile, many researchers recommend using S-curve trajectory planning. This approach meets the needs of fast and high-accuracy positioning operations with low computational costs. Fang et al. [4] briefly reviewed and discussed common S-curve models, which can be divided into two main classifications: polynomial S-curve models and trigonometric S-curve models. Wu [5] adopted the fourth-order S-curve method to create continuous trajectories up to the jerk level for a five-degree-of-freedom robotic manipulator. The second approach of the S-curve method involves deriving the jerk curve from a trigonometric function. This jerk function guarantees the smoothness of the jerk curve and ensures high-order continuity right up to the snap. This further improves the overall stability of the robot's motion. Valente et al. [6] adopted the S-curve model with a three-phase sine-jerk profile. This model enabled the 6-DOF serial robot ReRob I to generate smooth joint movements while respecting kinematic constraints. Fang et al. [7] studied the seven-segment sinusoidal jerk motion profile. They proposed an analytical optimization procedure to determine the optimal motion parameters that reduce both the execution time and residual vibration.

This improvement in movement smoothness requires a slightly longer time to reach the target position. To enable sufficient exploitation of the actuation capability, the constant jerk phase is included in motion profiles. As a result, the total motion duration can be minimized. In this case, the trajectory curves are extended to fifteen segments while maintaining the smoothness level of the trajectory. The constant jerk phase is introduced in the modified sinusoidal jerk model proposed by Fang et al. [8]. This approach generates smooth and time-optimal joint trajectories for robotic manipulators. The designed 15-phase sine jerk model achieves faster trajectories than the conventional 3-phase sine jerk trajectory profile. It reduces execution times by up to 24.5% and also leads to an average 23.4% reduction in jerk amplitudes. Fang et al. [4] presented a 15-segment S-curve trajectory planning method based on a piecewise sigmoid jerk function. The generated trajectories are infinitely continuously differentiable under given kinematic constraints. In the previous methods, enhancing the trajectory smoothness level came at the cost of longer execution times and more complex computations. However, the sigmoid and modified sinusoid jerk models strike a trade-off between speed, motion smoothness, and computational complexity. Even if the trajectory segments extend up to fifteen for these two models, the increase in complexity remains reasonable and easier to manage by the controller than the high-order polynomial trajectory.

We adopted the modified sinusoidal jerk model to generate the joint trajectories of the harvesting manipulator because the jerk function of this method is simple and easy to program compared to the sigmoid function. The corresponding time evolution of the acceleration, velocity, and displacement profiles can be derived directly from the integration of the jerk function. This method provides explicit mathematical formulas for acceleration, velocity, and displacement, offering a clear and precise understanding of the system's behavior. However, the expressions of acceleration, speed, and displacement are not available for the sigmoid S-curve model because its jerk function is not analytically integrable.

The study also aims to predict joint torque profiles at each joint throughout the motion profiles. Therefore, we integrate the dynamical model of the robotic system into the trajectory planning process. The dynamical model captures the relationship between joint torques, velocities, accelerations, and the resulting motion of the robot. In robotics, the common methods used for dynamic computations are Lagrange formulations and Newton-Euler methods [9–11]. The Euler-Lagrange equations of motion simplify the formulation of the dynamic equations for the 4-degree-of-freedom (DoF) articulated manipulator, enabling a comprehensive analysis of its motion and behavior by treating the manipulator as a whole [12, 13]. For that reason, the dynamic model of the robotic manipulator was presented based on the Lagrange formulations to compute the torque requirements at different points along the planned trajectory. This was achieved using Matlab software to evaluate the resulting torque profiles for each joint.

2   The Harvesting Robot Presentation

2.1   4-DOF Articulated Manipulator

The strawberry harvesting robot consists of two main subsystems: an articulated manipulator and a mobile platform. The manipulator is mounted on the mobile platform. The strawberry plants are arranged in parallel rows on a table-based system. The mobile platform traverses the aisles of a tabletop strawberry farm, stopping at designated picking locations. At each stop, the robot activates the manipulator to harvest the ripe fruits one by one. The robot manipulator is designed in SolidWorks, as shown in Fig. 1. The first articulation of the manipulator is the base joint, and the other three are the shoulder, elbow, and wrist joints. Each joint is controlled by its own motor. l_1, l_2, l_3, and l_4 represent the lengths of the first link, upper arm, lower arm, and end-effector, respectively. θ_1, θ_2, θ_3, and θ_4 are the angular positions of the waist, shoulder, elbow, and wrist, respectively.

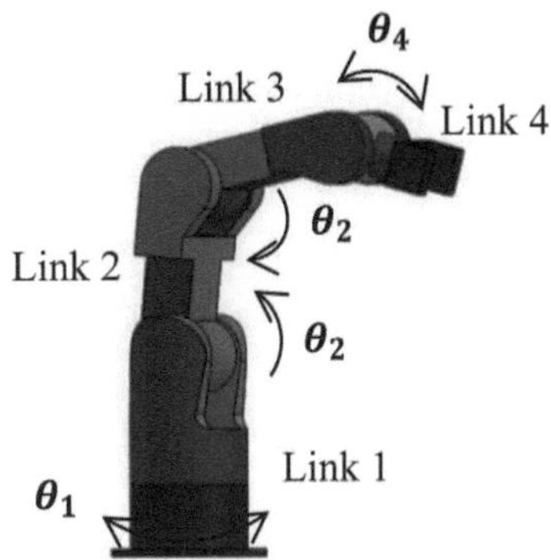

Fig. 1. SolidWorks design of the harvesting manipulator.

2.2 Picking Cycle of the Harvesting Manipulator

The harvesting process includes the following tasks: strawberry detection, localization, detachment, and placement. The vision system is responsible for the target perception operation. Once the fruit position is detected, the designed robot manipulator processes the picking cycle, which consists of the following steps as shown in Fig. 2: At the beginning, the manipulator moves towards the fruit location from the initial picking position at point P_0. When the fruit is reached, the end-effector is tasked with detaching the fruit from the plant, and then it steps back horizontally to avoid collision with an obstacle. Afterward, the fruit is transferred to the container, which is also placed on the mobile platform. To complete the picking cycle, the manipulator returns to the initial position.

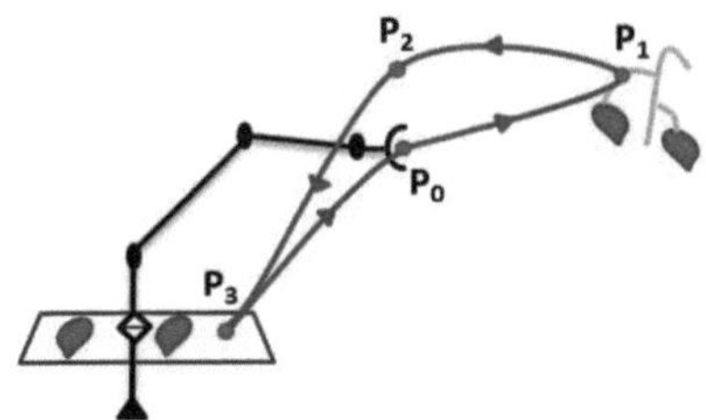

Fig. 2. Picking cycle steps.

3 Trajectory Planning

3.1 Modified Sine-Jerk Model Mathematical Formulation

Figure 3 presents the motion profiles of the designed 15-segment sinusoidal jerk model proposed in [8]. This model can be exactly defined with four time parameters: T_s, T_j, T_a, and T_v, which represent the duration of the sine jerk phase, the constant jerk phase, the constant acceleration phase, and the constant velocity phase, respectively. The overall duration of the motion is computed as follows:

$$T_J = 8T_{s,J} + 4T_{j,J} + 2T_{a,J} + T_{v,J} \tag{1}$$

204   I. Saoud et al.

$\dddot{\theta}_{peak}$, $\ddot{\theta}_{peak}$, and $\dot{\theta}_{peak}$ refer to the peak values of jerk, acceleration, and velocity, respectively. The jerk profile of this s-curve model is defined by a piecewise trigonometric function expressed below:

$$\dddot{\theta}(t) = \begin{cases} \dddot{\theta}_{peak} \sin\left(\frac{\pi}{2T_s}\tau_i\right), & t_0 \leq t < t_1, t_{12} \leq t < t_{13} \\ \dddot{\theta}_{peak}, & t_1 \leq t < t_2, t_{13} \leq t < t_{14} \\ \dddot{\theta}_{peak} \sin\left(\frac{\pi}{2}\left(1+\frac{\tau_i}{T_s}\right)\right), & t_2 \leq t < t_3, t_{14} \leq t \leq t_{15} \\ 0, & t_3 \leq t < t_4, t_7 \leq t < t_8, t_{11} \leq t < t_{12} \\ -\dddot{\theta}_{peak} \sin\left(\frac{\pi}{2T_s}\tau_i\right), & t_4 \leq t < t_5, t_8 \leq t < t_9 \\ -\dddot{\theta}_{peak}, & t_5 \leq t < t_6, t_9 \leq t < t_{10} \\ -\dddot{\theta}_{peak} \sin\left(\frac{\pi}{2}\left(1+\frac{\tau_i}{T_s}\right)\right), & t_6 \leq t < t_7, t_{10} \leq t < t_{11} \end{cases} \quad (2)$$

where t_i ($i = 0, 1, ..., 15$) is the time boundary of each segment, $\tau_i = t - t_i$ is the time relative to the commencement of the interval $[t_i, t_{i+1}]$ ($i = 0, 1, ..., 14$). The formulas for acceleration, velocity, and displacement with respect to time can be found by integrating the jerk function as given by:

$$\begin{cases} \ddot{\theta}(t) = \ddot{\theta}(t_i) + \int_{t_i}^{t} \dddot{\theta}(t)dt \\ \dot{\theta}(t) = \dot{\theta}(t_i) + \int_{t_i}^{t} \ddot{\theta}(t)dt \\ \Delta\theta(t) = \theta(t_i) + \int_{t_i}^{t} \dot{\theta}(t)dt \end{cases} \quad (3)$$

As illustrated in Fig. 3, at $t = t_3$, the acceleration attains its peak value. Using the formula of acceleration in the segment $[t_2, t_3]$ in Eq. (3), the peak acceleration is defined by:

$$\ddot{\theta}_{peak} = \dddot{\theta}_{peak}\left(\frac{4T_s}{\pi} + T_j\right) \quad (4)$$

Similarly, at $t = t_7$, the peak velocity is attained, and we use the formula of velocity in the segment $[t_6, t_7]$ from Eq. (3) to determine the peak velocity:

$$\dot{\theta}_{peak} = \ddot{\theta}_{peak}\left(2T_s + T_j + T_a\right) \quad (5)$$

Let us define $\Delta\theta$ as the angular displacement of a joint. The total displacement of the joint can be identified as follows:

$$\Delta\theta_t = \dot{\theta}_{peak}\left(4T_s + 2T_j + T_a + T_v\right) \quad (6)$$

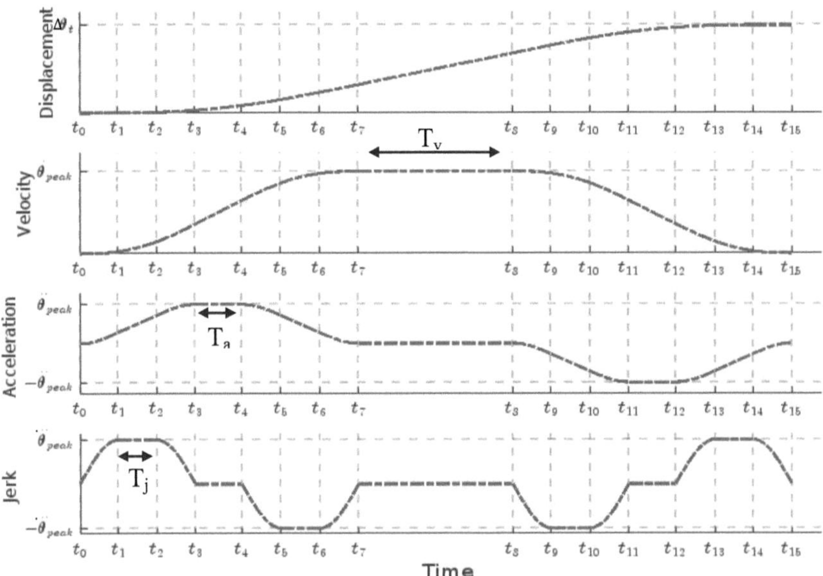

Fig. 3. Angular jerk, acceleration, velocity, and displacement profiles of the modified sinusoidal jerk model.

3.2 The Optimal Time Parameters

The aim of this section is to determine the minimum time required to displace the joint J. So we calculate the shortest time parameters T_s, T_j, T_a, and T_v within the given kinematic constraints without needing any optimization algorithms such as polynomials and splines methods [5]. The time periods T_a and T_v can disappear in cases of short angular displacement. More clearly, θ_{ref2} is the minimum rotation angle that allows the angular velocity to reach its maximal value, while θ_{ref1} represents the minimum rotation angle required to reach the maximum angular acceleration, with $\theta_{ref2} > \theta_{ref1}$. The expressions of the critical angles are defined as follows:

$$\theta_{ref2} = \frac{3\pi}{4+\pi} \times \frac{\ddot{\theta}_{max}\dot{\theta}_{max}}{\dddot{\theta}_{max}} + \frac{(\dot{\theta}_{max})^2}{\ddot{\theta}_{max}} \tag{7}$$

$$\theta_{ref1} = 2\left(\frac{3\pi}{4+\pi}\right)^2 \frac{(\ddot{\theta}_{max})^3}{(\dddot{\theta}_{max})^2} \tag{8}$$

The equations of the four time parameters T_s, T_j, T_a, and T_v depend on the maximum angular velocity, maximum angular acceleration, maximum angular jerk, and rotation angle. Their expressions change according to the joint rotation angle $\Delta\theta$. There are three cases in which the motion profiles change:

Case I: $\Delta\theta \geq \theta_{ref2}$. In this case, the acceleration and velocity can reach their maximum values ($|\ddot{\theta}_{peak}| = \ddot{\theta}_{max}$, $|\dot{\theta}_{peak}| = \dot{\theta}_{max}$) for a period of time T_v et T_a, respectively, because the angular displacement is sufficiently large. Thus, the motion profiles include all four time periods, i.e., the existence of fifteen trajectory segments. We take $T_s = T_j$, and according to Eq. (4), the expressions of T_s and T_j are obtained as follows:

$$T_s = T_j = \frac{\pi \ddot{\theta}_{max}}{(4 + \pi)\dddot{\theta}_{max}} \tag{9}$$

From Eq. (5), the formula for constant acceleration time can be written as:

$$T_a = \frac{\dot{\theta}_{max}}{\ddot{\theta}_{max}} - \left(2T_s + T_j\right) \tag{10}$$

After calculating the time periods T_s, T_j, and T_a, the duration of the constant velocity phase required by joint displacement $\Delta\theta$ can be directly given by Eq. (6):

$$T_v = \frac{\Delta\theta}{\dot{\theta}_{max}} - \left(4T_s + 2T_j + T_a\right) \tag{11}$$

Case II: $\theta_{ref1} \leq \Delta\theta < \theta_{ref2}$. In this instance, the acceleration can reach its limit value ($|\ddot{\theta}_{peak}| = \ddot{\theta}_{max}$) but the velocity cannot achieve its maximum value ($|\dot{\theta}_{peak}| < \dot{\theta}_{max}$) because the angular displacement is small. Thus, the period of time T_v disappears; $T_v = 0$ s. Under this condition, T_s and T_j maintain the same formula, and the expression of T_a is obtained by substituting Eq. (5) into Eq. (6) as follows:

$$T_a = -\left(3T_s + \frac{3T_j}{2}\right) + \sqrt{\left(T_s + \frac{T_j}{2}\right)^2 + \frac{\Delta\theta}{\ddot{\theta}_{max}}} \tag{12}$$

Case III: $\Delta\theta < \theta_{ref1}$. The maximum speed and acceleration cannot be reached because the angle of rotation is too small, so ($|\ddot{\theta}_{peak}| < \ddot{\theta}_{max}$ and $|\dot{\theta}_{peak}| < \dot{\theta}_{max}$). In this case, the constant velocity phase and the constant acceleration phase disappear in motion profiles; $T_v = T_a = 0$. The only periods that exist are T_s and T_j. In this case, the sine and constant jerk time periods are determined by the angular displacement $\Delta\theta$ and jerk limit:

$$T_s = T_j = \sqrt[3]{\frac{\pi \Delta\theta}{18(4 + \pi)\dddot{\theta}_{max}}} \tag{13}$$

Once the primary time periods have been determined, we pass to coordinate the motions of all active joints to guarantee a steady motion of the end-effector.

3.3 Coordinate the Robot's Motion

After identifying the four key periods for all joints, the overall duration of the motion for each joint is calculated using Eq. (1). It's the minimum trajectory duration T_J for a joint J with respect to kinematic constraints. However, the value of T_J can be different from one axis of rotation to another. As a result, the four rotation joints start at the same time but reach their end positions at different times.

Controlling each joint independently with respect to time may impose stress on the robot actuators, which decreases the precision of the mechanism's movements

[4]. Time synchronization of multi-joint motions is important for harvesting fragile fruit. Time-coordinated motion implies that all joints should complete their movements simultaneously, which can improve the steadiness of the manipulator's movements [5].

In this synchronization approach, the synchronization time is the longest of the execution times calculated for all joints, $T_{syn} = \max\{T_J\}$ ($J = 1, \ldots, 4.$). The previous calculated trajectory time of each actuator is readjusted to T_{syn}. Once we define the new common duration, we need to determine its corresponding time parameters as follows:

$$
\begin{cases}
T_{s,J}^{syn} = k_J T_{s,J} \\
T_{j,J}^{syn} = k_J T_{j,J} \\
T_{a,J}^{syn} = k_J T_{a,J} \\
T_{v,J}^{syn} = k_J T_{v,J}
\end{cases}
\tag{14}
$$

where $K_J = \frac{T_{syn}}{T_J}$ is the synchronization factor. In Eq. (14), the original time parameters will be scaled up by K_J to find the new time parameters. The peak values of angular jerk, acceleration, and velocity corresponding to the extended time parameters are given by the following formulas:

$$
\begin{cases}
\dddot{\theta}_{peak}^{syn} = \dfrac{\dddot{\theta}_{max}}{K_J^3} \\[2mm]
\ddot{\theta}_{peak}^{syn} = \dfrac{\ddot{\theta}_{peak}}{K_J^2} \\[2mm]
\dot{\theta}_{peak}^{syn} = \dfrac{\dot{\theta}_{peak}}{K_J}
\end{cases}
\tag{15}
$$

Finally, the new maximum values of the kinematic parameters are inserted into the jerk, acceleration, velocity, and displacement functions, $\dddot{\theta}(t)$, $\ddot{\theta}(t)$, $\dot{\theta}(t)$, and $\Delta\theta(t)$, respectively.

4 Dynamics Model

Determining the torque requirements for each joint of a robotic manipulator involves presenting the dynamic model of the system. The equation of motion is presented below:

$$
\frac{d}{dt}\left(\frac{\partial L}{\partial \dot{\theta}_i}\right) - \left(\frac{\partial L}{\partial \theta_i}\right) = \tau_i
\tag{16}
$$

where $L = K - P$ is the Lagrangian function, K and P are the total kinetic and potential energy, respectively. τ_i, θ_i, and $\dot{\theta}_i$ are joint i torque, position, and velocity, respectively, with $i = 1$ to 4. The expression of K is defined as follows:

$$
K = \frac{1}{2}\dot{q}^T D(q)\dot{q}
\tag{17}
$$

$q = [\theta_1\ \theta_2\ \theta_3\ \theta_4]^T$ is the vector of joint positions, $\ddot{q}$ and $\dot{q}$ are the vector of joint accelerations and velocities. $D \in R^{4\times4}$ is the inertia matrix, and its expression is given below:

$$
D = \sum_{i=0}^{4} m_i J_{v_i}(q)^T J_{v_i}(q) + J_{w_i}(q)^T R_i^0(q) I_i R_i^0(q)^T J_{w_i}(q)
\tag{18}
$$

J_v and J_w are the Jacobian linear and angular velocities, respectively. m_i represents the mass of the i-th link. I_i is the moment of inertia matrix in the body-attached frame of link i. The moment of inertia of each link in a mechanical system was calculated using Solidworks software. R_i^0 is the rotation matrix with respect to the base of the frame attached to link i. The total potential energy of the system is presented by the following formula:

$$P = \sum_{i=0}^{4} P_i = \sum_{i=0}^{4} g^T r_{ci} m_i \tag{19}$$

where $g = [0\ 0\ -9.81\ \text{m/s}^2]^T$ is the gravity vector in the base frame, and the vector $r_{ci} \in R^3$ is the coordinate vector of the center of mass of link i. The kinetic energy and potential energy were substituted into the Euler-Lagrange equation, and it was presented in matrix form without considering the effects of friction.

$$D(q)\ddot{q} + C(q, \dot{q})\dot{q} + G(q) = \tau \tag{20}$$

$\tau \in R^{4\times1}$ is the joint torque vector, $G \in R^{4\times1}$ is the gravity force vector, and the matrix C $\in R^{4\times4}$ is centrifugal and coriolis force. This dynamic model has very high nonlinearity, so it was implemented in a Matlab environment to calculate the torque requirements at each joint.

5   Results and Discussion

We simulate the trajectory generation in the joint space of one step of the picking cycle, from the fruit realization position P_3 ($\theta_1 = 1.27$ rad, $\theta_2 = 1.21$ rad, $\theta_3 = -2.43$ rad, $\theta_4 = 1.21$ rad) to the initial position P_0 ($\theta_1 = 0$ rad, $\theta_2 = 2.2$ rad, $\theta_3 = -2.7$ rad, $\theta_4 = 0.3$ rad). The parameter values of each joint are listed in Table 1 and incorporated into the equations for position, velocity, acceleration, and jerk to simulate the motion profiles of the four joints, as shown in Fig. 4.

In Fig. 4, all fifteen segments are present in the motion profiles of the first and second joints. However, for the fourth joint, the constant velocity segment disappears due to the relatively short rotation angle. For joint 3, both constant acceleration and velocity periods are absent because of the excessively small angular displacement.

Table 1. Optimal time parameters and peak kinematic parameters after motion synchronization.

	Peak value of the kinematic parameters				Optimal time parameters		
	$\lvert \dddot{\theta}_{peak}^{syn} \rvert$	$\lvert \ddot{\theta}_{peak}^{syn} \rvert$	$\lvert \dot{\theta}_{peak}^{syn} \rvert$	T_s^{syn}	T_j^{syn}	T_a^{syn}	T_v^{syn}
Joint 1	30	4.93	1.65	0.072	0.072	0.12	0.21
Joint 2	20.45	3.75	1.4	0.08	0.08	0.13	0.09
Joint 3	5	1.25	0.412	0.11	0.11	0	0
Joint 4	17.67	3.46	1.387	0.086	0.086	0.14	0

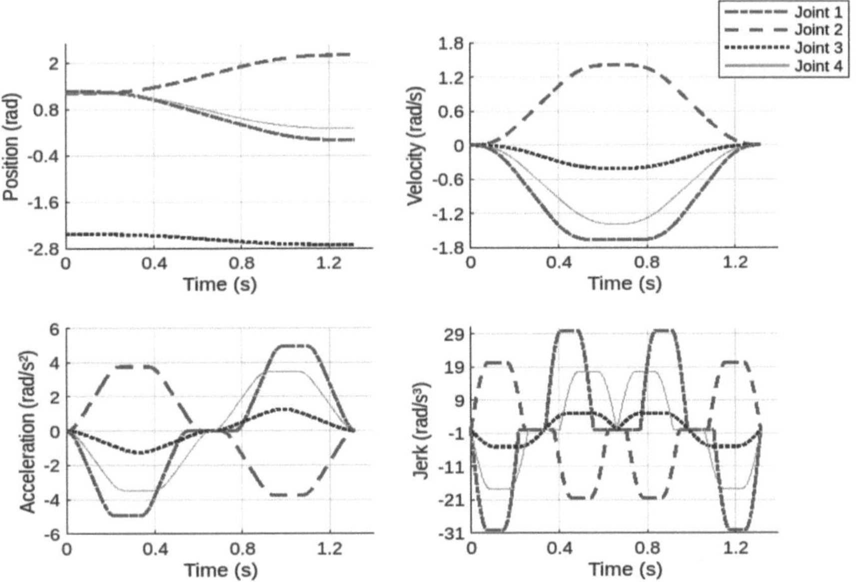

Fig. 4. The motion profiles of the four joints follow the planned trajectory.

We simulated three picking cycles using the 7-phase and 15-phase sine jerk trajectory planning methods. The execution time for each step of the picking cycles is presented in Tables 2 and 3. The average duration of one picking cycle is 4.9 s when using the 15-phase sine jerk trajectory model and 5.08 s when using the 7-phase sine jerk trajectory model. Compared with the existing harvesting manipulator, the duration of the picking cycle is shorter. The average cycle time for picking cherry tomatoes is 6.4 s for the harvesting robot proposed by Gao et al. [14]. The strawberry picking manipulator developed in [15] took about 6.1 s to finish one picking cycle. By adopting these trajectories planning methods, the total picking cycle duration is reduced by approximately 21.6% when taking the 15-phase sine jerk trajectory model and 18.7% when taking the 7-phase sine jerk trajectory model. This significant reduction in picking time translates to substantial gains in efficiency, potentially allowing for increased harvest yields. However, it's important to note that the 15-phase model offers a little more advantage in terms of time reduction.

Table 2. The execution time of the picking cycle using the 15-phase sine jerk trajectory model.

Picking cycle	Execution time of step (s)				Total duration (s)
	P_0 to P_1	P_1 to P_2	P_2 to P_3	P_3 to P_4	
1	0.99	0.88	1.38	1.32	4.57
2	1.04	1.03	1.32	1.32	4.71
3	1.45	1.17	1.4	1.4	5.42

Table 3. The execution time of the picking cycle using the 7-phase sine jerk trajectory model.

Picking cycle	Execution time of step (s)				Total duration (s)
	P_0 to P_1	P_1 to P_2	P_2 to P_3	P_3 to P_4	
1	1.04	0.93	1.42	1.36	4.75
2	1.09	1.08	1.36	1.36	4.89
3	1.49	1.21	1.45	1.45	5.6

Using MATLAB simulation, we present in Fig. 5 the torque profiles for each joint during the motion from position P_3 to P_0, based on the 15-phase trajectory planning approach. The torque profiles are smooth and rounded, with their value increasing during acceleration and deceleration phases. The desired motion was achieved without sudden jumps or drops in torque. A smoother torque profile puts less strain on the motor, potentially extending its lifespan.

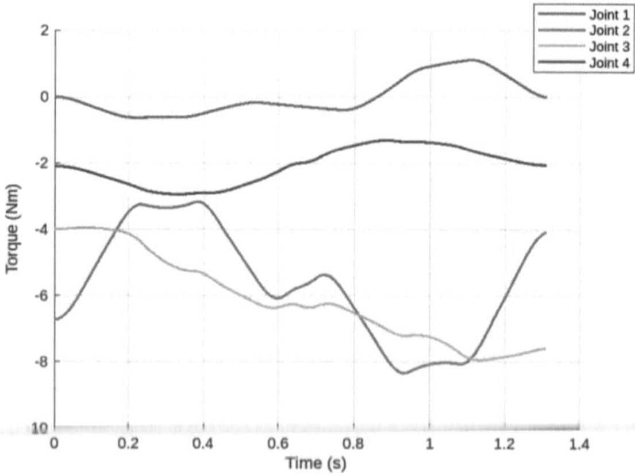

Fig. 5. The torque profile for each joint.

The 15-phase trajectory-planning approach has the ability to incorporate rapid and precise synchronized motion for the multi-axis manipulator. This method not only ensures a gentle and precise harvesting process but also minimizes losses, maintains the quality of the produce, and protects the manipulator mechanism itself. Moreover, this approach can be utilized for various other tasks in agriculture that require accuracy, such as precision planting, pesticide application, and even crop monitoring. Therefore, farmers can streamline operations, reduce labor costs, and ultimately improve overall crop yields and farm sustainability.

The chosen trajectory planning strategy significantly minimizes the jerk amplitudes of the robot's joints, resulting in smoother torque profiles with lower peak torque demands. However, despite minimizing jerk, there's no guarantee that the torque profile won't surpass the actuator's torque limitations.

6 Conclusion

In conclusion, this paper presents valuable insights into the application of the trigonometric S-curve trajectory planning methodology with a modified sine jerk profile for the 4-DOF harvesting manipulator and the way to synchronize motion for the manipulator joints. This optimal trajectory planning can effectively find a balance between speed and motion smoothness for the robotic manipulator. This approach yields picking cycle durations up to 21.6% shorter than previous harvesting robots. Then, we integrate the dynamic model of the manipulator into the trajectory planning approach using the Lagrange formulation. This approach presents a global view of torque variations throughout the joint motions. This trajectory planning method also generates smooth torque profiles. Consequently, the harvesting manipulator can enhance productivity and operate more efficiently without causing damage to the plants or crop.

This approach provides an effective solution for tasks that demand high precision while maintaining efficient operational speed. By incorporating dynamics, in future work we will integrate the dynamic constraints (torque limits) into time parameter optimization. This allows for the generation of trajectories that are not only kinematically feasible but also dynamically consistent with the manipulator's capabilities.

References

1. Lee, A., Choi, Y.: Smooth trajectory planning methods using physical limits. Proc. Inst. Mech. Eng. C J. Mech. Eng. Sci. **229**, 2127–2143 (2015). https://doi.org/10.1177/095440621 4553982
2. Lu, S., Ding, B., Li, Y.: Minimum-jerk trajectory planning pertaining to a translational 3-degree-of-freedom parallel manipulator through piecewise quintic polynomials interpolation. Adv. Mech. Eng. **12**, 168781402091366 (2020). https://doi.org/10.1177/1687814020913667
3. Fang, S., Ma, X., Qu, J., Zhang, S., Lu, N., Zhao, X.: Trajectory planning for seven-DOF robotic arm based on seventh degree polynomial. In: Jia, Y., Du, J., Zhang, W. (eds.) Proceedings of 2019 Chinese Intelligent Systems Conference, pp. 286–294. Springer, Singapore (2020). https://doi.org/10.1007/978-981-32-9686-2_34
4. Fang, Y., Hu, J., Liu, W., Shao, Q., Qi, J., Peng, Y.: Smooth and time-optimal S-curve trajectory planning for automated robots and machines. Mech. Mach. Theory **137**, 127–153 (2019). https://doi.org/10.1016/j.mechmachtheory.2019.03.019
5. Wu, G., Zhang, N.: Kinematically constrained jerk-continuous s-curve trajectory planning in joint space for industrial robots. Electronics **12**, 1135 (2023). https://doi.org/10.3390/electr onics12051135
6. Valente, A., Baraldo, S., Carpanzano, E.: Smooth trajectory generation for industrial robots performing high precision assembly processes. CIRP Ann. **66**, 17–20 (2017). https://doi.org/10.1016/j.cirp.2017.04.105
7. Fang, Y., Zhu, G.-N., Zhao, Y., Gu, C.: Design procedure for motion profiles with sinusoidal jerk for vibration reduction. Appl. Sci. **13**, 13320 (2023). https://doi.org/10.3390/app132 413320
8. Fang, Y., Qi, J., Hu, J., Wang, W., Peng, Y.: An approach for jerk-continuous trajectory generation of robotic manipulators with kinematical constraints. Mech. Mach. Theory **153**, 103957 (2020). https://doi.org/10.1016/j.mechmachtheory.2020.103957

9. Fass, T.H., Hao, G., Cantillon-Murphy, P.: Vectorized formulation of newton-euler dynamics for efficiently computing three-dimensional folding chains. J. Mech. Robot. **14**, (2022). https://doi.org/10.1115/1.4054311

10. Li, G., Huang, H., Guo, H., Li, B.: Dynamic modeling and control for a deployable grasping manipulator. IEEE Access **7**, 23000–23011 (2019). https://doi.org/10.1109/ACCESS.2019.2897689

11. Satya Durga Manohar Sahu, V., Samal, P., Kumar Panigrahi, C.: Modelling, and control techniques of robotic manipulators: a review. Mater. Today Proc. **56**, 2758–2766 (2022). https://doi.org/10.1016/j.matpr.2021.10.009

12. Lee, T.S., Alandoli, E.A.: A critical review of modelling methods for flexible and rigid link manipulators. J. Braz. Soc. Mech. Sci. Eng. **42**, 508 (2020). https://doi.org/10.1007/s40430-020-02602-0

13. Al-Qahtani, H.M., Mohammed, A.A., Sunar, M.: Dynamics and control of a robotic arm having four links. Arab. J. Sci. Eng. **42**, 1841–1852 (2017). https://doi.org/10.1007/s13369-016-2324-y

14. Gao, J., et al.: Development and evaluation of a pneumatic finger-like end-effector for cherry tomato harvesting robot in greenhouse. Comput. Electron. Agric. **197**, 106879 (2022). https://doi.org/10.1016/j.compag.2022.106879

15. Xiong, Y., Ge, Y., Grimstad, L., From, P.J.: An autonomous strawberry-harvesting robot: design, development, integration, and field evaluation. J. Field Robot. **37**, 202–224 (2020). https://doi.org/10.1002/rob.21889

Improving Machine Learning Accuracy in Detecting SQL Injection Attack Using NLP and Feature Engineering

Amjad Rattrout[1]([✉]) [iD], Majdi Jaradat[1,3] [iD], and Rashid Jayousi[2] [iD]

[1] Information Technology Engineering, AAUP, Jenin, Palestine
`amjad.rattrout@aaup.edu, m.saleh24@student.aaup.edu`
[2] Computer Science, Al-Quds University, Abu Dis, Palestine
`rjayousi@staff.alquds.edu`
[3] Ministry of Public Works and Housing, Al Bireh, Palestine
`mjaradat@mpwh.pna.ps`

Abstract. Traditional rule-based and signature-based methods face limitations in effectively identifying evolving attack techniques. To address this challenge, we propose a Detection SQL Injection Attack framework (DSQLIA), which enhances the accuracy of machine learning (ML) algorithms in detecting SQLIA. In the propose framework, we leverage Natural Language Processing (NLP) and feature engineering. NLP techniques applied to analyze the textual content of SQL queries and extract meaningful information for distinguishing between legitimate and malicious queries. Relevant features capturing the unique characteristics of SQL injection attacks identified and created through feature engineering. In the framework we evaluate different ML algorithms, including decision trees, support vector machines (SVM), and artificial neural networks (ANN) on a dataset. An accuracy, precision, recall, and F1-score performance metrics used to assess algorithm effectiveness. The results showed that the SVM algorithm achieves the highest accuracy of 0.994, followed by the decision tree with 0.975, and the ANN with 0.966. This highlights the improved performance of SVM in accurately classifying SQL queries. By combining feature engineering and NLP techniques, the DSQLIA model enhances ML accuracy in SQL injection detection, offering a valuable approach to mitigating the risks posed by these vulnerabilities in web applications.

Keywords: Machine learning · Natural Language Processing (NLP) · Web Application Security · Feature Engineering · SQL Injection

1 Introduction

With the growing importance of online applications across multiple domains, security has emerged as a vital problem. The confidentiality and integrity of sensitive data held in databases are seriously threatened by SQL injection attacks, one of the many vulnerabilities that these applications are susceptible to [1].

H. Badir et al. (Eds.): INTIS 2024, CCIS 2645, pp. 213–226, 2026.
https://doi.org/10.1007/978-3-032-14964-0_17

These attacks exploit vulnerabilities in web application input validation mechanisms, allowing unauthorized people to manipulate SQL queries and gain unauthorized access to the underlying database.

In the traditional ways of detecting and preventing SQL injection attacks used by signature-based or rule-based techniques, which often struggle to effectively identify new and evolving attack patterns. To overcome these limitations, we have turned to machine learning approaches, which have shown promise in detecting and mitigating various types of cyber threats.

To improve the effectiveness of ML algorithms in SQL injection attack detection, this research proposes the DSQLIA model. The model incorporates (NLP) and feature engineering techniques to capture the unique characteristics of SQL injection attacks and distinguish between legitimate and malicious queries. NLP techniques are employed to analyze the textual content of SQL queries. By extracting meaningful information from the queries, such as keywords, query structure, and patterns, the DSQLIA model can further improve the discrimination between normal and malicious queries. NLP techniques enable the model to understand the intent and context of SQL queries, allowing for more accurate detection of SQL injection attacks.

Furthermore, feature engineering involves the identification and creation of relevant features that provide insights into the syntax, semantic meaning, and execution behavior of SQL queries.

The research is structured into key sections. Section 3 provides a literature review, Sect. 4 SQL injection attacks overview, Sect. 5 Natural Language Processing (NLP), Sect. 6 Feature Engineering, Sect. 7 Proposed Model, Sect. 8 experimental setup and case study, Sect. 9 results and discussion and finally, Sect. 10 concludes and future work.

2   Literature Review

The detection of SQL Injection attacks using machine learning approaches has gained significant attention due to the increasing complexity and prevalence of such attacks. This literature review provides an overview of existing research and proposed solutions in this domain, along with their benefits and limitations.

The detection of SQL Injection attacks through machine learning methodologies has become a prominent area of research due to the rising complexity and prevalence of such cyber threats [2]. Utilizing machine learning algorithms enables the classification of network traffic, distinguishing between SQL Injection attacks and legitimate data, thus bolstering cybersecurity measures [3,4]. Studies have explored various classification techniques, with CNN emerging as particularly effective, boasting an accuracy rate of around 97% in detecting SQL Injection attacks [2]. Moreover, research has delved into the vulnerabilities posed by cloud computing, emphasizing the need for robust detection tools to combat SQL Injection attacks, with SVM showing promising accuracy rates, surpassing 99% in certain cases [3].

Furthermore, the intersection of SQL Injection attacks and artificial intelligence, particularly machine learning and deep learning models, has been extensively investigated to safeguard against cyber threats [5,6]. Such attacks pose significant risks to web applications, potentially compromising sensitive data and undermining system integrity. Consequently, there's a growing emphasis on leveraging machine learning algorithms to detect and prevent SQL Injection attacks, with the aim of fortifying cyber-physical systems against such vulnerabilities [5]. Additionally, the literature underscores the critical role of machine learning in addressing cybersecurity concerns, particularly in combating SQL Injection attacks, which are among the top security threats according to OWASP [7].

In parallel, research has explored innovative techniques to enhance the efficacy of SQL Injection attack detection, with a focus on integrating machine learning methods with traditional defense strategies [8]. The proposed approach involves training machine learning models to identify patterns indicative of SQL Injection attacks, thereby augmenting existing cybersecurity measures. Moreover, the literature highlights the persistent nature of SQL Injection attacks and the imperative of adopting machine learning techniques to bolster defense mechanisms [8]. These efforts underscore the ongoing pursuit of innovative solutions to mitigate the risks posed by SQL Injection attacks, with machine learning playing a pivotal role in enhancing cybersecurity protocols.

In summary, the literature review highlights the growing interest in using machine learning approaches for detecting SQL Injection attacks. Machine learning is a subfield of artificial intelligence that focuses on developing algorithms and models that enable computers to learn and make predictions or decisions without explicit programming. Many popular machine learning approaches used like Support Vector Machines (SVM) [9], Decision Trees, Artificial Neural Networks (ANN, Naive Bayes Classifier, Logistic Regression, Convolutional Neural Network (CNN) and deep learning approaches [2,3,6,10–13].

Overall, my DSQLIA model shares similarities with the existing literature in terms of leveraging ML algorithms for SQL Injection attack detection. However, it distinguishes itself by incorporating NLP and feature engineering techniques to enhance accuracy, and also the adoption of firewall (WAF). Additionally, the specific focus on the Ministry of Public Works and Housing in Palestine adds a practical and real-world context to the research.

3   SQL Injection Attacks-Overview

Confidentiality, integrity and availability considered as the safety valve in web applications. So, any focus on website functionality rather than security will cause susceptibilities in the web application, which allow the attacker to access unauthorized data [14], any stolen data will lose of confidentiality, any ability to modified in an unexpected data will lose integrity, and also Loss of availability takes place when denial of service is caused by an attacker. Based on OWASP's compilation of the top 10 web application attacks from 2013 to 2021, SQL injection remains the most prevalent type of attack targeting websites [10]. To avoid and mitigate SQL injection attacks, [6] we must know how it works and the different ways available to implement the SQL injection attack? SQL injection is a malicious query-based attack that provide information in the URL parameter, which the statement consists of SQL malicious query for information retrieval. The architecture of web application consists of three layers, presentation layer, business layer and database layer [2] (Fig. 1).

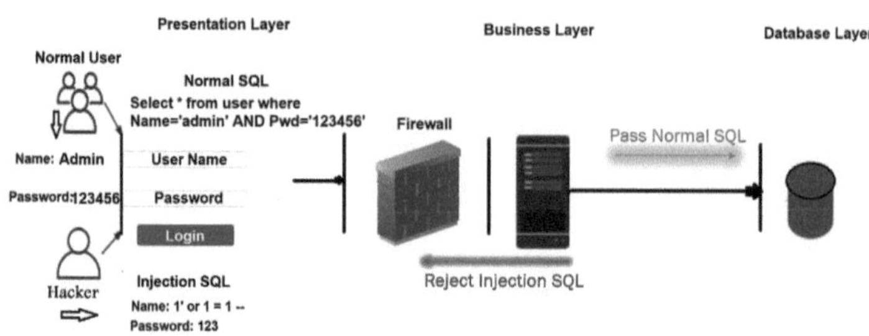

Fig. 1. The IT architecture of Ministry of Public Works and Housing

The user inputs the required information from login form, then these information's sent to the server in the form of parameter string and finally the user retrieves the information from the database [15]. That's from normal user. But unfortunately, Hacker also can access it over cyber world. The following example illustrate how SQL query execute in both normal SQL and malicious SQL. SELECT * from user where name = 'admin' AND Pwd = '123456'.

SELECT * from user where Name = '1' or 1 = 1– AND Pwd = '123' Because the injection statement (or = 1–) the list of users from user table will expose the whole database. To avoid and mitigate SQL injection attacks, we must do the following [14].

4   Natural Language Processing (NLP)

In the realm of Natural Language Processing (NLP) applied to SQL statements, the process of extracting features or variables involves transforming the textual representation of SQL queries into structured data that can be comprehended by machine learning algorithms [5]. This crucial step aims to capture pertinent information from SQL statements and represent it in a format conducive to machine learning model utilization. To extract features or variables from SQL statements, a variety of techniques can be employed. One commonly utilized approach is tokenization, wherein the SQL query is segmented into individual tokens or words [5]. This aids in identifying keywords, table names, column names, operators, and other relevant components. Additionally, syntactic analysis is employed to examine the grammatical structure of the query. This analysis identifies relationships between different elements, such as discerning the subject, predicate, and object within a SQL query [12]. Moreover, semantic analysis plays a pivotal role in understanding the meaning behind the SQL statement. This process involves mapping the SQL query to a semantic representation that encapsulates the intent or purpose of the query. For instance, it helps identify whether a query is retrieving data, updating data, or executing a specific action. Through the extraction of features or variables from SQL statements, NLP facilitates the conversion of textual SQL queries into a format effectively utilized by machine learning models. This enables the development of SQL injection detection systems, query classification models, and other applications reliant on SQL statement analysis.

5   Feature Engineering

Feature engineering plays a pivotal role in significantly enhancing the performance of machine learning models by deriving meaningful features from SQL statements, which include token frequencies, POS tags, and sentiment scores. A diverse range of techniques are employed, such as tokenization, lemmatization, POS tagging, named entity recognition (NER), sentiment analysis, topic modeling, and word frequency analysis. NER, for instance, identifies entities like database table names, which are crucial in detecting SQL injection attacks [13]. Sentiment analysis reveals the emotional tone associated with each statement, while topic modeling uncovers common themes within the dataset, and word frequency analysis identifies significant keywords. These extracted features enrich the information available to classifiers, enabling them to discern discriminative patterns and make accurate predictions. Ultimately, feature engineering enhances model accuracy, convergence speed, and generalization to unseen data, highlighting its pivotal role in various machine learning applications.

6   Proposed Model

The proposed model as shown in Fig. 2 for detecting SQL injection attacks (DSQLIA) using a machine learning approach aims to enhance web application security by analyzing user inputs and classifying them as either legitimate or potentially malicious. Traditional rule-based and signature-based methods have limitations in effectively identifying and preventing these attacks due to the constantly evolving attack techniques. To overcome these limitations, the model leverages feature engineering and Natural Language Processing (NLP) techniques to enhance its accuracy and efficiency. The process start from gathering textual data set for SQL statements from legitimate or potentially malicious, then pre-processing Cleans the data to ensure its quality and suitability for analysis [16]. Then NLP techniques are applied to analyze the textual content of SQL queries. NLP allows the model to extract meaningful information from the queries, such as identifying suspicious keywords, syntactic patterns, or unusual query structures. By incorporating NLP, the model gains a deeper understanding of the query content, enabling it to make more informed decisions in classifying queries as either legitimate or potentially malicious. Subsequently,

Feature engineering plays a crucial role in the model by extracting and creating relevant features that capture the unique characteristics of SQL injection attacks. This involves identifying and optimizing features related to SQL query syntax, semantic meaning, and execution behavior. By engineering these features, the model becomes more capable of distinguishing between normal and malicious queries, leading to improved accuracy in detecting SQL injection attacks.

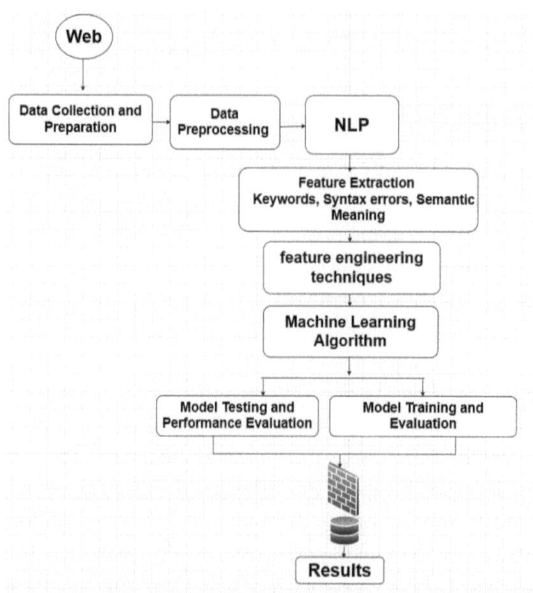

Fig. 2. DSQLIA Proposed Model

By combining feature engineering and NLP with machine learning algorithms, the proposed model enhances its ability to accurately detect SQL injection attacks. During the training phase, the model learns from a dataset that includes both legitimate and malicious queries, enabling it to identify and generalize the distinguishing characteristics of SQL injection attacks. The model can then be deployed in a production environment, where it continuously monitors incoming user inputs, applying the learned patterns to classify queries in real-time.

Overall, the integration of feature engineering, NLP techniques and firewall integration in the proposed model, strengthens its accuracy, efficiency, and adaptability in detecting SQL injection attacks. By leveraging these advanced techniques, the model provides an effective solution for enhancing web application security and mitigating the risks associated with SQL injection vulnerabilities.

7   Experiment and Case Study

Here, we aimed to detect SQL injection attacks using a machine learning approach. The following subsections explain how we implement the experiment.

7.1   Dataset

The dataset used for this study consisted nearly 23,000 SQL statements with both legitimate and malicious. The dataset were gathered from cloud records. We applied the pre-processing on data, this step involves handling missing values, removing duplicates, dealing with outliers, normalizing or scaling variables, and transforming data formats. Then Exploratory Data Analysis (EDA) were applied, to explore and visualize the data to gain a better understanding of its characteristics. Perform statistical summaries, data visualizations, and descriptive analyses to identify patterns, distributions, correlations, and outliers.

We employed natural language processing (NLP) techniques to pre-process and analyze the statements. By using tokenization technique, the textual data were splitting into individual words or tokens. We used python platform to execute the experiment, the extracted data set was saved in excel.csv file. Subsequently, Feature Engineering taken into account to Identify the most relevant features (variables) that contribute to the problem at hand. Perform feature selection techniques to choose the subset of features that are most informative, by combining or transforming existing features to improve predictive power.

The data set taken by implementing NLP techniques has been treated by Principal Component Analysis (PCA) technique to reduce dimensions. To implement PCA for dimensionality reduction, the reduced feature matrix obtained from PCA is applied as input to the classifier models, enabling improved model performance by reducing noise, eliminating redundant features, and focusing on the most informative aspects of the data as shown in Fig. 3.

7.2   Model Implementation

In this study, we employed a range of machine learning algorithms, such as decision trees, support vector machines (SVM), and Artificial neural networks, to identify SQL injection attacks.

Following the preprocessing stage, which involved applying various NLP techniques as discussed previously, we divided the dataset into training and testing sets. The training set was utilized to train the machine learning models, while the testing set was employed to assess their performance.

First, we implemented a decision tree classifier. Decision trees are a popular choice for classification tasks due to their simplicity and interpretability. The decision tree algorithm learned from the features extracted from the SQL statements and made predictions on whether a statement was vulnerable to SQL injection or not. The model equation is:

$$f(X) = \text{DecisionTree}(\text{NLP}(X)) \tag{1}$$

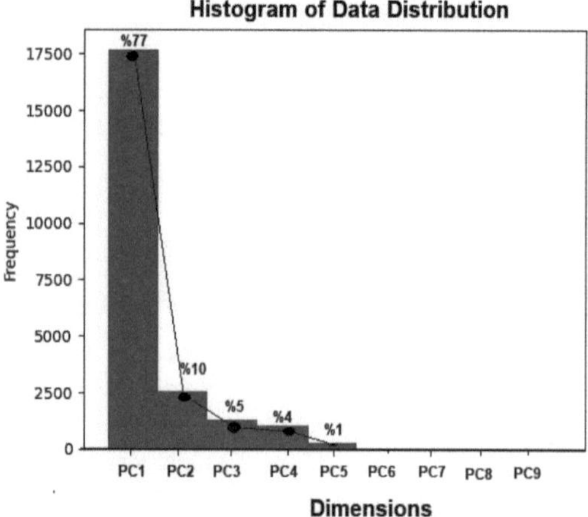

Fig. 3. Visualization for PCA that Represent most relative Data Point

where:

- X represents the input data (feature matrix).
- NLP(X) denotes the application of Natural Language Processing techniques to the input data X.
- DecisionTree($\cdot$) represents the Decision Tree model applied to the output of NLP.
- $f(X)$ is the model's output or prediction.

Next, we employed support vector machines (SVM) for classification. SVMs are known for their ability to handle high-dimensional data and nonlinear relationships. By training an SVM classifier on the features derived from the SQL statements, we aimed to classify statements as either vulnerable or non-vulnerable.

The model equation is:

$$f(X) = \text{SVM}(\text{NLP}(X)) \tag{2}$$

where:

- X represents the input data (feature matrix).
- NLP(X) denotes the application of Natural Language Processing techniques to the input data X.
- SVM($\cdot$) represents the Support Vector Machine model applied to the output of NLP.
- $f(X)$ is the model's output or prediction.

Furthermore, we utilized Artificial neural networks, specifically deep learning models, to perform the classification task. Neural networks are capable of learning complex patterns and relationships in the data. We designed a neural network architecture with appropriate layers and activation functions to capture the underlying patterns in the SQL statements and predict their vulnerability to SQL injection attacks. The model equation is:

$$f(X) = \text{ANN}(\text{NLP}(X; \Theta)) \tag{3}$$

where:

- X represents the input data (feature matrix).
- $\text{NLP}(X; \Theta)$ denotes the application of Natural Language Processing techniques to the input data X with model parameters Θ.
- $\text{ANN}(\cdot)$ represents the Artificial Neural Network model applied to the output of NLP.
- $f(X)$ is the model's output or prediction.

For each machine learning algorithm, we evaluated the model's performance using appropriate evaluation metrics such as accuracy, precision, recall, and F1 score. These metrics helped us assess the effectiveness of each algorithm in detecting SQL injection attacks [17].

By comparing the performance of different machine learning algorithms, we aimed to identify the most effective approach for detecting SQL injection vulnerabilities in the dataset. The results of this evaluation provided insights into the strengths and weaknesses of each algorithm and their suitability for this specific task.

7.3   Firewall Integration

To further strengthen our model, we integrated a firewall into the system. The firewall acted as a preventive measure by blocking or flagging suspicious SQL statements that exhibited patterns indicative of SQL injection attacks. This additional layer of security provided an added safeguard against potential vulnerabilities. In the Ministry of Public Works and Housing, we use Fortinet D500 to enhance the security measures and prevent SQL injection threats by implementing a web application firewall (WAF) feature. By comparing the inputs received by an application with a comprehensive database of known attack patterns, the WAF effectively identifies and blocks malicious SQL queries. Regular updates and patches to the signature list ensure that organizations stay proactive in mitigating the evolving threats in the cybersecurity landscape.

The integration of machine learning (ML) capabilities within Fortinet D500 empowers organizations to tailor their security measures for individual applications. Additionally, ML algorithms enable the system to differentiate between harmless anomalies and malicious activities, minimizing the impact of false positives and reducing any potential disruptions to business operations.

8   Results and Discussion

In this section, we present the results of our experiment and discuss the utilization of NLP techniques, feature engineering, and the use of a firewall to strengthen our model for detecting SQL injection attacks, finally, we implementing machine learning algorithms to evaluate our model.

By engineering meaningful features from the SQL statements, we provided rich information to the classifiers. These features enabled the models to learn discriminative patterns and make accurate predictions. By integration the firewall in our proposed model, which firewall acted as a preventive measure by blocking or flagging suspicious SQL statements that exhibited patterns indicative of SQL injection attacks. This additional layer of security provided an added safeguard against potential vulnerabilities. The results bellow for the model with using feature engineering (Table 1):

Table 1. Performance Comparison of SVM, Decision Tree, and Artificial Neural Network by Implement Feature Engineering

Measurement	SVM	Decision Tree	Artificial Neural Network
Accuracy	0.994	0.975	0.966
Precision	0.989	0.953	0.951
Recall	1.000	1.000	1.000
F1-score	0.995	0.987	0.983

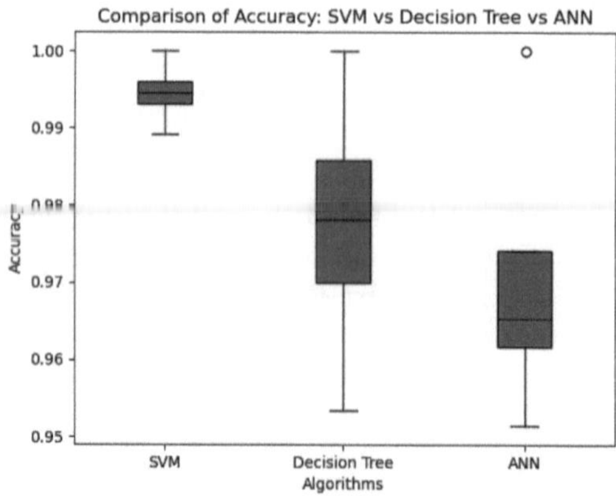

Fig. 4. The three classifiers accuracy after applying feature engineering

The table shows the comparison of classification performance among three different machine learning algorithms: Support Vector Machine (SVM), Decision Tree, and Artificial Neural Network (ANN). The performance metrics evaluated include Accuracy, Precision, Recall, and F1-score (Fig. 4).

Looking at the results, the SVM algorithm achieved the highest accuracy with a value of 0.994, followed by the Decision Tree with 0.975 and the ANN with

0.966. This indicates that SVM performed slightly better in correctly classifying the data compared to the other two algorithms.

In terms of precision, which measures the proportion of correctly predicted positive instances out of all predicted positive instances, SVM achieved a precision of 0.989, while the Decision Tree and ANN achieved 0.953 and 0.951, respectively. This suggests that SVM had a higher ability to accurately identify positive instances.

The recall metric, which measures the proportion of correctly predicted positive instances out of all actual positive instances, shows a perfect score of 1.000 for all three algorithms. This indicates that all algorithms were able to correctly identify all positive instances in the dataset.

The F1-score, which combines precision and recall into a single metric, also indicates a strong performance for all algorithms. The SVM achieved an F1-score of 0.995, followed by the Decision Tree with 0.981, and the ANN with 0.965. These scores indicate that SVM achieved the best overall balance between precision and recall.

Based on these results, it can be concluded that the SVM algorithm performed the best overall in terms of accuracy, precision, recall, and F1-score. However, both the Decision Tree and ANN algorithms also showed strong performance in classifying the data, with high recall and F1-scores.

It's worth noting that these results are specific to the dataset and evaluation metrics used in this analysis. The choice of algorithm may vary depending on the specific requirements of the problem, the nature of the data, and other factors such as computational efficiency and interpretability. Further analysis and experimentation may be needed to determine the most suitable algorithm for a particular task.

The results demonstrate that feature engineering has a positive impact on the performance of the classification models. Without feature engineering, the SVM model achieved an accuracy of 0.9738, the Decision Tree model achieved 0.9711, and the Artificial Neural Network achieved 0.9645. While with feature engineering, the SVM model improved to 0.994 accuracy, the Decision Tree model achieved 0.975, and the Artificial Neural Network achieved 0.966. The results demonstrate that feature engineering has a positive impact on the accuracy of all three models. The models with feature engineering consistently outperform the models without it. This suggests that the engineered features contribute valuable information that helps the models make more accurate predictions.

The results bellow taken from the model without applying feature engineering (Table 2 and Fig. 5):

Table 2. Performance Comparison of SVM, Decision Tree, and Artificial Neural Network without Implement Feature Engineering

Measurement	SVM	Decision Tree	Artificial Neural Network
Accuracy	0.9738	0.9711	0.9645
Precision	0.9843	0.9604	0.9515
Recall	0.9243	0.9302	0.9202
F1-score	0.9580	0.9410	0.9537

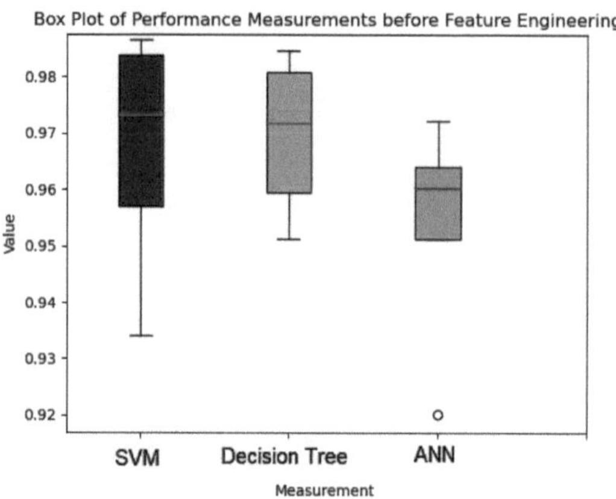

Fig. 5. The three classifiers accuracy before applying feature engineering

9   Conclusion and Future Work

SQL injection attacks pose a significant threat to web applications, necessitating the development of effective solutions. In this study, we propose a detection SQL injection model (DSQLIA) that leverages machine learning algorithms. Specifically, we applied three popular algorithms, namely Support Vector Machine (SVM), Decision Tree, and Artificial Neural Network (ANN).

To ensure the accuracy and efficiency of our detection model, we extracted meaningful features from a real-world dataset. The selected features have proven to be highly effective in distinguishing SQL injection attack requests from regular SQL queries and plain text. This indicates the robustness of the chosen feature set in identifying malicious activities.

The results obtained from evaluating our model on real-world detection systems demonstrate the efficacy of our suggested approach, which is based on machine learning and incorporates the selected attributes. The Support Vector Machine algorithm achieved the highest accuracy, with an impressive value of 0.994. The Decision Tree algorithm also exhibited strong performance, attaining an accuracy of 0.975. Additionally, the Artificial Neural Network algorithm achieved an accuracy of 0.966. These findings highlight the suitability of our model for effectively detecting SQL injection attacks.

In the future work, the Development an automated frameworks and tools should be worked with, to facilitate the integration and deployment of the SQL injection detection model into existing web application environments. This would ensure the practicality and widespread adoption of the proposed solution.

References

1. Hubskyi, O., Babenko, T., Myrutenko, L., Oksiiuk, O.: Detection of SQL injection attack using neural networks. In: Shkarlet, S., Morozov, A., Palagin, A. (eds.) MODS 2020. AISC, vol. 1265, pp. 277–286. Springer, Cham (2021). https://doi.org/10.1007/978-3-030-58124-4_27
2. Anandha Krishnan, S.S., Sabu, A.N., Sajan, P.P., Sreedeep, A.L.: SQL injection detection using machine learning. **11** (2021)
3. Jemal, I., Cheikhrouhou, O., Hamam, H., Mahfoudhi, A.: SQL injection attack detection and prevention techniques using machine learning. Int. J. Appl. Eng. Res. **15**(6), 569–580 (2020)
4. Alkhathami, J.M., Alzahrani, S.M.: Detection of SQL injection attacks using machine learning in cloud computing platform. J. Theor. Appl. Inf. Technol. **100**(15) (2022)
5. Alghawazi, M., Alghazzawi, D., Alarifi, S.: Detection of SQL injection attack using machine learning techniques: a systematic literature review. J. Cybersecurity Priv. **2**(4), 764–777 (2022)
6. Li, Q., Li, W., Wang, J., Cheng, M.: A SQL injection detection method based on adaptive deep forest. IEEE Access **7**, 145385–145394 (2019)
7. Al-Maliki, M.H.A., Jasim, M.N.: Review of SQL injection attacks: detection, to enhance the security of the website from client-side attacks. Int. J. Nonlinear Anal. Appl. **13**(1), 3773–3782 (2022)
8. Azman, M.A., Marhusin, M.F., Sulaiman, R.: Machine learning-based technique to detect SQL injection attack. J. Comput. Sci. (2021)
9. Chen, Z., Guo, M., et al.: Research on SQL injection detection technology based on SVM. In: MATEC Web of Conferences, vol. 173, p. 01004. EDP Sciences (2018)
10. Muhammad, T., Ghafory, H.: SQL injection attack detection using machine learning algorithm. Mesopotamian J. Cybersecurity **2022**, 5–17 (2022)
11. Pham, B.A., Subburaj, V.H.: An experimental setup for detecting sqli attacks using machine learning algorithms. J. Colloquium Inf. Syst. Secur. Educ. **8**, 5 (2020)
12. Al-Maliki, M.H.A., Jasim, M.N.: Comparison study for NLP using machine learning techniques to detecting SQL injection vulnerabilities. Int. J. Nonlinear Anal. Appl. (2023)
13. Xie, X., Ren, C., Fu, Y., Xu, J., Guo, J.: SQL injection detection for web applications based on elastic-pooling CNN. IEEE Access **7**, 151475–151481 (2019)
14. Alam, A., Tahreen, M., Alam, Md.M., Mohammad, S.A., Rana, S.: SCAMM: detection and prevention of SQL injection attacks using a machine learning approach. Ph.D. thesis, Brac University (2021)

15. Gautam, B., Tripathi, J., Singh, S.: A secure coding approach for prevention of SQL injection attacks. Int. J. Appl. Eng. Res. **13**(11), 9874–9880 (2018)
16. Liu, M., Li, K., Chen, T.: Deepsqli: deep semantic learning for testing SQL injection. In: Proceedings of the 29th ACM SIGSOFT International Symposium on Software Testing and Analysis, pp. 286–297 (2020)
17. Abdulmalik, Y.: An improved SQL injection attack detection model using machine learning techniques. Int. J. Innov. Comput. **11**(1), 53–57 (2021)

AI-Based Anomaly Detection for IoT Cybersecurity Events

Zineb Hidila[✉] and Mohamed Tabaa

LPRI: Multidisciplinary Research and Innovation Laboratory,
Moroccan School of Engineering Sciences (EMSI), Casablanca, Morocco
`{z.hidila,m.tabaa}@emsi.ma`

Abstract. Cyber security attacks has always been a big threat to any known smart and connected industry, not only the economical losses are great but also in term of data privacy, this is why it is essential to put in place preventive measures capable to detect those malicious attacks as reliable and as early as possible. For this matter anomaly detection comes handy as a technique of early prevention by stopping those attacks through a large set of methodologies such us machine learning and deep learning models. for this work we are going to focus on the elaboration a benchmarks of different solutions and focus on a new recent approach of detection using a Graph neural networks applied to a Bluetooth dataset, that contains many attacks such us the DOS and the DDOS and the Bluesmack. We will begin by analyzing the dataset through a set of methodologies starting with a baseline analysis and machine learning techniques: Isolation forest, support vector machines and continue with deep learning models: LSTM autoencoders and graph convolutional networks. The work is going to outline the different aspects of anomaly detection, a walk-through of the dataset with the different components of the Bluetooth stack layer, the injected attacks and the impact on the dataset, then we'll define each approach of machine learning and deep learning techniques,moving to an experimental section of each method and their evaluation performances. Finally a discussion of the potential improvements of those techniques and how it can be extended or optimized afterward.

Keywords: Machine Learning · Deep Learning · GCN · Anomaly · Bluetooth · Cybersecurity

1 Introduction

The growth of usage of IOT (Internet of things) devices implies a serious implication of the current trends and flaws. So far, we witness a lot of cybersecurity incidents [1,2] related to smart infrastructures, agriculture and so on, which indicated there's a lack of involvement in research areas dealing with anomalies instead of focusing more on new infrastructures and networks [3]. Anomaly detection, sometimes referred to as outliers detection is a technique employed in

© The Author(s), under exclusive license to Springer Nature Switzerland AG 2026
H. Badir et al. (Eds.): INTIS 2024, CCIS 2645, pp. 227–239, 2026.
https://doi.org/10.1007/978-3-032-14964-0_18

identifying data that fails to match the distribution. This issue impact greatly the results of any data analysis [4], or classification tasks [5]. Furthermore, those methods which are applied to IOT(Internet of things) involve a human expertise in the process known as feature engineering. Feature engineering [6,7] is used for the design of prepossessing pipelines and data transformation in a hope to organize the discriminative information from the data. Although, it has been used for so many years, there are some drawbacks in the process; first we always need a collaboration between the expert and the model developer; second the biased feature extraction knowing that the human factor can't be 100% sure which feature to extract for a high performance. From those limitations it was necessary to limit the involvement of feature engineering for learning algorithms to deal with anomaly. For this work, we will focus on applying a bench-marking of a Bluetooth dataset in the medical field linked to cybersecurity events [8]. For this matter, it is important to be able to detect the presence of malicious data and be used as a preventive measure. Anomaly detection is accomplished by using different methodologies from statistical analysis [9], machine learning [10,11] and deep learning techniques [12,13]. Most of the statistical and machine learning techniques aren't able to expend and connect the different features of the dataset, for such, switching to deep learning models has shown interesting results compared to the classical approaches [14–17] which will be discussed in the further sections. For this work, we are going to focus on the elaboration a benchmarks of different solutions and test a new recent approach of detection through the use of Graph neural networks applied to a Bluetooth dataset [8], that contains many attacks such us the DOS and the DDOS and the Bluesmack. The structure of the paper is as follows: Sect. 2 provides a discussion on the recent research of anomaly detection algorithms in IoT applied to cybersecurity, Sect. 3 is a walk-through of the dataset with the different components of the Bluetooth stack layer, the injected attacks and the impact on the dataset. In Sect. 4 we'll define each approach of machine learning and deep learning techniques, then we are going to experiments with different approaches described in the abstract. Finally a conclusion and perspectives for describing potential improvements of those techniques and how it can be extended or optimized afterward.

2   Related Work

Since the focus is on an IOT context applied to an Industry 4.0, it is necessary to have a formal definition of the anomaly. In literature, we define anomaly as deviation from the norms, rules, forms and so on. When we deal with anomaly in industrial events, it is more of a tangible effect observed on systems which alters their states by deviating from the norms (locally or globally). From this definition we can extract some insights:

1. The state of the anomaly is changeable, since in most cases we're dealing with time series data.
2. Anomaly focuses on small subsets, thus overlooking possible correlations.
3. The amount of noise is a significant factor.

To begin with, many researchers addressed the anomaly in a variety of industrial domains, starting with health monitoring on large scale power generation using a statistical signal processing technique known as independent component analysis [18]. The results of this research demonstrated that the suggested method can effectively discern the primary factors of abnormality from among the varied components comprising a typical turbine system. Away from the health domain, we have cybersecurity where [19] presented a comparative study of many machine learning methods for anomaly detection in cyberattacks on IoT networks. Their comparison was on including Support Vector Machine (SVM), Artificial Neural Network (ANN), Decision Tree (DT), Logistic Regression (LR), and k-Nearest Neighbours (k-NN). The result of their study showed that the neural network out performed all the other models. In the same topic [3], this research proposes an anomaly detection algorithm using inference aimed at identifying cyber-intrusions within the computer network environment of substations, and for an early detection. Moving to some machine learning techniques, we have the Isolation forest [20], the isolation forest is a continuum of the random forest algorithm, applied to anomaly detection [21]it showed some significant improvements with an accuracy rate of 95.4%. Another supervised machine learning technique for intrusion detection we have Support vector Machines (SVM) [22], the significant findings in their work demonstrated efficient detection capabilities for identifying short-duration intrusions and attacks within the network traffic. Next we have the LSTM autoencoders [23] and Variational autoencoders [24], where in the first work a comparative analysis was done on LSTM, GRU, Bi-LSTM and Neural Networks, for the second research the variational autoencoders method outperforms autoencoders based and the PCA based methods. Last but no least, the recent research focusing on graph neural networks for the outliers detection has gained attention, since the structure of the graphs captures the complexity of the data, and link the whole components that usually was nearly impossible with classical approaches. As an example [25], where the authors demonstrated with their experiments the outperforming capabilities of a graph representation learning.

3   Dataset

For this study, we chose to use the bluetack dataset [8] dealing with realistic generated data using the e-healthcare test-bed. When dealing with a Bluetooth dataset in such sensitive area, recognizing the smallest abnormalities has a great impact on securing the confidentiality of patients and having a correct diagnosis. But first lets described the Bluetooth protocol stack [26,27] and outline the choice on which the anomalies are going to focus on, note that the data provided in this research is already pre-processed.

3.1   Bluetooth Protocol Stack

As described in the Fig. 1, the Bluetooth protocol stack is a set of layers that describes the architecture and functionalities which is used in the Bluetooth com-

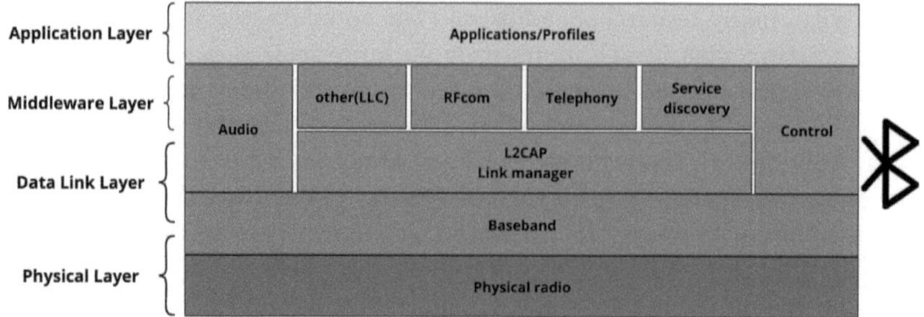

Fig. 1. The bluetooth protocol stack.

munication. We have: the architecture, middle-ware, data link and the physical layer. Each of those layers contribute in ensuring a reliable short-range wireless communication for facilitating interoperability between the devices. Here's a simplified explanation of some of the components of the Bluetooth stack layers:

1. **Radio (RF)/the physical layer**: It performs modulation/demodulation of the data into radio frequency signals. It outlines the physical characteristics of Bluetooth transceivers with two types of links: connection-less and connection-oriented.
2. **Link Layer/Baseband link layer**: Establishing the connectwith in a piconet, ensuring addressing, timing, packet format, and power control.
3. **Link Manager protocol layer**: Creation of links, dealing with monitoring to check the health and termination upon command and failure
4. **Logical Link Control and Adaption (L2CAP) Protocol layer**: Known as the heart of the Bluetooth stack. It is considered as a bridge between the lower and the upper layer of the Bluetooth protocol stack. The data packets received from upper layers are packaged and sent to lower layers for segmentation and multiplexing.
5. **Service Discovery Protocol (SDP) layer**: It allows detecting the services accessible on another Bluetooth-enabled device.
6. **RF comm (Radio Front end Component) layer**: It furnishes a serial interface with WAP and OBEX, providing emulation of serial ports over the logical link control and adaption protocol(L2CAP). This protocol is based on the ETSI standard TS 07.10 [28].
7. **SDP (Service Discovery Protocol)**: Discovering and understanding the different services provided by other Bluetooth devices within a range.
8. **TCS (Telephony Control Protocol)**: The primary function of this layer is setup and release within call control and group management for the gateway that serves many devices.
9. **Application layer**: Interaction of the users with the application.

For the anomaly scenario, the most relevant metrics in the dataset are describe in the table below (Table 1) with their Bluetooth protocol stack associated layer:

Table 1. Association between the bluetack metrics and Bluetooth Protocol Layers

Metric	Layer
HCI_ACL_count_per_100msec	HCI layer
HCI_CMD_count_per_100msec	
HCI_EVT_count_per_100msec	
ACL_Data_count_per_100msec	
Read_RSSI_count_per_100msec	
Read_Link_Quality_count_per_100msec	
Read_Tx_Power_Level_count_per_100msec	
Disconnect_complete_count_per_100msec	
Command_Complete_count_per_100msec	
HCI_Evnt_count_per_100msec	
Length_per_100msec	L2CAP layer
L2CAP_count_per_100msec	
Received_count_per_100msec	Data Link layer
Sent_count_per_100msec	
Destination_BDADDR_count_per_100msec	
Source_BDADDR_count_per_100msec	
Master_count_per_100msec	LMP layer
Slave_count_per_100msec	

3.2 Injected Attacks on the L2CAP Layer

Although many metrics are correlated in terms of injected attacks, the focus for this study is to analyse and detect the outliers on the l2CAP layer since the injections were applied directly on it. Before the bench-marking on the different models and approaches for this work, it is worth defining each type of attack [29, 30] (Fig. 2) and discuss their respective impacts on that layer. For the L2CAP it's usually flooded with those malignant intrusions to disrupt and exhaust the services.

- **DDos**: A distributed denial of services acts on compromising systems usually spread across many targets, leading to a disruption of the traffic. Usually the attack sends overloaded packets draining the resources such as memory, bandwidth, capacity and so on. The attack blocks access to the authorized users.
- **Dos**: Since a Bluetooth connection is based on the piconet network, which means that devices can be paired together respecting the master and the slave topology; makes the peered devices vulnerable to the flaw of sending oversized (malicious) data packets that blocks the users from accessing the services. Logically, this leads to a Denial of Services (DOS); in terms of the Bluetooth stack protocol, the L2CAP is the one responsible for establishing the connection oriented data services to the upper layer of the stack.

- **BlueSmack**: Is a type of a DOS attack, acts on IP based devices, Sending 600-byte pingsto the L2CAP that echos requests to Bluetooth devices, resulting in input buffer overflow.

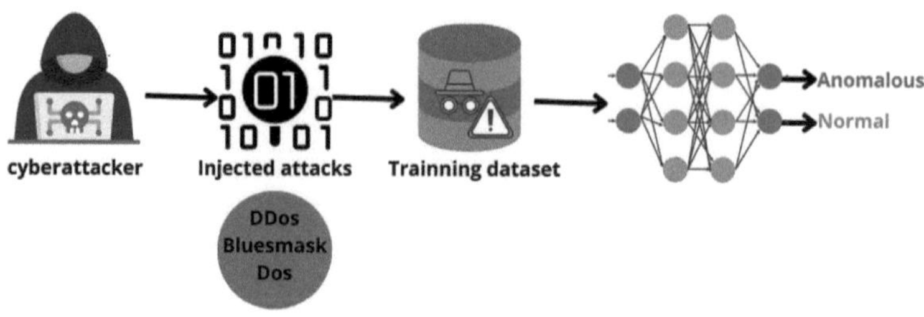

Fig. 2. Types of attacks performed on the training dataset.

4   Experiments

This section describes the different experiments done on the dataset to identify the anomalies based on the methods/models described in the background section. We first start by outlining each model with its parameters and results.

4.1   Statistical Analysis

The statistical analysis applied to anomaly detection is based on calculating the statistical properties of data to identify the data points or instances that are behaving out of the norm based on certain metrics like/mean, standards devia tion and quantiles. The first step of this technique is to perform an exploratory data analysis to comprehend the structure, the distribution to detect patterns and characteristics. Afterwards, it is necessary to calculate the standards score (Z-score) based on a threshold, to indicate how many standards deviations are far from the mean to detect the anomalous points. Some of the setbacks of using the z-score method, is not being adaptable to a small dataset; which is not the case for ours, but still even a larger dataset the mean behave sensitively to the outliers impacting the z-score and flagging data points. To address this issue, we use a modified z-score (see Eq. 1) using the median rather than the mean.

modified z-score

$$M_i = \frac{0.6745 * (X_i - \hat{X})}{MAD} \tag{1}$$

M_i = modified z score
0.6745 = is a constant used to approximate a median-equivalent of standard deviation

X_i = is the value to calculate a score for
$\hat{X}$ = is the median of the dataset
MAD = is the median absolute deviation of the dataset

In this analysis and based on the metrics shown in the Table 2, the results demonstrate a promising performance, with a precision of 0.801 and a recall of 0.9052. This presents that the algorithm adequately identifies anomalies while minimizing false labels, capturing approximately 90.52% of actual anomalies while classifying around 80.1% of flagged instances. However, there are areas for improvement, notably in reducing the false positive rate (0.202) and false negative rate (0.331). Overall, while the algorithm demonstrates strong performance in anomaly detection, further adjustment is necessary to improve its accuracy and reliability, like for example testing different values of the threshold (Fig. 3).

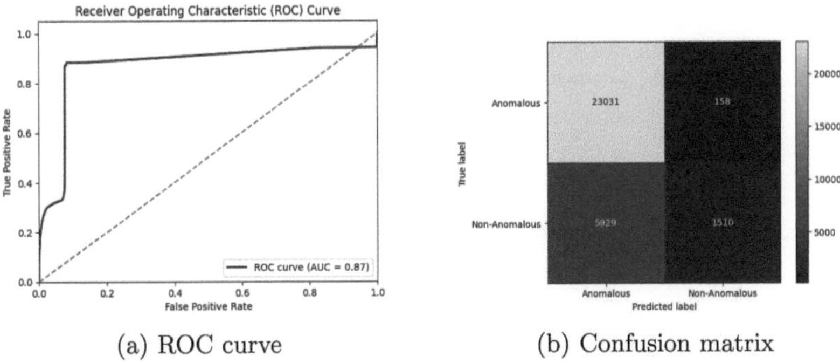

(a) ROC curve   (b) Confusion matrix

Fig. 3. The ROC curve and confusion matrix of the statistical analysis.

4.2   Isolation Forest

Isolation Forest (IF) is an unsupervised learning algorithm that detect anomalies based on isolating anomalies through a random split. The algorithm base his learning solely on the characteristics of the data without being labeled. The results shown in Table 2 clearly demonstrate how the isolation forest performed better than the statistical analysis. A noticeable metric is the value of the precision showing how the algorithm performed poorly at identifying false positives (Fig. 4).

4.3   Support Vecor Machine

Since our data is already pre-processed we opted to test the SVM instead of the one class one. We first applied the approach with the recommended parameters but after we tested with cross validation to find the exact parameters using a grid search to minimize the false positive and false negatives rates. Then we ended

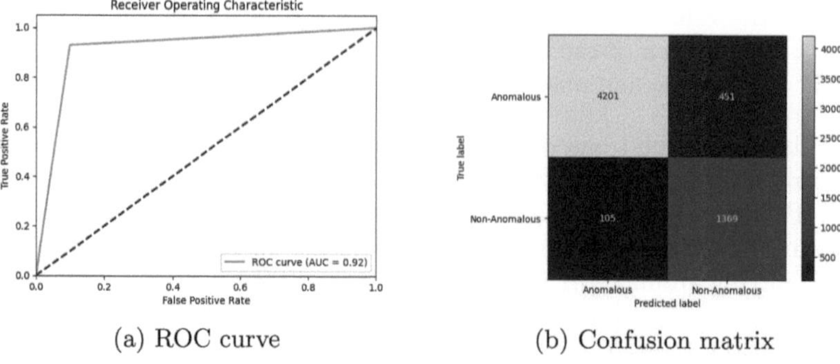

(a) ROC curve   (b) Confusion matrix

Fig. 4. The ROC curve and confusion matrix of IForest.

our analysis by applying a test via a transformed practical component analysis and projected features. The results obtained from the SVM (Table 2) collectively demonstrate the SVM's remarkable capability in accurately identifying positive instances while maintaining a high level of overall accuracy, making it a reliable and efficient tool for the anomaly detection (Figs. 5 and 6).

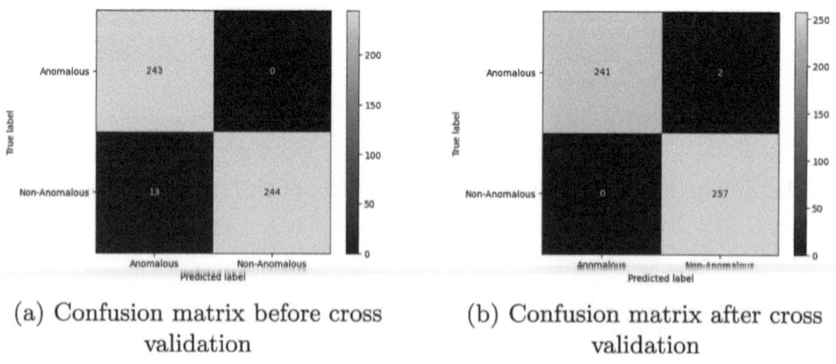

(a) Confusion matrix before cross   (b) Confusion matrix after cross
validation   validation

Fig. 5. confusion matrix SVM.

4.4   LSTM Autoencoders

For the deep learning models and since our data is a timeseries one (counts on every 100 ms), it is interseting to analyze the behavior of an LSTM autoencoder model in term of outliers detection. For this type of model, the autoencoder is capable of reconstructing normal sequences correctly using the recurrent architecture (Fig. 7).

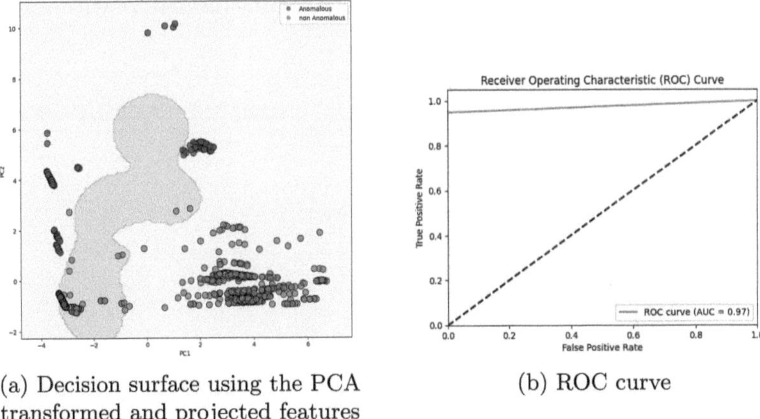

(a) Decision surface using the PCA transformed and projected features

(b) ROC curve

Fig. 6. SVM metrics.

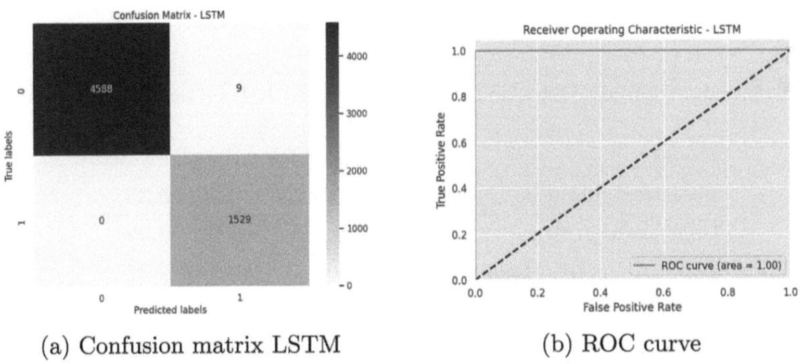

(a) Confusion matrix LSTM

(b) ROC curve

Fig. 7. LSTM metrics.

4.5   Graph Convolutional Networks

A graph convolutional network is a deep learning model that performs on graph data using convolutions. Graphs consist of nodes (vertices) and edges (connections between nodes), where nodes represent entities and edges represent relationships or interactions between entities. GCNs extend traditional convolutional neural networks (CNNs) to process graph-structured data, enabling them to learn representations of nodes that incorporate information from their local neighborhood.

In the context of anomaly detection, Graph Convolutional Networks (GCNs) leverage the graph structure of data to identify anomalies or unusual patterns within the network. For this type of structure, we applied the node classification technique for the anomaly where the malignant node represents data that had been injected by malicious packets in the Bluetooth network, below we have the evaluation metrics and the results for the confusion matrix within the ROC curve (Fig. 8).

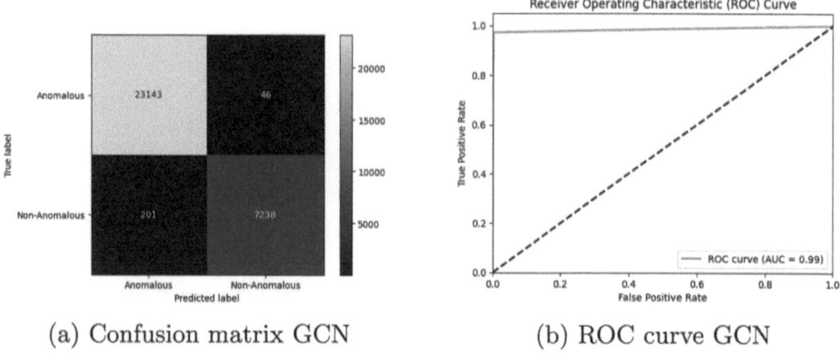

(a) Confusion matrix GCN   (b) ROC curve GCN

Fig. 8. GCN metrics.

Table 2. Anomaly Detection models results in IoT Cybersecurity events

Model	Accuracy	Precision	Recall	F1-Score
statistical analysis	0.80	0.9052	0.20	0.33
Isolation Forest	0.90	0.75	0.92	0.92
Support Vector Machine	0.97	1.0	0.949	0.97
LSTM Autoencoders	0.99	0.99	0.97	0.99
GCN	0.99	0.99	0.96	0.97

4.6   Analysis

From the benchmarking results we can say that Isolation Forest Achieves relatively high precision and reasonable recall, indicating a good balance between correctly identifying anomalies and minimizing false positives. The accuracy and F1-score are also high, demonstrating strong overall performance. For the SVM we have excellent precision and recall, indicating that it captures all anomalies in the dataset. The accuracy and F1-score are also high, reflecting the robustness of SVM in anomaly detection. On the other hand the LSTM autoencoder performs better than the previous models suggesting a robust performance in the anomaly detection. Finally for the GCN we also observe high scores in the evaluation metrics close to the LSTM. Overall, we can deduce that SVM, LSTM Autoencoders, and GCNs appear to be the most effective methods for anomaly detection in this scenario, with high precision, recall, accuracy, and F1-score. Isolation Forest also performs well, particularly in terms of precision and overall accuracy.

5   Conclusion and Perspective

In this study, we showed how important it is to identify the presence of malicious data in the context of cybersecurity in the industry 4.0 through an e-health dataset. The bench-marking results that we presented Table 2 shows that deep learning models outperformed the machine learning one. By means of this research, we went through many anomaly detection techniques, from the statistical approaches using z-scores, machine learning algorithms (Isolation forest and SVM), and deep learning architectures (LSTM autoencoders and GCN). For our use case, we saw that all the models performed well to some extents expect for the statistical one which is a straightforward technique. The reason for such outcome is the fact that those calculations fails exploring the complexity of data in depth.

Back to the machine learning algorithms, the results indicate a sophisticated learning pattern since it learns from both labeled and unlabeled data making it more adaptable to diverse patterns. On the contrast the deep learning techniques, the case of LSTM and GCN leverage the complexity of the representation learning of the data, capturing patterns and anomalies fluently, although the computational resources are higher.

This study is an initial step to find the appropriate models for the outliers detection, which results in two main ones, the LSTM, GCN and the SVM. From those starting models we are going to delve into hybrid architectures to maximize the efficiency of anomaly detection taking into count the resources management. For the ongoing research and development, the attention goes more into having architectures that are more robust and scalable on the long term facing some of the emerging challenges such as the adversarial attacks [31]. The implication of such architectures in the industry 4.0 has a huge impact since it touches all the main sectors, from healthcare, finance, industrial IOT and so on, where the early detection not only a certain guard for the data being shared but also a cost management to avoid losses in the operations. Another aspect to explore is the intersection of many other interdisciplinary domains from data analytics, cybersecurity to further improve the efficacy and reliability of anomaly detection methods, to have at the end secure resilient and adaptable systems in this data-driver world.

6   Future Work

Following the benchmark done on the methods described in Table 2, some of the potential future directions for extending the anomaly detection can involve:

- Transfer learning and context adaptation: includes investigating the potential of transfer learning implementation by the usage of pre-trained models and knowledge transfer to reduce the data scarcity issues.
- Hybrid integration: Combining multiple anomaly detection models could potentially leverage the capabilities and improve the overall accuracy, such as combining Isolation Forest with LSTM Autoencoders or GCNs with SVMs [32,33]

- Adversarial strategies: this approach can involve adversarial training strategies to strengthen the detection of malicious attacks.
- scalability and efficiency: to address the scalability of anomaly detection models, implementing light weighted components of the models to be distributed on a larger scale will potentially speed up the processes.

By addressing those different directions, we're going to develop more robust, broad and optimized solutions capable of mitigating the current issues in cybersecurity and efficiently solve the threats.

References

1. Temara, S.: The ransomware epidemic: recent cybersecurity incidents demystified. Asian J. Adv. Res. Rep. **18**(3), 1–16 (2024)
2. Kulkarni, A., Wang, Y., Gopinath, M., Sobien, D., Rahman, A., Batarseh, F.A.: A review of cybersecurity incidents in the food and agriculture sector. *arXiv preprint*arXiv:2403.08036 (2024)
3. Ten, C.-W., Manimaran, G., Liu, C.-C.: Cybersecurity for critical infrastructures: attack and defense modeling. IEEE Trans. Syst. Man Cybern. Part A Syst. Hum. **40**(4), 853–865 (2010)
4. Blázquez-García, A., Conde, A., Mori, U., Lozano, J.: A review on outlier/anomaly detection in time series data. ACM Comput. Surv. **54**(3) (2021)
5. Arif, I., Ackovska, N.: IoT aided smart home architecture for anomaly detection. In: Fortino, G., Liotta, A., Gravina, R., Longheu, A. (eds.) Data Science and Internet of Things. IT, pp. 1–19. Springer, Cham (2021). https://doi.org/10.1007/978-3-030-67197-6_1
6. Carta, S., Podda, A.S., Recupero, D.R., Saia, R.: A local feature engineering strategy to improve network anomaly detection. Future Internet, **12**(10), 177 (2020)
7. Jeyakumar, S., et al.: Feature engineering for anomaly detection and classification of blockchain transactions, Authorea Preprints (2023)
8. Unal, D.: Bluetack dataset. IEEE DataPort, 01/09/2021. https://ieee-dataport.org/documents/bluetack
9. Moustafa, N., Slay, J.: The evaluation of network anomaly detection systems: statistical analysis of the UNSW-NB15 data set and the comparison with the kdd99 data set. Inf. Secur. J. Glob. Perspect. **25**(1–3), 18–31 (2016)
10. Nassif, A.B., Talib, M.A., Nasir, Q., Dakalbab, F.M.: Machine learning for anomaly detection: a systematic review. IEEE Access **9**, 78658–78700 (2021)
11. Shon, T., Moon, J.: A hybrid machine learning approach to network anomaly detection. Inf. Sci. **177**(18), 3799–3821 (2007)
12. Chalapathy, R., Chawla, S.: Deep learning for anomaly detection: a survey. arXiv preprint arXiv:1901.03407 (2019)
13. Pang, G., Shen, C., Cao, L., Van Den Hengel, A.: Deep learning for anomaly detection: a review. ACM Comput. Surv. (CSUR) **54**(2), 1–38 (2021)
14. Wang, X., Wang, Y., Javaheri, Z., Almutairi, L., Moghadamnejad, N., Younes, O.S.: Federated deep learning for anomaly detection in the internet of things. Comput. Electr. Eng. **108**, 108651 (2023)
15. Wang, Y.-C., Houng, Y.-C., Chen, H.-X., Tseng, S.-M.: Network anomaly intrusion detection based on deep learning approach. Sensors **23**(4), 2171 (2023)

16. Landauer, M., Onder, S., Skopik, F., Wurzenberger, M.: Deep learning for anomaly detection in log data: a survey. Mach. Learn. Appl. **12**, 100470 (2023)
17. Li, G., Jung, J.J.: Deep learning for anomaly detection in multivariate time series: approaches, applications, and challenges. Inf. Fusion **91**, 93–102 (2023)
18. Ajami, A., Daneshvar, M.: Data driven approach for fault detection and diagnosis of turbine in thermal power plant using independent component analysis (ica). Int. J. Electr. Power Energy Syst. **43**(1), 728–735 (2012)
19. Inuwa, M.M., Das, R.: A comparative analysis of various machine learning methods for anomaly detection in cyber attacks on IoT networks. Internet Things **26**, 101162 (2024)
20. Xu, D., Wang, Y., Meng, Y., Zhang, Z.: An improved data anomaly detection method based on isolation forest. In: 2017 10th International Symposium on Computational Intelligence and Design (ISCID), vol. 2, pp. 287–291. IEEE (2017)
21. Sadaf, K., Sultana, J.: Intrusion detection based on autoencoder and isolation forest in fog computing. IEEE Access **8**, 167059–167068 (2020)
22. Zhang, Y., Yang, Q., Lambotharan, S., Kyriakopoulos, K., Ghafir, I., AsSadhan, B.: Anomaly-based network intrusion detection using SVM. In: 2019 11th International Conference on Wireless Communications and Signal Processing (WCSP), pp. 1–6. IEEE (2019)
23. Mirza, A.H., Cosan, S.: Computer network intrusion detection using sequential LSTM neural networks autoencoders. In: 2018 26th Signal Processing and Communications Applications Conference (SIU), pp. 1–4 (2018)
24. An, J., Cho, S.: Variational autoencoder based anomaly detection using reconstruction probability. Spec. Lect. IE **2**(1), 1–18 (2015)
25. Zheng, L., Li, Z., Li, J., Li, Z., Gao, J.: Addgraph: anomaly detection in dynamic graph using attention-based temporal GCN. In: IJCAI, vol. 3, p. 7 (2019)
26. Beutel, J., et al.: Overview of the bluetooth wireless technology. In: ERSA 2004: Engineering of Reconfigurable Systems & Algorithms, pp. 163–169 (2004)
27. Haartsen, J.: The bluetooth radio system. IEEE Pers. Commun. **7**(1), 28–36 (2000)
28. ETSI (European Telecommunications Standards Institute). ETSI Technical Specification TS 101 369. Technical report, European Telecommunications Standards Institute (1999)
29. Nateq Be-Nazir Ibn, M., Tarique, M.: Bluetooth security threats and solutions: a survey. Int. J. Distrib. Parallel Syst. **3**, 127 (2012)
30. Cope, P., Campbell, J., Hayajneh, T.: An investigation of bluetooth security vulnerabilities. In: Proceedings of the 7th IEEE Annual Computing and Communication Workshop and Conference (IEEE CCWC 2017), Las Vegas, NV, USA (2017)
31. Madry, A., Makelov, A., Schmidt, L., Tsipras, D., Vladu, A.: Towards deep learning models resistant to adversarial attacks. *arXiv preprint* arXiv:1706.06083 (2017)
32. Majjed Al-Qatf, Yu., Lasheng, M.A.-H., Al-Sabahi, K.: Deep learning approach combining sparse autoencoder with SVM for network intrusion detection. IEEE Access **6**, 52843–52856 (2018)
33. Kale, R., Lu, Z., Fok, K.W., Thing, V.L.: A hybrid deep learning anomaly detection framework for intrusion detection. In: 2022 IEEE 8th International Conference on Big Data Security on Cloud (BigDataSecurity), IEEE International Conference on High Performance and Smart Computing,(HPSC) and IEEE International Conference on Intelligent Data and Security (IDS), pp. 137–142. IEEE (2022)

A Concatenation Deep Learning Model for Photovoltaic Inspection Based on Aerial Infrared Images

Marwa Zerrouk[1]([⊠]), Toufik Enfissi[1], Zoubir Barraz[1,2], and Imane Sebari[1]

[1] Photogrammetry–Cartography Department, School of Geomatics and Surveying Engineering, IAV HASSAN II, Rabat, Morocco
`zerroukmarwa@iav.ac.ma`
[2] Green Energy Park, Benguerir, Morocco

Abstract. Photovoltaic (PV) systems have become a significant role player in the energy transition. However, they are subject to various external environmental factors, whether during manufacturing, installation, or throughout their lifetime. They need efficient, fast, and intelligent inspection, especially when it comes to large-scale farms. In this sense, the combination of UAV imagery with deep learning (DL) techniques will allow quality control while improving the performance of PV systems and minimizing operation and maintenance costs. The main objective of our study is to propose a deep-learning approach based on the concatenation of two DL models to automate the process of detecting and classifying PV panel anomalies from aerial Infrared thermal images. The proposed concatenation is based on the transfer learning of two CNN architectures, namely VGG19 and DenseNet201. We adopt the 'CAVIAR' strategy, which involves training several models in parallel and then selecting the most effective and best-performing one. We applied our approach to a set of images of real solar farms, including 20,000 images with six (06) classes of anomalies. The results show that the proposed concatenation-based model obtained the best accuracy by extracting features from two robust deep networks. The solution was able to predict the presence of anomalies with an F1 score of 86% and to correctly classify seven (07) classes with an average accuracy of 73%, providing an interesting improvement over the two models run individually.

Keywords: Photovoltaic system (PV) · deep learning (DL) · Anomaly · transfer learning · Concatenation · UAV · thermal images

1 Introduction

1.1 A Subsection Sample

The photovoltaic (PV) industry is rapidly developing as an alternative to fossil energy and an effective tool to help mitigate climate change [1, 2]. Hence, the use of PV systems. As the adoption of these latter is increasing, studying their deterioration is crucial

H. Badir et al. (Eds.): INTIS 2024, CCIS 2645, pp. 240–253, 2026.
https://doi.org/10.1007/978-3-032-14964-0_19

for effective intervention and preventing breakdowns [3]. Faults in panels can affect their effectiveness or cause extreme failures [4]. These faults include Hotspots, cracks, shadowing, soiling, and diode faults [3]. In this matter, techniques like thermography are used, considering their ability to test the system without affecting its integration and structure [5].

Nowadays, with recent advances in hardware and software as well as the emergence of autonomous monitoring [1], Unmanned Aerial Vehicles (UAVs) have been increasingly utilized since they ensure reliable condition monitoring of PV systems [6]. UAVs provide high-quality, accurate, and cost-effective maintenance and help improve the life of PV plants. Manual monitoring though useful, has its limitations; especially in large PV farms where a comprehensive inspection might be laborious and time-consuming [7].

Deep Learning (DL) models have also shown potential for efficient inspection by UAVs. However, overfitting and complex hyperparameter combinations pose challenges. This study aims to improve fault detection and classification in PV systems, combining and optimizing two prominent deep learning architectures: VGG19 [8] and DenseNet201 [9]. The research contributes significantly to green energy goals and the global shift towards renewable energy sources.

This paper is divided and organized into five sections. Section 2 provides a literature review on Deep Learning use cases for classification while focusing on ensemble models, while Sect. 3 describes the adopted methodology to detect and classify anomalies in PV systems. Section 4 illustrates the results of the final model and compares it with existing ones proposed in similar studies while providing a discussion of these results. Finally, the last and fifth section concludes the discussion and suggests some recommendations for future works.

2 Literature Review

Deep learning models have proven their efficiency in several domains, particularly in preventive diagnosis and maintenance. In the domain of PV systems inspection, [10] present in their paper a new method for detecting faults in photovoltaic systems using multi-output deep learning models like CNN, LSTM, and bi-directional networks. The method reduces the number of sensors per string by 50%, increases scalability, and achieves high accuracies of 99.94% and 99.54% for fault classification and location, respectively.

In their study, [11] developed a two-layer inspection solution for detecting overheated regions on photovoltaic (PV) arrays using aerial LWIR Multiview photogrammetry and deep learning. The solution generates a georeferenced orthomosaic of the site using SFM-MVS and uses deep semantic segmentation to extract and quantify affected regions. The FPN-DenseNet121 model achieved the best performance, with a mean of intersection over union of 93.44% and an F1-score of 96.39% on the test set, providing pixel-based and tile-based quantification of affected regions, making it efficient for large-scale PV plant monitoring.

To discuss the use of thermal images in PV fault monitoring, [12] used thermography along with the YOLOv3 deep learning-based convolutional neural network. The used model demonstrated the successful detection of the specified faults in the thermal images.

Another study [13] explores the use of Artificial Intelligence technologies in PV fault detection using RGB (Red Green Blue) images captured by UAVs. The experimentation went through two phases, the Deep Learning phase where they used six pre-trained networks: DenseNet-201, VGG19, ResNet-50, GoogLeNet, VGG16, and AlexNet, to extract features from the images. The Machine Learning phase used decision tree models for feature selection in the second phase. The goal was to choose the best extractor-classifier pair. Results show that DenseNet-201 combined with the K-nearest-neighbor worked best and achieved a classification accuracy of almost 100%.

To explore multi-source remote sensing, this paper [14] proposes a novel PV panel fault monitoring technology by combining optical and thermal infrared data with deep learning technology. The approach enables rapid and accurate identification and localization of PV panel faults. The use of high-resolution UAV optical and thermal infrared images allows for the detection of both surface and internal faults. The Mask RCNN algorithm is used for precise localization and numbering of PV panels, followed by fault scene classification using deep learning.

Furthermore, it is worth noticing that a limited number of studies have targeted Ensemble learning, especially in PV inspection. This approach has convincingly demonstrated its capacity to bring together the pros of multiple CNN models and minimize the limits that each one manifests [15]. Moreover, in the field of medicine, studies have confirmed the operability of concatenating different deep-learning models. Table 1 summarizes the usage of Deep learning for anomaly detection and classification in PV systems while displaying case studies of the usage of concatenation in other fields.

In Table 1, we provide an inventory of the different studies that explored Deep Learning in the PV monitoring field as well as concatenation models in other fields. By presenting this recap table, we aim to provide insights into the current state of research, showcase the potential benefits of Deep Learning and concatenation models, and identify areas where further investigation could lead to significant advancements in PV monitoring.

Table 1. Examples of Studies using Deep Learning for anomaly classification in PV and concatenation implementation in other fields

	Field	Image Nature	Results evaluation (Precision)	References
Deep Learning using different models	Photovoltaic anomaly detection	Thermal	83%	[16]
			97.67%	[17]
			Maximum Test Accuracy at 63.73% and an average accuracy of 59.53%	[18]
		RGB	90%	[19]
			99.5%	[10]

(*continued*)

Table 1. (*continued*)

	Field	Image Nature	Results evaluation (Precision)	References
		EL	-	[20]
			88.42%	[21]
			77.3%	[22]
Ensemble Learning (concatenation approach)	Biomedical imagery classification	RGB	93% Enhancement of 2.5%	[23]
	Pneumonia and COVID-19 detection	Radiographic	91.4%	[24]
	Brain tumor classification	MRI	99%	[25]

3 Methods and Experiments

In our study, a deep-learning approach based on the concatenation of two deep-learning models [26, 27] is proposed for automatic photovoltaic anomaly detection and classification. The studied anomalies are hot spots, dirt, cracks, diodes, shading, and offline modules. These are derived from IR images acquired by a UAV. First, an anomaly detector is established by a binary classification. Secondly, the nature of the anomaly affecting the PPV is detected with multi-class classification. For both types of classification, the "CAVIAR" strategy is adopted [28]. This latter involves training several models in parallel and then selecting the most effective one. Pre-trained DenseNet201 and VGG-19 are run individually and compared to the concatenated model (Fig. 1).

3.1 The Dataset

The Dataset used is "InfraredSolarModules". It is collected from January 1 to December 31, 2019, and contains 20,000 images of eleven anomalies found at the PPV (Table 2) [29]. Aerial photography was performed using medium- and long-wave IR cameras mounted on drones. The dataset was analyzed for visual similarities and imbalances, leading to the need for RGB images and re-distribution of classes with the same visual manifestation to reduce class sizes and improve classification effectiveness.

Table 2. The dataset used for model training

Class	Images	Description
No anomaly	10.000	Nominal solar Module
Hotspots	3663	Hot spots occur on a thin film module, or with a square geometry in single or multiple cells

(*continued*)

Table 2. (*continued*)

Class	Images	Description
Shadowing	2695	Sunlight obstructed by vegetation, man-made structures, or adjacent rows
Diode	1674	Activated bypass diode, typically 1/3 or 2/3 of the module
Cracking	941	Module anomaly caused by cracking on the module surface
Offline Module	828	The entire module is heated
Soiling	205	Dirt, dust, or other debris on the surface of the module

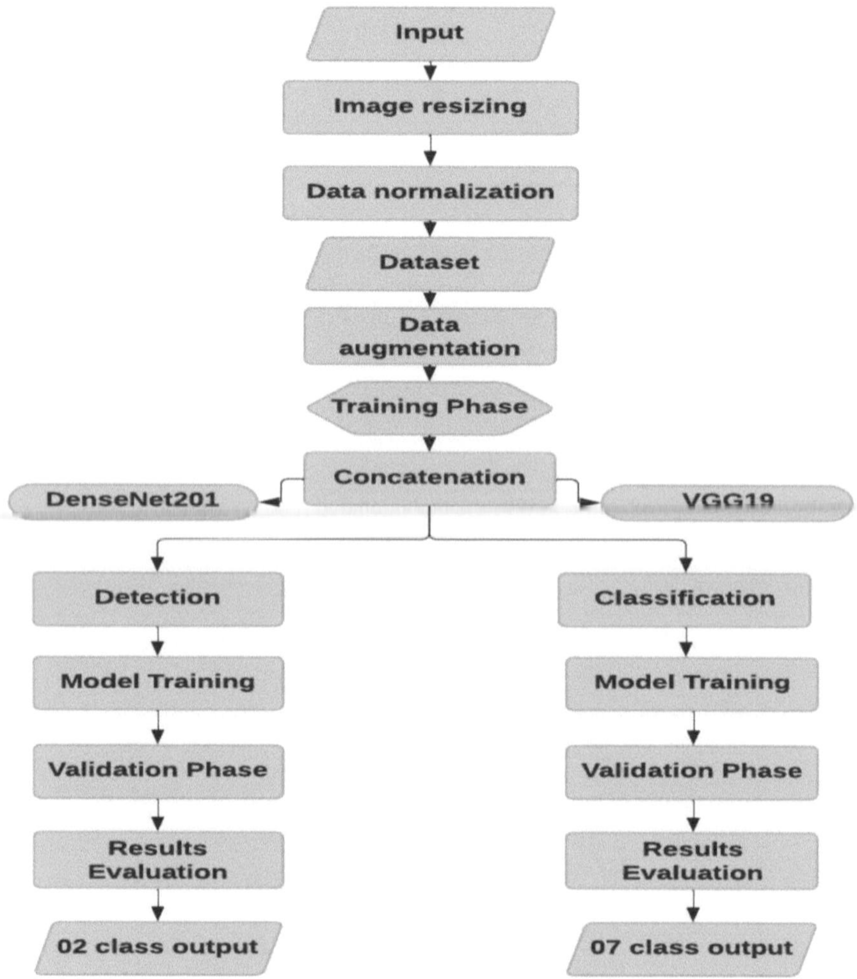

Fig. 1. Proposed methodology for the concatenated model training.

3.2 Data Preparation

The training phase of a model involves labeling, annotation, and normalization to ensure high performance. It consists in detecting anomalies and classifying them into six categories, and a seventh no-anomaly one (07 in total). The dataset is divided into training and test sets, with 20% for validation and the rest for training.

3.3 The Proposed Model

The proposed concatenated model is designed based on the features extracted by VGG19, a CNN known for its simplicity yet deeper than its deeper predecessors allowing to learn more complex features [30], and DenseNet201, as a densely-connected-layers model [31] as shown in Fig. 2. As the two networks generate feature maps of the same size, we can concatenate their features to test the effect of concatenating these two high-performance architectures on the results obtained and to see if their combination will improve the quality of the generated semantic features or not. Our concatenated neural network is designed from the features extracted by VGG-19 and DenseNet201. Then, we connect the concatenated features to two convolutional layers with 64 filters of dimension (3 × 3) to generate a feature map specific to each filter with steps of (3 × 3) pixels. These are followed by a MaxPooling layer with a pool size of (2 × 2) pixels, used to select the maximum elements from the feature map region covered by the filter window. At the next level, the CNN has two more convolutional layers with 128 filters of dimension (3 × 3) and a step of (3 × 3) pixels, with a MaxPooling layer (2 × 2) pixels that receives a feature map containing the most significant elements. Then, we add a fully connected dense layer with 140 neurons.

A Dropout of 0.2% is applied to randomly set the outgoing edges of the hidden units (neurons that constitute the hidden layers) to 0 at each update during the training phase to prevent overfitting of our model. A Flatten layer is used to convert the data into a one-dimensional array to be fed into the fully connected layer of seven neurons which presents the possible outputs of the network.

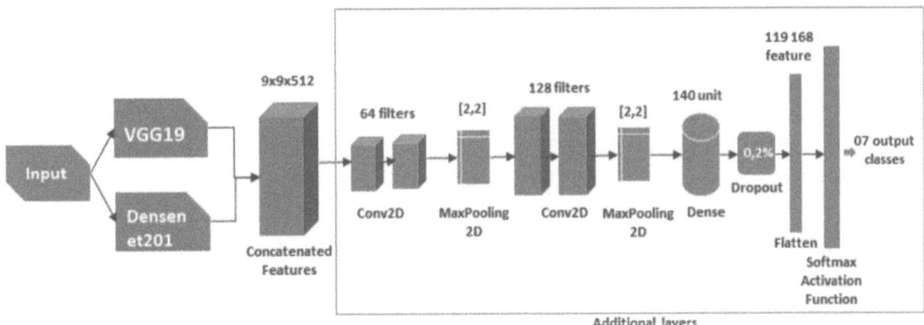

Fig. 2. The proposed concatenated DL model for the identification of anomalies in PV modules via UAV thermal images.

In our CNN, the ReLU non-linear activation function is used in the first convolutional layer and the intermediate layers. While the "Sigmoid" function is used in the last layer for binary classification and "Softmax" for multi-class classification.

The addition of these layers was inspired by the architecture presented in [18] with some modifications.

- Changing the location of the "Flatten" layer and the Dense layer;
- Reducing the number of units in the Dense layer (960 units → 140 units);
- Adding two regularizations L1 and L2.

4 Results

The practical part uses a 64 Go station with GeForce RTX 2080WDDM GPU and Intel® Core™ i7-9700F CPU [32]. For model fine-tuning [33], "Early Stopping" is used for optimization. Accuracy metrics and loss functions are used to monitor network results and find the best model.

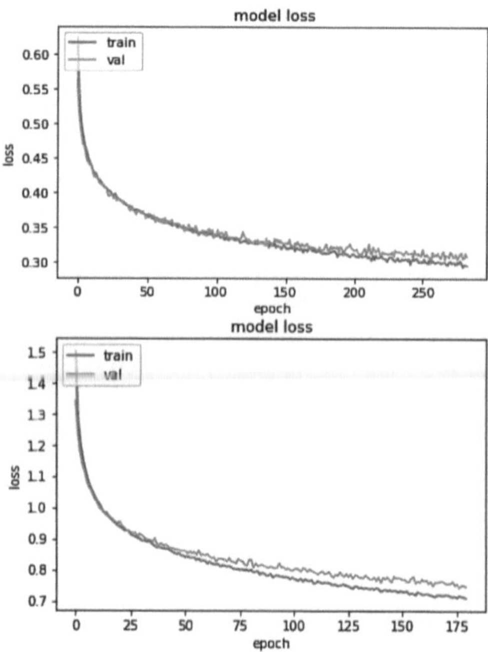

Fig. 3. Categorical loss of the training and validation dataset for 2-class (a) and 7-class (b) outputs using the concatenated model.

In Fig. 3, we display the loss curves of our concatenated model for both the fault identification (02 classes)(a) and the classification (06 anomaly classes and a non-anomaly one) (b). The curves allow us to deduce that the concatenated model, in both (a) and (b) generalizes faster. We can also notice that the validation loss is higher than the training one, with a minimal gap between the two.

Table 3 shows the training accuracy of models, with 2-class outputs at 87.84% and 7-class outputs at 75.75%. The concatenation technique improved accuracy by 7.76% and 12.84%, respectively.

To evaluate the performances of the different models applied, five different metrics are used: Confusion matrix, Accuracy, Precision, F1 score, and Precision-Recall Curve.

Figure 4 illustrates the confusion matrix of each of the three models during the detection phase. Predicting a panel as defective when it is not an error that an old-fashioned visual inspection can easily remedy. On the other hand, there is a significant risk that the PPV will be classified as intact when it is not, which will hinder the proper maintenance of the PV field. Thus, a good confusion matrix contains a minimum of (FP) and (FN). From the three confusion matrices, we can notice that the concatenated model has the least (FP) and (FN) compared to VGG-19 and DenseNet201, 870 (FN) by VGG-19, and 571 by DenseNet201 compared to 512 by concatenation. In addition, 311 (FP) by VGG-19 and 184 by DenseNet201 versus 113 by concatenation only.

Table 3. The accuracy values at the end of training for the three models for the 2-class output and 7-class output.

	VGG19	DenseNet201	Concatenated model
2-class output Accuracy in %	73.41	86.74	**87.84**
7-class output Accuracy in %	53.26	72.56	**75.75**

The performance in terms of accuracy, precision, and F1 score for the detection are presented in Table 4.

Table 4. Results of the evaluation of the three models based on accuracy, precision, and F1 score in the anomaly detection phase.

Metrics	VGG19	DenseNet201	Concatenation
Accuracy	70.47%	81.12%	**84.37%**
Precision	74.07%	80.41%	**85.32%**
F1 Score	65.44%	79.83%	**82.46%**

The Concatenation-based classifier and Dense-Net201 outperformed the VGG19 in terms of accuracy, precision, and F1 score. The concatenated model was more efficient in identifying anomalies like "Hotspots," "Shadowing," "Diode," "Offline Module," and "Soiling," with 214 correct predictions compared to 187 for Dense-Net201 and 56 for VGG-19.

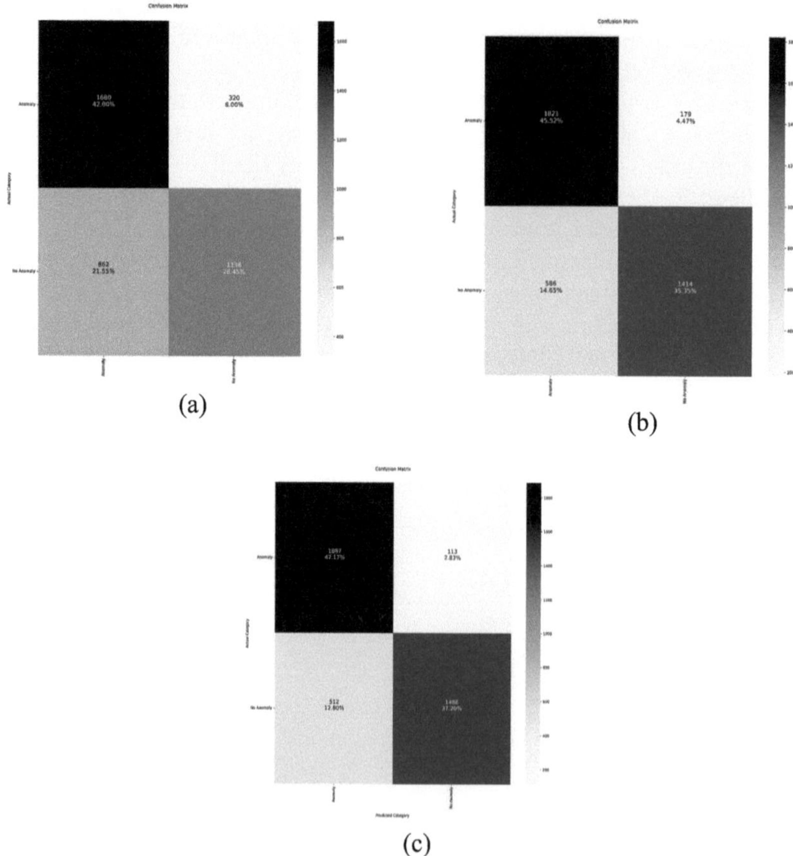

(a)

(b)

(c)

Fig. 4. Confusion matrix obtained from (a) VGG19, (b) DenseNet201, and (c) concatenated models in binary classification.

The values of the precision and F1 Score are detailed in Table 5. The analysis of Table 5 leads us to conclude that the concatenated model provides the best results, as it exceeds VGG-19 and denseNet201 in terms of the weighted average for both accuracy and F1 score.

Table 5. The evaluation metrics used for the three models.

	VGG19	DenseNet201	Concatenation
Precision	49%	68%	**70%**
F1 Score	44%	67%	**69%**

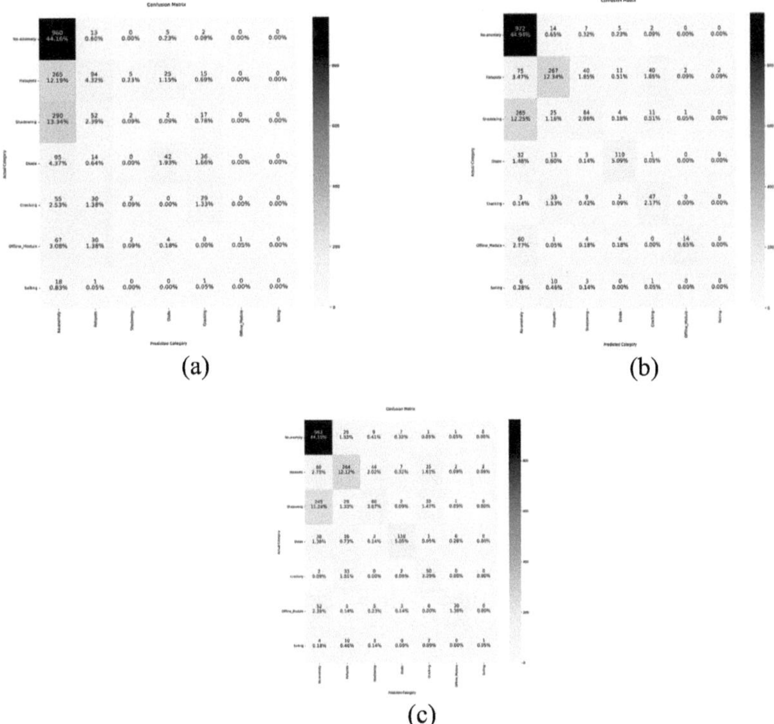

Fig. 5. Confusion matrix obtained from VGG19(a), DenseNet201(b), and concatenated model(c) in multiclass classification.

The study evaluated the performance of three models using precision-recall curves. The precision decreases with recall increase, a trade-off called the precision/recall trade-off. The VGG19 model had an accuracy rate (AP) of 55%, DenseNet201 (B) at 75%, and the Concatenated model (C) at 79%, confirming its effectiveness in minimizing false positives (Fig. 5).

The analysis established above shows that the concatenated model offered outstanding performance results and outperformed VGG-19 and DenseNet201, known to be very successful and strong models in the Deep Learning world.

The shading anomaly, characterized by spots with a high-temperature background, was predicted as No Anomaly twice with a probability of 37.19% and 48.49%. This probability remains low since the images appear devoid of clear spots, even to the naked eye. The offline module has a dark and uniform contrast. This was therefore predicted as shading, which seems absurd but tolerable due to the low prediction probability (29.56%).

The model was able to detect the hot spots on several examples with a probability between 67% and 84% (Fig. 6).

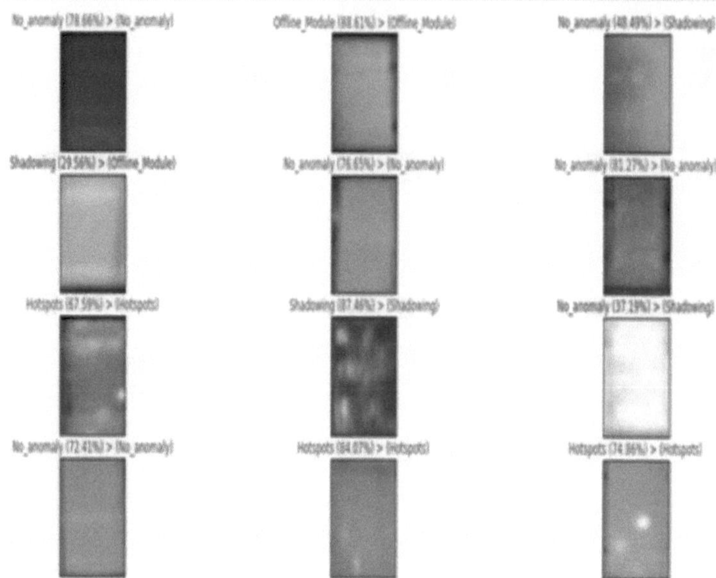

Fig. 6. Visualization of the predictions with their probabilities from the concatenation DL model: false predictions are in red and correct predictions are in green.

5 Discussion

The study focuses on anomaly detection and classification from thermal images using three architectures with transfer learning: VGG19, DenseNet201, and a concatenation of both with custom layers. The model achieved the highest accuracy among the three models and the lowest loss during the detection phase with an accuracy of 88% and a loss of 0.3036 and for classification with an accuracy of 76% and a loss of 0.7105.

The overall accuracy of the concatenated model outperformed DenseNet201 with a 2% difference for the classification of seven classes. The model identified most classes compared to the two models, with an average accuracy of 82% for the diode defect and 70% for the hot spots. However, it had difficulty in detecting certain classes due to poor image quality and data imbalance.

The addition of custom layers containing regularization, including Dropout and L1 and L2 regularizations, contributed to the reduction of overfitting and optimized classification results. These results show the interest of transfer learning in optimizing the detection of anomalies on PPVs on thermal images, showing the potential of concatenating CNN architectures for improving the automatic classification of various PPV anomalies.

Our study unveils promising prospects for future research and development. By integrating top-performing models in a single system, even greater accuracy and robustness can be achieved. The versatility of our approach ensures that as newer, more sophisticated models emerge, they can be effortlessly integrated into the existing framework. This adaptability not only maintains our inspection system at the cutting edge of technology but also encourages continuous innovation and improvement in automated photovoltaic (PV) system inspection.

6   Conclusion

The study proposes combining VGG19 and DenseNet201 architectures by concatenation to detect and classify PV anomalies. The model correctly identified 93% of healthy PV modules and 79% of faulty ones. The concatenated model outperformed VGG19 and DenseNet201 separately, with an average margin of over 9%. This suggests the potential of concatenation in improving CNN model performance. In this regard, we target through our future works to prepare a proper Database with the necessary Data and images in order to get a more efficient maintenance of the panels in field. We also aim to use the proposed solution as the subject of a real-time detection and classification application, which can be integrated into drone platforms to perform on-board inspections and monitor large-scale PV farms without having to interrupt their functioning.

Acknowledgments. This work was supported by the Green Energy Park in Benguerir (Morocco) [Reference: GEP-OCP-Digitalized PV plant project].

Data Availability Statement. The Infrared Solar Modules dataset by Raptor Maps is a third party dataset accessible at: https://github.com/RaptorMaps/InfraredSolarModules.

Competing Interests. The authors declare no competing interests.

References

1. Aghaei, M.: Autonomous monitoring and analysis of photovoltaic systems. Energies **15**, 4–9 (2022). https://doi.org/10.3390/en15145011
2. Lin, B., Chen, Y.: The rapid development of the photovoltaic industry in China and related carbon dioxide abatement costs. Reg. Environ. Chang. **20**, 49 (2020). https://doi.org/10.1007/s10113-020-01633-6
3. El-Banby, G.M., Moawad, N.M., Abouzalm, B.A., Abouzaid, W.F., Ramadan, E.A.: Photovoltaic system fault detection techniques: a review. Neural Comput. Appl. **35**, 24829–24842 (2023). https://doi.org/10.1007/s00521-023-09041-7
4. Baltacı, Ö., Kıral, Z., Dalkılınç, K., Karaman, O.: Thermal image and inverter data analysis for fault detection and diagnosis of PV systems. Appl. Sci. **14**, 3671 (2024). https://doi.org/10.3390/app14093671
5. Kandeal, A.W., et al.: Infrared thermography-based condition monitoring of solar photovoltaic systems: a mini review of recent advances. Sol. Energy **223**, 33–43 (2021). https://doi.org/10.1016/j.solener.2021.05.032
6. Li, X., Li, W., Yang, Q., Yan, W., Zomaya, A.Y.: An unmanned inspection system for multiple defects detection in photovoltaic plants. IEEE J. Photovolt. **10**, 568–576 (2020). https://doi.org/10.1109/JPHOTOV.2019.2955183
7. Sherozbek, J., Dadajon, J., Malrey, L.: Photovoltaics plant fault detection using deep learning techniques. Remote Sens. 149–160 (2022)
8. Mohbey, K.K., Sharma, S., Kumar, S., Sharma, M.: COVID-19 identification and analysis using CT scan images: deep transfer learning-based approach. Elsevier Inc. (2022)

9. Jaiswal, A., Gianchandani, N., Singh, D., Kumar, V., Kaur, M.: Classification of the COVID-19 infected patients using DenseNet201 based deep transfer learning. J. Biomol. Struct. Dyn. **39**, 5682–5689 (2021). https://doi.org/10.1080/07391102.2020.1788642

10. Mustafa, Z., Awad, A.S.A., Azzouz, M., Azab, A.: Fault identification for photovoltaic systems using a multi-output deep learning approach. Expert Syst. Appl. **211**, 118551 (2023). https://doi.org/10.1016/j.eswa.2022.118551

11. Zefri, Y., Sebari, I., Hajji, H., Aniba, G., Aghaei, M.: A layer-2 solution for inspecting large-scale photovoltaic arrays through aerial LWIR multiview photogrammetry and deep learning: a hybrid data-centric and model-centric approach. Expert Syst. Appl. **223**, 119950 (2023). https://doi.org/10.1016/j.eswa.2023.119950

12. Kayci, B., Demir, B.E., Demir, F.: Deep learning based fault detection and diagnosis in photovoltaic system using thermal images acquired by UAV. Politek Derg. **27**, 91–99 (2024). https://doi.org/10.2339/politeknik.1094586

13. Jerome Vasanth, J., Naveen Venkatesh, S., Sugumaran, V., Mahamuni, V.S.: Enhancing photovoltaic module fault diagnosis with unmanned aerial vehicles and deep learning-based image analysis. Int. J. Photoenergy **2023**, 8665729 (2023). https://doi.org/10.1155/2023/8665729

14. Zhang, W., Wang, G., Yao, G., Lu, C., Liu, Y.: Study on fault monitoring technology of photovoltaic panel based on thermal infrared and optical remote sensing. **XLVIII**, 13–17 (2024)

15. Li, W., Paffenroth, R.C., Berthiaume, D.: Neural network ensembles: theory, training, and the importance of explicit diversity. 1–27 (2021)

16. Pierdicca, R., Malinverni, E.S., Piccinini, F., Paolanti, M., Felicetti, A., Zingaretti, P.: Deep convolutional neural network for automatic detection of damaged photovoltaic cells. Int. Arch. Photogramm. Remote Sens. Spat. Inf. Sci. - ISPRS Arch. **42**, 893–900 (2018). https://doi.org/10.5194/isprs-archives-XLII-2-893-2018

17. Du, B., He, Y., He, Y., Duan, J., Zhang, Y.: Intelligent classification of silicon photovoltaic cell defects based on eddy current thermography and convolution neural network. IEEE Trans. Ind. Inform. **16**, 6242–6251 (2020). https://doi.org/10.1109/TII.2019.2952261

18. Fonseca Alves, R.H., de Deus Júnior, G.A., Marra, E.G., Lemos, R.P.: Automatic fault classification in photovoltaic modules using Convolutional Neural Networks. Renew. Energy **179**, 502–516 (2021). https://doi.org/10.1016/j.renene.2021.07.070

19. Zyout, I., Oatawneh, A.: Detection of PV solar panel surface defects using transfer learning of the deep convolutional neural networks. 1–4 (2020). https://doi.org/10.1109/aset48392.2020.9118384

20. Bartler, A., Mauch, L., Yang, B., Reuter, M., Stoicescu, L.: Automated detection of solar cell defects with deep learning. In: European Signal Processing Conference 2018, pp. 2035–2039 (2018). https://doi.org/10.23919/EUSIPCO.2018.8553025

21. Deitsch, S., et al.: Automatic classification of defective photovoltaic module cells in electroluminescence images. Sol. Energy **185**, 455–468 (2019). https://doi.org/10.1016/j.solener.2019.02.067

22. Nguyen, V.-K.: Realization and Verification of Deep Learning Models for Fault Detection and Diagnosis of Photovoltaic Modules (2020)

23. Nguyen, L.D., Gao, R., Lin, D., Lin, Z.: Biomedical image classification based on a feature concatenation and ensemble of deep CNNs. J. Ambient. Intell. Humaniz. Comput. **14**, 15455–15467 (2019). https://doi.org/10.1007/s12652-019-01276-4

24. Rahimzadeh, M., Attar, A.: A modified deep convolutional neural network for detecting COVID-19 and pneumonia from chest X-ray images based on the concatenation of Xception and ResNet50V2. Informatics Med Unlocked **19**, 100360 (2020). https://doi.org/10.1016/j.imu.2020.100360

25. Noreen, N., Palaniappan, S., Qayyum, A., Ahmad, I., Imran, M., Shoaib, M.: A deep learning model based on concatenation approach for the diagnosis of brain tumor. IEEE Access **8**, 55135–55144 (2020). https://doi.org/10.1109/ACCESS.2020.2978629
26. Saad, W., Shalaby, W.A., Shokair, M., El-Samie, F.A., Dessouky, M., Abdellatef, E.: COVID-19 classification using deep feature concatenation technique. J. Ambient. Intell. Humaniz. Comput. **13**, 2025–2043 (2022). https://doi.org/10.1007/s12652-021-02967-7
27. Ayadi, M., Ksibi, A., Al-Rasheed, A., Soufiene, B.O.: COVID-AleXception: a deep learning model based on a deep feature concatenation approach for the detection of COVID-19 from chest X-ray images. In: Healthcare, vol. 10 (2022). https://doi.org/10.3390/healthcare10102072
28. Serrano Bautista, R., Núñez Mora, J.A.: Value-at-risk predictive performance: a comparison between the CaViaR and GARCH models for the MILA and ASEAN-5 stock markets. J. Econ. Financ. Adm. Sci. **26**, 197–221 (2021). https://doi.org/10.1108/JEFAS-03-2021-0009
29. Matthew, M., Edward, O., Vadhavkar, N.: Infrared solar module dataset for anomaly detection. In: The International Conference on Learning Representations, pp. 1–5 (2020)
30. Wen, L., Li, X., Li, X., Gao, L.: A new transfer learning based on VGG-19 network for fault diagnosis. In: Proceedings of the 2019 IEEE 23rd International Conference on Computer Support Cooperative Work Design, CSCWD 2019, pp. 205–209 (2019). https://doi.org/10.1109/CSCWD.2019.8791884
31. Lu, T., Han, B., Chen, L., Yu, F., Xue, C.: A generic intelligent tomato classification system for practical applications using DenseNet-201 with transfer learning. Sci. Rep. **11**, 1–8 (2021). https://doi.org/10.1038/s41598-021-95218-w
32. Zeng, J., Yang, L.T., Ning, H., Ma, J.: A systematic methodology for augmenting. **50**, 81–87 (2015)
33. Too, E.C., Yujian, L., Njuki, S., Yingchun, L.: A comparative study of fine-tuning deep learning models for plant disease identification. Comput. Electron. Agric. **161**, 272–279 (2019). https://doi.org/10.1016/j.compag.2018.03.032

Where We are in Handling IoT and Robotics' Data for Agro-Ecology Applications?: An Architectural View

Houssam Bazza[4(✉)], Hassan Badir[4], Filippo Berto[1], Sandro Bimonte[2], Aldo Calcante[1], Paolo Ceravolo[1], Ali Hassan[7], Tahar Kechadi[6], Rim Moussa[3], Roberto Oberti[1], Sana Sellami[5], and Nicolas Tricot[2]

[1] Università degli studi di Milano, Milan, Italy
{filippo.berto,aldo.calcante,paolo.ceravolo,roberto.oberti}@unimi.it
[2] University Clermont Auvergne, TSCF, INRAE, Montoldre, France
{sandro.bimonte,nicolas.tricot}@inrae.fr
[3] University of Carthage, Tunis, Tunisia
rim.moussa@enicarthage.rnu.tn
[4] IDS, Abdelmalek Essaadi University, Tangier, Morocco
{houssam.bazza,hassan.badir}@etu.uae.ac.ma
[5] Aix Marseille Univ, CNRS, LIS, Marseille, France
sana.sellami@univ-amu.fr
[6] School of Computer Science, University College Dublin, Dublin, Ireland
tahar.kechadi@ucd.ie
[7] Digital Innovation Center, CGI, Montpellier, France
a.hassan@cgi.com

Abstract. Internet of Things (IoT) and robotics technologies have reached a good maturity and they are being used in several fields, such as healthcare, manufacturing, urban planning, and agriculture. In the agro-ecology context, some solutions based on robots and sensors were proposed, for example for monitoring the status of the crops, detecting nutritional and health stress, and for management operations (such as weeding, optimal application of fertilizers, and crops' protection treatments). Similar applications can be found in the animal farming domain. These solutions use Big Data technologies that require handling voluminous, real-time, and heterogeneous data generated by agricultural operations. Multiple architectures are proposed, with different characteristics specifically designed to address a particular farming application. Therefore, generic architecture guidelines for deploying agro-ecology application systems are missing. They could help researchers and engineers choose adequate data management tools for their farming applications. This paper discusses and presents a reference architecture of an agro-ecology application system to properly handle data needed in such a specific context.

Keywords: Internet of Things · Robots · Agro-ecology · System architecture

H. Badir et al. (Eds.): INTIS 2024, CCIS 2645, pp. 254–267, 2026.
https://doi.org/10.1007/978-3-032-14964-0_20

1   Introduction

Smart farming has gained significant attention in academic and industrial sectors in recent years, owing to advancements in the Internet of Things (IoT) and robotic technologies [12]. This has triggered a wave of new research projects focused on developing information technology (IT) solutions that leverage sensors and robots for optimal management of crop and animal agro-ecology practices. These IT systems have made it possible to conduct precise agricultural tasks, optimize the utilization of production input and natural resources, and automate repetitive and labor-intensive activities.

To achieve these goals, the IT systems used in smart farming are often based on data management and analytic frameworks for Big Data [9]. However, the architectural design of these systems varies depending on agro-ecology application specifications. While advanced data management and analysis tools are widely seen as essential for agro-ecology, there is still a lack of clear guidelines for deploying agro-ecology application systems, including the choice of data management and analytic systems. This makes developing and implementing smart farming solutions difficult.

Moreover, Big Data analytics in smart farming introduces new challenges around data security, privacy, and ethical implications [1]. The large volume, velocity, and variety of data generated from different sources, including sensors, robots, and other IoT devices, present challenges in keeping data private and accurate. Therefore, the need for strong data governance frameworks to tackle these challenges and guarantee proper data management in smart farming.

Despite these challenges, the potential benefits of smart farming are significant [2]. By leveraging the latest IoT and robotic technologies, farmers can boost crop yields, lower costs, use resources efficiently, and adopt sustainable practices. With the continued growth of smart farming, it is expected that more advanced data management frameworks will be developed to address the challenges associated with deploying these systems in practice.

Therefore, in this paper based on our previous works [4] [1] [25], we discuss the requirements that an agro-ecology system architecture should support in terms of data and operations. We also present a reference architecture that supports these requirements.

This paper is structured as follows: Sect. 2 presents related work, Sect. 3 details the context of our previous projects, and the data requirements are shown in Sect. 4. The reference architecture is described in Sect. 5. Finally, Sect. 6 concludes the paper.

2   Related Work

In this section, we provide an overview of recent works on smart farming based on robots and IoT data.

[28] presents an architecture based on the *Kappa* architecture for cow feeding. The authors detail the tuning of the broker component (i.e. Kafka) that

has an impact on the speed of treatment of sensor data. [27] presents (SFOBA), a big data architecture for smart farming, including complex IoT components, which enables a platform for batch and real-time processing of smart farming data. The proposed architecture is inspired by the *Lambda* architecture, and it uses a pipeline built on top of Hadoop for real-time data. Finally, Apache Kylin is used to perform fast multidimensional OLAP queries. [31] proposes WALLeS-MART, a cloud-based system framework for smart farming. The authors present a general architecture targeting IoT common problems (acquisition, processing, and storing) of batch and real-time data analysis. The architecture has been tested and applied in real-case scenarios. [16] proposes a multi-level architecture model enabling herders to better monitor their livestock, and farmers to protect their crops from natural events by predicting risks. The proposed architecture offers simplicity and flexibility and grants independence from technological tools or protocol constraints. The system is built on a five-layer, multi-level architecture. The data processing layer is considered to be the most important in their architecture. The authors 'suggest' the usage of Hadoop and MongoDB for data storage. [8] extends an open IoT platform and provides a cloud-based architecture for smart farming combining sensors, decision-support systems, and control systems over remote and autonomous devices. The authors provide a simulated case of a pest as proof of concept using Spark for the implementation. [26] provides a general overview of Big Data approaches and tools used in precision livestock farming. The architecture suggested in the paper uses ETL data flow for knowledge extraction, and Kafka is used for the pre-treatment phase coupled with Apache Storm for stream processing. Using LiDAR (Light Detection And Ranging). [18] Proposes a novel, fully automated methodology for generating multi-temporal synthetic point clouds. It leverages airborne topographic LiDAR data to calculate tree crown shading and simulate forest growth. Validation results demonstrate efficiency and accuracy exceeding baseline linear regression by 9.4%. In [24] a comprehensive framework is proposed for achieving environmental intelligence support in electrical power transmission corridor vegetation management. It facilitates the extraction of complementary features from (LiDAR) data, enabling predictive analytics with vegetation growth simulation.

[17] proposes a Big Data-based decision support framework to obtain efficient control over farm irrigation. The proposed architecture uses Kafka to collect IoT data and send them to AWS cloud. A study to reach uniform soil moisture content levels is performed to test the framework's usability. [22] proposes an aquaculture monitoring system for storing and processing aquacultural sensors. The system uses Apache Flink as a processing platform, Kafka as a distributed publishing-subscribing messaging system and MongoDB to store sensor data. In [36], an IoT architecture and platform based on microservices are proposed to manage different IoT devices. The platform supports a suite of features, including device management, robust security, seamless interoperability, reusability, and powerful big data handling capabilities. It consists of two layers: data and services. The services layer integrates four tools: *RabbitMQ* to allow interoperability with different protocols, *Micro Mu* to build and manage microservices

(e.g. alert, ingestion, query, and device), *Influx* framework for time series storage and analysis, and *Firebase* for hosting services (e.g. user authentication, real-time database). The platform has been validated in a smart farming scenario related to vineyards. In [40], a cloud robotic application platform is introduced. The application aims to migrate complex computations of robotic applications to the cloud to provide robots with various functional services. This system leverages a microservices architecture to make the application more flexible and compatible.

The above-described works present ad-hoc architectures to handle special cases of smart farming. However, all these proposals are based on common solutions. These intersections have been also pointed out in different survey works. A survey from an architectural point of view of the last 3 years is provided in [35]. This work is very relevant since it highlights the crucial role of Wifi and the Hadoop ecosystem for smart farming applications. Also, [11] provides a survey of existing recent works by highlighting the types of architectures used: cloud-based and distributed architecture (edge and fog). The authors stress the importance of data lake and lakehouse solutions for storing data. They also present osmotic and dew computing as new paradigms of distributed architectures. [33,39] provide a survey of existing work relating to crop management. In [39], authors confirm the effectiveness of a multi-layer architecture based on the perception layer, service layer, network layer, and application layer. In particular, the service layer is in charge of data ingestion, storage, transformation, and analysis. They present an overview of different kinds of data storage solutions and computation from edge to the cloud. The survey presented in [29] offers a literature review on advancements in the smart agriculture context based on IoT technologies and artificial intelligence (AI) techniques. Several challenges are described such as providing more AI-based solutions toward edge devices, the effect of data-driven decisions on smart farming, and the importance of open-source solutions for farmers. [38] provides a review of the applications of the Internet of Things in arable farming. The authors propose a general IoT architecture based on three layers: a device layer, which is composed of physical devices, a network layer, which enables data communication to the cloud by using communication protocols, and an application layer that offers different services such as data storage, advanced analytics, easy access through an API, and a user interface software application. Although these works provide a detailed panorama of existing architectures, they do not present the components' details and interactions.

3   Case Studies

In this section, we present the agro-ecology applications of our previous projects, which will be used to describe the data requirements that must be supported by our reference architecture for IoT&robots-based agro-ecology applications.

3.1 Mechanical Weeding

Agricultural robots are seen as a major contributor to sustainable agriculture, thanks to their ability to reduce workload or improve working conditions for farmers [23]. Therefore, [4] proposes the *LambdaAgrIoT* architecture for monitoring and scheduling autonomous agricultural robot tasks. It supports Big Data (real-time, analytics, and transactional) workloads and it is built upon the lambda architecture. Data used in this system come from robots and in-field sensors. Robots have been used for mechanical weeding operations. Also, other kinds of operations have been tested. *LambdaAgrIoT* architecture allows farmers to follow in real-time the advancement of agricultural tasks using a simple web-based user interface, where all data (i.e. robot positions, odometry data, and sensors data) are easily visualized. Moreover, also alerts generated by robots about their mechanical faults could be visualized.

3.2 Crop Phenotyping

Crop phenotyping is the science of measuring various plant characteristics using different methods. This helps us identify plants with the best responses to treatments and environmental conditions. Ultimately, the goal is to find plants with the most desirable traits, achieved through a combination of their genes, the environment they grow in, and how they are managed.

Phenotyping can dramatically benefit from sensors enabling multiple, traceable, high spatio-temporal resolution measurements of plant features along the growth. In such a context, sensor platforms are vital. They handle the physical sensors, manage how they take measurements, and make that data accessible to other software programs. In simple terms, a sensors platform is a software layer that abstracts the underlying hardware of a sensor and provides a standardized interface for data acquisition, processing, and communication.

In the case study [5], an IoT&robots based architecture for phenotyping of plants cultivated in a greenhouse environment is presented. In particular, two sensor platforms are used: an IoT platform for acquiring relevant environmental data and a robot mobile platform for accurate monitoring of the development of individual plants in response to different protocols of biostimulant and protection treatments and to environmental conditions. As IoT platform, the TIM ICON is used for aggregating several sensing devices deployed at fixed locations (indoor and outdoor) collecting relevant data on environmental conditions, such as air temperature and humidity, soil temperature and moisture, rainfall, and wind speed, along with light intensity (irradiation) and leaf wettability .... The TIM ICON platform provides a centralized data management system that allows users to access and analyze data from different sensors in a standardized way. The robot platform deploys plants' measurement missions in the cultivated area, revisiting the individual units of cultivation (mini-plots or single plants, depending on the considered crop) at different times during the growth. The robot is equipped with RGB, hyper-spectral, and depth cameras producing 2D, spectral, and 3D images of plants that can be analyzed to obtain accurate information on the evolution of individuals (growth rate, morphological features, accumulation of pigments, ...). The obtained data are stored in a purposely built Big Data engine, which provides a data lake storage, a time series DBMS and a query engine exposing each service through an API. Ingestion and transformation of the data are implemented using source-specialized connector-agents and a pipeline-based task-execution platform. These allow researchers to automate their data life-cycle processes, from measurement to analysis and visualization.

3.3 Crop Yield Monitoring

To achieve the desired grain yield, farmers must consider several crucial crop management factors: fertilizer application, organic manure for plant nutrition, weed control, pesticide use, and maintaining optimal plant population density [25]. On the other hand, various factors other than crop management could be major influencing factors such as weather conditions and soil type. Even if all crop management factors are set at the optimum levels, the final crop yield outcome could be influenced by extreme weather conditions, such as first and last frost, and continuous frost days during the growing stage [20]. Moreover, the crop yield is limited by the soil type and the spatial-temporal associated with the field. To investigate crop yield-limiting factors, an effective reference architecture is required to allow: (1) study of soil nutrient management, where various machine learning models on soil nutrient data along with weather data can be applied; (2) study of vegetation indices data by analyzing satellite imagery and observing how the weather factors contribute to the growth of crops, and whether we can predict the yield limits in the early stages. A system achieving these goals has been proposed in [25].

4 Requirements

In this section, based on our previous works (c.f. Sect. 3) and on existing works described in Sect. 2, we present the requirements for a data-centric architecture. Three main classes of data are usually used: *Transactional*, *Streaming*, and *Historical data*.

Transactional Data. Transactional data refers to data that can be updated and deleted. These data are used to describe the context of the applications and to analyze other types of data.

Transactional data are:

- *Alphanumeric*, such as the name of the farmer that is relevant for traceability of the processes, the characteristics of plants that are critical information to be kept for crop management, etc.
- *Spatial.* These data are geographical data that usually have a vector (such as boundaries of the plot, positions of obstacles in the fields, etc.) or a raster format (for example a soil humidity map).

- *Spatio-temporal.* These data are spatial data associated with temporal ones. In other terms, spatio-temporal data are spatial data that change over time. An example is a crop parcel, which geometry can vary over time from one year to another.
- *Trajectory.* A trajectory is an ordered sequence of points and timestamps. An example is the set of positions in time of the path that must be followed by an autonomous tractor or by a weeding robot.

The operators that can be applied to these data are: select, delete, and update.

Streaming Data. Streaming data are data produced in a continuous or episodic way, and does not need (or cannot) be stored permanently. Streaming data types are the same as Transactional data, plus multimedia data (such as videos and images). In particular, streaming data are:

- *Alphanumeric,* for example, air temperature, wind speed, tool depth or position, robot speed, etc.
- *Spatial,* for example, the GPS coordinates of a sensor.
- *Spatio-temporal,* for example, weather forecasts, grazing animals, etc.
- *Trajectory,* for example, the real-time movement of a robot.
- *Multimedia,* for example, the images or videos sent by a weeding robot to inform the farmer about its position and environment in a particular blocking condition.

Operators that are applied to streaming data are continuous queries. Continuous queries are queries that are triggered with a particular frequency and use a set of data defined by temporal or tuples windows. An example of a continuous query over meteorological data coming from a sensor can be: *"Each 1 h* (i.e. frequency), *provides the minimum temperature measured in the last 30 min* (i.e. time window)".

Usually, these data are used in combination with Transactional data, in order to contextualize the raw data coming from the streaming data sources (i.e. robots and sensors). For example, the geometries of the plots can be used to select and query the needed sensors. Therefore, common data operators for streaming data are *join* and *continuous queries.*

Moreover, more complex advanced analytical methods are applied to these data. For example, machine learning algorithms can be used to inform decisions about the next positions of a robot when it is evolving in the field.

Historical Data. Historical data are streaming and transactional data that are permanently stored. Historical data can be:

- *Alphanumeric,* for example, hourly average air temperature and solar irradiation intensity, daily rainfall, etc.
- *Spatial,* boundaries of fields or plots, boundaries of vulnerable or restricted zones, soil texture maps, fertility maps, infestation maps, prescription maps, yield maps, etc.
- *Spatio-temporal,* crop rotation maps, epidemiological maps, weed spreading maps, etc.

- *Trajectory*, time sampled position of the machine or of the robot during an operation, etc.
- *Multimedia*, for example, the images or videos acquired by machines, drones, or robots about weeds infestation at specific time-points, phenological stages of the crop at sample dates, images of crop diseases, etc.

Extendibility. As previously described, agro-ecology involves several kinds of data (e.g. meteorological, agronomic). "Hypothesis-driven" analysis is an approach that agro-ecology researchers use to develop their analyses. With this approach, all the data required by the models at design time are identified and selected, and in cases where they are not available, these data are removed from the analytical process. To avoid such limitation, "data-driven" analysis [15] enables deriving knowledge from data at design time. However, in the context of complex data domains such as agro-ecology, "data-driven" analysis approach is not very practical since the collection of data could be a very huge task. Therefore, by providing flexible data management tools, researchers in agro-ecology can easily explore and analyze their data, discover new patterns and correlations, and develop more accurate models and predictions (as pointed out in [10]). This, in turn, can lead to more effective and sustainable agricultural practices, better resource management, and improved crop yields.

5   Reference Architecture

In this section, we describe the reference architecture for agro-ecology applications focusing on data management and analysis systems. The data producers are usually sensors and robots. Sensors come with embedded operating systems that are very limited in storage and computation capabilities. On the contrary, robots are equipped with classical workstations or laptops, where the robot operating system is installed. An example is ROS^1. Therefore it is possible to provide robots with light data management systems.

In the following, we discuss the architecture components that can be deployed at the farm or cloud levels.

Data Pipelines. Multiple data pipelines execute on both raw data and organized data for different purposes including crucial data preparation steps like cleaning, enrichment, and loading into a particular store. Data pipelines fall into two categories (*i*) Batch pipelines that are triggered to execute upon the receipt of a data batch, and (*ii*) Stream pipelines that execute continuously. Data pipelines are designed as workflows. Workflows automate scientific and business processes. Workflows are a set of automated tasks. They are usually represented as a Directed Acyclic Graph (DAG), where each node is a task, and edges show which tasks must be completed first. Data pipelines are polyglot. They are coded in different languages (python, scala, java, or SQL) depending on the analytical DBMS back-end interfaces. *Apache Airflow* allows the execution of implemented

---

[1] https://www.ros.org/.

workflows as well as monitoring. Data pipelines can also be implemented using *Spark* and *Kafka* APIs or Extract Transformation Loading (ETL) tools such as *Talend*.

Messages Broker System. A message broker acts as a middleman for application communication. It ensures messages are valid, transforms and routes them if needed, and directs them to the correct recipient. This approach minimizes the need for applications to be aware of each other's specifics, promoting a decoupled architecture. A message broker system is then mandatory in smart farming since data are received from multiple sources (i.e. robots and sensors) and forwarded to other data management systems (and vice versa). *Apache Kafka* is an example of a message broker system. *Apache Kafka* is a powerful tool for managing real-time data. It is a distributed data streaming platform where various sources can publish data streams, which can then be subscribed to and processed by multiple consumers in real-time.

Streaming Engine. Streaming engines offer the ability to quickly, efficiently, and securely process huge volumes of real-time data. *Apache Flink* is an example of a streaming engine playing the role of a real-time analytical processor, enabling the processing of both stream and batch data. Moreover, *Flink* offers multiple operations on data streams such as joining, filtering, grouping, defining windows, aggregating, and supporting standard SQL. Spatial data types (e.g. point, polygon) are also supported by *GeoFlink*, a Flink extension that provides the ability to perform some types of continuous queries over spatial streams (range, KNN, and join queries) [34].

Raw Data Management System. This system is in charge of storing all data coming from sensors, robots, and other data sources. It must be scalable and flexible. It should be combined with tools to efficiently extract data. An example is *Hadoop Distributed File System* (HFDS). *HDFS* has been widely used to store sensors data, but also robotic data such as rosbag files[2] and odometry data [41]. [14] presents a survey of data lake systems. Authors point out that the storage of raw data is usually supported by *Hadoop*. Recently, an extension for spatial data in *Hadoop* has been proposed with *Spatial Parquet* [32]. Finally, *HDFS* storage is compatible with many DBMSs as well as Metadata Management and Data Governance systems.

Analytical DBMSs. It aims to store data extracted and transformed from raw data, in order to be analyzed. For example, *MobilityDb* is a relational DBMS that natively supports trajectory data [42]. Therefore, *MobilityDb* can be used to store and query trajectory data of robots, while *MongoDB* is suitable for GPS data of robots [30]. Another example is *InfluxDB* for the aggregation queries over time series data from sensors [21]. Also, special DBMS for handling raster data have been developed such as one presented in [3]. Moreover, there is a need for querying data stored in different systems. Then, a polyglot query engine system is needed [19], as discussed in the next.

---

[2] http://github.com/valtech/ros_hadoop.

Metadata Management and Data Governance System. A Metadata Management and Data Governance system helps organizations manage their data more effectively. It lets them create a data catalog, categorize their data, and ensure proper data governance. Catalog systems allow managing the extensibility needed by agro-ecology applications. Indeed, when new data arrive, it is possible to use this kind of system to look for them and discover new possible analysis possibilities associated with these new data, and consequently improve the analytical systems. An example of such a system is *Apache Atlas*, which allows to store and query metadata about data and transformation operations over them. Some tools, such as *GeoNetwork* are specially conceived for spatial data. *GeoNetwork* is a decentralized system for managing geographic information. It allows users to access and share geo-referenced databases, cartographic products, and detailed descriptions (metadata) from various sources.

Analytical System. An agro-ecology information system relies heavily on its ability to analyze data. This analysis is crucial for extracting valuable knowledge from the large amounts of information it collects. Due to the variability of the data types to be analyzed this function is composed of multiple components addressing particular needs.

- **Spatial analysis**: Spatial OLAP systems are designed to deal with large amounts of data and enable the analysis of multidimensional data. They are built on top of data warehouses, which are Analytical DBMSs components designed to store large amounts of data issued from various sources. Spatial OLAP servers and clients, such as GeoMondrian and Map4OLAP, are used to provide decision-makers with interactive displays of the data, including tabular, graphical, and map displays [6]. A major strength of Spatial OLAP systems is their ability to perform complex multidimensional analysis on large volumes of data. Additionally, Teaming up Spatial OLAP with GIS unlocks advanced capabilities for analyzing and mapping data with geographic context [7].
- **Artificial Intelligence**: Artificial intelligence (AI) is another technology that has great potential for smart farming. AI involves the simulation of human intelligence processes by machines. Machine learning and deep learning are commonly used in smart farming applications to determine crop growth and levels of plant stress using computer vision models [13]. For example, AI can detect pest risk in fruits at an early stage. In addition, AI can be applied to the entire farm to increase productivity by connecting farm devices to AI techniques [37]. AI techniques can also be applied to stream data, enabling real-time monitoring using libraries such as *Apache Spark MLib* and *Flink ML*. By using AI and machine learning techniques, farmers can make more informed decisions and improve their operations' efficiency and effectiveness.

Query Engine. To cope with data variety and different query patterns, data is analyzed in different Analytical DBMSs, as previously described. Each of these systems has its own data model and query language. This leads to a situation

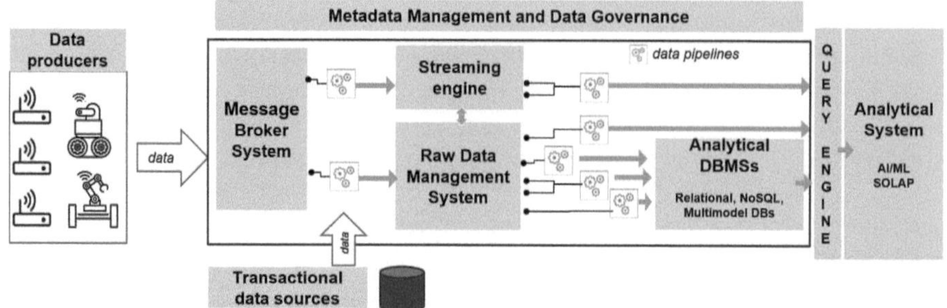

Fig. 1. Reference Architecture.

where data is stored in different formats and locations, making it difficult to query and join data from different sources. To address this challenge, a query engine is required that can transparently query and join data from different Analytical DBMSs. The query engine acts as an intermediate layer between the user and the analytical database management systems. It is responsible for query routing, query pre-processing, and query post-processing and should be capable of routing queries to a single Analytical DBMS or multiple systems. Several existing technologies provide query engines for querying and joining data from different analytical database management systems. *Apache Presto*, for example, is an open-source distributed SQL query engine that can query data from different sources, including *Hive*, *Hadoop Distributed File System* (HDFS), and *Cassandra*. It provides a unified SQL interface that enables users to query data from multiple data sources. Similarly, *Trino*, a fork of *Presto*, also provides a query engine that supports querying data from multiple and different analytical database management systems (Fig. 1).

6   Conclusion

Agro-ecology is a crucial social and economic academic and industrial issue for the next years. Several works are being conducted to evaluate and define new agricultural practices as more sustainable. Indeed, recently some works have investigated the usage of IoT and robots for smart farming and in particular for agro-ecology practices. These solutions provide complex data management and analysis systems issued from Big Data frameworks. However, there are no clear generic guidelines about the tools to use to implement such agro-ecology applications. Therefore, based on our different previous works on Big Data and agro-ecology, in this paper, we present the requirements in terms of data acquisition, data analytics, data governance, and data querying for agro-ecology applications. Then, we propose our view of a reference architecture that relies on these requirements, to offer a generic architectural framework that can be implemented by academic and industrial actors to set up their agro-ecology system application.

In terms of future work, we aim to implement our architecture based on microservices to make software development more flexible and deploy it in different agro-ecology applications. The objective is to provide an open-source tool for agro-ecology data management and analytics.

Acknowledgement. This work has been supported by the French National Research Agency under the IDEX-ISITE project, initiative 16-IDEX-0001 (CAP 20-25), and the project ANR-20-PCPA-0002.

References

1. Ardagna, C.A., Ceravolo, P., Damiani, E.: Big data analytics as-a-service: issues and challenges. In: 2016 IEEE International Conference on Big Data (Big Data), pp. 3638–3644. IEEE (2016)
2. Ayaz, M., Ammad-Uddin, M., Sharif, Z., Mansour, A., Aggoune, E.H.M.: Internet-of-things (IoT)-based smart agriculture: toward making the fields talk. IEEE Access **7**, 129551–129583 (2019)
3. Baumann, P., Misev, D., Merticariu, V., Huu, B.P.: Array databases: concepts, standards, implementations. J. Big Data **8**(1), 1–61 (2021). https://doi.org/10.1186/s40537-020-00399-2
4. Belhassena, A., et al.: Towards an architecture for agricultural autonomous robots' scheduling. In: 25th International Enterprise Distributed Object Computing Workshop, EDOC Workshop 2021, Gold Coast, Australia, 25–29 October 2021, pp. 194–203. IEEE (2021)
5. Berto, F., et al.: A 5G-IoT enabled big data infrastructure for data-driven agronomy. In: IEEE Globecom 2022 Workshops, Rio de Janeiro, Brazil, 4–8 December 2022, pp. 588–594. IEEE (2022)
6. Bimonte, S., Edoh-Alove, É., Coulibaly, F.A.: Map4olap: a web-based tool for interactive map visualization of OLAP queries. In: Chen, Y., et al. (eds.) 2021 IEEE International Conference on Big Data (Big Data), Orlando, FL, USA, 15–18 December 2021, pp. 3747–3750. IEEE (2021)
7. Bimonte, S., Miquel, M.: When spatial analysis meets OLAP: multidimensional model and operators. Int. J. Data Warehous. Min. **6**(4), 33–60 (2010)
8. Cadavid, H., Garzón, W., Pérez, A., López, G., Mendivelso, C., Ramírez, C.: Towards a smart farming platform: from IoT-based crop sensing to data analytics. In: Serrano C., J.E., Martínez-Santos, J.C. (eds.) CCC 2018. CCIS, vol. 885, pp. 237–251. Springer, Cham (2018). https://doi.org/10.1007/978-3-319-98998-3_19
9. Ceravolo, P., et al.: Big data semantics. J. Data Semant. **7**, 65–85 (2018)
10. Coulibaly Fagnine, A., Bimonte, S., Rizzi, S., Sylvie, M.M., Fabre, F.: Towards a multi-model approach to support user-driven extensibility in data warehouses: agro-ecology case study. In: DataPlat'23: 2nd International Workshop on Data Platform Design, Management, and Optimization, Ioannina, Greece, 28 March 2023. CEUR (2023)
11. Debauche, O., Mahmoudi, S., Manneback, P., Lebeau, F.: Cloud and distributed architectures for data management in agriculture 4.0: review and future trends. J. King Saud Univ.-Comput. Inf. Sci. **34**(9), 7494–7514 (2022)
12. Debauche, O., et al.: Data management and internet of things: a methodological review in smart farming. Internet Things **14**, 100378 (2021)

13. Ghosal, S., Blystone, D., Singh, A.K., Ganapathysubramanian, B., Singh, A., Sarkar, S.: An explainable deep machine vision framework for plant stress phenotyping. Proc. Natl. Acad. Sci. **115**(18), 4613–4618 (2018)
14. Hai, R., Quix, C., Jarke, M.: Data lake concept and systems: a survey. arXiv preprint arXiv:2106.09592 (2021)
15. Hartmann, P.M., Zaki, M., Feldmann, N., Neely, A.: Capturing value from big data: a taxonomy of data-driven business models used by start-up firms. Int. J. Oper. Prod. Manag. **36**(10), 1382–1406 (2016)
16. Houngue, P., Sagbo, R., Kedowide, C.: An hybrid novel layered architecture and case study: IoT for smart agriculture and smart livestock. In: Pereira, P., Ribeiro, R., Oliveira, I., Novais, P. (eds.) Society with Future: Smart and Liveable Cities, pp. 71–82. Springer, Cham (2020)
17. Keswani, B., Mohapatra, A.G., Keswani, P., Khanna, A., Gupta, D., Rodrigues, J.: Improving weather dependent zone specific irrigation control scheme in IoT and big data enabled self driven precision agriculture mechanism. Enterprise Inf. Syst. **14**(9–10), 1494–1515 (2020)
18. Kohek, Š., Žalik, B., Strnad, D., Kolmanič, S., Lukač, N.: Simulation-driven 3D forest growth forecasting based on airborne topographic lidar data and shading. Int. J. Appl. Earth Obs. Geoinf. **111**, 102844 (2022). https://doi.org/10.1016/j.jag.2022.102844. https://www.sciencedirect.com/science/article/pii/S1569843222000462
19. Kranas, P., et al.: Parallel query processing in a polystore. Distrib. Parallel Databases **39**(4), 939–977 (2021). https://doi.org/10.1007/s10619-021-07322-5
20. Kukal, M.S., Irmak, S.: U.S. agro-climate in 20th century: growing degree days, first and last frost, growing season length, and impacts on crop yields. Sci. Rep. **8**(1)
21. Liu, R., Yuan, J.: Benchmarking time series databases with IoTDB-benchmark for IoT scenarios. arXiv preprint arXiv:1901.08304 (2019)
22. Lou, Y., Chen, L., Ye, F., Chen, Y., Liu, Z.: Research and implementation of an aquaculture monitoring system based on Flink, MongoDB and Kafka. In: Rodrigues, J.M.F., et al. (eds.) ICCS 2019. LNCS, vol. 11538, pp. 648–657. Springer, Cham (2019). https://doi.org/10.1007/978-3-030-22744-9_50
23. Martin, T., et al.: Robots and transformations of work in farm: a systematic review of the literature and a research agenda. Agron. Sustain. Dev. **42**(4), 66 (2022)
24. Mongus, D., et al.: A complete environmental intelligence system for lidar-based vegetation management in power-line corridors. Remote Sens. **13**(24) (2021). https://doi.org/10.3390/rs13245159. https://www.mdpi.com/2072-4292/13/24/5159
25. Nabila, C., Tahar, K.M.: Data analytics for crop management: a big data view. J. Big Data **9**(1) (2022)
26. Nolack Fote, F., Mahmoudi, S., Roukh, A., Ahmed Mahmoudi, S.: Big data storage and analysis for smart farming. In: 2020 5th International Conference on Cloud Computing and Artificial Intelligence: Technologies and Applications (CloudTech), pp. 1–8 (2020)
27. Ouafiq, E.M., Elrharras, A., Mehdary, A., Chehri, A., Saadane, R., Wahbi, M.: IoT in smart farming analytics, big data based architecture. In: Zimmermann, A., Howlett, R.J., Jain, L.C. (eds.) Human Centred Intelligent Systems. SIST, vol. 189, pp. 269–279. Springer, Singapore (2021). https://doi.org/10.1007/978-981-15-5784-2_22
28. Penka, J.B.N., Mahmoudi, S., Debauche, O.: A new kappa architecture for IoT data management in smart farming. Procedia Comput. Sci. **191**, 17–24 (2021)

29. Qazi, S., Khawaja, B.A., Farooq, Q.U.: IoT-equipped and AI-enabled next generation smart agriculture: a critical review, current challenges and future trends. IEEE Access **10**, 21219–21235 (2022)
30. Ravichandran, R., Prassler, E., Huebel, N., Blumenthal, S.: A workbench for quantitative comparison of databases in multi-robot applications. In: 2018 IEEE/RSJ International Conference on Intelligent Robots and Systems (IROS), pp. 3744–3750. IEEE (2018)
31. Roukh, A., Fote, F.N., Mahmoudi, S.A., Mahmoudi, S.: Big data processing architecture for smart farming. In: Shakshuki, E.M., Yasar, A. (eds.) The 11th International Conference on Emerging Ubiquitous Systems and Pervasive Networks (EUSPN 2020)/The 10th International Conference on Current and Future Trends of Information and Communication Technologies in Healthcare (ICTH-2020)/Affiliated Workshops, Madeira, Portugal, 2–5 November 2020. Procedia Computer Science, vol. 177, pp. 78–85. Elsevier (2020)
32. Saeedan, M., Eldawy, A.: Spatial parquet: a column file format for geospatial data lakes [extended version]. arXiv preprint arXiv:2209.02158 (2022)
33. Saiz-Rubio, V., Rovira-Más, F.: From smart farming towards agriculture 5.0: a review on crop data management. Agronomy **10** (2020)
34. Shaikh, S.A., Kitagawa, H., Matono, A., Mariam, K., Kim, K.S.: Geoflink: an efficient and scalable spatial data stream management system. IEEE Access **10**, 24909–24935 (2022)
35. Thi, M.H., Vinh, N.T.Q., Quynh, N.T.H., et al.: Computing infrastructure of IoT applications in smart agriculture: a systematical review. In: 2021 6th International Conference on Innovative Technology in Intelligent System and Industrial Applications (CITISIA), pp. 1–9. IEEE (2021)
36. Trilles, S., González-Pérez, A., Huerta, J.: An IoT platform based on microservices and serverless paradigms for smart farming purposes. Sensors **20**(8), 2418 (2020)
37. Vasisht, D., et al.: Farmbeats: an IoT platform for data-driven agriculture. In: Proceedings of the 14th USENIX Conference on Networked Systems Design and Implementation, NSDI 2017, pp. 515–528. USENIX Association, USA (2017)
38. Villa-Henriksen, A., Edwards, G.T., Pesonen, L.A., Green, O., Sørensen, C.A.G.: Internet of things in arable farming: implementation, applications, challenges and potential. Biosys. Eng. **191**, 60–84 (2020)
39. Vitali, G., Francia, M., Golfarelli, M., Canavari, M.: Crop management with the IoT: an interdisciplinary survey. Agronomy **11**(1), 181 (2021)
40. Xu, B., Bian, J.: A cloud robotic application platform design based on the microservices architecture. In: CCRIS 2020: International Conference on Control, Robotics and Intelligent System, Xiamen, China, 27–29 October 2020, pp. 13–18. ACM (2020)
41. Yoo, A., Shin, S., Lee, J., Moon, C.: Implementation of a sensor big data processing system for autonomous vehicles in the c-its environment. Appl. Sci. **10**(21), 7858 (2020)
42. Zimányi, E., Sakr, M.A., Lesuisse, A.: Mobilitydb: a mobility database based on postgresql and postgis. ACM Trans. Database Syst. **45**(4), 19:1–19:42 (2020)

Synergizing Blockchain and Cloud: Elevating Decentralization and Scalability in Blockchain-Cloud Deployment Modes

Youness Bentayeb[✉] and Hassan Badir

IDS Research Team (Ingénierie des Données et des Systèmes-UAE) ENSAT, Abdelmalek Essaadi University Tangier, Tangier, Morocco
`youness.bentayeb@etu.uae.ac.ma`

Abstract. The intersection of blockchain and cloud technologies introduces transformative possibilities for reshaping business and organizational operations. Within this evolving landscape, the amalgamation of these technologies gives rise to novel deployment modes, referred to in this paper as Blockchain-Cloud Deployment Modes (BCDM). This paper provides an in-depth exploration and comparative analysis of these BCDM, emphasizing their capacity to enhance decentralization and scalability. The study investigates three distinct BCDM: Cloud over Blockchain (CoB), Blockchain over Cloud (BoC), and Mixed Blockchain Cloud (MBC). CoB leverages blockchain as a backend for storing and managing data within cloud applications, while BoC employs a cloud-based infrastructure for hosting and running blockchain applications. MBC, a hybrid approach, integrates CoB and BoC by deploying multiple blockchain instances on a cloud-based infrastructure. Critical parameters, including security, scalability, interoperability, and performance, serve as the basis for the comparative evaluation. Our findings unveil unique strengths within each BCDM. CoB excels in security and privacy, BoC demonstrates superior scalability and interoperability, and MBC emerges as a versatile architecture capable of addressing varied use cases. This research contributes valuable insights to the dynamic landscape of blockchain-cloud integration, empowering decision-makers to discern and adopt deployment modes tailored to their specific needs.

Keywords: Decentralized System · Blockchain · Cloud Computing · Security · Cloud Engineering · Blockchain Service Model

1 Introduction

The intersection of blockchain and cloud technologies marks a pivotal moment in the evolution of modern computing [1], offering transformative possibilities for reshaping business and organizational operations [2]. Blockchain technology, renowned for its decentralized and secure architecture, and cloud computing, recognized for providing scalable and flexible infrastructures, individually bring unique strengths to the technological landscape [3]. As organizations grapple with the increasing need for enhanced

H. Badir et al. (Eds.): INTIS 2024, CCIS 2645, pp. 268–275, 2026.
https://doi.org/10.1007/978-3-032-14964-0_21

security, scalability, and efficient data management, the integration of blockchain and cloud technologies emerges as a compelling solution [1]. In response to this paradigm shift, a new framework emerges. The amalgamation of blockchain and cloud technologies leads to the formation of novel deployment modes [4], collectively referred to in this paper as Blockchain-Cloud Deployment Modes (BCDM). These modes represent innovative approaches to deploying systems and applications, leveraging the complementary strengths of blockchain and cloud infrastructures [2, 4]. The primary purpose of this paper is to conduct a comprehensive exploration and comparative analysis of Blockchain-Cloud Deployment Modes (BCDM), with a particular emphasis on decentralization and scalability. The study focuses on three distinct BCDM: Cloud over Blockchain (CoB), Blockchain over Cloud (BoC), and Mixed Blockchain Cloud (MBC). Throughout the analysis, critical parameters including security, scalability, interoperability, and performance serve as the foundation for assessing the unique strengths and characteristics of each BCDM. By providing valuable insights, this research aims to assist decision-makers in making informed choices regarding the adoption of deployment modes that align with their specific organizational needs.

2 Background

In this section, we set the foundation for understanding the individual components of the study—blockchain technology and cloud computing. Here, we delve into the fundamental principles and features of each, highlighting their significance in the context of the emerging Blockchain-Cloud Deployment Modes (BCDM).

A. *Overview of Blockchain Technology*

Blockchain technology is renowned for its decentralized, tamper-resistant ledger system [3]. Originally devised as the underlying technology for cryptocurrencies, blockchain has evolved beyond its initial applications [5]. It operates on a distributed network, facilitating secure and transparent transactions without the need for a central authority. Key features, such as immutability, consensus mechanisms, and smart contracts, contribute to the robust and trustless nature of blockchain systems.

B. *Overview of Cloud Computing*

Cloud computing has revolutionized the way organizations handle data and deploy applications [6]. It provides on-demand access to a shared pool of configurable computing resources over the internet [7]. The cloud's scalability, flexibility, and cost- effectiveness make it a pivotal component of modern IT infrastructures. Various service models, including Infrastructure as a Service (IaaS), Platform as a Service (PaaS), and Software as a Service (SaaS), offer organizations diverse options for meeting their specific computing needs [8].

C. *Intersection and Synergy between Blockchain and Cloud*

The convergence of blockchain and cloud technologies represents a strategic alliance [7]. While blockchain ensures decentralized trust and security, cloud computing provides the necessary infrastructure for scalable and efficient deployment [4]. The symbiotic relationship between these technologies lays the groundwork for the exploration of Blockchain-Cloud Deployment Modes (BCDM). This intersection opens up new avenues for addressing challenges related to data management, security, and scalability, offering organizations a more holistic and adaptable approach to technological integration.

3   Blockchain-Cloud Deployment Modes

The synergy between blockchain technology and cloud computing unveils a plethora of possibilities, particularly in sectors where the paramountcy of security and transparency cannot be overstated [9]. This chapter delineates three principal deployment architectures that epitomize the integration of blockchain with cloud computing: Cloud over Blockchain (CoB), Blockchain over Cloud (BoC), and Mixed Blockchain Cloud (MBC), each catering to distinct requirements and offering unique advantages.

- **Cloud over Blockchain (CoB)**

    The CoB architecture leverages the cloud as a robust platform for hosting applications powered by blockchain technology [4]. This amalgamation harnesses the cloud's scalability and fault tolerance alongside blockchain's unparalleled security and data privacy features. In a CoB setup, while the cloud provider is tasked with infrastructure management, blockchain technology steps in to fortify security and ensure transparency. This model finds its utility in myriad applications, ranging from secure data sharing and supply chain management to safeguarding sensitive healthcare data.
- **Blockchain over Cloud (BoC)**

    Conversely, the BoC architecture utilizes blockchain technology to orchestrate the cloud infrastructure, introducing a layer of enhanced security and transparency to cloud computing services [8]. Blockchain's capability to meticulously track and authenticate all transactions related to the cloud infrastructure makes BoC particularly appealing. Benefits of this architecture include accelerated and more efficient cloud resource deployment, bolstered fault tolerance, and scalability [9]. BoC's applications are vast, including but not limited to, streamlining financial transactions, augmenting government services, and enhancing gaming experiences.
- **Mixed Blockchain Cloud (MBC)**

    The MBC architecture represents a harmonious blend of CoB and BoC, integrating the strengths of both to forge a more adaptable and customizable infrastructure [4]. This architecture facilitates granular control over aspects such as security, privacy, and scalability, making it suitable for applications that demand a high degree of flexibility [4, 9]. MBC's potential use cases span smart city development, the Internet of Things (IoT), and e-commerce platforms, showcasing its versatility.

The table (Table 1) below encapsulates the comparative advantages and potential applications of each architecture:

In essence, the fusion of blockchain with cloud computing not only elevates the security and transparency paradigms but also significantly enhances scalability across various industries, paving the way for innovative deployment architectures tailored to meet the evolving demands of the digital era.

Table 1. Summarizes the differences between CoB, BoC, and MBC.Deployment Modes.

Architecture	Cloud Utilization	Blockchain Functionality	Advantages	Use Cases
CoB	Hosts blockchain-based applications	Secures and brings transparency	Scalability, fault-tolerance, data privacy	Data sharing, supply chain, healthcare
BoC	Manages cloud infrastructure	Authenticates cloud transactions	Security, transparency, efficiency, scalability	Financial transactions, government, gaming
MBC	Integrates cloud and blockchain	Enables granular control over security and scalability	Customization, flexibility	Smart cities, IoT, e-commerce

4 Approach

In lieu of a traditional Methodology section, this article adopts a comprehensive approach to investigate and analyze Blockchain-Cloud Deployment Modes (BCDM). The chosen approach, blending qualitative and quantitative insights, aligns with the research objectives and emphasizes the practical exploration of CoB, BoC, and MBC.

4.1 Data Collection

Transparency in the data collection process is pivotal. Utilizing both primary and secondary sources, pertinent information about CoB, BoC, and MBC is gathered.

The focus is on real-world applications, user experiences, and industry use cases to provide authentic insights.

4.2 Comparative Framework

Rather than adhering to a rigid comparative analysis framework, a flexible and dynamic approach is embraced. This allows for an organic exploration of critical parameters such as security, scalability, interoperability, and performance. The aim is to capture the nuances of each BCDM without imposing preconceived notions.

4.3 Iterative Analysis

The analysis process is iterative, involving continuous refinement as new insights emerge. This dynamic approach accommodates the evolving nature of blockchain and cloud technologies, ensuring that the study captures the most current and relevant information.

This approach to the comparative analysis ensures a systematic and rigorous examination of Blockchain-Cloud Deployment Modes, providing valuable insights into their relative strengths and limitations.

5 Comparative Analysis

In our pursuit of a comprehensive understanding, we conducted a detailed comparative analysis of the Blockchain-Cloud Deployment Modes (BCDM), considering critical factors like scalability, performance, security, and ease of implementation. The findings are encapsulated in the following narrative:

- **Scalability**

  Scalability is a pivotal consideration in cloud computing architectures. The CoB deployment mode, reliant on a single blockchain, encounters limitations in scalability [10]. In contrast, the BoC deployment mode addresses this challenge adeptly by employing multiple blockchains. This not only enhances scalability but also boosts overall throughput. The MBC deployment mode takes a nuanced approach, achieving a balance between scalability and granular control. It employs a main blockchain for high-level transactions and sidechains for specific purposes [4]. Overall, both the BoC and MBC deployment modes outshine the CoB deployment mode in terms of scalability.

- **Performance**

  The performance metric is crucial for evaluating the efficiency of cloud computing architectures. The CoB deployment mode exhibits lower performance due to its reliance on a single blockchain, leading to potential delays in transaction processing [11]. In contrast, both the BoC and MBC deployment modes showcase higher performance. Their utilization of multiple blockchains enables the distribution of workload and optimization of transaction processing.

- **Security**

  Security is paramount in cloud computing architectures, and the integration of blockchain technology significantly enhances this aspect by providing decentralization and transparency. While all three deployment modes - CoB, BoC, and MBC - leverage blockchain for enhanced security, the BoC and MBC deployment modes may have a slight edge due to their use of multiple blockchains. This introduces redundancy and fault tolerance, bolstering overall security [12].

- **Ease of Implementation**

  The practical adoption of cloud computing architectures relies on the ease of implementation. The CoB deployment mode, with its reliance on a single blockchain, is relatively straightforward to implement [13]. On the other hand, both the BoC and MBC deployment modes may present higher complexity due to the utilization of multiple blockchains. However, leveraging established blockchain platforms and open- source tools can streamline the implementation process for both BoC and MBC deployment modes [12].

In summary, our comparative analysis indicates that both the BoC and MBC deployment modes offer distinct advantages over the CoB deployment mode, particularly in terms of scalability, performance, and security. While the CoB deployment mode may have an edge in ease of implementation, the ultimate choice of deployment mode depends on the specific needs and requirements of the cloud computing application.

The subsequent table (Table 2) outlines key factors across CoB, BoC, and MBC deployment modes, encapsulating distinct characteristics related to scalability, performance, security, and the complexity of implementation.

Table 2. Comparative analysis of CoB, BoC, and MBC Deployment Modes.

Factor	CoB Deployment Mode	BoC Deployment Mode	MBC Deployment Mode
Scalability	Limited due to reliance on a single blockchain	Better due to use of multiple blockchains	Balanced approach with main blockchain and sidechains
Performance	Lower due to reliance on a single blockchain	Higher due to use of multiple blockchains	Higher due to use of multiple blockchains
Security	Enhanced by use of blockchain technology	Enhanced by use of blockchain technology and redundancy/fault tolerance	Enhanced by use of blockchain technology and redundancy/fault tolerance
Ease of Implementation	Relatively easy due to reliance on a single blockchain	More complex due to use of multiple blockchains	More complex due to use of multiple blockchains but can be simplified with established blockchain platforms and open-source tools

This comparative analysis is structured to deliver a comprehensive understanding of the strengths and considerations associated with each Blockchain-Cloud Deployment Mode. Through a systematic assessment of security, scalability, interoperability, and performance, decision-makers can glean valuable insights to inform their choices and tailor deployment modes according to their specific organizational needs.

6 Discussion

Unveiling the insights garnered from the comparative analysis of Blockchain-Cloud Deployment Modes (BCDM), our focus now shifts to deciphering the practical implications inherent in each mode.

6.1 Interpretation of Findings

Diving into the results, we unravel the intricate dance of features within each BCDM. This exploration illuminates how the specific attributes of each mode contribute to its performance in terms of security, scalability, interoperability, and overall system efficiency [14]. The goal is to unearth insights that unveil the unique strengths within each deployment mode [4].

6.2 Implications for Deployment Decisions

Expanding on our interpretation, we navigate the practical implications for organizations contemplating the adoption of Blockchain-Cloud Deployment Modes. Decision-makers can find guidance here, emphasizing factors like organizational objectives, security requirements, and scalability needs [7]. This discussion serves as a compass for making judicious choices aligned with the distinctive operational contexts of diverse organizations.

6.3 Addressing Challenges and Opportunities

In the final leg, we critically confront the challenges and opportunities embedded in the adoption of BCDM. By acknowledging potential hurdles and highlighting pathways for improvement, organizations can navigate the integration of blockchain and cloud technologies more adeptly [7, 15]. This discussion not only unveils current challenges but also sets the groundwork for future advancements, contributing to the ongoing evolution of decentralized and scalable systems.

The Discussion phase amalgamates the research findings into a cohesive narrative, offering a bridge between empirical insights and practical considerations. It stands as a testament to how Blockchain-Cloud Deployment Modes can be strategically leveraged in diverse organizational landscapes, fostering a deeper understanding of their strategic implications.

7 Conclusion

In conclusion, this study explored the integration of blockchain and cloud technologies through the lens of Blockchain-Cloud Deployment Modes (BCDM). The comparative analysis revealed distinct strengths within each deployment mode—Cloud over Blockchain (CoB), Blockchain over Cloud (BoC), and Mixed Blockchain Cloud (MBC). CoB excelled in security and privacy, BoC demonstrated superior scalability and interoperability, while MBC emerged as a versatile architecture capable of addressing varied use cases [9]. The study contributes valuable insights to the dynamic landscape of blockchain-cloud integration. Decision-makers can leverage these findings to discern and adopt deployment modes that align with their specific needs. As organizations navigate the evolving terrain of technological integration, the nuanced understanding provided by this research serves as a guide for strategic decision-making [3]. Looking ahead, future research can further explore the intricacies of Blockchain- Cloud Deployment Modes, addressing potential challenges and refining the integration approaches [4]. By fostering continued inquiry, this study contributes to the ongoing evolution of decentralized and scalable systems in the contemporary technological landscape.

References

1. Khare, S., Sahay, R., Kumar, R.: Deployment of blockchain in cloud computing- a comprehensive review. In: 2023 2nd International Conference for Innovation in Technology (INOCON), Bangalore, India, pp. 1–6 (2023). https://doi.org/10.1109/INOCON57975.2023.10101317

2. Taherdoost, H., Madanchian, M.: Blockchain-based new business models: a systematic review. Electronics **12**(6), 14792023 (2023). https://doi.org/10.3390/electronics12061479
3. Nakamoto, S.: Bitcoin: a peer-to-peer electronic cash system (2008). https://bitcoin.org/bitcoin.pdf
4. Bentayeb, Y., Badir, H., En-Nahnahi, N.: Blockchain-based cloud computing: model-driven engineering approach. In: Kacprzyk, J., Ezziyyani, M., Balas, V.E. (eds.) AI2SD 2022. LNNS, vol. 637, pp. 639–650. Springer, Cham (2023). https://doi.org/10.1007/978-3-031-26384-2_55
5. Razia, B., Awwad, B.: A comprehensive review of blockchain technology and its related aspects in higher education. In: Hamdan, A., Hassanien, A.E., Mescon, T., Alareeni, B. (eds.) Technologies, Artificial Intelligence and the Future of Learning Post-COVID-19. Studies in Computational Intelligence, vol. 1019, pp. 553–571. Springer, Cham (2022). https://doi.org/10.1007/978-3-030-93921-2_29
6. Mansouri, Y., Ali Babar, M.: A review of edge computing: Features and resource virtualization. J. Parallel Distrib. Comput. **150**, 155–183 (2021). https://doi.org/10.1016/j.jpdc.2020.12.015. ISSN 0743-7315
7. Xue, H., Chen, D., Zhang, N., Dai, H.-N., Yu, K.: Integration of blockchain and edge computing in internet of things: a survey. Future Gener. Comput. Syst. (2022). https://doi.org/10.1016/j.future.2022.10.029, https://www.sciencedirect.com/science/article/pii/S0167739X22003521. ISSN 0167-739X
8. Blanco, D.F., Le Mouël, F., Lin, T., Escudié, M.-P.: A Comprehensive survey on software as a service (SaaS) transformation for the automotive systems. IEEE Access **11**, 73688–73753 (2023). https://doi.org/10.1109/ACCESS.2023.3294256
9. Gai, K., Choo, K.-K.R., Zhu, L.: Blockchain-enabled reengineering of cloud datacenters. IEEE Cloud Comput. **5**(6), 21–25 (2018). https://doi.org/10.1109/MCC.2018.064181116
10. Azzaoui, A.E.L., Sharma, P.K., Park, J.H.: Blockchain-based delegated quantum cloud architecture for medical big data security. J. Netw. Comput. Appl. **198**, 103304 (2022). https://doi.org/10.1016/j.jnca.2021.103304, https://www.sciencedirect.com/science/article/pii/S1084804521002952. ISSN 1084-8045
11. Gai, K., Guo, J., Zhu, L., Yu, S.: Blockchain meets cloud computing: a survey. IEEE Commun. Surv. Tutor. **22**(3), 2009–2030 (2020). https://doi.org/10.1109/COMST.2020.2989392
12. Murthy, C.V.N.U., Shri, M. L., Kadry, S., Lim, S.: Blockchain based cloud computing: architecture and research challenges. IEEE Access. **8** (2020). https://doi.org/10.1109/ACCESS.2020.3036812
13. Zhu, X., Badr, Y.: A survey on blockchain-based identity management systems for the internet of things. In: 2018 IEEE International Conference on Internet of Things (iThings) and IEEE Green Computing and Communications (GreenCom) and IEEE Cyber, Physical and Social Computing (CPSCom) and IEEE Smart Data (SmartData), Halifax, NS, Canada, pp. 1568–1573 (2018). https://doi.org/10.1109/Cybermatics_2018.2018.00263
14. Yang, X., Chen, A., Wang, Z., Li, S.: Cloud storage data access control scheme based on blockchain and attribute-based encryption. Secur. Commun. Netw. **2022**, 1–12 (2022). https://doi.org/10.1155/2022/2204832. Article ID 2204832
15. Hueber, O.: The blockchain and the sidechain innovations for the electronic commerce beyond the Bitcoin's framework. Int. J. Transit. Innov. Syst. **6**(1), 88–102 (2018). https://doi.org/10.1504/IJTIS.2018.090770

Towards Blockchain and Agile Methodology Synergy to Enhance Digital Transformation: The Case of SAFe Framework

Fatine Ziane[1]([⊠]), Afaf Ouaddah[2], Younes Laghouaouti[1]([⊠]), and Rabia Marghoubi[1]

[1] EVEREST, INPT, Temara, Morocco
`ziane.fatine@doctorant.inpt.ac.ma`
[2] RAISS, INPT, Rabat, Morocco

Abstract. In today's fast-changing business environment, avoiding the pervasive integration of digital solutions into all aspects of an enterprise is no longer a viable option. Instead, it is necessary to ensure that they become a standard and are used for survival in the modern business era. This paper elaborates on the factors contributing to the increasing significance of digital transformation and how it may help boost efficiency, customer experience, and innovation. Nonetheless, it is also necessary to address a wide range of potential roadblocks to comply.

This article suggests an innovative solution to tackle the above problems by uniting the potential of Blockchain technology and the SAFE Framework. Thanks to its main principles of decentralization, immutability, and transparency, Blockchain provides a secure and tamper-proof environment for data sharing. The SAFE Framework, which is based on learning, alignment, autonomy, and transparency, promotes collaboration and trust-building throughout the transformation process. Through the examination of how the forces mentioned above may complement each other, the paper investigates the possibility of a safer, more collaborative, and flexible path of digital transformation and the opportunity to discover the benefits of organizational expansion.

Keywords: Agile methodology · Blockchain · Digital Transformation · SAFe Framework · Resistance to change

1 Introduction

The digital landscape is undergoing a paradigm shift. Organizations across all industries are embracing **digital transformation**, a comprehensive integration of digital technologies into every facet of their operations. This transformation is driven by a multitude of factors, including globalization [1], technological advancements [3], and evolving customer expectations. By leveraging digital tools and platforms, organizations aim to achieve a multitude of benefits, including:

- **Increased Efficiency:** Automation of tasks, streamlined processes, and real- time data analysis empowers organizations to operate with greater efficiency [6].

H. Badir et al. (Eds.): INTIS 2024, CCIS 2645, pp. 276–287, 2026.
https://doi.org/10.1007/978-3-032-14964-0_22

- **Improved Customer Experience:** Digital transformation allows businesses to connect with customers on new levels, fostering loyalty and satisfaction [7].
- **Enhanced Innovation:** Digital tools and platforms break down silos, facilitate collaboration, and accelerate innovation cycles, enabling organizations to develop innovative products and services.

However, the path to successful digital transformation is not without its hurdles. Security concerns, a lack of trust among stakeholders, and inefficient data management can all hinder progress.

This delves into the concept of digital transformation, highlighting its growing importance and the potential challenges it presents. It then introduces two possible solutions that can help organizations overcome these challenges and unlock the full potential of digital transformation: **Blockchain technology** and the **SAFE Framework**. Blockchain, with its core principles of decentralization, immutability, and transparency, offers a secure and tamper-proof platform for data exchange. The SAFE Framework, emphasizing continuous learning, alignment, empowerment, and transparency, fosters collaboration and trust during the transformation process. By analyzing how these two forces can work in synergy, this exploration delves into the potential for a more secure, collaborative, and agile digital transformation journey, ultimately unlocking new opportunities for organizational growth.

At first in Sect. 2, the discussion delves into the background of the digital transformation, how SAFe Framework enhanced it, and the potential impact that Blockchain brings to this process. In Sect. 3, the synergy between SAFe and Blockchain is fully explained and illustrated. Finally, Sect. 4 is dedicated to the related work published about the fields cited above.

2 Background

2.1 Digital transformation: A Double-Edged Sword

Digital transformation, the comprehensive integration of digital technologies across all facets of an organization, is sweeping across the business landscape [2]. Driven by factors like globalization, technological advancements, and evolving customer expectations, organizations are embracing digital transformation to unlock a plethora of benefits [2].

Key Drivers:

- Evolving Customer Expectations: Customers today expect seamless, personalized, and omnichannel experiences. Digital transformation empowers businesses to leverage technology to meet these evolving needs, fostering stronger customer loyalty and satisfaction.
- Increased Competition and Market Disruption: The business landscape is constantly changing, with new technologies and competitors emerging rapidly. Digital transformation helps businesses stay ahead of the curve by improving efficiency, agility, and innovation, allowing them to adapt to changing market dynamics.

- Operational Inefficiencies and Data Silos: Traditional business processes can be slow, manual, and prone to errors. Data may be scattered across various systems, hindering effective decision-making. Digital transformation facilitates automation, data integration, and real-time insights, leading to improved operational efficiency and data-driven decision-making.

However, the path of digital transformation is not paved solely with roses. It also presents some potential drawbacks that require careful consideration.

Potential Drawbacks:

- **Security Concerns:** The growing reliance on digital technologies introduces new vulnerabilities. Cyberattacks and privacy violations pose significant risks that organizations must mitigate through robust cybersecurity measures and data governance strategies.
- **Data Breaches and Privacy Concerns:** The collection and analysis of vast amounts of customer data raise privacy concerns. Organizations must ensure transparency in data collection practices and implement robust data protection protocols to build trust with customers.
- **Resistance to Change:** Digital transformation can disrupt established workflows and require employees to adapt to new technologies and processes.

Managing change effectively, providing adequate training, and fostering a culture of continuous learning is crucial to overcoming resistance to change and ensuring collaboration among stakeholders.

Digital transformation, therefore, presents itself as a double-edged sword. While it unlocks significant opportunities for organizations to thrive in the digital age, it also necessitates careful navigation of potential pitfalls. By acknowledging both the benefits and drawbacks, organizations can develop comprehensive digital transformation strategies that enhance efficiency, drive innovation, and create a secure and customer-centric environment for success [8].

2.2   The SAFe Framework: Building Trust in the Digital Age

The Scaled Agile Framework (SAFe) is built on a foundation of core values that emphasize collaboration, alignment, transparency, and lean-agile principles. These values form the cornerstone of SAFe implementation and guide organizations in their journey toward achieving business agility at scale. Some of the key core values of SAFe include [4]:

1. **Alignment:** SAFe promotes alignment across all levels of the organization, ensuring that everyone is working towards common goals and objectives. This alignment fosters a sense of shared purpose and enables teams to work cohesively towards delivering value to customers.
2. **Transparency:** Transparency is a fundamental aspect of SAFe, enabling stakeholders to have visibility into the progress, impediments, and outcomes of initiatives. By promoting transparency, SAFe facilitates informed decision- making and fosters trust among team members and stakeholders.

3. **Collaboration:** SAFe encourages collaboration among cross-functional teams, promoting communication and knowledge sharing. Collaboration is essential for breaking down silos, fostering innovation, and delivering value to customers more effectively.
4. **Customer-Centricity:** SAFe places a strong emphasis on customer-centricity, prioritizing the delivery of value to end-users through iterative and incremental development cycles. By focusing on customer needs and feedback, organizations can ensure that their products and services meet user expectations and drive business success.

While the SAFe framework offers many benefits for organizations looking to scale agile practices, it is not without its drawbacks and limitations. Some of the common challenges associated with SAFe implementation include:

1. **Complexity:** SAFe is a comprehensive framework that encompasses multiple layers, roles, and processes, which can lead to bigger complexity, especially for organizations transitioning from traditional project management approaches.
2. **Rigid Structure:** SAFe's prescriptive nature can sometimes be perceived as rigid, limiting flexibility and adaptability in response to changing market dynamics or evolving customer needs.
3. **Resistance to Change:** Implementing SAFe often requires significant organizational change, which can be met with resistance from employees accustomed to traditional ways of working. Overcoming resistance to change and fostering a culture of agility can be a significant challenge for organizations adopting SAFe.

Despite its drawbacks, the SAFe framework provides a structured approach to scaling agile practices and fostering organizational agility. By embracing SAFe's core values and principles, organizations can build trust in the digital age by:

1. **Promoting Transparency:** Leveraging SAFe's emphasis on transparency, organizations can build trust by providing stakeholders with visibility into the progress, challenges, and successes of agile initiatives.
2. **Encouraging Collaboration:** SAFe encourages collaboration among cross-functional teams, fostering trust through open communication, shared goals, and collective problem-solving.
3. **Delivering Value Incrementally:** By prioritizing customer-centricity and delivering value incrementally, organizations can build trust with stakeholders by demonstrating tangible outcomes and responding quickly to feedback.
4. **Embracing Continuous Improvement:** SAFe promotes a culture of continuous improvement, where teams reflect on their processes, experiment with new ideas, and adapt to changing circumstances. By embracing continuous improvement, organizations can build trust by demonstrating a commitment to learning and growth.

In conclusion, the SAFe framework offers a structured approach to scaling agile and fostering organizational agility in the digital age. While it has its drawbacks and limitations, SAFe provides organizations with a framework for building its values including alignment, transparency, respect for people, and continuous improvement to create a climate of trust. Still, it does not specify the mechanisms to ensure its values.

2.3 Unveiling the Power of Blockchain

In the quest for a more secure and trustworthy digital transformation journey, Blockchain technology emerges as a potential game-changer. Blockchain is a distributed ledger technology offering a secure, transparent, decentralized platform for data exchange and record-keeping through multiple core principles:

- **Decentralization:** Unlike traditional databases controlled by a central authority, Blockchain data is distributed across a network of computers. This eliminates the risk of a single point of failure and empowers participants to verify transactions independently.
- **Immutability:** Once a transaction is recorded on a Blockchain, it becomes permanent and tamper-proof. Cryptographic hashing ensures the integrity of data, making it virtually impossible to alter or manipulate records.
- **Transparency:** All participants on the network have access to a complete and immutable record of transactions. This transparency fosters trust and accountability within the ecosystem.

These core principles of Blockchain hold immense potential to address the security concerns that often plague digital transformation initiatives, such as:

- **Secure Data Storage:** Blockchain offers a secure platform for storing sensitive data. Cryptographic hashing and immutability ensure the data's integrity and prevent unauthorized access.
- **Tamper-Proof Records:** The immutable nature of Blockchain transactions makes it virtually impossible to alter records retrospectively. This fosters trust and eliminates concerns about data manipulation.
- **Enhanced Traceability:** Blockchain enables real-time tracking of assets and transactions throughout a supply chain. This transparency offers greater visibility and reduces the risk of fraud or counterfeit products.

By harnessing the power of Blockchain, organizations can create a more secure and trustworthy digital environment, fostering collaboration, building trust with stakeholders, and paving the way for a successful digital transformation journey.

3 Synergy: Blockchain and SAFE for Enhanced Digital Transformation

The individual strengths of Blockchain and the SAFE Framework become even more potent when combined. An examination of this synergistic relationship will reveal its potential to mitigate challenges and propel successful digital transformation.

3.1 Overcoming Challenges

Digital transformation often faces hurdles like security concerns and data management challenges:

- **Security and Trust:** Blockchain's secure and transparent data management addresses concerns about data breaches and fosters trust among stakeholders. The SAFE Framework's emphasis on transparency and alignment further strengthens trust within the transformation team.
- **Data Management:** Blockchain provides an immutable and tamper-proof platform for data storage, improving data integrity and facilitating secure data sharing across the organization. The SAFE Framework promotes data governance by encouraging collaboration and clear ownership of data assets.
- **Resistance to Change:** The SAFE Framework's focus on continuous learning and empowerment equips teams to adapt to new Blockchain-based technologies. By fostering a culture of collaboration and open communication, the framework helps mitigate resistance and facilitates a smooth transition.

3.2 Benefits of Synergy

- **Increased Security:** The combined power of Blockchain's data security and the SAFE Framework's emphasis on clear ownership minimizes data vulnerabilities and fosters a secure digital transformation environment.
- **Improved Collaboration:** The SAFE Framework fosters communication and collaboration within the transformation team. This, coupled with Blockchain's ability to provide a transparent and shared view of data, enhances collaboration across the organization.
- **Faster Innovation:** By enabling secure data sharing and collaboration, the combined approach facilitates a more agile environment where teams can experiment, innovate, and develop new solutions faster [2].

As illustrated in Fig. 1, the blockchain can enhance the targeted challenges of any digital transformation.

Firstly, blockchain enables unparalleled transparency by providing a tamper-proof audit trail of all transactions and interactions within the agile ecosystem. This transparency fosters trust among stakeholders and enhances visibility into the flow of value across the organization, addressing concerns related to accountability and governance.

Secondly, blockchain enhances security by safeguarding sensitive data and ensuring data integrity throughout the agile lifecycle. The cryptographic techniques employed in blockchain technology mitigate the risk of data manipulation or unauthorized access, enhancing the confidentiality and reliability of information shared among agile teams.

Moreover, blockchain facilitates decentralized collaboration, allowing agile teams to interact and exchange information in a peer-to-peer manner without relying on centralized intermediaries. This decentralization promotes autonomy, resilience, and agility within the organization, enabling teams to adapt quickly to changing requirements and market conditions.

Furthermore, blockchain's smart contract functionality can automate various aspects of agile processes, such as task assignment, progress tracking, and incentive mechanisms, streamlining workflow management and reducing administrative overhead.

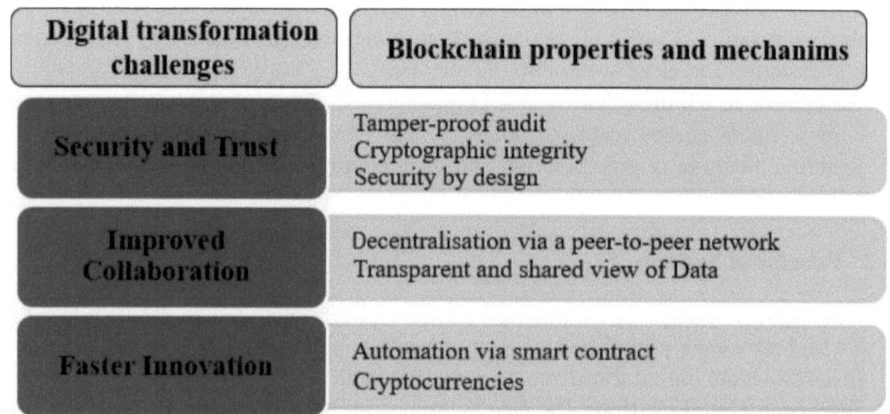

Fig. 1. How blockchain mechanism overcomes SAFE challenges

As an illustration, Supply Chain Management presents a smart implementation of Blockchain technology through securing the tracking of goods and materials while using the SAFe Framework to facilitate collaboration between suppliers, manufacturers, and distributors. This transparency streamlines communication, identifies bottlenecks, and fosters trust throughout the supply chain [5].

3.3   Integrating Blockchain with SAFe Framework

The Scaled Agile Framework (SAFe) can benefit significantly from blockchain integration. Here's how blockchain can be architected within the different levels of SAFe:

3.3.1   Portfolio Level

At the portfolio level, blockchain can be used to manage a shared record of investment decisions and track the progress of epics across different value streams. This fosters transparency and facilitates portfolio-level governance. A private blockchain can be implemented to restrict access to authorized stakeholders within the portfolio. Smart contracts can automate funding allocation based on predefined criteria and track the use of funds across epics.

By integrating blockchain at the portfolio level of the SAFe framework, organizations can reap a multitude of benefits:

- **Improved decision-making through transparent investment tracking.**
- **Increased efficiency in resource allocation and funding management.**
- **Enhanced governance with automated controls and audit trails**.

3.3.2 Large Solution Level

At the Large Solution level of the SAFe Framework, blockchain integration offers a compelling set of advantages:

- Enhanced Dependency Management: Blockchain can be used to create a secure and transparent record of dependencies between epics and features across all value streams contributing to the Large Solution. This improves visibility, facilitates communication, and streamlines overall program execution.
- Automated Compliance Enforcement: By leveraging smart contracts, SAFe can enforce program-wide policies and automate compliance checks at the Large Solution level. This reduces the risk of non-compliance with regulations and ensures all contributing value streams adhere to established standards.
- Improved Collaboration and Visibility: Establishing a consortium blockchain with participants from various value streams fosters a collaborative environment. This shared platform enhances communication, transparency, and visibility into the progress of the Large Solution.

3.3.3 Essential Level

Within the Essential SAFe level, blockchain can be crucial in managing the Program Backlog and ensuring data integrity.

- **Traceability and Trust:** By leveraging a private blockchain, the lifecycle of Epics and Features within the Program Backlog can be tracked transparently. This fosters team trust and collaboration by providing a tamper-proof record of changes and decision-making processes.
- **Enhanced Visibility and Control:** Smart contracts can be implemented to automate workflows associated with the Program Backlog, such as triggering reviews or approvals when dependencies are met. This enhances visibility and control over the overall program execution.
- **Hybrid Approach:** A hybrid approach can be considered for interactions with external stakeholders. A private blockchain can be used internally to manage the Program Backlog, while a public blockchain can be utilized for secure data sharing with external partners. This ensures data confidentiality while facilitating collaboration.

As illustrated in Fig. 2, Blockchain Integration could be performed through the 4 roles of the SAFe Framework by emphasizing the need to assign clear ownership and responsibilities for integrating blockchain technology within the SAFe structure.

3.4 Considerations

However, the integration of Blockchain with SAFe Framework presents several challenges to take into consideration, such as:

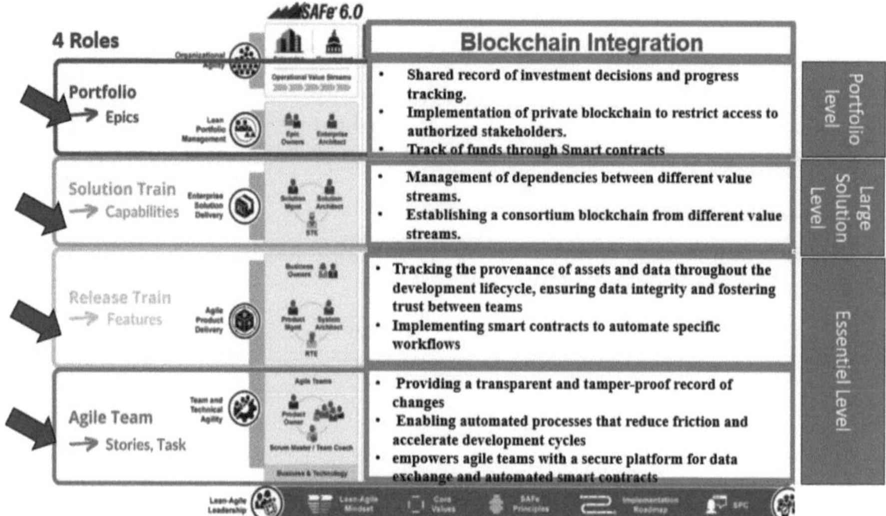

Fig. 2. Empowering SAFe Levels with Blockchain

- **Interoperability:** Ensuring compatibility between blockchain platforms used at different SAFe levels is crucial. This might involve using standardized protocols or custom integrations to facilitate seamless information flow across the portfolio, program, and value stream levels.
- **Cost and Resource Requirements:** Implementing and maintaining blockchain solutions can be resource-intensive. Organizations need to carefully evaluate the cost-benefit analysis and identify resource requirements for successful integration.
- **Governance and Regulatory Issues:** Current regulatory frameworks surrounding blockchain are still evolving. Organizations need to stay informed and ensure their blockchain integration adheres to relevant regulations and governance structures within the SAFe context.
- **Scalability:** Choosing a blockchain solution that can scale to meet the growing needs of the SAFe implementation is vital. Public blockchains might face scalability limitations, so exploring private or consortium blockchains might be necessary.
- **Security and Data Privacy:** Implementing robust security measures is essential to protect sensitive data stored on the blockchain. This includes addressing potential vulnerabilities and ensuring compliance with data privacy regulations and the choice of the private Blockchain to ensure maximum security.
- **Latency and Performance:** Transaction processing times on some blockchain platforms can be slower compared to traditional systems. Organizations need to consider the impact of latency on their specific SAFe workflows and choose a solution that meets their performance requirements.

This is a high-level overview, and the specific architecture of blockchain integration will vary depending on the specific needs of the organization and the SAFe implementation.

Security considerations are crucial throughout the architecture design process. Exploring existing tools and frameworks that facilitate blockchain integration with SAFe can further streamline implementation.

In conclusion, by harnessing the strengths of both Blockchain technology and the SAFE Framework, organizations can embark on more secure, collaborative, and agile digital transformation journeys. This synergy releases a climate of trust that will allow not only the improvement of collaboration but also unlock the potential for enhanced operational efficiency, improved customer experiences, and the creation of innovative products and services that position them for success in the digital age.

4   Related Works

In recent years, the intersection of blockchain technology and software development has given rise to innovative frameworks and methodologies. This section reviews and compares four notable articles that explore distinct aspects of employing blockchain in software engineering.

Authors in [1] investigate the implementation of the Scaled Agile Framework (SAFe) in organizations, with a particular emphasis on its shortcomings and the proposal of an AI-based solution for tracking team performance. The study delves into the challenges faced during the Software Enlargement Period and emphasizes the need for responsive and timely software delivery.

Furthermore, the work in [12] explores the application of agile development methodologies within the context of blockchain. It highlights the potential of Agile principles for recording workflow and enhancing product development, specifically through the integration of Smart Contracts for payment support.

Another interesting study [10] scrutinizes the impact of existing software engineering processes and models, including Agile and DevOps, in the realm of blockchain-oriented software engineering. The article assesses the adaptability of conventional techniques to futuristic technologies and emphasizes the essentiality of evolving software engineering processes for blockchain-oriented systems.

Finally, a recent paper [11] introduces a blockchain-based framework named Testing-Plus, focusing on optimizing the software testing process. It addresses challenges related to transparency, trust, coordination, and communication in software testing by leveraging blockchain technology. The framework ensures a secure and transparent platform for acceptance testing and payment verification through the use of smart contracts.

Below is a summarized comparison presented in Table 1:

From the above literature, we noticed that all articles recognize the significance of agility in software development, whether it is in the context of project management (**papers 1 and 3**), blockchain integration (**papers 2 and 4**), or team performance tracking (**papers 1 and 4**). The studies emphasize the importance of overcoming challenges such as trust, transparency, and coordination, and propose innovative solutions, ranging from AI-based performance tracking to the utilization of blockchain and smart contracts. While **papers 2 and 4** specifically focus on the integration of blockchain technology in software development, **papers 1 and 3** explore broader aspects of software engineering methodologies and processes, with **paper 3** addressing the adaptability of conventional techniques to emerging technologies.

Table 1. Comparative Analysis of Blockchain Integration in Software Development Methodologies

Paper number	Paper	Key Focus	Innovation	Technology Integration	Noteworthy Aspect
1	Ameta et al. [9]	SAFe implementation, AI-based team performance tracking	AI application for team tracking	SAFe	Emphasis on Adaptation and challenges during the Software Enlargement Period
2	Lenarduzzi et al. [12]	Agile principles in blockchain, Smart Contracts	Smart Contracts for enhanced workflow	Blockchain	Integration of agile principles with blockchain
3	Md Jobair Hossain et al. [10]	Impact of conventional processes on blockchain	Evolution of processes for futuristic technologies	Blockchain, Agile, DevOps	Comprehensive study on evolving software engineering processes
4	Shoaib Farooq et al. [11]	Testing optimization using TestingPlus framework	Use of blockchain for testing, smart contracts	Blockchain, Ethereum, Smart Contracts	Addressing challenges in testing through blockchain integration

5   Conclusion

In conclusion, while the Scaled Agile Framework (SAFe) offers a robust structure for implementing agile practices at scale, organizations often encounter challenges related to transparency, trust, and security during the transition process. These limitations can impede the effectiveness of agile transformations and hinder the realization of desired outcomes.

Blockchain technology presents a compelling solution to address these limitations and enhance the implementation of the SAFe framework. By leveraging blockchain's inherent properties of transparency, immutability, and decentralized consensus, organizations can overcome key challenges encountered in agile transitions.

By harnessing the power of blockchain technology, organizations can unlock new opportunities for innovation, efficiency, and value creation in their agile transformations. Whether it's enhancing transparency, ensuring security, or fostering decentralized collaboration, blockchain offers a transformative solution to augment the implementation of the SAFe framework and drive successful agile transitions in today's digital era.

Future work consists of implementing blockchain technology in the different levels of the SAFE framework namely Portfolio, Large Solution, and Essential. This implementation will initially create a climate of trust and transparency between the different stakeholder's roles at different levels: Agile Team, Release Train, Solution Train Engineering, and Epis Owners, and secondly ensure the sharing of data securely and transparently between the different workflows: starting with the portfolio level for good governance and effective management of the company's value Stream management until the essential level based on the principles of operational agility.

References

1. Wieland, J., et al.: The Globalization Reader, 7th edn. Routledge (2019)
2. Verhoef, P.C., et al.: Digital transformation: A multidisciplinary reflection and research agendan (2019)
3. McKinsey & Company. What is Digital Transformation? McKinsey & Company
4. Leffingwell, D.: Scaled agile framework for enterprise (SAFE). Scaled Agile Framework for Enterprise (2020). https://scaledagileframework.com/
5. Hohns, R., et al.: Scaled Agile Framework (SAFe) for Lean Enterprises: Applying Principles and Patterns. Apress (2021)
6. Abrahams, M., et al.: Blockchain for agile supply chain management: a use case for traceability and information sharing. Logistics **5**(1) (2022)
7. McKinsey & Company. What is Digital Transformation? McKinsey & Company (2023). https://www.mckinsey.com/featured-insights/mckinsey-explainers/what-is-digital-transformation
8. Saleh, A., et al.: The impact of digital transformation on customer experience in retail banking. J. Islamic Mark. **11**(2), 278–294 (2020)
9. Ameta, U., Patel, M., Sharma, A.K.: Scaled agile framework implementation in organizations', its shortcomings and an AI-based solution to track team's performance. In: 2022 IEEE 3rd Global Conference for Advancement in Technology (GCAT). IEEE (2022)
10. Faruk, M.J.H., et al.: Software engineering process and methodology in blockchain-oriented software development: a systematic study. In: 2022 IEEE/ACIS 20th International Conference on Software Engineering Research, Management and Applications (SERA). IEEE (2022)
11. Shoaib Farooq, M., Ahmed, F.: A blockchain-based framework for distributed agile software testing life cycle. arXiv e-prints: arXiv-2307 (2023)
12. Lenarduzzi, V., et al.: Blockchain applications for agile methodologies. In: Proceedings of the 19th International Conference on Agile Software Development: Companion (2018)

Leader- Similarity for Community Detection in Complex Networks

Sara Ahajjam[1(✉)], Jamal Ghaffour[2], and Hassan Badir[1]

[1] Technologies of Information and Communications Laboratory (LabTIC), NationalSchoolof Applied Sciences of Tangier, Abdelmalek Essaadi University, Tangier, Morocco
ahajjamsara@gmail.com

[2] Monitoring Laboratory for Emerging Technologies, Hassan 1st University of Settat, Tangier, Morocco

Abstract. Community detection is a fundamental task in the study of complex networks, enabling the partitioning of nodes into distinct clusters to enhance network organization and analysis. However, many existing methods suffer from a common limitation: they require prior knowledge of the number of communities or a predefined community structure, hindering their applicability to diverse network scenarios. To overcome this challenge, we introduce a novel approach termed Leader-Similarity Community Detection (LSCD) algorithm for community detection in complex networks, leveraging leader nodes and considering the entire network structure. Our experimental evaluations on real-world networks demonstrate that LSCD outperforms state-of-the-art methods in terms of accuracy and robustness.

Keywords: Centrality · Community detection · Relative entropy · Similarity · complex networks

1 Introduction

Complex networks are pervasive, modeling intricate systems across domains like biology, neuroscience, and the internet. Represented as graphs, nodes symbolize entities such as proteins in biological networks, profiles in social networks, or accounts in financial networks, while edges denote interactions between them. Despite their varied origins, these networks often share non-trivial properties, such as the "small world" phenomenon observed in Milgram's experiment, where the average distance between any two nodes is relatively short compared to the overall network size. [1]. Moreover, nodes tend to have a heterogeneous degree distribution, which can often be well approximated by a power law. This means that there are many highly connected nodes acting as hubs, surrounded by less connected nodes. Furthermore, complex networks often exhibit a community structure, with tightly interconnected groups of nodes and fewer connections to external nodes. This structure poses algorithmic challenges, making community detection algorithms essential for uncovering hidden structures within these networks.

H. Badir et al. (Eds.): INTIS 2024, CCIS 2645, pp. 288–301, 2026.
https://doi.org/10.1007/978-3-032-14964-0_23

Identifying communities enhances the understanding of network structures across various fields. Communities, as mesoscopic structures, consist of nodes strongly connected internally and weakly connected externally, representing similar topics in web pages, social groups, or protein sets in biological networks. This understanding is crucial for analyzing and interpreting the structure of complex and small-world networks [2].

Another phenomenon of significant interest in complex networks is diffusion. Disease spread serves as a prime example where an infected individual can transmit a virus to others, causing a cascade effect. This concept extends to information and influence in social networks, the spread of computer viruses in digital networks, and other domains. Studying diffusion models helps understand why some trends or innovations are adopted more rapidly than others. Analyzing network structures is crucial for examining the impact of these models on human behavior. In social media, certain individuals with numerous connections can exert greater influence or achieve higher notoriety. This prominence of key nodes is not limited to social networks but is also evident in communication networks, where specific nodes facilitate crucial interactions. Understanding the centrality and influence of nodes in networks reveals the mechanisms behind diffusion processes and their implications for societal dynamics. This phenomenon is attributed to the intrinsic nature of complex networks, characterized by a power-law distribution of nodes, where a few nodes, known as hubs, have a disproportionately high number of connections compared to the majority.

Community detection, closely related to graph partitioning in mathematics and clustering in data mining, poses a challenging NP problem [3]. Despite numerous proposed methods, the challenge of detecting communities remains unresolved to a satisfactory degree, as highlighted in Fortunato's review [2]. The complexity is compounded by variations in the definition of a community; while some define it as a set of similar nodes, others view it as a group of densely connected nodes. Moreover, most research combining community and leader detection typically starts by identifying communities, then detecting the leader nodes within each [4–8]. However, in addition to the example of the spread of the epidemic cited above, several examples can demonstrate that the leader builds his community: in political elections, the president of the political party is responsible for the constitution of his community. Building upon these insights, to contribute to the advance of scientific research in the field of data analysis; we propose in this context to explore the issues mentioned above, according to an approach to detect nodes leaders, and detect communities that will be formed around these leaders.

This paper is organized as follow: an overview of the related works is discussed in Sect. 2. In Sect. 3, the proposed algorithm is elaborated. The results of the LSCD algorithm and its discussion are illustrated in Sect. 4.

2 Related Works

Analysis of complex networks has consistently revealed that within each community, a central member, or leader, plays a pivotal role. This leader orchestrates the dissemination of information and attracts new members. Proposed methodologies integrate community detection and leader identification to better understand these networks. Initially, algorithms identify cohesive groups of nodes as communities [9]. Then, using metrics such as centrality measures, central nodes within each community are identified as potential leaders. This combined approach offers a comprehensive understanding of the organizational structure and dynamics of complex networks, enabling researchers to delineate communities and pinpoint influential leaders who drive their evolution and behavior.

The "TopLeaders" algorithm [8] offers a novel approach for identifying leader nodes while handling outliers. Inspired by the k-means algorithm, TopLeaders begins by randomly selecting k nodes and forming communities based on proximity. Each member's centrality is then evaluated, with the node having the highest degree designated as the leader. This leader initiates the next community formation. This iterative process continues until convergence. In the "Follow the Leader" algorithm, a new guided clustering centrality is proposed for the detection of leader nodes and communities. The nodes with a high centrality are chosen as a starting point. The approach is carried out in three stages: initially group the vertices of G into different groups, then merge the groups with a large percentage of overlap, and finally contract the vertices in the same groups to form a new vertex [10]. Fang et al. propose a new LDA algorithm [11] for detecting communities based on leaders, involving through three main stages: leaders' identification, follower class identification, and leader assignment to clusters. Leaders are selected using leadership centrality, where a node is deemed a leader if its leadership centrality exceeds that of at least one neighbor. Followers are also identified using leadership centrality, where the follower with the highest leadership value and his neighbors form the first class of followers. The follower classes are used to form communities, where each leader is assigned to the class that contains their neighbors. This approach of assigning leaders to different follower classes allows for the identification of overlapping communities. The Leiden Algorithm, developed by Traag et al. in 2019, enhances community detection in networks by improving upon the Louvain Algorithm's limitations. It achieves this through smart local moves, fast local move approaches, and refined aggregation processes, resulting in faster and higher-quality community detection. The algorithm ensures well-connected and optimally partitioned communities, making it a valuable tool for analyzing complex network structures [12]. The fast label propagation algorithm (FLPA) builds upon the principles of the traditional label propagation algorithm (LPA) but introduces optimizations to enhance computational speed. Inspired by the fast local move in the Leiden algorithm, FLPA maintains a queue of nodes to be considered for label updates, reducing unnecessary computations. However, it only considers neighbors with different labels that are not already in the queue, reducing redundant computations [13]. LPA-HM, proposed by Wu et al. introduces an innovative approach to community detection in highly mixed networks. It improves upon traditional label propagation algorithms by preprocessing node labels based on common neighbors, leading to more stable assignments. During label propagation, LPA-HM strategically assigns labels considering both neighborhood prevalence and overall label influence, enhancing accuracy. Additionally, it incorporates early stopping criteria to prevent over propagation, especially effective in networks with high mixing parameters. Experimental evaluations demonstrate LPA- HM's superior performance in detecting complex community structures, making it a significant advancement in network analysis, with potential applications across various domains [14].The proposed algorithm (TI-SC) that has 4 phases: (a) community detection using the Louvain algorithm, (b) community merging based on relationships between cores nodes, (c) selecting the primary seed node with the highest score of neighborhood of order 1 and 2, d) updating the scoring criteria by decreasing the scores of neighbors of seed nodes [30]. In the same perspective, El Kouni et al. propose NI- LPA, an enhanced version of the LPA, designed for detecting overlapping communities in networks. It introduces a novel measure of node importance based on degree and clustering coefficient, aiming to improve stability and accuracy. NI-LPA assigns unique importance values to nodes and refines community detection through specialized propagation and filtering processes. Experimental evaluations demonstrate NI-LPA's superior performance in identifying overlapping communities, with notable improvements in efficiency and precision across various network datasets. Overall, NI-LPA offers a robust method for analyzing complex network structures with overlapping community memberships [15].

3 LSCD Approach

The Leader-Similarity Community Detection (LSCD) approach consists of detecting communities in complex networks using leaders. The leaders nodes are followed by others nodes of the networks, and are responsible for the diffusion and the dissemination of information and influence in networks. Based on this assumption, we consider that leaders are the identifiers of the communities, and are attracting new nodes to join their communities. Therefore, our approach has three parts: first, detects the leaders' nodes of the network. Second, compute the similarity between the selected leaders' nodes. Third, detect the communities. The Leader-Similarity Community Detection (LSCD) approach aims to detect communities in complex networks by leveraging leader nodes. These leader nodes play a pivotal role in diffusing and disseminating information and influence throughout the network. Building on this premise, we posit that leaders act as community identifiers, attracting new nodes to join their respective communities. Consequently, our approach consists of three main components:

Step1: Leaders' nodes detection

This initial phase involves identifying the leader nodes within the network. These leaders are nodes that exhibit significant influence and connectivity, serving as focal points for community formation. To capture both their power and position, leader nodes are identified using the HybridRank algorithm proposed in [16]. This algorithm utilizes hybrid centrality to rank network nodes and select a subset of leader nodes, collectively maximizing information diffusion throughout the network. The hybrid centrality leverages the global topology of the network without relying on any specific structure. It is computed for all network nodes, and nodes are ranked in decreasing order based on their hybrid centrality scores. This ranking approach enables the identification of influential leader nodes essential for effective information dissemination across the network.

The hybrid centrality is defined as follows:

$$HC(v) = ICC(v) * EC(v) \tag{1}$$

With ICC(v) is the Improved Coreness Centrality defined as:

$$ICC(v) = \sum_{u \in \Gamma(v)} C(u) \tag{2}$$

EC(v) is the eigenvector centrality of node v.

Thus, the initial leader is the node with the highest hybrid centrality score. Subsequently, additional leader nodes are selected by excluding the neighborhood of previously chosen leaders. Specifically, the adjacent neighbors of the first leader are removed from the ranked list, and the next leader is selected from the remaining nodes. This iterative process continues until all nodes have been considered, resulting in a final list of leader nodes being selected. By systematically excluding the neighborhoods of previous leaders, the algorithm ensures a diverse selection of influential nodes across the network.

Step 2: Similarity computation

After identifying the leader nodes, the selected list is refined by aggregating similar nodes into the same community, thereby optimizing the community structure.

Utilizing the leaders, influence propagates to a significant number of members within the network, thereby defining the initial number of communities. Inspired by the research of Zhang et al. [17], the Relative Entropy Similarity measure is employed to compute the similarity between the selected leaders. The Relative Entropy Similarity incorporates the local network of each node, defined as follows:

a. Local Network

The local network of a node comprises its adjacent nodes, i.e., the selected node and its neighborhood of order 1. The local network is calculated as the sum of the degrees of the studied node and each of its adjacent neighbors. Figure 1. Illustrated the local network of the node 6 and node 7 belonging to the initial graph.

$$RL(i) = \sum_{i}^{\Gamma(i)} d(i) \tag{3}$$

With: d(i) is the degree of node i.

Considering the network below (Fig. 1) G = (V, E), the local network of node 6 is formed by nodes [9, 3, 8], is equal to:

RL(6) = d(6) + d(9) + d(3) + d(8) = 3 + 4 + 6 + 3 = 16

The local network of node 7 is formed by nodes [1, 5] is equal to: RL(7) = d(7) + d(1) + d(5) = 9

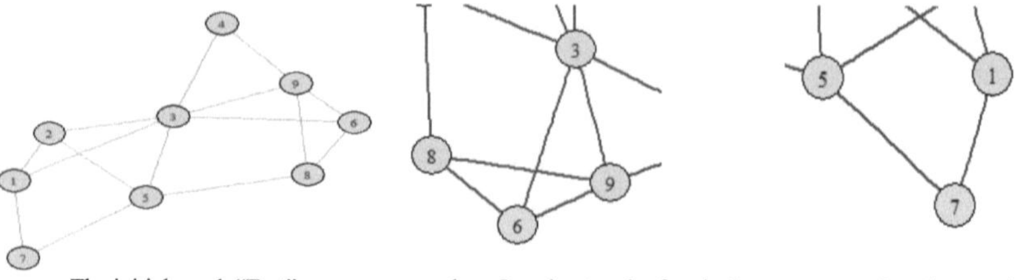

| a. The initial graph "Test" | b. Local network of node 6 | c. Local network of node 7 |

Fig. 1. The network of test

b. Relative Entropy

Relative Entropy or the Kullback Leibler divergence is an important concept in information theory. It is a measure of the distance between two probability distributions. Assume two probability distributions P and Q, where the relative entropy (RE) is represented as follows:

$$ER(P/Q) = \sum_{i=1}^{n} P(i) \cdot \ln\left(\frac{P(i)}{Q(i)}\right) \tag{4}$$

This formula calculates the difference between the expected log likelihood of data under the true distribution P and the expected log likelihood of the same data under the approximate distribution Q. The Relative Entropy measures the information lost when using Q to approximate P, and it is non-negative and equal to zero if and only if P and Q are identical.

With P and Q have the same number of component n.

- The Relative Entropy is an asymmetric measure, where: $ER(P/Q) = ER(Q/P)$ is not really correct.
- The Relative Entropy is always non-negative: $ER(P/Q) \geq 0$
- If P is greater than Q, we replace the missing values of i with zeros so that P and Q have the same number of components n, and the same length.

For the node 6 (Fig. 1b.), the probability distribution is defined by the degree of the node and its adjacent related to local network LN. The degree of node 6 is equal to 3, and the degree of each of its neighbours $\{3, 8, 9\}$ is successively equal to [3, 4, 6] compared to local network that is equal to 16.

For that, the probability of node 6 is represented as follow:

$$P(6) = \left(\frac{d(6)}{RL(6)}, \frac{d(3)}{RL(6)}, \frac{d(8)}{RL(6)}, \frac{d(9)}{RL(6)}\right) = \left(\frac{3}{16}, \frac{6}{16}, \frac{3}{16}, \frac{4}{16}\right)$$

Next, the probability is ranked decreasingly:

$$P(6) = \left(\frac{6}{16}, \frac{4}{16}, \frac{3}{16}, \frac{3}{16}\right)$$

For the node 7, the probability is as follows:

$$P(7) = \left(\frac{d(7)}{RL(7)}, \frac{d(1)}{RL(7)}, \frac{d(5)}{RL(7)}\right) = \left(\frac{4}{9}, \frac{3}{9}, \frac{2}{9}\right)$$

when comparing the probabilities of two nodes that have a different number of neighbors, adjustments need to be made to ensure that the compared probabilities have the same number of components.

In our graph, node 7 has three neighbors and node 6 has four neighbors, we need to add one component to the probability distribution of node 7 to make it comparable to node 6. This adjustment involves adding zeros to the probability distribution of node 7 so that it matches the number of components in the probability distribution of node 6.

$$P(7) = \left(\frac{4}{8}, \frac{3}{8}, \frac{2}{8}, 0\right)$$

For that, the relative entropy of node 6 compared to node 7 is:

$$ER(P(6), P(7)) = \sum_{i}^{4} P(6)[i] \ln\left(\frac{P(6)[i]}{P(7)[i]}\right)$$

c. *Relative Entropy Similarity*

Relative Entropy Similarity [18] measure the similarity between two probability distribution P and Q. While the Relative Entropy is an asymmetric measure, so, the two entropies are considered. For that, the similarity between two leaders i and j is defined as follows:

$$Si,j = 1 - \left(ER\left(\frac{P(i)}{P(j)}\right) + ER\left(\frac{P(j)}{P(i)}\right) \right) \tag{5}$$

The sum of the similarity of each node to the others nodes in the network is used for identifying the nodes similarity. While the similarity value between two nodes is high, the nodes are more similar. The similarity between the network nodes (Fig. 2) is presented below:

```
> ERSimilarity
          [,1]      [,2]      [,3]      [,4]      [,5]      [,6]      [,7]      [,8]      [,9]
[1,] 1.0000000 0.9928465 0.8906628 0.9037506 0.9760653 0.9928465 0.9760653 1.0000000 0.9760653
[2,] 0.9928465 1.0000000 0.9397512 0.9493169 0.9950924 1.0000000 0.9950924 0.9928465 0.9950924
[3,] 0.8906628 0.9397512 1.0000000 0.9995918 0.9693396 0.9397512 0.9693396 0.8906628 0.9693396
[4,] 0.9037506 0.9493169 0.9995918 1.0000000 0.9760265 0.9493169 0.9760265 0.9037506 0.9760265
[5,] 0.9760653 0.9950924 0.9693396 0.9760265 1.0000000 0.9950924 1.0000000 0.9760653 1.0000000
[6,] 0.9928465 1.0000000 0.9397512 0.9493169 0.9950924 1.0000000 0.9950924 0.9928465 0.9950924
[7,] 0.9760653 0.9950924 0.9693396 0.9760265 1.0000000 0.9950924 1.0000000 0.9760653 1.0000000
[8,] 1.0000000 0.9928465 0.8906628 0.9037506 0.9760653 0.9928465 0.9760653 1.0000000 0.9760653
[9,] 0.9760653 0.9950924 0.9693396 0.9760265 1.0000000 0.9950924 1.0000000 0.9760653 1.0000000
```

Fig. 2. Similarity matrix using relative entropy of « Test » network

According to the similarity matrix (Fig. 2), we notice that the node 1 is similar to node 8, node 2 is similar to node 6, and nodes {5, 7, 9} are similar.

The relative entropy similarity is used to measure the similarity between all the selected leaders' nodes using HybridRank algorithm. If the similarity between two leaders is higher than a certain threshold β, so those leaders are attributed to the same community. If not, the node will be the unique leader of the community. This step defines the number of the communities in the network.

Step 3: community detection

The community detection consists of grouping similar nodes into the same community. To achieve this, the similarity between nodes is assessed using a novel similarity measure. Nodes are selected for inclusion in a community based on a predetermined similarity threshold, denoted as γ. This proposed similarity metric considers both the number of leaders in the community C and the proximity of the node under consideration j to the leader(s) of the community.

The primary objective of this proposed similarity measure is to strike a balance among the leaders within the community, ensuring that each leader holds equal importance within the community. By considering both the number of leaders and the proximity of nodes to these leaders, the proposed similarity measure aims to create cohesive communities where each leader contributes equally to the community's structure and influence.

The similarity between the community C and the node j is defined as follow:

$$Sc_j = \frac{Int_{C,v}}{NL \cdot K_j} \tag{6}$$

With: Kj is the degree of the node j, NL is the number of leaders in the community C, IntC,v is the intersection of the neighborhood of leaders of community C and node v, defined as follow:

$$Int_{C,v} = \sum_{i=1}^{NL} \Gamma(v) \cap \Gamma(L_i) \tag{7}$$

With: $\Gamma(v)$ is the neighbourhood of order 1of node v, L is the list of the leaders of the community C

If the similarity between node v and community C exceeds a certain threshold γ (i.e., SC,v $\geq \gamma$), then node v is assigned to the community. Otherwise, the similarity for other nodes in the network is calculated until all nodes are processed. The number of communities in the network is predetermined. Each community is identified by its leaders. In this step, we select similar nodes for each community.

Starting with the first community, consisting of the leader node with the highest hybrid centrality and its similar leaders, if any, we compute the similarity between community leaders and other nodes in the network. Nodes with a similarity value greater than or equal to the threshold γ are assigned to the community and removed from the network. This process is repeated for all communities detected previously. In cases where a community contains only one leader, we identify adjacent nodes (neighbors) of this leader in the initial network. The leader is then assigned to the community to which the majority of its adjacent neighbors belong. Our approach does not allow for overlapping communities; thus, the detected communities are disjoint, meaning each node belongs to one and only one community (Figs. 3 and 4).

```
> Similarity
          [,1]      [,2]      [,3]      [,4]      [,5]      [,6]      [,7]      [,8]      [,9]
[1,] 1.0000000 0.3333333 0.3333333 0.3333333 1.0000000 0.3333333 0.0000000 0.0000000 0.3333333
[2,] 0.3333333 1.0000000 0.6666667 0.3333333 0.3333333 0.3333333 0.6666667 0.3333333 0.3333333
[3,] 0.1666667 0.3333333 1.0000000 0.1666667 0.1666667 0.1666667 0.3333333 0.5000000 0.3333333
[4,] 0.5000000 0.5000000 0.5000000 1.0000000 0.5000000 1.0000000 0.0000000 0.5000000 0.5000000
[5,] 0.7500000 0.2500000 0.2500000 0.2500000 1.0000000 0.5000000 0.0000000 0.0000000 0.5000000
[6,] 0.3333333 0.3333333 0.3333333 0.6666667 0.6666667 1.0000000 0.0000000 0.3333333 0.6666667
[7,] 0.0000000 1.0000000 1.0000000 0.0000000 0.0000000 0.0000000 1.0000000 0.5000000 0.0000000
[8,] 0.0000000 0.3333333 1.0000000 0.3333333 0.0000000 0.3333333 0.3333333 1.0000000 0.3333333
[9,] 0.2500000 0.2500000 0.5000000 0.2500000 0.5000000 0.5000000 0.0000000 0.2500000 1.0000000
```

Fig. 3. Matrix similarity of « Test» network

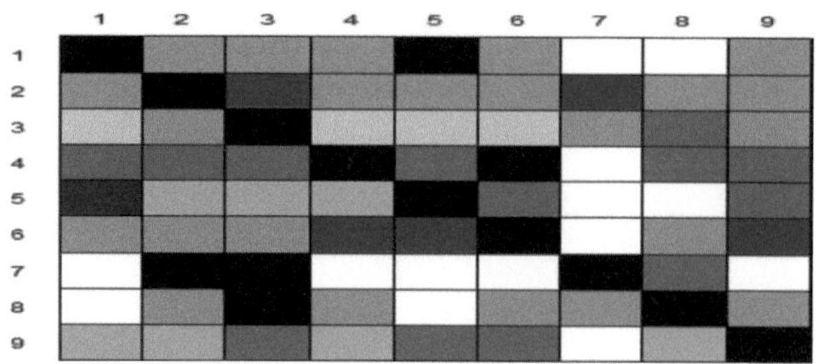

Fig. 4. Socio-matrix of « Test » network similarity

4   Results

Leader-Similarity Community Detection (LSCD) algorithm seeks to detect communities using the leaders selected by the HybridRank algorithm. This process involves reducing the list of leaders by merging similar ones into the same community, employing relative entropy similarity that accounts for the local network of each leader. Subsequently, other nodes in the network are assigned to communities based on their similarity with the leaders, using a novel similarity measure.

To validate the efficacy of the LSCD algorithm, we compared its results with other algorithms addressing similar challenges. Experimentation with the LSCD algorithm was conducted on datasets with known ground truth, including the Zachary Karate Club [19], American College Football [20], and Political blogs datasets [21].

Table 1. Topological properties of real-world networks.

Datasets	N	M	kmax	<k>	<k2>	<cc>
Zachary Karate Club	34	78	17	4.588	35.647	0.587
American College Football	115	616	13	10.713	115.61	0.403
Political blogs	1490	19090	468	25.624	1824.6	0.360

Table 1 represents the topological features of the used datasets: n and m are the total number of nodes and edges, respectively, $<k>$ is the average degree of nodes, $kmax$ is the maximal degree and $<cc>$ is the average of clustering coefficient

We evaluate the performance of our algorithm using two key metrics: Normalized Mutual Information (NMI) and Adjusted Rand Index (ARI). NMI measures the statistical dependence between two partitions by considering the mutual information shared between them and their individual entropies. A higher NMI indicates a stronger similarity between partitions [22]. ARI is an extension of the Rand Index that provides a stable measure of similarity between partitions. It compares pairs of data points in two partitions and calculates the agreement between them [23]. These metrics help assess the effectiveness of our algorithm in detecting communities by comparing the detected partitions with ground-truth partitions in datasets like the Zachary Karate Club, American College Football, and Political blogs datasets.

The experiments are structured into three main parts:

- **Threshold Variation Experiment:** This part assesses the algorithm's performance by varying the number of communities to detect and the corresponding number of leaders to be used for community formation. It measures the algorithm's efficiency by adjusting the thresholds β and γ, which determine the fusion of similar leader nodes into the same community and the assignment of similar nodes to community leaders, respectively.
- **Full Leader Set Experiment:** In this experiment, the LSCD algorithm utilizes all the detected leaders during the leader detection step. The communities are then formed based on these leaders, with the threshold γ being varied to observe its impact on the results.
- **Algorithm Comparison:**
- The final part involves comparing the results obtained from the LSCD algorithm with those from other established algorithms. This comparison evaluates the effectiveness and performance of the LSCD algorithm in community detection against existing methods.

The outcomes of the LSCD algorithm are depicted in Fig. 5 and Fig. 6, where the influence of the number of leaders on community detection is explored. By maintaining the threshold $\beta = 1$ for leader similarity and varying γ within the range [0.3, 0.7], the NMI and ARI metrics are evaluated across different datasets: Zachary Karate Club, American College Football, and Political blogs. The clustering coefficient (cc) values of 0.58, 0.403, and 0.36 correspond to Zachary, Football, and Blogs datasets, respectively. Notably, the LSCD algorithm shows higher efficiency when γ is considerably smaller than the clustering coefficient.

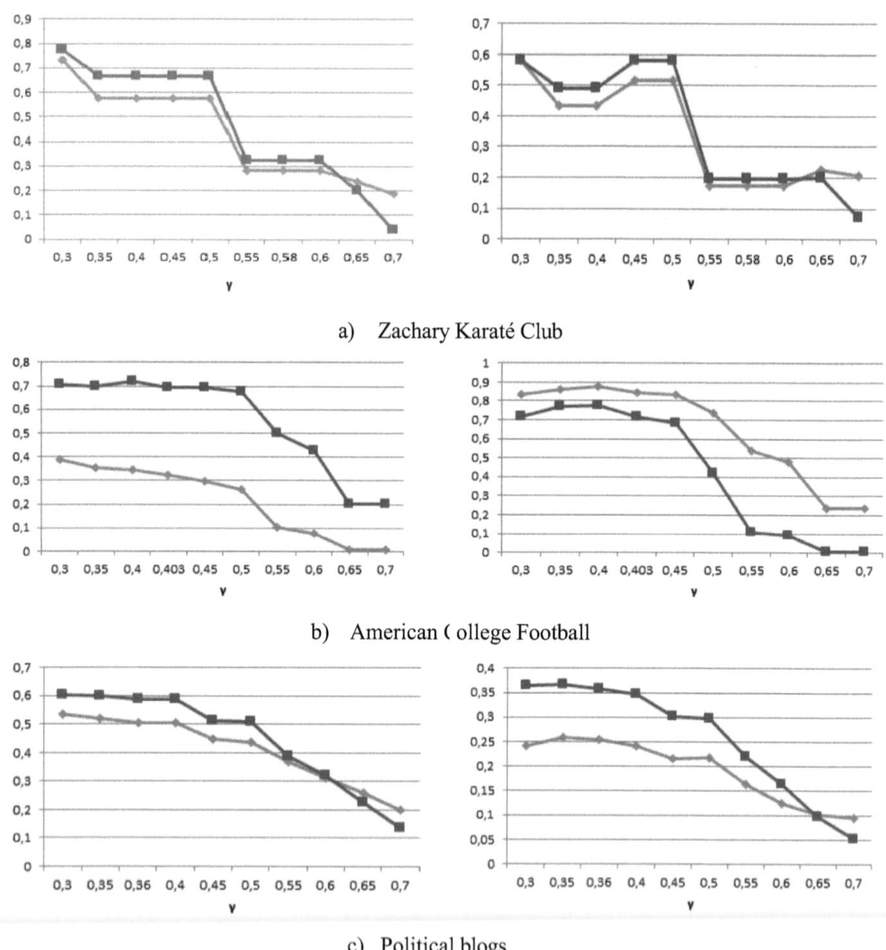

a)   Zachary Karaté Club

b)   American College Football

c)   Political blogs

Fig. 5. NMI and ARI for LSCD algorithm with predefined number of leaders (left) and $\beta = 1$ (right)

Further analysis involves measuring NMI and ARI values for LSCD using all detected leaders, with β set to 1 and γ varying within [0.3, 0.7], as mentioned in Fig 6 and Fig 7. In the case of Zachary, the number of leaders reduces from four to three communities after merging based on relative entropy similarity. Similarly, American Football sees a reduction from 19 to 16 communities, while Political blogs maintain the same community count. Notably, LSCD exhibits greater efficiency when γ aligns closer to the average clustering coefficient. Validation of LSCD's performance involves comparing its NMI and ARI values with those of established algorithms such as Walktrap [24], Leading eigenvector [25], Infomap [26], Multi-level or Louvain [27], Edge betweenness [28] and Fast Greedy [29], label propagation [14]. For Zachary and Political blogs datasets, LSCD outperforms other algorithms in terms of both NMI and ARI. While competitive for American Football, the algorithm's effectiveness is influenced by the network's degree distribution, which deviates from a power law. However, LSCD excels in detecting communities within scale-free networks characterized by most of low-degree nodes and few high-degree nodes.

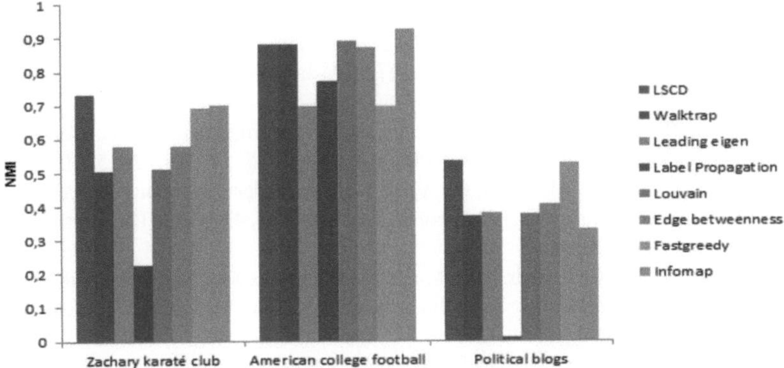

Fig. 6. NMI results for different algorithms

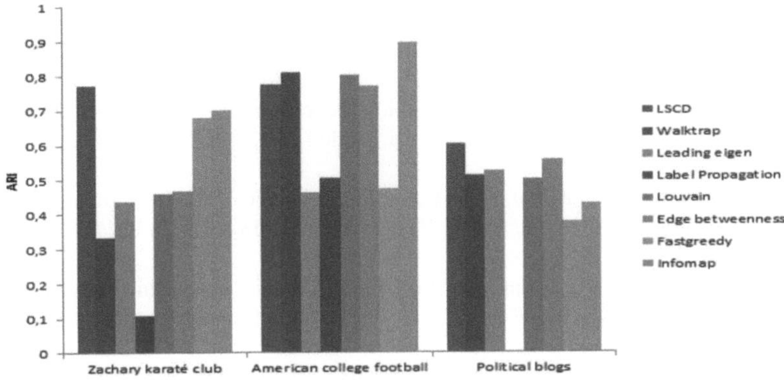

Fig. 7. ARI results for different algorithms

5   Conclusion

In this paper, we have introduced the Leader-Similarity Community Detection (LSCD) algorithm, designed for detecting communities and leaders in complex networks. The algorithm comprises three main steps: leader detection using the HybridRank algorithm, leader similarity to merge similar leaders into the same community, and community detection to assign the remaining nodes to their respective communities. Notably, our method does not require prior knowledge of the number of leaders or communities to be detected, nor does it rely on pre-defined community structures. To validate the effectiveness of our algorithm, we tested it using ground-truth datasets and compared its performance to state-of-the-art methods using various metrics. Across all datasets, the LSCD algorithm demonstrated notable efficiency compared to other methods, underscoring its effectiveness in community detection within complex networks.

References

1. Milgram, S.: The Small World Problem (1967)
2. Fortunato, S.: Community detection in graphs. Phys. Rep. **486**, 75–174 (2011). https://doi.org/10.1016/j.physrep.2009.11.002
3. Ahajjam, S., Badir, H.: Community detection in social networks. In: Biswas, A., Patgiri, R., Biswas, B. (eds.) Principles of Social Networking: The New Horizon and Emerging Challenges, pp. 91–107. Springer, Singapore (2022). https://doi.org/10.1007/978-981-16-3398-0_5
4. Ahajjam, S., El Haddad, M., Badir, H.: LeadersRank: towards a new approach for community detection in social networks. In: Proceeding AICCSA 2015. AICCSA 2015 (2015)
5. Ahajjam, S., El Haddad, M., Badir, H.: A new scalable leader-community detection approach for community detection in social networks. Soc. Netw. **54**, 41–49 (2018). https://doi.org/10.1016/j.socnet.2017.11.004
6. Helal, N.A., Ismail, R.M., Badr, N.L., Mostafa, M.G.M.: Leader-based community detection algorithm for social networks. Wiley Interdiscip. Rev. Data Min. Knowl. Discov. **7** (2017). https://doi.org/10.1002/widm.1213
7. Fu, J., Wu, J., Liu, C., Xu, J.: Leaders in communities of real-world networks. Phys. Stat. Mech. Appl. **444**, 428–441 (2016). https://doi.org/10.1016/j.physa.2015.09.091
8. Khorasgani, R.R., Chen, J., Zaïane, O.R.: Top leaders community detection approach in information networks. In: Proceedings of the 4th Workshop on Social Network Mining and Analysis, p. 228 (2013). ISSN 2319-7323
9. Li, J., et al.: A comprehensive review of community detection in graphs (2024). http://arxiv.org/abs/2309.11798, https://doi.org/10.48550/arXiv.2309.11798
10. Wu, Q., Qi, X., Fuller, E., Zhang, C.-Q.: Follow the leader: a centrality guided clustering and its application to social network analysis. Sci. World J. **2013**, e368568 (2013). https://doi.org/10.1155/2013/368568
11. Fang, C., Mu, D., Deng, Z., Hu, J., Yi, C.-H.: Fast detection of the fuzzy communities based on leader-driven algorithm. Int. J. Mod. Phys. B **32**, 1850058 (2017). https://doi.org/10.1142/S0217979218500583
12. Traag, V.A., Waltman, L., van Eck, N.J.: From Louvain to Leiden: guaranteeing well-connected communities. Sci. Rep. **9**, 5233 (2019). https://doi.org/10.1038/s41598-019-41695-z
13. Traag, V.A., Šubelj, L.: Large network community detection by fast label propagation. Sci. Rep. **13**, 2701 (2023). https://doi.org/10.1038/s41598-023-29610-z
14. Wu, Q., Chen, R., Wang, L., Guo, K.: A label propagation algorithm for community detection on high-mixed networks. Concurr. Comput. Pract. Exp. **33**, e6141 (2021). https://doi.org/10.1002/cpe.6141
15. Ben El Kouni, I., Karoui, W., Romdhane, L.B.: Node importance based label propagation algorithm for overlapping community detection in networks. Expert Syst. Appl. **162**, 113020 (2020). https://doi.org/10.1016/j.eswa.2019.113020
16. Ahajjam, S., Badir, H.: Identification of influential spreaders in complex networks using HybridRank algorithm. Sci. Rep. **8**, 11932 (2018). https://doi.org/10.1038/s41598-018-30310-2
17. Zhang, Q., Li, M., Deng, Y., Mahadevan, S.: Measure the similarity of nodes in the complex networks. ArXiv150200780 Phys (2015)
18. Qian, H.: Relative entropy: free energy associated with equilibrium fluctuations and nonequilibrium deviations. Phys. Rev. E. **63** (2001). https://doi.org/10.1103/PhysRevE.63.042103

19. Zachary, W.W.: An information flow model for conflict and fission in small groups. J. Anthropol. Res. **33**, 452–473 (1977)
20. Newman, M.E.J.: Modularity and community structure in networks. Proc. Natl. Acad. Sci. **103**, 8577–8582 (2006). https://doi.org/10.1073/pnas.0601602103
21. Adamic, L.A., Glance, N.: The political blogosphere and the 2004 U.S. election: divided they blog. In: Proceedings of the 3rd International Workshop on Link Discovery, pp. 36–43. ACM, New York (2005). https://doi.org/10.1145/1134271.1134277
22. Ghosh, J., Strehl, A., Merugu, S.: A consensus framework for integrating distributed clusterings under limited knowledge sharing. In: In Proceedings of the NSF Workshop on Next Generation Data Mining, pp. 99–108 (2002)
23. Hubert, L., Arabie, P.: Comparing partitions. J. Classif. **2**, 193–218 (1985). https://doi.org/10.1007/BF01908075
24. Pons, P.: Détection de communautés dans les grands graphes de terrain. Paris 7 (2010)
25. Newman, M.E.J.: Community detection and graph partitioning. EPL Europhys. Lett. **103**, 28003 (2013). https://doi.org/10.1209/0295-5075/103/28003
26. Rosvall, M., Axelsson, D., Bergstrom, C.T.: The map equation. Eur. Phys. J. Spec. Top. **178**, 13–23 (2009). https://doi.org/10.1140/epjst/e2010-01179-1
27. Blondel, V.D., Guillaume, J.-L., Lambiotte, R., Lefebvre, E.: Fast unfolding of communities in large networks. J. Stat. Mech. Theory Exp. **2008**, P10008 (2008). https://doi.org/10.1088/1742-5468/2008/10/P10008
28. Newman, M.E.J., Girvan, M.: Finding and evaluating community structure in networks. Phys. Rev. E Stat. Nonlin. Soft Matter Phys. **69**, 026113 (2004). https://doi.org/10.1103/PhysRevE.69.026113
29. Liu, W., Pellegrini, M., Wang, X.: Detecting communities based on network topology. Sci. Rep. **4** (2014). https://doi.org/10.1038/srep05739
30. Beni, H.A., Bouyer, A. TI-SC: top-k influential nodes selection based on community detection and scoring criteria in social networks. J. Ambient Intell. Human Comput. **11**, 4889–4908 (2020). https://doi.org/10.1007/s12652-020-01760-2

Short Papers

Enhancing Academic Success: Performance Early Prediction Using Machine Learning Algorithms

Abderrazek Hachani[1], Maha Mallek[1,2], and Yosra Jmal[1,3]([⊠])

[1] ESPRIT School of Engineering, Cebalat, Tunisia
{Abderrazek.hachani,Maha.mallek,Yosra.Jmal}@esprit.tn
[2] LARIA, National School of Computer Science (ENSI), Manouba, Tunisia
[3] LTSIRS, National Institute of Applied Science and Technology (INSAT), Tunis, Tunisia

Abstract. Emerging technologies, particularly artificial intelligence (AI) and machine learning (ML) algorithms, present valuable opportunities to analyse learning management system data (LMS) and considered as the corner stone of Learning analytics (LA). The aim is to analyse student performance during a course or a whole academic year. In particular, it identifies at risk students and enables educators to timely support this student's category and can provide clear guidance to improve teaching and learning strategies. This is why implementing an Early-Warning System is very crucial in this context to alert at risk student with weak performance, during first course sessions, to mitigate potential failures. The primary objective of this paper is to develop and implement an early-warning system that assists educators in identifying these students requiring attention and prompts them to be aware of their academic progress, thereby facilitating timely interventions to reduce the risk of failure. This study target web technologies course for the third-year engineering level in Esprit school of engineering, Tunisia. The experiments involve testing and comparing the performance of various classifiers, with a focus on Logistic Regression (LR), Random Forest (RF), Naive Bayes (NB) and K-Nearest Neighbours (KNN). The classification process considers factors such as students' engagement in different activities over time, the scores obtained in these activities, class attendance, and final results. The ultimate goal is to early predict student performance by categorizing them into two groups: those requiring additional support (convocation) and those who achieve well, the initial weeks of the course.

Keywords: Learning Management System (LMS) · Machine Learning · Learning Analytics · Early Prediction · Academic Success · Educational Technology

1 Introduction

When determining a student's knowledge, skills, and talents, learning evaluation in education entails a methodical procedure of obtaining and analyzing information. Accreditation programs and standards offer structures to guarantee uniformity and quality in

H. Badir et al. (Eds.): INTIS 2024, CCIS 2645, pp. 305–311, 2026.
https://doi.org/10.1007/978-3-032-14964-0_24

education. Institutions can uphold high standards and show accountability by using these frameworks.

The measure of the extent to which each student achieves the intended specified learning outcomes, if we value personal and interpersonal skills, and product, process, system, and service building skills, and incorporate them into curriculum and learning experiences, then we must have effective assessment processes for measuring them. Different categories of learning outcomes require different assessment methods. For example, learning outcomes related to disciplinary knowledge may be assessed with oral, online and written tests, while those related to design-implement skills may be better measured with recorded observations. Using a variety of assessment methods accommodates a broader range of learning and increases the reliability and validity of the assessment data.

The future of learning experiences in the ever-changing field of education can be greatly shaped by the efficient use of data. Learning Management Systems (LMS) have emerged as crucial instruments for gathering enormous volumes of data about students, offering a previously unheard-of chance to learn more about the factors that predict academic success. The abundance of data created by learning management system (LMS) platforms has created opportunities for utilizing machine learning approaches to predict and comprehend student progress as educational institutions move more and more towards digital platforms.

This article presents a novel project at esprit school of engineering that uses data from Google classroom to forecast student performance by utilizing machine learning techniques. This project is driven by the goal of providing educators with proactive insights that will allow them to recognize students who might need more assistance and adjust their teaching methods to meet their specific needs. We expect to explore the complex patterns hidden in LMS data, which goes beyond conventional evaluation techniques.

The remainder of this paper is organized as follows: Related work on early-warning systems is presented in the Section II. Section III presents the research methodology. Using our purpose-built dataset, the experimental results of our system are presented in section IV. Finally, Section V concludes this paper and outlines future work.

2 Related Work

There is a large body of literature relevant to explore machine learning techniques for predicting students' performance. In this section, we review the most recent and accurate works dealing with this problem.

Llanos et al. [1] have proposed a model for forecasting student success in a 16-week CS1 programming course. Grades, delivery time and the total number of attempts in exams are all used by the model. The model was trained and assessed using 8 algorithms and Week three saw the best results for the gradient boosting classifier.

In order to identify students who are at risk of failing in blended learning environments, the authors of Fahd et al. [2] suggests a novel strategy that makes use of machine learning models. According to the research, random forest algorithm obtained an accuracy of 85%.

The prediction of student performance by data mining and artificial intelligence is covered in paper [3] 16 features from 480 students make up the dataset extracted from Kalboard LMS, and the trained model's accuracy was 0.76.

In [4] the authors have asserted that Business Understanding, Data Understanding, Data Preprocessing, and Modelling constituted the four stages of the study project that were conducted. Decision tree, Bayesian, and k-Nearest Neighbor classifiers were the types of classifiers employed in the testing process, with the accuracy of predictions ranging between 52% and 67%.

The effectiveness of ML and LSTM-based models in forecasting student performance is assessed in paper [5] The study used the LIME method for interpretability analysis and focused on online teaching and learning using a virtual learning environment. The authors' main conclusions showed that deep learning techniques perform better at predicting grades than traditional regression techniques. Conversely, interpretability decreases with increasing prediction model sophistication.

To evaluate students' success in the course, Zangooei et al. [6] have employed learning analytics technologies. The LSTM neural network model was utilised to forecast pupils' academic achievement. In terms of prediction accuracy, the authors demonstrated that LSTM network performs better than the SVM method.

3 Research Methodology

As shown in Fig. 1, the research methodology for this study follows a structured approach to predict early risk students based on Google Classroom data. The methodology encompasses several key stages, beginning with the clear definition of the research objective. A comprehensive review of existing literature on student risk prediction, machine learning, and educational data mining was conducted to establish a foundation for the study.

Data collection involved obtaining LMS data, ensuring compliance with data privacy regulations and ethical considerations. The collected data underwent rigorous preparation, including cleaning, handling missing values, and preprocessing tasks such as normalization and encoding.

Feature extraction was performed to identify and extract relevant features from the LMS data, which would serve as input for the prediction models. Subsequently, Pearson correlation analysis was conducted to assess relationships between variables and their correlation with early student risk.

The predictive models were built using Logistic Regression, Random Forest, Naïve Bayes and K-Nearest Neighbors. The data was split into training and testing sets, and the models were trained and evaluated using appropriate performance metrics such as accuracy.

3.1 Data Collection

The dataset utilised in this study consists of information derived from the web technologies course classroom for third-year engineering students conducted in the 2023

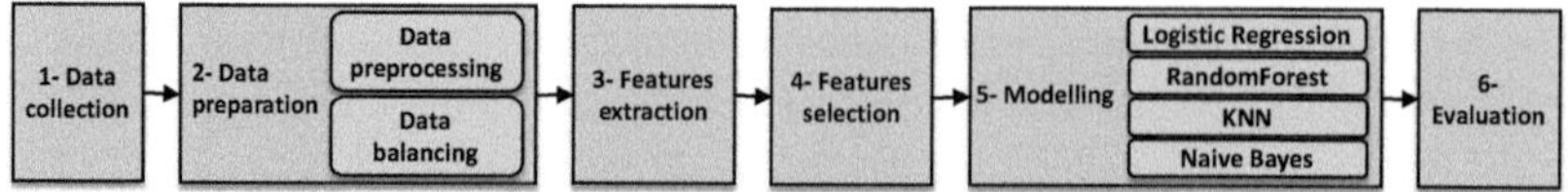

Fig. 1. Overview of the different steps in our proposed method.

academic year at Esprit School of Engineering, Tunisia. This dataset includes details regarding students' assessments and Student Attendance.

The classroom setting facilitates flexible curriculum delivery, giving teachers the freedom to assign and review content with their pupils. With this flexibility, students can take advantage of opportunities to participate in online activities, access course materials, and take tests, all of which can improve their overall learning experience.

After analysis, a csv file is produced from the data collection. There are 120 rows and 15 columns of gathered records in this file. Students' names and identifiers are included in the columns along with the dates of submission for assessments 1, 2, 3, and 4. In a similar vein, all seven class periods' worth of student attendance is included. The overall average and the final exam mark for this module come next. Every row represents a student record. To train, validate, and test the prediction models, these data were used. A total of 120 students took the course; 24 students, or 80% of the data, were set aside for testing, while the remaining 96 students, or 20% of the data, were randomly assigned for training and validation.

3.2 Data Preparation

Any data mining method must start with data preparation. This is the initial stage of data preparation for early student performance prediction. Two primary tasks are involved: (i) **Data anonymization** that aim to make the data anonymous, the two columns that contained the names and identities of the students were deleted. (ii) **Data pre-processing** that first use df.isna(), sum() to find the missing values in the DataFrame. The.dropna() function was then used to eliminate these records. The following stage was to convert the results of the four evaluations' submission dates into a numerical representation according to how those results related to a target date. This was accomplished by using the convert_to_float function. Following was the encoding of the assessment results: There are four categories for student submissions: three for those turned in before the deadline, two for those sent in on time, one for those turned in after the deadline, and zero for those that are missing. Furthermore, the attendance of students was converted into a percentage for every individual student. The last stage of data preprocessing was creating values that represented success and failure from the student's final exam and total grade columns.

3.3 Features Extraction

Activities conducted by students within the Learning Management System (LMS) classroom involve diverse tasks, including the completion of four homework assignments with specified deadlines. To capture this information, the first feature extracted is the submission date for each student's assessment in the classroom. Additionally, we incorporated other pertinent features such as student attendance across the seven sessions, the grade obtained in the final exam for the module, and the overall grade achieved. This analysis revealed the identification of four key features: submission date for each assessment, final grade, student attendance during the seven sessions, and overall grade.

3.4 Features Selection

Selecting features with correlations close to zero. The Pearson method was employed to calculate the linear correlation between pairs of features, producing results between -1 and $+1$. Upon conducting these calculations, it was observed that the overall grade feature exhibited a correlation coefficient of 1 with other features. Consequently, the overall average was eliminated as it does not contribute significantly.

3.5 Modelling

Modelling is a fundamental step of the presented method which follows the preprocessing of the dataset and the features selection. This task requires two steps: **(i) Selected algorithms:** The suggested model incorporates four algorithms: K-Nearest Neighbours (KNN) [7] Random Forest (RF) [8], Logistic Regression (LR) [9] and Naive Bayes (NB) [10, 11]. The selection of RF, LR, and NB algorithms is based on their ability to accurately forecast student performance in the initial phases, as suggested by baseline articles. Furthermore, this choice is driven by the unique benefits that each algorithm provides in this situation. The construction of the prediction model comes after the algorithm selection. In order to do this, the model is trained using 80% of the data produced during the data preparation step, with the remaining 20% set aside for testing. The final predictions are then produced using the selected features, and the results for specific metrics during weeks 2, 4, and 7 of the courses are obtained.

   (ii) Selected metrics: In order to evaluate the performance of the used algorithms, we adopt the official evaluation metric, which is based on F1-score. The F1 score can be interpreted as a weighted average of the precision and recall.

3.6 Evaluation

The goal of this research is to forecast student performance beginning in week two of the course by achieving an F1 score metric value of more than 70%.

4 Results

In this study, a total of four traditional classification algorithms were utilized for early prediction student performance: Naive Bayes, Logistic Regression (LR), k-Nearest Neighbors (KNN) and Random Forest (RF). Various tests were conducted to determine the performance of these algorithms using F1 score. This metric is evaluated for weeks 2, 4, and 7 of the study as shown in Table 1.

   Across the weeks, the algorithm with the highest performance result was the LR. The LR predicted the student performance with F1 score 72.56% in the week 2, while

76.37% in the week 4 and 84.61% in the seventh week. It can be remarked, that F1 score increases during the weeks and the loss values decrement with increasing weeks, which indicates the strength of the model. Conversely, KNN and RF achieved the lowest results. These models could be a potentially good method, but it need a much higher number of students to produce better and relevant results.

Table 1. Results of Prediction algorithms in Weeks 2, 4, and 7.

Week	Metrics	KNN (%)	LR (%)	RF (%)	NB (%)
Week2	F1-Score	47.30	**72.56**	63.37	47.30
Week4		56.09	**76.37**	68.91	56.09
Week7		59.80	**84.61**	71.64	59.80

5 Conclusion

In conclusion, this study has demonstrated the potential of machine learning algorithms in predicting early risk students based on Learning Management System (LMS) data. The research methodology employed a systematic approach, encompassing data collection, preparation, feature extraction, correlation analysis, and the implementation of predictive models using Logistic Regression, Random Forest, and Naïve Bayes algorithms.

Ethical concerns about student data protection and appropriate use were considered in this work. The study of the implementation outcomes highlighted performance of each classification algorithm and provided insightful information about how well it performed. Despite the short dataset in this study, the Logistic Regression (LR) approach outperforms Random Forest (RF), k-Nearest Neighbours (KNN), and Naive Bayes.

We are thinking about including new aspects in this study, like student psychologies, personal data, and additional weekly activities, to improve it. We'll also broaden the study to include early risk pupils in a variety of academic programmes in addition to a particular class.

References

1. Llanos, J., Bucheli, V.A., Restrepo-Calle, F.: Early prediction of student performance in CS1 programming courses. PeerJ Comput. Sci. **9**, e1655 (2023)
2. Fahd, K., Miah, S.J., Ahmed, K.: Predicting student performance in a blended learning environment using learning management system interaction data. Appl. Comput. Inform. (2021)
3. Bhusal, A.: Predicting student's performance through data mining. arXiv preprint arXiv:2112. 01247 (2021)
4. López Zambrano, J., Lara Torralbo, J.A., Romero Morales, C.: Early prediction of student learning performance through data mining: a systematic review. Psicothema (2021)
5. Chen, H.C., Prasetyo, E., Tseng, S.S., Putra, K.T., Kusumawardani, S.S., Weng, C.E.: Week-wise student performance early prediction in virtual learning environment using a deep explainable artificial intelligence. Appl. Sci. **12**(4), 1885 (2022)

6. Zangooei, H., Fatemi, O.: Predicting students at risk of academic failure using learning analytics in the learning management system. Q. Iran. Dist. Educ. J. **3**(2), 32–44 (2021)
7. Syed, M. E.: Attribute weighting in k-nearest neighbor classification (master;s thesis) (2014)
8. Siemens, G.: Learning analytics: envisioning a research discipline and a domain of practice. In: Proceedings of the 2nd International Conference on Learning Analytics and Knowledge, pp. 4–8 (2012)
9. Hosmer, D.W., Hosmer, T., Le Cessie, S., Lemeshow, S.: A comparison of goodness-of-fit tests for the logistic regression model. Stat. Med. **16**(9), 965–980 (1997)
10. Domingos, P., Pazzani, M.: On the optimality of the simple Bayesian classifier under zero-one loss. Mach. Learn. **29**, 103–130 (1997)
11. Levine, R.R.: Factors affecting gastrointestinal absorption of drugs. Am. J. Dig. Dis. **15**, 171–188 (1970)

Advancements in Arabic Handwritten Text Recognition: A Comprehensive Study of End-to-End Deep Learning Architecture with a Focus on Decoding Techniques

I. Bounour[1(✉)], A. Ammour[2], G. Khaissidi[1], and M. Mrabti[1]

[1] Laboratory LIPI ENS, USMBA Fez, Fez, Morocco
imane.bounour@usmba.ac.ma

[2] Euromed Research Centre, School of Engineering in Digital and Artificial Intelligence, Euromed University of Fes, Eco-Campus, Fes-Meknes Road, 30030 Fez, Morocco

Abstract. Optical Character Recognition (OCR) serves as a pivotal technology, permitting the conversion of text within images or scanned documents into machine-readable and editable formats. While OCR has demonstrated success across various languages, tackling Arabic OCR remains a significant challenge due to the intricate nature of the Arabic graphical writing system.

Among the most employed architectures in Arabic word recognition is one that combines Convolutional Neural Network (CNN), Recurrent Neural Network (RNN), and Connectionist Temporal Classification (CTC). This architecture involves a decoding operation that transforms the network's output into meaningful words.

This paper utilizes IFN/ENIT database to assess and compare the results of three decoding methods, namely: Best Path Decoding (BPD), Token Passing (TP), and Word Beam Search (WBS). This aims to understand to what extent the decoding method can influence recognition results, then to identify the method that leads to high accuracy, specifically in the case of Arabic Handwriting.

Keywords: Arabic Handwriting recognition · END-TO-END based-architecture · Decoding algorithms · INF/ENIT database

1 Introduction

Optical Character Recognition (OCR) falls within the domain of computer vision, seeking to automate the conversion of printed or handwritten text into a machine- readable digital format [1]. Given its widespread applications in various sectors such as education, communication, banking, legal documentation, historical preservation, and beyond, this technology holds significant importance [2].

In the recent past, OCR technology has achieved levels of accuracy and speed, comparable to human reading abilities, particularly in recognizing printed texts [3]. However, the effectiveness of OCR is not always high when dealing with handwritten

H. Badir et al. (Eds.): INTIS 2024, CCIS 2645, pp. 312–318, 2026.
https://doi.org/10.1007/978-3-032-14964-0_25

texts. In fact, languages with complex writing systems like Arabic generally require more advanced methods to establish a reliable handwriting recognition system [5].

Arabic handwritten-text recognition has been addressed following either holistic and segmentation approaches. In the holistic approach, each word is treated as a cohesive entity, enabling the capture of overall patterns and features within its morphological structure [3]. The recognition task in this case can be performed through various classifiers, including k-nearest neighbors (KNN), Support Vector Machines (SVM) [4] and, more recently, architectures based on CNNs. On the other hand, segmentation approach entails breaking down words into characters or smaller meaningful units, known as graphemes, either explicitly or implicitly [5]. Recognition of words is then achieved by identifying these graphical units using classifiers as Hidden Markov Models (HMMs) [6], Recurrent Neural Networks (RNNs), including RNN-Long Short-Term Memory (LSTM) and RNN-Bidirectional Long Short-Term Memory (BLSTM, and in certain configurations a combination between A CNN and an RNN followed by a temporal connectionist classification (CTC) layer.

The CNN-RNN-CTC end-to-end architecture has demonstrated remarkable results, particularly in recognizing and transcribing cursive Arabic handwriting [7], where the interconnected nature of characters poses a challenge for traditional recognition methods. In this configuration, the entire recognition process, from the input image to the final text output, is integrated into a single model. The model learns to extract features [8], understand sequential dependencies [9], and produce the final text representation in a consistent and streamlined manner, without the need for intermediate steps such as explicit segmentation.

The decoding operation plays a central role in this architecture. it allows the transformation of raw model outputs-typically presented as probabilities, into a format that aligns with the intended representation of the recognized text. This crucial step involves interpreting the predictions generated by the model, considering the overall context of the output sequence and taking into account sequential dependencies.

Alongside the introduction of a novel end-to-end Arabic handwritten training model, this article undertakes a comparative analysis of three decoding methods-Best Path Decoding (BPD), Token Passing (TP), and Word Beam Search (WBS). The objective is to systematically evaluate the influence of theses decoding techniques on the performance of the recognition system, then identify the technique most conducive to achieving high accuracy in the case of Arabic handwriting recognition.

The remainder of this paper is structured as follows: Sect. 2 details the methodology employed in our study, outlining the applied approaches and techniques. Section 3, presents the experimental configurations and discuss the obtained results. Section 4, evaluates the performance of the trained models. The final section encapsulates our conclusions drawn from the findings and outlines plans for future work.

2 Methodology

2.1 IFN/ENIT Database and Preprocessing

We utilize the IFN/ENIT database, introduced by Pechwitz and Maergner, as a foundational resource for our research in handwritten Arabic text recognition [10]. This database includes 1000 forms written by 411 unique contributors and is divided into six sets for training and testing. It comprises approximately 27,000 handwritten Arabic names representing Tunisian city names, supported by a lexicon of 937 place names and Ground Truth files for detailed analysis.

To enhance the quality and consistency of the word images, we employ preprocessing techniques [11] such as binarization, which minimizes noise and improves the distinction between characters and backgrounds, and resizing, which standardizes image sizes. Additionally, data augmentation methods, including rotation and shearing, are applied to further enrich the dataset and improve model training efficacy.

2.2 Deep Learning Model

In our approach, we utilized an end-to-end architecture combining a CNN, RNN, and the connectionist temporal classification (CTC) layer [12]. The CNN acts as a feature extractor, capturing complex spatial patterns in word images. The RNN, specifically a Bi-LSTM network, captures sequential dependencies, understanding contextual relationships between characters. The CTC layer aligns the RNN's predictions with ground truth labels, accommodating variable-length sequences without explicit character segmentation [13]. During prediction, the CTC generates a probability matrix for each character at each time step, which is decoded to obtain the predicted sequence, including handling sequences of varying lengths with a "blank" symbol for flexible alignment [14].

2.3 Decoding Algorithms

The common decoding techniques in Arabic handwritten recognition include "BPD" [15], "TP-Decoder" [16], and "WBS" [17]. The difference between these decoding methods lies in how they interpret the outputs of the text recognition model to obtain the final text sequence. Each method adopts a specific approach to handle the output probabilities and align them with the predicted text sequence.

In the presence of this multitude algorithms, evaluating the relevance and effectiveness of each algorithm in the Arabic text recognition process becomes of paramount importance. Indeed, the challenges posed by the interconnectedness of characters and the variability in writing styles in Arabic handwriting necessitate a careful examination of how the decoding approach output addresses these specific complexities.

3 Experiment Configuration

In the initial stage of model construction, a CNN architecture is used, starting with an input layer followed by a convolutional block that includes a depthwise convolution [18] with a 3×3 kernel, batch normalization, and ReLU activation. This block is repeated with varying filters and pooling configurations: 64 filters, 128 filters with 2×2 max-pooling, 256 filters with 1×2 max-pooling, and 512 filters without max-pooling, each followed by dropout at a rate of 0.1. In the second part, a Bi-LSTM with 128 units is applied, with reshaping to connect the CNN and Bi-LSTM. The final layer uses the CTC loss function with a Dense layer and softmax activation. The model is optimized with the Adam optimizer (learning rate of 0.001), a batch size of 64 images, and 40 training epochs.

4 Performance Evaluation and Experiment Results

The performance of the training models is evaluated using two metrics: Character Accuracy Rate (CAR) [19] and Word Accuracy Rate (WAR) [20]. These metrics provide valuable insights into the precision of the model's predictions at both the character and word levels. The CAR measures the accuracy of individual character predictions within a sequence using the Levenshtein distance, ranging from 0% (no correct characters) to 100% (perfect character-level prediction). The WAR evaluates the correctness of word-level predictions by comparing the entire predicted word sequence against the ground truth, with a score of 0% indicating no matches and 100% indicating perfect alignment of all words.

The following table (Table 1) presents the obtained results for the Bi-LSTM-CTC constructed models on the IFN/ENIT database under different train-test configurations and decoding algorithms.

Table 1. Experimental results for the Bi-LSTM-CTC models across various train-test configurations on the IFN/ENIT database

Train-test configurat ion	Bi-LSTM-CTC (BPD)		Bi-LSTM-CTC (TP-decoder)		Bi-LSTM-CTC (WBS)	
	CAR%	WAR%	CAR%	WAR%	CAR%	WAR%
abc-d	88,6	86,5	93,3	92,7	96,6	94,8
bcd-a	86,1	85	91,4	90,5	95,5	94,1
abcd-e	84,3	83,9	92,5	92	96,8	94,9
abcde-f	84,8	82,3	94,1	92,3	96	95,1
ebdf-c	85,6	84,1	94,6	93,1	97,9	96,3

The results show that Bi-LSTM-CTC with BPD achieved moderate to high CAR% and WAR% across various configurations (abc-d, bcd-a, abcd-e, abcde-f, ebdf-c). However, it appears that this decoder is not consistently the most efficient one, as its CAR% and WAR% values vary across different configurations. Bi-LSTM-CTC with TP-decoder offers more stable and improved performance compared to BPD. The values are consistently higher across different configurations in terms of both CAR% and WAR%. Notably, Bi-LSTM-CTC with WBS consistently outperforms both BPD and TP-decoder.

The values of CAR% and WAR% are consistently the highest across all configurations, indicating superior recognition accuracy.

This results suggest that the BPD may not be the most efficient for the Bi-LSTM-CTC recognition model. TP-decoder shows improvement, but the most notable gains in both CAR% and WAR% are achieved with WBS, making it the preferred decoding algorithm for enhancing recognition accuracy in the context of Arabic handwriting.

Several hypotheses can be proposed to explain these findings. Indeed, the interconnected and cursive nature of Arabic handwriting poses a unique challenge for recognition models. BPD, while providing a simple and rapid solution, may struggle with the complexity of capturing intra-word connections and contextual variations. TP-decoder, on the other hand, introduces a level of flexibility in handling variable-length sequences and exploring different hypotheses. This adaptability could contribute to its improved performance compared to BPD in capturing the nuances of Arabic cursive writing. WBS emerges as the most successful decoding method, consistently outperforming both BPD and TP-decoder. This could be attributed to WBS's explicit consideration of word-level information, enabling it to navigate through the cursive structure with a better understanding of contextual relationships between characters.

5 Conclusion

This article aimed to comprehensively explore and evaluate various decoding methods within the context of Arabic handwritten text recognition. The study utilized the IFN/ENIT database and employed the Bi-LSTM-CTC model with Best Path Decoding, Token Passing, and Word Beam Search as decoding strategies.

Considering the varied performance of decoding algorithms, a promising avenue for further improvement lies in the exploration of a Hybrid Decoding Approach. This approach involves the deliberate integration of Token Passing and Word Beam Search decoding algorithms in a synergistic manner to amplify their respective strengths and collectively enhance overall recognition accuracy. This proposed hybrid methodology represents an innovative extension of our current investigation into decoding methods. By systematically designing and rigorously evaluating this hybrid approach, we aim to provide a comprehensive understanding of its impact on recognition performance. This research direction not only builds upon the insights gleaned from individual decoding methods but also presents a novel solution to potentially address their inherent limitations. The subsequent incorporation of this hybrid decoding strategy into our study has the potential to significantly contribute to the advancement of efficient Arabic recognition systems, and we intend to conduct thorough experiments and analyses to validate its efficacy and relevance within the scope of this paper.

References

1. Mittal, R., Garg, A.: Text extraction using OCR: a systematic review. In: 2020 Second International Conference on Inventive Research in Computing Applications (ICIRCA), pp. 357–362. IEEE (2020). https://doi.org/10.1109/ICIRCA48905.2020.9183326

2. Hamad, K., Kaya, M.: A detailed analysis of optical character recognition technology. Int. J. Appl. Math. Electron. Comput. **4**, 244–244 (2016). https://doi.org/10.18100/ijamec.270374

3. Malakar, S., Sahoo, S., Chakraborty, A., Sarkar, R., Nasipuri, M.: Handwritten Arabic and Roman word recognition using holistic approach. Vis. Comput. **39**, 2909–2932 (2023). https://doi.org/10.1007/s00371-022-02500-7

4. Lawgali, A., Angelova, M., Bouridane, A.: A framework for arabic handwritten recognition based on segmentation. Int. J. Hybrid Inf. Technol. **7**, 413–428 (2014). https://doi.org/10.14257/ijhit.2014.7.5.38

5. Adiguzel, H., Sahin, E., Duygulu, P.: A hybrid for line segmentation in handwritten documents. In: 2012 International Conference on Frontiers in Handwriting Recognition, pp. 503–508. IEEE (2012). https://doi.org/10.1109/ICFHR.2012.156

6. Ahmad, I., Fink, G.A.: Multi-stage HMM based Arabic text recognition with rescoring. In: 2015 13th International Conference on Document Analysis and Recognition (ICDAR), pp. 751–755. IEEE (2015). https://doi.org/10.1109/ICDAR.2015.7333862

7. Gader, T., Chibani, I., Echi, A.: Arabic handwriting off-line recognition using ConvLSTM-CTC: In: Proceedings of the 12th International Conference on Pattern Recognition Applications and Methods (SCITEPRESS - Science and Technology Publications), pp. 529–533 (2023). https://doi.org/10.5220/0011794700003411

8. Ballester, P., Araujo, R.: On the performance of GoogLeNet and AlexNet applied to sketches. In: Proceedings of the AAAI Conference on Artificial Intelligence, vol. 30 (2016). https://doi.org/10.1609/aaai.v30i1.10171

9. Li, C., Zhan, G., Li, Z.: News text classification based on improved Bi-LSTM-CNN. In: 2018 9th International Conference on Information Technology in Medicine and Education (ITME), pp. 890–893. IEEE (2018). https://doi.org/10.1109/ITME.2018.00199

10. El Abed, H., Margner, V.: The IFN/ENIT-database - a tool to develop Arabic handwriting recognition systems. In: 2007 9th International Symposium on Signal Processing and its Applications, pp. 1–4. IEEE (2007). https://doi.org/10.1109/ISSPA.2007.4555529

11. Farooq, F., Govindaraju, V., Perrone, M.: Pre-processing methods for handwritten Arabic documents. In: Eighth International Conference on Document Analysis and Recognition (ICDAR 2005), vol. 1, pp. 267–271. IEEE (2005). https://doi.org/10.1109/ICDAR.2005.191

12. Lorigo, L.M., Govindaraju, V.: Offline Arabic handwriting recognition: a survey. IEEE Trans. Pattern Anal. Mach. Intell. **28**, 712–724 (2006). https://doi.org/10.1109/TPAMI.2006.102

13. Graves, A., Fernández, S., Gomez, F., Schmidhuber, J.: Connectionist temporal classification: labelling unsegmented sequence data with recurrent neural networks. In Proceedings of the 23rd international conference on Machine learning - ICML 2006, pp. 369–376. ACM Press (2006). https://doi.org/10.1145/1143844.1143891

14. Hou, J., Wang, P., Zhang, J., Yang, M., Feng, M., Yin, J.: CTC blank triggered dynamic layer-skipping for efficient CTC-based speech recognition. In: 2023 IEEE Automatic Speech Recognition and Understanding Workshop (ASRU), pp. 1–5. IEEE (2023). https://doi.org/10.1109/ASRU57964.2023.10389635

15. Katerynych, L., Safarov, E.: Increasing accuracy of recognition systems using decoding algorithms. In: 2021 IEEE 3rd International Conference on Advanced Trends in Information Theory (ATIT), pp. 236–240. IEEE (2021). https://doi.org/10.1109/ATIT54053.2021.9678690

16. Chen, Z., Jain, M., Wang, Y., Seltzer, M.L., Fuegen, C.: End-to-end contextual speech recognition using class language models and a token passing decoder. In: ICASSP 2019 - 2019 IEEE International Conference on Acoustics, Speech and Signal Processing (ICASSP) (IEEE), pp. 6186–6190 (2019). https://doi.org/10.1109/ICASSP.2019.8683573

17. Scheidl, H., Fiel, S., Sablatnig, R.: Word beam search: a connectionist temporal classification decoding algorithm. In: 2018 16th International Conference on Frontiers in Handwriting Recognition (ICFHR), pp. 253–258. IEEE (2018). https://doi.org/10.1109/ICFHR-2018.2018.00052
18. Zhang, R., Zhu, F., Liu, J., Liu, G.: Depth-wise separable convolutions and multi-level pooling for an efficient spatial CNN-based steganalysis. IEEE Trans. Inf. Forensics Secur. **15**, 1138–1150 (2020). https://doi.org/10.1109/TIFS.2019.2936913
19. Manwatkar, P.M., Singh, K.R.: A technical review on text recognition from images. In: 2015 IEEE 9th International Conference on Intelligent Systems and Control (ISCO) (IEEE), pp. 1–5 (2015). https://doi.org/10.1109/ISCO.2015.7282362
20. Elliman, D.G., Lancaster, I.T.: A review of segmentation and contextual analysis techniques for text recognition. Pattern Recognit. **23**, 337–346 (1990). https://doi.org/10.1016/0031-3203(90)90021-C

A Prediction Model Based On Recurrent Neural Network To Predict Freezing Of Gait Related To Parkinson's Disease

Yurub Awwad[1(✉)] , Amjad Rattrout[1] , and Rashid Jayousi[2]

[1] Arab American University, Jenin, Palestine
y.awwad5@student.aaup.edu, amjad.rattrout@aaup.edu
[2] Alquds University, Abu Dis, Palestine
rjayousi@staff.alquds.edu

Abstract. Patients of Parkinson's Disease may suffer movement difficulty. They may fall down. Therefore, they should be monitored all the time. A monitoring system which detects such difficulty and notify family or doctors will help protecting patients. In this paper we propose a model which may be used in such system to predict the happening of this difficulty. The model is based on Recurrent Neural Network trained on dataset collected for this purpose. The model achieved 99% of accuracy.

Keywords: Parkinson's Disease · RNN · Freezing of Gait · Datamining

1 Introduction

About 10 million people around the world are suffering Parkinson's Disease. In Epidemiology; Parkinson's Disease is a degenerative neurological disorder where the dopamine levels in the brain are decreased. This disorder is responsible for some difficulty in speech, walk, and some impairments in cognitive. This disease was described as depression by James Parkinson which eventually named by his name [1].
Parkinson's Disease diagnosis are traditionally made by observing the movement skills of the patient. The neurological history of the patient could also help in Parkinson's Disease diagnosis [2].
Freezing of Gait FoG is a difficulty of Parkinson's Disease. There are three types of FoG difficulties; StartHesitation, Turn, and Walk. Each of them has its own properties. [3]. And for sure this type of difficulty adversely affects quality of life [4]. This work is to build a model to predict FoG.

2 Literature Review

Authors in [5] work proposed two models to identify Parkinson's disease using Deep Learning based on Neural Networks. They used two datasets one for each model. The VGFR spectrogram Detector dataset and Voice Impairment Classifier dataset. The first is based on the endothelium in blood vessels. This model is

H. Badir et al. (Eds.): INTIS 2024, CCIS 2645, pp. 319–327, 2026.
https://doi.org/10.1007/978-3-032-14964-0_26

based on Convolutional Neural Network CNN. While the second is a dataset of recorded Vocal Fundamental Frequency of patient's voice. This model is based on Artificial Neural Network ANN. Their classification models scored 88.1% and 89.15% respectively.

The work In [6] is a system to monitor status of Parkinson's Disease Patients. The Model is proposed using Gated Recurrent Neural Network trained on a dataset collected from smartphones. The input data is a set of information gathered from smart phone using it's sensors like position and speed of patient. The aim of the system is to keep an eye on patients with Parkinson's Disease so doctors can see the effect of the current treatment. The proposed model reached a 88% of accuracy.

Authors in [7] proposed a comprehensive model to enhance the prediction of Parkinson's disease diagnosis using dataset based on voice recording of patients. For feature selection they tested four methods; Filtered-based Features Selection, Correlation-based Feature Subset Selection, Principle Component Analysis, and Wrapper-based Features Selection. While for classification they tested Naive Bayes, Support Vector Machine, Multi-layer Perceptron , K-Nearest Neighbor, and Random Forest. Their best results were using wrapper-based for feature selection stage and K-Nearest Neighbor For Prediction stage. Their best accuracy was 88.33% in classification of whether the person is a Parkinson Disease Patient or not.

in [8] authors built a classification model to diagnose whether a Patient is having Parkinson's Disease or not. Their model is using Machine Learning based on Multi-Layer Preceptron and K-Nearest Neighbor. The used Dataset to train their network is consist of 195 subject with 24 features, all are attributes of voice recording for patients with and without a Parkinson's Disease. the best accuracy achieved by this model is 91.28%.

All related work above are to diagnose the Parkinson's Disease, but they do not identify the symptom of Freezing of Gait except [6] which is built to predict the Freezing of Gait but they used a different dataset than the one in this study, and they reached 88% accuracy. Our contribution in this work is to achieve a better accuracy, And also we are using different dataset.

3   Dataset

The dataset which is used in this work is the "Parkinson's Freezing of Gait Prediction" obtained from Kaggle web site [9]. It comprises lower-back 3D accelerometer data from 65 subjects. Each subject was equipped with three sensors. These sensors are recording data synchronously and sending it as 128 data frame per second. The total records in our dataset is 7062672 records. For train, test and validate purposes a portion of data is selected from the whole dataset. This portion has 634203 records which are divided into three groups in 332928, 188841 and 112434 for train, test, and validation respectively.

The dataset which is used in this study is categorized and described as follow:
A. Sensors Data

- AccV: Acceleration from a lower-back sensor on first axes: V - Vertical.

- AccML: Acceleration from a lower-back sensor on second axes: ML - MedioLateral.

- AccAP: Acceleration from a lower-back sensor on third axes: AP - AnteroPosterior.

- In addition to Timesteps in which the data was sensed.

  B. Subjects Data

- Age: Subject's Age.

- Sex: Gender of Subject.

- YearsSinceDx: Number of years since Subject diagnosed as Parkinson's Disease patient.

- UPDRSIIIOn: Unified Parkinson's Disease Rating Scale score during on medication.

- UPDRSIIIOff: Unified Parkinson's Disease Rating Scale score during off medication.

- NFOGO: Self-report FoG questionnaire score [9].

- Visit: which is the number of the current treatment exercise.

  C. Labels

The Labels were originally three columns to identify each type of FoG; StartHesitation, Turn and Walk. For the purpose of our study they were merged into one Label to identify any happening of FoG. This dataset is first normalized and cleaned from duplicates.

4   Methodology

The Proposed model shown in Fig. 1 illustrates the process flow of data into the model. which is divided into two main processes. The first is to normalize data into two manners. the first is to normalize data regarding the patient information using normal data normalization process. The second is to normalize data regarding the accelerometer which is subjected to some constrains on the values that accelerometer generates. the second main process is to input the data into the trained network to classify or predict the output.

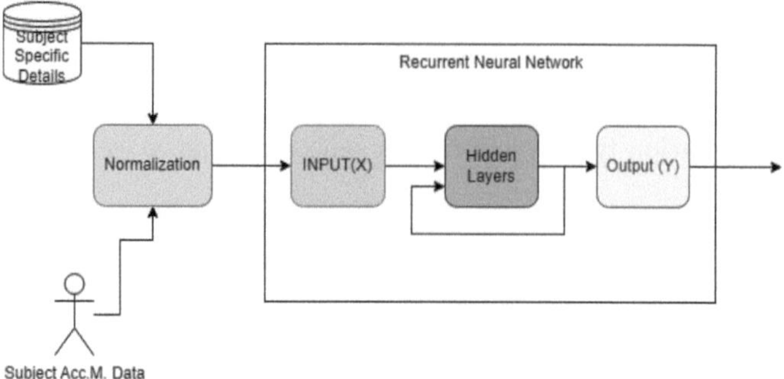

Fig. 1. Proposed Model using RNN.

5   Data Pre-processing

The pre-processing on data is done in two stages. The first one is to convert non-numerical values into numerical values, such as on/off to 1, 0. And the True/False into 1,0 both respectively. The second stage is to scale all numerical values into $[0, 1]$ range using Eq. 1

$$f(x) = \frac{x - min(x)}{max(x) - min(x)} \tag{1}$$

where x is the value to be normalized, $min(x)$ the minimum value for this column, $max(x)$ the maximum value for this column. Data such as Age, Test Result, Visits could be normalized with no problem. But the sensor's data are different. The Accelerometer specification data sheet defined the data range for its values to be in range between -16 to $+16$ (g). Therefore, the normalize Eq. 2 is used for Accelerometer data.

$$x' = \begin{cases} 16 & if\,x > 16 \\ -16 & if\,x < -16 \\ x & otherwise \end{cases} \tag{2}$$

Now the data are ready to be exported as a flat file for further investigations.

6   Prediction Model

Because of the multi dimensional of the data, and the targeted data are a classification whether a FOG occurred or not. Also. Data are arriving in a time series. The prediction model needs to be built on an algorithm that supports this type of prediction.

Artificial Neural Network is a candidate for this type of prediction. But which type of Neural Network is best for this dataset. The normal multi-layer neural network is first tested and it showed a good accuracy varies between (74%) and (94%) which is shown in Fig. 2.

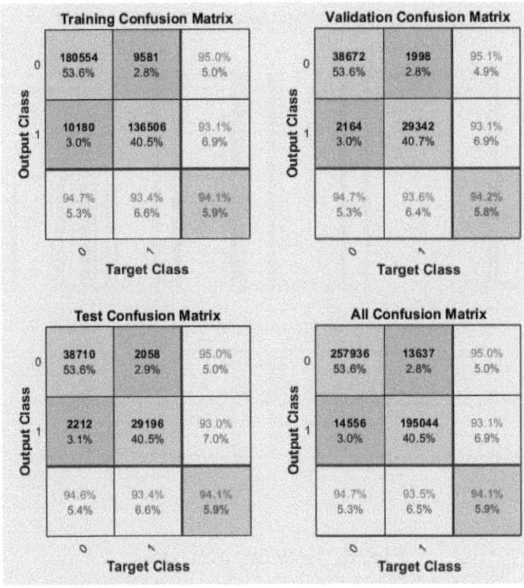

Fig. 2. Result of Trained Multi-Layer Neural Network with larger amount of data.

Recurrent Neural Network is then selected and tested. The result was promising. And therefore a further testing and tuning on the network is done.

The proposed model in Fig. 1. Is consist of two types of normalized data one for the subject specific data like Age, Sex, Test results. Visit number etc. While the other one is for the Accelerometer data AccV, AccML and AccAP.

The RNNs allow to get benefit from the hidden state (H). This hidden state allows the network to store variables from the last (T) states in addition to the current input(X). This is useful for our model because data is a time series which the current state or the output (Y) is affected by some previous states. (T) is also called a delay [10].

7   Training RNN on Dataset

After building the proposed model. The RNN is trained using the subset of the dataset which is prepared and normalized for this purpose. Figure 3 shows response of the network.

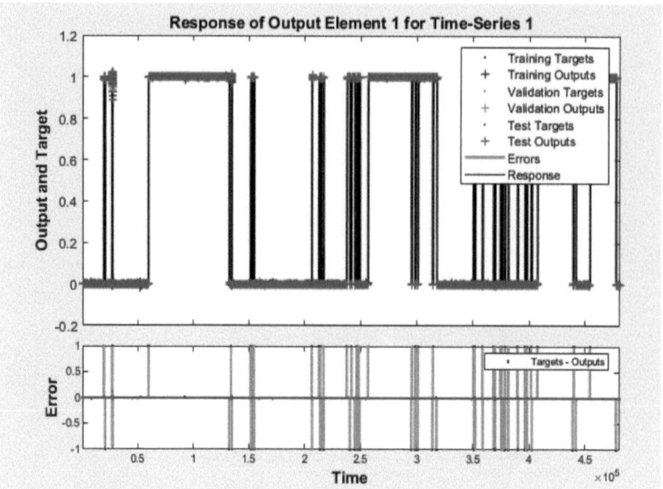

Fig. 3. Network Response.

The response curve in Fig. 3 is illustrating the predicted values and the actual values during the training, testing and validating the network. The bottom section is showing the error. It is clear that most errors occurs at the beginning or ending of the difficulty event. To validate this result. Another data which were not seen by the network in the training process were exposed to the RNN, and the result is shown in Fig. 4.

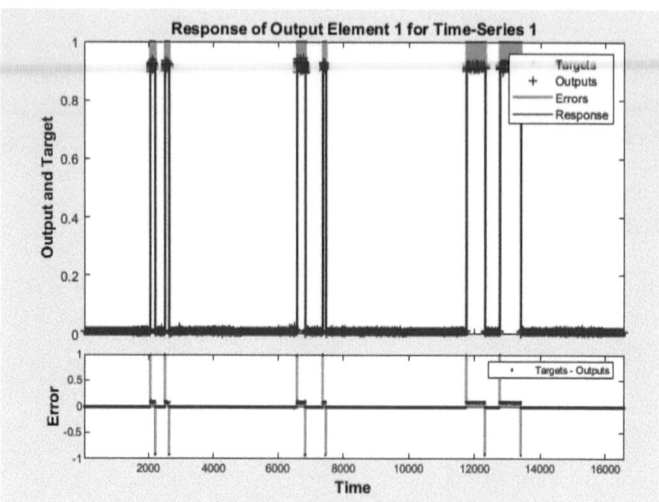

Fig. 4. Response of unseen data by network.

The response curve in Fig. 4, shows the same characteristic of the training response when it is applied on the unseen data.

To achieve the best training result of our model. The network is trained using different configurations parameters. The configuration parameters and the MSE results are listed in the Table 1.

Table 1. RNN Configuration Parameters

Network	Layers	Neurons	Delay	MSE
RNN	2	10	7	2.2×10^{-4}
RNN	2	6	7	1.8×10^{-4}
RNN	2	5	7	2.6×10^{-4}
RNN	2	7	3	1.5×10^{-4}
RNN	2	10	2	1.9×10^{-4}
RNN	2	6	2	2.5×10^{-4}
RNN	2	5	2	2.9×10^{-4}

The RNN configured with two layers using 7 neurons and a delay parameter of 2 which is highlighted in gray achieved the minimum MSE.

8 Generalization

Due to the high accuracy achieved by the proposed model, the Recurrent Neural Network is further investigated to avoid any kind of bias that could appear using the selected training data. Therefore, a new portion of data with about 872 thousands of records is used to test the network. this portion is encompass new 8 Patients and included data for 115 sessions. This test is used to double check the validation of the network. The result which is shown in Fig. 5 supports this high accuracy.

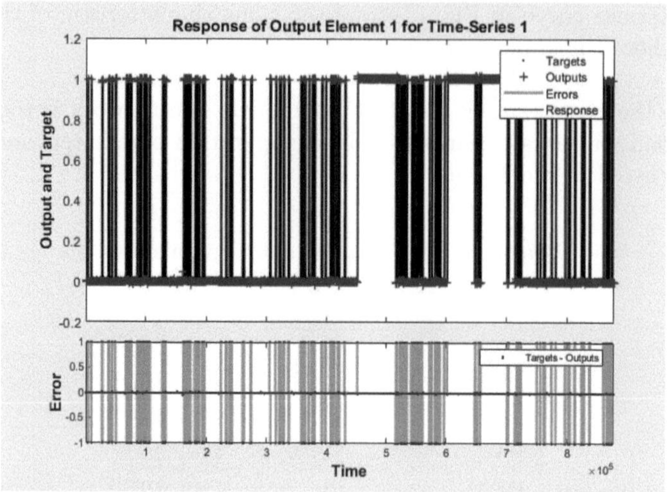

Fig. 5. Testing network with new data for generalization.

The total number of records used in the experiment is about 1.4 Million records which encompasses more than 20% of the total records of the dataset. Therefore we believe that the result we achieved is valid on all dataset.

9   Conclusion

In this article we proposed a prediction model to classify whether the patient is facing a Freezing of Gait or not. We used a Recurrent Neural Network. The RNN is trained on a dataset of ten features and included about 600K of records. The proposed model achieved accuracy of 99%. The results were validated twice. One using a specified dataset at the training stage. While the other is using a larger number of records to a void any possible bias.

10   Future Work

The proposed model can predict whether a FOG is happening or not to patient, but it does not classify which type of FOG it is. Therefore any future work should consider building a network to classify what type of FOG is happening.

Acknowledgment. The Dataset is downloaded with thanks to Kaggle Web Site. The authors are very thankful to Dan Jackson and the Open Movement team at Newcastle University. A special thanks to Vanessa Gossage at Axixity Co. for their help.

References

1. Weintraub, D., Mamikonyan, E.: The neuropsychiatry of Parkinson disease: a perfect storm. Am. J. Geriatr. Psychiatry **27**(9), 998–1018 (2019)
2. Ellis, T.D., et al.: Evidence for early and regular physical therapy and exercise in parkinson's disease. In *Seminars in neurology*, volume 41, pages 189–205. Theme Medical Publishers, Inc. 333 Seventh Avenue, 18th Floor, New York, NY (2021)
3. Mancini, M., Weiss, A., Herman, T., Hausdorff, J.M.: Turn around freezing: community-living turning behavior in people with Parkinson's disease. Front. Neurol. **9**, 18 (2018)
4. Rukavina, K., et al. Ethnic disparities in treatment of chronic pain in individuals with Parkinson's disease living in the united kingdom. Movement Disorders Clin. Prac. **9**(3), 369–374 (2022)
5. Johri, A., Tripathi, A., et al.: Parkinson disease detection using deep neural networks. In: 2019 twelfth International Conference on Contemporary Computing (IC3), pages 1–4. IEEE (2019)
6. Shichkina, Y., Irishina, Y., Stanevich, E., de Jesus, A., Salgueiro, P.: The main aspects of creating a system of data mining on the status of patients with Parkinson's disease. Proc. Comput. Sci. **186**, 161–168 (2021)
7. Saeed, F., et al.: Enhancing Parkinson's disease prediction using machine learning and feature selection methods. Comput. Mater. Continua **71**(3), 5639–5658 (2022)
8. Mathur, R., Pathak, V., Bandil, D.: Parkinson disease prediction using machine learning algorithm. In: Emerging Trends in Expert Applications and Security: Proceedings of ICETEAS 2018, pages 357–363. Springer (2019)
9. Nieuwboer, A., et al.: Reliability of the new freezing of gait questionnaire: agreement between patients with Parkinson's disease and their Carers. Gait & posture, **30**(4),459–463 (2009)
10. Medsker, L., Jain, L.C.: Recurrent neural networks: design and applications. CRC press (1999)

Protein-Protein Interaction Prediction Using Graph Neural Networks

Othmane Boumya, Hamza Hraiche, and Kaouter Karboub[✉]

LPRI, Ecole Marocaine des Sciences de L'Ingénieur (EMSI), 23300 Casablanca, Morocco
kaouter.karboub@gmail.com

Abstract. The paper describes a new approach to use Graph Neural Networks (GNNs) to predict protein-protein interactions (PPIs). This method tries to improve the accuracy and speed of PPI predictions by using the expressivity of graphs and language models. In particular, the paper describes two graph-based methods, GCN-based and GAT-based. Pre-trained language models were leveraged for feature extraction, which yielded better results than standard encoding methods like one-hot encoding. The results show that the GATv2 model performed better than both GCN and GAT with an accuracy of 98.31%, an f-score of 98.85%, a sensitivity of 99.01%, and a precision of 98.68%. A comparison with other works based on similar PPI datasets showed that the GATv2 approach is better based on several metrics.

Keywords: Graph Neural Networks · Protein-Protein Interactions · Pan's dataset

1 Introduction

Proteins are large, complex molecules that play crucial roles in the body. Proteins are composed of amino acids, of which there are 20 common ones, each having a unique side chain. These combinations of amino acids are called amino sequences, where each amino acid is called a residue. The protein graph represents the amino acid network, also known as the residue contact network, where each node is a residue. The sequence of amino acids determines the protein's unique 3D structure and specific function. A protein structure follows a specific hierarchy. Its primary structure is the sequence of amino acids. Its secondary structure is the folding pattern exhibited by a protein over a few dozen residues. The tertiary structure is the 3D structure of a protein determined by the interactions of the side chains. Proteins do not function alone, they must interact with other proteins to perform their functions. This makes the study of protein-protein interactions (PPIs) necessary to understand biological processes beyond the direct physical binding of proteins.

The accurate prediction of unknown PPIs provides an important theoretical basis for discovering the mechanisms of disease prevention, disease treatment, and novel drug discovery. Identifying the residues involved in the physical contacts in PPI complexes helps with constructing protein-protein interaction networks (PPINs) [1], predicting protein functions, and designing novel drugs.

H. Badir et al. (Eds.): INTIS 2024, CCIS 2645, pp. 328–334, 2026.
https://doi.org/10.1007/978-3-032-14964-0_27

Deep learning algorithms can process large amounts of data and learn the hidden patterns present in our data. Newer studies on PPI have used the 3D structure of the protein as a source of protein information, which proved to be successful, as proven by Jha et Saha [2]. However, graphs are a very convenient abstraction for molecules. Current works on PPIs utilize graph neural networks (GNNs) to make these predictions. Attention-based approaches are a key factor behind the power of GNN models.

In this paper, we propose a GNN-based method that leverages the expressiveness of graphs and a language model. We represent each protein as a graph where each node is a residue from its amino acid sequence. We utilize the language model SeqVec [3] to extract features for every node in the graph (the protein's residues). We use a Graph Attention Network [4] (GAT) model to learn the hidden representation from the protein's structure and sequence information.

2 Literature Review

Baranwal et al. [5] introduce Struct2Graph, a novel approach for predicting PPIs based on the 3D structural data of folded protein globules. They employ a GAT model, to directly analyze the structural information of proteins and predict PPIs.

Jha and Saha proposed an approach for predicting PPIs using multimodal information. It combines both sequence-based and 3D structural information of proteins. A deep learning classifier is used to predict the correct labels for the PPIs problem based on these multimodal features.

Sun et al. [6] utilize a Stacked Auto-Encoder (SAE) to develop a deep-learning model for sequence-based PPI prediction. The study employed two coding methods, autocovariance (AC) and conjoint triad (CT), to represent protein sequences. A one-hiddenlayer SAE model with 400 neurons using the AC coding method performed best.

Fang et al. [7] use an S-VGAE model to embed protein nodes. The benchmark dataset is Pan's dataset. The node features consist of both structural and sequence information. First, the CT method transforms the amino acid sequence into a fixed-length encoding. They employed the S-VGAE model to get the embeddings for every protein based on their encoded sequences and structural information. These embeddings were then fed to a classifier.

3 Implementation

The protein-protein dataset was extracted from Pan's Human Dataset [8]. This raw dataset was pre-processed by removing homologous proteins using the CD-HIT tool. We obtained the 3D structure of each protein from PDB to generate the graphs. The sequences of the proteins were encoded using two LMs, ProtBERT [9] and SeqVec. The later proved to be more accurate, so we used the SeqVec encoded sequences for the rest of our experiments. The encoded sequences were then fed to GAT and GCN-based classifiers. As evident by our results, the GAT-based classifier yielded better results than the GCN-based.

The pairwise interaction data was first assembled from Pan's Human dataset. An ID mapping was later performed to access the PDB archive and obtain the 3D structure to build the graph. The model is developed by firstly performing an encoding of the residues for each protein. The embedded graphs are then fed to a GNN-based classifier GAT-based and GCN-based (Fig. 1).

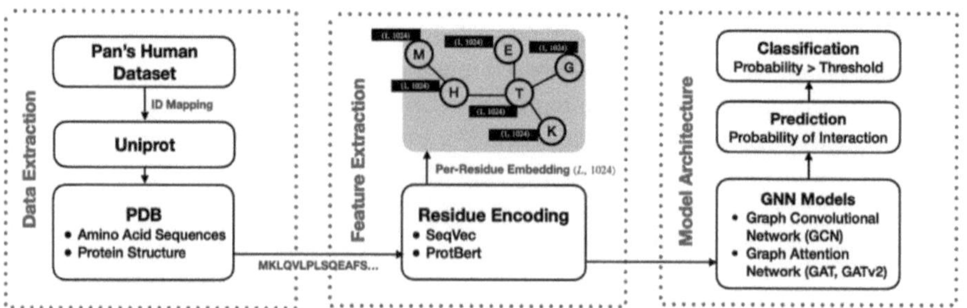

Fig. 1. The proposed approach

3.1 Feature Extraction

Pan's Human Dataset, containing both positive and negative samples, is used as our benchmark dataset. Pan et al. obtained 36,630 positive PPI pairs from the HPRD database. The 9,476 negative PPI pairs were constructed from Negatome Swiss-Prot by pairing the proteins from different subcellular localizations. We combined both the positive, and negative datasets, which contain 36,480 protein pairs from 2,184 proteins. Preprocessing consisted of removing protein pairs that are considered homologous with a 40% cut using the CD-HIT tool.

In order to obtain the amino acid sequences and the 3D structures of the proteins, we used the Uniprot ID mapping tool to create a mapping from RefSeq identifiers to PDB identifiers, using UniprotKB identifiers as an intermediate. We then retrieved the 3D protein structures from the RCSB Protein Data Bank. Every graph is a protein, and every node is an amino acid. Node features are extracted from the amino acid sequence and its structure using two pre-trained language models: SeqVec (LSTM-based).

SeqVec. A model that captures the biophysical characteristics of protein sequences. The resulting output vector from its two bi-LSTM layers has dimensions of $[L \times 3 \times 1024]$, where L signifies the length of the amino acid sequence. Notably, SeqVec can generate embeddings either per-protein or per-residue within the protein. Given the representation of proteins as graphs of residues in this context, the latter option was chosen. To derive per-residue embeddings, the output of the three layers is summed, yielding an embedding vector of dimension $[L \times 1024]$ per protein.

ProtBert. Similar to SeqVec, ProtBert is a pre-trained language model designed for protein sequences, employing a masked language modeling objective. The BERT [10] based model's self-attention layer produces embeddings, each possessing a dimensionality of 1024, corresponding to each residue within the protein sequence. This process culminates in comprehensive and contextually rich representations of protein sequences, facilitating various downstream tasks within the domain of protein analysis and prediction.

3.2 Model Architecture

Since we are working with non-Euclidian, graph data, we used three GNN-based architectures (GCN, GAT, GATv2) to learn node representations that model the relationships between the obtained residue embeddings. We then applied global mean pooling to the resulting embeddings for each protein, and obtained a vector per protein. These two vectors are then concatenated to obtain the final representation for the protein interactions. These outputs are then fed to a classifier that outputs the final probability of interaction. Two proteins are classified as interacting if their probability of interaction exceeds the specified threshold.

Graph Convolutional Networks (GCN). GCNs [11] are used to learn features from our graph protein data. The connections between pairs of nodes are encoded in the adjacency matrix A. The node features are encoded in the feature matrix X, then every GCN layer takes the adjacency matrix A and the previous node embedding $H^{(l)}$ to output the next layer embedding $H^{(l+1)}$. The entire process can be expressed as:

$$H^{(l+1)} = GCN(H^{(l)}, A) = ReLU\left(\widetilde{D^{-\frac{1}{2}}} \cdot \widetilde{A^{T}} \cdot \widetilde{D^{-\frac{1}{2}}} \cdot H^{(l)} \cdot W^{(l)^{T}}\right) \qquad (1)$$

Graph Attention Networks (GAT). GAT and GATv2 are improvements over GCNs where the normalized weight coefficients are calculated using a self-attention process. The process is similar to that of a GCN, where the layer $H^{(l)}$ takes the previous node embeddings, the adjacency matrix, and the attention matrix. The entire process can be expressed as:

$$H^{(l+1)} = GAT(H^{(l)}, A) = ReLU(\widetilde{A^{T}} \cdot W_{\alpha} \cdot H^{(l)} \cdot W^{T})$$

3.3 Evaluation Metrics

Since our final PPI task counts as binary classification, we must categorize our output into one of four groups: true positives, false positives, false negatives, and true negatives. These metrics were used to assess the model's performance: accuracy, sensitivity, specificity, precision, f-score, and Matthews correlation coefficient (MCC).

4 Results and Discussion

Our method consists of representing each protein as a graph, combining it with its encoded sequence information, and then feeding it to three different GNN architectures (GCN, GAT, GATv2). Our best performance was achieved by using the LSTM-based SeqVec language model and the improved GATv2 model. It yielded an accuracy of 98.31%, an f-score of 98.85%, a sensitivity of 99.01%, and a precision of 98.68%. Our best hyperparameter values are heads: 2, dropout rate: 0.2, learning rate: 0.001. During training, the mean squared error loss was minimized with the Adam optimizer. We chose 50 as the maximum number of epochs, with an early stopping method to reduce overfitting. Table 1 shows our results with the evaluation metrics. Figure 2 illustrates the comparison of the GCN, GAT and GATv2 models with the different metrics.

Table 1. Results with metrics

	Sensitivity	Specificity	Accuracy	Precision	F-score	MCC
GCN	100%	N/A	73.4%	72.4%	84.7%	N/A
GAT	98.83%	96.77%	98.28%	98.83%	98.83%	95.61%
GATv2	99.01%	96.35%	98.31%	98.68%	98.85%	95.65%

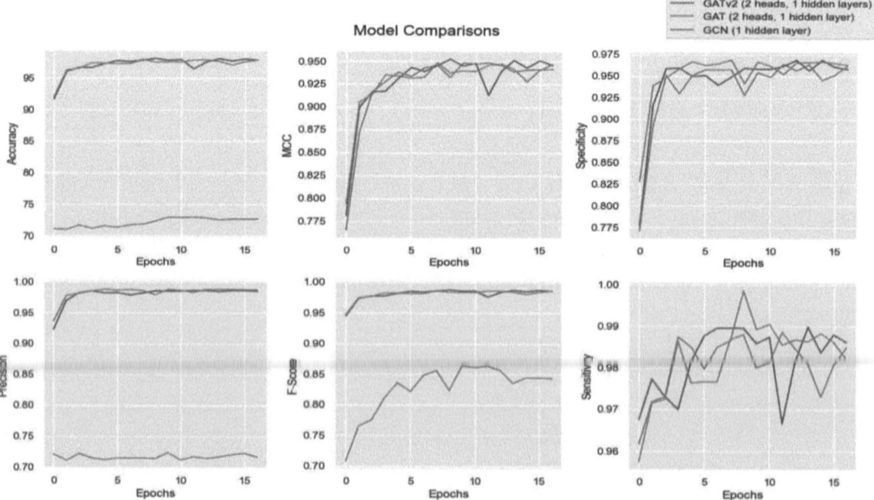

Fig. 2. Model comparison GCN, GAT and GATv2

The added self-attention aspect in the GAT and GATv2 architectures allows our models to create more expressive node representations. This resulted in better performances than other methods, including our GCN model. To further evaluate our model's performance, we compared its results with state-of-the-art deep learning-based PPI prediction methods, such as Stacked Auto-Encoder (SAE), CNN [12] (Table 2).

Table 2. Comparison with other works based on the same or different datasets.

	Sensitivity	Specificity	Accuracy	Precision	F-score	MCC
GATv2	99.01%	96.35%	98.31%	98.68%	98.85%	95.65%
Fang et al. [7]	98%	99.58%	98.78%	99.57%	98.78%	N/A
Sun et al. [6]	98.06%	96.34%	97.19%	96.27%	N/A	N/A
Jha and Saha [2]	98.07%	95.04%	97.20%	97.99%	98.03%	93.16%
Pan et al.[8]	94.2%	98%	96.4%	N/A	N/A	92.8%
Jiang et al. [12]	96.3%	98.0%	97.1%	98.4%	97.3%	94.1%

5 Conclusion

This study investigates the important area of using Graph Neural Networks (GNNs) to predict protein-protein interactions (PPIs). Recognizing that traditional PPI identification methods have their limits, the study focuses on how GNNs might be able to better capture the complexities of protein interactions. By representing proteins as graphs and using pre-trained language models to extract features, the suggested method shows a potential way to predict PPIs. In particular, the GAT-based algorithm performed better than the GCN-based one. The method, which was tested on Pan's Human Dataset, offers a new way to predict PPIs by emphasizing how structure, order, and computing methods work together. As the field of bioinformatics continues to grow, these kinds of high-tech computer techniques will be very helpful in figuring out how complex biological relationships work.

References

1. De Las Rivas, J., Fontanillo, C.: Protein-protein interaction networks: unraveling the wiring of molecular machines within the cell. Brief. Funct. Genomics **11**, 489–496 (2012)
2. Jha, K., Karmakar, S., Saha, S.: Graph-BERT and language model-based framework for protein–protein interaction identification (2023)
3. Heinzinger, M., Elnaggar, A., Wang, Y., Dallago, C., Nechaev, D., Matthes, F., Rost, B.: Modeling aspects of the language of life through transfer-learning protein sequences. BMC Bioinform. **20** (2019)
4. Veličković, P., Cucurull, G., Casanova, A., Romero, A., Liò, P., Bengio, Y.: Graph attention networks. arXiv:1710.10903 [cs, stat] (2018)
5. Baranwal, M., et al.: Struct2Graph: a graph attention network for structure based predictions of protein–protein interactions. BMC Bioinform. **23** (2022)
6. Sun, T., Zhou, B., Lai, L., Pei, J.: Sequence-based prediction of protein protein interaction using a deep-learning algorithm. BMC Bioinform. **18** (2017)
7. Fang, Y., Fan, K., Song, D., Lin, H.: Graph-based prediction of protein-protein interactions with attributed signed graph embedding. BMC Bioinform. **21** (2020)
8. Pan, X.-Y., Zhang, Y.-N., Shen, H.-B.: Large-scale prediction of human protein–protein interactions from amino acid sequence based on latent topic features. J. Proteome Res. **9**, 4992–5001 (2010)

9. Elnaggar, A., et al.: ProtTrans: towards cracking the language of life's code through self-supervised deep learning and high performance computing (2021)
10. Devlin, J., Chang, M.-W., Lee, K., Toutanova, K.: BERT: pre-training of deep bidirectional transformers for language understanding (2019)
11. Kipf, T.N., Welling, M.: Semi-supervised classification with graph convolutional networks (2016)
12. Jiang, Y., Wang, Y., Shen, L., Adjeroh, D.A., Liu, Z., Lin, J.: Identification of all-against-all protein–protein interactions based on deep hash learning. BMC Bioinform. **23** (2022)

Enhancing Human-Robot Collaboration in Disassembly Processes Through Vision-Based Hardware Detection

Ameur Soufiane[1,2,3](✉), Tabaa Mohammed[2], Hamlich Mohamed[1], Hidila Zineb[2], and Bearee Richard[3]

[1] CCPS Laboratory, ENSAM, University of Hassan II, Casablanca, Morocco
ameursoufiane00@gmail.com
[2] Multidisciplinary Laboratory of Research and Innovation (LPRI), Moroccan School of Engineering Sciences (EMSI), 20250 Casablanca, Morocco
[3] Arts Et Métiers Institute of Technology, LISPEN, HESAM Université, 59000 Lille, France

Abstract. In the interests of efficient remanufacturing, this paper provides an overview of the most effective approach for disassembling end-of-life products through a comparison of available methods, involving the use of computer vision and robots. It also outlines a very flexible approach to locating hardware components in electronic waste (e-waste). This case study focuses on the process of extracting components with a view to recycling or reusing them. Using computer hardware as an illustration, the aim is to find the right disassembly method and to allocate tasks appropriately. Prioritizing the HRC method, is particularly effective for disassembling the computer, as both the human and the robot can work simultaneously on it. In addition, the object detection system connected to the robot was trained using a dataset of computer hardware. The YOLO (You Only Look Once) has been chosen as the most appropriate algorithm. This enables our robot to detect the components it needs at the extraction station.

Keywords: Remanufacturing · Computer Vision · Human-Robot Collaboration

1 Introduction

The increasing demand for sustainable manufacturing practices has led to a growing focus on the efficient disassembly of end-of-life products. Disassembly is a critical step in the recycling and remanufacturing of products, as it allows for the recovery of valuable materials and components. However, the disassembly process is often complex and time-consuming, particularly when dealing with products of varying designs and structures. Human-robot collaboration (HRC) [1], has emerged as a promising approach to optimize disassembly time and improve the overall efficiency of the process. This article discusses the potential of HRC in enhancing disassembly processes through the integration of vision-based hardware detection. Non-destructive disassembly allows for the isolation of reusable or recyclable materials, components, and toxic substances. Once the optimal disassembly process was identified, a dataset was utilized for training purposes, The

H. Badir et al. (Eds.): INTIS 2024, CCIS 2645, pp. 335–341, 2026.
https://doi.org/10.1007/978-3-032-14964-0_28

YOLO (You Only Look Once) algorithm [2], emerged as the most suitable for integration into disassembly approaches. This enabled the robot to efficiently recognize specific components. For instance, considering computers as EOLP, it is noteworthy that between 1997–2007 in the United States and in 2010 in Japan more than 500 million tons of electronic waste were generated [3]. Additionally, approximately 68% of e-waste in India consists of computer accessories [4]. Using a real simulation with a robot simulator, the paper aims to prove that harnessing HRC with computer vision integration takes the least time and effort to implement.

2 Related Work

Human-robot collaboration has enhanced the efficiency and adaptability of disassembly tasks, assigning repetitive or physically demanding tasks to robots while utilizing human problem-solving abilities. For instance, R. Gerbers et al. [5], centers on creating instruments for human-robot teamwork, concentrating on control structure, cost-effectiveness, and sensor technology. The study underscores the significance of uniform interfaces and streamlined instrument development to enhance efficient collaboration between humans and robots. Another study by W. H. Chen et al. [6], used a comprehensive state diagram to train a robot for new bit positions, enabling it to return to its initial position multiple times using joint control for improved accuracy in approaching the bits. This research offers valuable insights into developing robotic systems for unscrewing during disassembly processes, addressing the need for adaptability and flexibility in industrial automation. Another innovative case study by Huang Jun et al. showcased the use of a KUKA LBR IIWA two-finger gripper robot to separate pressure-assembled components with active compliance monitoring and impedance monitoring for safe interaction with human operators. Additionally, J.P Jacomini Prioli et al. [7], focused on cyber-physical architecture that utilizes human-robot interaction within collaborative robots as an adaptable automated disassembly system designed to address challenges associated with large-scale disassembly processes necessary for managing uncertainties related to end-of-life product quality. Similarly, J. Huang et al. [8], consisted in designing a cognitive robotic agent with multisensory systems for disassembly tasks, by proposing robot-driven disassembly sequences. The study focused on optimizing the distribution of tasks between robots and human operators to improve the efficiency and productivity of disassembly processes.

3 Methodology

3.1 Overview

The current disassembly process for end-of-life products, like computers, is known to be inefficient and time-consuming. The manual disassembly line, comprising multiple stations with varying extraction times for components, often leads to an imbalance in task distribution and underutilization of resources. In this section, we will use computers as an example to identify the most efficient disassembly approach. The first step involves preparing the workspace with necessary tools like screwdrivers, gloves, and a mask due to dust accumulation in EOL computers. By incorporating computer vision technology into the disassembly process, it will allow for real-time recognition of components, enabling a more precise and efficient disassembly workflow. Integrating computer vision technology in the disassembly of end-of-life products like computers can lead to improved resource management, sustainability, and cost-effectiveness, maximizing resource utilization and minimizing environmental impact. Subsequently, we still need to make a comparison to find out which type of disassembly is the most appropriate for this integration. A mathematical model developed for this specific objective is to identify the least time-consuming disassembly approach, in which it's presented as:

$$T_{td} = \sum T + \sum S + Cpt \tag{1}$$

$$T_{td} = T_{srw} + T_{hdd} + T_{ps} + S_{srw/ps} + S_{ps/hdd} + Cpt \tag{2}$$

where:

T_{td}: Overall time taken for disassembly.

T_{srw}: Duration to remove the screw.

T_{ps} : T_{hdd}: time dedicated to removing the power supply unit or the hard disk drive.

$S_{srw/ps}$: $S_{ps/hdd}$: Switch between each extraction.

Cpt: time taken for the camera system to detect an object.

3.2 Dataset

For perfect results in the model, we are training a dataset called YoloDatasetsMerged [9], which contains 7 classes of hardware as indicated in Table 1. The database contains 10011 images with an image ratio of 640 × 640.

Table 1. Several classes of the proposed dataset.

Dataset	Classes	Images
YoloDatasetsMerged Computer Vision Project [9]	HDD	2597
	PSU	1497
	Other components (5 classes)	5917

4 Case Studies

This case study will be carried out using three different techniques to disassemble an end-of-life computers: manual, robotic, and human-robot collaborative. The disassembly procedure will be divided into two main stages: one for removing screws and another for extracting components. Manual disassembly will act as a reference point, relying entirely on human labor to accomplish the tasks. For the robotic and HRC disassembly methods, we will simulate and assess the processes using Robodk software. The robotic approach involves programming industrial robots to independently handle component extraction (task2) and (task3). In contrast, the HRC method integrates a collaborative workspace where a human operator and a robot work together utilizing their respective strengths. In The HRC method, both the operator and the robot are responsible for component extraction (Fig. 1).

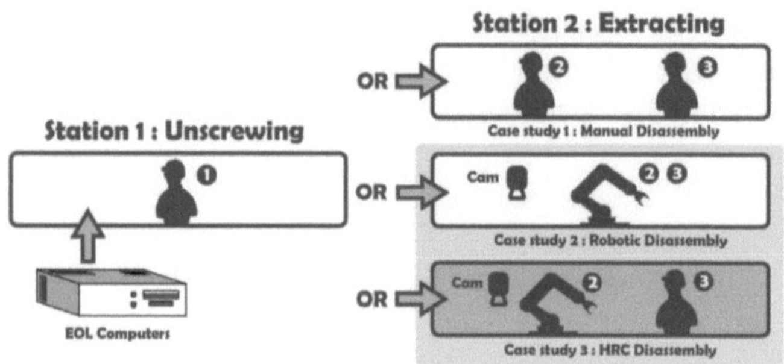

Fig. 1. Process flow of the disassembly line containing two stations.

To simulate the robotic and human-robot collaborative disassembly processes, the RoboDK software [10], is integrated with a vision system comprising cameras. In the setup shown, an OAK-D camera is employed to provide visual feedback and guidance to the UR10-e robot during the component extraction phase. This camera captures detailed images of the end-of-life computer, allowing RoboDK to analyze the spatial information and generate precise trajectories for the robot to follow. Additionally, a separate camera is utilized for manual disassembly, enabling the recording and analysis of the process for comparison purposes. The seamless integration of vision technology with RoboDK plays a crucial role in ensuring accurate and efficient disassembly operations, whether performed autonomously by the robot or in collaboration with humans (Fig. 2).

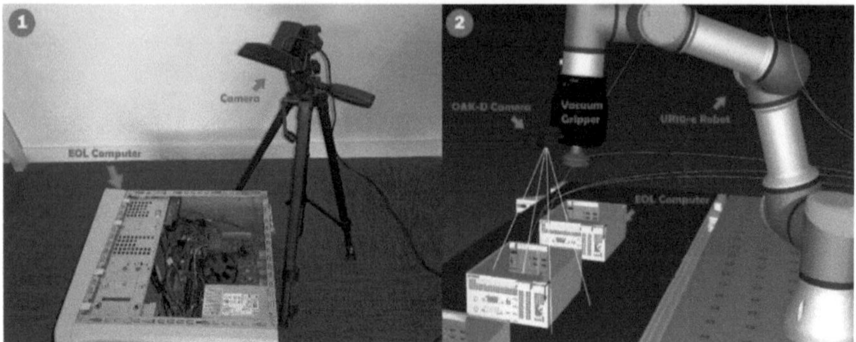

Fig. 2. Simulation of the disassembly line using Robodk with real-time camera.

In this case study, we used five versions of the YOLO-v5 object detection model to train the dataset for identifying components within end-of-life computers. The models ranged from the lightweight YOLO-v5n to the more computationally expensive YOLO-v5x. Table 2 presents the results obtained from evaluating these models on our dataset. The precision was highest for the YOLO-v5l and YOLO-v5x models at 0.97733 and 0.97721, respectively. However, other metrics revealed that the YOLO-v5l model achieved a good balance between accuracy and BFLOPs compared to v5x.

Table 2. Results of the YOLO-v5 models.

Model	Precision	mAP@0.5	mAP@0.5:0.95	BFLOPs
YOLO-v5n	0.95084	0.96159	0.78235	4.5
YOLO-v5s	0.95175	0.97650	0.82477	16.5
YOLO-v5m	0.97458	0.98341	0.81603	49.0
YOLO-v5l	0.97746	0.98375	0.87482	109.1
YOLO-v5x	0.97721	0.98354	0.86524	205.7

After completing all three case studies, Table 3 displays the disassembly time for each scenario. It is evident that the robotic approach (case 2) required a longer duration for extraction due to the overall increase caused by the system camera's time (3 s) and the robot's path planning. In contrast, with the HRC method, a shorter disassembly time is observed due to the simultaneous work by both the operator and the robot facilitated by collaboration techniques.

Table 3. Disassembly time of each case.

Task	CASE 1	CASE 2	CASE 3
Task 1	18	18	18
Switch 1	3	3	3
Task 2	13	17 +3	17 +3
Switch 2	3	0	0
Task 3	14	25 +3	14 +3
Total	51	66	41

5 Result Assessment

The YOLO-v5l model was trained on 100 epochs of the previous dataset containing computer parts, with the aim of enabling efficient object detection. After training, the model achieved an average precision (mAP) of 0.97 with an intersection threshold above union of 0.514. Precision and recall values were recorded at 0.97 and 0.944 respectively, indicating its ability to accurately identify and classify computer parts. These results underline the effectiveness of the YOLOv5 architecture in rapidly detecting and classifying randomly positioned computer parts, making it fundamental requirement for automating disassembly processes and promoting efficient recycling practices (Fig. 3).

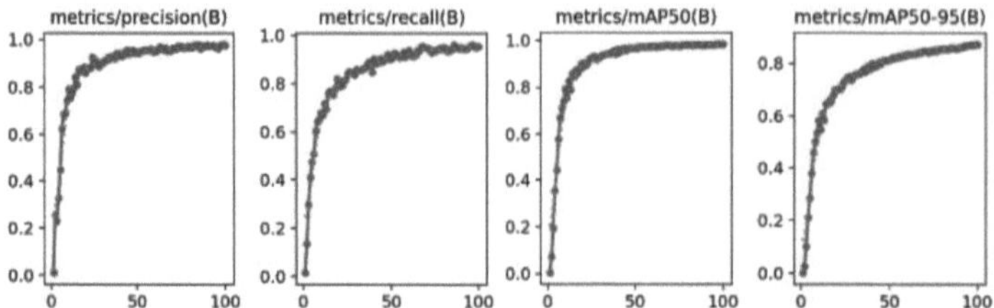

Fig. 3. The evolution in the 100 training epochs of the YOLO-v5m

Our results demonstrate the significant benefits of human-robot collaboration in improving computer disassembly efficiency. When a human operator and a robot worked in parallel to disassemble computers, total disassembly time was reduced by an average of 22% compared with the human operator alone. The robot was able to complete task 2 efficiently, using object detection which helped the robot to find the right path, while the human operator 2 concentrated on more complex and delicate operations, while waiting the robot to finish his task $MAX\{T_{ps}, T_{hdd}\}$. Our results highlight the potential of human-robot collaboration to streamline e-waste disassembly and recycling operations, with man and robot complementing each other's strengths to optimize the process (Fig. 4).

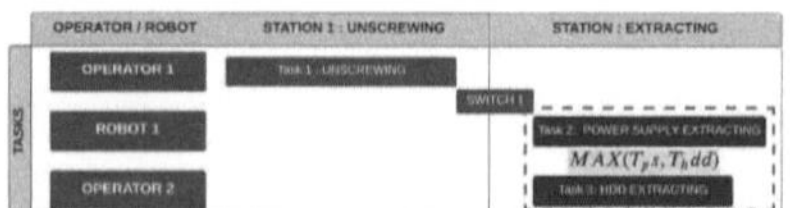

Fig. 4. Gantt Chart of HRC Disassembly tasks.

6 Conclusion and Future Research

This article discusses a global approach for disassembling computer waste, highlighting the potential of human-robot collaboration in optimizing disassembly time. The integration of object detection using YOLOv5 has significantly improved the robotic system's ability to accurately identify and process components, resulting in increased efficiency. Training the YOLOv5 dataset showed promising results in real-life disassembly scenarios. The overall approach has demonstrated significant potential for improving the efficiency, safety and sustainability of disassembly operations. As automation and robotics continue to advance, exploring how robots can collaborate with human operators in the disassembly of end-of-life products is an exciting and highly promising field. Future research will focus on enhancing the capabilities of the robotic system by incorporating advanced algorithms for trajectory optimization to minimize disassembly time while ensuring safety and accuracy.

References

1. Green, S.A., Billinghurst, M., Chen, X., Chase, J.G.: Human-robot collaboration: a literature review and augmented reality approach in design. Int. J. Adv. Robot. Syst. **5**(1) (2008). https://doi.org/10.5772/5664
2. Redmon, J., Divvala, S., Girshick, R., Farhadi, A.: You only look once: unified, real-time object detection. In: 2016 IEEE Conference on Computer Vision and Pattern Recognition (CVPR), Las Vegas, NV, USA, pp. 779–788 (2016). https://doi.org/10.1109/CVPR.2016.91
3. Bushehri, F.I.: UNEP's role in promoting environmentally sound management of e-waste. In: 5th ITU Symposium on "ICTs, the Environment and Climate Change", Cairo, Egypt (2010)
4. Islam, M.T., Huda, N.: Material flow analysis (MFA) as a strategic tool in E-waste management: applications, trends and future directions. J. Environ. Manage. **244**, 344–361 (2019). https://doi.org/10.1016/j.jenvman.2019.05.062
5. Gerbers, R., Wegener, K., Dietrich, F.: Safe, flexible and productive human-robot-collaboration for disassembly of lithium-ion batteries. In: Kwade, A., Diekmann, J. (eds.) Recycling of Lithium-Ion Batteries (2018). https://doi.org/10.1007/978-3-319-70572-9_6
6. Chen, W.H., Wegener, K., Dietrich, F.: A robot assistant for unscrewing in hybrid human-robot disassembly. In: 2014 IEEE International Conference on Robotics and Bio-mimetics (ROBIO 2014), Bali, Indonesia, pp. 536–541 (2014). https://doi.org/10.1109/ROBIO.2014.7090386
7. Prioli, J.P.J., Rickli, J.L.: Collaborative robot based architecture to train flexible automated disassembly systems for critical materials. Procedia Manuf. **51**, 46–53 (2020). https://doi.org/10.1016/j.promfg.2020.10.008
8. Huang, J., et al.: An experimental human-robot collaborative disassembly cell. Comput. Ind. Eng. **155**, 107189 (2021).https://doi.org/10.1016/j.cie.2021.107189. ISSN 0360-8352
9. La Salle University. YoloDatasetsMerged Dataset. Open-Source Dataset. Roboflow Universe. Roboflow (2023). https://universe.roboflow.com/la-salle-university/yolodatasets merged. Accessed 27 Mar 2024
10. RoboDK. (n.d.). RoboDK Documentation. https://robodk.com/doc/en/

Empowering Earthquake Management Through Advanced Machine Learning in Social Media Analytics and Facebook Data for Good Utilization: A 2023 Case Study

Mohamed Mastir[✉], Ali Dahbi, and Khalil El-Hami

Mohammed V University in Rabat, Scientific Institute, Av. Ibn Batouta, B.P. 703, Agdal, Rabat, Morocco
mastirmohamed@gmail.com

Abstract. The earthquakes that occurred in Turkey, Syria, and Morocco in 2023 had an impact, leading to casualties and damage. Infrastructure and widespread human suffering. This research focuses on how social media was utilized during these disasters, specifically examining the sentiment expressed in tweets related to the earthquakes in Turkey and Syria. The study explores techniques such as machine learning, lexical analysis, and hybrid strategies for sentiment analysis. Additionally, it looks into Facebook's Population During Crisis datasets to gain insights into population movements during emergencies. By defining regions of interest and analyzing location, data from users' posts on Facebook proves valuable for assessing impact, allocating resources efficiently, and tracking evacuation patterns. The use of this data during the Morocco earthquake is also discussed to show how it complements reports. The discussion section touches upon both the advantages and challenges of using media for disaster communication. While social platforms allow for real-time updates, user engagement, and the amplification of information, they also present obstacles like misinformation spread, network congestion, a lack of verification mechanisms, and emotional repercussions. The paper presents an innovative solution, the employment of AI techniques like machine learning and social media analysis, as both can offer comprehensive insight and improve strategic preparation for better management of natural disasters, especially when responding to earthquakes.

Keywords: Natural disasters · Social media · Sentiment analysis · Facebook · Crisis response · Machine Learning

1 Introduction

In the year 2023, Turkey, Syria, and Morocco faced seismic events that led to a high number of human and infrastructure casualties. On February 6, 2023, several earthquakes hit Turkey and Syria. A powerful tremor measuring 7.8 on the Richter scale struck near Gaziantep. Later that day, another 7.5-magnitude earthquake struck at 1:30 PM [1]. On September 8, 2023, a powerful earthquake measuring 6.8 on the Richter scale struck

H. Badir et al. (Eds.): INTIS 2024, CCIS 2645, pp. 342–347, 2026.
https://doi.org/10.1007/978-3-032-14964-0_29

Morocco [2]. Social media, particularly Facebook and X, significantly aided communication during the 2023 seismic events in Turkey, Syria, and Morocco. The use of advanced technologies like machine learning in disaster management is promising [3]. Social media platforms, especially X, play a crucial role in sharing real-time information during disaster crises. They provide a valuable source of data in various formats, such as text, images, and audio-visual content [4]. Social media platforms significantly enhance disaster management by providing first-hand information, enhancing communication, and improving emergency response. The study highlights the increasing attention focused on the social media aspect of disaster management, indicating a growing interest in this field [5]. Indonesia is implementing a new approach to natural disaster management using social media data mining techniques. This system analyzes posts related to floods, landslides, and tornadoes, aiming to gather real-time data on disaster impacts, calculate damages, and identify areas requiring immediate attention [6]. This study aims to investigate the potential for enhancing social media use in natural disaster management. We will explore the pivotal role played by social media platforms. From sentiment analysis of tweets to the remarkable initiatives of Facebook For Good, we unravel the impact of digital connectivity during times of crisis.

2 Methods

2.1 Sentiment Analyses for Turkey and Syria Earthquakes

Search Keywords Method
Social media, especially X, significantly aids in natural disaster management by facilitating real-time information sharing, crowdsourcing incident reports, enhancing emergency responder awareness, aiding early warning systems, integrating with GIS modeling, and promoting community engagement. X's rapid dissemination of information, user-generated content analysis, and collaborative features contribute to improved communication, coordination, and response efforts, ultimately enhancing the resilience of communities in the face of emergencies [7]. The Double Ranking (DR) approach is a novel technique used in social media analytics to efficiently identify relevant search keywords for analyzing tweets related to citizens' feelings during earthquakes in Turkey and Syria [8].

Sentiment Analyses
Sentiment analysis is crucial for understanding public opinion during natural disasters. Combining user behavior and emotional analysis, researchers can track emotional trends on platforms like Sina Weibo and X. This helps identify key groups and factors affecting public sentiment, providing insights for disaster response strategies and emergency management efforts [9]. Sentiment analysis is a crucial research field in social media post-audits, identifying emotions in content. Despite being primarily used in English, its application extends to other languages. The research identifies multiple techniques for providing accurate results in sentiment analysis, such as machine learning techniques, lexical approaches, and hybrid strategies.

Related Study

Researchers have used various algorithms, including hybrid heterogeneous SVM, attention-graph neural networks, and recurrent memory neural networks, to analyze sentiments in social media tweets. These algorithms have been evaluated based on dataset quality, feature selection, and classification techniques, revealing the importance of selecting appropriate algorithms for effectively capturing and interpreting sentiments in online conversations [10]. Among the above sentiment analysis techniques, we suggest the best algorithms that have been applied, especially for social media platform data such as X, and produced accurate results in multiple tweet niches such as: hybrid heterogeneous support vector machine (H-SVM) [11], attentional-graph neural network [12], recurrent memory neural network [13], corpus-based approach, and SVM [14].

Result

Sentiment Analysis of Turkey and Syria Earthquake Tweets

The study analyzes emotions in tweets about earthquakes in Turkey and Syria using the "ranking approach," a search method that efficiently locates and gathers relevant tweets for seismic assessment during such occurrences.

Data Preprocessing

Before conducting sentiment analysis, an important initial stage was preparing the dataset. This essential step was focused on improving data quality by eliminating elements and details and establishing a consistent format for analysis. Data preprocessing is a crucial step in data mining, involving steps like descriptive data summarization, cleaning, integration, transformation, and discretization. It addresses issues like missing values, outliers, and noise, ensuring data is clean, integrated, and transformed for analysis. This process enhances data quality, removes inconsistencies, and ensures accurate pattern evaluation and decision-making in real-world applications across industries [15].

Machine Learning Algorithm Selection: Support Vector Machine (SVM)

The sentiment analysis task utilized the Support Vector Machine (SVM) algorithm from machine learning, known for its accuracy in classifying tasks. The model was trained on labeled data to forecast sentiment by analyzing emoticons, hashtags, and language patterns in tweets. The sentiment analysis reveals that many people are expressing emotions about the earthquakes in Turkey and Syria, with the SVM classifier identifying many emotions in the tweets, indicating their impact on those affected. Emotion analysis in datasets underscores the significance of understanding emotions in disaster response, aiding in efficient communication and tailored support resources during and after seismic events.

The research examines 179,432 tweets discussing the earthquakes in Turkey and Syria (Fig. 1). It shows that emotions ran high at the onset of the earthquakes but gradually subsided. Initially, there were tweets, especially right after the earthquakes struck, but these decreased as time passed. The upheaval and damage caused by the earthquakes resulted in people feeling frustrated and critical of how government agencies handled the rescue operations. However, as time went on, negative tweets decreased as people started to regain their balance after the shock and frustration.

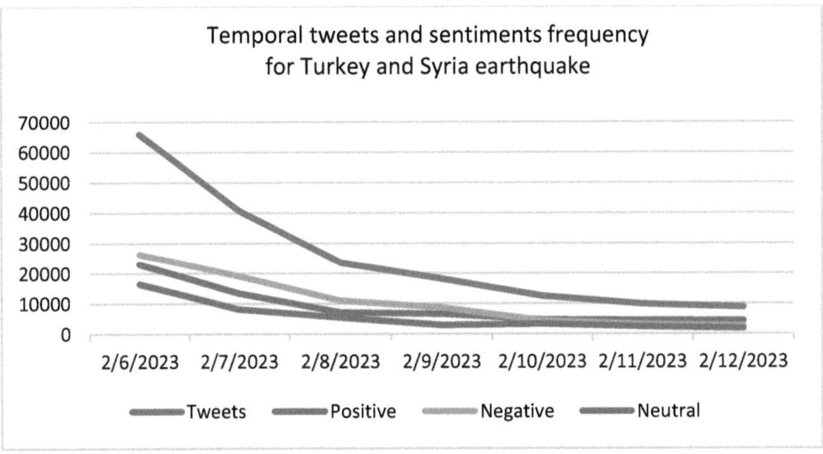

Fig. 1. A temporal tweets and sentiments frequency for Turkey and Syria earthquake.

2.2 Facebook Population During Morocco Earthquake

Data for Good is a crucial aspect of modern research and societal advancement, utilizing data science and analytics to tackle social issues, promote equity, and drive positive change. Platforms like dataforgood.facebook.com provide valuable insights for evidence-based decision-making, humanitarian efforts, and contributing to the greater good. [16]. In the realm of disaster response and humanitarian aid, understanding population movements during crises is paramount. Facebook, as an omnipresent social media platform, offers a novel lens through which to observe these dynamics. This section delves into the concept of Facebook Population During Crisis [17], draws insights from official sources, and explores its applications in the context of the devastating Morocco earthquake.

Understanding Facebook Population During Crisis
Facebook Disaster Maps are a valuable tool for humanitarian organizations in crisis response and recovery, using aggregated and anonymized data from Facebook usage to provide insights into population movements, resource needs, and situational awareness. Collaborative projects address specific responder needs, enhancing informed decisions and resulting in more efficient interventions [18]. Facebook's Population During Crisis datasets provide a glimpse into the behavior of users who have enabled Location Services during emergencies.

Applications for the Morocco Earthquake
Facebook's data plays a crucial role in disaster response:

- Impact Assessment and Resource Allocation: *By analyzing Facebook Population During Crisis data*, responders can assess impact zones. Areas with reduced Facebook activity may indicate evacuation centers or severe damage. Conversely, spikes in Facebook users can guide resource allocation. Aid delivery can be prioritized in areas experiencing increased activity.

- Tracking Evacuation Patterns: Monitoring z-scores over time allows us to track evacuation patterns. Sudden increases in Facebook activity may signal mass evacuations from affected regions. This information informs evacuation routes and strategic resource deployment.
- Complementing Official Reports: While Facebook data provides valuable insights, it should complement official government reports and ground assessments. Integrating these sources enhances disaster preparedness and response strategies.

3 Discussion

Social media platforms are crucial for spreading information during natural disasters, but they face challenges such as false information, public confusion, and disparities in social group and geographic usage. Technical issues arise in processing and analyzing large amounts of data, especially regarding tweet location accuracy. Here are a few aspects: Instant Updates; User Contributions; Amplification of Official Messages; Misinformation and Rumors; Strained Networks; Lack of Verification; Emotional Impact; Limited Access and Connectivity; Selective Exposure and Privacy Concerns. Balancing communication and privacy during emergencies is crucial. Prioritizing data privacy and user consent while utilizing media for disaster response reduces risks and maintains trust. Research shows AI and social media can improve natural disaster management, but relief agencies haven't fully utilized them. Instant updates, user-generated content, and machine learning algorithms are effective for rescue and earthquake response. Further exploration is needed to improve disaster management, rescue planning, aid distribution, damage assessment, subsidies, and misinformation. The study on the use of media and AI in disaster management has limitations, such as its limited scope and potential outdated findings. Future research should focus on understanding social media usage during disasters, developing reliable AI frameworks, improving internet accessibility in remote areas, and assessing long-term perspectives. By addressing these limitations, we can advance our understanding and utilization of media and AI technologies for risk management.

4 Conclusion

Social media plays a huge role in managing disasters, especially when paired with artificial intelligence (AI). Despite obstacles and the risk of misuse, platforms like X and Facebook contribute to disaster response by enabling information sharing, raising awareness of the situation, and facilitating emergency communication. AI-powered systems can analyze social media data to identify disasters, evaluate their impact, and support recovery efforts. However, challenges include dealing with unorganized content, ensuring privacy protection, and addressing ethical issues. Future studies should concentrate on refining AI methods, enhancing data preparation processes, and exploring ways to apply AI in disaster management.

References

1. 2023 Turkey and Syria earthquake: one year on, https://www.redcross.org.uk/stories/disasters-and-emergencies/world/turkey-syria-earthquake
2. Rafferty, J.P.: Morocco earthquake of 2023 | Description, Geology, Deaths, & Facts, https://www.britannica.com/event/Morocco-earthquake-of-2023
3. Acıkara, T., Xia, B., Yiğitcanlar, T., Hon, C.K.H.: Contribution of social media analytics to disaster response effectiveness: a systematic review of the literature. Sustainability. **15**, 8860 (2023). https://doi.org/10.3390/su15118860
4. Vishwanath, T., Shirwaikar, R.D., Jaiswal, W.M., Yashaswini, M.: Social media data extraction for disaster management aid using deep learning techniques. Remote Sens. Appl. Soc. Environ. **30**, 100961 (2023). https://doi.org/10.1016/j.rsase.2023.100961
5. Wang, W.: A review of natural disaster management trends in social media from 2009 to 2018. J. Eng. Sci. Technol. Rev. **15**, 210–219 (2022). https://doi.org/10.25103/jestr.153.23
6. Arianto, R., Warnars, H.L.H.S., Gaol, F.L., Trisetyarso, A.: Mining unstructured data in social media for natural disaster management in Indonesia. In: IEEE. (2018).https://doi.org/10.1109/inapr.2018.8627045
7. Athanasis, N., Themistocleous, M., Kalabokidis, K., Παπακωνσταντίνου, A., Soulakellis, N., Palaiologou, P.: The emergence of social media for natural disasters management: a big data perspective. The international archives of the photogrammetry. Remote Sens. Spat. Inf. Sci. **XLII-3/W4**, 75–82 (2018). https://doi.org/10.5194/isprs-archives-xlii-3-w4-75-2018
8. Wang, S., Chen, Z., Liu, B., Emery, S.: Identifying search keywords for finding relevant social media posts. In: Proceedings of the AAAI Conference on Artificial Intelligence, vol. 30, (2016). https://doi.org/10.1609/aaai.v30i1.10387
9. Ma, X., et al.: Evolution of online public opinion during meteorological disasters. Environ. Hazards **19**, 375–397 (2019). https://doi.org/10.1080/17477891.2019.1685932
10. Al-Otaibi, S., Al-Rasheed, A.: A review and comparative analysis of sentiment analysis techniques. Informatica. **46** (2022). https://doi.org/10.31449/inf.v46i6.3991
11. Kaur, H., Ahsaan, S.U., Alankar, B., Chang, V.: A proposed Sentiment Analysis deep learning algorithm for analyzing COVID-19 tweets. Inf. Syst. Front. **23**, 1417–1429 (2021). https://doi.org/10.1007/s10796-021-10135-7
12. Wang, M., Hu, G.: A novel method for X sentiment analysis based on attentional-graph neural network. Information **11**, 92 (2020). https://doi.org/10.3390/info11020092
13. Liu, N., Shen, B.: ReMemNN: a novel memory neural network for powerful interaction in aspect-based sentiment analysis. Neurocomputing **395**, 66–77 (2020). https://doi.org/10.1016/j.neucom.2020.02.018
14. Abdulla, N., Ahmed, N.A., Shehab, M.A., Al-Ayyoub, M.: Arabic sentiment analysis: lexicon-based and corpus-based. IEEE. (2013). https://doi.org/10.1109/aeect.2013.6716448
15. Yang, H.: Data preprocessing. Pennsylvania State Univ. Citeseer (2018)
16. View https://dataforgood.facebook.com
17. View https://dataforgood.facebook.com/dfg/tools/facebook-population-maps
18. Maas, P.: Facebook Disaster Maps. --. (2019). https://doi.org/10.1145/3292500.3340412

Towards Advanced Modeling of Road User Behaviors for Urban Congestion Management: A Framework Based on Neural Networks

Mohamed Laamimach[(✉)] and Aziz Mabrouk

Information Security, Intelligent Systems and Applications (ISISA), Abdelmalek Essaadi University, Tetouan, Morocco
Mohamed.laamimach@etu.uae.ac.ma, amabrouk@uae.ac.ma

Abstract. Urban congestion is a major issue for cities around the world, causing detrimental effects on the economy, environment, and quality of life. Faced with the urgency of finding sustainable solutions, this research introduces a revolutionary approach using neural networks for advanced modeling of road user behavior. Our goal is to provide an analytical framework capable of accurately predicting congestion and offering effective management strategies. Through an exhaustive literature review, we identify the gaps in current methods and propose a model that integrates behavioral data with traffic flows to anticipate variations in urban congestion. This study illustrates how a deep understanding of movement dynamics, combined with the power of artificial intelligence, can contribute to smarter and more adaptive transport systems. We also discuss methodological challenges and future perspectives, highlighting the potential impact of our approach on urban planning and sustainable mobility. Ultimately, this research aims to enhance our ability to manage congestion, paving the way towards more fluid, safe, and environmentally friendly cities.

Keywords: Urban congestion · Neural networks · Behavior modeling · Traffic management · Artificial intelligence · Intelligent transportation systems

1 Introduction

In our increasingly urbanized world, traffic congestion is a major issue, leading to wasted time, pollution, and declining urban life quality. Artificial Intelligence (AI), especially neural networks, offers promise in addressing this challenge by mimicking human pattern recognition.

However, applying AI to traffic management faces hurdles due to diverse human behaviors, environmental changes, and complex urban dynamics. Our study aims to explore how neural networks, combined with detailed behavioral and environmental data, can transform congestion prediction and management. It should be noted that this article is at this stage conceptual and exploratory, aiming to lay the theoretical foundations for future research. Empirical results will be obtained in later phases of the project, once the theoretical approach has been more firmly established.

© The Author(s), under exclusive license to Springer Nature Switzerland AG 2026
H. Badir et al. (Eds.): INTIS 2024, CCIS 2645, pp. 348–353, 2026.
https://doi.org/10.1007/978-3-032-14964-0_31

Our goal is twofold: demonstrate neural networks' effectiveness in modeling road user behavior and highlight their potential impact on urban planning. Ultimately, we aim for AI-driven congestion management to create smoother, safer, and more sustainable cities.

2 Literature Review

In addressing urban congestion, AI and neural networks offer innovative solutions for traffic prediction and management. This review explores their advancements and lingering challenges. Despite their potential, issues like adaptability and human perception integration remain. We highlight the importance of diverse data and widespread AI use while outlining future directions for urban congestion management.

2.1 Innovative AI Approaches for Traffic Prediction and Management

The work of Achemlal and al. (2020) marked a significant milestone by applying neural networks to the SUMO traffic simulation to predict user behavior and optimize traffic light control. Their approach demonstrates the potential of neural networks to improve the flow of urban traffic. However, the main limitation of this research lies in its application to simulated environments, raising questions about its viability in real and more unpredictable traffic conditions.

2.2 The Impact of Risk Perception on User Behavior

Ndeme and al. (2023) focused on the perception of risk among road users and its influence on their behavior. Through a survey-based methodology, they explored how communication about road safety can alter this perception and, potentially, reduce congestion. Although promising, this research suggests a need for a more systematic integration of these behavioral perceptions into traffic predictive models, to develop more effective congestion management strategies.

2.3 The Use of LSTM Models and the Integration of Diverse Data

Samonte et al. (2022) proposed an innovative approach utilizing LSTM models to integrate environmental data and social network data for enhanced urban traffic prediction. This method emphasizes the importance of diverse data in congestion prediction, while also acknowledging challenges in data collection, processing, and analysis for accurate forecasts.

2.4 CNNs and Their Application to Traffic Data Analysis

Pi et al. (2022) showed (Convolutional Neural Networks) CNNs' efficacy in analyzing traffic data during events, achieving high accuracy in vehicle counting. This research extends their findings to daily urban traffic, aiming to improve traffic prediction and congestion management through AI and neural networks, considering real-time data and road user behaviors.

2.5 Synthesis of Contributions and Gaps

Current research shows AI's potential to enhance urban traffic prediction and management, yet applying it faces hurdles:

Integration of Heterogeneous Data:
Handling diverse data types (behavioral, environmental, real-time) is complex, requiring rigorous methods for quality assurance.

Complexity of Neural Network Models:
Designing and interpreting neural networks demands expertise, balancing accuracy with explainability.

Validation in Real Conditions:
Testing models in varied urban contexts is crucial for robustness,demanding evaluation.
  Despite progress, overcoming these challenges can significantly improve urban traffic management, enhancing city life.

3 Research Proposal

Our research aims to use neural networks for accurate congestion prediction by integrating diverse data sources. We seek to improve congestion management in real urban settings, enhancing reliability and applicability across various contexts.

3.1 Originality and Justification of the Topic

This project uniquely combines deep neural networks with behavioral and environmental data for urban congestion prediction. Unlike past studies focusing on historical data or simple simulations, it uses real-time data and advanced models to offer more accurate and adaptive congestion forecasts.

3.2 Research Objectives

The primary objective is to develop a predictive system capable of effectively integrating road users behaviors and environmental data with the aim of significantly improving the management of urban congestion.
  The specific objectives include:

- **Integrating behavioral and environmental data:** Leverage the wealth of data from social networks and urban sensors to enhance the accuracy of predictions.
- **Developing a predictive model based on deep neural networks:** Utilize the most advanced network architectures, such as Long Short-Term Memory (LSTM) and Convolutional Neural Network (CNN), to model the complex patterns of urban traffic.
- **Validating the model in real traffic scenarios:** Evaluate the model's performance in varied conditions to ensure its reliability and generalizability.

3.3 Research Questions

The key questions guiding this research include:

– How can the integration of diverse data sources be optimized to enhance the accuracy and reliability of predictive models for congestion management?
– What neural network architectures demonstrate superior performance in modeling the complex dynamics of urban traffic, considering the challenges associated with neural network complexity?
– What methodologies can be employed to assess the real-world impact of developed predictive models on congestion management under varied urban conditions?

3.4 Methodology

This project adopts a rigorous and holistic methodology to ensure the reliability and applicability of our results in real urban contexts.

- **Data collection and preprocessing:**

Acquisition of Multi-Source Data: Gather diverse datasets from urban sensors, GPS devices, social media platforms, and traffic cameras.

Cleaning and normalization: Address data inconsistencies, missing values, and outliers, and apply standardization techniques for a consistent dataset ready for analysis.

- **Analysis of user behaviors:**

Behavioral Pattern Identification: Identify key behavioral patterns and factors influencing mobility decisions.

Integration into Model Design: Use insights from behavioral analysis to inform AI model design, ensuring accurate capture of urban traffic dynamics.

Acquisition of Multidisciplinary Skills: Include experts from psychology, sociology, and engineering to understand user behaviors and traffic dynamics comprehensively.

- **Model development and training:**

Architecture Exploration: Design and optimize models based on deep neural networks, exploring Long Short-Term Memory (LSTM) and convolutional neural networks (CNN) architectures.

Iterative Training Approach: Employ multiple training cycles with varied hyperparameters and optimization techniques to maximize prediction performance and accuracy.

- **Validation and evaluation:**

Real Urban Environment Testing: Conduct rigorous testing in real urban environments to assess model performance and ensure robustness.

Benchmark Comparison: Evaluate model performance against existing benchmarks using metrics such as MAE and RMSE to quantify prediction accuracy and reliability.

3.5 Model Architecture

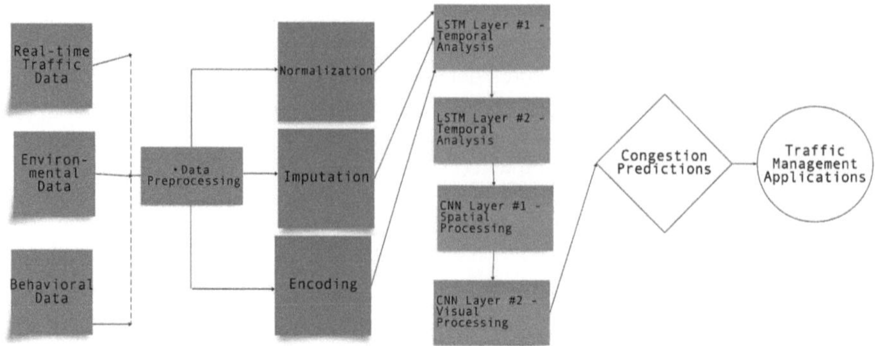

Fig. 1. Predictive model architecture for modeling road user behaviors and managing urban congestion

This Fig. 1 illustrates the complex architecture of the predictive model developed to integrate and analyze real-time behavioral and environmental data, using deep neural networks, to predict urban congestion with improved accuracy.

Technical Architecture: The predictive model will utilize advanced deep learning architectures like LSTM and CNNs, implemented using TensorFlow or PyTorch for flexibility and scalability.

4 Potential Impact and Application

This research aims to revolutionize urban congestion management using deep neural networks, integrating behavioral and environmental data for more accurate forecasts and sustainable mobility solutions.

- **Impact on urban congestion management:** Enhancing prediction accuracy enables effective traffic management, optimizing signals, and minimizing disruptions during events, resulting in reduced congestion, improved efficiency, and lower emissions.
- **Applications in intelligent navigation systems:** Predictive analytics in navigation platforms offer optimized routes, reducing travel times and stress by diverting drivers from congestion hotspots and ensuring smoother traffic flow.
- **Contribution to Sustainable Urban Mobility** This research improves urban mobility by refining transport policies, integrating AI into planning, and emphasizing road user behavior modeling for adaptive traffic management.

5 Perspectives

This project also introduces exciting perspectives for future research in urban traffic management, including:

Improvement of Data Processing Methods: can enhance the accuracy of neural network models by handling diverse data efficiently.

Advances in AI Model Explainability: bridge the gap between technical complexity and practical utility, aiding their acceptance and adoption.

Innovative Validation Strategies: ensure the reliability of AI models in real urban settings, paving the way for effective deployment.

Interdisciplinary Integration: Collaboration between AI experts, urban planners, transportation psychologists, and policymakers could enrich the modeling of user behaviors and congestion management. This interdisciplinary approach could lead to more comprehensive and humanized urban mobility solutions.

Adoption of Emerging Technologies: Incorporating emerging technologies, such as the Internet of Things (IoT) and autonomous vehicles, into traffic management models offers significant potential to transform how cities manage and anticipate congestion.

6 Conclusion

This research proposal offers a fresh approach to urban congestion using neural networks. By integrating real-time data and advanced AI techniques, it aims to enhance congestion prediction and develop user-centric traffic interventions. Despite challenges, successful implementation could revolutionize navigation systems and urban planning for sustainability, setting a model for future studies.

References

Achemlal, B., Chaqroun, A.: A tutorial on traffic prediction and control in urban areas using SUMO and artificial neural networks (2020)

Akhtar, M., Moridpour, S.: A review of traffic congestion prediction using artificial intelligence. J. Adv. Transp. **2021**(30), 1–18 (2021).https://doi.org/10.1155/2021/8878011

Boua, M.: Comportements des usagers de la route au Maroc : rôle des croyances, de la perception des risques et de l'explication naïve des accidents. Université Grenoble Alpes, Thèse de doctorat (2021)

Buch, N., Velastín, S.A., Orwell, J.: A review of computer vision techniques for the analysis of urban traffic. IEEE Trans. Intell. Transp. Syst. **2011** (2011)

Deep learning in traffic flow control and prediction for traffic management. (2022). In Proceedings of the International Conference on Industrial Engineering and Operations (pp. 4026–4035). Istanbul, Turkey: IEOM Society International

Liu, X., Liu, W., Mei, T., Ma, H.: A deep learning-based approach to progressive vehicle re-identification for urban surveillance (2016)

Lu, D., Weng, Q.: A survey of image classification methods and techniques for improving classification performance. Int. J. Remote Sens. **28**(5) (2007)

Mikulski, J.: Introductionoftelematicsfortransport (2012). https://doi.org/10.1109/elektro.2012.6225616

Ndeme, R.N., Mbassi, J.C., Mayouotain, N.M.: Les Cahiers Scientifiques du transport-scientific papers transportation, 2021, 76–77 (2023).https://doi.org/10.46298/cst-10953

Reed, T.: INRIX Global Traffic Scorecard. Global Traffic Scorecard (2019). https://trid.trb.org/view/1456836

Development of Cyber-Space Vulnerabilities Online Monitoring Solution Using Machine Learning

Tizniti Douae[1]([✉]), Kabachi Nadia[2], and Satir Abdellatif[3]

[1] IDS Research Structure, Applied Science National School, Tangier, Morocco
Tizniti.douae@etu.uae.ac.ma
[2] Claude Bernard University Lyon, Lyon, France
nadia.kabachi@univ-lyon1.fr
[3] Applied Science National School, Tangier, Morocco
satir.abdellatif@etu.uae.ac.ma

Abstract. In this article, we will address the problem of automatic classification of security vulnerabilities by detecting those that target critical infrastructures from those who are not, through the classification of vulnerabilities existing in the CVE database. The existing issue is the complexity to detect vulnerabilities targeting only critical infrastructure, based uniquely on the CVE data base, reason why it is necessary to use data analysis, domain knowledge, NLP, and machine learning techniques such as clustering, labeling, word embedding, classification, modeling and evaluation, in order to represent an efficient solution for this problem.

Keywords: Cyber security · Vulnerabilities · Machine learning · NLP · CVE · Critical infrastructure

1 Introduction

Today's cybersecurity landscape is marked by emerging threats that specifically target critical infrastructures. Cyber attackers have demonstrated an increasing capacity to exploit vulnerabilities in systems especially those located in critical infrastructures [6], for example hospitals, Electrical grid, water distribution remote control system, etc. Successful attacks can have devastating consequences, ranging from the interruption of vital services to massive economic losses and risks to public safety. Cyber security aims to guarantee the confidentiality of information, by preventing unauthorized access. Preserve the integrity of data by ensuring that it is not altered by unauthorized actions. By protecting them against interruptions and disruption, reason behind the need to develop advanced vulnerability detection strategies targeting critical infrastructures since it is more urgent than ever. Traditional approaches to treat vulnerabilities databases are essential, but not sufficient to cope with the growing

Supported by IDS research structure.

increasing amount of vulnerabilities. That why it become necessary to include Machine learning into the process of vulnerabilities treatment, using data analysis we became able to treat and classify vulnerabilities targeting critical infrastructures only, since the CVE platform is exposing a large number of vulnerabilities that covers a multitude of targeted sectors. This technological watch allows organizations to monitor cyber vulnerabilities targeting different types of business sectors, in order to implement appropriate security measures by identifying potential vulnerabilities, then organizations can take preventive measures to strengthen their defenses and reduce the risk of cyber-attacks. The presented model through this article addresses this important concern by harnessing the power of Machine Learning, Deep Learning, data analysis, natural language processing NLP and predictive modeling. [8–11]

2   State of Art

Cyber security refers to all measures and practices designed to protect computer systems, networks, data, and users against attacks and malicious activities on the Interne These help to ensure trust, data protection, and businesses activities continuity, in a digital environment that is increasingly interconnected and exposed to cyber threats. Vulnerabilities are progressing remarkably over time, and their severity and impact are becoming ever more significant, threatening infrastructures more deeply, reason why vulnerabilities technological watch is highly required. Technological watch is the process of collecting, analyzing, and disseminating information on technological advances, new trends, and innovations in a specific field. Its aim is to keep abreast of the latest technological developments in order to be integrated into professional or personal activities. It involves several stages: Gathering Information analysis, Interpreting trends, Disseminating results. There are several vulnerability databases available that provide detailed information about security flaws. These databases are regularly updated to include new vulnerabilities and provide up-to-date information on security measures. those databases are widely used by security researchers, cyber security professionals and organizations to keep informed of vulnerabilities and take steps to mitigate them. Among the most popular databases: Exploit-DB, OSVDB (Open Source Vulnerability Database, SARD (Software Assurance Reference Dataset)NVD (National Vulnerability Database). NVD is a public database maintained by the National Institute of Standards and Technology (NIST) in the USA. It contains information on software vulnerabilities, including descriptions, severity levels cross-references and patches. NVD serves as a central repository for vulnerability information and is a valuable resource for researchers, developers and security professionals. [12] Each vulnerability entry in NVD is directly connected to CVE (Common Vulnerabilities and Exposures) [1], which is a publicly accessible database.

Machine learning techniques are increasingly being applied into cybersecurity field especially for vulnerabilities classification and identification, below are represented some works that are exploiting machine learning algorithm, for different cyber-security purposes.

B. Verma R. Chernis, in their article focused on the classification of vulnerable functions in C programs using machine learning techniques, and revealed that trivial features performed better than complex features, achieving an accuracy of 74%, compared with 69% for n-grams and 60% for suffix trees. [2]
B., Li H. Li M. Zhang Q. Tang C. Shuai suggested a smart approach for automatic vulnerability classification using the Latent Dirichlet Allocation (LDA) model and the Support Vector Machine (SVM). [3]
M., Kanehara H. Kubo M. Murata N. Sun B. Takahashi T. Aota discuss in their article the misclassification results of the proposed system and identifies cases where vulnerabilities were easily misclassified, even by humans. The proposed scheme achieved an Accuracy of 96.92 % experiments using real CVE inputs. [5]
M., Cheng F. Meinel C. Gawron discussed the need for automated vulnerability classification. The study revealed that automated classification is viable, with single-attribute accuracy on a single attribute ranging from 70% to 90%, depending on the attribute and the dataset. Even combined attributes resulted in lower accuracy, it was still acceptable, with an accuracy of around 60% to 70% on test data and around 50% on validation data. This result is particularly remarkable given the multitude of attribute combinations. [4]
In summary, this survey has enabled us to learn about the various references and databases used in the field of cyber security. These resources are essential for monitoring, detecting and responding to cyber-attacks. Through the use of these references and databases, organizations can strengthen their security posture and react proactively to cyber threats.

3   Methodology and Results

Among the most important features of the Common Vulnerabilities and Exposures (CVE) database, it is standardized, and globally recognized, reliable format for documenting vulnerabilities, thus facilitating effective communication and information sharing between cybersecurity professionals and organizations. The purpose of our work is to develop a predictive model capable to categorize vulnerabilities found in the CVE database as those that specifically target critical infrastructures, through the adoption of a comprehensive approach exploiting the power of machine learning, natural language processing NLP. This solution involves eight key stages:

3.1   Data Collection and Preparation

collection of representative vulnerability data scenarios, cleaning and preprocessing the data, creating a suitable appropriate dataset for training and evaluation. Using two of the most python's popular libraries used for this purpose 'Requests' and 'BeautifulSobsup'. These libraries enable developers to extract data from websites and store it locally for further processing or analysis. Once extracted, it can be saved under CSV, JSON or SQLite database. [7]

3.2   Feature Extraction and Clustering

implementation of feature extraction techniques application of clustering algorithms to group similar vulnerabilities according to their characteristics. To help discover patterns and obtain information from data. The extraction of CVE data provides a complete and accurate set of data, which can be used for research, risk assessment and for implementation of appropriate cyber security measures.

We proceeded according to five tasks as explained bellow:

- Aggregation: First, we aggregate all the datacollected into a single CSV file

- Cleaning: analysis of missing values (NaN) in our data, to be deleted, to avoid potential errors and reduce computational complexity.

- Encoding: Encoding categorical variables, we need to convert them into numerical form using methods such as One Hot Encoding

- Scaling: Scaling is a pre-processing technique used to normalize the digital characteristics of a dataset.

- Clustering: is a step performed after having extracted and prepared the data, that aims to perform a series of processing tasks before creating a model. we need to test different clustering algorithms to assign the correct label to each data point. K=2 was defined for cluster numbers because we have a binary problem.
  the common internal evaluation measures used for clustering models assessment are Silhouette Score, Davies-Bouldin Index, Calinski-Harabasz Index: also known as the Variance Ratio Criterion.

Table 1. Clustring Algorithms Results.

Metric	Silhouette Score	Davies-Bouldin Index	Calinski-Harabasz Index
Kmeans	0.803	0.172	236 171
Kmodes	0.412	1.404	23 442
Birch	0.610	0.632	94 827
FCM	0.803	0.172	236 171
KPrototypes	0.803	0.172	236 171

Based on these measures obtained for the five algorithms, it can be concluded that K-Means, FCM and K-Prototypes are providing the best performance for our data, as they achieved the highest scores on all three evaluation measures.

3.3   Labels Assignment

Assign appropriate labels to each group. This step involves classifying vulnerabilities into groups, one group targeting critical infrastructure and one that does not (Table 1).

3.4   Feature Importance Analysis

Analyze the importance of the different features contribution to the classification. For an overview of the aspects of vulnerabilities that are most indicative of their potential impact on critical infrastructures.

3.5   Model Evaluation

Performance evaluation of the trained classification model using evaluation measures. This step ensures that the model's predictions are in line with the real labels. For the evaluation of our model we considered two metrics Accuracy and F1 - Score that are calculated using equations bellow :

$$Accuracy = (TP + TN)/(TP + TN + FP + FN) \tag{1}$$

$$F1 - Score = 2(Precision Recall)/(Precision + Recall) \tag{2}$$

where :

$$Precision = TP/(TP + FP) \tag{3}$$

and

$$Recall = TP/(TP + FN) \tag{4}$$

considering that "Class 0" is the positive class and "Class 1" is the negative class, according to our model we get 1733 True Positive (TP), 1731 True Negative (TN), 39 False Positive (FP): 39, 24 False Negative (FN). which means that the model has in one side correctly predicted that 1733 instances were positive (class 0), and 1731 instances were negative (class 1). And in the other side incorrectly predicted that 39 instances were positive when in fact they were negative, and incorrectly predicted 24 instances as negative when they were actually positive (Table 2).

Accuracy: is the ratio between the correctly predicted instances and the total number instances in the dataset. In our case, this is approximately 0.98, which means that our model correctly predicts about 98 % of all the samples.

F1-Score: is the weighted average (harmonic) of precision and recall.

These results indicate that our model is working in a satisfying way, so we are now able to deploy our model to test and predict new data selection.

Table 2. Result of model evaluation.

Metric	undersampling	Oversampling
TP	1733	8514
TN	1731	8692
FP	39	159
FN	24	163
Accuracy	98,21 %	98,16 %
precision	97,80 %	98,17 %
recall	97,80 %	98,17 %
F1-scor	97,80 %	98,17 %

3.6 Tuning and Optimization

Fine-tune hyperparameters and model parameters to optimize classification performance. This process aims to strike balance between minimizing false positives and false negatives.

3.7 Vulnerabilities Classification

the purpose of our project consists of using supervised learning techniques to train the model on labeled data Before applying the classification algorithms, we first need to select the most important features of our data using Random Forest Feature Importance. Which measures the importance of each feature by observing how much the model's performance decreases when that feature is removed. As we have an unbalanced dataset (one class has many more samples than the other), we first need to balance the data using resampling techniques. The Oversampling technique serve to Increase the number of instances in the minority class by duplicating existing samples or by generating synthetic samples using method such as SMOTE (Synthetic Minority Over-sampling Technique). The Under-sampling technique that we used in our project to balance our data. Reduce the number of instances in the majority class by deleting samples at a random basis. We used Voting Classifier to train our model, combining the predictions of several individual classifiers to make a final prediction. It aggregates the predictions of each classifier and generates the class label with the highest number of votes (in the case of a Hard vote) or the highest average probability (in the case of a soft vote). The training and validation curves converge to a low error rate and remain close to each other, indicating a good fit where the model generalizes well.

3.8 Solution Deployment

The developed solution was deployed into web application composed of two major interfaces, The first one is an interactive EDA (exploratory data analysis) interface, dedicated to the analyses of the CVE database and visualizing various graphs. Through which users can easily filter for vulnerabilities by date, types, scores and CWE-IDs, and visualize the data results. The second interface is used to test the predictions of new input data, by means of which users can easily enter vulnerability variables for specific requirements and visualize the prediction result, based on the classification algorithms, and steps, and indicate if the new vulnerability might target a critical infrastructure or not.

4   Discusion and Conclusion

In conclusion, it's true that this work can be extended even further aiming to get more refined, and precise results, and enhance the user experience throughout the exploration of vulnerabilities targeting critical infrastructures. However, the proposed solution, can be considered as satisfying since the provided results are responding to our project goals. Through the flow of data extraction and preparation, data analysis, clustering and classification techniques, culminating in the deployment of our final model under a web application. This project represents a considerable step forward in the automation of vulnerability classification contributing to the improvement of cybersecurity practices and providing a basis for future research in the field.

References

1. CVE Homepage. https://www.cvedetails.com. Last accessed january2024
2. B., Chernis, V.R.: Machine Learning Methods for Software Vulnerability Detection, In: Proceedings of the Fourth ACM International Workshop on Security and Privacy Analytics - IWSPA 18 (2018)
3. B., Li, H., Li, M., Zhang, Q., Shuai, T.C.: Automatic classification for vulnerability based on machine learning., In. IEEE International Conference on Information and Automation (ICIA), (2013)
4. Gawron, M., Cheng, F., Meinel, C.: Automatic vulnerability classification using machine learning. In: Cuppens, N., Cuppens, F., Lanet, J.-L., Legay, A., Garcia-Alfaro, J. (eds.) CRiSIS 2017. LNCS, vol. 10694, pp. 3–17. Springer, Cham (2018). https://doi.org/10.1007/978-3-319-76687-4_1
5. M., Kanehara, H., Kubo, M., Murata, N., Sun, B.: Takahashi T.Aota, Automation ofVulnerability Classification from its Description using Machine Learning., In: IEEE Symposium on Computers and Communications (ISCC) (2020)
6. CIP, Critical Infrastructure Protection Standards, North American Electric Reliability Corporation (NERC)
7. H., Md Nasir, M.H.N., Ab Razak, M.F., Firdaus, A., Hanif, A.N.B.: The rise of software vulnerability: Taxonomy of software vulnerabilities detection and machine learning approaches., J. Network Comput. Appl. **179**, 103009 (2021)
8. IEC62443, Network and system security. Int. Electr. Commission
9. ISO/IEC, ISO/IEC 27000, 27001 and 27002 for Information Security Management, J. Inf. Secur. (2013)
10. maCERT, Moroccan Computer Emergency Response Team.https://www.dgssi.gov.ma/fr/macert.html. Visited at 06/2023

11. NIST, A framework for improving the Cybersecurity of critical infrastructures., J. Inf. Secur. (2014)
12. NVD, National Vulnerability Database. https://nvd.nist.gov/. Visited at 06/2023
13. R., Kim, L., et al.: Automated Vulnerability Detection in Source Code Using Deep Representation Learning., In: 2018 17th IEEE International Conference on Machine Learning and Applications (ICMLA), (2018)

Enhanced Road Object Detection for ADAS Using YOLOv8 and Hyperparameter Evolution

Omar Bouazizi[1(✉)], Chaimae Azroumahli[2], and Aimad El Mourabit[1]

[1] Systems, and Data Engineering Team, ENSAT, Abdelmalek Essaadi University, Tangier, Morocco
omar.bouazizi@etu.uae.ac.ma

[2] Laboratory of Intelligent Systems and Applications (LSIA), Moroccan School of Engineering Sciences (EMSI), Tangier, Morocco

Abstract. Road object detection is crucial for enhancing the safety of Advanced Driver Assistance Systems (ADAS). This paper presents a model fine-tuned with YOLOv8 and the BDD dataset, specifically designed for road object detection using monocular camera input from moving vehicles. The model leverages the YOLOv8 architecture and transfer learning to accurately identify road objects in video streams captured by these vehicles. Additionally, it employs genetic evolution and mutation techniques for the systematic optimization of hyperparameters governing the YOLOv8 model. The integration of this hyperparameter evolution technique underscores the importance of optimizing model parameters to achieve superior performance for ADAS, aligning with recent advancements in the field. Through extensive experimentation, our model demonstrates significant efficacy in real-time road object detection, achieving a mean Average Precision (mAP) of 0.629 and an impressive F1 score of 0.95. Furthermore, the model processes video data at 56 frames per second (FPS), highlighting its suitability for real-time ADAS applications.

Keywords: Road Object Detection · CNN · Transfer Learning · YOLOv8 · ADAS · Evolve

1 Introduction

In recent years, ADAS has gained considerable attention in enhancing road safety. It encompasses diverse applications to boost situational awareness and prevent accidents [1]. However, at the core of ADAS functionalities lies the fundamental task of object detection [2]. Convolutional Neural Networks (CNNs) has seen a surge in popularity in the development of object detection models [3, 4]. They are used to autonomously learn spatial hierarchies of features from input images and spatial relationships essential for identifying objects [5]. Among CNN-based algorithms, the YOLO series has gained significant attention in literature [6]. Models such as YOLOv5, YOLOv7, and the latest iteration, YOLOv8, have become instrumental in real-time object detection tasks due to their higher reported FPS [4, 7–10]. YOLOv8, in particular, has undergone

H. Badir et al. (Eds.): INTIS 2024, CCIS 2645, pp. 362–368, 2026.
https://doi.org/10.1007/978-3-032-14964-0_33

continual refinement, showcasing advancements in computational efficiency and accuracy compared to its predecessors. Unlike previous models like YOLOv7, which relied on anchor boxes to predict bounding boxes (BBox) and object classes directly from input images in a single step, YOLOv8 introduces the use of free anchor boxes [11]. This innovation allows the network to autonomously learn optimal parameters during training, enhancing adaptability across diverse scenarios [8]. Moreover, the integration of transfer learning with YOLOv8 offers substantial advantages in the development of domain-specific object detection models.

In this study, we adapted YOLOv8 and BDD100k dataset [12] to create a road object detection model. In addition, we used Genetic evolution and mutation methods, integrated into YOLOv8 for fine-tuning the training hyperparameters. This approach ensures that the model's parameters are dynamically adjusted to better suit the characteristics of the used BDD dataset, ultimately enhancing its accuracy and effectiveness for real-time road object detection tasks. The rest of this paper is organized as follows: Sect. 2 presents related works on creating road object detection models for real-time applications. Section 3 illustrates the steps followed to create the road object detection model. Section 4 summarizes the experimentation and evaluation steps, and then discusses the results obtained. The conclusion brings this work to a close.

2   Related Works

Several approaches and architectures have been proposed for real-time road object detection models. The most relevant to this work employ one-stage detector CNNs, such as SSD [5] and YOLO [6] architecturess. In recent years, numerous researchers have made notable contributions to the field of road object detection models for ADAS. For example, the authors of [13] proposed a lightweight CNN model for classifying 43 traffic signs from the German Traffic Sign Recognition Benchmark dataset. They implemented Faster R-CNN and YOLOv4 networks for traffic sign recognition, achieving a mAP of 59.88% at 35 FPS. Similarly, the authors of [14] introduced DK_YOLOv5, an object detection model for low-light scenes. This model achieved superior accuracy compared to mainstream models, with a mAP.5 of 71.9% on the Mine_Exdark dataset, surpassing the standard YOLOv5, which achieved 67.5%.

In the same context, the authors of [15] presented a one-stage detector-based approach for detecting road damage. They utilized the Multi-level Feature Pyramids method based on M2det to overcome limitations of existing methods like serie of R-CNN and RetinaNet. Their method incorporats an attention mechanism to enhance the precision of local BBox, achieving an mAP score of 63.96% on their dataset. Another notable contribution is described in [16], where the authors introduced M-YOLO, a traffic sign detection algorithm designed for complex road scenes. Using the CCTSDB dataset and a pre-trained YOLOv8 model, they demonstrated superior performance with an average accuracy of 97.8%. Correspondingly, the authors of [17] introduced MYOLO-lite, an object detection model for detecting trains and railway damages. They used YOLOv4, MobileNet, and K-means clustering to detect railways damages. They reported an mAP score of 95.74% and 42.04 FPS.

Given the advancements of YOLO architectures in real-time object detection, it is clear that these models are highly beneficial for ADAS. However, with the coutinuous development of newer versions, such as YOLOv8, there is a compelling need to test and evaluate these latest iterations to further enhance road object detection models.

3   Road Object Detection Model

Our methodology revolves around retraining the YOLOv8 pre-trained model using the extensive BDD100k dataset. Figure 1 provides a visual representation of the following approach.

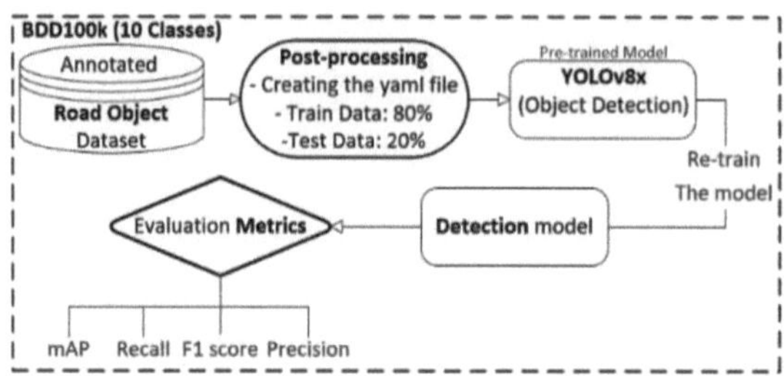

Fig. 1. Retraining the Road Object Detection Model through Hyperparameter Evolution

3.1   Data Description

Our approach relied on the use of the BDD100k annotated datasets. This dataset facilitated a reduction in the number of classes from the original 80 classes in the YOLOv8-n pre-trained model [3, 9]. Table 1 presents an overview of its characteristics. Originally, this dataset provided BBox coordinates in four dimensions: x_{min}, x_{max}, y_{min}, y_{max}. To align with the requirements of YOLO, we transformed these coordinates into its specified format, comprising the width $w_{B.Box}$, the height $h_{B.Box}$, and the BBox coordinates x_{center} and y_{center}. Additionally, we partitioned the dataset into training, validation, and testing sets. In terms of image dimensions, we resized the BDD100k images from 1 280 × 720 pixels to a fixed shape of 640 × 360 pixels.

3.2   Transfer Learning with YOLOv8

In this study, we employed transfer learning to construct an object detection model based on the pre-existing YOLOv8-n architecture, the lightweight scale model with the highest FPS among the different scales offerd by Yolov8 [19]. In this phase, the feature extraction process begins, where pretraining involves freezing the lower layers to retain valuable learned features. During retraining, we start by removing the top layers of the pre-trained models and replacing them with a new set of convolutional layers designed to predict the BBox coordinates and confidence scores of road objects. The updated weights of the final detection models are then fine-tuned through backpropagation, utilizing the target dataset. The majority of the objects are well represented in the training dataset (see Table 1).

Table 1. Transfer learning Datasets Statistics.

Label Name	Train	Val	Label Name	Train	Val
Car	713 211	102 506	Rider	4 517	649
Person	11 672	1 597	Truck	186 117	26 885
Bike	100 797	7 210	Train	239 686	34 908
Motor	3 002	452	Traffic sign	136	15
Bus	91 349	130 262	Traffic Light	29 971	4 245

3.3 YOLOv8 Hyperparameters' Evolution

The process of hyperparameter evolution is the utilization of genetic evolution and muta-tion techniques to refine the hyperparameters of YOLOv8 model. This revolves around exploring an optimal set of hyperparameters by iteratively making random adjustments to the initial configuration. Through this iterative process, the mAP score emerges as the primary metric for evaluating the model's performance. In our work, hyperparam-eter evolution allows us to systematically optimize parameters such as learning rate, batch size, and augmentation methods to enhance the model's efficacy in discerning and accurately localizing various road objects.

3.4 Training Road Object Detection Model

During the development of our road object detection model, several critical factors were taken into consideration. The training hardware configuration used comprised an NVIDIA GeForce RTX 2060 GPU with 12 workers and 16 GB of RAM. The initial hyperparameters consisted of a batch size of 50 epochs and a learning rate of 0.001.

Figure 2 provides an overview of the training results. Figure 2(a) showcases sam-ple output images with their corresponding BBox from a training instance. Meanwhile, Fig. 2(b) illustrates the distribution of the F1 score and the confidence score. They were calculated using Eq. (1). These visualizations offer valuable insights into the model's per-formance. The training process yielded high-density regions around specific confidence values for different classes, affirming the model's exceptional detection performance. Furthermore, Fig. 3(a) presents the confusion matrix generated by YOLO after training both detection models. Through an analysis of the confusion matrix, specific classes that posed challenges for accurate prediction, such as the "train" class, were identified. To refine our model's performance, we can apply a data augmentation strategy to enhance the prediction accuracy for the train class.

$$F1 = \frac{2 * (Precison * Recall)}{(Precison + Recall)}, \text{Confidence} = \frac{sum\,of\,Trust\,(Obj)}{sum\,of\,Trust\,(All)} \tag{1}$$

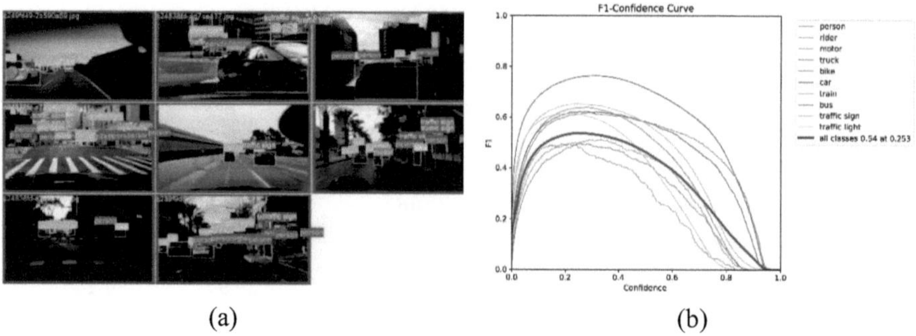

(a)   (b)

Fig. 2. Training process of the Object Detection Model

4   Results and Discussion

To assess the efficacy of our model, we conducted an evaluation of our model accuracy and FPS. Figure 3(b) provides a visual representation of the inference test using our model. The evaluation of our model involves the use of precision, recall, F1 score, and the mAP as delineated in Eq. (2).

$$mAP = \frac{\sum_i^n AP_i}{n}, AP_i \text{ is average precision for class i and n} \tag{2}$$

Table 2 presents the evaluation metrics of our model after 50 epochs. These findings are considered highly competitive as discussed in the related works section. Overall, the results highlight the efficacy of our approach and the advantages of utilizing the latest YOLOv8 architecture for road object detection tasks.

Table 2. Evaluation of the Object Detection Model

mAP	Precision	Recall	F1	FPS
0.6295	0.974	0.9383	0.9558	56

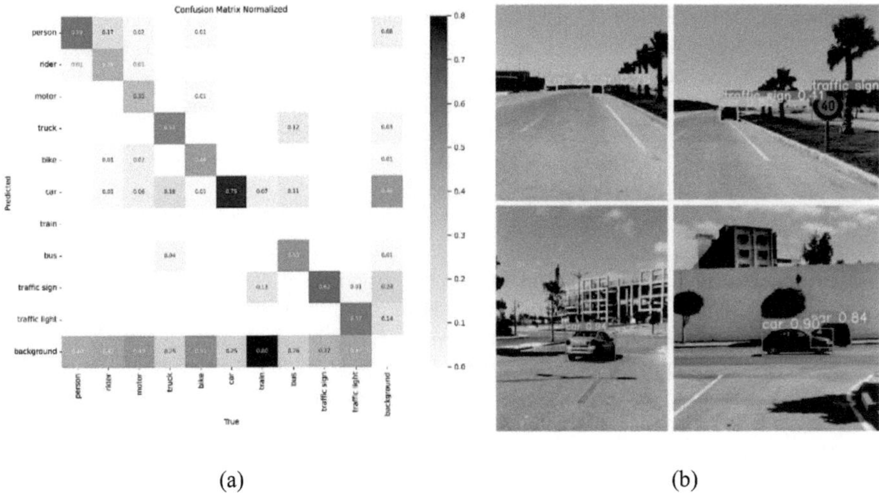

(a)   (b)

Fig. 3. (a) Confusion Matrix for the Detection Classes. (b) Inference results of our model

5 Conclusion

In this paper, we created and evaluated the performance of a YOLOv8-based road object detection model aimed at enhancing road safety and navigation capabilities within autonomous and assisted driving systems. This model provides essential data for ADAS applications, including road object classification, Bbox coordinates, and confidence scores, thereby facilitating the recognition and classification of various on-road entities such as vehicles, pedestrians, and traffic signals. Our model demonstrated strong performance metrics, achieving a mAP score of 0.629 and an F1 score of 0.95 and 56 FPS. These results enable more precise and timely decision-making, which is crucial for navigating dynamic and often unpredictable road environments. The high accuracy and efficiency of our model underscore its potential for real-world implementation, contributing significantly to the advancement of autonomous and assisted driving technologies.

References

1. Malligere Shivanna, V., Guo, J.I.: Object detection, recognition, and tracking algorithms for ADASs—a study on recent trends. Sensors **24**, 249 (2024)
2. Shunmuga Perumal, P., Wang, Y., Sujasree, M., et al.: LaneScanNET: a deep-learning approach for simultaneous detection of obstacle-lane states for autonomous driving systems. Expert Syst. Appl. **233**, 120970 (2023). https://doi.org/10.1016/j.eswa.2023.120970
3. Mohammed, G.S.A., Diah, N.M., Ibrahim, Z., Jamil, N.: Vehicle detection and classification using three variations of you only look once algorithm. Int. J. Reconfigurable Embedded Syst. **12**(3), 442 (2023). https://doi.org/10.11591/ijres.v12.i3.pp442-452
4. Veluchamy, S., Muthukrishnan, R., Karthi, S.: HY-LSTM: a new time series deep learning architecture for estimation of pedestrian time to cross in advanced driver assistance system. J. Vis. Commun. Image Representation **97**, 103982 (2023). https://doi.org/10.1016/j.jvcir.2023.103982

5. Bouazizi, O., Azroumahli, C., El Mourabit, A., Oussouaddi, M.: Road object detection using SSD-MobileNet algorithm: case study for real-time ADAS applications. J. Robot. Control (JRC) **5**(2), 551–560 (2024). https://doi.org/10.18196/jrc.v5i2.21145

6. Redmon, J., Divvala, S., Girshick, R., Farhadi, A.: You only look once: unified, real-time object detection. In: Proceedings of IEEE Comput Soc Conf Comput Vis Pattern Recognit 2016-Decem, pp. 779–788 (2016). https://doi.org/10.1109/CVPR.2016.91

7. Wang, Z., Hua, Z., Wen, Y., et al.: E-YOLO: recognition of estrus cow based on improved YOLOv8n model. Expert Syst. Appl. **238**, 122212 (2024). https://doi.org/10.1016/j.eswa.2023.122212

8. Zhai, X., Huang, Z., Li, T., et al.: YOLO-Drone: an optimized YOLOv8 network for tiny UAV object detection. Electron **12**, 3664 (2023). https://doi.org/10.3390/electronics12173664

9. Oh, G., Lim, S.: One-stage brake light status detection based on YOLOv8. Sensors (Basel) **23**, 1–18 (2023). https://doi.org/10.3390/s23177436

10. Reis, D., Kupec, J., Hong, J., Daoudi, A.: Real-Time Flying Object Detection with YOLOv8 (2023)

11. Wang, C.-Y., Bochkovskiy, A., Liao, H-YM.: YOLOv7: Trainable bag-of-freebies sets new state-of-the-art for real-time object detectors, pp. 7464–7475 (2023). https://doi.org/10.1109/cvpr52729.2023.00721

12. Yu, F., Chen, H., Wang, X., et al.: BDD100K: A Diverse driving dataset for heterogeneous multitask learning. In: Proceedings of IEEE Computer Society Conference on Computer Vision and Pattern Recognition, pp. 2633–2642 (2018).https://doi.org/10.1109/CVPR42600.2020.00271

13. Youssouf, N.: Traffic sign classification using CNN and detection using faster-RCNN and YOLOV4. Heliyon **8**, e11792 (2022). https://doi.org/10.1016/j.heliyon.2022.e11792

14. Wang, J., Yang, P., Liu, Y., et al.: Research on improved YOLOv5 for low-light environment object detection. Electron **12**, 1–22 (2023). https://doi.org/10.3390/electronics12143089

15. Yin, J., Qu, J., Huang, W., Chen, Q.: Road damage detection and classification based on multi-level feature pyramids. KSII Trans. Internet Inf. Syst. **15**, 786–799 (2021). https://doi.org/10.3837/tiis.2021.02.022

16. Liu, Y., Shi, G., Li, Y., Zhao, Z.: M-YOLO: traffic sign detection algorithm applicable to complex scenarios. Symmetry (Basel) **14**, 952 (2022). https://doi.org/10.3390/sym14050952

17. Liu, Y., Gao, M., Zong, H., et al.: Real-time object detection for the running train based on the improved YOLO V4 neural network. J. Adv. Transp. **2022**, 4377953 (2022). https://doi.org/10.1155/2022/4377953

18. Talaat, F.M., ZainEldin, H.: An improved fire detection approach based on YOLO-v8 for smart cities. Neural Comput. Appl. **35**, 20939–20954 (2023). https://doi.org/10.1007/s00521-023-08809-1

19. Wang, G., Chen, Y., An, P., et al.: UAV-YOLOv8: a small-object-detection model based on improved YOLOv8 for UAV aerial photography scenarios. Sensors **23**, 7190 (2023). https://doi.org/10.3390/s23167190

Automation Synergy: Intrusion Detection Through Deep Learning via a DevOps Pipeline in a Cloud Environment

Oumaima Lifandali[(✉)], Zouhair Chiba, Noreddine Abghour, Khalid Moussaid, and Mounia Miyara

Mathematics and Computing Department, LIS Labs, Faculty of Sciences Ain Chock, Hassan II University, Casablanca, Morocco
`oumaima.lifandali@gmail.com`, `{zouhair.chiba,noreddine.abghour,`
`khalid.moussaid,mounia.miyara}@univh2c.ma`

Abstract. DevOps is vital for intrusion detection, especially when integrating Deep Learning (DL) algorithms to boost system security. Its importance lies in creating a collaborative environment where development, operations, and security teams automate and streamline these processes. Manual handling of DL algorithms is time-consuming and error-prone due to the vast data volumes and the need for constant model updates to counter evolving threats. The complexity of modern IT environments further complicates rapid detection of malicious behaviors. DevOps addresses these challenges through continuous integration and delivery (CI/CD), automating development, testing, and deployment. This automation allows seamless integration of DL-based intrusion detection solutions into workflows, facilitating quick adaptation to new threats and ensuring continuous security. DevOps tools automate data collection, model training, algorithm deployment, and result integration into monitoring systems, enabling faster intrusion detection and response. In summary, DevOps enhances intrusion detection by creating an agile, collaborative ecosystem that integrates deep learning to strengthen IT system security and resilience.

Keywords: Cloud Computing · DevOps · Deep Learning · IDS

1 Introduction

DevOps is crucial in the modern technological landscape, particularly for anomaly detection using deep learning algorithms. Manual methods for ML-based anomaly detection are prone to errors and inefficiency due to the vast data volumes and the need for constant model updates. DevOps addresses these challenges by automating and streamlining processes, enhancing collaboration between development, operations, and security teams. This automation is vital for deploying ML-based detection solutions effectively. Intrusion Detection Systems (IDS), enhanced with AI and deep learning and integrated through DevOps, offer advanced, adaptive security measures. This integration allows for continuous data collection, model training, and deployment, enabling proactive threat

H. Badir et al. (Eds.): INTIS 2024, CCIS 2645, pp. 369–374, 2026.
https://doi.org/10.1007/978-3-032-14964-0_34

detection. DevOps thus automates and optimizes security processes, helping organizations stay ahead of cybersecurity challenges and fostering continuous improvement and resilience. We propose combining the strengths of security, AI, and DevOps by using deep learning for automated intrusion detection (Fig. 1).

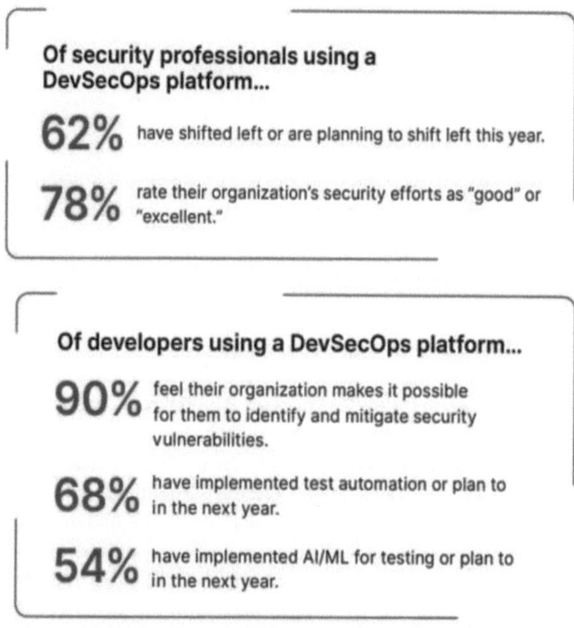

Fig. 1. DevSecOps & Improved Security

Gitlab's 2023 [1] report indicates that DevSecOps platforms and shift-left approaches enhance collaboration between development and security teams, automate security tasks, and promote developer accountability for code security. 90% of developers using DevSecOps platforms believe their organizations effectively identify and mitigate security vulnerabilities. Additionally, 68% have implemented or plan to implement test automation within the next year, while 62% have adopted or plan to adopt shift-left practices. Furthermore, 54% have implemented or plan to implement AI/ML for testing within the next year. Overall, 78% of respondents rate their organization's security efforts as 'good' or 'excellent'. The structure of this work includes listing relevant papers in Sect. 2, defining approaches in Sect. 3, proposing a solution in Sect. 4, completing the task in Sect. 5, and references.

2   Related Work

To reduce resource usage and computational complexity in detection, this research [2] examines key traffic features for reliable intrusion detection. The proposed method uses the Random Forest algorithm, ranking features by relevance through Recursive Feature Elimination. On the NSL-KDD dataset, results show 99.83% accuracy for binary detection and 99.69% for multiclass classification, with execution times of 20 and 39 s, respectively. However, the NSL-KDD dataset, created in 2009, may not reflect current threat landscapes, lacking sensitivity to modern attack tactics. The dataset's age underscores the need for contemporary data to train effective intrusion detection models that address current cybersecurity challenges.

This article [3] introduces μDetector, an intrusion detection tool for microservice-based systems. It automates prior intrusion detection algorithms for Kubernetes and KubeEdge deployments. Users provide a configuration file, and surveillance agents collect system calls, forwarding them to the IDS for anomaly detection. Anomalies trigger alarms indicating potential intrusions. Users interact with the tool via an online board or command line interface. μDetector, based on deep learning, offers accuracy and usability but may have limitations, such as false positives and complex configuration.

Network and cloud security are critical due to increasing data transmissions, cloud elasticity, and global resource distribution. A survey of 300 North American organizations spending at least one million dollars on cloud infrastructure revealed 79% experienced at least one cloud data breach. AWS leads the market with a 34% share. This research [4] highlights the need for enhanced intrusion detection using the AWS cloud dataset. The proposed hybrid approach uses deep learning, preprocessing data, normalizing with PCA, and categorizing with the SMO-FCM algorithm, providing data for analysis with an AutoEncoder. However, despite these measures, the high prevalence of breaches indicates potential gaps in security systems and the need for further scrutiny of the hybrid approach's effectiveness.

This article [5] addresses the rising vulnerability of the Internet to security attacks, emphasizing the importance of Intrusion Detection Systems (IDS). Traditional IDS detect attacks post-execution, causing damage. The proposed early detection IDS identifies attacks before significant harm, using various deep neural network architectures. The approach uses supervised learning to extract features from raw network traffic, avoiding manual selection. Tested on web applications and IoT datasets, it shows high performance. A limitation is the lack of integration with DevOps, which could enhance deployment and management, aligning with continuous development processes for better adaptability and quick response to network changes.

We propose adapting DevOps practices to automate anomaly detection in IDS using deep learning algorithms. Integrating DevOps facilitates continuous development, deployment, and operation of IDS, enhancing efficiency and agility. Automation through DevOps allows quick updates and improvements to detection algorithms, keeping IDS adaptable to evolving threats. Deep learning benefits from DevOps' iterative nature, enabling continuous learning and model refinement based on real-time data. This approach promotes collaboration between development and operations teams, accelerating issue resolution and enhancing security. In summary, DevOps automation in IDS leads to increased efficiency, rapid threat response, and a more collaborative security framework.

3 Preliminaries

In this section, we elaborate on the concepts of the approaches we have adopted for our solution, defining them in depth.

3.1 DevOps

DevOps [6] is a set of tools and practices that enable organizations to develop, test, and deploy software more quickly and reliably. By using DevOps, organizations can deliver products faster than traditional development cycles, gaining a competitive advantage. This approach allows for daily feature updates and rapid bug fixes, compared to traditional release cycles of several days. DevOps offers agility, with multiple versions released weekly, monthly, or even daily, depending on needs. Automated tests and reviews ensure that flawed versions are caught early, preventing issues in production. Automating infrastructure provisioning and testing enhances deployment reliability and reduces operational problems. Continuous logging and metrics provide visibility for developers and operations teams. The primary benefit of DevOps is the automation of repetitive tasks, allowing developers to focus on coding rather than manual deployments.

3.2 IDS

Intrusion Detection Systems (IDS) are essential for securing computer systems by detecting and responding to suspicious or malicious activities [7]. They continuously monitor network traffic, event logs, and other data sources to identify potential intrusions. There are two main types of IDS: Network-based IDS (NIDS) and Host-based IDS (HIDS). NIDS monitors network traffic for unusual patterns or known attack signatures, identifying activities like port scans and DDoS attempts but may struggle with internal threats. HIDS, deployed on individual machines, analyzes event logs and system files to detect abnormal activities such as unauthorized access or suspicious user actions, but might miss attacks that don't alter the machine visibly. The integration of artificial intelligence (AI) into IDS enhances detection accuracy by automating complex pattern recognition. Deep learning models enable IDS to adapt to new threats, improving their ability to identify emerging attacks. IDS are crucial for cybersecurity, providing a first line of defense and preserving the integrity of networks and computer systems.

3.3 Deep Learning

Deep learning, a subset of artificial intelligence, employs deep neural networks with multiple layers to model and comprehend intricate data. Its notable feature is the capacity to extract hierarchical representations, enabling the capture of increasingly abstract features as data moves through network layers. This capability is pivotal for tackling complex tasks in computer vision, natural language processing, and pattern recognition. The deep learning process involves forward propagation, where data traverses the network to produce predictions, and backpropagation, which adjusts network weights to minimize errors. Various neural network architectures cater to specific application needs: Convolutional Neural Networks (CNNs) excel in image processing, Recurrent Neural Networks (RNNs) in sequential data analysis like text or speech, Generative Adversarial Networks (GANs) in generating realistic data, and Autoencoder Neural Networks (AEs) in learning compressed data representations.

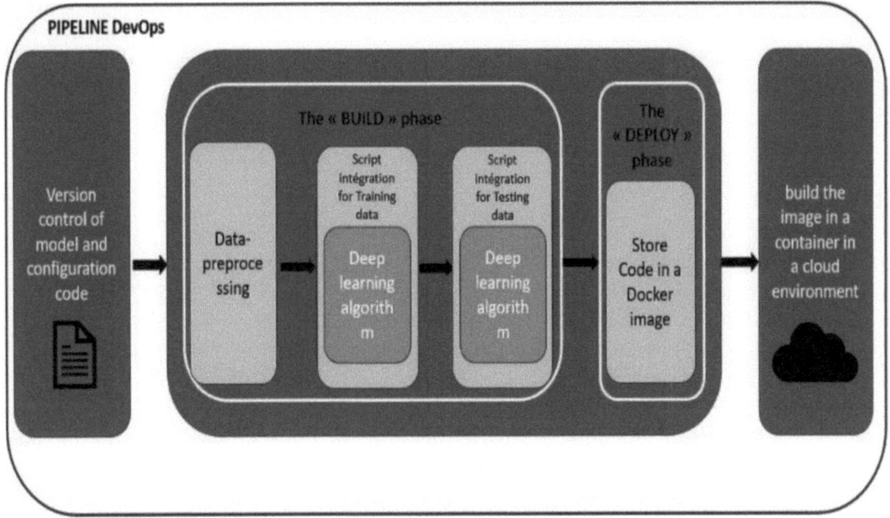

Fig. 2. The intrusion detection automation pipeline

4   Proposed System

At this crucial stage, we illustrate a schema using a sophisticated DevOps pipeline to automate anomaly detection with deep learning algorithms (Fig. 2).

Our system, divided into three strategic components, orchestrates the entire automation process holistically. The first part emphasizes version control for the model's code, ensuring robust management, traceability, rollback capability, and team collaboration. The second part, with four sub-components, covers data preprocessing, automated model training, automated testing, and storing the final code in a Docker image. This containerization ensures portability, reproducibility, and isolation. The third section focuses on building the Docker image, transitioning the code to a cloud environment for flexibility and scalability, thus enabling proactive and automated anomaly detection. The goal is to develop an anomaly detection system powered by deep learning, seamlessly integrated with DevOps principles, creating an efficient and practical framework tailored to business needs.

5   Conclusion

Integrating deep learning-powered intrusion detection into the DevOps pipeline transforms IT security. This innovative approach combines advanced models with DevOps practices, enhancing automated threat detection and proactive prevention. It creates a seamless integration of security within the development and operational lifecycle. This synergy offers a dynamic, adaptive response to emerging threats, accelerating anomaly detection and enabling instant responses through intelligent automation. Consequently, intrusion detection becomes more agile and effective, strengthening IT systems' robustness and resilience. This seamless integration marks a new era where cybersecurity aligns with operational efficiency, ensuring proactive protection against future challenges. As a future direction and next steps, we aim to implement our proposed system with various types of Intrusion Detection Systems (IDS) and different deep learning algorithms in a cloud environment.

References

1. GitLab 2023 Global DevSecOps Report: Security Without Sacrifices. (n.d.).Accessed 1 Apr 2024.https://learn.gitlab.com/devsecops-survey-2023?mkt_tok=MTk0LVZZWQy0yMjEAAA GSORBxqSUAjddUVbKOeuOPiNNWS3s48w0Be3ZL1a7CzCRPNjjpXaFPMcd00II5FHtf 4THV0S1f1TyZTClVvdS-cg_r1g4ngH0Y9bRr_3fZaipn_G4&utm_campaign=devsecops plat&utm_content=developersurvey2023_ai&utm_medium=email&utm_source=marketo&_ pfses=hyP7Q4g7Qtgb8jvcWVNyqvob
2. Flora, J., Teixeira, M., Antunes, N.: µDetector: automated intrusion detection for microservices. In: Proceedings - 2023 IEEE International Conference on Software Analysis, Evolution and Reengineering,SANER2023, pp. 748–752 (2023).https://doi.org/10.1109/SANER56733. 2023.00084
3. Kannari, P.R., Chowdary, N.S., Laxmikanth Biradar, R.: An anomaly-based intrusion detection system using recursive feature elimination technique for improved attack detection. Theor. Comput. Sci. **931**, 56–64 (2022). https://doi.org/10.1016/J.TCS.2022.07.030
4. Rm, B., Mk, J.K.: Intrusion Detection on AWS Cloud through Hybrid Deep Learning Algorithm. Electronics **12**(6), 1423 (2023). https://doi.org/10.3390/electronics12061423
5. Ahmad, T., Truscan, D., Vain, J.: EARLY: a tool for real- time security attack detection. In: Sadovykh, A., Truscan, D., Mallouli, W., Cavalli, A.R., Seceleanu, C., Bagnato, A. (eds.) CyberSecurity in a DevOps Environment : From Requirements to Monitoring, pp. 225–252. Springer (2023)
6. Battina, D.S.: Devops, a new approach to cloud development & testing (2020). International Journal of Emerging Technologies and Innovative Research (www.jetir.org), ISSN:2349–5162, Vol.7, Issue 8, page no.982–985, August-2020, Available :http://www.jetir.org/papers/JETIR2 008432.pdf , Available at SSRN: https://ssrn.com/abstract=4004330
7. Jabez, J., Muthukumar, B.: Intrusion detection System (IDS): anomaly detection using outlier detection approach. Procedia Comput. Sci. **48**(C), 338–346 (2015). https://doi.org/10.1016/J. PROCS.2015.04.191

Explainable AI for Energy Prediction in Smart Building

Nisrine Bajja[1,2,3]($\boxtimes$), Mohamed Hamlich[1], and Franck Dufrenois[3]

[1] Complex Cyber Physical Systems Laboratory, ENSAM, II University, Casablanca, Hassan, Morocco
bajjanisrine@gmail.com
[2] Pluridisciplinary Laboratory of Research and Innovation (LPRI), EMSI Casablanca, Casablanca, Morocco
[3] LISIC, ULCO Calais, 50 rue F. Buisson, Calais, France

Abstract. Many researchers have taken an interest in climate change and environmental issues, as they have a significant impact on people's well-being. Artificial Intelligence have been integrated in the field of energy, which is considered as an essential resource to our daily lives, to predict energy consumption and manage energy resources in order to attain a sustainable and durable future. The development of machine learning models has become an essential part of this process. However, these models are often viewed as black boxes, making it difficult to gain insights from them. Explainable Artificial Intelligence (XAI) has emerged to address this concern. In this paper, our goal is to develop an explanatory approach that explains each part of the machine learning pipeline, from the collection of data to the building of models. Machine learning models and explainable artificial intelligence (XAI) tools will be used to achieve this. Three datasets, namely electrical energy consumption, solar radiation production and weather, have been used to build models using SVR, MLP and XGB. The most influential features that affect the increase in energy consumption have been retrieved using SHAP, LIME and Eli5.

Keywords: eXplainable AI · Smart building · energy prediction · Smart city · LIME · SHAP · Machine Learning · Interpretability · Explainability -Transparency

1 Introduction

Over the past few years, artificial intelligence has significantly impacted sectors such as healthcare and finance, improving efficiency. The increasing urban population is expected to reach over 4 billion by 2050, leading to a rise in transportation, water, and energy consumption. This has sparked interest among researchers exploring Smart Cities to enhance urban infrastructure and promote equitable resource management. Smart cities utilize advanced IoT technologies to connect different urban areas and collect real-time data for processing using big data techniques. Additionally, smart transportation aims to reduce environmental impact through electrification to decrease gas emissions,

H. Badir et al. (Eds.): INTIS 2024, CCIS 2645, pp. 375–381, 2026.
https://doi.org/10.1007/978-3-032-14964-0_35

while the Energy Performance of Buildings Directive introduced Nearly Zero Energy Building adoption aiming at managing energy consumption and reducing greenhouse emissions by up to 90% by 2050. Another concept presented under the European Green Deal is transitioning from NZEBs to zero-emission buildings (Atanasiu et al., 2011) [1]. In order to take actions, predictions made by AI based models should be understood to the stakeholders. For this purpose, many studies highlight the use of interpretable and explainable models to make AI models more understood, this notion is known in the literature review as eXplainable Artificial Intelligence [2, 3]. The integration of artificial intelligence and eXplainable Artificial Intelligence techniques holds great potential for improving energy management in smart cities [4, 5]. Therefore, in order to gauge the willingness of users to prioritize better explanations over accuracy in AI model predictions, a user study should be conducted within the context of XAI. In this paper, we present a novel predictive model for daily energy consumption using machine learning models within three datasets, and explaining the founded prediction using XAI techniques.

2   Related Works

In recent years, there has been a growing interest in the field of energy consumption forecasting to predict the energy use, (Wei et al.,2019) [6] presents a review paper on Energy consumption used model from 1990 to 2019, reviewing 116 papers. In this regard, there are several studies that conducts a thorough research on building AI models to predict energy consumption, (Olu Ajayi et al., 2022) [7] presents the use of many ML models ANN, SVM, RF, DT, LR to predict the annual building energy consumption using a large dataset of residential building, DNN, Gradient Boosting, SVM and RF outperformed other models. In study [8] (Geoffrey et al., 2007) conducted a comparison between decision tree and neural networks in predicting electricity energy consumption, elucidating the accurate performance of Decision Tree than other model. Pham et al. 2020 [10] introduced a RF based model to predict short-term energy use in hourly resolution using 5 different datasets for 1-year energy consumption. (Shapi et al., 2021) [11] introduces an energy consumption predictive model for smart building based on three supervised model KNN, SVM and ANN with MLP using a collected dataset from June 2018 to December 2018. SVM shows a promising result in the prediction accuracy. Exploring the previous studies, it's shown that ANN and SVM are the widely used model for energy consumption forecasting [9]. All the research on this field aim to provide early forecasting of energy consumption to provide the managers of buildings with insights to take further actions to reduce the overuse of energy.

3   Methodologies

This study aims to predict the electricity consumed in smart buildings using ML models and XAI techniques to explain the resulting predictions. The dataset, methods and results are discussed in this section.

3.1 Dataset

In this study, we used energy use, solar energy production and weather dataset (As shown in Table 1 from a 328 m2 all-electric, zero-energy commercial building with 2 floors in Virginia, USA. Table 2 shows the merged set:

Table 1. Table of data description.

Category	Data Description	Data Resolution
Energy use	HVAC Lighting Plug & process loads Whole building	Daily-Monthly-Hourly-By circuit Daily-Monthly-Hourly Daily-Monthly-Hourly Daily-Monthly-Hourly
Energy production	Discharged Energy	Daily-Monthly
Weather	Solar Radiation Energy Daily weather	Daily-Monthly-Hourly Daily-Monthly

Table 2. Feature Description of final dataset.

Id	Description	Type	Id	Feature	Type
1	Date	datetime64	16	Avg.2	float64
2	Total HVAC Energy Use (Wh)	float64	17	Min.2	int64
3	Total Hot Water Energy Use (Wh)	float64	18	Max.3	int64
4	HVAC - 1st Floor (Wh)	float64	19	Avg.3	float64
5	HVAC - 2st Floor (Wh)	float64	20	Min.3	int64
6	Interior Lights (Wh)	int64	21	Max.4	float64
7	Exterior Lights (Wh)	int64	22	Min.4	int64
8	1st flr Lights (Wh)	int64	23	Avg.4	float64
9	2nd flr Lights (Wh)	int64	24	Total	float64
10	Max x	int64	25	Energy Discharged (Wh)	float64
11	Avg	float64	26	Ave	float64
12	Max.1	int64	27	Min y	float64
13	Avg.1	float64	28	Max y	float64
14	Min.1	int64	29	StD	float64
15	Max.2	int64	30	Daily Electricity Use (Wh)	float64

3.2 Our Approach

During the model building phase, we adopted for an explanatory approach from data collection to the prediction phase. In the next subsection, we present the initial step in the ML pipeline Data preprocessing.

3.2.1 Data Preprocessing

This step involves merging the three datasets into a unified data set. Feature engineering techniques are applied, including handling missing values using interpolation and normalizing and standardizing the dataset due to its normal distribution. The distribution of each feature per season is visualized to gain insights about electricity overuse during the year, as well as specific distributions for Lighting, HVAC, and solar radiation production per season.

3.2.2 Model Building

During the model building phase, it is important to choose appropriate models for our case study and dataset. We consider the presence of outliers in our dataset when selecting models. To address this, we analyze the characteristics, strengths, and limitations of regression models suitable for handling outliers. As a result, we utilize robust regression models such as decision trees, Random Forests, and gradient boosting machines.

4 Explainability Tools

In the final prediction stage, explainability tools are used to clarify why a certain model makes specific predictions. There are two aspects: local explainability focuses on individual predictions, while global explainability covers the entire model. The following models have been employed for generating both types of explanations (Fig. 1).

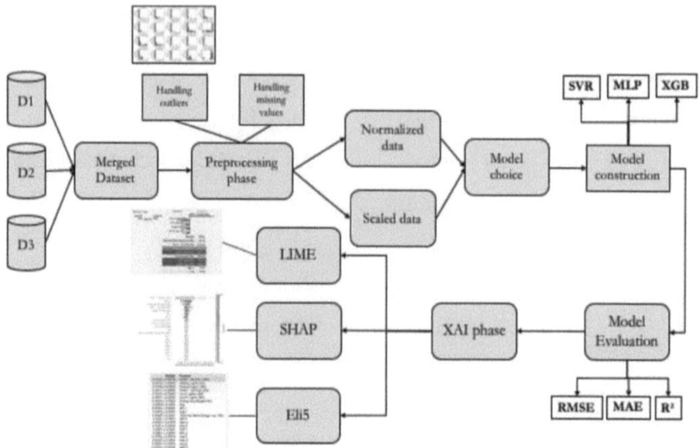

Fig. 1. Our XAI approach architecture

5 Discussions

5.1 ML Experiment Results

Table 3 Table 4 and Table 5 provide a comparison of errors used to evaluate the MLP, SVR, and XGBR models across three scenarios: original dataset, normalized dataset, and scaled dataset. The results demonstrate that using a normalized dataset yields good performance with RMSE values of 0.042 for MLP and 0.043 for XGBR. These models outperformed SVR in all three scenarios.

Table 3. Model performance Original dataset

model	RMSE	MAE	R^2
MLP	**4633.39**	**3509.13**	**0.9975**
XGB	4707.78	3626.96	0.9852
SVR	16964.20	13060.29	0.0288

Table 4. Results of Normalized

model	RMSE	MAE	R^2
MLP	**0.0423**	**0.0314**	**0.9979**
XGB	0.0431	0.0332	0.9820
SVR	0.0533	0.0454	0.9060

Table 5. Results of scaled Dataset

model	RMSE	MAE	R^2
MLP	**0.2522**	**0.1916**	**0.9989**
SVR	0.2577	0.1969	0.9857
XGB	0.2588	0.1993	0.9252

5.2 XAI Tools Experiment Results

We use SHAP, LIME, and Eli5 for local and global explainability with the MLP model. Figure 2 shows the results of this approach. For a specific sample (row 4), HVAC-2nd Floor has a positive impact on the prediction while Interior Lights, 1st flr lights, Energy discharged, and 2nd flr lights have negative effects. In global explanations SHAP in the middle shows that HVAC-2nd Floor contributes most to the model's prediction with a positive influence on the output.

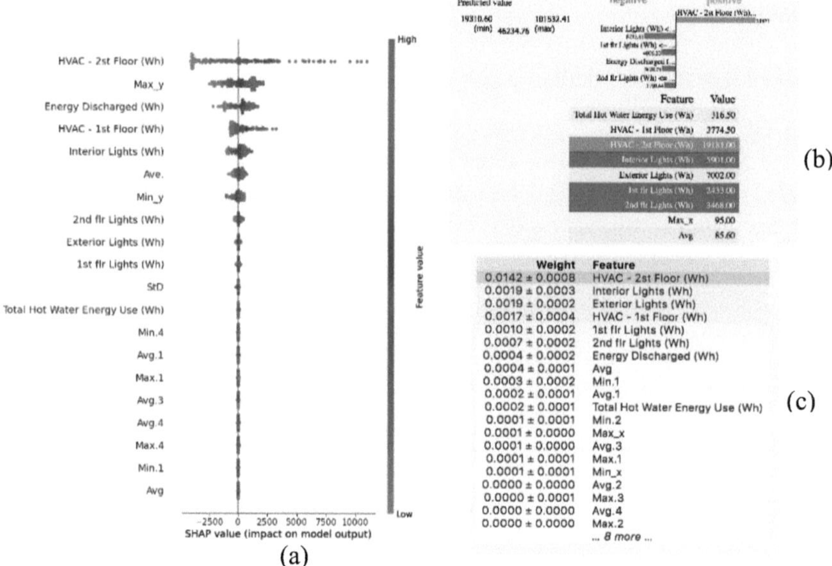

Fig. 2. Comparison of explainability methods using MLP model (a) SHAP, (b) LIME, (c) ELI5

6 Conclusion and Perspectives

In this study, our main goal was to develop a transparent approach using ML models and XAI techniques. We utilized three datasets and experimented with three models: MLP, SVR, and XGB. The MLP model outperformed the others across all scenarios with the original dataset as well as normalized and scaled versions. By implementing local and global explanations, we aimed to generate recommendations that effectively communicate results to end-users and assist decision-making managers in managing energy resources more effectively. Our approach stands out due to its emphasis on explainability from the outset. Despite differences in the methods used for XAI at both local and global levels, there were similarities in identifying influential features. For future directions, we intend to incorporate generative AI to translate visualized explanations into understandable text formats and extend the applications.

References

1. Atanasiu, B.: Principles for nearly zero-energy buildings: paving the way for effective implementation of policy requirements. 9789491143021 (2011)
2. Arrieta, A.B., et al.: Explainable Artificial Intelligence (XAI): Concepts, taxonomies, opportunities and challenges toward responsible AI. Inf. Fusion **58**, 82–115 (2020)
3. Gunning, D., Aha, D.: DARPA's explainable artificial intelligence (XAI) program. AI Mag. **40**(2), 44–58 (2019)
4. De Bock, K.W., et al.: Explainable AI for operational research: a defining framework, methods, applications, and a research agenda. Eur. J. Oper. Res. (2023)

5. Ahmed, I., Jeon, G., Piccialli, F.: From artificial intelligence to explainable artificial intelligence in industry 4.0: a survey on what, how, and where. IEEE Trans. Ind. Inform. **18**(8), 5031–5042 (2022)
6. Wei, N., Li, C., Peng, X., Zeng, F., Lu, X.: Conventional models and artificial intelligence-based models for energy consumption forecasting: a review. J. Petrol. Sci. Eng. **181**, 106187 (2019)
7. Olu-Ajayi, R., Alaka, H., Sulaimon, I., Sunmola, F., Ajayi, S.: Building energy consumption prediction for residential buildings using deep learning and other machine learning techniques. J. Build. Eng. **45**, 103406 (2022)
8. Tso, G.K., Yau, K.K.: Predicting electricity energy consumption: a comparison of regression analysis, decision tree and neural networks. Energy **32**(9), 1761–1768 (2007)
9. Yang, L., Yan, H., Lam, J.C.: Thermal comfort and building energy consumption implications– a review. Appl. Energy **115**, 164–173 (2014)
10. Pham, A.D., Ngo, N.T., Truong, T.T.H., Huynh, N.T., Truong, N.S.: Predicting energy consumption in multiple buildings using machine learning for improving energy efficiency and sustainability. J. Clean. Prod. **260**, 121082 (2020)
11. Shapi, M.K.M., Ramli, N.A., Awalin, L.J.: Energy consumption prediction by using machine learning for smart building: Case study in Malaysia. Dev. Built Environ. **5**, 100037 (2021)

Exploration of Semantic Segmentation Algorithms Through Deep Learning for Extracting Water Bodies from Wetland Areas

Mehdi Kechna, Yousra Achemlal[✉], Kenza Ait El Kadi[✉], Siham Fellahi[✉], Marwa Zerouk[✉], and Hicham Hajji[✉]

Hassan 2 Agronomic and Veterinary Institute, 10000 Rabat, Morocco
mehdikechna01@gmail.com

Abstract. Predicting the introduction of avian influenza remains a sensitive issue, with a direct impact on humans and animals' health, which requires considerable efforts to prevent and limit its spread within the Moroccan territory. This is due to the inability to interrupt the natural phenomenon of wild birds' migration, which carries the disease and consequently contaminates other species, including poultry. Since the spread of this disease primarily occurs in wetland areas, experts are keen to identify and border these regions. To address this, our study provides a decision aid tool based on segmentation of water bodies within these ecosystems, which are susceptible sites for contamination. This is achieved through three deep learning-based semantic segmentation algorithms, namely the UNet, Attention UNet, and TransUNet models, trained on Sentinel-2 satellite imagery. The aim is to achieve optimal predictions and select the most adept model among these three with the best ability to recognize and extract water bodies. The process includes data preprocessing, hyperparameter tuning, qualitative and quantitative validation, and model performance enhancement through augmentation techniques using the Segment Anything model. Finally, the resulting model is deployed through a local web application. The results achieved by the most performant model are as follows: An F1 score of 87.21%, the average of the Intersection over Union (mIoU) of 74.31%, and an accuracy of 69.68%, which proved competitive with previous approaches to water body extraction.

Keywords: Avian Influenza · Semantic segmentation · Deep Learning · Wetlands · Water Bodies · Wild birds migrating · U-Net · Attention UNet · TransUNet · Segment Anything Model

1 Introduction

Wetlands are spatial units covered with water or intermittently wetted, forming a living system characterized by a trophic network established and maintained mainly by internal components and factors within this space, not exceeding a depth of six meters (HCEFLCD, 2015). Serving as vital biodiversity support, they host a wide variety of natural habitats and species, but also serve as a migration site for wild birds, which, in the event of contamination, poses a pandemic threat such as avian influenza (Stevens et al., 2010).

H. Badir et al. (Eds.): INTIS 2024, CCIS 2645, pp. 382–391, 2026.
https://doi.org/10.1007/978-3-032-14964-0_36

Research into the epidemiological forecast of avian influenza in Morocco has demonstrated that the niches of migratory birds, originating from this disease, focus on wetlands (FAO, 2007).

In this regard, we have focused on establishing a decision support tool to guide experts in identifying and delineating wetlands most likely to introduce this disease, through the segmentation of water bodies, the main component of these ecosystems, using satellite imagery and deep learning techniques. In addition to the decision support provided, mapping water bodies and extracting them from satellite images play a significant role in various applications such as monitoring changes in water bodies (Sarp et Ozczlik, 2017), analyzing water quality (Chen et al., 2018), and categorizing types of water bodies (Artibi et al., 2021).

To achieve this goal, recent research in this field has focused on improving the accuracy of water body extraction from satellite images either by using pre-built models or creating their own models. However, transformer mechanisms have not been tested or introduced in this context despite their success in other areas. Hence the choice was made for the TransUNet model, which has benefited from attention mechanisms in its construction as well as the architecture of the UNet model, which is why we have selected it for comparison with the UNet and Attention UNet models, while seeking the best performance achievable by these models.

To further improve the performance of our approach, we are exploring a less explored avenue in terms of data augmentation. Traditionally, augmentation techniques such as GANs are widely recognized and used for semantic segmentation applied to other case studies. However, the SAM model, recently introduced by MetaAI, opens up a new perspective on DataAugmentation. Its application in this context, still underexplored, represents an exciting opportunity for improving the accuracy and robustness of our model.

2 Methodology

2.1 General Methodology

Like any semantic segmentation process based on deep learning, a general methodology, as illustrated in (Fig. 1), is followed.

Firstly, the acquisition and preparation of the dataset, then the training of the deep learning model with the adjustment of its hyperparameters, and finally the validation of the results qualitatively by comparing predictions with the validation dataset and quantitatively by evaluation metrics.

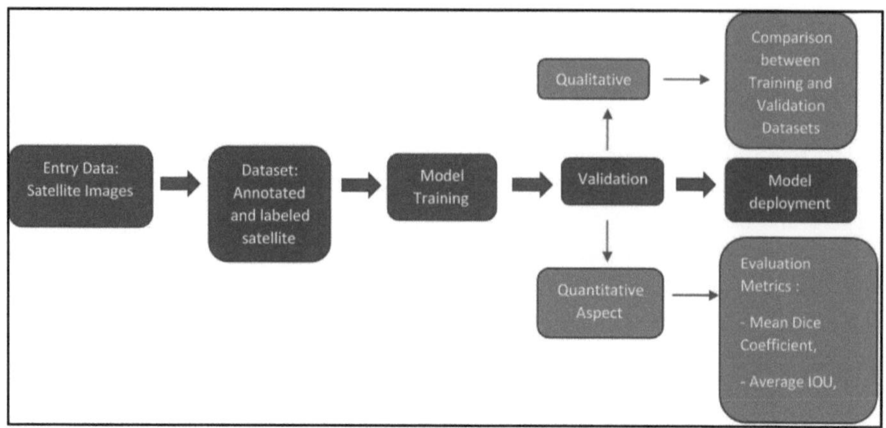

Fig. 1. General Methodology

3 Data

3.1 Data Acquisition

This is a collection of 2841 satellite images of water bodies taken by the Sentinel-2 satellite over the United States. Each image has a mask that distinguishes between areas where water exists (white pixels) and areas where water is absent (black pixels).

The masks were generated by calculating the Normalized Difference Water Index (NDWI) derived from the near-infrared (NIR) band 8 and the green band 3. This index maps free water masses in a satellite image, allowing water bodies to stand out from the ground and vegetation. It is calculated as follows:

$$NDNNI = \frac{Green - NIR}{Green + NIR} \tag{1}$$

The data is published as Open Data through the Kaggle interface, using the Creative Commons CC BY-NC-SA 4.0 license. The directory in question is divided into a folder of RGB images and a folder of masks, with.jpg extensions. It is accessible on Kaggle via the following link: https://www.kaggle.com/datasets/franciscoescobar/satellite-images-of-water-bodies.

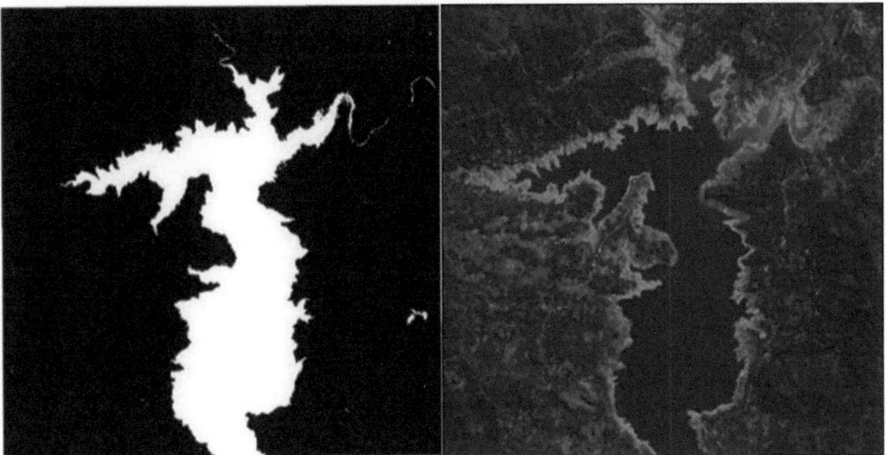

Fig. 2. Example of used data (Image and its mask)

Before integrating this database into subsequent processes, it was crucial to correct it for various imperfections such as the presence of masks incompatible with the expected prediction, or images bordered by black-colored pixels, which consequently produce masks incorrectly identifying these pixels as water.

From Copernicus, the images are downloaded in the form of 13 separate bands, among which we have grouped bands B02, B03, and B04, corresponding respectively to the blue, green, and red bands.

3.2 Data Augmentation

The band grouping is performed in ArcGIS using the 'Composite Bands' tool from the ArcToolBox menu - Data Management Tools - Raster - Raster Processing - Composite Bands, in the following order (B04, B03, B02), thus providing a three-band RGB image that will feed our SAM model to predict binary masks of water bodies from these input images.

4   Results

We have summarized in Table 1 the competitive combinations allowing each of the three models to achieve maximum efficiency in segmenting water bodies in wetland areas.

Table 1. Hyperparameter combinations offering the best performances for the three models

ID	Epoque	Batch	α	Temps de Calculs	Loss	Val Loss	Acc	Val Acc	mIoU	Dice	Val Dice
U13	40	4	10^{-3}	26min 55s	0.0782	0.1950	0.7536	0.7402	0.7045	0.9235	0.8601

(continued)

Table 1. (*continued*)

ID	Epoque	Batch	α	Temps de Calculs	Loss	Val Loss	Acc	Val Acc	mIoU	Dice	Val Dice
A25	**50**	**8**	$10{-}3$	**26min 28s**	0.0702	0.2316	0.7543	0.7380	0.7093	0.9348	0.8660
T26	**50**	**8**	$10{-}4$	**2h 13min**	0.0637	0.2197	0.7550	0.7395	0.7052	0.9410	0.8708

Firstly, the maximum performance of the three models was noted respectively via configurations T26, A25, and U13. The T26 combination recorded the highest value achieved by the Dice coefficient compared to all the trials of the three models.

Subsequently, the predictions produced by the TransUNet model are more consistent with the provided masks than those of Attention UNet followed by UNet. Indeed, the TransUNet model demonstrated an ability to better capture the edges of large water bodies despite their discontinuities, as well as good recognition of small isolated water bodies.

For all trials of the three models, we observed especially in the loss function graphs, the successive oscillations of the curve corresponding to the validation set, mainly stemming from some imperfections in the data used, which also influence other metrics. Since this defect slightly affects all three models, we focused on their performances and behavior despite this issue. However, the TransUNet model offers the best performance, especially with the hyperparameter combination adopting the Binary Cross Entropy function as the loss function, the Adam optimization function with a batch size set to 8, a learning rate of 10–4, and over 50 epochs.

Despite the costly time component, the TransUNet model proves to be the most optimal approach for water body extraction from satellite images by achieving the best performance qualitatively and quantitatively compared to the UNet and Attention UNet models. This will allow for better identification of water bodies and the establishment of a decision support tool for its qualification as a wetland or not, aiming to identify the ecological niches of migratory birds and reduce or even prevent the spread of avian influenza in the national territory.

4.1 Improvement of Results

In order to improve the metrics and the learning of the TransUNet model, we attempted to adjust and augment our database by feeding our model with more training data, as the performance of transformers in general and TransUNet specifically improves with the increase in data size (Dosovitskiy et al., 2021).

As explained in the tools and methodology section, augmentation is carried out through the Segment Anything model on RGB satellite images captured by Sentinel-2, representing wetland sites at the national level. This allows the model to adapt to the nature of existing water bodies in Morocco and better predict them.

To extract binary masks from the images prepared via the SA model, we chose to work in the Google Colab environment due to the availability of Jupyter widgets, which are interactive interfaces that allow us in our case to delineate the area or areas of interest, which are the water bodies.

First, we install the Segment Anything model and the corresponding weights, then import the SamPredictor module and apply our spatial delineation or Bounding Box in the form of [x_min, y_min, x_max, y_max], using the mask prediction command: Predict (Fig. 3).

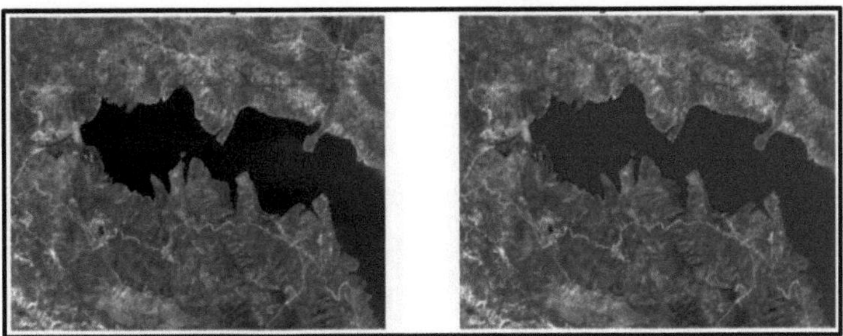

Fig. 3. Image segmentation by SAM via a Bounding Box (original image and segmented image)

The output of the SamPredictor module provides three probable predictions of the mask that the model deems suitable, based on a score it calculates due to the ambiguity encountered in identifying the prompt, and it is up to the user to subsequently choose the most effective prediction. (Fig. 4).

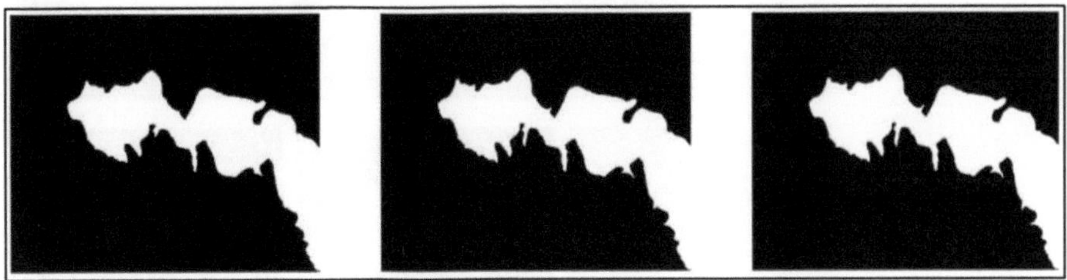

Fig. 4. Segmentation predictions provided by SAM

By repeating the same process on the acquired satellite images, we obtained a dataset of 154 images and their corresponding masks, which will be subject to augmentation for the TransUNet model to improve our results. Subsequently, we retrained our model using the previously qualified most performing hyperparameter configuration, namely Adam optimizer, a batch size of 8, a learning rate of 10–4, and a number of epochs of 50, along with an augmented dataset (Fig. 5).

The resulting metrics are presented below.

Table 2. Quantitative results achieved by TransUNet before and after database augmentation.

	Epoque	Batch	α	Temps de Calculs	Loss	Val Loss	Acc	Val Acc	mIoU	Dice	Val Dice
Avant Augmentation	**50**	**8**	10^{-4}	**2h 13min**	0.0637	0.2197	0.7550	0.7395	0.7052	0.9410	0.8708
Après Augmentation	**50**	**8**	10^{-4}	**2h 29min**	0.0630	0.2598	0.7673	0.7431	0.6998	0.9415	0.8721

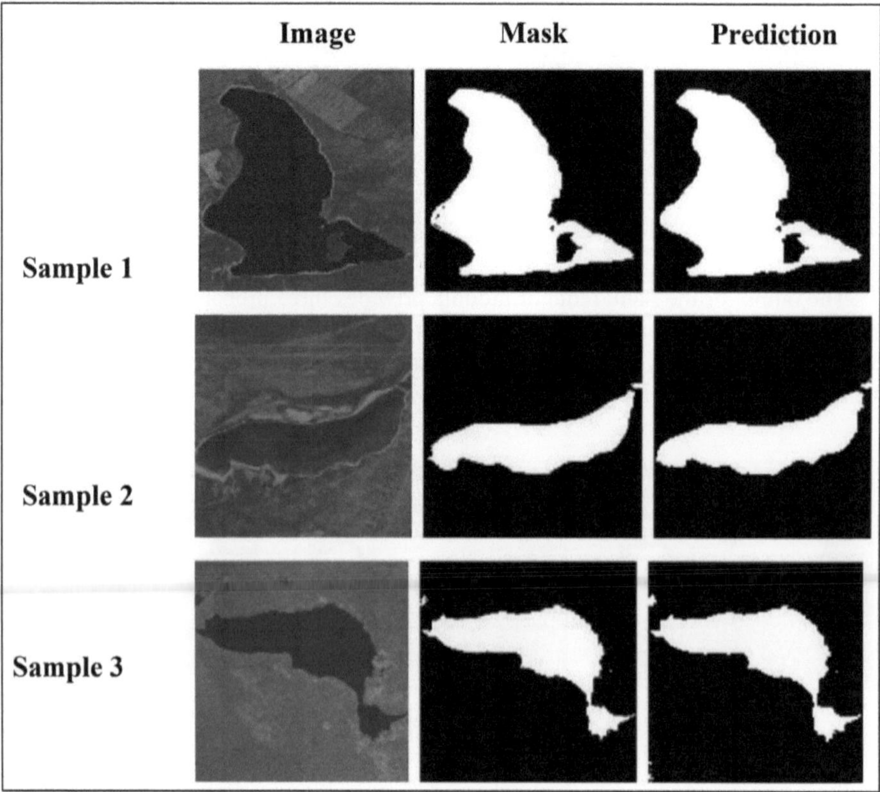

Fig. 5. Qualitative results achieved by TransUNet after database augmentation.

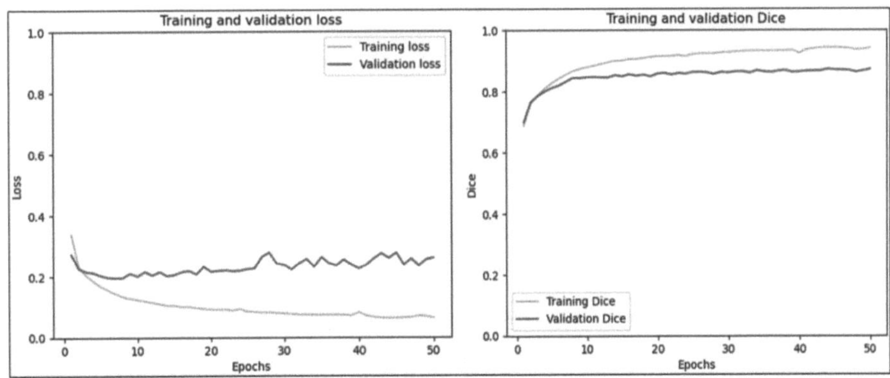

Fig. 6. Graphs of the cost function and Dice coefficient of the augmented TransUNet model.

We can conclude that following the introduction of the augmentation technique outlined, the results have improved both quantitatively and qualitatively, which supports the hypothesis made about the necessity of feeding the TransUNet model with more data.

Firstly, the evaluation metrics, including the F1 score and accuracy, corresponding to the validation set have improved from 87.08% and 73.95% to 87.21% and 74.31%, respectively, while the mean IoU value has slightly decreased from 70.52% to 69.68% due to the increase in the number of training and validation data, indicating that the calculation of mIoU takes into account more data. (Table 2).

Secondly, the predictions are very satisfactory in terms of resemblance to the masks of the images and demonstrate a good quality of adaptation and identification of water bodies regardless of their length or area. (Fig. 6).

Finally, the graphs illustrating the behavior of the TransUNet model over epochs no longer show severe oscillations, which were previously justified by defects in the database that have been further rectified and augmented by the new Sentinel-2 images and their corresponding masks generated via SAM. However, the remaining imperfections have created a slight divergence of the loss function curve relative to the validation set from the curve of the training data. (Fig. 6).

Despite the imperfections identified in the database, the augmented TransUNet model has offered good qualitative and quantitative performance, demonstrating its effectiveness in the context of segmenting water bodies in wetland areas from satellite images.

5   Conclusion

The prediction of the introduction of avian influenza is a vital concern due to its effects on human and animal health. This disease primarily spreads through wetland areas due to the natural phenomenon of wild bird migration. This study aims to provide a decision support tool dedicated to experts for identifying wetland areas with a higher risk of contamination through the automatic extraction of water bodies from these ecosystems.

To achieve this goal, we opted to use semantic segmentation algorithms through deep learning as they have proven their considerable benefits in water body extraction. Recent research in this field has focused on improving the accuracy of water body extraction from satellite images, either by using pre-built models or creating their own models.

However, the potential of transformer mechanisms has not been explored or applied in the field of water body extraction, despite their proven success in other sectors. It is in this context that we chose the TransUNet model. This model capitalizes on the strengths of attention mechanisms and relies on the architecture of the UNet model. Due to this combination, we considered the UNet and Attention UNet models as comparable benchmarks to TransUNet. This approach aims to identify the optimal performance that these models can offer while seeking to achieve the most successful results. Taking into account the imperfections identified in the dataset used for training our models, we noted that the results offered by the UNet model, with an mIoU of 70.45%, an F1 score of 86.01%, and an accuracy of 75.36%, and by Attention UNet with 70.93%, 86.60%, and an accuracy of 75.43%, respectively, are competitive with the values achieved by previous research. These values include an mIoU of 74.53% (Joshua et al., 2023), an F1 score of 92% using an FCN with very high-resolution images (Li et al., 2019), and an accuracy of 90% for the modified UNet architecture (Yan et al., 2022).

Meanwhile, TransUNet has proven its ability to produce good predictions compared to the two models used, achieving an F1 score of 87.08%, an mIoU of 70.52%, and an accuracy of 73.95%, which we were able to improve with the augmentation technique to finally reach values of 87.21%, 69.68%, and 74.31%, respectively. However, this improvement comes despite a costly execution time and a remarkable sensitivity to the volume of input data; indeed, the more data it is fed, the better its results become.

In addition to the exploration of vision transformers through the TransUNet model, our study offers a qualitative and quantitative analysis of the effect of hyperparameter variation on the quality of expected predictions, allowing the reader to decide on the choice to make regarding the training of the three models for similar applications to ours. Thus, it can be exploited for other purposes such as monitoring changes in water bodies, analyzing water quality, and categorizing types of water bodies.

References

High Commission for Water and Forests and the Fight Against Desertification (HCEFLCD). Dakki, M.; Menioui, M.; Amhaouch, Z. "National Strategy and Action Plan 2015–2024 for Wetlands in Morocco". Climate Change Adaptation and Biodiversity Valuation Program / Nagoya Protocol (GIZ-ACCN) (2015)

Stevens, K.B., Costard, S., Métras, R., Theuri, W., Hendrickx, S., Pfeiffer, D.U.: Improving surveillance of H5N1 avian influenza - Mapping the risk of H5N1 avian influenza in Africa: Final report and maps of H5N1 avian influenza risk". (2010). EDRSAIA (Early Detection, Reporting and Surveillance for Avian Influenza in Africa) project. Nairobi, Kenya: ILRI. [Lien](https://cgspace.cgiar.org/handle/10568/2510)

Food and Agriculture Organization of United Nations FAO. 'The global strategy for prevention and control of H5N1 highly pathogenic avian influenza'(2007). https://www.fao.org/3/a1145e/a1145e00.html

Chen, J., et al.: TransUNet: transformers make strong encoders for medical image segmentation (2021). https://arxiv.org/abs/2102.04306

Artibi, Y., Bouaaddi, A.: Exploration des architectures Deep Learning et Google Earth Engine pour Une Analytique Urbaine (2021)

Yan, K., et al.: Deep learning-based automatic extraction of cyanobacterial blooms from Sentinel-2 MSI satellite data. Remote Sens. **14**, 4763 (2022). https://doi.org/10.3390/rs14194763

Weathering the Storm: Evaluating the Generalization of Recent Object Detection Models for UAV Power Line Inspection of Insulators in Challenging Meteorological Conditions

Rita Aitelhaj, Badr-Eddine Benelmostafa[(✉)], and Hicham Medromi

System Architecture Team (EAS), EngineeringResearchLaboratory(LRI, Hassan II University
Casablanca, Casablanca, Morocco
phd.benel@gmail.com

Abstract. Unmanned aerial vehicles (UAVs) have demonstrated substantial improvements in the efficiency of power line inspections. The application of sophisticated deep learning object detection algorithms facilitates automated anomaly identification through drone imagery, significantly expediting inspection processes. This not only enhances operational efficiency but also leads to cost reductions and diminished associated risks. Nonetheless, challenges arise, particularly in the face of adverse weather conditions. Images captured by drones showing snow, rain, or fog introduce noise, compromising image clarity and quality, which is expected to be a significant obstacle for object detection models. Our research is centered on two main objectives: (i) assessing the impact of weather disturbances on the model's efficacy, and (ii) determining the necessity of training the model in a noisy context for detecting broken porcelain insulators—a critical component of power line infrastructure. The study evaluates model performance metrics trained on clear images, tested on noise-free datasets, and those with simulated noise (snow, fog, and rain). Additionally, recent object detection models (YOLOV8 and RTDETR) trained on three noisy datasets (snow, fog, and rain) are tested on their respective noisy test datasets, with benchmarking against a model exclusively trained on clear images. The findings reveal a slight superiority of the model trained in a clear context over its noisy counterpart in the corresponding test environment. However, marginal efficiency gains are observed when training a model in a noisy environment and testing it in the same context. Ultimately, the results affirm the model's generalization ability, indicating that training in a noisy context is not imperative, considering the limited added value compared to potential risks associated with data collection operations in extreme conditions. The code and dataset can be accessed at: https://github.com/phd-benel/weather_p owerline_insulator.

Keywords: UAV Power Line Inspection · Automated anomaly identification · Object detection algorithms · YOLOV8 · RTDETR · Simulated weather conditions · Generalization ability · Computer Vision

H. Badir et al. (Eds.): INTIS 2024, CCIS 2645, pp. 392–408, 2026.
https://doi.org/10.1007/978-3-032-14964-0_38

1   Introduction

The utilization of unmanned aerial vehicles (UAVs) for power line inspection holds considerable potential for enhancing operational efficiency within the energy sector. Integrating sophisticated object detection algorithms into drone-based systems offers an avenue for automating the identification and recognition of anomalies in power lines, thereby accelerating the inspection process [1–4]. However, the influence of weather conditions on the efficacy of power line inspections is a critical consideration for optimizing the deployment of drones in this context.

Establishing a resilient pipeline for power line inspection necessitates a nuanced understanding of whether image collection should occur under diverse weather conditions. This strategic approach serves to mitigate risks associated with investing in such initiatives, given that adverse weather elements such as rain, snow, and atmospheric disturbances can impede the acquisition of clear and accurate images, potentially leading to operational complications or accidents.

A pivotal inquiry emerges: Do contemporary object detection methods exhibit a decline in performance when confronted with environmental noise, particularly in adverse weather conditions like rain, snow, and fog? Should these methods be trained with images captured under specific weather conditions?

The primary contribution of this study lies in addressing these fundamental questions concerning the impact of adverse weather conditions on the performance of object detection methods employed in UAV-based power line inspections.

Through a systematic evaluation and analysis of the sensitivity of recent object detection algorithms to noise induced by diverse weather phenomena, this research aims to furnish valuable insights into the viability and dependability of deploying drones for electrical line inspections under varying environmental circumstances. The outcomes of this study will inform the development of a resilient and adaptive pipeline for power line inspection, ensuring optimal performance and minimizing risks associated with inclement weather.

2   Related Works

The examination of power line infrastructure through unmanned aerial vehicles (UAVs) has garnered considerable attention, particularly in the development of object detection models aimed at identifying anomalies in insulators. Despite extensive research in this domain [5–8], few studies have ventured into detecting insulator anomalies under adverse weather conditions, primarily due to the challenges associated with collecting data in such settings, including safety risks. Nevertheless, notable studies have risen to this challenge, with a specific emphasis on foggy environments, considered less perilous. For example, Liu et al. [9] introduced the Dark-Center algorithm to address challenges in outdoor insulator detection during low visibility in foggy conditions. This methodology, amalgamating the dark channel prior, optimized defogging modules, and an enhanced CenterNet network, markedly enhanced target detection accuracy, achieving 96.76% on the CPILD dataset. Transitioning to another study, Xin et al. [10] proposed a two-stage detection model incorporating a defogging algorithm for accurate detection of insulator umbrella disc shedding in foggy weather. This approach achieved a precision of 0.925 and a recall of 0.841, showcasing a 5.9% and 8.6% improvement over the original model, respectively. Subsequently, Zhang et al. [11] introduced the SFID dataset for insulator and self-explosive defects detection, developing the Foggy Insulator Network (FINet), an enhanced YOLOv5 object detection model (SE-YOLOv5) trained on foggy images, achieving a robust 96.2% F1 score for insulator and defect detection. Moreover, Li et al. [12] constructed the Power Line Components Detection (PLCD) dataset, encompassing adverse weather scenarios like rain, snow, and haze. They introduced the CSUNet image restoration model, effective in noise removal and image restoration, significantly enhancing downstream object detection performance. Addressing challenges in snowy environments, Hao et al. [13] proposed an icing monitoring dataset from China Southern Power Grid. Utilizing Yolov5, they introduced a weakly supervised and phased transfer learning method to recognize insulators and ice types, achieving high recognition precision (86.6%), recall (91.3%), and mean average precision (90.1%), with a rapid recognition speed of 8 ms/image. Despite commendable efforts in the field of power line inspection, research has always been conducted with a predominant focus on objectives such as noise suppression [910,12] and training models in noisy conditions [11, 13]. However, no attention has been directed towards the specific inquiries addressed in this paper, to the best of available knowledge. These include (i) an assessment of the impact of noise associated with meteorological disturbances on the effectiveness of models, and (ii) an evaluation of the necessity of training models within a noisy context in the powerline inspection domain. Notably, extant literature within the powerline inspection domain has yet to delve into these nuanced aspects, despite analogous explorations having taken place in other domains [14]. This study seeks to contribute novel insights to the existing body of knowledge by addressing these research gaps and elucidating the implications of meteorological noise on the performance and training requirements of models in the context of powerline inspection. Specifically, our study focuses on addressing multiple problematic aspects across various weather conditions, which are pivotal for the development of business and management projects in this domain.

3 Methodology

To address the identified research questions, this manuscript presents a methodological framework, as depicted in Fig. 1. The initial phase involves dataset preparation, comprising two distinct sets: (a) an Original one, devoid-of-noise dataset denoted as the Insulator Defect Image Dataset (IDID) [15] and (b) a variant termed "Noisy," derived from the Original dataset. The Noisy dataset is created by introducing simulated noise effects, specifically simulating snow, rain, or fog individually. Consequently, four datasets are established: Original, Snowy, Rainy, and Foggy. Subsequently, two analytical scenarios are delineated to facilitate pertinent deductions: 1-Object Detection models are trained on the original dataset and subsequently evaluated on both Original and Noisy datasets. This approach aims to quantify the impact of noise on model performance by scrutinizing outcomes on distinct test sets. 2- Models are trained on each distinct noise type (snow/rain/fog) and evaluated on corresponding data categories. This comparison gauges the efficacy of training models under adverse weather conditions against models unexposed to any form of noise. The outlined steps collectively constitute our methodological approach, providing a systematic framework to address the research questions at hand.

1. Results comparison of a model trained on the original dataset, without noise, then tested on both datasets: original and noisy, to evaluate the noise impact on the model's performance.
2. Results comparison of a model trained on the original dataset, without noise, then tested on noisy dataset, and another model trained and tested on noisy dataset to evaluate the necessity to train models in noisy environment.

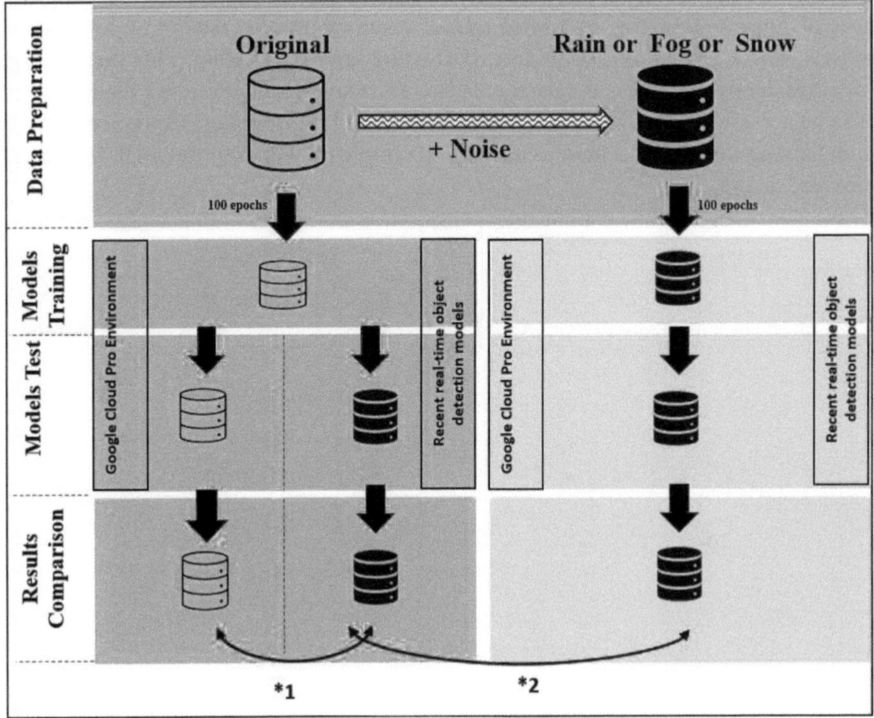

Fig. 1. Methodological Framework for Assessing Noise Impact on Model Performance and Evaluating the Need for Training in Noisy Environments.

4 Materials and Experimentations

4.1 Dataset Preparation

The investigation is anchored in the comprehensive Insulator Defect Images Dataset (IDID) [15], which comprises meticulously labeled, high-quality images depicting defects in transmission line insulators. This research specifically centers on the insulator chain, identified as the primary subject and parent class within the images. The dataset encompasses 1,600 images, categorizing them into three subclasses: 1. Flashover-damaged insulator shell, 2. Broken insulator shell, and 3. Good insulator shell. For experimental rigor, only subclasses 1 and 2 were considered, with the goal of anomaly detection, resulting in a refined dataset of 1,584 images after the exclusion of non-interesting images by using the Roboflow platform. This dataset is meticulously stratified into three primary subsets. The initial subset, constituting 70% of the data, is allocated for training, 10% serves as a validation dataset, and the remaining 20% of images are designated for testing. Consequently, the first dataset is denoted as "IDID_Original." Subsequently, to introduce meteorological noise into the images, the "IDID_Original" dataset was employed, and substantial noise was incorporated using the Python library "imgaug" [16] for each subset. To ensure equitable evaluation, consistent dataset distributions were maintained. For example, the Test subset of "IDID_Original" had three types of noise (snow, fog, and rain) added, resulting in the creation of four distinct datasets: IDID_Original, IDID_Snow, IDID_Fog, and IDID_Rain. This methodology was consistently applied to the other subsets. The parameters governing the introduced artificial noise are meticulously documented in Table 1, representing the optimal settings for achieving the most accurate rendering. Examples illustrating the final datasets are presented in Fig. 2.

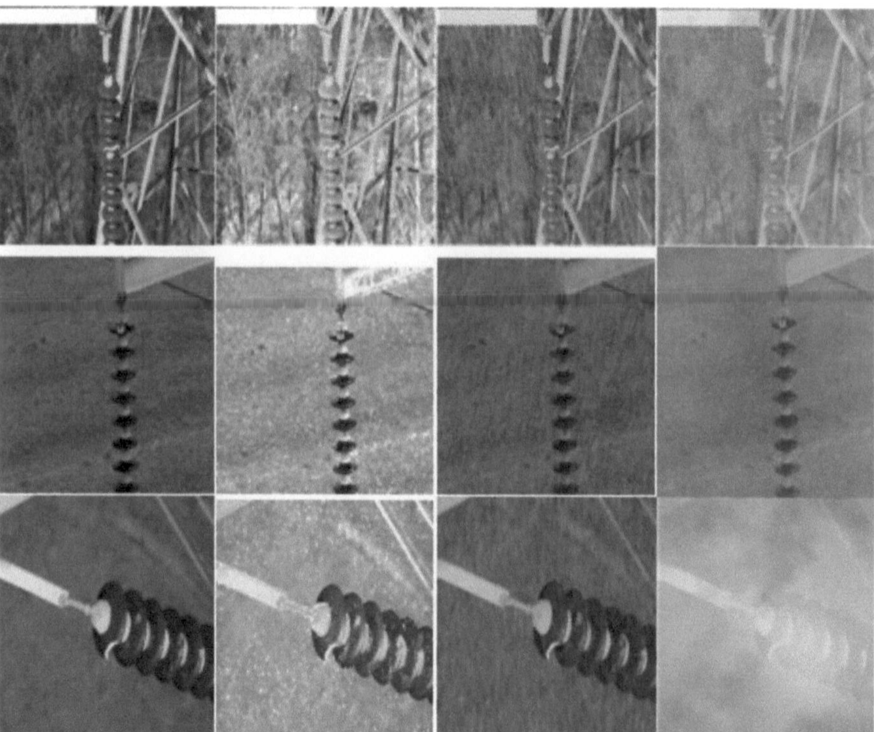

Fig. 2. Illustrative Images of Datasets: Sequential Column Display of IDID_Original (first column), IDID_Snow, IDID_Rain, and IDID_FOG (last column).

Table 1. Meteorological noise parameters introduced using imgaug python library.

Dataset Name	Type of Noise Added	Imgaug Parameters	Value
IDID_Original	-	-	-
IDID_Snow	Snow	lightness_threshold	180
		lightness_multiplier	1.5
		flake_size	0.7
		speed	0.02
IDID_Rain	Rain	drop_size	(0.4,0.6)
		speed	(0.05,0.1)
IDID_Fog	Fog	Default	Default

4.2 Experimental Environment and Training Process

Environment Setup. The investigation was conducted within an optimized computational framework utilizing Google Colab, a cloud-based platform known for its streamlined and resource-efficient features. The Tesla T4 Graphics Processing Units (GPU), recognized for its parallel processing capabilities, was employed to harness GPU acceleration, significantly expediting both the training and inference phases of the object detection models. PyTorch, specifically version 1.10.0, coupled with CUDA version 12.1, served as the software framework for model implementation.

Object Detection Models. To conduct a rigorous investigation, this study employs a thorough analysis utilizing two contemporary and robust object detection models, namely Yolov8-m [17] and RTDETR-L [18]. The evaluation is conducted using The Insulator Defect Image Dataset (IDID), with a specific focus on exploring deployment solutions within drones or ground stations. These models, distinguished by the 'm' and 'l' indicators, have been tailored for deployment on conventional consumer-grade GPUs, aligning with the overarching objectives of the research. Furthermore, it is pertinent to highlight that the selected models demonstrate a notable degree of parameter uniformity, as detailed in Table 2. This consistency in parameter counts establishes a robust foundation for conducting a comprehensive and equitable comparative analysis.

Table 2. Comparative information of recent object detection models: rtdetr-l and yolov8m.

Models	Parameters	Inference Time (A100 GPU–BS = 32)	Frame per Second	Model size in mega-bity	Released Date
RTDETR-L	31,9 M	26.3 ms	38	63,1 Mb	April 2023
YOLOv8m	25,8 M	7,9 ms	127	52 Mb	January 2023

Training Process.   The models underwent training adhering to the established settings and hyperparameters as prescribed by the original authors of the respective models [19]. Transfer learning was implemented, initializing the neural network weights based on the pre-trained model supplied by the original authors. This strategy aimed to optimize performance and expedite training processes, particularly in distinct scenarios. The training protocol extended over 20 h, spanning 100 epochs with a consistent batch size of 20 across all models. A total of eight models were trained, consisting of four yolov8-m models trained on IDID_original, IDID_rain, IDID_fog, and IDID_snow, and an equivalent set of four models for RTDETR-L. Additionally, to mitigate overfitting in machine learning models, a common practice involves monitoring the validation loss. This metric reflects the model's error on a separate dataset not utilized during training, offering insights into the model's generalization capacity. Instances of overfitting manifest when the training loss diminishes, yet the validation loss commences an ascent, indicating a potential lack of generalization to new, unseen data. Examination of the provided curves in the Fig. 3 reveals an absence of overfitting in our models, thereby bolstering the interpretability and reliability of our analyses and results. In fact, Fig. 3 here focuses on the validation loss examination for YOLOv8-M and RTDETRL models across diverse meteorological datasets. The initial pair of graphs elucidates the assessment of loss functions, namely giou_loss and l1_loss, pertaining to the RTDETR-L model, which encompasses three distinct loss functions. It is pertinent to note that cls-loss is excluded from the visual representation due to the amalgamation of classes 1 and 2 within the IDID dataset, resulting in a singular "anomaly" class. Subsequently, the latter pair of graphs delineates the evolution of the loss functions, specifically dfl_loss and box_loss, for the YOLOv8-M model, which similarly incorporates three loss functions. Notably, Yolov8's loss of cls is also not shown for the same reason.

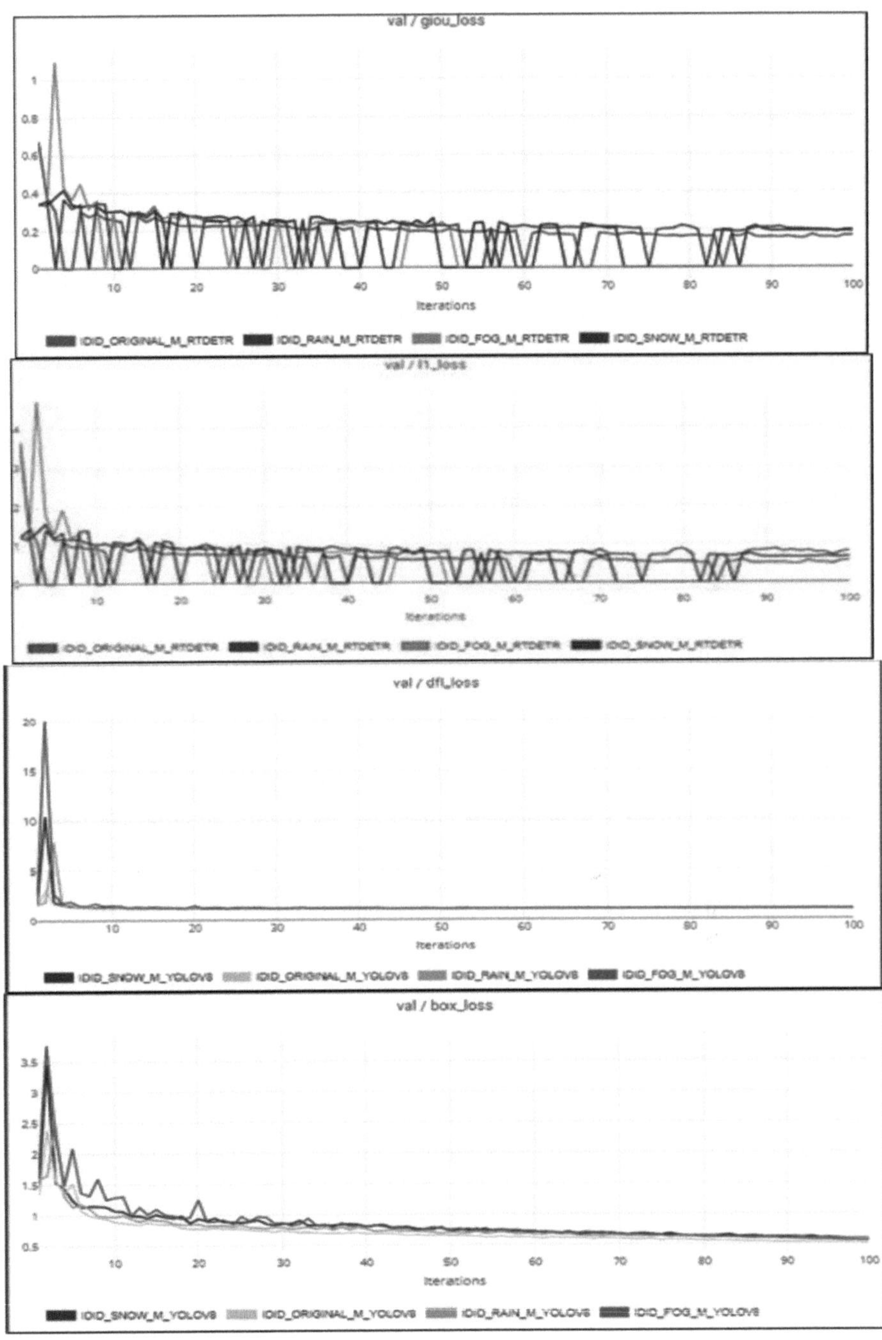

Fig. 3. Analysis of Validation Loss for YOLOv8-M and RTDETR-L Models in Different Meteorological Datasets.

Metrics Evaluation.   In the domain of insulator anomaly detection, wherein safety and system stability hold paramount importance, meticulous metric selection is imperative for a comprehensive evaluation. Notably, the metric of recall assumes a critical role, delineating the model's proficiency in capturing all instances of insulator anomalies within the dataset. The heightened emphasis on recall aligns seamlessly with the safetycritical nature of insulator anomalies in power systems, wherein any oversight could potentially lead to severe operational ramifications. Concomitantly, the metric mAP@50 assumes significance by virtue of its capacity to gauge the precision-recall trade-off at a specific Intersection over Union (IoU) threshold. This nuanced evaluation is pivotal in optimizing the balance between precision and recall, particularly pertinent in the context of insulator anomaly detection. Given the potential consequences of false positives leading to unnecessary maintenance interventions, mAP@50 plays a pivotal role in fine-tuning the model's performance, ensuring a judicious equilibrium between precision and recall for the effective and efficient identification of anomalies within the intricate domain of insulator anomaly detection in power systems. Both metrics are widely acknowledged within the field of computer vision.

5   Results

5.1   Problematic 1: Measuring the Impact of the Noise Related to Meteorological Disturbances on the Effectiveness of the Models

The investigation into the initial problem seeks to assess the generalization capacity of models when exposed to a novel environment depicted through synthetic imagery featuring diverse meteorological conditions, encompassing snow, rain, and fog. The objective is to compare the outcomes of models trained on the IDID_original dataset and evaluate their performance on two distinct datasets—original and noisy (inclusive of rain, snow, and fog datasets). The findings presented in Table 3 and Fig. 4 underscore the models' robust adaptability, showcasing noteworthy performances across various meteorological scenarios. A nuanced examination of the performance deterioration emerges when transitioning from original to noisy test sets. On the original test sets, both the RTDETR_original and YOLOV8_original models exhibit commendable performance, achieving respective Recall scores of 0.935 and 0.934, coupled with mAP@50 values of 0.971 and 0.963. However, on noisy test sets, a discernible performance decrement is observed, albeit remaining relatively moderate. In rainy conditions (IDID_Rain), RTDETR_original experiences a reduction of 0.135 in Recall and 0.073 in mAP@50 in comparison to its original test set performance. Similarly, YOLOV8_original demonstrates a decrease of 0.137 in Recall and 0.077 in mAP@50 under analogous conditions. In snowy conditions (IDID_Snow), RTDETR_original registers a decrease of 0.141 in Recall and 0.106 in mAP@50 relative to its original test set performance, while YOLOV8_original exhibits a reduction of 0.124 in Recall and 0.083 in mAP@50. Conversely, in foggy scenarios (IDID_Fog), RTDETR_original records a decrease of 0.075 in Recall and 0.037 in mAP@50 compared to the original test set, while YOLOV8_original manifests a decrease of 0.109 in Recall and 0.048 in mAP@50. It is noteworthy that the noise induced by fog appears to impact the models' performance less severely compared to snow and rain, both of which generate nearly identical effects on the two models. These results underscore that despite the reduction in performance under adverse weather conditions, the models exhibit considerable stability and efficiency, with a maximum decrease of 0.141 in Recall and 0.106 in mAP@50. This resilience underscores the models' remarkable capacity to maintain robust performance even in challenging environments. This consistent performance across diverse environments instills confidence in the potential real-world applicability of these models, warranting further exploration in this research direction.

Table 3. Assessing model generalization and performance in meteorological conditions: a comparative study on recall and map@50 metrics across original and noisy test sets.

TrainSet	TestSet	Models	Recall	mAP@50
IDID_Original	IDID_Original	RTDETR	0.935	0.971
		YOLOV8	0.934	0.963
IDID_Original	IDID_Rain	RTDETR	0,8	0,898
IDID_Original	IDID_Fog	YOLOV8	0,797	0,886
		RTDETR	0,86	0,934
IDID_Original	IDID_Snow	YOLOV8	0,825	0,915
		RTDETR	0,794	0,865
		YOLOV8	0,81	0,88

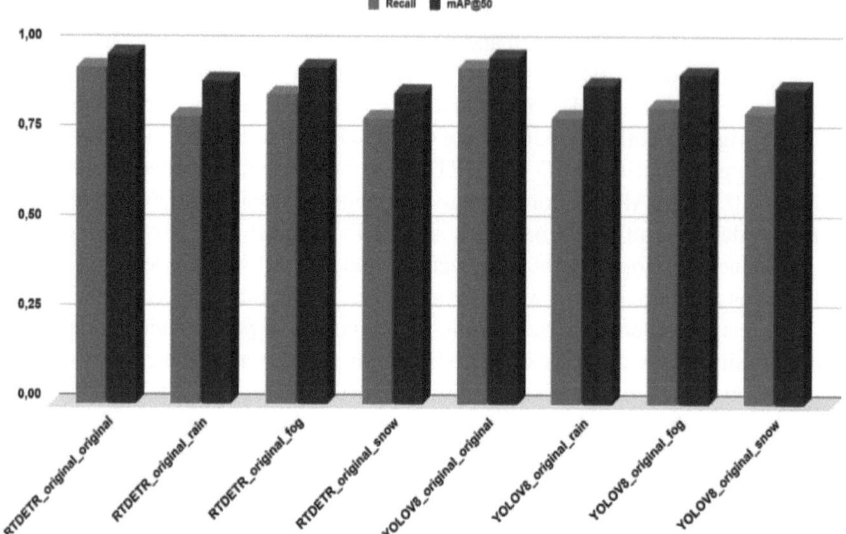

Fig. 4. Graphical representation illustrating a comparative analysis of model performance based on the Recall and mAP@50 metrics across original and noisy test sets. The labels on the horizontal axis legend are specified as "ModelName_TrainSet_TestSet".

Moreover, these findings are quantitatively evident. Specifically, Fig. 5 illustrates the inference outcomes of models trained on original datasets and subsequently tested in novel environmental contexts. The figure vividly portrays the models' generalization capabilities, demonstrating their adeptness in detecting anomalies (depicted by red rectangles) in extreme weather conditions, despite lacking prior exposure to rain, fog, or snow. A comparison with the ground truth (referenced in column 1) indicates that the models exhibit remarkable performance in identifying anomalies. Nevertheless, the models exhibit occasional false positives, particularly in snowy conditions, a phenomenon attributed to the transformative effect of snow on object shapes. Interestingly, the introduction of noise through fog and rain appears to exert minimal impact on anomaly detection in this context. In conclusion, the commendable generalization proficiency of the models amidst challenging weather conditions presents a promising outlook.

(a)   Ground Truth   (b) YOLOV8   (c) RTDETR

Fig. 5. Illustrative comparison of model inferences trained on IDID_Original on representative images in multiple test environment.

5.2 Problematic 2: Assessing the Necessity to Train the Model in a Noisy Context

The second problem aims to assess the need to train models in a noisy context, by asking whether it is essential to acquire data in difficult weather conditions. The aim is to compare test results on noisy data with models trained on two separate datasets: the original and noisy datasets, encompassing rain, snow and fog scenarios. The results, presented in Table 4 and Fig. 6, highlight that even if the models trained on noisy data show an overall improvement, the performance differences are small. This suggests that the need to train on noisy images may be negligible, especially when considering the potential risks associated with data collection, such as drone accidents. A careful examination of the data highlights several key observations. In the IDID_Rain scenario, the RTDETR model demonstrates substantial improvement in recall (0.122 increase) and mAP@50 (0.057 increase) when trained in rainy conditions (IDID_Rain) compared to its set. Original drive (IDID_Original). Similarly, the YOLOV8 model shows improvements in recall (0.024 increase) and mAP@50 (0.071 increase) during rain-specific training. The IDID_Snow scenario demonstrates notable improvements for both models when trained in snowy conditions, with the RTDETR model showing an increase in recall (0.115) and mAP@50 (0.098), and the YOLOV8 model showing improvements in 0.093 in recall and 0.072 in mAP@ 50. This highlights the positive impact of contextual training in snowy environments. Conversely, when transitioning to the IDID_Fog test set, the RTDETR model unexpectedly experiences a decrease in recall (0.064) and mAP@50 (0.042) when trained in fog conditions (IDID_Fog), which means potential challenges in adapting to this environment. The YOLOV8 model, however, displays a marginal decrease in recall (0.009) but an increase in mAP@50 (0.016), indicating a more resilient response to fog-induced noise. This intriguing result suggests that models not exposed to fog during training perform better in foggy conditions. A plausible explanation is that models exposed to fog might have acquired characteristics specific to the foggy environment, which, while improving performance in fog, could compromise generalization to clearer conditions. This finding provides valuable insights into model behavior and suggests avenues for optimizing training strategies, potentially minimizing the need for explicit exposure to harsh weather conditions during the training phase. Overall, the encouraging results, such as the increase in mAP@50 (0.098) and Recall (0.122) across all datasets, highlight the added value of contextualized training to improve anomaly detection. However, given the modest nature of this increase, it is crucial to weigh the costs and risks associated with collecting data in various weather conditions, including possible drone accidents. Depending on the circumstances, using models trained on clear data may be more prudent, although the final decision rests on project managers' full assessment of the pros and cons.

Table 4. Comparative analysis of model performance on recall and map@50 metrics across different weather conditions and training sets.

TestSet	Model	TrainSet	Recall	mAP@50
IDID_Rain	RTDETR	IDID_Original	0,8	0,898
		IDID_Rain	0,922	0,955
	YOLOV8	IDID_Original	0,797	0,886
		IDID_Rain	0,821	0,957
IDID_Fog	RTDETR	IDID_Original	0,86	0,934
		IDID_Fog	0,796	0,892
	YOLOV8	IDID_Original	0,825	0,915
		IDID_Fog	0,834	0,931
IDID_Snow	RTDETR	IDID_Original	0,794	0,865
		IDID_Snow	0,909	0,963

(continued)

Table 4. (*continued*)

TestSet	Model	TrainSet	Recall	mAP@50
	YOLOV8	IDID_Original	0,81	0,88
		IDID_Snow	0,903	0,952

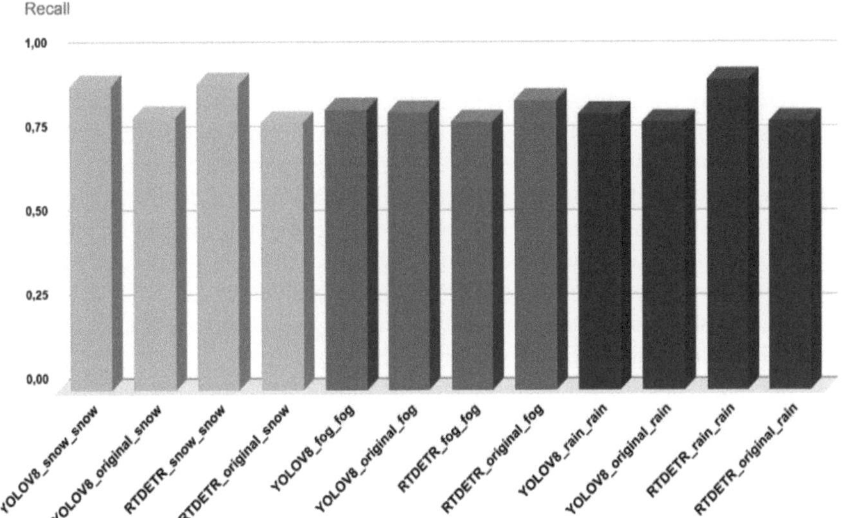

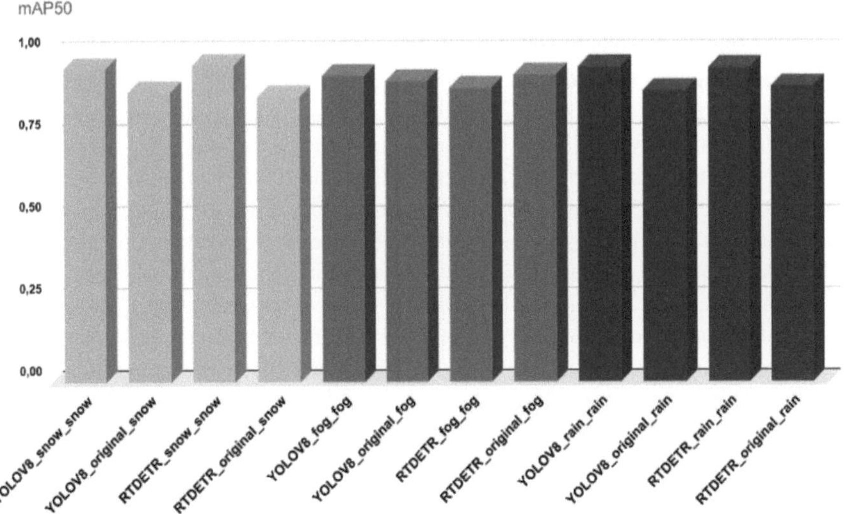

Fig. 6. Graphical representation illustrating a comparative analysis of model performance based on the Recall and mAP@50 metrics across original and noisy training and test sets. The labels on the horizontal axis legend are specified as "ModelName_TrainSet_TestSet".

6 Limitations

Several limitations are inherent in this study that warrant consideration. Firstly, the utilization of simulated weather images introduces a degree of abstraction, deviating from the complexities and nuances inherent in real-world scenarios. While the simulated conditions provide a controlled environment for evaluating model performance, the translatability of findings to authentic, dynamic weather conditions may be limited. Secondly, the study focuses on the detection of a single anomaly, thereby simplifying the complexity of powerline inspection tasks. In actual powerline infrastructure assessments, various anomalies such as corrosion, structural damage, or foreign object interference may coexist, each presenting distinct challenges for detection algorithms. The oversimplification of anomaly types in this study may not fully capture the multifaceted nature of anomalies encountered in practical powerline inspection scenarios. Moreover, the study does not encompass the full spectrum of diverse weather conditions that powerline infrastructure may encounter. Weather phenomena like sandstorms, dust, and extreme temperature fluctuations, which are prevalent in certain regions, are not accounted for. These unaddressed conditions represent additional challenges in real-world scenarios, where the environmental variability could impact the robustness and adaptability of anomaly detection models.

In essence, while the study contributes valuable insights into anomaly detection in simulated weather conditions, it is imperative to acknowledge these limitations when extrapolating the results to real-world applications, where the complexity and variability of weather conditions and anomaly types are considerably more extensive.

7 Conclusion

Unmanned aerial vehicles (UAVs) or drones have showcased significant advancements in optimizing the efficiency of power line inspections. The deployment of sophisticated deep learning object detection algorithms enables automated anomaly identification through drone imagery, leading to expedited inspection processes, cost reductions, and reduced associated risks. However, challenges arise, particularly in adverse weather conditions. Drone-captured images with snow, rain, or fog introduce noise, compromising image clarity and quality, posing a substantial obstacle for object detection models. This study focuses on two primary objectives: (i) assessing the impact of weather disturbances on model efficacy and (ii) determining the necessity of training the model in a noisy context for detecting broken porcelain insulators—a crucial component of power line infrastructure. The research evaluates model performance metrics trained on clear images, tested on noise-free datasets, and those with simulated noise (snow, fog, and rain). Additionally, recent object detection models (YOLOV8 and RTDETR) trained on three noisy datasets (snow, fog, and rain) are tested on their respective noisy test datasets, benchmarked against a model exclusively trained on clear images. The findings reveal several noteworthy insights contributing to the overall understanding of anomaly detection model effectiveness under extreme weather conditions. Primarily, concerning the first problem, the deployed models exhibit noteworthy robustness, demonstrating a considerable generalization capacity even in previously unencountered environments. This resilience suggests that additional measures, such as noise removal, may not be indispensable, showcasing the models' inherent ability to handle diverse sources of disturbance. Secondarily, the study underscores that collecting images in extreme weather conditions may not be necessary to enhance model performance. By avoiding the collection of real images by drones in challenging climatic conditions, potential risks associated with accidents during data collection are mitigated, while maintaining the models' effective generalization. In conclusion, this investigation indicates that existing models have achieved a level of robustness that minimizes the need for incorporating complex steps into the process. They can be effectively deployed even without image collection in extreme weather conditions. In addition, it is clear that future models will be more and more robust. This positive development is promising for the practical application of these models in real-world situations, where variability in weather conditions is unavoidable, thus facilitating management and implementation for developers of power line inspection projects using drones equipped with computer vision technologies.

References

1. Xu, B., et al.: Development of power transmission line detection technology based on unmanned aerial vehicle image vision. SN Appl. Sci. **5**, 72 (2023). https://doi.org/10.1007/s42452-023-05299-7
2. Nguyen, V.N., Jenssen, R., Roverso, D.: Intelligent monitoring and inspection of power line components powered by UAVs and deep learning. IEEE Power and Energy Technol. Syst. J. **6**(1), 11–21 (2019). https://doi.org/10.1109/JPETS.2018.2881429
3. Cheng, X.: Research on the application of computer vision technology in power system UAV line inspection. E3S Web Conf. **358**, 01030 (2022). https://doi.org/10.1051/e3sconf/202235801030
4. Liu, X., et al.: Review of data analysis in vision inspection of power lines with an in-depth discussion of deep learning technology, ArXiv:2003.09802. https://api.semanticscholar.org/CorpusID:214612507
5. He, M., Qin, L., Liu, K., et al.: MFI-YOLO: multi-fault insulator detection based on an improved YOLOv8. IEEE Trans. Power Delivery **39**(1), 168–179 (2024)
6. Liu, X., Rao, Z., Zhang, Y., Zheng, Y.: UAVs images based real-time insulator defect detection with transformer deep learning. In: 2023 IEEE International Conference on Robotics and Biomimetics (ROBIO), pp. 1–6 (2023)
7. Zou, X., Zhou, Y.: DeFCN-nano: an end-to-end real-time object detection for insulator defects. In: 2023 IEEE International Conference on Robotics and Biomimetics (ROBIO), pp. 1–6 (2023)
8. Zhang, Z., et al.: BS-YOLOv5s: insulator defect detection with attention mechanism and multi-scale fusion. In: 2023 IEEE International Conference on Image Processing (ICIP), pp. 2365–2369 (2023)
9. Liu, L., Ke, C., Lin, H.: Dark-center based insulator detection method in foggy environment. Appl. Sci. **13**, 7264 (2023). https://doi.org/10.3390/app13127264
10. Xin, R., et al.: Insulator umbrella disc shedding detection in foggy weather. Sensors **22**, 4871 (2022). https://doi.org/10.3390/s22134871
11. Zhang, Z.-D., et al.: FINet: an insulator dataset and detection benchmark based on synthetic fog and improved YOLOv5. IEEE Trans. Instrum. Meas. **71**, 1–8 (2022). https://doi.org/10.1109/TIM.2022.3194909

12. Li, Y., et al.: Boosting power line inspection in bad weather: Removing weather noise with channel-spatial attention-based UNet. Multimed Tools Appl. (2023). https://doi.org/10.1007/s11042-023-17554-5

13. Hao, Y., et al.: Methods of image recognition of overhead power line insulators and ice types based on deep weakly-supervised and transfer learning. IET Gener. Transm. Distrib. **16**, 2140–2153 (2022)

14. Tremblay, M., et al.: Rain rendering for evaluating and improving robustness to bad weather. Int. J. Comput. Vis. **129**, 341–360 (2021). https://doi.org/10.1007/s11263-020-01366-3

15. Lewis, D., Kulkarni, P.: Insulator defect detection (2021). https://doi.org/10.21227/vkdw-x769

16. https://imgaug.readthedocs.io/en/latest/

17. Jocher, G., Chaurasia, A., Qiu, J.: YOLO by ultralytics (Version 8.0.0) (2023). https://github.com/ultralytics/ultralytics

18. Lv, W., et al.: DETRs beat YOLOs on real-time object detection (2023). arXiv:2304.08069. https://arxiv.org/abs/2304.08069

19. https://github.com/ultralytics/ultralytics/blob/main/ultralytics/cfg/default.yaml

Author Index

A

Abdellatif, Satir   354
Abdelwahed, El Hassan   149
Abghour, Noreddine   369
Abid, Meryem   163
Achemlal, Yousra   382
Achhab, Nizar Ben   80, 200
Ahajjam, Sara   288
Aitelhaj, Rita   392
Aitelmahjoub, Abdelhafid   177
Aitouhanni, Imane   31
Amar, Oumkeltoum   149
Ammour, A.   312
Assaf, Rasha   94
Awwad, Yurub   319
Azroumahli, Chaimae   362
Azyat, Abdelilah   80

B

Badir, Hassan   254, 268, 288
Bajja, Nisrine   375
Barraz, Zoubir   240
Bazza, Houssam   254
Bendaouia, Ahmed   149
Benelmostafa, Badr-Eddine   392
Benlahmar, El Habib   42
Benmallouk, Ilham   149
Benmamoun, Zoubida   3
Bentayeb, Youness   268
Benzakour, Intissar   149
Berqia, Amine   31
Berto, Filippo   254
Bimonte, Sandro   254
Borrohou, Sanae   105
Bouazizi, Omar   362
Bouchra, Adnane   177
Boudia, Mohamed Amine   186

**Boumya, Othmane   328
Bounour, I.   312
Boussetta, Abdelmalek   149

C

Calcante, Aldo   254
Ceravolo, Paolo   254
Chahboun, Asaad   200
Chiba, Zouhair   369

D

Dahbi, Ali   342
Dandache, Abbas   177
Daraghmeh, Yousef   132
Daraghmi, Yousef-Awwad   15
Douae, Tizniti   354
Dufrenois, Franck   375

E

El Filali, Sanaa   42
El Idrissi Saik, Imane   67
El Jiani, Laila   42
El-Hami, Khalil   342
El-hmous, Naima   3
Elyan, Derar   132
Enfissi, Toufik   240
Ezzaher, Fatima Ezahrae   80

F

Fellahi, Siham   382
Fissoune, Rachida   67
Fissoune, Rachida   105

G

Ghaffour, Jamal   288

H

Hachani, Abderrazek   305
Hachimi, Hanaa   3, 163
Hajji, Hicham   382
Haloum, Ihsane   42
Hamlich, Mohamed   375
Hassan, Ali   254
Hidila, Zineb   227
Hraiche, Hamza   328

J

Jaafari, Hatim Idriss   200
Jaradat, Majdi   213
Jayousi, Rashid   53, 94, 213, 319
Jebbor, Ikhlef   3
Jmal, Yosra   305

K

Kabachi, Nadia   105
Kadi, Kenza Ait El   382
Karboub, Kaouter   328
Kechadi, Tahar   254
Kechna, Mehdi   382
Khaissidi, G.   312
Khalilia, Mohammed   94
Khamayseh, Faisal   132

L

Laamimach, Mohamed   348
Laghouaouti, Younes   276
Latifa, Er-rajy   119
Lemrani, Meryem   67
Lifandali, Oumaima   369

M

Mabrouk, Aziz   348
Mallek, Maha   305
Marghoubi, Rabia   276
Mastir, Mohamed   342
Medromi, Hicham   392
Mezroui, Soufiane   200
Miyara, Mounia   369
Mohamed, El Ghazouani   119
Mohamed, Hamlich   335
Mohammed, Tabaa   335

Mourabit, Aimad El   362
Moussa, Rim   254
Moussaid, Khalid   369
Mrabti, M.   312
My Ahmed, El Kiram   119

N

Naciri, Hafssa   80
Naciri, Zaynab   149
Nadia, Kabachi   354
Naji, Areen   53

O

Oberti, Roberto   254
Ouaddah, Afaf   276
Oussama, Lahihab   119

Q

Qassimi, Sara   149

R

Raissouni, Naoufal   80, 200
Rattrout, Amjad   15, 53, 94, 213, 319
Richard, Bearee   335

S

Sabha, Muath   15, 132
Saffarini, Muhammed   15
Saffarini, Rasha   132
Saoud, Inas   200
Sebari, Imane   240
Sellami, Sana   254
Soufiane, Ameur   335

T

Tabaa, Mohamed   163, 227
Talimi, Hasnaa   67
Tricot, Nicolas   254

Z

Zerouk, Marwa   382
Zerrouk, Marwa   240
Ziane, Fatine   276
Zineb, Hidila   335